Microsoft® SQL Server® 2012

REPORTING
SERVICES

Fourth Edition

Brian Larson

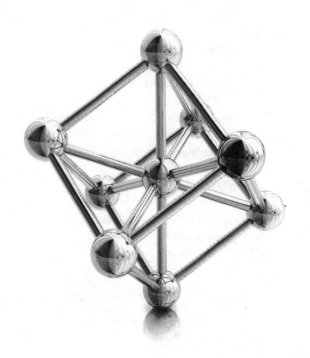

Mc
Graw
Hill

New York Chicago San Francisco Lisbon
London Madrid Mexico City Milan
New Delhi San Juan Seoul Singapore
Sydney Toronto

The McGraw·Hill Companies

Library of Congress Cataloging-in-Publication Data

Larson, Brian.
  Microsoft SQL Server 2012 reporting services / Brian Larson. — 4th ed.
      p.   cm.
   ISBN-13: 978-0-07-176047-8 (alk. paper)
   ISBN-10: 0-07-176047-4 (alk. paper)
   1. SQL server.   2. Client/server computing.   I. Title.
   QA76.9.C55L376   2012
   004'.36—dc23   2012001223

McGraw-Hill books are available at special quantity discounts to use as premiums and sales promotions, or for use in corporate training programs. To contact a representative, please e-mail us at bulksales@mcgraw-hill.com.

Microsoft® SQL Server® 2012 Reporting Services, Fourth Edition

234567890   DOC DOC   109876543

ISBN   978-0-07-176047-8
MHID   0-07-176047-4

Sponsoring Editor Wendy Rinaldi	**Proofreader** Bev Weiler
Editorial Supervisor Patty Mon	**Indexer** Karin Arrigoni
Project Editor Deepti Narwat, Cenveo Publisher Services	**Production Supervisor** James Kussow
Acquisitions Coordinator Joya Anthony	**Composition** Cenveo Publisher Services
Technical Editors Dan English Paul Purington	**Illustration** Cenveo Publisher Services
Copy Editor Lisa McCoy	**Art Director, Cover** Jeff Weeks
	Cover Designer Jeff Weeks

This book is dedicated to my family. To my children, Jessica and Corey, who gave up many hours of "dad time" during the writing of this book. And especially to my wife, Pam, who, in addition to allowing me to commit to this project, gave countless hours of her own time to make sure things were done right.

About the Author

Brian Larson served as a member of the original Reporting Services development team as a consultant to Microsoft. In that role, he contributed to the original code base of Reporting Services. Brian is currently the Vice President of Technology for Superior Consulting Services in Minneapolis, Minnesota, a Microsoft Managed Partner.

Brian has presented at national conferences and events, including the SQL Server Magazine Connections Conference, the PASS Community Summit, and the Microsoft Business Intelligence Conference, and has provided training and mentoring on Reporting Services across the country. He has been a contributor and columnist for *SQL Server Magazine*. In addition to this book, Brian is the author of *Delivering Business Intelligence with Microsoft SQL Server 2012* and co-author of *Visualizing Data with Microsoft Power View*, both from McGraw-Hill Professional.

Brian is a Phi Beta Kappa graduate of Luther College in Decorah, Iowa, with degrees in physics and computer science. He has 26 years of experience in the computer industry, and 22 years of experience as a consultant creating custom database applications. Brian is an MCITP: Business Intelligence Developer 2008 and a Microsoft Certified Database Administrator (MCDBA).

Brian and his wife Pam have been married for 26 years. Pam will tell you that their first date took place at the campus computer center. If that doesn't qualify someone to write a computer book, then I don't know what does. Brian and Pam have two children, Jessica and Corey.

About the Technical Editors

Dan English, MVP, MCITP, is a Microsoft SQL Server MVP, an MCITP Business Intelligence Developer for Microsoft SQL Server 2005 and 2008, and an MCTS for Microsoft Office SharePoint Server 2007 – Configuring. Dan is a Principal BI consultant at Superior Consulting Services. He currently helps to lead the Minnesota Business Intelligence User Group and is an avid blogger (http://denglishbi.wordpress.com), Microsoft forums helper, and tweeter (@denglishbi).

Paul Purington, MCITP, is a partner and member of the management team at Superior Consulting Services. As a BI consultant, Paul has experience with both large- and small-scale business intelligence environments.

Contents at a Glance

Contents

Part I   Getting Started

Part II   Report Authoring

Foreword

I t's been only eight years since the first release of Reporting Services, but during this time, the Reporting Services team delivered five releases (SSRS 2000, SSRS 2005, SSRS 2008, SSRS 2008 R2, and SSRS 2012) covering three high-volume product lines (SQL Server, Visual Studio, and Office). Although the focus was on developers, independent software vendors, and database administrators initially, the needs and expectations have evolved and expanded to information workers as well.

Business intelligence is an area in constant evolution, as is reporting. BI is not just about operational reporting or ad hoc reporting, or even embedded reporting with every operational and business application anymore. Dashboarding, visual analytics, scorecarding, and real-time data analysis, as well as traditional reporting, are all evolving toward each other, and lines are starting to blur between them. Nowadays, users expect their dashboard to be as interactive as their analytical experiences, or expect to build visual analysis within sophisticated report designs. So with all these techniques coming together, Reporting Services has also been evolving through the years to support all of these types of needs.

The other change that has been happening in recent years is the democratization and consumerization of reporting and analysis practices throughout every enterprise area and regardless of an organization's size. Information is the new business currency, identifying insights in vast amounts of data, sharing information, and collaborating across departments on this information in order to identify key business trends and turn data into a strategic advantage.

With data sources forever becoming larger, more diverse, more dynamic, and more rapid, BI is not just for IT anymore. Users are becoming more impatient—their business needs require answers now, not in a few weeks when IT will be able to deliver for them, so BI is becoming more agile. BI is about allowing anyone and everyone to take advantage of this new currency at the time when they need to use it.

In a world that is seeing economic crises following each other at an unprecedented pace in all parts of the world, BI is more important than ever. It is the technology area that is enabling businesses to remain competitive or even take competitive advantage in this tormented world. It is about optimizing business, taking streams of data and information and turning them into insights and actions. Users at all levels of technical or business savvy now need to be proactively alerted when events happen in the vast sea of data they now have within their reach. They need to be able to navigate this data visually and simply without having to learn a programming language or sophisticated tools.

This is why through the years we have been building a single platform that allows a full continuum of experiences and capabilities for all these needs—from proactive to reactive analysis, from high-end sophisticated report designs to full ad hoc interactive experiences.

I met Brian during my first year as the Group Program Manager for Reporting Services in 2007 during a DevConnections conference. Brian has been an SSRS aficionado and practitioner since the early days of the product. Very few people know the product in all its various aspects and have used it as much as Brian has. His books provide an exceptionally complete and exhaustive tour of all aspects of Reporting Services. But one of the things I find particularly valuable and interesting in the book are the real-life examples that are described throughout the chapters. They are not just focusing on flashy examples, but are describing numerous tips and techniques that will be directly and immediately useful for the reader in many business scenarios and industries.

If you are new to Reporting Services, plan to expand your expertise, have specific questions in mind, or just want to learn about the most recent feature additions to the latest release, this book is for you. Don't plan to put it on a shelf; it probably will not stay there very much or very long...

—Thierry D'Hers
Principal Group Program Manager for Microsoft SQL Server Reporting Services
Microsoft Corporation

Acknowledgments

A journey of a thousand miles begins with a single step." Perhaps this book project was not a journey of a thousand miles, although it seemed that way in the early hours of the morning with a deadline approaching. Be that as it may, it is possible to identify the first step in this whole process. A coworker of mine at Superior Consulting Services, Marty Voegele, was between assignments, on the bench, in consultant-speak. Marty was bored, so he decided to take matters into his own hands. Marty had previously consulted to Microsoft and still had contacts in the SQL Server area. He made a few phone calls, and before long, Marty was again consulting to Microsoft, this time creating something called Rosetta.

As work was added, I had the opportunity to take on part of this assignment as well. It was both challenging and exciting working on code that you knew would be part of a major product from a major software company. What was perhaps most exciting was that Rosetta seemed to be a tool that would fill several needs we had identified while developing custom applications for our own clients.

As the beta version of what was now called Reporting Services was released, a brief introductory article on Reporting Services appeared in *SQL Server Magazine*. One of the sales representatives here at Superior Consulting Services, Mike Nelson, decided this would be a nice bit of marketing material to have as we trumpeted our involvement with Reporting Services. One thing led to another, and before we knew it, Mike had offered Marty's and my services to write a more in-depth article for *SQL Server Magazine*. This article became the cover article for the December 2003 issue and has become known as the "Delightful" article.

This was where I grabbed the map and compass and decided on the next path. Because the magazine article came out fairly well, I decided to write a book on the topic. Marty informed me that writing a 700-page book would probably make his fingers fall off, so I could take this next step on my own. So, here we are today, one book and three revisions later. All of this is a rather lengthy way of saying that I owe a big thank you to Marty and Mike. Without a shadow of a doubt, this book would not have happened without them.

I also want to thank John Miller, the owner of Superior Consulting Services. John hired me as his first employee 15 years ago to be Superior's Chief of Technology. He has supported our efforts on Reporting Services and made it a focus area at Superior Consulting. Without John's founding of Superior Consulting Services and his bringing together people such as Marty and Mike, none of this would have come into being.

I also want to thank the entire group at McGraw-Hill Professional, especially Wendy Rinaldi, who has worked with me through a number of books and revisions. The assistance, guidance, professionalism, and humor of the editorial staff have made this project much easier. The attention that McGraw-Hill Professional has given this project has been truly overwhelming.

Last, but certainly not least, I want to thank my wife, Pam, for all her efforts and understanding. Not only did she agree to my taking personal time to write and revise this book, but she took it upon herself to proofread every page and work through every sample report. You, as a reader, are greatly benefiting from her efforts.

I also want to thank you, the reader, for purchasing this book. My hope is that it will provide you with an informative overview, steady guide, and quick reference as you use Reporting Services.

Best wishes,
Brian Larson
blarson@teamscs.com

Introduction

It's hard to believe that Microsoft SQL Server Reporting Services is now in its fifth version (counting SQL Server 2008 R2). We have already seen a number of advances in the product, from the rearchitecting of the rendering engine to the addition of the tablix and mapping. Never has there been a product with so much potential for sharing business information with such ease of use and at such a reasonable price. Anyone who has ever struggled to find a way to efficiently share database information across an enterprise will see a reason to be delighted with this product.

Now I will admit that I may not be unbiased when expressing this opinion. I did have the opportunity to create a small piece of what has now become Reporting Services. But my excitement goes beyond that.

The main reason I get excited about Reporting Services is because I have been a database application developer for 22 years. I have fought with various reporting tools. I have struggled to find a way to efficiently share data between far-flung sales offices and the corporate headquarters. I have researched enterprise-wide reporting systems and started salivating when I saw the features they offered, only to have my hopes dashed when I looked at the licensing fees. I have shaken my fist at the computer screen and screamed, "There must be a better way!"

With Reporting Services, there is. During the past nine years, my colleagues and I at Superior Consulting Services have had the opportunity to incorporate Reporting Services into custom database solutions. We have worked with a number of organizations, helping them get up-to-speed on the product. We have seen how quickly and easily Reporting Services can improve the data analysis and data distribution capabilities within an enterprise.

At one client, we began implementing Reporting Services on Monday morning. By Wednesday afternoon, reports were being e-mailed around the company. Information was being shared as never before. On Thursday morning, the president of the company emerged from his office to see what all the hoopla was about. As he stared at a newly created Reporting Services report, he began saying things like, "So that's why we're having a problem in this area" and "Now I see why our end-of-month's totals went that direction."

At another client, I was working with a manager to mock up a report in Reporting Services. He seemed to be taking a long time going over the layout, so I assumed we did not have things quite right. When I asked what was wrong with the report, he said, "Nothing's wrong. I'm just seeing information about this year's production that I hadn't seen before." Scenarios like these are enough to make even the most cynical data processing professional sit up and take notice!

This book is designed to help you and your organization achieve those same results. As you work through the examples in this book, I hope you have several of those "ah-ha!" moments—not only moments of discovering new capabilities in Reporting Services, but also moments of discovering how Reporting Services can solve business problems in your organization.

One note about the structure of the book: This book is meant to be a hands-on process. You should never be far from your Reporting Services development installation as you read through these chapters. The book is based on the philosophy that people understand more and remember longer when the learning takes place in an interactive environment. Consequently, the majority of the book is based on business needs and the reports, code, and configurations you will create to fulfill those needs.

The book is dedicated to offering examples demonstrating complete solutions. I have tried to stay away from code snippets as much as possible. Nothing is worse than seeing five lines of code and knowing they are exactly the solution you need, but being unable to implement them because you do not know what code is supposed to come before or after those five lines to make the whole thing work. With the examples in this book, along with the supporting materials available from the book's webpage, you should always see a solution from beginning to end, and you should be able to turn around and implement that solution to fulfill your organization's business needs.

I have also tried to have a little fun in the book when appropriate. That is why the business scenarios are based on Galactic Delivery Services (GDS), an interplanetary package delivery service. (You might call it the delivery service to the stars.) While GDS is a bit fanciful with its antimatter transports and robotic employees, the business needs discussed will ring true for most organizations.

I hope you find this book a worthwhile tool for getting up-to-speed on this exciting product. I hope you get a chuckle or two from its GDS examples. Most of all, I hope the book enables you to unlock the potential of Reporting Services for your organization.

The Galactic Database and Other Supporting Materials

All of the samples in this book are based on business scenarios for a fictional company called Galactic Delivery Services. The data for these examples comes from the Galactic database. You can download the Galactic database, as well as the image files and other supporting materials, from the book's webpage on the McGraw-Hill Professional website. This download also includes the complete source code for all of the reports and .NET code seen in the book.

The download is found on this book's webpage at www.mhprofessional.com. Search for the book's webpage using the ISBN, which is 0071760474. Use the "Sample Code" link to download the Zip file containing the book's material. Follow the instructions in the Zip file to install the Galactic database and the other sample code as needed.

Part I

Getting Started

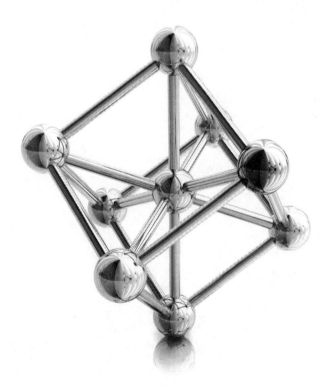

Chapter 1

Let's Start at the Very Beginning

In This Chapter

▶ **Sharing Business Intelligence**

▶ **Report Authoring Architecture**

▶ **Report-Serving Architecture**

▶ **Diving In**

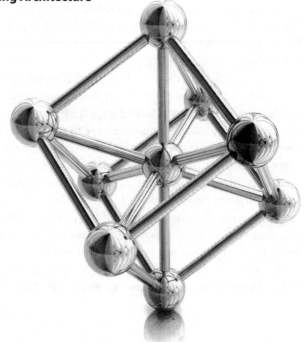

SQL Server 2000 Reporting Services was Microsoft's entry into the web-based reporting arena. This first version of Reporting Services enabled you to easily share business information—what is commonly known as "business intelligence" these days—with management, co-workers, business partners, and customers throughout the world. In an interconnected workplace, it makes sense that your reporting solution should offer company-wide, nationwide, and even worldwide communication.

SQL Server 2005 Reporting Services built on the success of the original. Where almost every other aspect of the SQL Server 2005 release represented a completely new platform, Reporting Services simply added to the solid foundation provided by the earlier version to make a great product even better. The 2005 release provided an additional report-authoring environment, improved report-development features, and enhanced capabilities for distributing reports.

The SQL Server 2008 release brought major changes to Reporting Services. The report processing and rendering engine was completely rewritten. This allowed Reporting Services to be more robust, especially when rendering large reports. This overhaul allowed for major changes to the report definition structure and a simplification of the inner workings of the report-rendering engine.

The interim SQL Server release, SQL Server 2008 R2, which came out in 2010, added more data visualizations and report authoring enhancements. Data bars, sparklines, indicators, and maps were added to the array of tools available for presenting information on reports in a graphical format. Individual report items could be saved in a report part gallery for reuse by other report authors.

All that brings us to the latest release of Reporting Services, delivered as part of SQL Server 2012. A release that, once again, brings exciting new features to the product. But before we dive in to the latest release, let's take a quick look back at Reporting Services' beginnings.

Reporting Services was code-named Rosetta during its original development at Microsoft. This name comes from the Rosetta Stone, a stone slab found in 1799 that contains an inscription in both Egyptian hieroglyphics and Greek. This stone provided the key piece of information necessary to unlock the mystery of Egyptian hieroglyphics for the modern world. Just as the Rosetta Stone brought key information across 1,400 years of history, Rosetta, or Reporting Services, is designed to bring key information across distances to unlock the mystery of success for your business.

The Rosetta project, which I was privileged to play a very, very small part in, was originally conceived as a feature of SQL Server 2005. However, as Microsoft told prospective customers about the features in Rosetta and demonstrated the first alpha versions, the reaction was strong: "We need this product and we need it now!" Because of this reaction, Microsoft decided that Rosetta would not wait for 2005, but, instead, would be made its own product to work with SQL Server 2000.

Just what are the features of Reporting Services that got everyone so excited? *Reporting Services* provides an environment for creating a number of different types of reports from a number of different data sources. The reports are previewed and refined using one of several authoring tools. Once completed, the reports are deployed to a *report server*, which makes the reports available via the Internet in a structured, secure environment. Last, but not least, the report management and distribution portion of Reporting Services is free of charge when installed on a server already running SQL Server.

Why did this set of features generate so much excitement? When you put them all together, the result is a product that facilitates the creation, management, and timely use of business intelligence.

Sharing Business Intelligence

Because you are reading this book, you are probably the keeper of some type of information that is important to your organization. You may have information on sales, finance, production, delivery, or one of a hundred other areas. All this information makes up the business intelligence necessary to keep today's corporate, academic, nonprofit, and governmental entities humming along.

The Need to Share

In addition to maintaining this information, you have a need to share this information with others. This need to share may have come from an important lesson you learned in kindergarten ("The world would be a much happier place if we all learned to share") or, more likely, this need to share your information was probably suggested to you by a manager or executive somewhere higher up the food chain. See if any of these situations sound familiar.

The Production Manager

Your company's order-entry system automatically updates the inventory database every four hours. In your company's line of business, some orders can require a large quantity of a given product. Because of this, it is important that the production manager knows about these changes in the inventory level in a timely manner so he can adjust production accordingly.

The production manager has asked you to provide him with an up-to-date inventory report that is created immediately following each update to the inventory database occurring during business hours. He would like this report to arrive on his PC as quickly as possible so he can make changes to the production schedule within an hour of the updates. He would also like to be able to print this report so he can add his own notations to it as he works out his new production schedule.

One more fact to keep in mind: your company's inventory system is in Cleveland, but the production facility is in Portland!

The Vice President of Sales

You are responsible for maintaining information on the amount of credit your company will extend to each of its clients. This information is updated daily in the company database. A report containing the credit information for all clients is printed weekly at corporate headquarters and mailed to each sales representative.

The vice president of sales has requested that the credit information be made available to the sales staff in a more timely manner. He has asked that this report be accessible over the Internet from anywhere across the country. The sales representatives will print the report when they have access to the Internet, and then carry it with them for those times when they cannot get online. He has also asked that this online version of the report be as up-to-date as possible.

The Chief Executive Officer

The chief executive officer (CEO) for your company has a hands-on management style. She likes to participate in all facets of the decision-making process and, therefore, needs to stay well informed on all aspects of the company. This includes the corporate balance sheet, inventory and production, and the company's stock price.

The CEO expects all this information to be available on her desktop when she arrives for work each morning at 7:00 A.M. The information must be in a format that's appropriate to print and share with the corporate vice presidents at their meeting each morning at 9:00 A.M. As you search for solutions to this one, remember no budget is allocated for this project—and, of course, your job is on the line.

Possible Solutions

These situations, and a thousand others just like them, confront businesses each day. In our world of massive connectivity, these types of requests are not unreasonable; even if that is the case, it does not mean these requests are easy to fulfill.

An HTML Solution

The first candidate to explore when you're looking to move information across the Internet is, of course, Hypertext Markup Language (HTML). You could use one of a number of tools for creating data-driven HTML pages. This would include Microsoft's ASP.NET, any of a number of Java environments, PHP—the list goes on and on.

Each of these environments is good at creating dynamic web content. However, they all take time and a certain level of programming knowledge. With deadlines looming, you may not have the time to create custom web applications to solve each of these problems. If you are used to manipulating data with Crystal Reports or Access reporting, you may not be ready to jump into full-blown application development, and you may not have a desire to do so at any time in the near future.

Even if you did create an application for each of these scenarios, one important requirement in each case is this: the information must be printable. HTML screens can look great in a browser window, but they can cause problems when printed. The content can be too wide to fit on the page, and there can be problems with page breaks. These types of formatting issues could make the output difficult for the sales representatives and the production manager to read. Asking the CEO to take this type of a report to the executive meeting could get you fired.

Let's look for another option!

A PDF Solution

Because the capability to control the printed output is important, Adobe PDF should be considered. Portable Document Format (PDF) files look good, both on the screen and in print. You can control where the page breaks occur and make sure everything looks great. However, several issues need to be overcome with PDF files.

First of all, you need some type of utility to produce output in a PDF format. This could be Adobe's full version of Acrobat or some other utility. Once this has been obtained, a document must be created that contains the desired database information. This is usually a report created with a reporting tool or development software. After this document is created, it is converted into a PDF document using an export function or a special printer driver.

Once the PDF document has been created, it can be copied to a website for access through the Internet. However, as soon as the PDF document is created, it becomes a static entity. It does not requery the database each time it is requested from the website. To remain up-to-date, the PDF document must be re-created each time the source data is changed. In addition, you may have to return to your programming environment to control access to the PDF documents on the website.

Perhaps there is a better way.

A Third-Party Reporting Environment

Reporting environments from other companies certainly overcome the limitations of our first two options. These third-party products allow reports to be built without requiring large amounts of programming. They can also dynamically generate output in a format such as Adobe PDF that will perform well onscreen and in print.

The problem with third-party reporting environments is the cost. Some products can run into the thousands or tens of thousands of dollars. This can be enough to break the budget—if indeed there is a budget—for reporting projects such as the ones discussed previously.

Microsoft Reporting Services

Now you can begin to see why companies get so excited about Reporting Services. It provides an elegant solution for all three of your demanding users—the production manager, the vice president of sales, and the chief executive officer. Reporting Services does not have the drawbacks inherent in the possible solutions considered previously.

No Programming Required

Reporting Services provides a simple, drag-and-drop approach to creating reports from database information. You can use a number of different tools to author reports. The Report Builder and the Report Designer in Visual Studio/SQL Server Data Tools let you truly unlock the power of Reporting Services to convey complex information.

You do not need to be a programmer to create Reporting Services reports. However, if you are comfortable with programming constructs, Chapters 8 and 9 include some simple Visual Basic expressions that can be used to spice up your report's presentation. Note, however, these expressions are not necessary to create useful reports. They are also simple enough that even those who are totally new to Visual Basic can master them with ease.

A Server with a View

With Reporting Services, you can view reports in your browser. Reporting Services provides a high-quality presentation of each report using dynamic HTML. Reports are presented in multiple pages with "VCR button" controls for navigating between pages.

Because Reporting Services uses dynamic HTML, it does not require any additional programs to be downloaded on your PC. There is no ActiveX control to install, no Java applet to download. Any browser that supports HTML 4.0 can view reports.

Plays Well with Printers

In addition to presenting reports in your browser using dynamic HTML, Reporting Services can *render* a report in a number of additional formats. These include an Adobe PDF document, a Tagged Image File Format (TIFF) image, an Excel spreadsheet, and even a Word document. All these formats look great onscreen when they are viewed, or on paper when they are printed.

NOTE

When Reporting Services renders a report, it gathers the most recent data from the database, formats the data in the manner the report's author specifies, and outputs the report into the selected format (that is, HTML, PDF, TIFF, and so on).

Even when being output in the PDF or TIFF format for printing, a report can be configured to requery the database every time it is accessed. This ensures the report is always up-to-date.

Special Delivery

Reporting Services provides several different ways to deliver reports to end users. Using either the Report Manager website or SharePoint users can access reports via an intranet or the Internet. Reporting Services also includes security features, which ensure that users access only the reports they should.

Users can also subscribe to reports they would like to receive on a regular basis. Reporting Services will send out a copy of the report as an e-mail attachment to each subscriber on a regularly scheduled basis. Alternatively, a Reporting Services administrator can send out a copy of the report as an e-mail attachment to a number of recipients on a mailing list. If that isn't enough, reports can be embedded right in .NET applications.

The Price Is Right

For anyone who has a licensed copy of SQL Server 2012, the price of Reporting Services is certainly right. Free! As long as the report server is installed on the same computer as the SQL Server database engine, your SQL Server 2012 license covers everything. With this single server architecture, it will not cost you one additional penny to share your reports with others using Reporting Services.

Reporting Services to the Rescue

Let's take one more look at the three scenarios we considered earlier—the production manager, the vice president of sales, and the chief executive officer. How can you use the features of Reporting Services to fulfill the requests made by each of them?

The production manager wants a report showing the current inventory. It is certainly not a problem to query the inventory data from the database and put it into a report. Next, he wants to get a new copy of the report every time the inventory is updated during business hours. The production manager can subscribe to your inventory report and, as part of the subscription, ask that a new report be delivered at 8:15 A.M., 12:15 P.M., and 4:15 P.M. Finally, the inventory system is in Cleveland, but the production manager is in Portland. Because a subscription to a report can be delivered by e-mail, the Reporting Services server can be set up in Cleveland, produce the report from the local data source, and then e-mail the report to Portland.

The solution for the vice president of sales is even more straightforward. He wants a report with credit information for each client. No problem there. Next, he wants the report available to his sales staff, accessible via the Internet. To achieve this, you can publish the report on the Report Manager website. You can even set up security so only sales representatives with the appropriate user name and password can access the report.

In addition, the vice president of sales wants the report to look good when printed. This is achieved with no additional work on the development side. When the sales representatives retrieve the report from the website, it is displayed as HTML. This looks good in the browser, but it may not look good on paper. To have a report that looks good on paper every time, the sales representatives simply need to export the report to either the PDF or TIFF format and then display and print the exported file. Now they are ready to go knocking on doors!

For the CEO, you can build a report or, perhaps a series of reports, that reflects the state of her company. This will serve to keep her informed on all facets of her business. To have this available on her desktop at 7:00 A.M., you can set up a subscription that will run the reports and e-mail them to her each morning at 6:15 A.M.

Finally, because she wants to print this report and share it with the corporate vice presidents, you can make sure the subscription service delivers the report in either PDF or TIFF format. The best part is that because you already have a SQL Server 2012 license, the Reporting Services solution costs the company nothing. You have earned a number of bonus points with the big boss, and she will make you the chief information officer before the end of the year!

Report Authoring Architecture

As mentioned previously, Reporting Services reports are created using either the Report Builder or the Report Designer. The *Report Builder* supports the construction of full-featured Reporting Services reports. It features a user interface similar to that of Microsoft Word 2010 or Microsoft Excel 2010, so it should be familiar for users comfortable with those products. The *Report Designer,* found in SQL Server Data Tools and Visual Studio, also supports all of the features of Reporting Services. In addition, it provides tools for project organization and source-code management for those reporting projects that have a lifecycle similar to that of a software development project (version control, check-in/check-out, etc.).

This book can help you get the most from the incredibly rich report-authoring features available in Report Builder and the Report Designer. These environments contain everything necessary to create a wide variety of reports for Reporting Services. Everything you need to select information from data sources, create a report layout, and test your creation is right at your fingertips.

Report Structure

Each Reporting Services report contains two distinct sets of instructions that determine what the report will contain. The first is the data definition. The *data definition* controls where the data for the report will come from and what information will be selected from that data. The second set of instructions is the report layout. The *report layout* controls how the information will be presented on the screen or on paper. Both of these sets of instructions are stored using the Report Definition Language (RDL).

Figure 1-1 shows this report structure in a little more detail.

Data Definition

The data definition contains two parts: the data source and the dataset. The *data source* is the database server or data file that provides the information for your report. Of course, the data source itself is not included in the report. What is included is the set of instructions the report needs to gain access to that data source. These instructions include the following:

▶   The type of source you will be using for your data (for example, Microsoft SQL Server 2012, Oracle, DB2, Informix, or Microsoft Access). Reporting Services will use this information to determine how to communicate with the data source.

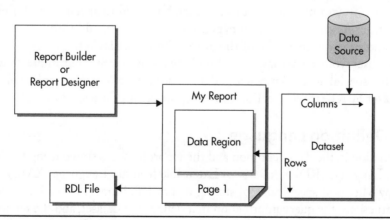

Figure 1-1   *Report structure*

▶ The name of the database server or the path to the data file.

▶ The name of the database.

▶ The login for connecting to this data source, if a login is required.

When the report is executing, it uses the data source instructions contained in the report to gain access to the data source. It then extracts information from the data source into a new format that can be used by the report. This new format is called a *dataset*.

The content of the dataset is defined using a tool called the Query Designer. The *Query Designer* helps you build a database query. The database query may be in Transact-Structured Query Language (T-SQL) for querying relational data, Multidimensional Expression language (MDX) for querying multidimensional data, or Data Mining Expression language (DMX) for querying data-mining data. The query provides instructions to the data source, telling it what data you want selected for your report. The query is stored in the report as part of the data definition.

The data selected by the query into the dataset consists of rows and columns. The rows correspond to the records the query selects from the data source. The columns correspond to the fields the query selects from the data source. (MDX queries are flattened into a table of rows and columns.) Information on the fields to be selected into the dataset is stored in the report as part of the data definition. Only the information on what the fields will be called and the type of data they will hold is stored in the report definition. The actual data is not stored in the report definition, but instead is selected from the data source when the report is run.

Report Layout

The data that the report has extracted into a dataset is not of much use to you unless you have some way of presenting it to the user. You need to specify which fields go in which locations on the screen or on paper. You also need to add things such as titles, headings, and page numbers. All of this forms the report layout.

In most cases, your report layout will include a special area that interacts with the dataset. This special area is known as a data region. A *data region* displays all the rows in the dataset by repeating a section of the report layout for each row.

Report Definition Language

The information in the data definition and the report layout is stored using the Report Definition Language (RDL). *RDL* is an Extensible Markup Language (XML) standard designed by Microsoft specifically for storing report definitions. This includes the data source instructions, the query information that defines the dataset, and the report layout. When you create a report in the Report Designer, it is saved in a file with an .rdl extension.

If you have not worked with XML, or are not even sure what it is, don't worry. The Report Designer, Report Builder, and Reporting Services will take care of all the RDL for you. For those of you who want to learn more about RDL, we'll take a quick peek under the hood in Chapter 8.

Report Designer

Figure 1-2 shows the Report Designer. This is one of the tools you can use for creating and editing reports throughout this book. We will look at some features of the Report Designer now and discuss them in more detail in Chapter 5 through Chapter 9.

Design Surface

The design surface, in the center of Figure 1-2, is where you create your report layout. To do this, you use four of the other areas visible in Figure 1-2: the Report Data window, the Toolbox, the Properties window, and the Grouping pane. You will learn how these work in the following sections. The design surface shares space with the Preview tab. The Preview tab will show you how the report layout and the data combine to create an honest-to-goodness report.

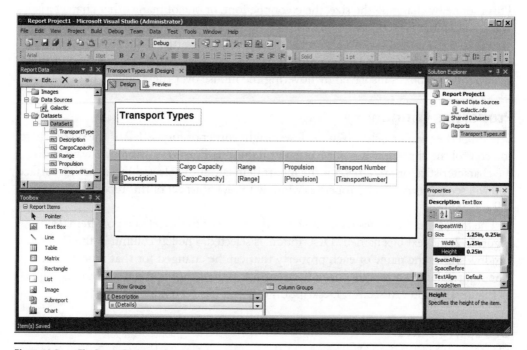

Figure 1-2   *The Report Designer*

Report Data Window

The Report Data window, in the upper-left corner of Figure 1-2, provides a list of database and other types of fields you can use in your report. The Report Data window makes it easy to add database information to your report layout. Simply drag the desired field from the Report Data window and drop it in the appropriate location on your report layout. The Report Designer takes care of the rest.

Toolbox

The *Toolbox* contains all the report items you use to build your reports. These report items, sometimes called controls, are responsible for getting the text and graphics to show up in the right place on your reports. As with any construction project, you can only construct reports properly *after* you learn how to use the tools (report items) in the Toolbox. You learn how to use each of the report items in the Toolbox in Chapters 4, 5, 6, 7, 8, and 9.

As with the fields in the Report Data window, the report items in the Toolbox are placed on the report layout with a simple drag-and-drop. However, whereas fields are pretty much ready to go when they are dropped onto the design surface, report items almost always need some formatting changes to get them just the way you want them. This is done by changing the size, the color, the font, or one of many other characteristics of the report item.

Unlike the layout shown in Figure 1-2, the Toolbox is often hidden on the left side of the screen. This is the default configuration for the Report Designer. When in this layout, the Toolbox is displayed by hovering the mouse over the Toolbox tab.

Properties Window

The Properties window, shown in the lower-right corner of Figure 1-2, is the place where you control the characteristics of each report item. The Properties window always shows the characteristics, or *properties,* for the report item currently selected in the design surface. You will see an entry in the Properties window for every aspect of this report item that you can control.

The top of the Properties window shows the name of the selected report item. In Figure 1-2, the text box named "Description" is selected. The left column in the Properties window shows the name of each property that can be changed for that report item. The right column shows the current setting for each of those properties. For example, in Figure 1-2, you can see the Description text box has a Height of 0.25in.

Grouping Pane

The Grouping pane is at the bottom of the design surface in Figure 1-2. This pane, made up of the Row Groups area and the Column Groups area, is where you control how grouping operates within the report. The advanced row grouping and column grouping that are now possible in a report are what make Reporting Services a powerful tool for creating complex report layouts.

Report Builder

The Report Builder functions similar to the Report Designer. Figure 1-3 shows a report being created using the Report Builder.

The Report Builder uses the ribbon-style user interface found in Microsoft Office 2010. This is the main difference between the Report Designer and the Report Builder. The Report Builder does not have a Toolbox. Instead, the report items are found on the Insert tab of the ribbon. The other tabs on the ribbon provide additional controls for formatting report items placed on the design surface.

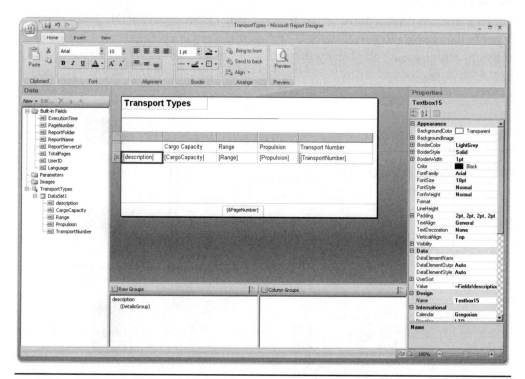

Figure 1-3   *The Report Builder*

Report-Serving Architecture

Once you finish building your report and have it looking exactly the way you want, it is time to share that report with others. This is the time when your report moves from its safe, childhood life inside the Report Designer or Report Builder to its adult life on a report server. This is known as *deploying* or *publishing the report*. Let me assure you, reports pass through deployment much easier than you and I passed through adolescence!

Report Server

The *report server* is the piece of the puzzle that makes Reporting Services the product it is. This is the software environment that enables you to share your report with the masses—at least, those masses who have rights to your server. Figure 1-4 shows the basic structure of the report server.

Report Catalog

When a report is deployed to a report server, a copy of the report's RDL definition is put in that server's Report Catalog. The *Report Catalog* is a set of databases used to store the definitions for all of the reports available on a particular report server. It also stores the configuration, security, and caching information necessary for the operation of that report server.

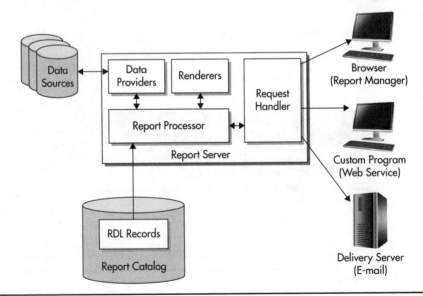

Figure 1-4   *Report server architecture*

Even though you may use any ODBC- or OLE DB-compliant data source to supply data to your reports, the Report Catalog database can only exist in SQL Server 2005, SQL Server 2008, or SQL Server 2012. The Report Catalog database is created as part of the Reporting Services installation process. Except for creating regular backups of any Report Catalog databases, it is probably a good idea to leave the Report Catalog alone.

Report Processor

When a report needs to be executed, the report processor component of the report server directs the show. The *report processor* retrieves the report from the Report Catalog and orchestrates the operation of the other components of the report server as the report is produced. It takes the output from each of the other components and combines them to create the completed report.

Data Providers

As the report processor encounters dataset definitions in the report RDL, it retrieves the data to populate that dataset. It does this by first following the instructions in the report's data source for connecting to the database server or file that contains the data. The report processor selects a *data provider* that knows how to retrieve information from this type of data source.

The data provider then connects to the source of the data and selects the information required for the report. The data provider returns this information to the report processor, where it is turned into a dataset for use by the report.

Renderers

Once all the data for the report has been collected, the report processor is ready to begin processing the report's layout. To do this, the report processor looks at the format requested. This might be HTML, PDF, TIFF, or one of several other possible formats. The report processor then uses the *renderer* that knows how to produce that format.

The renderer works with the report processor to read through the report layout. The report layout is combined with the dataset, and any repeating sections of the report are duplicated for each row in the dataset. This expanded report layout is then translated into the requested output format. The result is a report ready to be sent to the user.

Request Handler

The *request handler* is responsible for receiving requests for reports and passing those requests on to the report processor. Once the report processor has created the requested report, the request handler is also responsible for delivering the completed report. In the next section, you will learn about the various methods the request handler uses for delivering reports.

Report Delivery

We have discussed how a report is created by the report server. What we have not discussed is where that report is going after it is created. The report may be sent to a user through the Report Manager website. It may be sent in response to a web service request that came not from a user, but from another program. It may also be e-mailed to a user who has a subscription to that report.

Report Manager Website

One way for users to request a report from the report server is through the *Report Manager* website. This website is created for you when you install Reporting Services in Native mode. Figure 1-5 shows a screen from the Report Manager website.

The Report Manager website organizes reports into folders. Users can browse through these folders to find the report they need. They can also search the report titles and descriptions to locate a report.

The Report Manager also includes security that can be applied to folders and reports. With this security, the site administrator can create security roles for the users who will be accessing the site. These security roles control which folders and reports a user

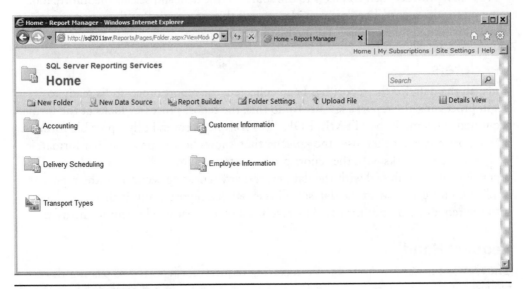

Figure 1-5 *The Report Manager website*

is allowed to access. You will learn about security when we look at the Report Manager in Chapter 10.

In the Report Manager, reports are always displayed using the HTML format. Once a report has been displayed as an HTML page, the user can then export the report into any of the other available formats.

SharePoint

SharePoint may also be set up to serve as a means for users to request reports. This can be done in two ways. The first uses the Report Explorer and Report Viewer web parts. These web parts can be used in a SharePoint web application to allow users to navigate report folders and to view reports on a Reporting Services report server.

The Report Explorer and Report Viewer web parts were originally made available as part of SQL Server 2000 Reporting Services Service Pack 2. They were part of SQL Server 2005 Reporting Services and SQL Server 2008 Reporting Services as well. The web parts continue to be available in the 2012 release, but they have not been upgraded to take advantage of new features and functionality.

The second means of utilizing Reporting Services through SharePoint involves a tight integration of the two products. In this configuration, a SharePoint 2010 installation will actually become the host for the report server's Report Catalog. In addition, the SharePoint user interface replaces the Report Manager website as the user interface for locating and viewing reports, as well as for managing the report server. Accessing reports through SharePoint integration is as easy and intuitive as accessing any other document on the SharePoint site.

Subscription Delivery

If the users do not want to go to the report, the request handler can make the report go to them. In other words, users do not necessarily need to come to the Report Manager website to receive a report. They can have the report delivered to them through a subscription service. The Report Manager enables users to locate a report on the site and then subscribe to it so it will be delivered to them in the future.

When users subscribe to a report, they provide an e-mail address to which the report will be delivered. The content of the report can either be embedded in the body of the e-mail or be included as an e-mail attachment, depending on the requested format. Users can specify the format for the report at the time they create their subscription.

The site administrator can also set up report subscriptions. These function like a mass mailing, using a list of e-mail addresses. Rather than requiring each user to access the Report Manager to create their own subscription, the site administrator can create one subscription that is delivered to every user in a list.

Web Service Interface

In addition to delivering reports to humans, either at their request or on a subscription basis, the request handler can deliver reports to other software applications. This is done through a series of web services. A *web service* is a mechanism that allows programs to communicate with each other over the Internet.

A program calls a web service on the report server, requesting a particular report in a particular format. The request handler relays this request to the report processor, just like any other request for a report. The completed report is returned as the response to the web service request to the program that originated it.

Web services use a standard called Simple Object Access Protocol (SOAP). *SOAP* is supported by both Windows and non-Windows environments, so a program running on a non-Windows computer that supports SOAP can receive a report created by Reporting Services.

Diving In

Now that you have been introduced to all of the capabilities of Reporting Services, I hope you are ready to dive in and make it work for you. In the next chapter, you will learn about the installation and setup of Reporting Services. If Reporting Services has already been installed, you can skip ahead to Chapter 3.

In Chapter 3, we make sure you have a firm understanding of database basics before getting to the actual building of reports in Chapter 4. Chapter 3 also introduces you to Galactic Delivery Services (GDS), the company we use as a case study throughout the remainder of the book. Even if your database skills are tip-top, you should spend a few minutes in Chapter 3 getting to know GDS.

Chapter 2

Putting the Pieces in Place: Installing Reporting Services

In This Chapter

- ▶ Preparing for the Installation
- ▶ The Installation Process
- ▶ Common Installation Issues

- ▶ Spending Some Time in Basic Training

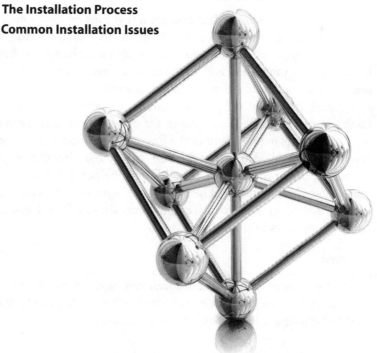

Before you can begin to enjoy all the benefits of Reporting Services discussed in Chapter 1, you of course have to install the Reporting Services software. Reporting Services installs as part of the SQL Server 2012 installation. Before you begin the installation process, however, it is important to understand the structure of Reporting Services.

In this chapter, you will learn about the components that make up Reporting Services and the five editions of Reporting Services offered by Microsoft. Next, you will find out how the components are combined in different types of Reporting Services installations and see how to plan for each installation type. As part of that planning, you will learn about the software that must be in place prior to installing Reporting Services. After considering these preliminaries, we will walk you through the installation process.

Preparing for the Installation

The most important part of the Reporting Services installation is not what you do as you run the setup program, but what you do before you begin. In this section, we discuss the knowledge you need and the steps you should take to prepare for installation. With the proper plan in place, your Reporting Services installation should go smoothly and you can create reports in no time.

The Parts of the Whole

Reporting Services is not a single program that runs on a computer to produce reports. Instead, it is a number of applications, utilities, and databases that work together to create a report management environment. As you plan your Reporting Services installation, it is important that you understand a little bit about each piece of the puzzle and how all these pieces work together to create a complete system.

Figure 2-1 shows all the parts that make up a complete Reporting Services installation. Each part has a specific role to play in the development, management, and delivery of reports, or in the management of the Reporting Services environment itself. All of these items can be installed as part of the SQL Server 2012 installation process.

It is important to note that not all Reporting Services installations include all of the items shown in Figure 2-1. The subsequent sections of this chapter discuss the various types of installations and which components they include. Let's take a look at each part and see how it fits into the whole.

NOTE

Unless specifically stated, the text and diagrams in this chapter are describing a Native mode Reporting Services installation. The other type of installation, a SharePoint Integrated mode Installation, is described in the section "SharePoint Integrated Mode Installation" later in this chapter.

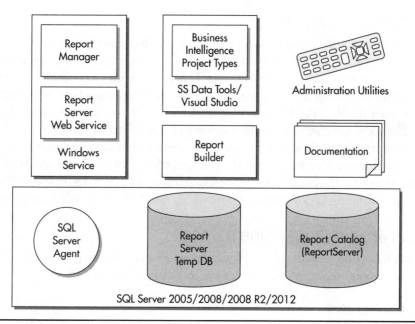

Figure 2-1   *Reporting Services component parts*

The Windows Service

The Reporting Services *Windows service* is the heart of Reporting Services and is, of course, included as part of the Reporting Services installation. This service is responsible for the two main interfaces with the report server. First, it contains the application that implements the Report Manager website. Second, it provides a web service interface for programmatic interaction with the report server.

As discussed in Chapter 1, the Report Manager website provides a user interface for requesting reports and managing the report server. The Report Server web service provides a programmatic interface for requesting reports. It also provides an interface for report server administration.

In addition to these two interfaces, the Reporting Services Windows service provides the engine responsible for report rendering. This is true whether the report is requested through the Report Manager website, the report server web service, or subscription delivery. As you saw in Figure 1-4 of Chapter 1, this includes fetching the report definition, retrieving the data used in the report, and rendering the report in the desired format.

Administration Utilities

The administration utilities are tools for managing the Reporting Services Windows service and for making changes to its configuration. The main administration utility is the *Reporting Services Configuration Manager*. This tool provides a convenient method for examining and modifying the configuration settings of a Reporting Services installation. You learn about the Reporting Services Configuration Manager in more detail in the section "The Reporting Services Configuration Manager," later in this chapter.

The administration utilities can be run on the computer that is hosting the Reporting Services Windows service to manage the configuration on that computer. Most of the administrative utilities can also be used to manage a Reporting Services Windows service that is running on another computer. This is called *remote administration*.

SQL Server 2005/2008/2008 R2/2012

One of the following versions of the SQL Server database engine is required to hold the database where Reporting Services stores its Report Catalog database:

- ▶ SQL Server 2005
- ▶ SQL Server 2008
- ▶ SQL Server 2008 R2
- ▶ SQL Server 2012

Reporting Services also uses the SQL Server Agent, which you will learn about shortly. In addition, databases in SQL Server can be used as data sources for Reporting Services reports.

SQL Server Agent

SQL Server Agent is part of SQL Server and is created as part of the SQL Server installation process. It is used by SQL Server to execute jobs scheduled to run at a certain time. These jobs might back up a database or transfer information from one database to another. Jobs may be scheduled to run once, or they may run on a regular basis, such as once a day or once a week.

Reporting Services also uses the SQL Server Agent to execute scheduled jobs. These jobs are used to run reports and distribute the results. In Chapter 1, you learned about users who subscribe to a report. When users subscribe to a report, they ask for it to be run and delivered to them on a regular basis. When a user creates a subscription, Reporting Services creates a SQL Server Agent job to handle that subscription.

For example, our production manager in Chapter 1 wanted to receive a copy of the inventory report shortly after each update to the inventory database. We'll assume these updates happen at 8:00 A.M., 12:00 P.M., and 4:00 P.M. each day. To get the report he wants, the production manager subscribes to the inventory report and creates a delivery schedule of 8:15 A.M., 12:15 P.M., and 4:15 P.M. When this subscription is created, Reporting Services creates a SQL Server Agent job scheduled to run at 8:15 A.M., 12:15 P.M., and 4:15 P.M. each day. When the job runs, it instructs the Reporting Services Windows service to run the report and e-mail it to the production manager.

The Report Server and Report Server Temp DB Databases

During the Reporting Services installation process, two databases are created within SQL Server: the Report Server and Report Server Temp DB databases. The *Report Server database* is used to store the Report Catalog. (Recall from Chapter 1 that the Report Catalog holds the information about all of the reports deployed to a report server.) The Report Server database also holds information about the virtual structure that contains these reports. This includes such things as the folder structure displayed by the Report Manager and the security settings for each folder and report.

As the name implies, the *Report Server Temp DB database* is used as temporary storage for Reporting Services operations. Information can be stored here to track the current users on the Report Manager website. Short-term copies of some of the most recently executed reports are also stored here in what is known as the *execution cache*.

Sample Reports and the AdventureWorks Database

In previous versions of SQL Server, the sample code and sample database could be installed as part of the SQL Server installation process. Beginning with SQL Server 2008, the samples are now downloaded from the Internet. From the Start menu, select All Programs | Microsoft SQL Server 2012 | Documentation & Community | Community Projects & Samples for instructions on downloading and installation.

SQL Server Data Tools/Visual Studio/Report Builder

As discussed in Chapter 1, Reporting Services reports are created using SQL Server Data Tools, Visual Studio, or the Report Builder. All of these report development environments produce the same result. There is no difference between a report created in SQL Server Data Tools, a Visual Studio development environment, or the Report Builder.

If you are going to use SQL Server Data Tools for creating reports, you need to install it as part of the Reporting Services installation process. Report Builder can be accessed through Report Manager. It can also be downloaded from Microsoft and installed separately. If you plan to create reports using a Visual Studio development environment, you need to purchase and install it separately.

Documentation

The final piece of Reporting Services is the documentation. The bulk of this documentation is found in the SQL Server Books Online. After Reporting Services is installed, you can view the SQL Server Books Online through your Start menu. You'll find it under All Programs | Microsoft SQL Server 2012 | Documentation & Community | SQL Server Documentation. There is also a set of help screens for the Report Manager interface that can be accessed through the Report Manager user interface.

Editions of Reporting Services

Reporting Services comes in seven different editions:

- ► Express Edition
- ► Standard Edition
- ► Business Intelligence Edition
- ► Enterprise Edition
- ► Developer Edition

There is also an Evaluation Edition, which does not require a license, but it can only be used for a limited time. We won't be discussing the Evaluation Edition in this book, but you can think of it as essentially being a Developer Edition you get to try out for free.

Reporting Services is licensed as part of your SQL Server 2012 license. Therefore, in a production environment, the Reporting Services edition you are licensed to use is the same as the SQL Server 2012 edition you are licensed to use. For example, if you have a Standard Edition of SQL Server 2012, you are only licensed for the Standard Edition of Reporting Services.

The Express Edition

All editions of Reporting Services provide a rich environment for report authoring, report management, and report delivery. The Express Edition does not require a SQL

Server license. It is intended to be distributed with packaged applications that require a SQL Server database. The Express Edition does not include many of the SQL Server management tools, such as SQL Server Management Studio.

The Express Edition has some limitations compared to the other editions. It does not include all of the business intelligence and high-availability features you find in the Standard, Business Intelligence, and Enterprise Editions. When it comes to the reporting environment, they do not support e-mail and file share subscriptions, and report caching. They also do not support SharePoint Integration mode. In addition, Reporting Services in these editions can only access 4GB of memory.

The Standard Edition

Standard Edition, as one might expect, provides the features needed by most "standard" SQL Server implementations. It includes the features excluded from the Express Edition. Reporting Services in the Standard Edition can access as much memory as the operating system can make available.

Just a few of the more advanced features of Reporting Services are not included in the Standard Edition. These advanced features are listed in the following section, "The Business Intelligence and Enterprise Editions."

The Business Intelligence and Enterprise Editions

The Business Intelligence and Enterprise Editions of Reporting Services includes the following advanced features:

▶ **Data-Driven Subscriptions**   Send a report to a number of users from a predefined mailing list. Data-driven subscriptions are discussed in Chapter 11.

▶ **Scale-Out Deployment**   Configure several Reporting Services Windows services running on multiple computers to point to a single SQL Server database engine hosting the Report Catalog. The scale-out deployment is discussed in the section "Types of Reporting Services Installations."

The Enterprise Edition includes a number of features for handling large volumes of data and for implementing high availability that are not available in the Business Intelligence Edition.

The Developer Edition

The Developer Edition provides support for all of the features of the Enterprise Edition. The Developer Edition does not, however, require that you have an Enterprise Edition license of SQL Server 2012. Of course, the Developer Edition is only for development and testing. It cannot be used in a production environment.

Types of Reporting Services Installations

Now that you are familiar with the components that make up Reporting Services and the ways that Microsoft licenses it, you can give some thought to just what your Reporting Services installation will look like. The first decision you need to make is which of the components you want to install. Although you can choose to include or exclude items in any combination you like, in the end, only three combinations make sense: the full installation, the server installation, and the report author installation.

In addition to these are a couple of specialized installation types. These are the distributed installation and the scale-out installation. These installations are for high-end, high-volume Reporting Services sites. We will discuss these configurations briefly so you are familiar with the variety of ways that Reporting Services can be configured.

Finally, there is one installation type that allows you to tightly couple Reporting Services with a SharePoint server.

The Full Installation

The full installation, as the name implies, is the "everything including the kitchen sink" installation. All of the items shown in Figure 2-1 and discussed previously are included in this installation. Nothing is left out.

The full installation is most likely to be used in a development environment. This might be on a server used by a group of developers or on a workstation used by a single developer. In either case, we want to have all the bells and whistles available to us as we figure out how to best use Reporting Services to suit our business needs.

The Server Installation

The server installation is most likely used when we're setting up Reporting Services on a production server. On a production server, we only want those items that are going to be used to deliver reports or to help us manage Reporting Services. We don't want to include anything that will take up space unnecessarily. Figure 2-2 shows the items included in the server installation.

The server installation includes the Reporting Services Windows service and the administration utilities used to manage it. As we discussed earlier, the Reporting Services Windows service provides the Report Manager website and the Report Server web service for managing and delivering reports. In addition, Reporting Services will

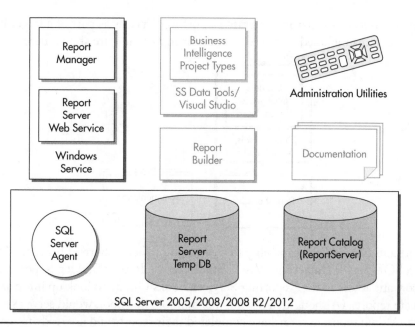

Figure 2-2   *The server installation*

need the SQL Server Agent, the Report Server database, and the Report Server Temp DB database for its operations.

We won't be doing any development work on the production server, so we will not need SQL Server Data Tools, Visual Studio, or the Report Builder. It is possible that you would want the documentation on the production server for questions on managing Reporting Services. Probably a better idea, though, is to have the documentation handy on a development computer and to keep the production installation as uncluttered as possible. The same can be said for the sample reports and the AdventureWorks database. You may want these on your production server for demonstration purposes, but, again, it is probably better to do this on a different computer and reserve your production server for reports and data required by your users.

The Report Author Installation

The report author installation is for individuals who are creating Reporting Services reports but not doing heavy-duty development. Report authors will not be creating full-blown applications that incorporate Reporting Services as part of a larger business system. The items included in the report author installation are shown here.

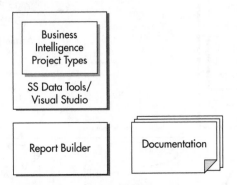

Report authors need the capability to create and preview reports. This capability is found in SQL Server Data Tools, Visual Studio, or the Report Builder. Report authors may also want access to the Reporting Services Books Online to look up information as they create reports. (Although, in my humble opinion, this book would serve as a better resource.) When report authors have completed their reports and are ready to have others use them, they will deploy the reports to a production Reporting Services server.

The Distributed Installation

In a distributed installation, the Reporting Services items discussed are not installed on a single computer. Instead, they are split between two computers that work together to create a complete Reporting Services system. One computer runs the SQL Server database engine and hosts the Report Catalog databases. This is the database server. The other computer runs the Reporting Services Windows service. This is the report server.

Figure 2-3 shows a distributed installation. Note that this figure shows the servers and the Report Designer workstations. It does not show computers used for viewing reports.

The distributed installation has advantages when it comes to scalability. Because the workload of the server applications—SQL Server and the Reporting Services Windows service—is divided between two servers, this installation can serve reports to a larger number of simultaneous users. The disadvantage of this type of installation is that it is more complex to install and administer. However, if you need a high-volume solution, it is certainly worth the effort to obtain one that will provide satisfactory response times under a heavy workload.

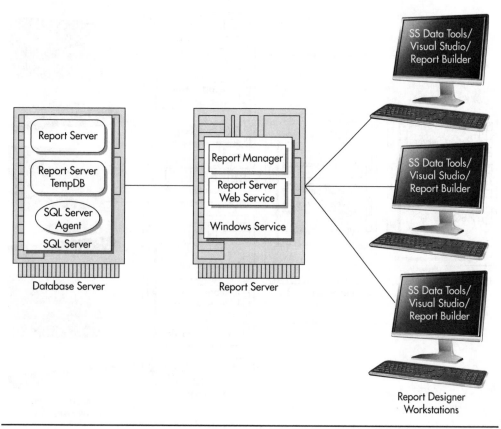

Figure 2-3   *A distributed installation of Reporting Services*

The Scale-Out Installation

The scale-out installation is a specialized form of the distributed installation, as shown in Figure 2-4. In a scale-out installation, a single database server interacts with several report servers. Each of the report servers uses the same Report Catalog databases for its information. By using additional report servers, we can handle even more simultaneous users with the scale-out installation than we could with the distributed installation.

Again, note that Figure 2-4 shows only the servers and the Report Designer workstations. It does not show computers used for viewing reports.

When report designers create reports, they can deploy them to any of the report servers. No matter which server is used, the reports will end up in the single Report Server database. Once the reports are in the Report Server database, they can be delivered by any of the report servers. In addition, because all of the information about

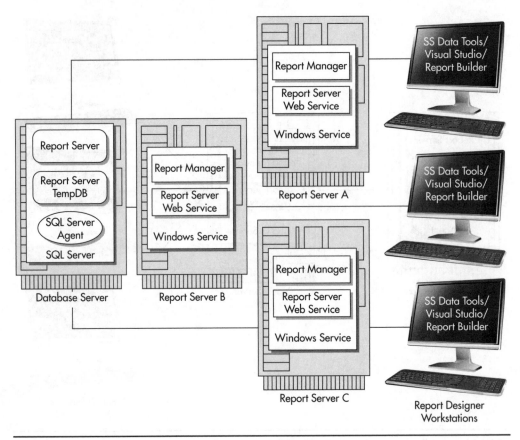

Figure 2-4 *A scale-out installation of Reporting Services*

the Report Manager is stored in the Report Server database, any changes to the Report Manager configuration made on one server will take effect on all the servers.

For example, suppose an administrator uses the Report Manager website to access the Reporting Services through Report Server A. The administrator creates a new folder called Sales Forecasts 2012, sets the security so the sales staff can access this folder, and places the Sales Forecast report in the folder. Immediately after the administrator is finished, a salesperson brings up Report Manager through Report Server C. The salesperson can browse the contents of the Sales Forecasts 2012 folder and will be able to run the Sales Forecast report.

As with the distributed installation, the scale-out installation provides a way to handle a large number of simultaneous requests for reports. Even though the scale-out installation uses a number of servers to deliver reports, it allows the Reporting Services to be administered without duplication of effort. The scale-out installation may take additional effort to get up and running, but once it is ready to go, it provides an efficient means of serving a large number of users.

SharePoint Integrated Mode Installation

For all of the types of Reporting Services installations previously mentioned, the Report Manager user interface, provided by Reporting Services itself, facilitates the interaction of users with the reports. It is also possible to install Reporting Services so that a SharePoint server provides the interface for interaction with the reports. This is known as Reporting Services SharePoint Integrated mode.

When operating in SharePoint Integrated mode, reports are stored as documents on a SharePoint Server. This allows you to manage reports in the same way you would manage Word documents and Excel spreadsheets. Many of the SharePoint features available for document management, such as searching and version control, can be applied to Reporting Services reports. In addition, existing SharePoint security can be applied to reports rather than requiring the creation of a second security structure in Report Manager.

In SharePoint Integrated mode, reports are executed and managed through the SharePoint Web Application. Reporting Services is configured through the SharePoint Central Administration Web Application. A report's RDL definition is stored in the SQL Server Reporting Services (SSRS) Service database. Communication between SharePoint and the SSRS Service database is handled by the Reporting Services Add-in and the SQL Server Reporting Services Shared Service Instance.

The architecture of a Reporting Services SharePoint Integrated mode installation is shown in Figure 2-5.

Installation Requirements

In this section, we itemize the software requirements for each of the installation types just discussed. Before we get to that, however, let's take a look at the hardware requirements for Reporting Services.

Hardware Requirements

The first thing to keep in mind when considering what computer hardware to use for Reporting Services is this: bigger and faster is better. With Reporting Services, we are dealing with a server application that will be handling requests from a number of users at the same time. In most installations, the Reporting Services Windows service will be sharing processor time and computer memory with the SQL Server database engine. We need to have enough server power so both of these systems can happily coexist.

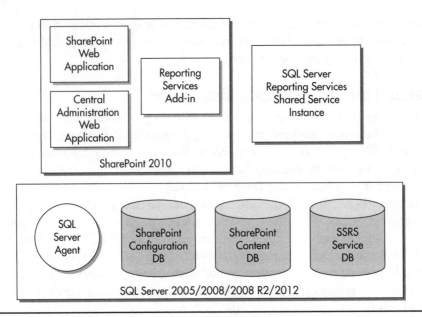

Figure 2-5   *A Reporting Services SharePoint Integrated mode installation*

Processor   Microsoft's stated minimum processor is a 1 gigahertz (GHz) Pentium III–compatible processor. You should install Reporting Services on this type of computer only if you are a patient person. A more realistic low end is probably a Pentium Dual-core at 1.6 GHz. This is true even for the report author installation. SQL Server Data Tools and Visual Studio demand a fair amount of horsepower to keep them from being sluggish.

Computer Memory   Microsoft's minimum requirement for computer memory is 512 megabytes (MB). This is, indeed, a bare minimum. If you are running the Reporting Services Windows service on the same server with SQL Server, that minimum should probably go up to 2GB. Again, these are the absolute minimums—4GB or more is a much better place to start.

Disk Space   A server installation of Reporting Services requires a minimum of 120MB of disk space. This does not include the space required for SQL Server 2012. Consult the Microsoft website for information on the disk space requirements for these items.

A report author installation requires a minimum of 1.1GB of disk space. Plan on using an additional 145MB if you are downloading and installing the sample reports.

Taken all together, you are going to need a minimum of 1.3GB of disk space for a full installation of Reporting Services.

Remember, these requirements are minimums. Also, keep in mind that they do not include the space required for reports to be deployed to the server or project files created by the Report Designer. A Reporting Services installation is not useful if there is no room for reports.

Software Requirements

SQL Server 2012 Reporting Services will run on the following operating systems:

- ▶ Windows 7 (32-bit or 64-bit)
- ▶ Vista (32-bit or 64-bit)
- ▶ Windows Server 2008 SP2 (32-bit or 64-bit)
- ▶ Windows Server 2008 R2

The following software must be installed and running properly on your computer before you can complete a server installation:

- ▶ Microsoft Windows Installer 4.5 or later
- ▶ Windows PowerShell 2.0
- ▶ Microsoft .NET Framework version 4.0

Microsoft .NET Framework 4.0 will be installed as the first step in the SQL Server 2012 installation process if it is not already present on the target computer.

Other Installation Considerations

You need to keep several other tidbits of information in mind as you plan your Reporting Services installation. Many of these items are listed here.

Distributed Installation and Scale-Out Installation Considerations

If you create a distributed installation, the report server and the database server must be in the same domain or in domains that have a trust relationship. If you create a scale-out installation, all the report servers and the database server must be in the same domain or in domains that have a trust relationship.

SharePoint Integrated Mode Considerations

Of course, for a SharePoint Integrated mode installation, you must have an instance of SharePoint running on the server where you will be installing Reporting Services. The following versions of SharePoint are supported:

- ▶ SharePoint Foundation 2010

- ▶ SharePoint Server 2010

- ▶ Windows SharePoint Services 3.0

- ▶ Office SharePoint Server 2007

Note that SharePoint 2010 requires Windows Server 2008 SP2 or Windows Server 2008 R2, and is only available as a 64-bit install.

Database Server Considerations

The following are a couple of things to keep in mind as you are determining which server will host the Reporting Services databases:

- ▶ The Report Server and Report Server Temp DB databases must be hosted by SQL Server 2005, SQL Server 2008, SQL Server 2008 R2, or SQL Server 2012. They cannot be hosted by an earlier version of SQL Server.

- ▶ If you do not want to use the default name for the Reporting Services database (ReportServer), you can specify a different name. The database name you specify must be 117 characters or fewer.

E-mail (SMTP) Server

If you are going to allow users to subscribe to reports and have them e-mailed, you need to specify the address of a Simple Mail Transfer Protocol (SMTP) server using the Reporting Services Configuration Manager. *SMTP* is the standard for exchanging e-mail across the Internet. You need to specify the address of an e-mail server that will accept e-mail messages from the report server and send them to the appropriate recipients.

In many cases, the address of your e-mail server is the same as the portion of your e-mail address that comes after the @ sign, prefaced by www. For example, if your e-mail address is MyEmail@Galactic.com, your e-mail server's address is probably either www.Galactic.com or smtp.Galactic.com. Be sure to verify the address of your e-mail server with your e-mail administrator. Also, make sure this e-mail server supports the SMTP protocol and that it will accept and forward mail originating from other servers on your network.

Encrypting Reporting Services Information

One of the options you may specify in the Reporting Services Configuration Manager is a requirement to use a Secure Sockets Layer (SSL) connection when accessing the Report Manager website and the Report Server web service. When an SSL connection is used, all of the data transmitted across the network is encrypted so it cannot be intercepted and read by anyone else. This is important if your reports contain sensitive personal or financial information.

To use SSL on a server, the server must have a server certificate. Server certificates are purchased from a certificate authority and installed on your server. You can find information on certificate authorities on the Internet.

Each server certificate is associated with a specific Uniform Resource Locator (URL). To use SSL with the Report Manager website and the Report Server web service, your server certificate must be associated with the URL that corresponds to the default website on the server. If www.MyRSServer.com takes you to the default website on your server, then the server certificate must be associated with www.MyRSServer.com. If you plan to require an SSL connection, you should obtain and install the appropriate server certificate prior to installing Reporting Services.

When you require the use of an SSL connection to access the Report Manager website and the Report Server web service, your users must specify a slightly different URL to access these locations. For instance, if the users would normally use http://www.MyRSServer.com/Reports to get to the Report Manager website, they will now have to use https://www.MyRSServer.com/Reports. The https in place of the http creates the SSL connection.

Login Accounts

The login account you are logged in as when you run the setup program must have administrative rights on the computer where the installation is being done. If you are doing a distributed or scale-out installation, the login account must have administrative rights on the computer that will be the report server, and also have SQL Server administrator rights on the database server.

The login account you are logged in as must also have system administration rights in the SQL Server installation that will contain the Report Catalog. The setup program uses this login to access SQL Server and create the items necessary for the Report Catalog. You may specify a different login, either a SQL login or a Windows login, for the Report Server to use when accessing the Report Catalog after the installation is complete.

You will be asked to specify two other login accounts during the Reporting Services installation and in the Reporting Services Configuration Manager. Make your choices ahead of time and track down any passwords you may need before you begin the installation process.

The Reporting Services Windows Service Account During the installation process, you will be asked to specify the login account used by the Reporting Services Windows service. If you are installing the SQL Server database engine or other SQL components as part of the same installation, you will be asked for login accounts for each of the necessary Windows services at the same time. You can choose from the following types of accounts:

▶ **The built-in LocalSystem account** The LocalSystem account has access to almost all resources on the local computer and may or may not have access to resources on other computers in the network. You do not need to supply a password if you use this account.

▶ **The built-in NetworkService account** This account exists on Windows server operating systems for running services. The difference between this account and the LocalService account is that this account has rights on the network and can access other servers on the network. You do not need to supply a password if you use this account.

▶ **The built-in LocalService account** This account exists on Windows server operating systems for running services. The difference between this account and the NetworkService account is that this account does not have rights on the network and cannot access other servers on the network. You do not need to supply a password if you use this account.

▶ **A domain user account** This is a regular user account that exists in the domain in which this server resides. You will need to know both the login name and the password.

Microsoft recommends a dedicated domain account be used as the login account for the Report Server service. By default, the installation program will create a domain account called ReportServer as the login account for this service.

The Report Server Database Credentials In the Reporting Services Configuration Manager, you can specify the Report Server database credentials. These credentials are used by the Reporting Services Windows service to log in to SQL Server and to access the Report Server database, the Report Server Temp DB database, and the SQL Server Agent. As noted earlier, this login account is used after the installation is complete. It is not used to access SQL Server during the installation process.

You have two options:

▶ The login account used by the Reporting Services Windows service

▶ A SQL Server login

You need to work with the database administrator of your SQL Server to determine which of these options to use.

NOTE

If a SQL Server login is used, it is recommended that you not use the sa login. The SQL Server login must be added to the RSExecRole role in the ReportServer, ReportServerTempDB, master, and msdb databases. This will be done automatically by the Reporting Services Configuration Manager.

Running the SQL Server Installation Program

You need to run the SQL Server installation program under a login that is a member of the local system administrators group. In addition, your login needs to have administrator permissions in SQL Server so you can perform the following tasks:

▶ Create SQL logins

▶ Create SQL roles

▶ Create databases

▶ Assign roles to logins

The Installation Process

Now that you have worked through all of the preparation, it is finally time to install Reporting Services. This is done through the SQL Server 2012 setup program, either at the time SQL Server 2012 is originally installed or later, as an addition to an existing SQL Server installation. In this section, you will see the portions of the SQL Server 2012 installation dealing with Reporting Services and learn about the option selections necessary for the various types of Reporting Services installations discussed earlier in this chapter. You will also look at the Reporting Services configuration, which must be done after the installation is complete. This additional configuration is done using the Reporting Services Configuration Manager.

The SQL Server 2012 Installation

If you are doing a full, server, distributed, or scale-out installation of Reporting Services, the setup program must be run on the computer that will serve as the report server. This is the computer that will be running the Reporting Services Windows service and hosting Report Manager and the Report Server web service. If you are doing a report author installation, the setup program must be run on the computer you will be using for report authoring.

If you are doing a distributed or scale-out installation, you do not need to run the Reporting Services setup program on the database server. You will, of course, need to install SQL Server 2005, SQL Server 2008, SQL Server 2008 R2, or SQL Server 2012 on the database server prior to doing the Reporting Services installation, but you do not need to run the Reporting Services portion of the setup program on that computer. The Reporting Services setup program on the report server will access the database server and take care of all the necessary installation and setup remotely.

Begin the installation by inserting the SQL Server 2012 installation CD into the CD or DVD drive. In most cases, the autorun process should take you to the Start screen. If this does not happen automatically, double-click the setup.exe file in the Servers folder on the installation CD. Use the Planning page to ensure you have all the necessary hardware and software prerequisites.

When you are ready to begin the actual installation, select "New SQL Server stand-alone installation or add features to an existing installation" from the Installation page as shown in Figure 2-6.

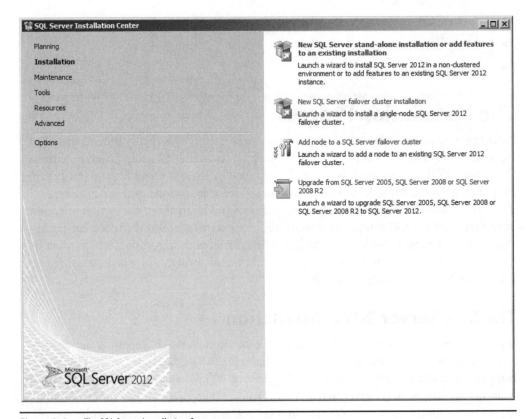

Figure 2-6   *The SQL Server Installation Center screen*

Preliminaries

The setup process begins with the usual preliminaries. You must read and accept the SQL Server licensing agreement. The setup will also double-check to make sure all the prerequisite software is installed and properly configured. Of course, you also need to enter the product key.

The Feature Selection Page

Once all this groundwork is complete, you get to the good stuff. On the Feature Selection page of the Installation Wizard, you can determine which components of SQL Server to install. The following sections show which items to select on the Feature Selection page for each type of installation.

Reporting Services Full Installation   On the Feature Selection page, select the following for a Reporting Services full installation:

▶ Database Engine Services, if you do not already have an appropriate version of the SQL Server database engine available to host the Report Catalog

▶ Reporting Services - Native

▶ SQL Server Data Tools

▶ Client Tools Connectivity

▶ Documentation Components

▶ Management Tools - Basic and Management Tools - Complete

The Feature Selection page should appear as shown in Figure 2-7. Click Next to continue with the SQL Server Installation Wizard.

NOTE

You may want to select other items on the Feature Selection page if you are installing other SQL Server components as part of this process. The items documented here represent the minimum for a Reporting Services full installation.

Reporting Services Server Installation   On the Feature Selection page, select the following for a Reporting Services server installation:

▶ Database Engine Services, if you do not already have an appropriate version of the SQL Server database engine available to host the Report Catalog

▶ Reporting Services - Native

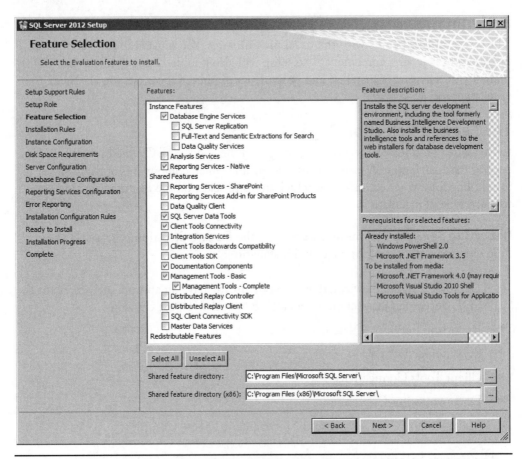

Figure 2-7   *The Feature Selection page of the SQL Server 2012 Installation Wizard for a Reporting Services full installation*

▶   Client Tools Connectivity

▶   Management Tools - Basic and Management Tools - Complete

The Feature Selection page should appear as shown in Figure 2-8. Click Next to continue with the SQL Server Installation Wizard.

NOTE

You may want to select other items on the Feature Selection page if you are installing other SQL Server components as part of this process. The items documented here represent the minimum for a Reporting Services server installation.

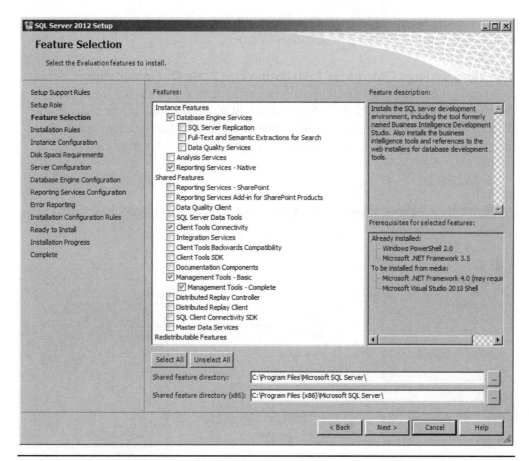

Figure 2-8   *The Feature Selection page of the SQL Server 2012 Installation Wizard for a Reporting Services server installation*

Reporting Services Report Author Installation   On the Feature Selection page, select the following for a Reporting Services report author installation:

▶ SQL Server Data Tools

▶ Client Tools Connectivity

▶ Documentation Components

▶ Management Tools - Basic and Management Tools - Complete

The Feature Selection page should appear as shown in Figure 2-9. Click Next to continue with the SQL Server Installation Wizard.

Reporting Services Distributed Installation and Scale-Out Installation   Before completing the Reporting Services portion of a distributed or scale-out installation, you must have SQL Server 2005, SQL Server 2008, SQL Server 2008 R2, or SQL Server 2012 running on the computer that will serve as the database server. Remember, either the Business Intelligence Edition or the Enterprise Edition of Reporting Services

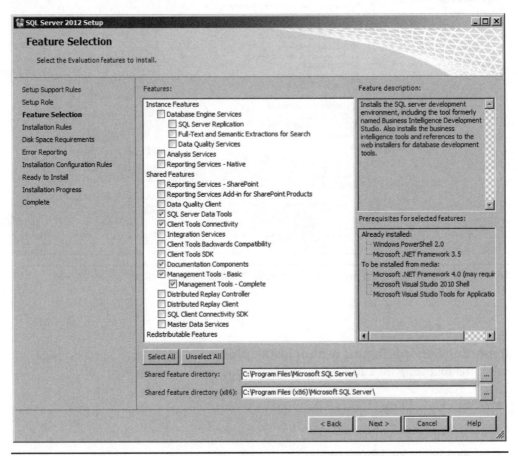

Figure 2-9   *The Feature Selection page of the SQL Server 2012 Installation Wizard for a Reporting Services report author installation*

is required for a scale-out installation. On the Feature Selection page, select the following for a Reporting Services distributed installation or a scale-out installation:

▶ Reporting Services - Native

▶ Client Tools Connectivity

▶ Management Tools - Basic and Management Tools - Complete

The Feature Selection page should appear as shown in Figure 2-10. Click Next. The wizard will check the installation rules to ensure everything is valid. Once this is complete, click Next to continue with the SQL Server Installation Wizard.

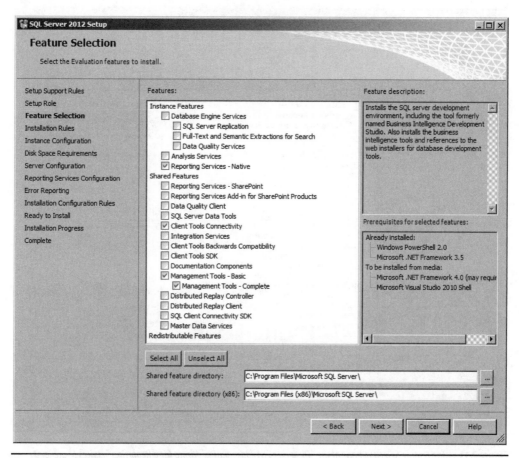

Figure 2-10   *The Feature Selection page of the SQL Server 2012 Installation Wizard for a Reporting Services distributed installation or scale-out installation*

Reporting Services SharePoint Integrated Mode Installation   On the Feature Selection page, select the following for a Reporting Services SharePoint Integrated mode installation:

▶   Reporting Services - SharePoint

▶   Reporting Services Add-in for SharePoint Products

The Feature Selection page should appear as shown in Figure 2-11. Click Next to continue with the SQL Server Installation Wizard.

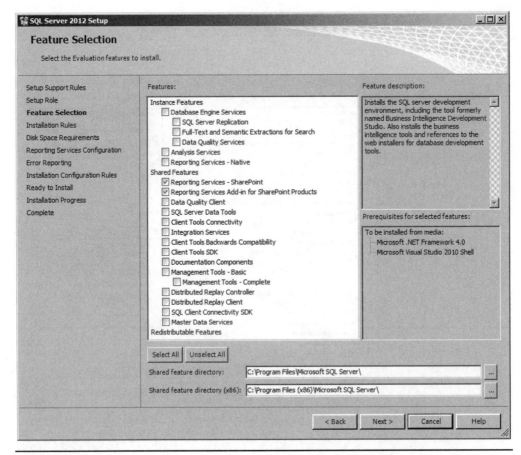

Figure 2-11   *The Feature Selection page of the SQL Server 2012 Installation Wizard for a Reporting Services SharePoint integrated mode installation*

Instance Configuration Page

The Instance Configuration page, shown in Figure 2-12, enables you to choose the name assigned to this instance of the components you are installing, including Reporting Services. The default instance will use Reports as the name of the Report Manager website and ReportServer as the name of the Reporting Services web service. If you specify an instance name, by default an underscore (_) followed by the instance name is appended to the end of the website and web service name. For example, if you specify an instance name of "RS2012," the website will be "Reports_RS2012" and the web service will be "ReportServer_RS2012."

You can see all the instances of SQL Server components currently installed on this computer in the grid at the bottom of the Instance Configuration page. Of course, your new instance name cannot be exactly the same name as any existing instance. Unless you have a reason to change the instance name from the default, such as multiple Reporting Services instances on a single server, it is probably a good idea to stick with the default.

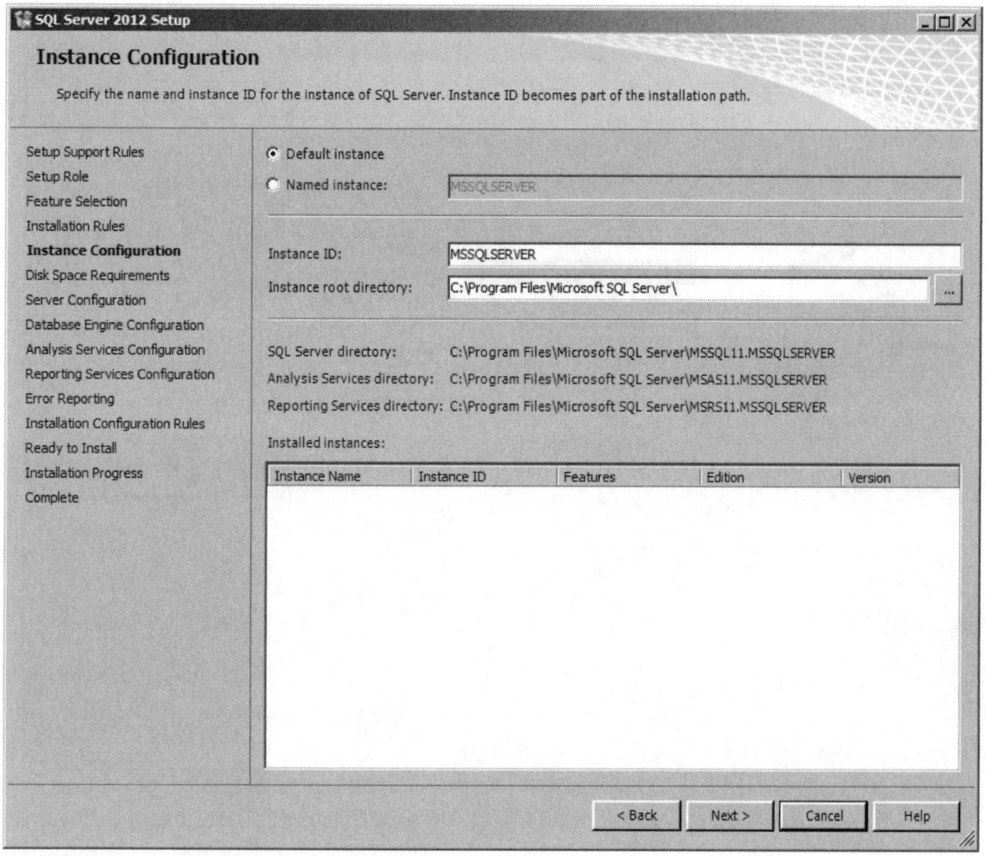

Figure 2-12 *The Instance Configuration page*

After you have entered the instance name, or if you have decided to use the default instance, click Next. The wizard will check the disk space requirements for your selected configuration. Once this is complete, click Next to continue with the SQL Server Installation Wizard.

Server Configuration Page

The Server Configuration page is shown in Figure 2-13. This page enables you to specify the Windows credentials the Reporting Services Windows service is to run under. The content of this screen will vary, depending on the SQL Server 2012 components you chose to install. The options available here were discussed previously in the "The Reporting Services Windows Service Account" section of this chapter. This page also enables you to select the startup type of each of the services being installed. If SQL Server was included as part of this install, SQL Server Agent should be changed to the Automatic startup type.

After you make your selections on this page, click Next to continue with the SQL Server Installation Wizard.

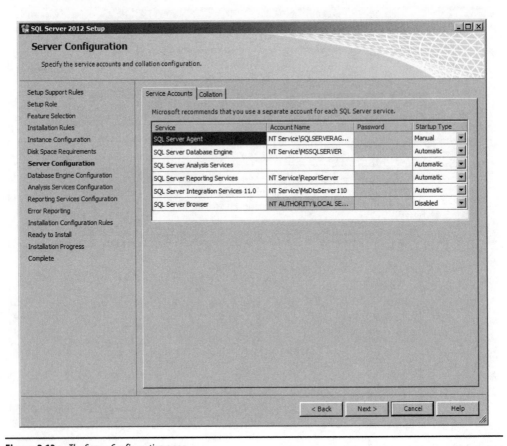

Figure 2-13   *The Server Configuration page*

The Reporting Services Configuration Page

After leaving the Server Configuration page, you may encounter several pages that deal with the setup of the SQL Server database engine and other SQL Server components, depending on the items you selected on the Feature Selection page. Make the appropriate choices for your SQL Server installation. Click Next to move from one page to the next.

Eventually, you will come to the Reporting Services Configuration page, shown in Figure 2-14. If SQL Server was selected on the Feature Selection page and you are installing the default instance, this page provides you with two choices for configuring your Reporting Services installation:

▶ Install and configure

▶ Install only

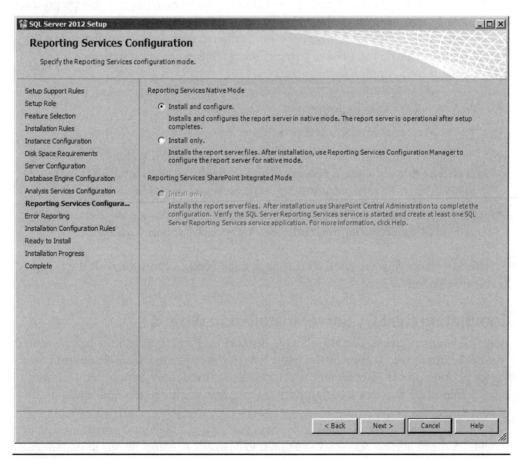

Figure 2-14 *The Reporting Services Configuration page*

If SQL Server was not selected on the Feature Selection page, or if you are not installing the default instance, you will not have a choice; the Install only option will be selected for you.

NOTE

If you are installing Reporting Services in SharePoint Integrated mode, the SharePoint Install only option will be selected for you. Configuration must be completed using SharePoint Central Administration.

If the Install only option is chosen, your new Reporting Services installation will need to be configured using the Reporting Services Configuration Manager utility program. You will learn more about this utility program in the upcoming section, "The Reporting Services Configuration Manager."

This may seem like a rather limiting set of choices, sort of an all-or-nothing proposition, but it is not. For the majority of Reporting Services installations, the Native mode default configuration will do just fine. Only rarely, for distributed or scale-out installations, or for nondefault instances, do you need to change the default configuration settings.

The default configuration settings are:

▶ Web service name is ReportServer.

▶ Report Manager website is Reports.

▶ The Report Catalog is hosted by the default instance of SQL Server 2012 being created by this installation process. (This is why the choice Install and configure is disabled when you are not installing SQL Server at the same time.)

▶ The login account used by the Reporting Services Windows service is used as the credentials for accessing the report server database (Report Catalog).

After you make your selection on this page, click Next to continue with the SQL Server Installation Wizard.

Completing the SQL Server Installation Wizard

After a few more screens, the SQL Server Installation Wizard has all the information it requires to install the components of SQL Server you requested. Click Install to finish the installation process. Remember, if you chose the Install only option, you will need to run the Reporting Services Configuration Manager to complete the final configuration of Reporting Services.

Even if you did use the Reporting Services Native mode default configuration, you should run the Reporting Services Configuration Manager to complete one important task.

You should always create a backup of the Reporting Services encryption key as the final step of a Reporting Services installation. See the later section, "Backing Up the Encryption Key," for instructions on completing this task.

The Reporting Services Configuration Manager

As you learned in the previous section of this chapter, the SQL Server Installation Wizard is geared completely toward installing Reporting Services with the default configuration. If you want to deviate from the default configuration, you must use another tool to make these nondefault configuration settings. When installing Reporting Services in Native mode, that tool is the Reporting Services Configuration Manager.

The Reporting Services Configuration Manager is found on the Start menu under All Programs | Microsoft SQL Server 2012 | Configuration Tools | Reporting Services Configuration Manager. When this utility starts up, it asks for the name of a server to connect to, as shown in Figure 2-15. Once you enter a server name and click Find, the program finds all instances of Reporting Services 2012 running on that server and displays them in the Report Server Instance drop-down box, as shown in Figure 2-16. You need to select an instance and click Connect to enter the utility program with the configuration information for that Reporting Services instance loaded.

The Reporting Services Configuration Manager contains a number of pages, each geared toward configuring a different aspect of Reporting Services. Let's take a look at each of these pages and learn what they are used for.

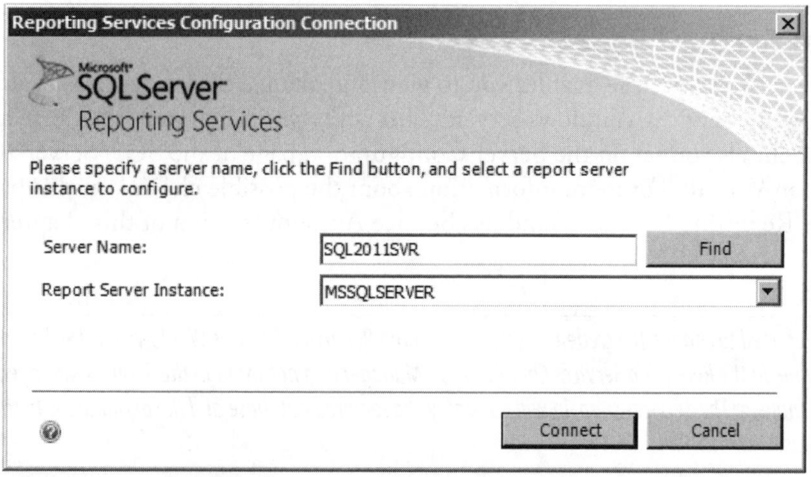

Figure 2-15 *The Reporting Services Configuration Connection dialog box*

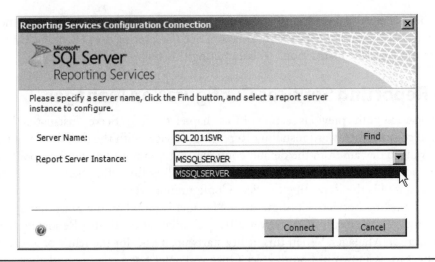

Figure 2-16 *Selecting an instance in the Reporting Services Configuration Connection dialog box*

Server Status Page

The Report Server Status page displays status information about the Report Server instance you selected, as shown in Figure 2-17. There is no configuration information to change on this page. This page does provide buttons to start or stop this instance of Reporting Services.

Service Account Page

The Service Account page enables you to view and change the credentials used to run the Reporting Services Windows service. This is shown in Figure 2-18. These are the same credentials you set on the Server Configuration page of the SQL Server 2012 Installation Wizard. For more information about the possible choices on this page, see the "The Reporting Services Windows Service Account" section of this chapter.

NOTE

If you ever need to change the credentials used to run the Reporting Services Windows service, be sure to make that change in the Reporting Services Configuration Manager and not through the Services Management Console snap-in. The Services snap-in will not apply the required database and file permissions to the new credentials.

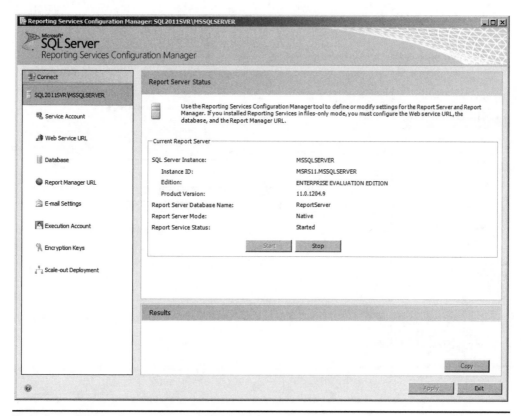

Figure 2-17   *The Report Server Status page of the Reporting Services Configuration Manager*

Web Service URL Page

The Web Service URL page enables you to view and change the URL used by the Reporting Services web service. This page is shown in Figure 2-19. As mentioned previously, if this is the default instance of Reporting Services on the server, the default name for this virtual directory is ReportServer.

The Web Service URL page also enables you to select the Internet Protocol (IP) address and Transmission Control Protocol (TCP) port used by the Report Server web service. You need to make sure the Report Server web service does not conflict with any other TCP/IP addresses on the network. The IP address setting will default to all IP addresses assigned to the computer, and the TCP port will default to port 80 for Hypertext Transfer Protocol (HTTP) and port 443 for Hypertext Transfer Protocol Secure (HTTPS).

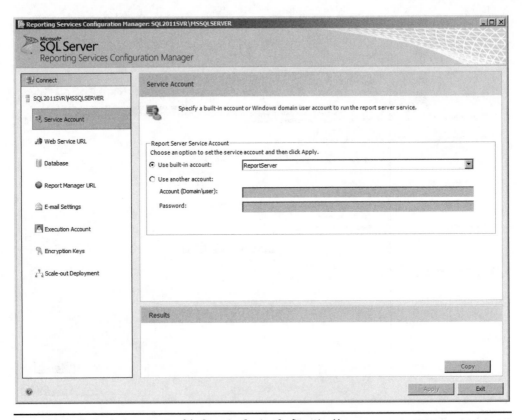

Figure 2-18 *The Service Account page of the Reporting Services Configuration Manager*

NOTE

Internet Information Services (IIS) also defaults to using ports 80 and 443. If you are running IIS and Reporting Services on the computer, make sure to select ports that do not conflict.

Finally, the Web Service URL page enables you to select whether or not you want to require an SSL connection when retrieving data from the Report Server web service. If you have any questions on this option, refer to the section "Encrypting Reporting Services Information." Because a server certificate is required for SSL, this option is disabled if you do not have a server certificate.

Report Server Database Page

The Report Server Database page, shown in Figure 2-20, enables you to select the set of databases that will serve as the Report Catalog. You can select the database server

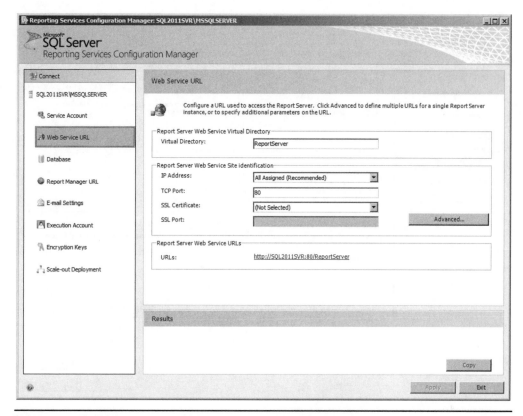

Figure 2-19   *The Web Service URL page of the Reporting Services Configuration Manager*

name, the name of the database on that server, and the credentials used to connect to that server. If you are performing a distributed or scale-out installation, this is where you will select the remote database server for hosting the Report Catalog. Remember, the database server hosting the Report Catalog must be SQL Server 2005, SQL Server 2008, SQL Server 2008 R2, or SQL Server 2012.

Click the Change Database button to change the database server or database to be used by the report server. You will have the option of creating a new Report Server database or choosing an existing Report Server database. In either case, you will need to complete the following steps:

▶   Specify the database server and the credentials to be used to complete the current operation. These credentials are not necessarily the same as those that will be used by the Reporting Services Windows service to connect to the database.

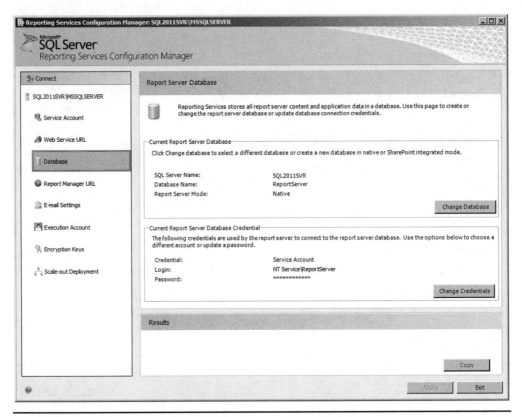

Figure 2-20 *The Report Server Database page of the Reporting Services Configuration Manager*

▶ Provide the name of the database.

▶ Specify the credentials used by the Reporting Services Windows service to connect to the database.

Click the Change Credentials button to change only the credentials used by the Reporting Services Windows service to connect to the database.

When you click the Apply button, the following tasks are performed:

▶ **Grant access rights to report server accounts** This task will set the appropriate rights in the databases for the credentials specified to be used by the Reporting Services Windows service.

▶ **Set the connection information** This task will set this Reporting Services instance to use the specified Report Catalog.

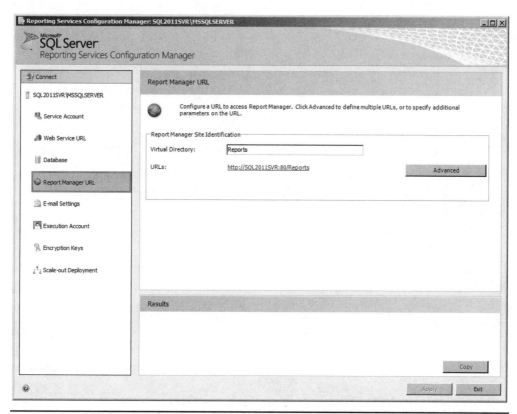

Figure 2-21   *The Report Manager URL page of the Reporting Services Configuration Manager*

Report Manager URL Page

The Report Manager URL page enables you to view and change the name of the virtual directory used by the Report Manager website. This page is shown in Figure 2-21. As mentioned previously, if this is the default instance of Reporting Services on the server, the default name for this virtual directory is Reports. Clicking the URL shown on this page will open Internet Explorer and take you to the Report Manager website.

E-mail Settings Page

The E-mail Settings page, shown in Figure 2-22, enables you to identify an SMTP server that can be used by Reporting Services. The SMTP server is used for delivering report subscriptions via e-mail. If an SMTP server is not specified, the e-mail delivery option will be unavailable when creating report subscriptions.

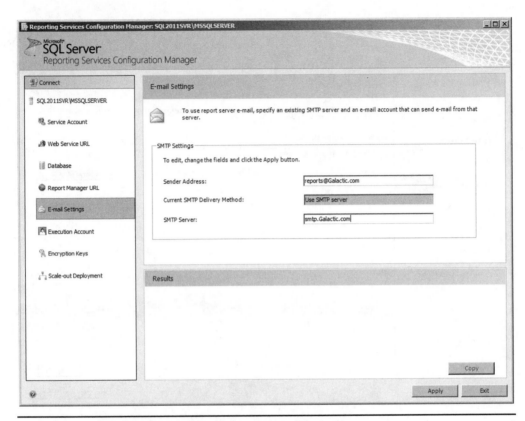

Figure 2-22   *The E-mail Settings page of the Reporting Services Configuration Manager*

Enter the name of an SMTP server that will accept mail from Reporting Services. You can also enter an e-mail address for Sender Address. This e-mail address will appear in the From line of any report subscriptions e-mailed from Reporting Services.

Execution Account Page

The Execution Account page, shown in Figure 2-23, enables you to specify a set of login credentials to be used by Reporting Services when it needs to access a file or other resource. For example, suppose you have a report that uses an Access database as its data source. When it is time for the report to query the data from the Access database, the Execution Account credentials are used to gain rights to the Access MDB file.

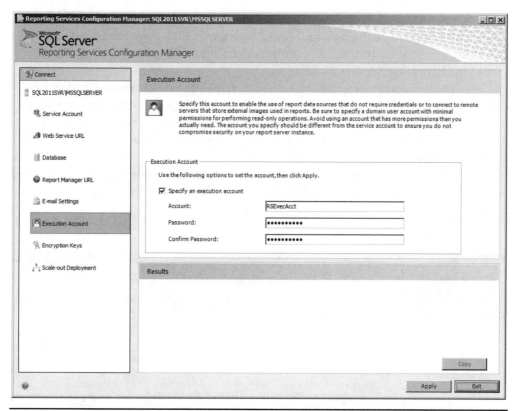

Figure 2-23   *The Execution Account page of the Reporting Services Configuration Manager*

The Execution Account is also used to gain access to image files, which are pulled from the file system for use in your report.

Using the Execution Account page, you can specify the login account and the password to be used. Make sure this account has the appropriate rights to access any directories that might contain data sources or images. However, this account should have limited rights throughout the network to prevent it from being used in a malicious manner. If you do not anticipate the need to allow access to data sources or image files in the file system, you do not need to specify an execution account.

Encryption Keys Page

As you have seen, Reporting Services uses various sets of credentials for its operation. Whenever a login account and a password are specified, these credentials are stored as encrypted text. In addition, any credentials you specify in a report or shared data source are encrypted. To encrypt and, more importantly, to decrypt these credentials, Reporting Services needs to use an encryption key. This encryption key is created as part of the Reporting Services installation.

If this encryption key ever becomes corrupt, none of these encrypted credentials can be decrypted. The credentials become useless, and Reporting Services becomes inoperable. To remedy this situation, you need to have a backup of the encryption key, which can be restored over the top of the corrupt key. This is the purpose of the Encryption Keys page, shown in Figure 2-24.

Use the Backup button to create a backup copy of the encryption key. Use the Restore button to restore a previously created encryption-key backup. Use the Change button to

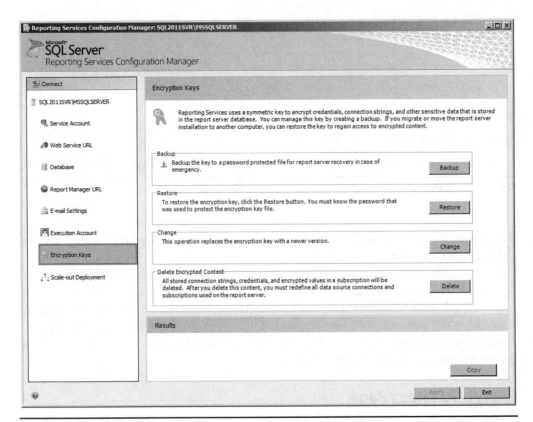

Figure 2-24 *The Encryption Keys page of the Reporting Services Configuration Manager*

create a new encryption key for Reporting Services. This should be done if your current encryption key becomes compromised. The current encryption key must be operable (that is, not corrupt) to use the Change function.

If your Reporting Services encryption key does become corrupt and you do not have a current backup, use the Delete button. This will remove all the encrypted credentials and create a new encryption key. After using this option, you will need to use the Report Server Database page of the Reporting Services Configuration Manager to reenter the database credentials. When the Delete button is used, Reporting Services will be inoperable until you enter a new set of database credentials. You will also need to reenter the data source credentials for each report and shared data source deployed on the server.

Backing Up the Encryption Key   To create a backup copy of the encryption key, click the Backup button. Enter a path and a filename for storing the key, and then enter a password to protect the encryption key. You may want to put the key backup on removable media so it can be stored in a safe place. Make sure you keep the password in a safe place as well. The password helps protect your encryption key backup and is required by the restore process.

NOTE

In previous versions of Reporting Services, the Reporting Services encryption keys had a bad habit of becoming corrupted. If the key does become corrupted, Reporting Services ceases to function and all the encrypted credential information on the server must be reentered. Therefore, it is important to maintain a current backup of your Reporting Services encryption key in a secure location.

Scale-out Deployment Page

The Scale-out Deployment page, shown in Figure 2-25, is used to add servers to a scale-out installation of Reporting Services. Each server added to the scale-out list uses the same encryption key. In this way, encrypted data stored in the common Report Catalog can be decrypted by any report server in the scale-out installation.

Menu Bar

The Connect button, at the top of the page's menu area, lets you connect to a different server and then select a Reporting Services instance on that server.

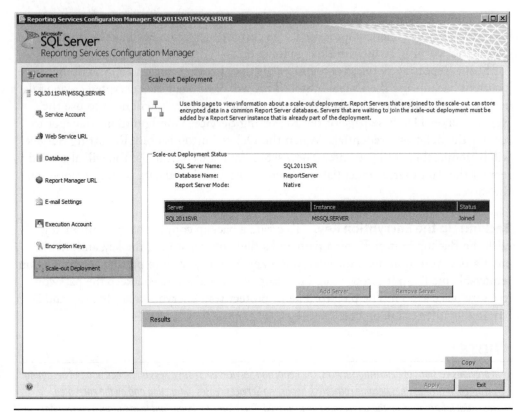

Figure 2-25   *The Scale-out Deployment page of the Reporting Services Configuration Manager*

Completing a Reporting Services SharePoint Integrated Mode Installation

In order to complete an installation of Reporting Services in SharePoint Integrated mode, you must configure SharePoint to work with Reporting Services. This is done through the SharePoint Central Administration site. This is found on the Start menu under All Programs | Microsoft SharePoint 2010 Products | SharePoint 2010 Central Administration. The main page of the SharePoint Central Administration site is shown in Figure 2-26.

Creating a Reporting Services Service Application

In order to use Reporting Services in SharePoint Integrated mode, you must create a Reporting Services service application. This is done by selecting the Manage service

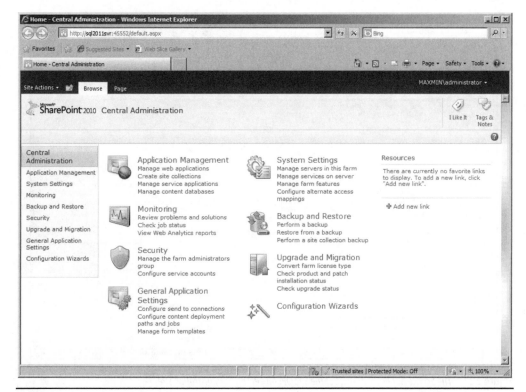

Figure 2-26   *The main page of the SharePoint Central Administration site*

applications link under the Application Management heading on the main page of the SharePoint Central Administration site.

This link takes you to the Service Applications page shown in Figure 2-27. On this page, click the New button in the upper-left part of the page. This will open a drop-down list showing types of items you can create. Select SQL Server Reporting Services Service Application as shown in Figure 2-28.

You will see a dialog box that enables you to enter the information necessary to create a Reporting Services Service Application. Enter a name for the service application. You can select an existing application pool to use for this new service application, but it is best to create a new one to isolate Reporting Services from other web services.

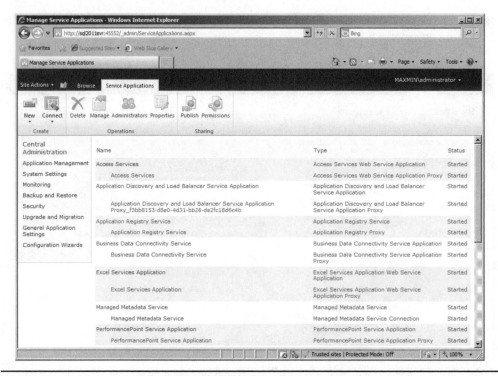

Figure 2-27 *The Service Applications page of the SharePoint Central Administration site*

Figure 2-28 *The New options on the Service Application page*

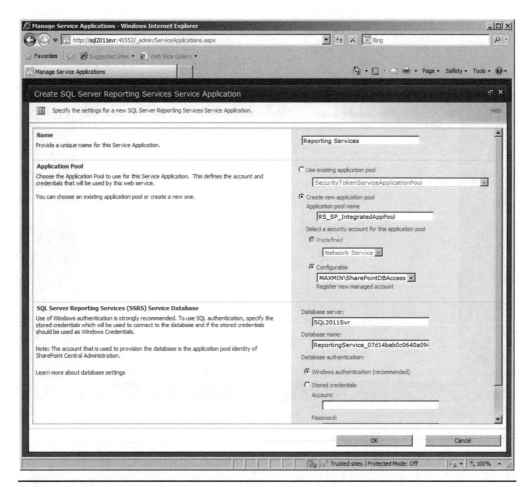

Figure 2-29   *The completed Create SQL Server Reporting Services Service Application dialog box*

The service application must create a database for its own use. You need to specify the instance of SQL Server where this database will be created. You also need to specify the credentials that will be used to connect to that instance of SQL Server. Use of Windows authentication is recommended.

The completed dialog box is shown in Figure 2-29. When you have filled in the required information, click OK to create the service application.

Making the Service Application Part of the Default Application Proxy Group

With the Reporting Services service application created, we must make it a part of the default application proxy group. In the Central Administration menu on the left side

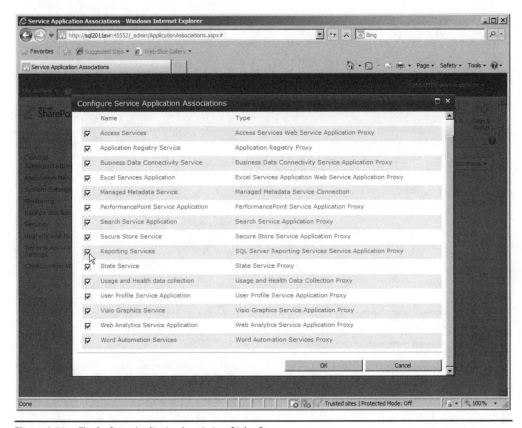

Figure 2-30   *The Configure Application Associations Dialog Box*

of the screen, click Application Management. On the Application Management page, click the Configure service application associations link under Service Applications. On the Service Application Associations page, click the default link under Application Proxy Group.

You will see a dialog box that allows you to select default service application associations. Click to check the box next to Reporting Services. The Configure Service Application Associations dialog box is shown in Figure 2-30. Scroll down, if necessary, and click OK and exit the dialog box.

Starting the Reporting Services Service Application

As your final step, you need to start the Reporting Services Service Application that you just created. In the Central Administration menu on the left side of the screen, click Application Management. On the Application Management page, click the Manage services on server link under Service Applications.

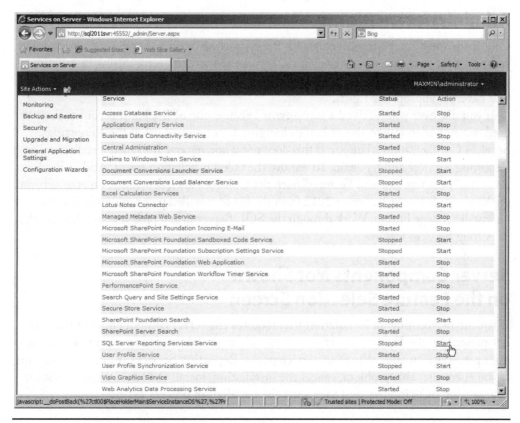

Figure 2-31   *The Start link for the SQL Server Reporting Services Service*

On the Services on Server page, scroll down, if necessary, to find the SQL Server Reporting Services Service. Click the Start link next to the SQL Server Reporting Services Service as shown in Figure 2-31. After a few moments, the page should refresh showing the SQL Server Reporting Services Service as Started.

Your Reporting Services SharePoint Integrated mode installation is now ready to go. We will talk more about managing Reporting Services reports in SharePoint Integrated mode in Chapter 10.

Common Installation Issues

This section lists some of the common problems you may encounter while installing Reporting Services. Suggested solutions are provided to help you resolve these problems.

Administrative Rights

One of the most frequent problems with the Reporting Services setup is not using login accounts that have the appropriate rights. If you encounter an error during installation, refer to the earlier section, "Login Accounts," and make sure you are using login accounts that have the appropriate rights.

If you discover you received a setup error because one of the login accounts you used was not adequate to the task, try changing that account using the Reporting Services Configuration Manager. If this does not work, remove the failed installation of Reporting Services and try again. To remove the failed installation, select "Add or Remove Programs" or "Programs and Features" from the Control Panel, depending on your version of Windows. Select SQL Server 2012 from the list of installed programs and click the Uninstall/Change button. Work through the SQL Server install program and deselect the Reporting Services features.

Server Components Not Shown on the Feature Selection Screen

If you are performing an installation that requires the server components but they are not present on the Feature Selection screen, this is probably an indication that you are not up-to-date on your Windows service packs. Reporting Services is finicky about this. If you encounter this problem, cancel the installation, install the latest service pack for your version of Windows, and then start the installation process again.

Installation Error 2755

You may receive Error 2755 if you are installing Reporting Services using a Terminal Server session. This will occur if you are using a mapped drive to access the setup files. The Windows Installer service that performs the setup operation is running in a different Windows session, so it may not have the same drive mappings. The error occurs because certain files needed by the installer cannot be found.

To remedy this problem, use a Universal Naming Convention (UNC) path to access the setup files, rather than a mapped drive. Alternatively, you may put the installation CD in a drive that is local to the computer on which you are performing the installation or copy the setup files to a drive that is local to that computer.

Reporting Services and IIS on the Same Server

If you are installing the report server on a computer that is already running IIS, care must be taken to ensure that these two services are not using the same TCP/IP port.

Both IIS and the report server will default to using port 80 for HTTP requests and port 443 for HTTPS requests. If this occurs, IIS and the report server will compete to handle traffic on these ports, resulting in neither service working correctly. If this occurs, simply use the Reporting Services Configuration Manager to direct the report server to a different port.

The Repair Utility and Installation Log File

If your installation does not complete successfully, you can try the Repair utility on the Maintenance page of the SQL Server Installation Center. If none of these suggestions solve your installation issues, you may want to consult the installation log files for more information.

The default location for the log files is

```
C:\Program Files\Microsoft SQL Server\110\Setup Bootstrap\Log
```

The log files will be in a folder named for the date and time of the installation.

Spending Some Time in Basic Training

You now have Reporting Services installed and ready to go. As mentioned at the end of Chapter 1, we will take time to ensure that you understand the basics of database architecture and querying before we begin creating reports. Chapter 3 gives you this database basic training. This basic training won't be as tough as Army boot camp, but it will get you ready to attack all those tough data-reporting challenges.

Chapter 3 also introduces you to Galactic Delivery Services (GDS): what it does, how it is structured, and what its data processing systems look like. We use GDS and its business needs for all our sample reports throughout the book.

Part II

Report Authoring

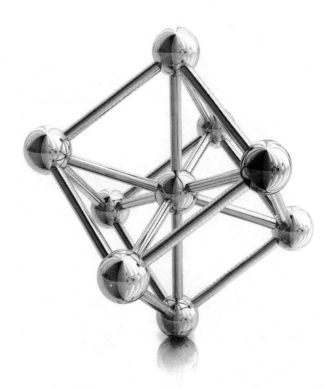

Chapter 3

DB 101: Database Basics

In This Chapter

► **Database Structure**
► **Galactic Delivery Services**
► **Querying Data**
► **On to the Reports**

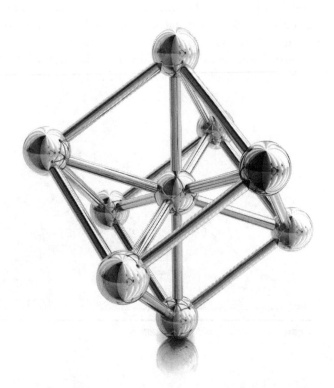

Before you begin creating reports, it is important that you have a good understanding of relational databases. In the first part of this chapter, you will see the tables, rows, and columns that make up relational databases. You will also learn about concepts such as normalization and relationships. These are the characteristics that make a relational database … well, relational.

Once you cover the basics, you are introduced to Galactic Delivery Services (GDS). The business needs of GDS serve as the basis for all the sample reports throughout this book. Even though GDS is a unique company in many respects, you will discover its reporting needs and its uses of Reporting Services are typical of most companies in this galaxy.

For the remainder of the chapter, you will explore the ins and outs of the *SELECT query*, which is what you use to extract data from your data sources for use in your reports. Even though Reporting Services helps you create SELECT queries through a tool called the Query Designer, it is important that you understand how SELECT queries work and how they can be used to obtain the correct data. A report may look absolutely stunning with charts, graphics, special formatting, and snappy colors, but it is completely useless if it contains the wrong data!

Database Structure

Databases are basically giant containers for storing information. They are the electronic crawlspaces and digital attics of the corporate, academic, and governmental worlds. For example, anything that needs to be saved for later use by payroll, inventory management, or the external auditor is placed in a database.

Just like our crawlspaces and attics at home, the information placed in a database needs to be organized and classified. Figure 3-1 shows my attic in its current state. As you can

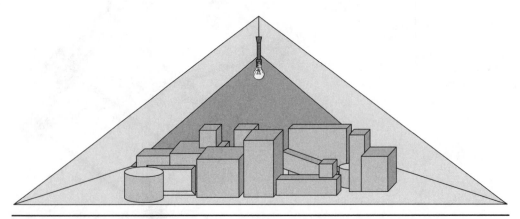

Figure 3-1   *My attic, with no organization*

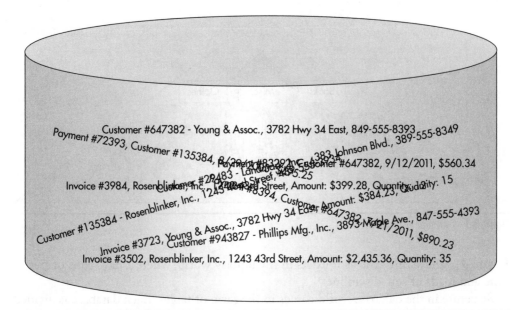

Figure 3-2   *An unorganized database*

see, it is going to be pretty hard to find those old kids' clothes for the thrift store clothing drive! I know they are up there somewhere.

Without some type of order placed on it, all the stuff in our home storage spaces becomes impossible to retrieve when we need it. The same is true in the world of electronic storage, as shown in Figure 3-2. Databases, like attics, need structure. Otherwise, we won't be able to find anything!

Getting Organized

The first step in getting organized is to have a place for everything and to have everything in its place. To achieve this, you need to add structure to the storage space, whether this is a space for box storage, like my attic, or a space for data storage, like a database. To maintain this structure, you also need to have discipline of one sort or another as you add items to the storage space.

Tables, Rows, and Columns

To get my attic organized, I need some shelves, a few labels, and some free time so I can add the much-needed structure to this storage space. To keep my attic organized, I also need the discipline to pay attention to my new signs each time I put another box into storage.

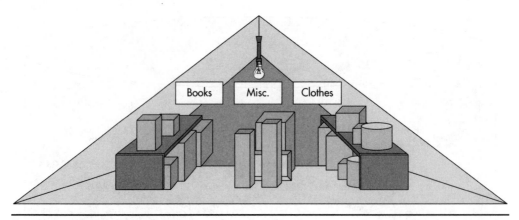

Figure 3-3   *My attic in my fantasy world*

Figure 3-3 shows my attic as it exists in my fantasy world, where I have tons of free time and loads of self-discipline.

Structure in the database world comes in the form of tables. Each database is divided into a number of tables. These tables store the information. Each table contains only one type of information. Figure 3-4 shows customer information in one table, payment information in another, and invoice header information in a third.

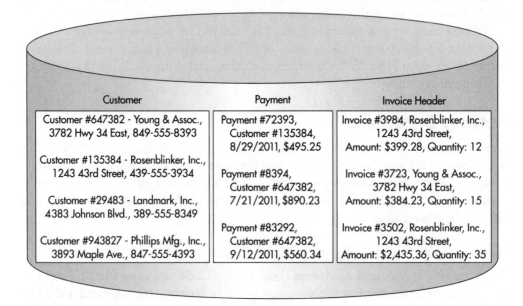

Figure 3-4   *A database organized by tables*

NOTE

Invoice Header is used as the name of the third table for consistency with the sample database that will be introduced in the section "Galactic Delivery Services" and used throughout the remainder of the book. The Invoice Header name helps to differentiate this table from the Invoice Detail table that stores the detail lines of the invoice. The Invoice Detail table is not discussed here, but it will be present in the sample database.

Dividing each table into rows and columns brings additional structure to the database. Figure 3-5 shows the Customer table divided into several rows—one row for each customer whose information is being stored in the table. In addition, the Customer table is divided into a number of columns. Each column is given a name: Customer Number, Customer Name, Address, and Phone. These names tell you what information is being stored in each column.

With a database structured as tables, rows, and columns, you know exactly where to find a certain piece of information. For example, it is pretty obvious that the customer name for customer number 135384 will be found in the Name column of the second row of the Customer table. We are starting to get this data organized, and it was a lot easier than cleaning out the attic!

NOTE

Rows in a database are also called records. Columns in a database are also called fields. Reporting Services uses the terms "rows" and "records" interchangeably. It also uses the terms "columns" and "fields" interchangeably. Don't be confused by this!

Customer

Customer #	Customer Name	Address	Phone
647382	Young & Assoc.	3782 Hwy 34 East	849-555-8393
135384	Rosenblinker, Inc.	1243 43rd Street	439-555-3934
29483	Landmark, Inc.	383 Johnson Blvd.	389-555-8349
943827	Phillips Mfg., Inc.	3893 Maple Ave.	847-555-4393

Figure 3-5   *A database table organized by rows and columns*

Columns also force some discipline on anyone putting data into the table. Each column has certain characteristics assigned to it. For instance, the Customer Number column in Figure 3-5 may only contain strings of digits (0–9); no letters (A–Z) are allowed. It is also limited to a maximum of six characters. In data design lingo, these are known as *constraints*. Given these constraints, it is impossible to store a customer's name in the Customer Number column. The customer's name is likely too long and contains characters that are not legal in the Customer Number column. Constraints provide the discipline to force organization within a database.

Typically, when you design a database, you create tables for each of the things you want to keep track of. In Figure 3-4, the database designer knew that her company needed to track information for customers, payments, and invoices. Database designers call these things *entities*. The database designer created tables for the customer, payment, and invoice header entities. These tables are named Customer, Payment, and Invoice Header.

Once the entities have been identified, the database designer determines what information needs to be known about each entity. In Figure 3-5, the designer identified the customer number, customer name, address, and phone number as the things that need to be known for each customer. These are *attributes* of the customer entity. The database designer creates a column in the Customer table for each of these attributes.

Primary Key

As entities and attributes are being defined, the database designer needs to identify a special attribute for each entity in the database. This special attribute is known as the primary key. The purpose of the *primary key* is to uniquely identify a single entity or, in the case of a database table, a single row in the table.

Two simple rules exist for primary keys. First, every entity must have a primary key value. Second, no two rows in an entity can have the same primary key value. In Figure 3-5, the Customer Number column can serve as the primary key. Every customer is assigned a customer number, and no two customers can be assigned the same customer number.

For most entities, the primary key is a single attribute. However, in some cases, two attributes must be combined to create a unique primary key. This is known as a *composite primary key*. For instance, if you were defining an entity based on presidents of the United States, the first name would not be a valid primary key. John Adams, John Quincy Adams, and John Kennedy all have the same first name. You would need to create a composite key combining first name, middle name, and last name to have a valid primary key.

Normalization

As the database designer continues to work on identifying entities and attributes, she will notice that two different entities have some of the same attributes. For example, in

Customer

Customer #	Customer Name	Address	Phone
647382	Young & Assoc.	3782 Hwy 34 East	849-555-8393
135384	Rosenblinker, Inc.	1243 43rd Street	439-555-3934
29483	Landmark, Inc.	383 Johnson Blvd.	389-555-8349
943827	Phillips Mfg., Inc.	3893 Maple Ave.	847-555-4393

Invoice Header

Invoice #	Customer Name	Address	Amount	Quantity
3984	Rosenblinker, Inc.	1243 43rd Street	$399.28	12
3723	Young & Assoc.	3782 Hwy 34 East	$384.23	15
3502	Rosenblinker, Inc.	1243 43rd Street	$2,435.36	35

Figure 3-6   *Database tables with duplicate data*

Figure 3-6, both the customer entity and the invoice header entity have attributes of Customer Name and Address. This duplication of information seems rather wasteful. Not only are the customer's name and address duplicated between the Customer and Invoice Header tables, but they are also duplicated in several rows in the Invoice Header table itself.

The duplicate data also leads to another problem. Suppose that Rosenblinker, Inc. changes its name to RB, Inc. Then, Ann in the data-processing department changes the name in the Customer table because this is where we store information about the customer entity. However, the customer name has not been changed in the Invoice Header table. Because the customer name in the Invoice Header table no longer matches the customer name in the Customer table, it is no longer possible to determine how many invoices are outstanding for RB, Inc. Believe me, the accounting department will think this is a bad situation.

To avoid these types of problems, database tables are normalized. *Normalization* is a set of rules for defining database tables so each table contains attributes from only one entity. The rules for creating normalized database tables can be quite complex. You can hear database designers endlessly debating whether a proper database should be in 3rd normal form, 4th normal form, or 127th normal form. Let the database designers debate all they want. All you need to remember is this: a normalized database avoids data duplication.

Relations

A *relation* is a tool the database designer uses to avoid data duplication when creating a normalized database. A relation is simply a way to put the duplicated data in one place and then point to it from all the other places in the database where it would otherwise occur. The table that contains the data is called the *parent* table. The table that contains a pointer to the data in the parent table is called the *child* table. Just like parents and children of the human variety, the parent table and the child table are said to be *related*.

In our example, the customer name and address are stored in the Customer table. This is the parent table. A pointer is placed in the Invoice Header table in place of the duplicate customer names and addresses it had contained. The Invoice Header table is the child table.

As mentioned previously, each customer is uniquely identified by their customer number. Therefore, the Customer Number column serves as the primary key for the Customer table. In the Invoice Header table, we need a way to point to a particular customer. It makes sense to use the primary key in the parent table, in this case the Customer Number column, as that pointer. This is illustrated in Figure 3-7.

Each row in the Invoice Header table now contains a copy of the primary key of a row in the Customer table. The Customer Number column in the Invoice Header table is called the foreign key. It is called a *foreign key* because it is not one of the native attributes of the invoice header entity. The customer number is a native attribute of the customer entity. The only reason the Customer Number column exists in the Invoice Header table is to create the relationship.

Let's look back at the name change problem, this time using our new database structure that includes the parent-child relationship. When Rosenblinker, Inc. changes its name to RB, Inc., Ann changes the name in the Customer table as before. In our new structure, however, the customer name is not stored in any other location. Instead, the Invoice Header table rows for RB, Inc. point back to the Customer table row that has the correct name. The accounting department stays happy because it can still figure out how many invoices are outstanding for RB, Inc.

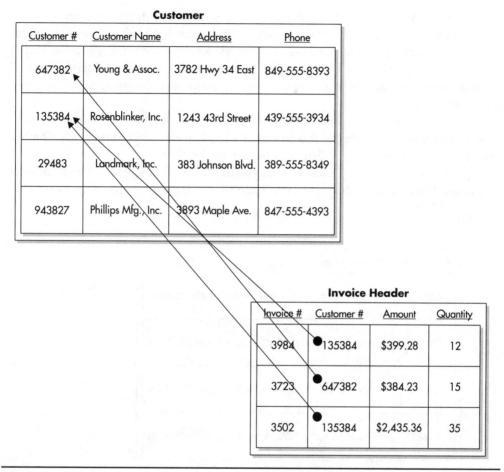

Figure 3-7   *A database relation*

Cardinality of Relations

Database relations can be classified by the number of records that can exist on each side of the relationship. This is known as the *cardinality* of the relation. For example, the relation in Figure 3-7 is a *one-to-many relation* (in other words, one parent record can have many children). More specifically, one customer can have many invoices.

It is also possible to have a *one-to-one relation*. In this case, one parent record can have only one child. For example, let's say our company rewards customers with a customer loyalty discount. Because only a few customers will receive this loyalty discount, we do not want to set aside space in every row in the Customer table to store the loyalty discount information. Instead, we create a new table to store this information. The new table is related to the Customer table, as shown in Figure 3-8. Our company's business rule says that a given customer can only receive one loyalty discount. Because the Loyalty Discount table has only one Customer Number column, each row can link to just one customer. The combination of the business rule and the table design makes this a one-to-one relation.

It is also possible to have a *many-to-many relation*. This relation no longer fits our parent/child analogy. It is better thought of as a brother/sister relationship. One brother can have many sisters, and one sister can have many brothers.

Suppose we need to keep track of the type of business engaged in by each of our customers. We can add a Business Type table to our database, with columns for the

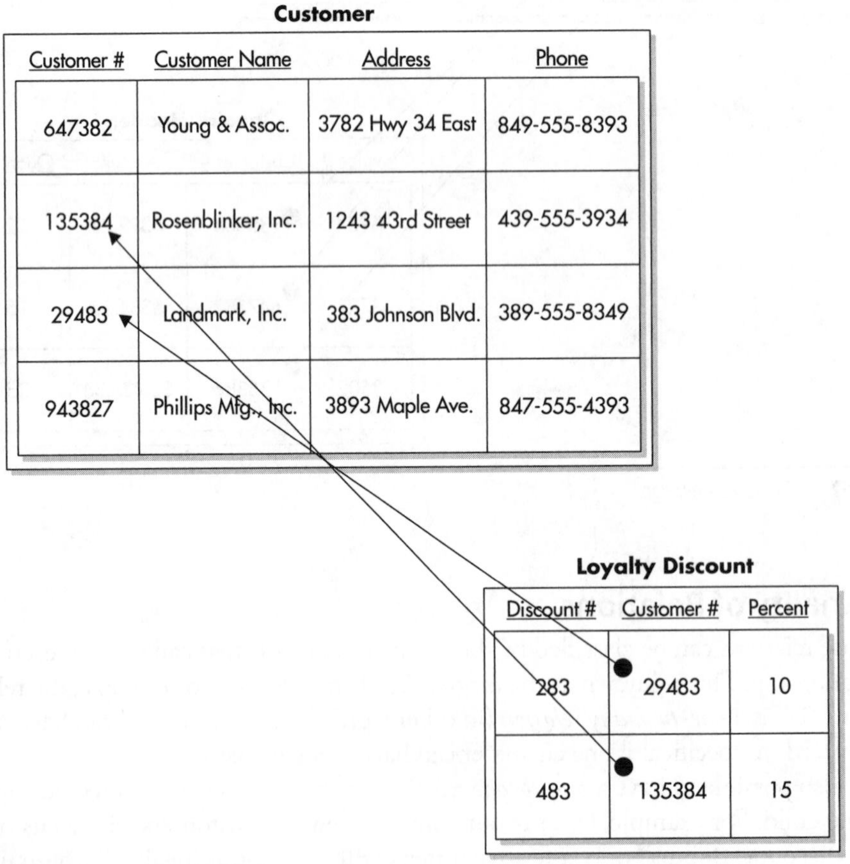

Customer

Customer #	Customer Name	Address	Phone
647382	Young & Assoc.	3782 Hwy 34 East	849-555-8393
135384	Rosenblinker, Inc.	1243 43rd Street	439-555-3934
29483	Landmark, Inc.	383 Johnson Blvd.	389-555-8349
943827	Phillips Mfg., Inc.	3893 Maple Ave.	847-555-4393

Loyalty Discount

Discount #	Customer #	Percent
283	29483	10
483	135384	15

Figure 3-8 *A one-to-one relation*

business type code and the business type description. We can add a column for the business type code to the Customer table. We now have a one-to-many relation, where one business type can be related to many customers. This is shown in Figure 3-9.

The problem with this structure becomes apparent when we have a customer that does multiple things. If Landmark, Inc. only produces paper products, there isn't a problem. We can put the business type code for paper products in the Customer table row for Landmark, Inc. We run into a bit of a snag, however, if Landmark, Inc. also produces plastics. We could add a second business type code column to the Customer table, but this still limits a customer to a maximum of two business types. In today's world of national conglomerates, this is not going to work.

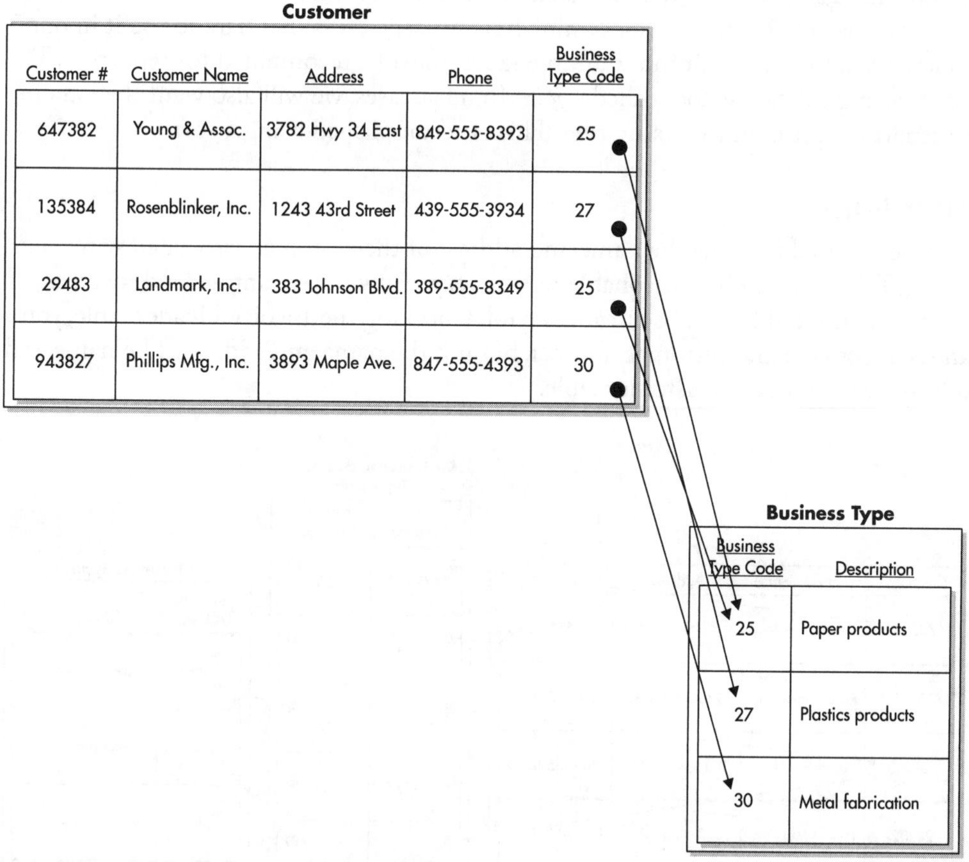

Figure 3-9   *Tracking business type using a one-to-many relation*

The answer is to add a third table to the mix to create a many-to-many relation. This additional table is known as a *linking table.* Its only purpose is to link two other tables together in a many-to-many relation. To use a linking table, you create the Business Type table just as before. This time, however, instead of creating a new column in the Customer table, we'll create a new table called Customer To Business Type Link. The new table has columns for the customer number and the business type code. Figure 3-10 shows how this linking table relates the Customer table to the Business Type table. By using the linking table, we can relate one customer to many business types. In addition, we can relate one business type to many customers.

Retrieving Data

We now have all the tools we need to store our data in an efficient manner. With our data structure set, it is time to determine how we can access that data to use it in our reports. Data that was split into multiple tables must be recombined for reporting. This is done using a database tool called a *join.* In most cases, we will also want the data in the report to appear in a certain order. This is accomplished using a sort.

Inner Joins

Suppose we need to know the name and address of the customer associated with each invoice. This is certainly a reasonable request, especially if we want to send invoices to these clients and have those invoices paid. Checking the Invoice Header table, you can see it contains the customer number, but not the name and address. The name and address is stored in the Customer table.

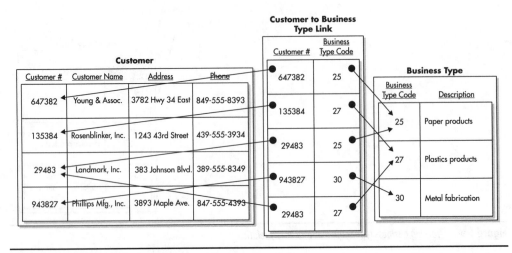

Figure 3-10   *Tracking the business type using a many-to-many relation*

To print our invoices, we need to join the data in the Customer table with the data in the Invoice Header table. This join is done by matching the customer number in each record of the Invoice Header table with the customer number in the Customer table. In the language of database designers, we are joining the Customer table to the Invoice Header table on the Customer Number column.

The result of the join is a new table that contains information from both the Customer table and the Invoice Header table in each row. This new table is known as a *result set*. The result set from the Customer table-to-Invoice Header table join is shown in Figure 3-11. Note that the result set table contains nearly the same information that was in the Invoice Header table before it was normalized. The result set is a *denormalized* form of the data in the database.

It may seem like we are going in circles, first normalizing the data and then denormalizing it. There is, however, one important difference between the denormalized form of the Invoice Header table that we started with in Figure 3-6 and the result set in Figure 3-11. The denormalized result set is a temporary table: it exists only as long as it is needed; then it is automatically deleted. The result set is re-created each time we execute the join, so the result set is always current.

Let's return once more to Ann, our faithful employee in data processing. We will again consider the situation where Rosenblinker, Inc. changes its name to RB, Inc. Ann makes the change in the Customer table, as in the previous example. The next time we execute the join, this change is reflected in the result set. The result set has the new company name because our join gets a new copy of the customer information from the Customer table each time it is executed. The join finds the information in the Customer table based on the primary key, the customer number, which has not changed. Our invoices are linked

Customer/Invoice Header Join Result Set

Customer #	Customer Name	Address	Phone	Invoice #	Customer #	Amount	Quantity
135384	Rosenblinker, Inc.	1243 43rd Street	439-555-3934	3984	135384	$399.28	12
647382	Young & Assoc.	3782 Hwy 34 East	849-555-8393	3723	647382	$384.23	15
135384	Rosenblinker, Inc.	1243 43rd Street	439-555-3934	3502	135384	$2,435.36	35

Data from the Customer table   Data from the Invoice Header table

Figure 3-11   *The result set from the Customer table-to-Invoice Header table join*

to the proper companies, so accounting can determine how many invoices are outstanding for RB, Inc., and everyone is happy!

Outer Joins

In the previous section, we looked at a type of join known as an inner join. When you do an inner join, your result set includes only those records that have a representative on both sides of the join. In Figure 3-11, Landmark, Inc. and Phillips Mfg., Inc. are not represented in the result set because they do not have any Invoice Header table rows linked to them.

Figure 3-12 shows another way to think about joins. Here, the two tables are shown as sets of customer numbers. The left-hand circle represents the set of customer numbers in the Customer table. It contains one occurrence of every customer number present in the Customer table. The right-hand circle represents the set of customer numbers in the Invoice Header table. It contains one occurrence of each customer number present in the Invoice Header table. The center region, where the two sets intersect, contains one occurrence of every customer number present in both the Customer table and the Invoice Header table. Looking at Figure 3-12, you can quickly tell that no customer numbers are present in the Invoice Header table that are not also present in the Customer table. This is as it should be. We should not have any invoice headers assigned to a customer that does not exist in the Customer table.

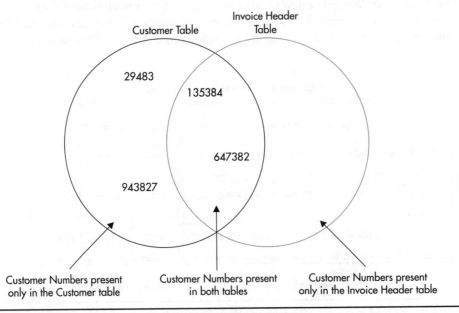

Figure 3-12   *The set representation of the Customer and Invoice Header tables*

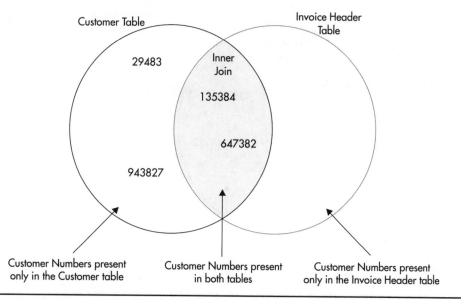

Figure 3-13   *The set representation of the inner join of the Customer table and the Invoice Header table*

Figure 3-13 shows a graphical representation of the inner join in Figure 3-11. Only records with customer numbers that appear in the shaded section will be included in the result set. Remember, two rows in the Invoice Header table contain customer number 135384. For this reason, the result set contains three rows—two rows for customer number 135384 and one row for customer number 647382.

The result set in Figure 3-11 enables us to print invoice headers that contain the correct customer name and address. Now let's look at customers and invoice headers from a slightly different angle. Suppose we have been asked for a report showing all customers and the invoice headers that have been sent to them. If we were to print this customers/invoice headers report from the result set in Figure 3-11, it would exclude Landmark, Inc. and Phillips Mfg., Inc. because they do not have any invoices and, therefore, would not fulfill the requirements.

What we need is a result set that includes all the customers in the Customer table. This is illustrated graphically in Figure 3-14. This type of join is known as a *left outer join*, so named because this join is not limited to the values in the intersection of both circles. It also includes the values to the left of the inner, overlapping sections of the circles.

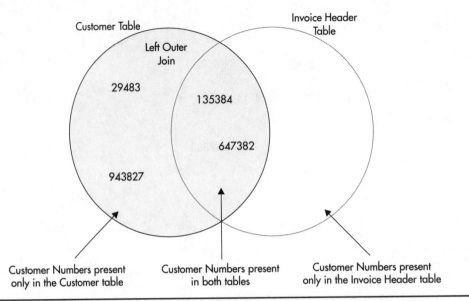

Figure 3-14 *The set representation of the left outer join of the Customer table and the Invoice Header table*

We can also perform a right outer join on two tables. In our example, a *right outer join* would return the same number of rows as the inner join. This is because no customer numbers are to the right of the intersection.

The result set produced by a left outer join of the Customer table and the Invoice Header table is shown in Figure 3-15. Notice the columns populated by data from the Invoice Header table are empty in rows for Landmark, Inc. and Phillips Mfg., Inc. The columns are empty because these two customers do not have any Invoice Header rows to provide data on the right side of the join.

Joining Multiple Tables

Joins, whether inner or outer, always involve two tables. However, in Figure 3-10, you were introduced to a many-to-many relation that involved three tables. How do you retrieve data from this type of relation? The answer is to chain together two different joins, each involving two tables.

Figure 3-16 illustrates the joins required to reassemble the data from Figure 3-10. Here, the Customer table is joined to the Customer To Business Type Link table using the Customer Number column common to both tables. The Customer To Business Type Link table is then joined to the Business Type table using the Business Type Code column present in both tables. The final result set contains the data from all three tables.

Customer/Invoice Header Left Outer Join Result Set

Customer #	Customer Name	Address	Phone	Invoice #	Customer #	Amount	Quantity
135384	Rosenblinker, Inc.	1243 43rd Street	439-555-3934	3984	135384	$399.28	12
647382	Young & Assoc.	3782 Hwy 34 East	849-555-8393	3723	647382	$384.23	15
135384	Rosenblinker, Inc.	1243 43rd Street	439-555-3934	3502	135384	$2,435.36	35
29483	Landmark, Inc.	383 Johnson Blvd.	389-555-8349				
943827	Phillips Mfg, Inc.	3893 Maple Ave.	847-555-4393				

Data from the Customer table   Data from the Invoice Header table

Figure 3-15   *The result set from the left outer join of the Customer table and the Invoice Header table*

**Customer/Customer to Business Type Link/Business Type
Join Result Set**

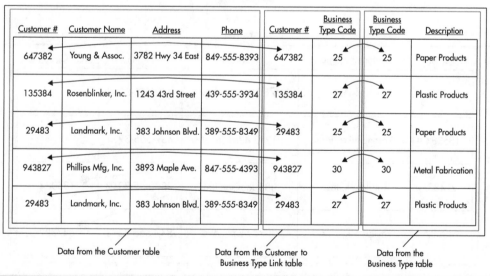

Customer #	Customer Name	Address	Phone	Customer #	Business Type Code	Business Type Code	Description
647382	Young & Assoc.	3782 Hwy 34 East	849-555-8393	647382	25	25	Paper Products
135384	Rosenblinker, Inc.	1243 43rd Street	439-555-3934	135384	27	27	Plastic Products
29483	Landmark, Inc.	383 Johnson Blvd.	389-555-8349	29483	25	25	Paper Products
943827	Phillips Mfg, Inc.	3893 Maple Ave.	847-555-4393	943827	30	30	Metal Fabrication
29483	Landmark, Inc.	383 Johnson Blvd.	389-555-8349	29483	27	27	Plastic Products

Data from the Customer table   Data from the Customer to Business Type Link table   Data from the Business Type table

Figure 3-16   *The result set from the join of the Customer table, the Customer To Business Type Link table, and the Business Type table*

Self-Joins

In our previous example, we needed to join three tables to get the required information. Other joins may only require a single table. For instance, we may have a customer that is a subsidiary of another one of our customers. In some cases, we'll want to treat these two separately so both appear in our result set. This requires us to keep the two customers as separate rows in our Customer table. In other cases, we may want to combine information from the parent company and the subsidiary into one record. To do this, our database structure must include a mechanism to tie the subsidiary to its parent.

To track a customer's connection to its parent, we need to create a relationship between the customer's row in the Customer table and its parent's row in the Customer table. To do this, we add a Parent Customer Number column to the Customer table, as shown in Figure 3-17. In the customer's row, the Parent Customer Number column will contain the customer number of the row for the parent. In the row for the parent, and in all the rows for customers that do not have a parent, the Parent Customer Number column is empty.

When we want to report from this parent/subsidiary relation, we need to do a join. This may seem like a problem at first because a join requires two tables and we only have one. The answer is to use the Customer table on one side of the join and a "copy" of the Customer table on the other side of the join. The second occurrence of the Customer table is given a nickname, called an *alias,* so we can tell the two apart. This type of join, which uses the same table on both sides, is known as a *self-join.* Figure 3-18 shows the results of the self-join on the Customer table.

Customer

Customer #	Customer Name	Address	Phone	Parent Customer #
647382	Young & Assoc.	3782 Hwy 34 East	849-555-8393	
135384	Rosenblinker, Inc.	1243 43rd Street	439-555-3934	
29483	Landmark, Inc.	383 Johnson Blvd.	389-555-8349	135384
943827	Phillips Mfg., Inc.	3893 Maple Ave.	847-555-4393	647382

Figure 3-17   *The customer/parent customer relation*

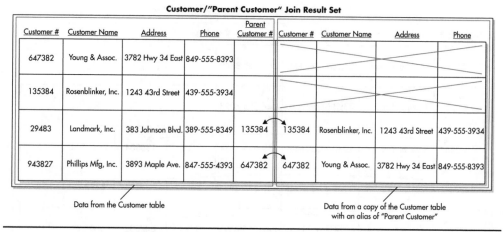

Figure 3-18   *The result set from the Customer table self-join*

Sorting

In most cases, one final step is required before our result sets can be used for reporting. Let's go back to the result set produced in Figure 3-15 for the customer/invoice header report. Looking back at this result set, notice the customers do not appear to be in any particular order. In most cases, users do not appreciate reports with information presented in this unsorted manner. This is especially true when two rows for the same customer do not appear consecutively, as is the case here.

We need to sort the result set as it is being created to avoid this situation. This is done by specifying the columns that should be used for the sort. Sorting by customer name probably makes the most sense for the customer/invoice header report. Columns can be sorted either in ascending order, smallest to largest (A–Z), or descending order, largest to smallest (Z–A). An ascending sort on Customer Name would be most appropriate.

We still have a situation where the order of the rows is left to chance. Because two rows have the same customer name, we do not know which of these two rows will appear first and which will appear second. A second sort field is necessary to break this "tie." All the data copied into the result set from the Customer table will be the same in both of these rows. We need to look at the data copied from the Invoice Header table for a second sort column. In this case, an ascending sort on Invoice Number would be a good choice. Figure 3-19 shows the result set sorted by Customer Name, ascending, and then by Invoice Number, ascending.

Customer/Invoice Header Left Outer Join Result Set

Customer #	Customer Name	Address	Phone	Invoice #	Customer #	Amount	Quantity
29483	Landmark, Inc.	383 Johnson Blvd.	389-555-8349				
943827	Phillips Mfg, Inc.	3893 Maple Ave.	847-555-4393				
135384	Rosenblinker, Inc.	1243 43rd Street	439-555-3934	3502	135384	$2,435.36	35
135384	Rosenblinker, Inc.	1243 43rd Street	439-555-3934	3984	135384	$399.28	12
647382	Young & Assoc.	3782 Hwy 34 East	849-555-8393	3723	647382	$384.23	15

Data from the Customer table   Data from the Invoice Header table

Figure 3-19 *The sorted result set from the left outer join of the Customer table and the Invoice Header table*

Galactic Delivery Services

Throughout the remainder of this book, you will get to know Reporting Services by exploring a number of sample reports. These reports will be based on the business needs of a company called Galactic Delivery Services (GDS). To better understand these sample reports, here is some background on GDS.

Company Background

GDS provides package-delivery service between several planetary systems in the near galactic region. It specializes in rapid delivery featuring same-day, next-day, and previous-day delivery. The latter is made possible by its new Photon III transports, which travel faster than the speed of light. This faster-than-light capability allows GDS to exploit the properties of general relativity and deliver a package on the day before it was sent.

Package Tracking

Despite GDS's unique delivery offerings, it has the same data-processing needs as any more conventional package-delivery service. It tracks packages as they are moved from one interplanetary hub to another. This is important, not only for the smooth operation of the delivery service, but also to allow customers to check on the status of their delivery at any time.

To remain accountable to its clients and to prevent fraud, GDS investigates every package lost en route. These investigations help to find and eliminate problems throughout the entire delivery system. One such investigation discovered that a leaking antimatter valve on one of the Photon III transports was vaporizing two or three packages on each flight.

GDS stores its data in a database called Galactic. Figure 3-20 shows the portion of the Galactic database that stores the information used for package tracking. The tables and their column names are shown. A key symbol in the gray square next to a column name indicates this column is the primary key for that table. The lines connecting the tables show the relations that have been created between these tables in the database. The key symbol at the end of the line points to the primary key column used to create the relation. The infinity sign, at the opposite end of the line to the key symbol, points to the foreign key column used to complete the relation. (The infinity sign looks like two circles or a sideways number 8.)

Each relation shown in Figure 3-20 is a one-to-many relation. The side of the relation indicated by the key is the "one" side of the relation. The side indicated by the infinity sign is the "many" side of the relation. For example, if you look at the line between the Customer table and the Delivery table, you can see that one customer may have many deliveries.

You may want to refer to these diagrams as we create sample reports from the Galactic database. Don't worry if the diagrams seem a bit complicated right now. They will make more sense as we consider the business practices and reporting needs at GDS. Also, our first report examples will contain only a few tables and the corresponding relations, so we will start simple and work our way up.

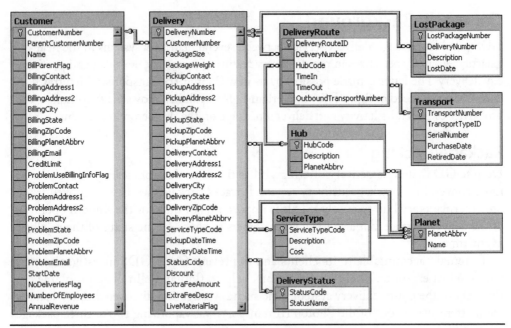

Figure 3-20   *The package tracking tables from the Galactic database*

Personnel

Every business needs a personnel department to look after its employees. GDS is no different. The GDS personnel department is responsible for the hiring and firing of all the robots employed by GDS. This department is also responsible for tracking the hours put in by the robotic laborers and paying them accordingly. (Yes, robots get paid at GDS. After all, GDS is an equal-opportunity employer.)

The personnel department is also responsible for conducting annual reviews of each employee. At the annual review, goals are set for the employee to attain over the coming year. After a year has passed, several of the employee's co-workers are asked to rate the employee on how well it did in reaching those goals. The employee's manager then uses the ratings to write an overall performance evaluation for the employee and establish new goals for the following year.

Figure 3-21 shows the tables in the Galactic database used by the personnel department. Notice that the Rating table has key symbols next to both the EvaluationID column name and the GoalID column name. This means the Rating table uses a composite primary key that combines the EvaluationID column and the GoalID column.

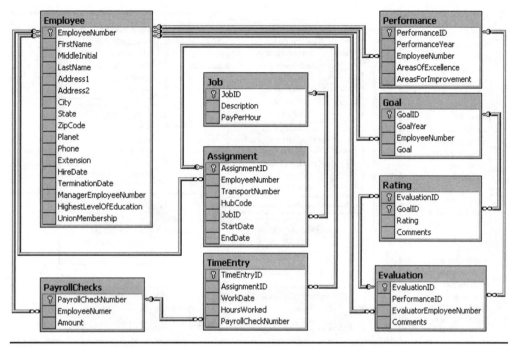

Figure 3-21 *The personnel department tables from the Galactic database*

Accounting

The GDS accounting department is responsible for seeing that the company is paid for each package it delivers. GDS invoices its customers for each delivery completed. The invoices are sent to the customer, and payment is requested within 30 days.

Even though GDS delivers its customers' packages at the speed of light, those same customers pay GDS at a much slower speed. "Molasses at the northern pole of Antares Prime" was the analogy used by the current chief financial droid. Therefore, GDS must track when invoices are paid, how much was paid, and how much is still outstanding.

Figure 3-22 shows the tables in the Galactic database used by the accounting department. Notice the Customer table appears in both Figure 3-20 and Figure 3-22. This is the same table in both diagrams. This table is shown in both because it is a major part of both the package tracking and the accounting business processes.

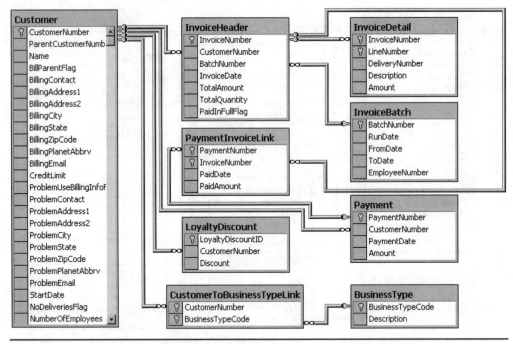

Figure 3-22 *The accounting department tables from the Galactic database*

Transport Maintenance

In addition to all this, GDS must maintain a fleet of transports. Careful records are kept on the repair and preventative maintenance work done on each transport. GDS also has a record of each flight a transport makes, as well as any accidents and mishaps involved.

Maintenance records are extremely important, not only to GDS itself, but also to the Federation Space Flight Administration (FSFA). Without proper maintenance records on all its transports, GDS would be shut down by the FSFA in a nanosecond. You may think this is an exaggeration, but the bureaucratic androids at the FSFA have extremely high clock rates.

Figure 3-23 shows the transport maintenance tables in the Galactic database.

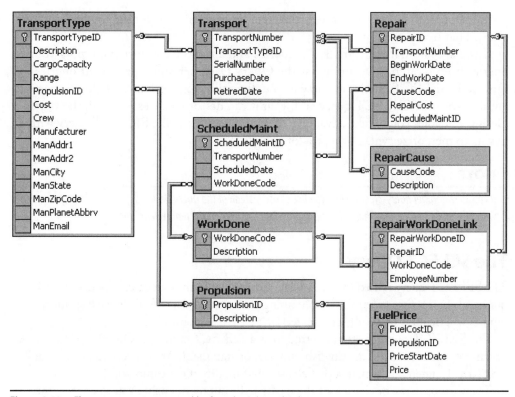

Figure 3-23   *The transport maintenance tables from the Galactic database*

Querying Data

You have now looked at the database concepts of normalization, relations, and joins. You have also been introduced to the Galactic database. We use this relational database throughout the remainder of this book for our examples. Now, it is time to look more specifically at how you retrieve the data from the database into a format you can use for reporting. This is done through the database query.

A *query* is a request for some action on the data in one or more tables. An *INSERT query* adds one or more rows to a database table. An *UPDATE* query modifies the data in one or more existing rows of a table. A *DELETE* query removes one or more rows from a table. Because we are primarily interested in retrieving data for reporting, the query we are going to concern ourselves with is the *SELECT query*, which reads data from one or more tables (it does not add, update, or delete data).

We will look at the various parts of the SELECT query. This is to help you become familiar with this important aspect of reporting. The good news is Reporting Services provides a tool to guide you through the creation of queries, including the SELECT query. That tool is the Query Designer.

If you are familiar with SELECT queries and are more comfortable typing your queries from scratch, you can bypass the Query Designer and type in your queries directly. If SELECT queries are new to you, the following section can help you become familiar with the SELECT query and what it can do for you. Rest assured: the Query Designer enables you to take advantage of all the features of the SELECT query without having to memorize syntax or type a lot of code.

NOTE

If you have another query-creation tool you like to use instead of the Query Designer, you can create your queries with that tool and then copy them into the appropriate locations in the report definition.

The SELECT Query

The SELECT query is used to retrieve data from tables in the database. When a SELECT query is run, it returns a result set containing the selected data. With few exceptions, your reports will be built on result sets created by SELECT queries.

The SELECT query is often referred to as a *SELECT statement*. One reason for this is because it can be read like an English sentence or statement. As with a sentence in English, a SELECT statement is made up of clauses that modify the meaning of the statement.

The various parts, or clauses, of the SELECT statement enable you to control the data contained in the result set. Use the *FROM clause* to specify which table the data will be selected from. The *FIELD LIST* permits you to choose the columns that will appear in the result set. The *JOIN clause* lets you specify additional tables that will be joined with the table in the FROM clause to contribute data to the result set. The *WHERE clause* enables you to set conditions that determine which rows will be included in the result set. Finally, you can use the *ORDER BY clause* to sort the result set, and the *GROUP BY clause* and the *HAVING clause* to combine detail rows into summary rows.

NOTE

The query statements shown in the remainder of this chapter all use the Galactic database. If you want to try out the various query statements as they are being discussed, open a query window for the Galactic database in SQL Server Management Studio. If you are not familiar with SQL Server Management Studio, you can try out the queries in the Reporting Services Generic Query Designer. To do this, turn to Chapter 5 and follow the steps for Task 1 of the Transport List Report. For SQL Server Data Tools and Visual Studio, stop after Step 29, and then click the Edit as Text button. For Report Builder, stop after Step 13, and then click the Edit As Text button. You will be in the Generic Query Designer. You can enter the query statements in the upper portion of the Generic Query Designer and execute them by clicking the toolbar button with the exclamation point (!). When you are finished, close the application without saving your changes.

The FROM Clause

The SELECT statement in its simplest form includes only a FROM clause. Here is a SELECT statement that retrieves all rows and all columns from the Customer table:

```
SELECT *
FROM dbo.Customer
```

The word "SELECT" is required to let the database know this is going to be a SELECT query, as opposed to an INSERT, UPDATE, or DELETE query. The asterisk (*) means all columns will be included in the result set. The remainder of the statement is the FROM clause. It says the data is to be selected from the Customer table. We will discuss the meaning of "dbo." in a moment.

As stated earlier, the SELECT statement can be read as if it were a sentence. This SELECT statement is read, "Select all columns from the Customer table." If we run this SELECT statement in the Galactic database, the results would appear similar to Figure 3-24. The SELECT query is being run in the Query Designer window of SQL Server Data Tools. Note the scroll bars on the right and on the bottom of the result set area indicate that not all of the rows and columns returned can fit on the screen.

The table name, Customer, has "dbo." in front of it. The dbo is the name of the schema the table is associated with. At its simplest, a schema is a way to group tables together inside a database. The default schema for tables in most cases is dbo. (The dbo stands for database owner, meaning the user who owns the database. This harkens back to a time in earlier versions of SQL Server where this prefix was tied to the user who created the table.)

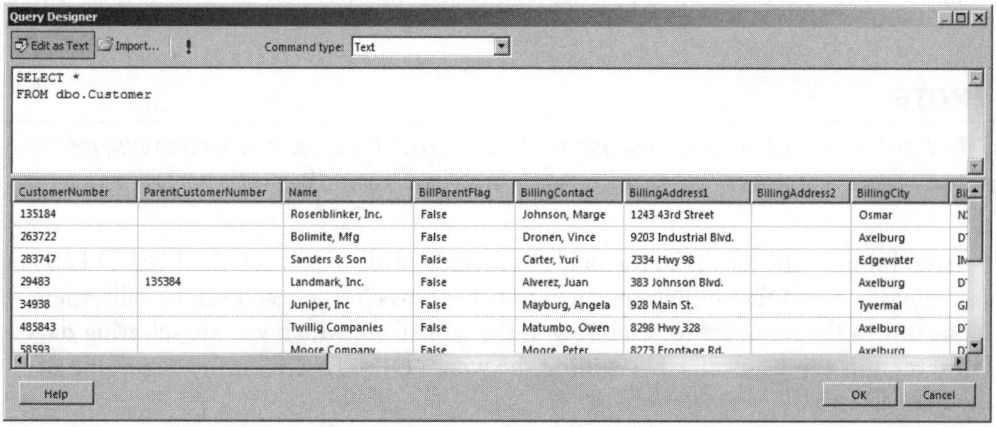

Query Designer

Edit as Text Import... !   Command type: Text

```
SELECT *
FROM dbo.Customer
```

CustomerNumber	ParentCustomerNumber	Name	BillParentFlag	BillingContact	BillingAddress1	BillingAddress2	BillingCity	Bil
135184		Rosenblinker, Inc.	False	Johnson, Marge	1243 43rd Street		Osmar	N:
263722		Bolimite, Mfg	False	Dronen, Vince	9203 Industrial Blvd.		Axelburg	D'
283747		Sanders & Son	False	Carter, Yuri	2334 Hwy 98		Edgewater	IN
29483	135384	Landmark, Inc.	False	Alverez, Juan	383 Johnson Blvd.		Axelburg	D'
34938		Juniper, Inc	False	Mayburg, Angela	928 Main St.		Tyvermal	GI
485843		Twillig Companies	False	Matumbo, Owen	8298 Hwy 328		Axelburg	D'
58593		Moore Company	False	Moore, Peter	8273 Frontage Rd.		Axelburg	D'

Help   OK   Cancel

Figure 3-24 *The SELECT statement in its simplest form*

In the Galactic database, the dbo.Customer table is part of the dbo schema. It would be possible for another Customer table, associated with a different schema, to be created in the Galactic database. For example, we could have an "xyz" schema and a table associated with that schema called xyz.Customer.

This situation, with two tables of the same name in the same database, does not happen often and is probably not a great idea. It can quickly lead to confusion and errors. Even though this is a rare occurrence, the Query Designer needs to account for this situation. The Query Designer uses both the name of the schema and the name of the table itself in the queries it builds and executes for you.

The FIELD LIST

In the previous example, the result set created by the SELECT statement contained all of the columns in the table. In most cases, especially when creating reports, you only need to work with some of the columns of a table in any given result set. Including all of the columns in a result set when only a few columns are required wastes computing power and network bandwidth.

A FIELD LIST provides the capability you need to specify which columns to include in the result set. When a FIELD LIST is added to the SELECT statement, it appears similar to the following:

```
SELECT CustomerNumber, Name, BillingCity
FROM dbo.Customer
```

The bold portion of the SELECT statement indicates changes from the previous SELECT statement.

This statement returns only the CustomerNumber, Name, and BillingCity columns from the Customer table. The result set created by this SELECT statement is shown in Figure 3-25.

NOTE

It is a good idea to get in the habit of always specifying a FIELD LIST in your queries rather than using the "". It will produce much more efficient queries, especially for tables that have a large number of columns.*

In addition to the names of the fields to include in the result set, the FIELD LIST can contain a word that influences the number of rows in the result set. Usually, there is one row in the result set for each row in the table from which you are selecting data. However, this can be changed by adding the word "DISTINCT" at the beginning of the FIELD LIST.

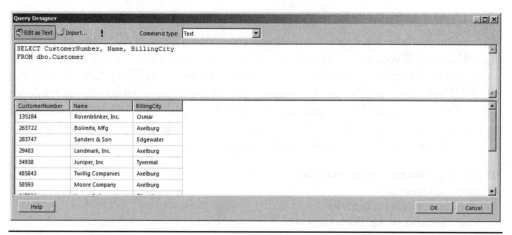

Figure 3-25   *A SELECT statement with a FIELD LIST*

When you use DISTINCT in the FIELD LIST, you are saying that you only want one row in the result set for each distinct set of values. In other words, the result set from a DISTINCT query will not include any two rows that have exactly the same values in every column. Here is an example of a DISTINCT query:

```
SELECT DISTINCT BillingCity
FROM dbo.Customer
```

This query returns a list of all the billing cities in the Customer table. A number of customers have the same billing city, but these duplicates have been removed from the result set, as shown in Figure 3-26.

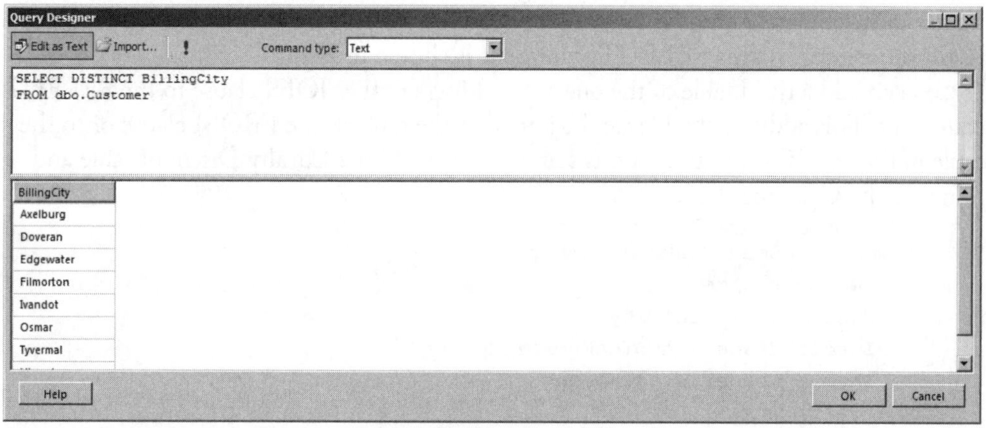

Figure 3-26   *A DISTINCT query*

The JOIN Clause

When your database is properly normalized, you are likely to need data from more than one table to fulfill your reporting requirements. As discussed earlier in this chapter, the way to get information from more than one table is to use a join. The JOIN clause in the SELECT statement enables you to include a join of two or more tables in your result set.

The first part of the JOIN clause specifies which table is being joined. The second part determines the two columns that are linked to create the join. Joining the Invoice Header table to the Customer table looks like this:

```
SELECT dbo.Customer.CustomerNumber,
    dbo.Customer.Name,
    dbo.Customer.BillingCity,
    dbo.InvoiceHeader.InvoiceNumber,
    dbo.InvoiceHeader.TotalAmount
FROM dbo.Customer
INNER JOIN dbo.InvoiceHeader
  ON dbo.Customer.CustomerNumber = dbo.InvoiceHeader.CustomerNumber
```

With the Customer table and the Invoice Header table joined, you have a situation where some columns in the result set have the same name. For example, a CustomerNumber column is in the Customer table and a CustomerNumber column is in the Invoice Header table. When you use the FIELD LIST to tell the database which fields to include in the result set, you need to uniquely identify these fields using both the table name and the column name.

If you do not do this, the query will not run and you will receive an error. Nothing prevents you from using the table name in front of each column name, whether it is a duplicate or not, as in this example. Using the table name in front of each column name makes it immediately obvious where every column in the result set is selected from. The result set created by this SELECT statement is shown in Figure 3-27.

You can add a third table to the query by adding another JOIN clause to the SELECT statement. This additional table can be joined to the table in the FROM clause or to the table in the first JOIN clause. In this statement, we add the Loyalty Discount table and join it to the Customer table:

```
SELECT dbo.Customer.CustomerNumber,
    dbo.Customer.Name,
    dbo.Customer.BillingCity,
    dbo.InvoiceHeader.InvoiceNumber,
    dbo.InvoiceHeader.TotalAmount,
    dbo.LoyaltyDiscount.Discount
FROM dbo.Customer
```

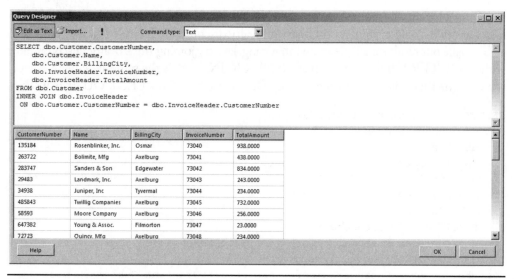

Figure 3-27   *A SELECT statement with a JOIN clause*

```
INNER JOIN dbo.InvoiceHeader
 ON dbo.Customer.CustomerNumber = dbo.InvoiceHeader.CustomerNumber
INNER JOIN dbo.LoyaltyDiscount
 ON dbo.Customer.CustomerNumber = dbo.LoyaltyDiscount.CustomerNumber
```

The result set from this SELECT statement is shown in Figure 3-28. Notice that the result set is rather small. This is because Landmark, Inc. is the only customer currently

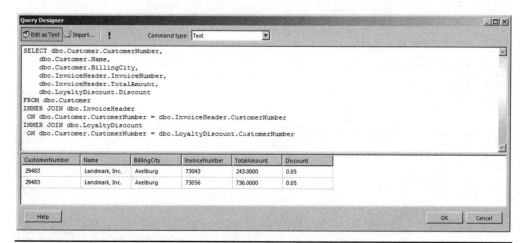

Figure 3-28   *A SELECT statement with two JOIN clauses*

receiving a loyalty discount. Because an INNER JOIN was used to add the Loyalty Discount table, only customers that have a loyalty discount are included in the result set.

To make our result set a little more interesting, let's try joining the Loyalty Discount table with an OUTER JOIN rather than an INNER JOIN. Here is the same statement, except the Customer table is joined to the Loyalty Discount table with a LEFT OUTER JOIN:

```
SELECT dbo.Customer.CustomerNumber,
    dbo.Customer.Name,
    dbo.Customer.BillingCity,
    dbo.InvoiceHeader.InvoiceNumber,
    dbo.InvoiceHeader.TotalAmount,
    dbo.LoyaltyDiscount.Discount
FROM dbo.Customer
INNER JOIN dbo.InvoiceHeader
 ON dbo.Customer.CustomerNumber = dbo.InvoiceHeader.CustomerNumber
LEFT OUTER JOIN dbo.LoyaltyDiscount
 ON dbo.Customer.CustomerNumber = dbo.LoyaltyDiscount.CustomerNumber
```

The result set for this SELECT statement is shown in Figure 3-29. Notice that the value for the Discount column is blank in the rows for all of the customers except for Landmark, Inc. (It is actually NULL, but this is being changed to a blank in the Query Designer display.) This blank value is to be expected, because there is no record in the Loyalty Discount table to join with these customers. When no value is in a column, the result set will contain a NULL value.

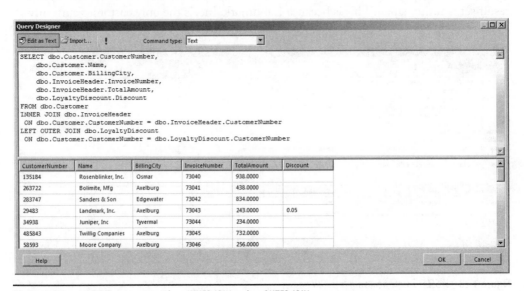

Figure 3-29   *A SELECT statement with an INNER JOIN and an OUTER JOIN*

The WHERE Clause

Up to this point, the result sets have included all of the rows in the table or all of the rows that result from the joins. The FIELD LIST limits which columns are being returned in the result set. Nothing, however, placed a limit on the rows.

To limit the number of rows in the result set, you need to add a WHERE clause to your SELECT statement. The WHERE clause includes one or more logical expressions that must be true for a row before it can be included in the result set. Here is an example of a SELECT statement with a WHERE clause:

```
SELECT dbo.Customer.CustomerNumber,
    dbo.Customer.Name,
    dbo.Customer.BillingCity,
    dbo.InvoiceHeader.InvoiceNumber,
    dbo.InvoiceHeader.TotalAmount,
    dbo.LoyaltyDiscount.Discount
FROM dbo.Customer
INNER JOIN dbo.InvoiceHeader
 ON dbo.Customer.CustomerNumber = dbo.InvoiceHeader.CustomerNumber
LEFT OUTER JOIN dbo.LoyaltyDiscount
 ON dbo.Customer.CustomerNumber = dbo.LoyaltyDiscount.CustomerNumber
WHERE (dbo.Customer.BillingCity = 'Axelburg')
```

The word 'Axelburg' (enclosed in single quotes) is a string constant. A *string constant*, also known as a *string literal*, is an actual text value. The string constant instructs SQL Server to use the text between the single quotes as a value rather than the name of a column or a table. In this example, only customers with a value of Axelburg in their BillingCity column will be included in the result set, as shown in Figure 3-30.

NOTE

Microsoft SQL Server 2012, in its standard configuration, insists on single quotes around string constants, such as 'Axelburg' in the previous SELECT statement. SQL Server 2012 assumes that anything enclosed in double quotes is a field name.

To create more complex criteria for your result set, you can have multiple logical expressions in the WHERE clause. The logical expressions are linked together with an AND or an OR. When an AND is used to link logical expressions, the logical expressions on both sides of the AND must be true for a row in order for that row to be included in the result set. When an OR is used to link two logical expressions, either one or both of the logical expressions must be true for a row in order for that row to be included in the result set.

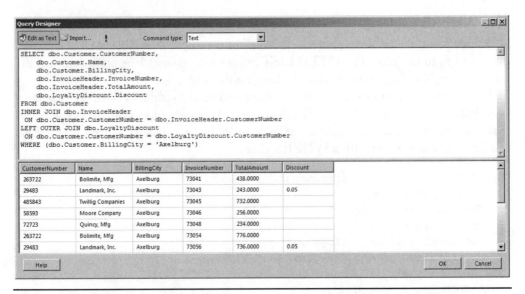

Figure 3-30 *A SELECT statement with a WHERE clause*

This SELECT statement has two logical expressions in the WHERE clause:

```
SELECT dbo.Customer.CustomerNumber,
    dbo.Customer.Name,
    dbo.Customer.BillingCity,
    dbo.InvoiceHeader.InvoiceNumber,
    dbo.InvoiceHeader.TotalAmount,
    dbo.LoyaltyDiscount.Discount
FROM dbo.Customer
INNER JOIN dbo.InvoiceHeader
 ON dbo.Customer.CustomerNumber = dbo.InvoiceHeader.CustomerNumber
LEFT OUTER JOIN dbo.LoyaltyDiscount
 ON dbo.Customer.CustomerNumber = dbo.LoyaltyDiscount.CustomerNumber
WHERE (dbo.Customer.BillingCity = 'Axelburg')
AND (dbo.Customer.Name > 'C')
```

Only customers with a value of Axelburg in their BillingCity column *and* with a name that comes after C will be included in the result set. This result set is shown in Figure 3-31.

The ORDER BY Clause

Up to this point, the data in the result sets has shown up in any order it pleases. As discussed previously, this will probably not be acceptable for most reports. You can add

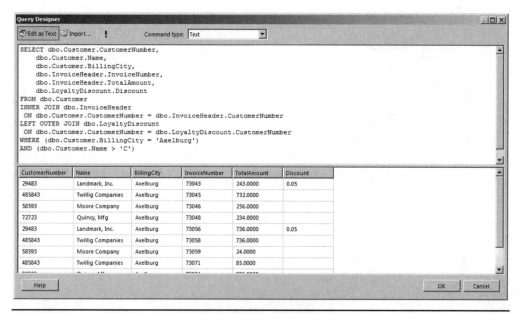

Figure 3-31 *A SELECT statement with two logical expressions in the WHERE clause*

an ORDER BY clause to your SELECT statement to obtain a sorted result set. This statement includes an ORDER BY clause with multiple columns:

```
SELECT dbo.Customer.CustomerNumber,
    dbo.Customer.Name,
    dbo.Customer.BillingCity,
    dbo.InvoiceHeader.InvoiceNumber,
    dbo.InvoiceHeader.TotalAmount,
    dbo.LoyaltyDiscount.Discount
FROM dbo.Customer
INNER JOIN dbo.InvoiceHeader
 ON dbo.Customer.CustomerNumber = dbo.InvoiceHeader.CustomerNumber
LEFT OUTER JOIN dbo.LoyaltyDiscount
 ON dbo.Customer.CustomerNumber = dbo.LoyaltyDiscount.CustomerNumber
WHERE (dbo.Customer.BillingCity = 'Axelburg')
AND (dbo.Customer.Name > 'C')
ORDER BY dbo.Customer.Name DESC, dbo.InvoiceHeader.InvoiceNumber
```

The result set created by this SELECT statement, shown in Figure 3-32, is first sorted by the contents of the Name column in the Customer table. The DESC that follows dbo.Customer.Name in the ORDER BY clause specifies the sort order for

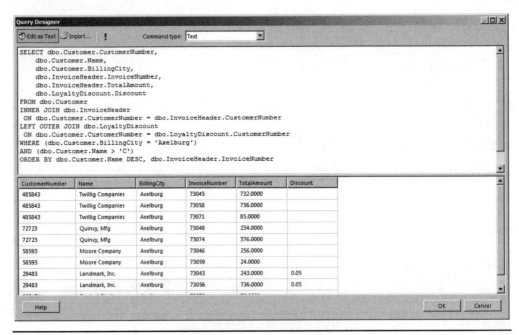

Figure 3-32   *A SELECT statement with an ORDER BY clause*

the customer name sort. DESC means this sort is done in descending order. In other words, the customer names will be sorted from the end of the alphabet to the beginning.

Several rows have the same customer name. For this reason, a second sort column is specified. This second sort is only applied within each group of identical customer names. For example, Twillig Companies has three rows in the result set. These three rows are sorted by the second sort, which is invoice number. No sort order is specified for the invoice number sort, so this defaults to an ascending sort. In other words, the invoice numbers are sorted from lowest to highest.

Constant and Calculated Fields

Our SELECT statement examples thus far have used an asterisk symbol or a FIELD LIST that includes only columns. A FIELD LIST can, in fact, include other things as well. For example, a FIELD LIST can include a constant value, as is shown here:

```
SELECT dbo.Customer.CustomerNumber,
    dbo.Customer.Name,
    dbo.Customer.BillingCity,
```

```
        dbo.InvoiceHeader.InvoiceNumber,
        dbo.InvoiceHeader.TotalAmount,
        dbo.LoyaltyDiscount.Discount,
        'AXEL' AS ProcessingCode
FROM dbo.Customer
INNER JOIN dbo.InvoiceHeader
  ON dbo.Customer.CustomerNumber = dbo.InvoiceHeader.CustomerNumber
LEFT OUTER JOIN dbo.LoyaltyDiscount
  ON dbo.Customer.CustomerNumber = dbo.LoyaltyDiscount.CustomerNumber
WHERE (dbo.Customer.BillingCity = 'Axelburg')
AND (dbo.Customer.Name > 'C')
ORDER BY dbo.Customer.Name DESC, dbo.InvoiceHeader.InvoiceNumber
```

The string constant 'AXEL' has been added to the FIELD LIST. This creates a new column in the result set with the value AXEL in each row. By including AS ProcessingCode on this line, we give this result set column a name of ProcessingCode. Constant values of other data types, such as dates or numbers, can also be added to the FIELD LIST. The result set for this SELECT statement is shown in Figure 3-33.

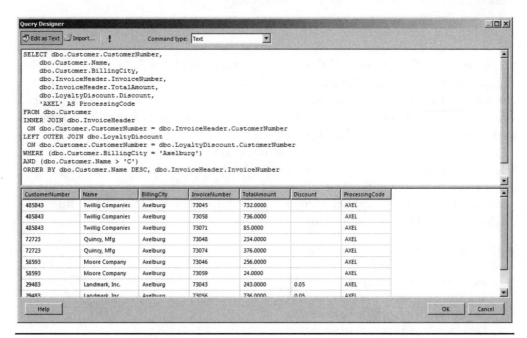

Figure 3-33   *A SELECT statement with a constant in the FIELD LIST*

In addition to adding constant values, you can include calculations in the FIELD LIST. This SELECT statement calculates the discounted invoice amount based on the total amount of the invoice and the loyalty discount:

```
SELECT dbo.Customer.CustomerNumber,
    dbo.Customer.Name,
    dbo.Customer.BillingCity,
    dbo.InvoiceHeader.InvoiceNumber,
    dbo.InvoiceHeader.TotalAmount,
    dbo.LoyaltyDiscount.Discount,
    dbo.InvoiceHeader.TotalAmount -
      (dbo.InvoiceHeader.TotalAmount *
            dbo.LoyaltyDiscount.Discount)
                AS DiscountedTotalAmount
FROM dbo.Customer
INNER JOIN dbo.InvoiceHeader
 ON dbo.Customer.CustomerNumber = dbo.InvoiceHeader.CustomerNumber
LEFT OUTER JOIN dbo.LoyaltyDiscount
 ON dbo.Customer.CustomerNumber = dbo.LoyaltyDiscount.CustomerNumber
WHERE (dbo.Customer.BillingCity = 'Axelburg')
AND (dbo.Customer.Name > 'C')
ORDER BY dbo.Customer.Name DESC, dbo.InvoiceHeader.InvoiceNumber
```

The result set for this SELECT statement is shown in Figure 3-34. Notice the value for the calculated column, DiscountedTotalAmount, is blank (actually NULL) for all the rows that are not for Landmark, Inc. This is because we are using the value of the Discount column in our calculation. The Discount column has a value of NULL for every row except for the Landmark, Inc. rows.

A NULL value cannot be used successfully in any calculation. Any time you try to add, subtract, multiply, or divide a number by NULL, the result is NULL. The only way to receive a value in these situations is to give the database a valid value to use in place of any NULLs it might encounter. This is done using the ISNULL( ) function, as shown in the following statement:

```
SELECT dbo.Customer.CustomerNumber,
    dbo.Customer.Name,
    dbo.Customer.BillingCity,
    dbo.InvoiceHeader.InvoiceNumber,
    dbo.InvoiceHeader.TotalAmount,
    dbo.LoyaltyDiscount.Discount,
    dbo.InvoiceHeader.TotalAmount -
      (dbo.InvoiceHeader.TotalAmount *
        ISNULL(dbo.LoyaltyDiscount.Discount, 0.00))
                AS DiscountedTotalAmount
```

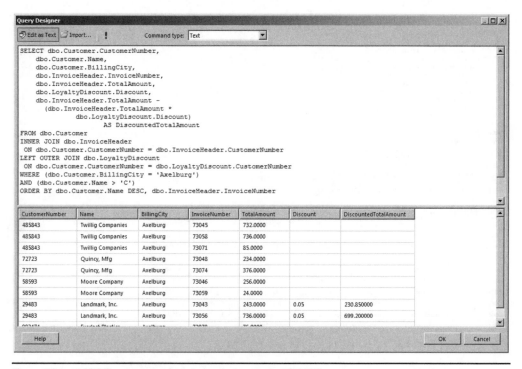

Figure 3-34   *A SELECT statement with a calculated column in the FIELD LIST*

```
FROM dbo.Customer
INNER JOIN dbo.InvoiceHeader
 ON dbo.Customer.CustomerNumber = dbo.InvoiceHeader.CustomerNumber
LEFT OUTER JOIN dbo.LoyaltyDiscount
 ON dbo.Customer.CustomerNumber = dbo.LoyaltyDiscount.CustomerNumber
WHERE (dbo.Customer.BillingCity = 'Axelburg')
AND (dbo.Customer.Name > 'C')
ORDER BY dbo.Customer.Name DESC, dbo.InvoiceHeader.InvoiceNumber
```

Now, when the database encounters a NULL value in the Discount column while it is performing the calculation, it substitutes a value of 0.00 and continues with the calculation. The database only performs this substitution when it encounters a NULL value. If any other value is in the Discount column, it uses that value. The result set from this SELECT statement is shown in Figure 3-35.

The GROUP BY Clause

Our sample SELECT statement appears to resemble a run-on sentence. You have seen, however, that each of these clauses is necessary to change the meaning of the statement

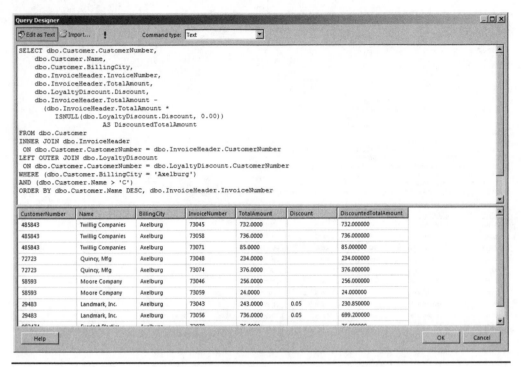

Figure 3-35 *A SELECT statement using the ISNULL() function*

and to provide the desired result set. We will add just two more clauses to the sample SELECT statement before we are done.

At times, as you are analyzing data, you only want to see information at a summary level, rather than viewing all the detail. In other words, you want the result set to group together the information from several rows to form a summary row. Additional instructions must be added to our SELECT statement in two places for this to happen.

First, you need to specify which columns are going to be used to determine when a summary row will be created. These columns are placed in the GROUP BY clause. Consider the following SELECT statement:

```
SELECT dbo.Customer.CustomerNumber,
    dbo.Customer.Name,
    dbo.Customer.BillingCity,
    COUNT(dbo.InvoiceHeader.InvoiceNumber) AS NumberOfInvoices,
    SUM(dbo.InvoiceHeader.TotalAmount) AS TotalAmount,
    dbo.LoyaltyDiscount.Discount,
    SUM(dbo.InvoiceHeader.TotalAmount -
        (dbo.InvoiceHeader.TotalAmount *
            ISNULL (dbo.LoyaltyDiscount.Discount, 0.00)) )
                AS DiscountedTotalAmount
```

```
FROM dbo.Customer
INNER JOIN dbo.InvoiceHeader
  ON dbo.Customer.CustomerNumber = dbo.InvoiceHeader.CustomerNumber
LEFT OUTER JOIN dbo.LoyaltyDiscount
  ON dbo.Customer.CustomerNumber = dbo.LoyaltyDiscount.CustomerNumber
WHERE (dbo.Customer.BillingCity = 'Axelburg')
AND (dbo.Customer.Name > 'C')
GROUP BY dbo.Customer.CustomerNumber, dbo.Customer.Name,
    dbo.Customer.BillingCity, dbo.LoyaltyDiscount.Discount
ORDER BY dbo.Customer.Name DESC
```

The CustomerNumber, Name, BillingCity, and Discount columns are included in the GROUP BY clause. When this query is run, each unique set of values from these four columns will result in a row in the result set.

Second, you need to specify how the columns in the FIELD LIST that are not included in the GROUP BY clause are to be handled. In the sample SELECT statement, the InvoiceNumber and TotalAmount columns are in the FIELD LIST, but are not part of the GROUP BY clause. The calculated column, DiscountedTotalAmount, is also in the FIELD LIST, but it is not present in the GROUP BY clause. In the sample SELECT statement, these three columns are the non-group-by columns.

The SELECT statement is asking for the values from several rows to be combined into one summary row. The SELECT statement needs to provide a way for this combining to take place. This is done by enclosing each non-group-by column in a special function called an *aggregate function*, which performs a mathematical operation on values from a number of rows and returns a single result. Aggregate functions include:

- ▶ **SUM( )**   Returns the sum of the values
- ▶ **AVG( )**   Returns the average of the values
- ▶ **COUNT( )**   Returns a count of the values
- ▶ **MAX( )**   Returns the largest value
- ▶ **MIN( )**   Returns the smallest value

The SELECT statement in our GROUP BY example uses the SUM( ) aggregate function to return the sum of the invoice amount and the sum of the discounted amount for each customer. It also uses the COUNT( ) aggregate function to return the number of invoices for each customer. The result set from this SELECT statement is shown in Figure 3-36. Note when an aggregate function is placed around a column name in the FIELD LIST, the SELECT statement can no longer determine what name to use for that column in the result set. You need to supply a column name to use in the result set, as shown in this SELECT statement.

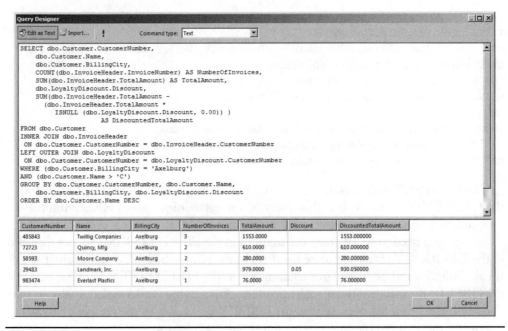

Figure 3-36 *A SELECT statement with a GROUP BY clause*

NOTE

When you're using a GROUP BY clause, all columns in the FIELD LIST must either be included in the GROUP BY clause or be enclosed in an aggregate function. In the sample SELECT statement, the CustomerNumber column is all that is necessary in the GROUP BY clause to provide the desired grouping. However, because the Name, BillingCity, and Discount columns do not lend themselves to being aggregated, they are included in the GROUP BY clause along with the CustomerNumber column.

The HAVING Clause

The GROUP BY clause has a special clause that can be used with it to determine which grouped rows will be included in the result set. This is the HAVING clause. The HAVING clause functions similarly to the WHERE clause. The WHERE clause limits the rows in the result set by checking conditions at the row level. The *HAVING* clause limits the rows in the result set by checking conditions at the group level.

Consider the following SELECT statement:

```
SELECT dbo.Customer.CustomerNumber,
    dbo.Customer.Name,
    dbo.Customer.BillingCity,
    COUNT(dbo.InvoiceHeader.InvoiceNumber) AS NumberOfInvoices,
    SUM(dbo.InvoiceHeader.TotalAmount) AS TotalAmount,
```

```
      dbo.LoyaltyDiscount.Discount,
      SUM(dbo.InvoiceHeader.TotalAmount -
        (dbo.InvoiceHeader.TotalAmount *
          ISNULL(dbo.LoyaltyDiscount.Discount,0.00)))
                    AS DiscountedTotalAmount
FROM dbo.Customer
INNER JOIN dbo.InvoiceHeader
 ON dbo.Customer.CustomerNumber = dbo.InvoiceHeader.CustomerNumber
LEFT OUTER JOIN dbo.LoyaltyDiscount
 ON dbo.Customer.CustomerNumber = dbo.LoyaltyDiscount.CustomerNumber
WHERE (dbo.Customer.BillingCity = 'Axelburg')
AND (dbo.Customer.Name > 'C')
GROUP BY dbo.Customer.CustomerNumber, dbo.Customer.Name,
    dbo.Customer.BillingCity, dbo.LoyaltyDiscount.Discount
HAVING COUNT(dbo.InvoiceHeader.InvoiceNumber) >= 2
ORDER BY dbo.Customer.Name DESC
```

The WHERE clause says that a row must have a BillingCity column with a value of Axelburg and a Name column with a value greater than C before it can be included in the group. The HAVING clause says a group must contain at least two invoices before it can be included in the result set. The result set for this SELECT statement is shown in Figure 3-37.

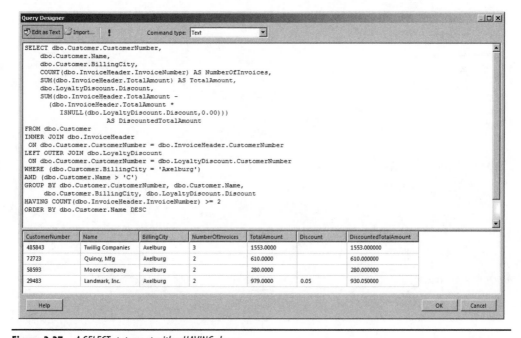

Figure 3-37   *A SELECT statement with a HAVING clause*

On to the Reports

Good reporting depends more on getting the right data out of the database than it does on creating a clean report design and delivering the report in a timely manner. If you are feeling a little overwhelmed by the workings of relational databases and SELECT queries, don't worry. Refer to this chapter from time to time if you need to.

Also, remember Reporting Services provides you with the Query Designer tool to assist with the query-creation process. You needn't remember the exact syntax for the LEFT OUTER JOIN or a GROUP BY clause. What you do need to know are the capabilities of the SELECT statement so you know what to instruct the Query Designer to create.

Finally, when you are creating your queries, use the same method that was used here: in other words, build them one step at a time. Join together the tables you will need for your report, determine what columns are required, and then come up with a WHERE clause that gets you only the rows you are looking for. After that, you can add in the sorting and grouping. Assemble one clause, and then another and another, and pretty soon, you will have a slam-bang query that will give you exactly the data you need!

Now, on to the reports....

Chapter 4

A Visit to Emerald City: The Report Wizard

In This Chapter

- ► **Obtaining the Galactic Database**
- ► **Getting Started with the Authoring Environment**
- ► **Your First Report**

- ► **An Interactive Table Report**
- ► **Creating Matrix Reports**
- ► **Report Parameters**
- ► **Flying Solo**

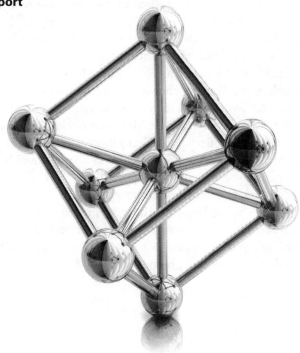

If the relational database concepts of Chapter 3 were new to you, you may feel like you have been through a twister and are not in Kansas anymore. You can take heart, however, knowing you have completed the preliminaries and are now ready to start building reports. So, without further ado, strap on your ruby slippers and follow the yellow-brick road, because you are off to see the wizard!

That wizard is, of course, the Report Wizard. Like the ruler of the Emerald City, the Report Wizard is not all-powerful. For example, the Report Wizard will not let you make use of all the features available in Reporting Services. The wizard is, however, a great place to get a feel for the way reports are constructed.

Obtaining the Galactic Database

Beginning with this chapter, we will create sample reports using the Galactic database. If you have not done so already, download the sample code from this book's webpage at www.mhprofessional.com. Search for the book's webpage using the ISBN, which is 0071760474, and then use the "Sample Code" link to download the zip file containing the book's material. Follow the instructions in the zip file to install the Galactic database and the other sample code as needed.

Getting Started with the Authoring Environment

In Chapter 1, we talked about the two different report authoring environments available for Reporting Services—the Report Designer and the Report Builder. Both environments provide access to all of the features of Reporting Services. The exercises in this book can be completed with either the Report Designer, found in SQL Server Data Tools (SSDT) and Visual Studio (VS), or the Report Builder, which is its own stand-alone application. You can choose whichever environment you are most comfortable with. You may wish to try a few of the exercises using SSDT or VS, and a few of the exercises using Report Builder to decide which works best for you.

Report Builder approaches report authoring similar to the way you would author a document in Word or Excel. SSDT and Visual Studio approach report authoring more like software development. (In fact, SSDT is a special version of the Visual Studio development environment operating under a different name.)

When using Report Builder, it is up to you to save your reports in an organized manner. You must create folders, either on the Report Server or in the file system that will group your reports in a meaningful manner. When using SSDT or Visual Studio, multiple reports are grouped together for you inside a project.

Creating a Project Using the Report Designer

SQL Server Data Tools and Visual Studio can be used for a number of business intelligence and software development tasks. *SQL Server Data Tools* is used to create Integration Services packages for data extract, transform, and load (ETL). It also is used to create Analysis Services BI Semantic Models. Visual Studio is used to create Windows applications, web applications, and web services.

To facilitate this variety of capabilities, these development environments support many different types of projects. These project types organize the multitude of solutions that can be created within the development environment into related groups. Reporting Services reports are created using the Business Intelligence | Reporting Services project template.

Project Templates

When you choose to create a new project in SSDT or in Visual Studio, you will see the New Project dialog box shown in Figure 4-1. The Installed Templates area of the screen shows the group of project templates you will be concerned with: Business Intelligence. The *Business Intelligence* group includes templates for a number of different projects.

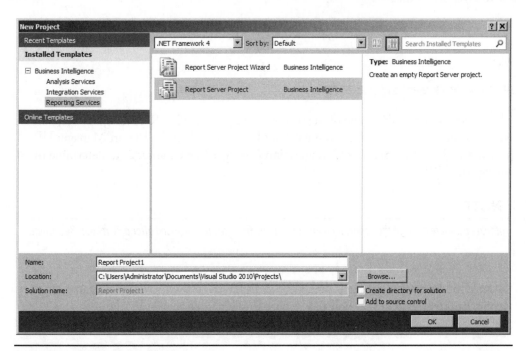

Figure 4-1   *The New Project dialog box*

NOTE

If you are using Visual Studio, you may see other groupings of project templates in addition to Business Intelligence for other types of software development.

You will look at two project templates in this book: Report Server Project Wizard, and Report Server Project. Either one will, ultimately, create a report project. The *Report Server Project Wizard* template uses the Report Wizard to guide you through the process of creating the first report in your new report project. The *Report Server Project* template simply creates an empty report project and turns you loose.

Launching the Report Builder

The Report Builder is available as a free download from Microsoft. If you download and install the Report Builder in this manner, you can launch it from the Start menu in the same way you launch any other software package. If you do not download and install the Report Builder, you will have to launch it from the Report Manager.

To do this, open a browser and navigate to the Report Manager. By default, the URL for the Report Manager is:

```
http://localhost/Reports
```

or

```
http://{servername}/Reports
```

where *{servername}* is the name of the server where you installed Reporting Services. If the Report Manager is not installed in the default location, look at the Report Manager URL page of the Reporting Services Configuration Manager (see Chapter 2) to determine the appropriate URL.

NOTE

It takes a minute or so for the Report Manager to load the first time it is accessed after a PC reboot. Be patient.

Once the Report Manager Home page is displayed in the browser, you can click the Report Builder button to launch the Report Builder, as shown in Figure 4-2.

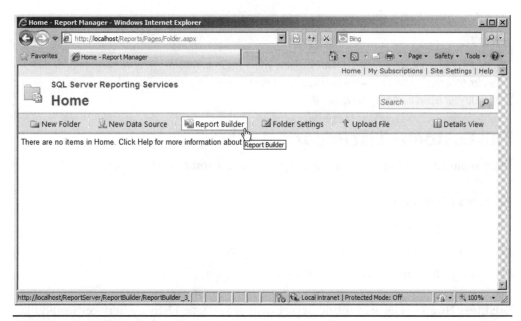

Figure 4-2   *Launching the Report Builder from the Report Manager*

Your First Report

Once you have installed the Galactic database, you are ready to build your first Reporting Services report. Of course, few people build reports just for the fun of it. Usually, there is some business reason for this endeavor. In this book, as stated in the previous chapter, we use the business needs of Galactic Delivery Services (GDS) as the basis for our sample reports.

Each of the sample reports used in this book is presented in a manner similar to what you see in this section. The report is introduced with a list of the Reporting Services features it highlights. This is followed by the business need of our sample company, Galactic Delivery Services, which this report is meant to fill. Next is an overview of the tasks that must be accomplished to create the report.

Finally, there are the steps to walk through for each task. In addition to the step-by-step description, each task includes a few notes to provide additional information on the steps you just completed. Follow the step-by-step instructions to complete the task, and then read through the task notes to gain additional understanding of the process you have just completed. You can complete the step-by-step instructions using SSDT, Visual Studio, or the Report Builder.

NOTE

Some tasks have one set of instructions for SSDT and Visual Studio and another set of instructions for Report Builder. Other tasks have the same set of steps for all environments. Be sure to follow only those sets of steps that apply to your report authoring environment.

The Customer List Report

Here is our first attempt at creating a report: the Customer List Report.

Features Highlighted

► Creating a data source

► Using the Query Designer to create a dataset

► Using the Report Wizard to create a table report

Business Need   The accounting department at Galactic Delivery Services would like an e-mail directory containing all the billing contacts for its customers. The directory should be an alphabetical list of all GDS customers. It must include the customer name, along with a billing contact and a billing e-mail address for each customer.

Task Overview

1. Begin a New Project in the SSDT or Visual Studio, or Preparing to Create a New Report in the Report Builder
2. Create a Data Source
3. Create a Dataset
4. Choose the Report Layout

Customer List Report, Task 1: Begin a New Project in SSDT or Visual Studio, or Preparing to Create a New Report in the Report Builder

DT **SSDT and Visual Studio Steps**
If you are using SSDT or Visual Studio, follow these steps. If you are using the Report Builder, skip ahead to the Report Builder instructions.

1. Run SSDT or Visual Studio. The Start page appears, as shown here.

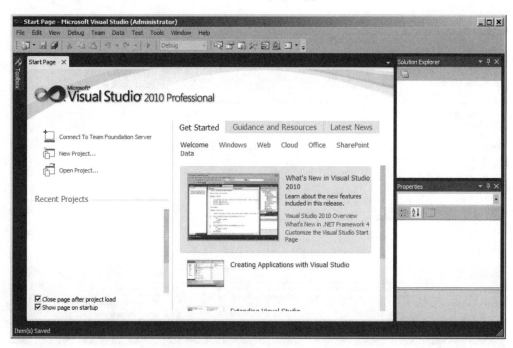

NOTE

The first illustration shows the default configuration of SSDT. Your screen may vary if this configuration has been changed.

2. Click the New Project toolbar button to create a new project. This displays the New Project dialog box, as shown in the following illustration. (You can create a new project in three different ways: Select File | New | Project from the Main

menu; click the New Project toolbar button; or click the New: Project link on the Start page.)

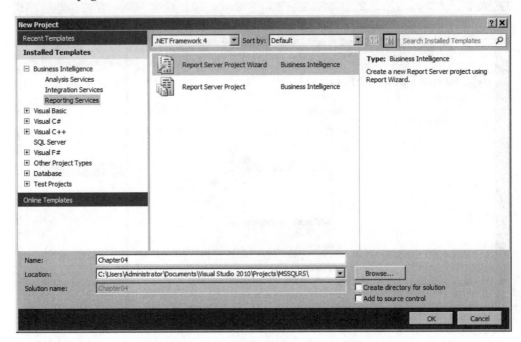

3. Expand Business Intelligence and select Reporting Services in the Installed Templates area of the dialog box.

4. Select Report Server Project Wizard in the center area of the dialog box.

5. Type **Chapter04** for the project name. This project will contain all the reports you create in this chapter using SSDT or Visual Studio.

6. Click Browse to open the Project Location dialog box.

7. The dialog box should default to the My Documents/Visual Studio 2010/Projects folder. If it does not, navigate to this folder.

8. Click the New folder button.

9. Enter **MSSQLRS** for the name Chapter04 of the new folder. This folder will contain all the projects you create for this book. Press ENTER.

10. Click Select Folder in the Project Location dialog box.

11. Make sure the Create directory for solution check box is unchecked. The New Project dialog box should now look like the second illustration.

Task Notes for SSDT and Visual Studio   We have now established a name and location for this project. This must be done for every project you create. Because SSDT and Visual Studio use the project name to create a folder for all the project files, the project name must be a valid Windows folder name. You can use the Browse button to browse to the appropriate location, as we did here, or you can type the path in the Location text box.

NOTE

Valid folder names can contain any character, except the following:
  */ ? : & \ * " < > | # %*
In addition, a folder cannot be named "." or "..."

The project name is appended to the end of the location path to create the full path for the folder that will contain the new project. In our example, a folder called Chapter04 will be created inside the folder MSSQLRS. All the files created as part of the Chapter04 project will be placed in this folder.

RB | **Report Builder Steps**
If you are using the Report Builder, follow these steps.

1. Open a browser and navigate to the Report Manager as discussed earlier in this chapter.
2. Click the New Folder button as shown here.

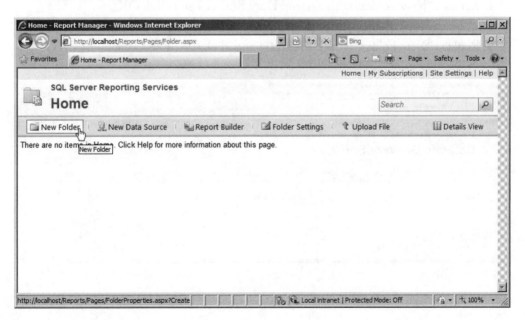

3. The New Folder page appears. Replace "New Folder" with **Galactic Deliver Services**. The New Folder page will appear as shown.

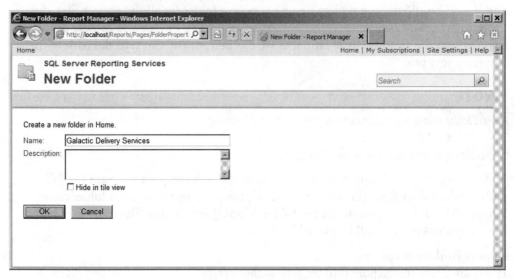

4. Click OK.

5. Click the entry for the Galactic Delivery Services folder to navigate into that folder.

6. Click the New Folder button again.

7. Replace "New Folder" with **Shared Data Sources** and click OK.

8. Click the New Folder button once more.

9. Replace "New Folder" with **Chapter04** and click OK. The Galactic Delivery Services folder appears as shown here.

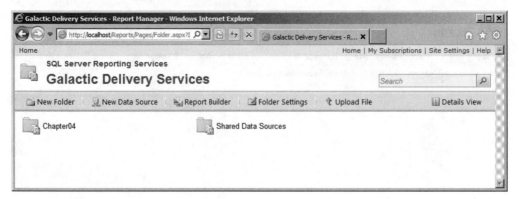

Task Notes for Report Builder   When using Report Builder for these exercises, we are going to save the resulting reports right on the report server. It is possible to save Report Builder reports directly to the file system. However, working with the report server and the Report Manager user interface on that report server allows us to work with a shared data source, which is a Reporting Services best practice.

If you do not have access to a report server, you can still create and save reports using Report Builder. You will first need to install Report Builder as its own application, rather than launching it from Report Manager. You can then launch Report Builder from your PC and save your reports in the file system. You will also have to create a data source in each report rather than using a shared data source.

Customer List Report, Task 2: Create a Data Source

DT   **SSDT and Visual Studio Steps**

1. Click OK in the New Project dialog box to start the Report Wizard. The Welcome to the Report Wizard page appears, as shown here.

2. Click Next. The Select the Data Source page appears.

3. Type **Galactic** for the data source name.

4. Select Microsoft SQL Server from the Type drop-down list, if it is not already selected.

5. Click Edit. The Connection Properties dialog box appears.

6. Type the name of the Microsoft SQL Server database server that is hosting the Galactic database. If the Galactic database is hosted by the default instance of SQL Server on the computer you are currently working on, you may type **(local)** for the server name.

7. Click the Use SQL Server Authentication radio button.

8. Type **GalacticReporting** for the User name.

9. Type **G@l@ct1c** for the Password. (The third character of the password is a lowercase l. The seventh character of the password is the number 1.)

10. Check the Save my password check box.

11. Select Galactic from the Select or enter a database name drop-down list. The Connection Properties dialog box should now look like what is shown here.

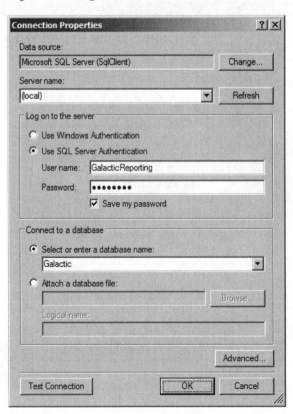

12. Click the Test Connection button. If the message "Test connection succeeded" appears, continue with Step 13. If an error message appears, make sure the name of your database server, the user name, the password, and the name of your database were entered properly. If your test connection still does not succeed, make sure you have correctly installed the Galactic database.

13. Click OK to return to the Select the Data Source page of the Report Wizard.

14. Check the Make this a shared data source check box. This page should now look like what is shown here.

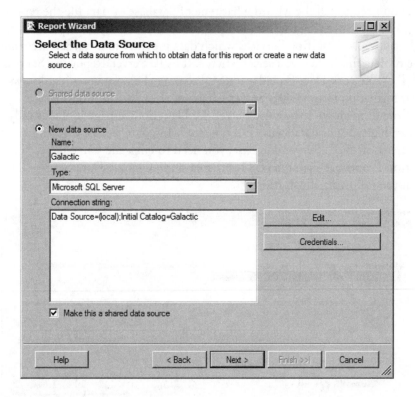

Task Notes for SSDT and Visual Studio　As discussed in Chapter 1, the data source is a set of instructions for connecting to the database server or the data file that will provide the information for your report. This set of instructions is also known as a connection string. In this sample report, we used the Connection Properties dialog box to build the connection string.

CAUTION

If you are manually entering a connection string, do not include the login and password information. The connection string is stored as plain text in the report definition file, so a password stored as part of the connection string is easy to discover. Instead, use the Credentials button on the Select the Data Source page to enter the login and password so they are stored in a more secure fashion.

Reporting Services can utilize data from a number of different databases and data files, but you need to tell the wizard what type of database or data file the report will be using. You did this using the Type drop-down list in Step 4 of the previous task. This selection tells Reporting Services which data provider to use when accessing the database or data file. When you select Microsoft SQL Server, Reporting Services uses the .NET Framework Data Provider for SQL Server. This data provider knows how to retrieve information from a SQL Server database.

The Type drop-down list on the Select the Data Source page includes only a few of the possible types of data sources. If you are using data from a data source other than a Microsoft SQL Server database, you need to click the Change button on the Connection Properties dialog box. This displays the Change Data Source dialog box shown in the following illustration.

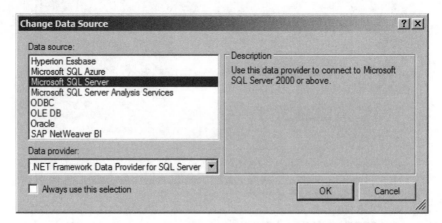

Use this dialog box to select the appropriate data source type.

Each data provider requires slightly different bits of information to create the connection string. The Connection Properties dialog box changes to suit the selected data provider. This means Steps 6 through 11 will vary when you use a data source type other than Microsoft SQL Server. Simply provide the information requested in the

Connection Properties dialog box. Be sure to use the Test Connection button to make sure everything is entered properly before leaving the Connection Properties dialog box.

Checking the Save My Password check box on the Connection Properties page allows the data source credentials to be saved with the data source definition. The *data source credentials* are the user name and password information required to access that data source. The credentials are encrypted before they are saved to help protect them. If you are not comfortable having the credentials stored in this manner, leave both the user name and password fields blank. You will be prompted for the credentials every time you execute the report or modify the dataset.

NOTE

If you leave the data source credentials blank and your selected data source requires a login, you will be prompted for database credentials when you click Next on the Select the Data Source page. The credentials you enter here are used to create a connection to the data source for the Design the Query page and for the Query Designer. These credentials are not stored with the data source.

A data source can be used by a single report, or it can be shared by several reports in the same project or on the same report server. Checking the Make this a shared data source check box allows this data source to be used by many reports. Shared data sources are stored separately from the reports that use them. Nonshared, or *embedded*, data sources are stored right in the report definition. If you have a number of reports in the same project that utilize data from the same database or the same data files, you will save time by using a shared data source.

CAUTION

Even though the data source credentials are encrypted, it is never a good idea to use the system administrator account or any other database login with system administrator privileges to access data for reporting. Always create a database login that has only the privileges required for reporting operations, and use this login as the reporting credentials.

Some companies require that reports use data from a development database server while they are being developed and a production database server when the reports are completed. Using a shared data source in this type of an environment makes it easier to switch a number of reports from the development database server to the production database server. The change is made once to the shared data source, and all the reports are ready to go.

RB **Report Builder Steps**

1. In Report Manager, click the Shared Data Sources folder to navigate into that folder.

2. Click on the New Data Source button as shown here.

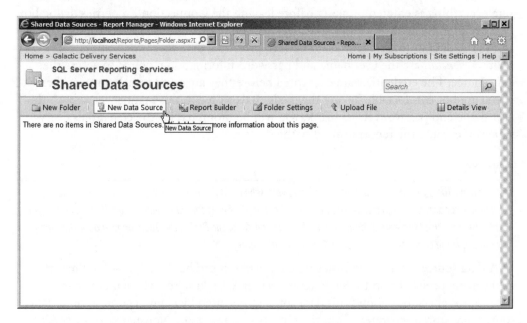

3. The New Data Source page appears. In the Name area, enter **Galactic** as the data source name.

4. Select Microsoft SQL Server from the Data source type drop-down list, if it is not already selected.

5. Type the following for the Connection string:

```
Data Source={servername}; Initial Catalog=Galactic
```

where *{servername}* is the name of the Microsoft SQL Server database server that is hosting the Galactic database. If the Galactic database is hosted by the default instance of SQL Server on the computer you are currently working on, you may use **(local)** for the server name.

6. Click the Credentials stored securely in the report server radio button.

7. Type **GalacticReporting** for the User name.

8. Type **G@l@ct1c** for the Password. (The third character of the password is a lowercase l. The seventh character of the password is the number 1.)

9. Click the Test Connection button. If the message "Connection created successfully" appears near the bottom of the page, continue with Step 10. If an error message appears near the bottom of the page, make sure the connection string (including the correct database server name), the user name, and the password were entered properly. If your test connection still does not succeed, make sure you have correctly installed the Galactic database. When correct, the New Data Source page appears as shown.

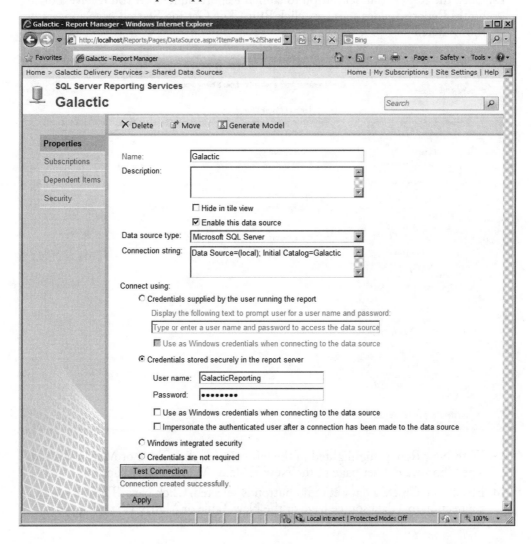

10. Click OK to create the data source.

11. Click the Galactic Delivery Services link in the upper-left corner of the page to return to that folder.

12. Click the Report Builder button to launch Report Builder. (If you receive a dialog box as Report Builder starts up, click Run.) The Getting Started page appears, as shown here.

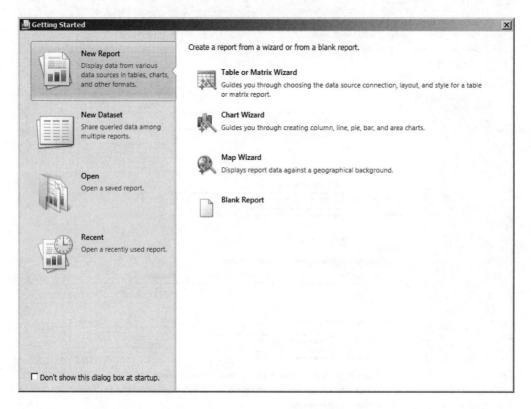

13. With New Report highlighted in the left column, click Table or Matrix Wizard. The Choose a dataset page of the New Table or Matrix Wizard appears.

14. Ensure the Create a dataset radio button is selected. Click Next. The Choose a connection to a data source page of the New Table or Matrix Wizard appears.

15. Click Browse. The Select Data Source dialog box appears.

16. Double-click the Galactic Delivery Services folder, and then double-click the Shared Data Sources folder. The Select Data Source dialog box appears as shown.

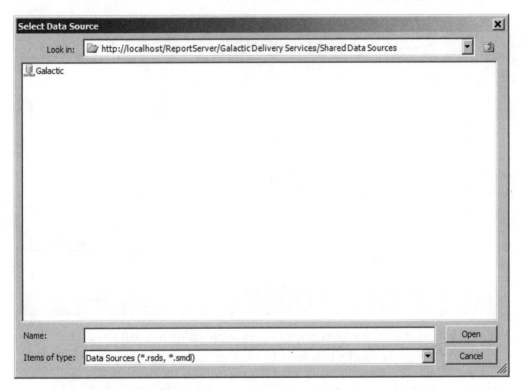

17. Double-click the Galactic shared data source to select it. This is the shared data source that you just created. The Choose a connection to a data source page of the New Table or Matrix Wizard will now appear as shown here.

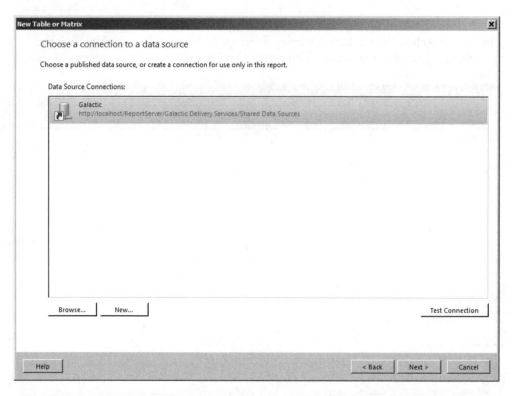

18. Click Next. The Enter Data Source Credentials dialog box will open.

19. Enter **G@l@ct1c** for the Password. (The third character of the password is a lowercase l. The seventh character of the password is the number 1.)

20. Check the Save password with connection check box. The Enter Data Source Credentials dialog box will appear as shown.

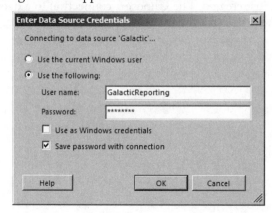

21. Click OK to exit the Enter Data Source Credentials dialog box. You will be taken to the Design a query page of the New Table or Matrix Wizard.

Task Notes for Report Builder   As discussed in Chapter 1, the data source is a set of instructions for connecting to the database server or the data file that will provide the information for your report. This set of instructions is also known as a connection string. In this sample report, we had to enter the connection string on the Shared Data Sources page in Report Manager. Fortunately, we only need to provide the two items, Data Source (server name) and Initial Catalog (database).

CAUTION

When you are manually entering a connection string, do not include the login and password information. The connection string is stored as plain text in the report definition file, so a password stored as part of the connection string is easy to discover. Instead, use the Connect using area of the Shared Data Sources page to enter the login and password so they are stored in a more secure fashion.

Reporting Services can utilize data from a number of different databases and data files, but you need to tell the wizard what type of database or data file the report will be using. You did this using the Data Source type drop-down list in Step 4. This selection tells Reporting Services which data provider to use when accessing the database or data file. When you select Microsoft SQL Server, Reporting Services uses the .NET Framework Data Provider for SQL Server. This data provider knows how to retrieve information from a SQL Server database.

Each data provider requires slightly different bits of information to make a connection. That means the connection string will vary for different data providers. Connection string information for other data providers is beyond the scope of this book. That information can be found on the Internet.

The information entered in the Connect using area is known as the data source credentials. The *data source credentials* are the user name and password information required to access that data source. The credentials are encrypted before they are saved to help protect them. If you are not comfortable having the credentials stored in this manner, leave both the user name and password fields blank. You will be prompted for the credentials every time you execute the report or modify the dataset.

A data source can be used by a single report, or it can be shared by several reports on the same report server. Shared data sources are stored separately from the reports that use them. Nonshared, or *embedded,* data sources are stored right in the report definition. If you have a number of reports in the same project that utilize data from the same database or the same data files, you will save time by using a shared data source.

While the New Table or Matrix Wizard in Report Builder can utilize a shared data source, it cannot, unfortunately, create a shared data source. That was why we manually created the shared data source in Report Manager before we started to create our first report in the Report Builder.

CAUTION

Even though the data source credentials are encrypted, it is never a good idea to use the system administrator account or any other database login with system administrator privileges to access data for reporting. Always create a database login that has only the privileges required for reporting operations, and use this login as the reporting credentials.

Some companies require that reports use data from a development database server while they are being developed and a production database server when the reports are completed. Using a shared data source in this type of an environment makes it easier to switch a number of reports from the development database server to the production database server. The change is made once to the shared data source, and all the reports are ready to go.

Customer List Report, Task 3: Create a Dataset

DT   **SSDT and Visual Studio Steps**

1. Click Next. The Design the Query page of the Report Wizard appears.
2. Click Query Builder. The Query Designer window opens with the Graphical Query Designer active.
3. The Graphical Query Designer is divided into four horizontal sections. The top section is called the *diagram pane.* Right-click in the diagram pane. You see the context menu, as shown here.

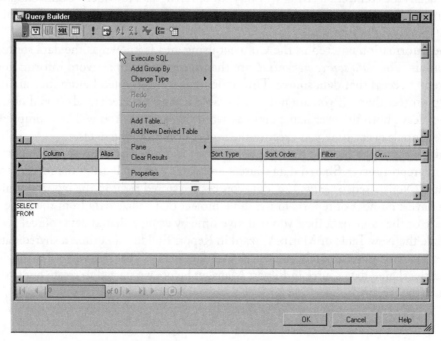

4. Select Add Table from the context menu. This displays the Add Table dialog box shown here. This dialog box contains a list of all the tables, views, and functions that return datasets, which are found in the data source.

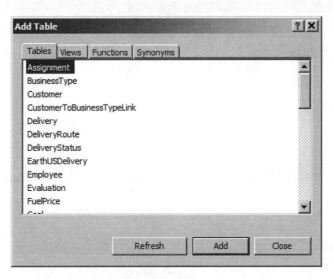

5. Double-click Customer in the list of tables. The Customer table is added to the query.

6. Click Close to exit the Add Table dialog box.

7. A list of the fields in the Customer table is displayed. Check the check box next to the Name field.

8. Scroll down the list of fields, and check the BillingContact and BillingEmail fields as well.

9. The section of the Query Designer directly below the diagram pane is called the *criteria pane*. In the criteria pane, type **1** in the Sort Order column across from the Name field. Or, you can click in the Sort Order column across from the Name field and select 1 from the drop-down list.

10. The section of the Query Designer directly below the criteria pane is the *SQL pane*. Right-click in the SQL pane. You see the context menu shown here.

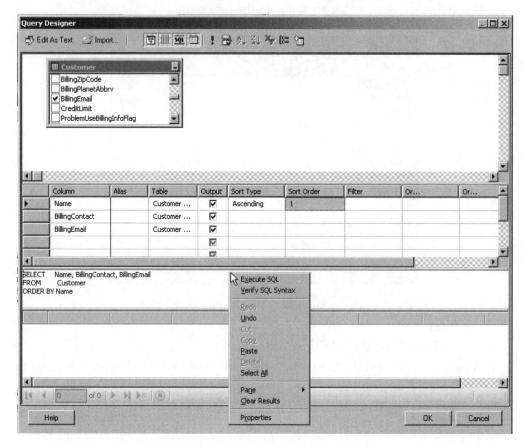

11. Select Execute SQL from the context menu. This runs the query and displays the results in the bottom section of the Query Designer. This bottom section is called the *results pane.* The Query Designer should now look like the illustration shown here.

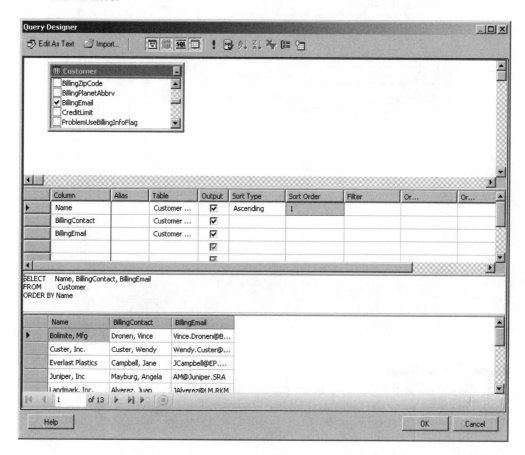

12. Click OK to return to the Design the Query page of the Report Wizard. This page should now look like the following illustration. Be sure to read the Task Notes for this task found after the Report Builder steps.

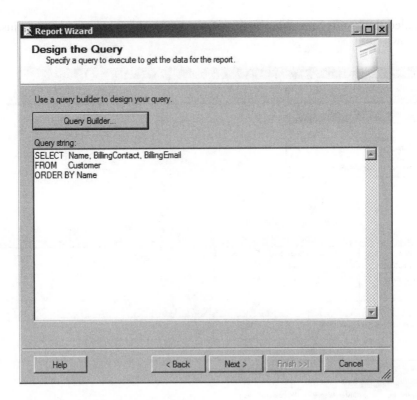

Report Builder Steps

1. We left off at the Design a query page of the New Table or Matrix Wizard. This page holds the Graphical Query Designer. The Graphical Query Designer is divided into several panes. The left side is the *Database view pane*. In the Database view pane, expand the Tables folder.

2. Expand the entry for the Customer table.

3. Check the boxes next to the following fields in the Customer table:

   ▶ Name

   ▶ BillingContact

   ▶ BillingEmail

The selected fields appear in the *Selected fields pane.* The Design a query page of
the New Table or Matrix Wizard should appear as shown here.

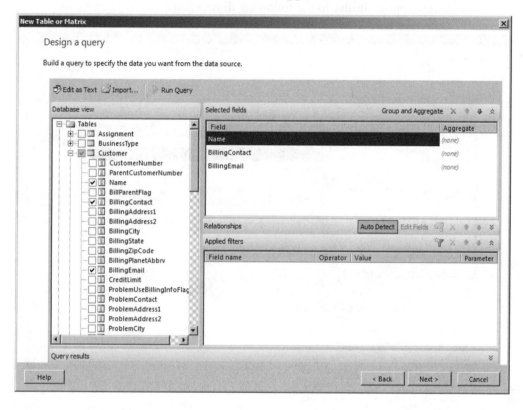

4. Click Run Query from the toolbar. This runs the query and displays the results in the bottom section. This bottom section is called the *Query results pane*. The page should now appear similar to the following illustration.

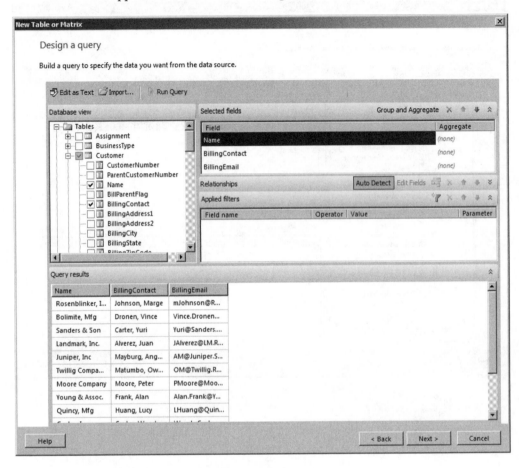

Task Notes The dataset represents the information to be retrieved from the data source and used in your report. The dataset consists of two parts. The first part is the database command used to retrieve data. This is the SELECT statement you created using the Query Designer. (The SELECT statement is created behind the scenes. It is not visible in the query designer.) This database command is called the query string.

The second part is the list of the columns in the result set created by executing the query string. This list of columns is called the *structure* or *schema* of the result set. The Query Designer determines the field list by executing the query string in a special manner so it returns the structure of the result set, but it does not return any rows in the result set.

When using the Query Designer with SQL Server Data Tools/Visual Studio, those of you familiar with your data source and also familiar with the SELECT statement can type your SELECT statement in the Query String text box on the Design the Query page. This is especially appropriate when you are executing a stored procedure to retrieve data rather than using a SELECT statement. A *stored procedure* is a program saved inside the database itself that can be used to modify or retrieve data. Using stored procedures in a query string is discussed more in Chapter 8.

It is a good idea to run the query yourself before exiting the Query Designer. We did this in Steps 10 and 11 of the SSDT/Visual Studio steps for this task and in Step 4 of the Report Builder steps for this task. Running the query ensures no errors exist in the SQL statement the Query Designer created for you. It also lets you look at the result set so you can make sure you are getting the information you expected.

Customer List Report, Task 4: Choose the Report Layout

DT **SSDT and Visual Studio Steps**

1. Click Next. The Select the Report Type page of the Report Wizard appears.

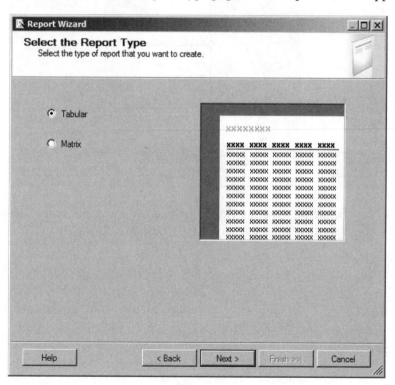

2. Make sure the Tabular radio button is selected, and click Next. The Design the Table page of the Report Wizard appears.

3. With the Name field highlighted in the Available fields list, click Details. The Name field moves to the Displayed fields list.

4. Do the same thing with the BillingContact and BillingEmail fields. The Design the Table page should now look like the following illustration.

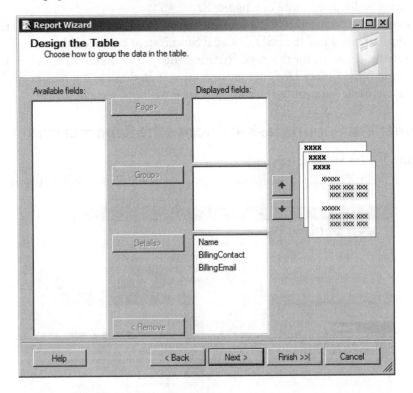

5. Click Next. Select the Ocean style in the style list. The Choose the Table Style page of the Report Wizard appears as shown here.

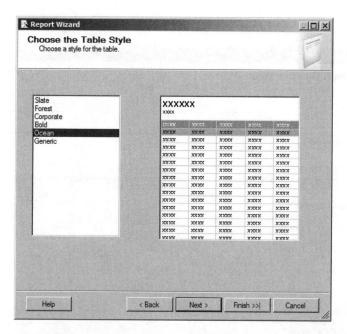

6. Click Next. The Choose the Deployment Location page of the Report Wizard appears. (This page of the wizard will be skipped under certain circumstances. See the Task Notes for this task.)

7. Click Next. The Completing the Wizard page appears.

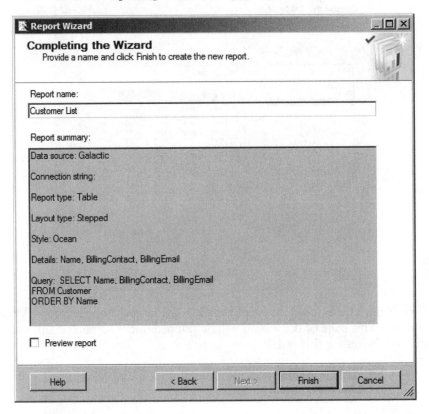

8. Type **Customer List** for the report name.

9. Click Finish. The SQL Server Data Tools or Visual Studio window appears with the Report Designer active.

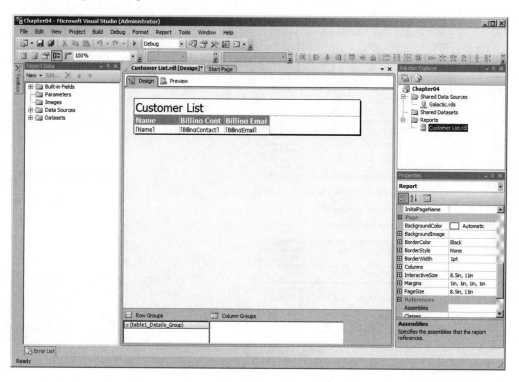

10. Click the Preview tab located just above the report layout. A preview of your report appears.

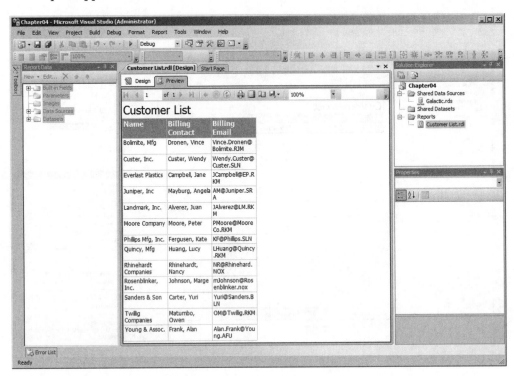

11. Click the Design tab.
12. The Report Wizard created columns in our report that seem a bit too narrow. We can improve the report by widening the columns. Click the Name heading ("Name" in a cell without square brackets around it).
13. Place your mouse pointer on the line separating the gray box above the Name heading and the gray box above the Billing Contact heading. Your mouse pointer changes to a double-headed arrow, as shown here.

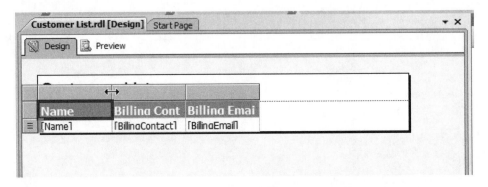

14. Hold down the left mouse button, and move the mouse pointer to the right. This makes the Name column wider.

15. Follow the technique described in Step 13 of this task to widen the Billing Contact and Billing Email columns as well.

16. Click the Preview tab. Your report should appear as shown here.

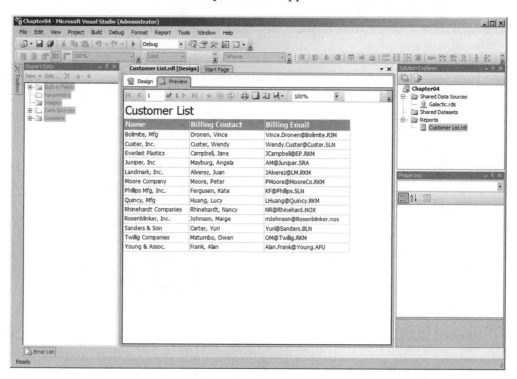

17. Repeat Steps 11 through 16 until you are satisfied with the appearance of the report.

18. When you are satisfied with the report, click the Save All button on the toolbar. This saves the project, the shared data source, and the report files. The Save All button is highlighted in the following illustration. Be sure to read the Task Notes for this task found after the Report Builder steps.

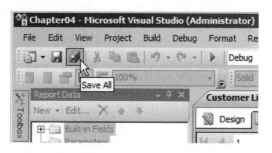

RB **Report Builder Steps**

1. Click Next. The Arrange fields page of the New Table or Matrix Wizard appears.
2. Drag the Name field from the Available fields list and drop it in the Values area.
3. Do the same thing for the BillingContact and BillingEmail fields. The Arrange fields page should now look like the following illustration.

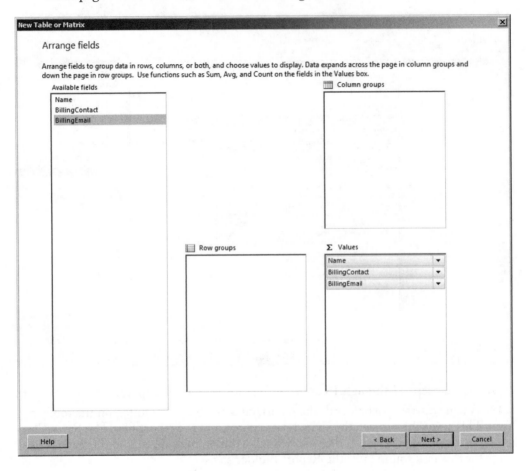

4. Click Next. The Choose the layout page of the wizard appears as shown here.

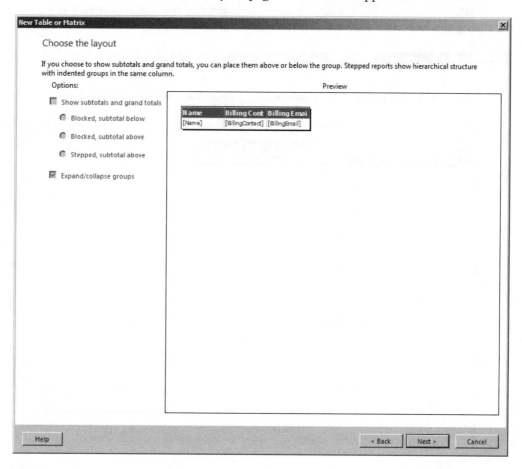

5. Our report layout is too basic to allow us any options here, so everything is disabled. Click Next. The Choose a style page of the wizard appears as shown here.

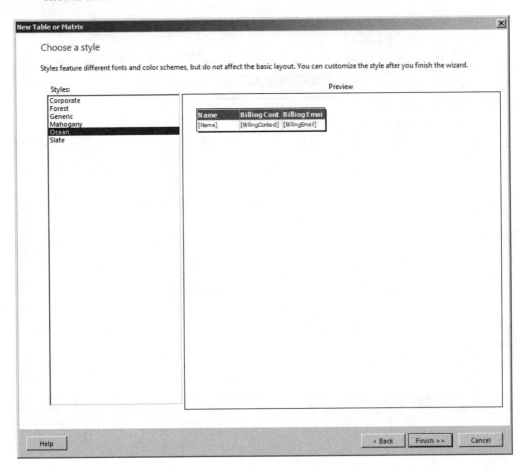

6. Select the Ocean style in the style list.

7. Click Finish. Report Builder shows the completed report design.

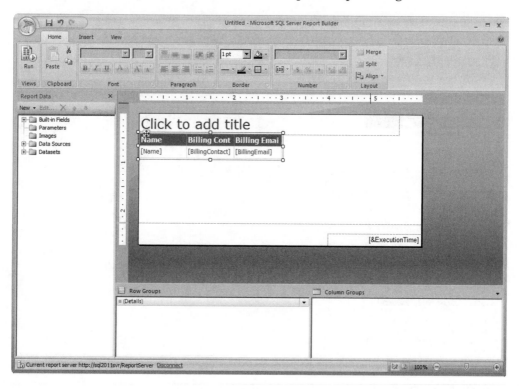

8. Click the Run button located in the upper-left corner. After a moment, a preview of your report appears.

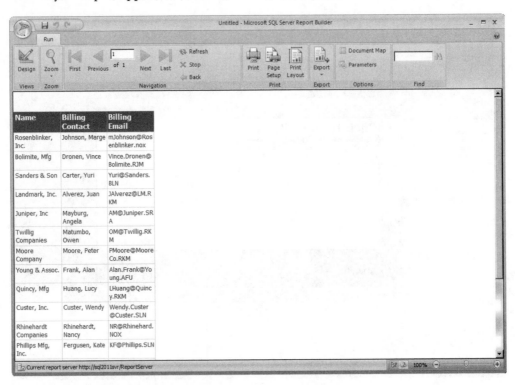

9. Click the Design button in the upper-left corner.

10. The Report Wizard created columns in our report that seem a bit too narrow. We can improve the report by widening the columns. Click the Name heading ("Name" in a cell without square brackets around it).

11. Place your mouse pointer on the line separating the gray box above the Name heading and the gray box above the Billing Contact heading. Your mouse pointer changes to a double-headed arrow, as shown here.

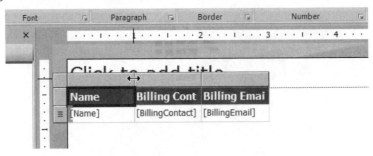

12. Hold down the left mouse button, and move the mouse pointer to the right. This makes the Name column wider.

13. Follow the technique described in Step 12 of this task to widen the Billing Contact and Billing Email columns as well.

14. Click the Run button. Your report should appear as shown here.

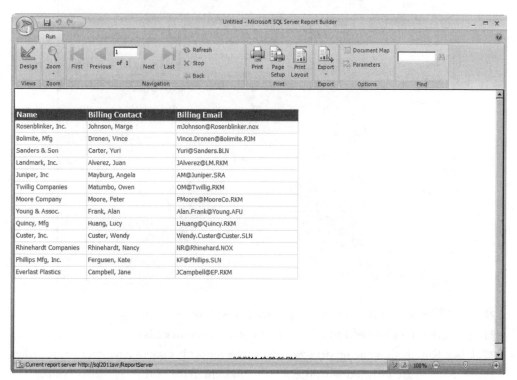

15. Repeat Steps 9 through 14 until you are satisfied with the appearance of the report.

16. As you view the report, notice the customer names are in a random order. The Design a query page of the wizard did not allow us to add an ORDER BY clause to the query. Instead, we will sort the data in the report. While viewing the report design, find the Row Groups area. Click the drop-down arrow next to the "= (Details)" entry and select Group Properties from the list. The Group Properties dialog box appears.

17. Click the entry for the Sorting page of the dialog box.

18. Click Add to add a Sort by column.

19. From the Sort by drop-down list, select "[Name]" to sort by customer name. The Group Properties dialog box should appear as shown.

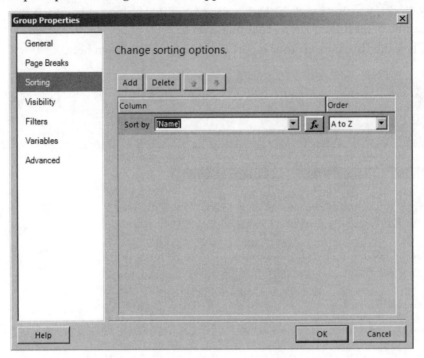

20. Click OK to exit the Group Properties dialog box.
21. Click the "Click to add title" area, and enter **Customer List**.
22. Click Run to view the report again. Note the report is now in customer name order.
23. When you are satisfied with the report, click the Save button at the top of the window. This saves the report design. The Save button is highlighted in the following illustration.

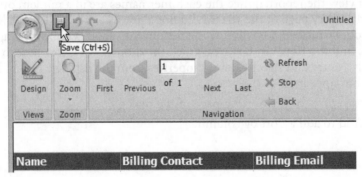

24. The Save As Report dialog box appears. Because you launched Report Builder from the Report Manager, the Save As Report dialog will default to the Home folder of the report server. If you want to save the report to the file system, use the My Documents or My Computer button on the left side of the dialog box. As discussed, we will save the reports directly to the report server when creating reports with Report Builder. Double-click the Galactic Delivery Services folder, and then double-click the Chapter04 folder.

25. Enter **Customer List** for the report Name. The Save As Report dialog appears as shown.

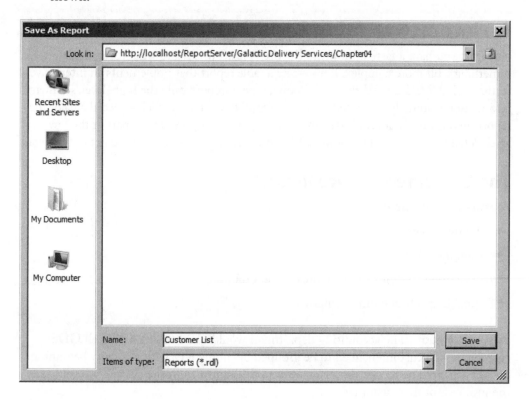

26. Click Save.

Task Notes   If you completed the SSDT and Visual Studio steps, you encountered the Choose the Deployment Location page (refer to the illustration in Step 6 for SSDT and Visual Studio). The information entered on this page is used when the report is moved from the SSDT or Visual Studio environment to a report server. These items are saved with the project, not with an individual report. For this reason, the Deployment

Location page is only displayed by the SSDT and Visual Studio Report Wizard for the first report created in a project. We discuss report deployment in Chapter 10.

For SSDT, Visual Studio, and Report Builder, you probably had to adjust the column widths several times to get the report just the way you wanted it to look. This is not a problem. Most reports you create require multiple trips between the Design and Preview/Run modes before everything is laid out as it should be. Knowing you can move back and forth with such ease is a real plus of the Report Designer and the Report Builder.

Congratulations! You have now completed your first report.

An Interactive Table Report

Now that you have a taste of how the Report Wizard works and what it can do, let's try something a bit more complex. Let's create a table report that implements an interactive feature called *drilldown*. With the drilldown type of report, only the high-level, summary information is initially presented to the viewers. They can then click a special area of the report (in our case, that area is designated by a plus [+] sign) to reveal part of the lower-level, detail information. The viewers drill down through the summary to get to the detail.

The Customer-Invoice Report

Features Highlighted

▶ Using a shared data source

▶ Linking tables

▶ Assigning columns for page breaks and grouping

▶ Enabling subtotals and drilldown

Business Need   The accounting department would like a report listing all GDS customers. The customers need to be grouped by billing city, with each city beginning on a new page. The report allows a viewer to drill down from the customer level to see the invoices for that customer.

Task Overview

1. Prepare to Create a Second Report
2. Create a New Report, Select the Shared Data Source, and Create a Dataset
3. Choose the Report Layout

Customer-Invoice Report, Task 1: Prepare to Create a Second Report

DT **SSDT and Visual Studio Steps**

If you have not closed the Chapter04 project since working on the previous section of this chapter, skip to Step 8. Otherwise, follow these steps, starting with Step 1:

1. Run SQL Server Data Tools or Visual Studio.
2. If a link to the Chapter04 project is visible on the Start page, click this link, and the Chapter04 project opens. Proceed to Step 8. If a link to the Chapter04 project is not visible on the Start page, continue with Step 3.
3. Select File | Open | Project/Solution.
4. Click Projects.
5. Double-click MSSQLRS.
6. Double-click Chapter04.
7. Double-click Chapter04.sln. (This is the file that contains the solution for Chapter04.)
8. If the Customer List report is displayed in the center of the screen, click the X on the "Customer List.rdl [Design]" tab to close this report.

Task Notes for SSDT and Visual Studio Steps   Opening the Chapter04 solution (Chapter04.sln) and opening the Chapter04 project (Chapter04.rptproj) produce the same end result, so you can do either. Only one project is in the Chapter04 solution, so that project is automatically opened when the solution is opened. When the Chapter04 project is opened, the last report you worked on is displayed in the center of the screen. In this case, it is probably the Customer List report.

You do not need to close one report before working on another. In fact, you can have multiple reports open at one time and use the tabs containing the report names to move among them. In most cases, however, I find that a philosophy of "the less clutter, the better" works well when creating reports. For this reason, I recommend you close all unneeded reports as you move from one report to the next.

RB **Report Builder Steps**

1. If the Report Builder was closed, open a browser and navigate to the Report Manager as discussed earlier in this chapter. Click the Report Builder button to launch Report Builder. The Getting Started page appears.
2. If the Report Builder is open, click the icon button in the upper-left corner and select New from the drop-down menu.

Customer-Invoice Report, Task 2: Create a New Report, Select the Shared Data Source, and Create a Dataset

DT SSDT and Visual Studio Steps

1. In the Solution Explorer on the right side of the screen, right-click the Reports folder. You see the context menu shown here.

2. Select the Add New Report command from the context menu. This starts the Report Wizard, enabling you to create another report in the current project.

3. Click Next. The Select the Data Source page appears.

4. Make sure the Shared data source radio button is selected and the Galactic data source is selected in the drop-down list, as shown here. Click Next. The Design the Query page appears.

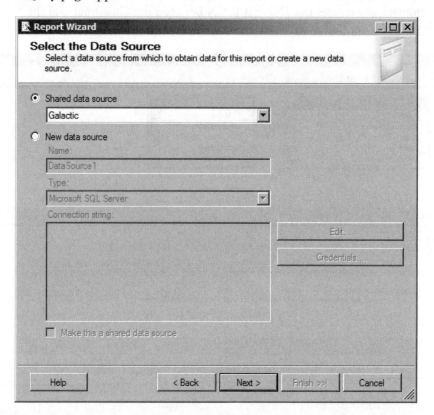

5. Click Query Builder. The Graphical Query Designer appears.

6. Right-click in the diagram pane (the upper area) of the Query Designer screen. You see the Diagram Pane context menu.

7. Select Add Table from the context menu.

8. Double-click Customer in the list of tables. The Customer table is added to the query.

9. Double-click InvoiceHeader in the list of tables. Make sure you select InvoiceHeader and *not* InvoiceDetail. The InvoiceHeader table is added to the query.

10. Click Close to exit the Add Table dialog box. Notice the Query Designer automatically creates the INNER JOIN between the Customer and the InvoiceHeader tables, as shown in the following illustration.

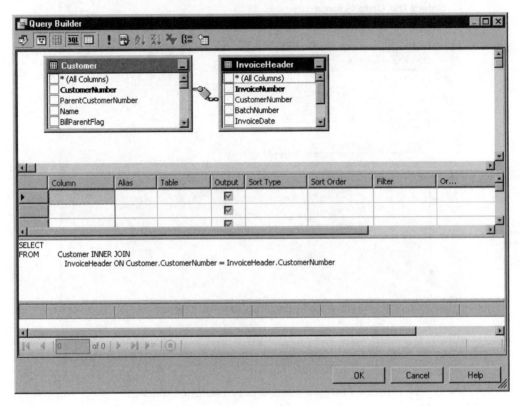

11. Right-click the gray diamond in the middle of the link joining the Customer and the InvoiceHeader tables. The Join Context menu is displayed, as shown in the following illustration.

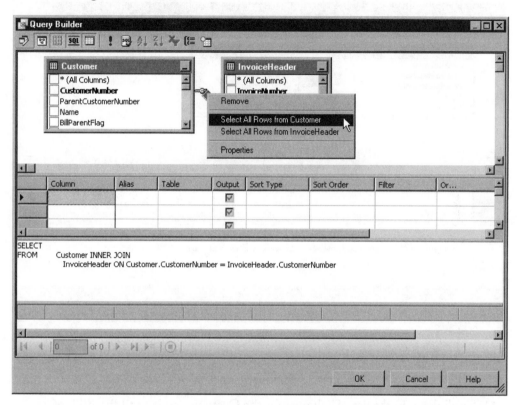

12. Choose the Select All Rows from Customer option from the context menu. The diamond symbol changes, as shown in the next illustration.

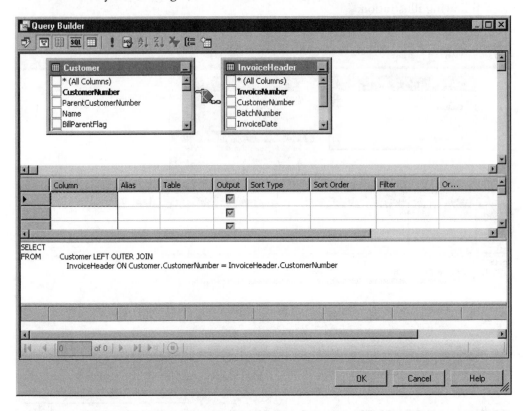

13. Scroll down in the list of columns for the Customer table until the BillingCity column name is visible.

14. Check the box next to the BillingCity column in the Customer table.

15. Scroll up in the list of columns for the Customer table, and check the box next to the Name column. This places the Name field after the BillingCity field in the resulting SQL query.

16. In the list of columns for the InvoiceHeader table, check the boxes next to the InvoiceNumber, InvoiceDate, and TotalAmount columns.

17. Place a 1 in the Sort Order column for the BillingCity field either by typing in the cell or using the drop-down list.

18. Place a 2 in the Sort Order column for the Name field.

19. Place a 3 in the Sort Order column for the InvoiceNumber field.

20. Right-click in the SQL pane, and select Execute SQL from the context menu. The query executes, and the result set is displayed in the results pane. The Query Designer should appear similar to the following illustration.

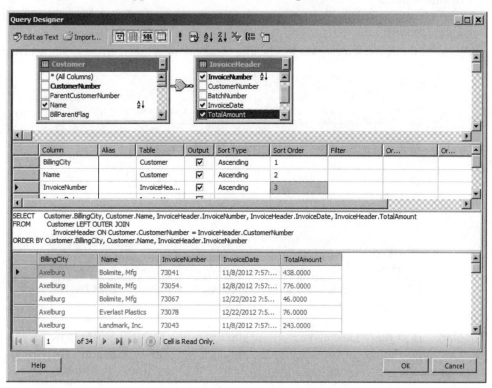

21. Click OK. This returns you to the Design the Query page. Be sure to read the Task Notes for this task found after the Report Builder steps.

RB Report Builder Steps

1. With New Report highlighted in the left column, click Table or Matrix Wizard. The Choose a dataset page of the New Table or Matrix Wizard appears.

2. Ensure the Create a dataset radio button is selected. Click Next. The Choose a connection to a data source page of the New Table or Matrix Wizard appears.

3. The Galactic shared data source should be selected by default. Click Next. The Graphical Query Designer on the Design a query page of the New Table or Matrix wizard appears.

4. Expand the Tables folder in the Database view pane.

5. Expand the entry for the Customer table.

6. Check the boxes next to the following fields in the Customer table in this order:
BillingCity
Name

7. Scroll down and expand the entry for the InvoiceHeader table.

8. Check the boxes next to the following fields in the InvoiceHeader table:
   InvoiceNumber
   InvoiceDate
   TotalAmount

9. Expand the *Relationships pane* by clicking on the double down arrow as shown here.

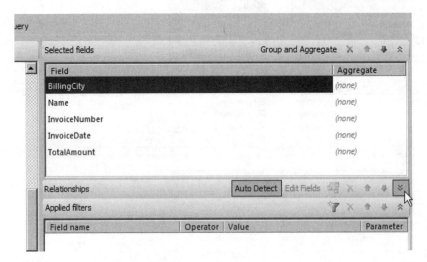

10. Notice the Query Designer automatically creates an INNER JOIN between the Customer and the InvoiceHeader tables. Click the Join Type column entry to activate the context menu as shown. Select Left Outer from the context menu.

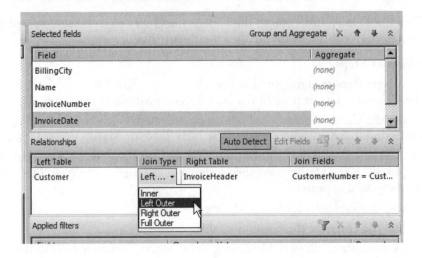

11. Click Run Query. The Design a query page should appear similar to the following illustration.

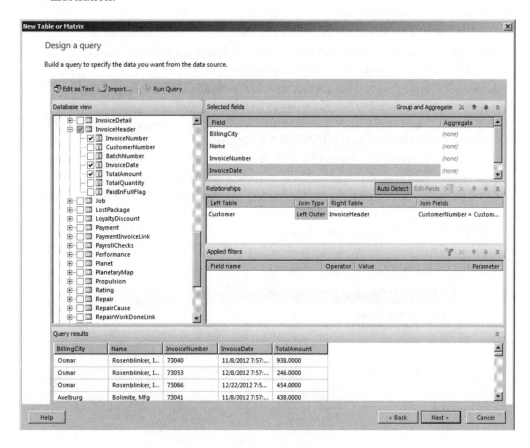

Task Notes   The Galactic data source you created in the first report is a shared data source. As such, the wizard defaults to using this shared data source any time a new report is created.

In the Query Designer, when a second table is added to the query, the Query Designer looks at the structure of the database. If there is a relationship defined between the new table and any of the tables already present in the query, a JOIN will be created based on that relationship.

The business need for this report states that the report should include all GDS customers. As you saw in Chapter 3, some customers may not have invoices, so to include all the customers in the report, you need to use a LEFT OUTER JOIN between the Customer table and the InvoiceHeader table.

Customer-Invoice Report, Task 3: Choose the Report Layout

DT | **SSDT and Visual Studio Steps**

1. Click Next. The Select the Report Type page of the Report Wizard appears.
2. Make sure the Tabular radio button is selected, and click Next. The Design the Table page of the Report Wizard appears.
3. With the BillingCity field highlighted in the Available fields list, click Page. The BillingCity field is moved to the Displayed fields list.
4. With the Name field highlighted in the Available fields list, click Group. The Name field is moved to the Displayed fields list.
5. With the InvoiceNumber field highlighted in the Available fields list, click Details. The InvoiceNumber field is moved to the Displayed fields list.
6. With the InvoiceDate field highlighted in the Available fields list, click Details. The InvoiceDate field is moved to the Displayed fields list.
7. With the TotalAmount field highlighted in the Available fields list, click Details. The TotalAmount field is moved to the Displayed fields list. The Design the Table page appears as shown here.

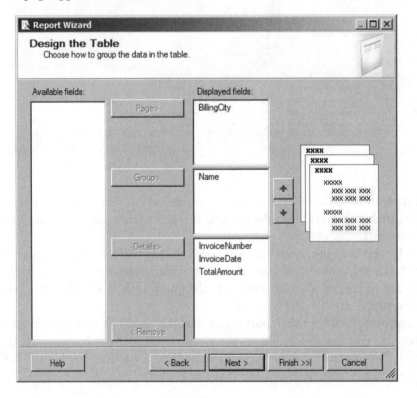

8. Click Next. The Choose the Table Layout page of the Report Wizard appears. This page appears in the Report Wizard because we put fields in the Group area on the Design the Table page.

9. Check the Include subtotals check box.

10. Check the Enable drilldown check box. The Choose the Table Layout page appears as shown.

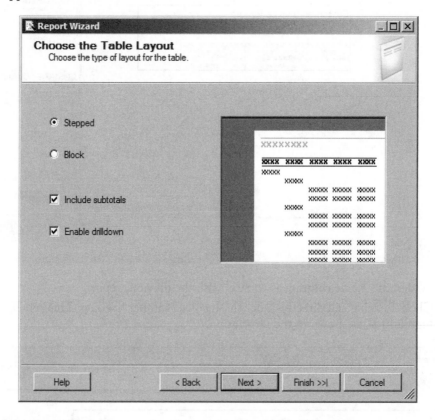

11. Click Next. The Choose the Table Style page of the Report Wizard appears.

12. Select Ocean in the style list, and then click Next. The Completing the Wizard page appears.

13. Type **Customer-Invoice Report** for the report name.

14. Click Finish. The Report Designer window opens as shown here.

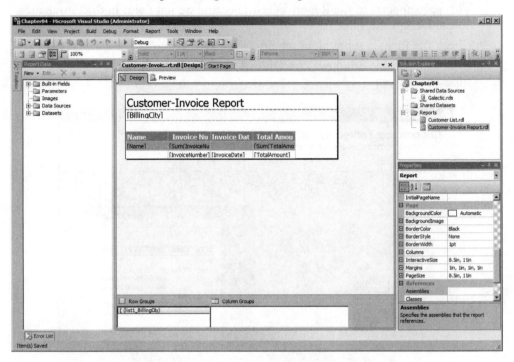

15. Widen the Name column, as you did with the previous report.

16. Click the table cell directly under the Invoice Number heading. This cell is highlighted, as shown in the illustration.

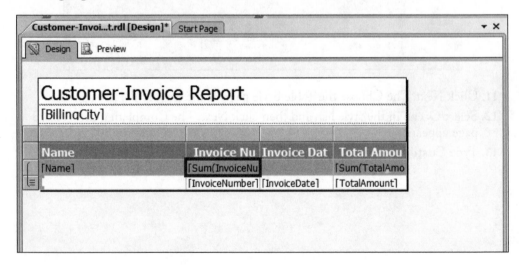

17. Press DELETE on your keyboard to remove the nonsensical totaling of the invoice numbers.

18. Click the Preview tab. A preview of your report appears.

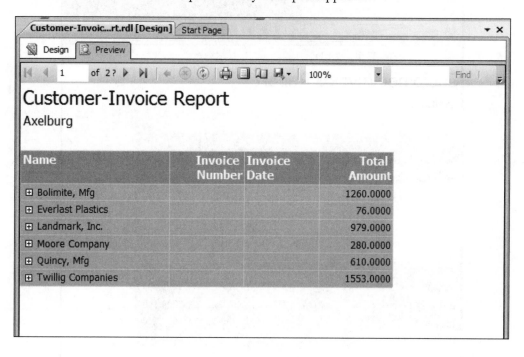

19. Click the plus sign in front of Bolimite, Mfg to view the invoices for this company, as shown here.

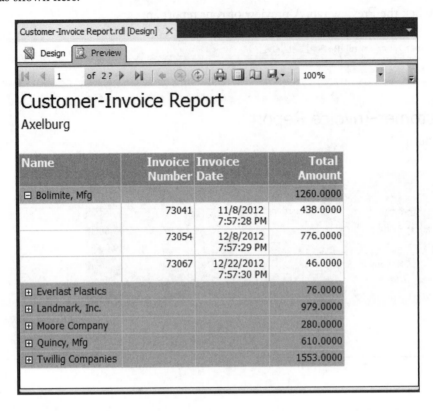

20. Click the Next Page button (the blue triangle just below the Preview tab) to advance to the next page of the report. The Next Page button is highlighted in the following illustration.

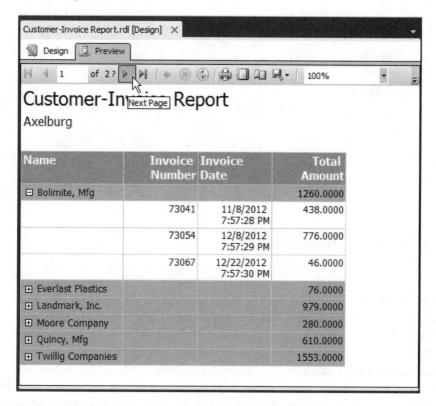

21. You can continue to work with the report preview to get a feel for the way report navigation and drilldown works. (For instance, you may want to try clicking the minus [–] sign.)

22. Click the Save All button on the toolbar.

Task Notes for SSDT and Visual Studio   When we created the Customer List report, we put all the columns from the dataset into the detail line of the report. This time, we put the BillingCity column in the Page area of the table layout. Because of this, the Report Wizard created a report that begins a new page every time there is a new value in the BillingCity column. In addition, the value of the BillingCity column appears at the top of each report page.

Groupings on the Customer-Invoice Report

Page Grouping on BillingCity	Table Grouping on Name	Billingcity	Name	InvoiceNumber	InvoiceDate	TotalAmount
				Dataset		
	Bolimite, Mfg	Axelburg	Bolimite, Mfg	73041	11-08-2011	438.00
		Axelburg	Bolimite, Mfg	73054	12-08-2011	776.00
		Axelburg	Bolimite, Mfg	73067	12-22-2011	46.00
	Everlast Plastics	Axelburg	Everlast Plastics	73078	12-22-2011	76.00
	Landmark, Inc.	Axelburg	Landmark, Inc.	73043	11-08-2011	243.00
Page 1: Axelburg		Axelburg	Landmark, Inc.	73056	12-08-2011	736.00
	Moore Company	Axelburg	Moore Company	73046	11-08-2011	256.00
		Axelburg	Moore Company	73059	12-08-2011	24.00
	Quincy, Mfg	Axelburg	Quincy, Mfg	73048	11-08-2011	234.00
		Axelburg	Quincy, Mfg	73074	12-22-2011	376.00
	Twillig Companies	Axelburg	Twiling Companies	73045	11-08-2011	732.00
		Axelburg	Twiling Companies	73058	12-08-2011	736.00
		Axelburg	Twiling Companies	73071	12-22-2011	85.00
Page 2: Doveran	Custer, Inc.	Doveran	Custer, Inc.	73049	11-08-2011	273.00
		Doveran	Custer, Inc.	73062	12-08-2011	243.00
		Doveran	Custer, Inc.	73075	12-22-2011	368.00
		Edgewater	Sanders & Son	73042	11-08-2011	834.00

Figure 4-3   *Groupings on the Customer-Invoice Report*

Figure 4-3 shows the dataset used in the Customer-Invoice report. The first 13 rows have a value of Axelburg for the BillingCity column. Therefore, Axelburg appears at the top of Page 1 of the report. All the rows with Axelburg in the BillingCity column will be on Page 1 of the report.

Using the Report Wizard, we put the Name column in the Group area of the table layout. This means the report will create a new group each time the value of the Name column changes. Again, looking at the preceding illustration, you can see the first three rows have a value of Bolimite, Mfg in the Name column. Therefore, these three rows will be combined in the first group on Page 1 of the report.

By checking the Enable drilldown check box, you told the Report Wizard to create a report in which the detail lines for each grouping are initially hidden. The detail lines for a group become visible when the plus sign for that group is clicked. By checking the Include subtotals check box, you told the Report Wizard to total any numeric columns in the detail and to show those totals in the group header for each group.

Let's look again at the first few rows of the dataset shown in Figure 4-3. The first three rows have a value of Bolimite, Mfg in the Name column. Because of this, these three rows are grouped together for the report shown after Step 18 in Task 3. In this report, the number 1260.0000 appears across from Bolimite, Mfg. This is the total of all the invoices in the detail rows for Bolimite, Mfg.

Because the Report Wizard tried to add up any and all numeric columns, it also created an entry in the grouping for a total of the invoice numbers. Adding up the invoice numbers does not result in a meaningful value, so we deleted this grouping entry in Steps 16 and 17 of this task.

RB **Report Builder Steps**

1. Click Next. The Arrange fields page of the New Table or Matrix Wizard appears.
2. Drag the BillingCity and Name fields to the Row groups area.
3. Drag the InvoiceNumber, InvoiceDate, and TotalAmount fields to the Values area. The Arrange fields page of the New Table or Matrix Wizard appears as shown here.

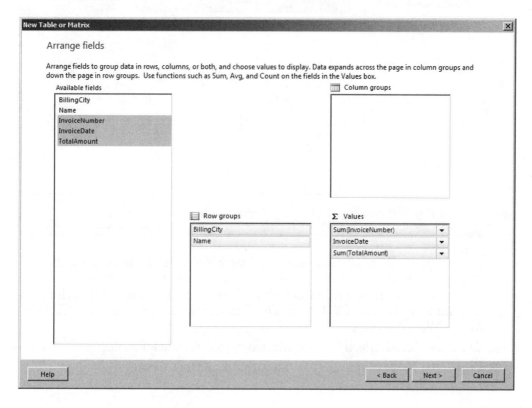

4. Click Next. The Choose the layout page of the New Table or Matrix Wizard appears.

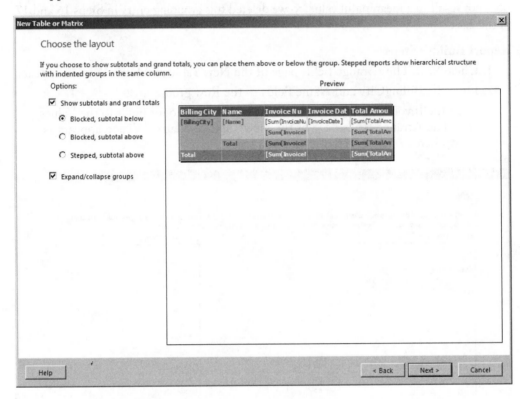

5. By default, the Show subtotals and grand totals check box is checked and the Blocked, subtotal below radio button is selected. In addition, the Expand/collapse groups check box is checked by default as shown here. These are all the selections we want for our report. Click Next. The Choose a style page of the New Table or Matrix Wizard appears.

6. Select the Ocean style, if it is not selected by default. Click Finish.

7. Widen the Name column, as you did with the previous report.

8. Click the second table cell below the Invoice Number heading (only "Invoice Nu" is visible) as shown here.

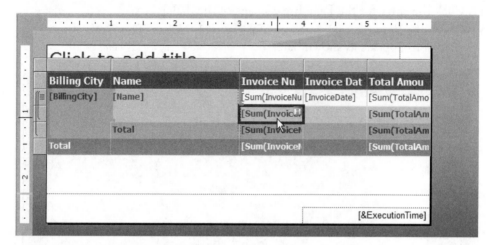

9. Hold down SHIFT and click the bottom table cell below the Invoice Number heading.

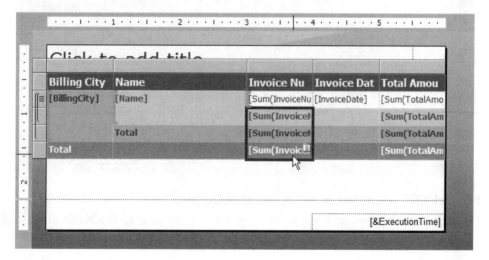

10. Press DELETE on your keyboard to remove the nonsensical totaling of the invoice numbers.

11. In the Row Groups area, click the drop-down arrow next to the BillingCity entry, and select Group Properties from the list. The Group Properties dialog box appears.

12. Click the entry for the Page Breaks page of the dialog box.

13. Check the Between each instance of a group check box. The Group Properties dialog box appears as shown here.

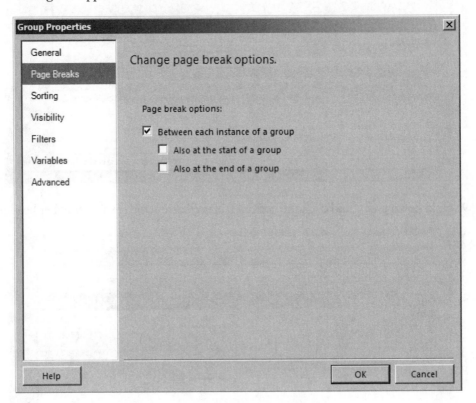

14. Click OK to exit the Group Properties dialog box.

15. In the Row Groups area, click the drop-down arrow next to the Name entry, and select Group Properties from the list. The Group Properties dialog box appears.

16. Click the entry for the Visibility page of the dialog box.

17. Select the Show radio button.

18. Uncheck the Display can be toggled by this report item check box. The dialog box should appear as shown.

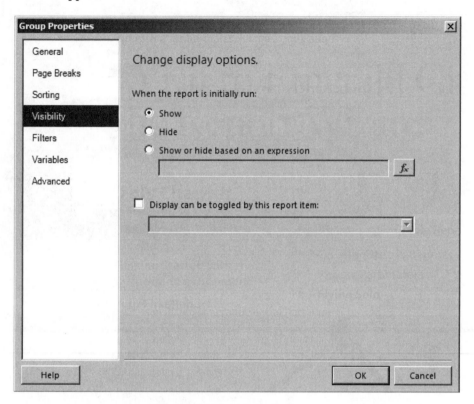

19. Click OK to exit the Group Properties dialog box.

20. Click the "Click to add title" area, and enter **Customer-Invoice Report**. The completed report layout should appear similar to the following illustration.

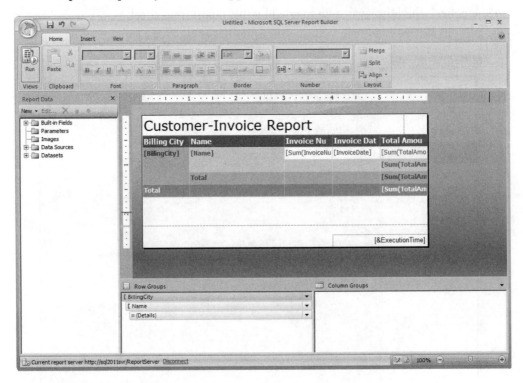

21. Click the Run button. A preview of your report appears.

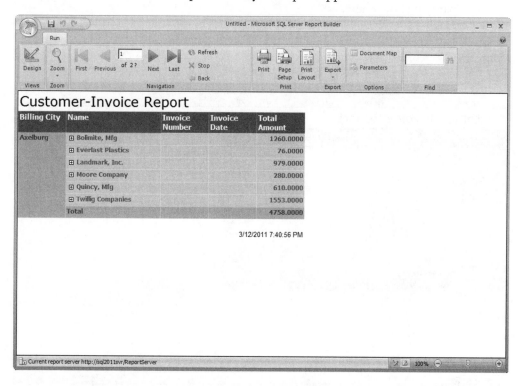

22. Click the plus sign in front of Bolimite, Mfg to view the invoices for this company, as shown here.

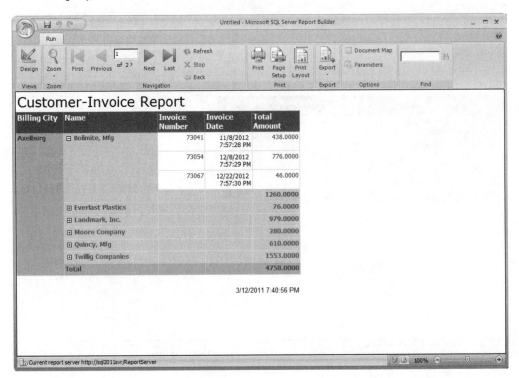

23. Click the Next Page button (the blue triangle in the ribbon) to advance to the next page of the report.

24. You can continue to work with the report preview to get a feel for the way report navigation and drilldown works. (For instance, you may want to try clicking the minus [–] sign.)

25. Click the Save button on the toolbar. The Save As Report dialog box appears.

26. Double-click the Galactic Delivery Services folder, and then double-click the Chapter04 folder.

27. Replace Untitled.rdl with **Customer-Invoice Report** for the Name.

28. Click Save.

Task Notes for Report Builder   When you created the Customer List report, you put all the columns from the dataset into the Values area of the report. This time, you put the BillingCity in the Row groups area. This created a row grouping for each billing city. You later modified the properties for this group to have the report create a page break between each group.

Figure 4-3 (in the previous Task Notes for SSDT and Visual Studio) shows the dataset used in the Customer-Invoice report. The first 13 rows have a value of Axelburg for the BillingCity column. Therefore, Axelburg appears at the top of Page 1 of the report. All the rows with Axelburg in the BillingCity column will be on Page 1 of the report.

You put the Name column in the Row groups area as well. This means the report will create a new group each time the value of the Name column changes. Again, looking at Figure 4-3, you can see the first three rows have a value of Bolimite, Mfg in the Name column. Therefore, these three rows will be combined in the first group on Page 1 of the report.

By leaving the Expand/collapse groups check box checked, you told the Report Wizard to create a report in which the detail lines for each grouping are initially hidden. The detail lines for a group become visible when the plus sign for that group is clicked. However, we only want the lowest-level group (the Details group) to be initially hidden. We do not want the Name group to be initially hidden. This is why we used the Group Properties dialog box to change the initial value of this group from Hide to Show.

By leaving the Show subtotals and grand totals check box checked, you told the Report Wizard to total any numeric columns in the detail and to show those totals in the group footer for each group.

Let's look again at the first few rows of the dataset shown in the preceding illustration. The first three rows have a value of Bolimite, Mfg in the Name column. Because of this, these three rows are grouped together for the report shown after Step 21 in Task 3. In this report, the number 1260.0000 appears across from Bolimite, Mfg. This is the total of all the invoices in the detail rows for Bolimite, Mfg.

Because the Report Wizard tried to add up any and all numeric columns, it also created an entry in the grouping for a total of the invoice numbers. Adding up the invoice numbers does not result in a meaningful value, so we deleted this grouping entry in Steps 8 through 10 of this task.

Finally, if you have been paying close attention, you will have noticed we did not specify any sort order for the groups and yet they appear properly sorted. When the wizard created the BillingCity and Name row groups, it automatically added sorting to the groups as well. (The Detail group is not sorted. You can add sorting to the Detail group on your own, if you would like extra credit.)

Creating Matrix Reports

You have now seen much of what the Report Wizard can do for you when it comes to tabular reports. Now, let's look at another report type the Report Wizard can produce for you. Prepare yourself. You are going to enter the matrix.

What Reporting Services calls a matrix report is referred to as a *crosstab* or a *pivot table report* elsewhere. In a tabular report, you have columns from a result set across the top and rows from a result set going down the page. In a matrix report, you have row values going across the top and down the page. Matrix reports are much easier to grasp once you have seen one in action, so let's give it a try.

The Invoice-Batch Number Report

Feature Highlighted

▶ Using the matrix report type

Business Need The accounting department processes invoices in batches. Once a week, the accounting department creates invoices to send to their customers for the deliveries made over the previous week. A batch number is assigned to each invoice as it is created. All the invoices created on the same day are given the same batch number.

The new report requested by the accounting department shows the total amount of the invoices created in each batch. The report also allows batches to be broken down by billing city and by customer. To allow this type of analysis, you need to use a matrix report.

Task Overview

1. Create a New Report, Select the Shared Data Source, and Create a Dataset
2. Choose the Report Layout

Invoice-Batch Number Report, Task 1: Create a New Report, Select the Shared Data Source, and Create a Dataset

DT **SSDT and Visual Studio Steps**

1. If you closed the Chapter04 project, reopen it. (If you need assistance with this, see Task 1 of the previous report.) If you have not yet done so, close the Customer-Invoice Report.
2. In the Solution Explorer on the right side of the screen, right-click the Reports folder.
3. Select the Add New Report command from the context menu. This starts the Report Wizard, enabling you to create an additional report in the current project.
4. Click Next. The Select the Data Source page appears.
5. Make sure the Shared Data Source radio button is selected and the Galactic data source is selected in the drop-down list. Click Next.
6. Click Query Builder. The Graphical Query Designer appears.
7. Right-click in the diagram pane (the upper area) of the Query Designer screen. You see the Diagram pane context menu.

8. Select Add Table from the context menu.

9. Add the following tables to the query:

Customer
InvoiceHeader

10. Click Close to exit the Add Table dialog box.

11. Check the following columns in the Customer table in the order shown here:

BillingCity
Name

12. Check the following columns in the InvoiceHeader table in the order shown here:

BatchNumber
InvoiceNumber
TotalAmount

13. Right-click in the SQL pane, and select Execute SQL from the context menu. The query executes, and the result set is displayed in the results pane. The Query Designer should appear similar to the illustration.

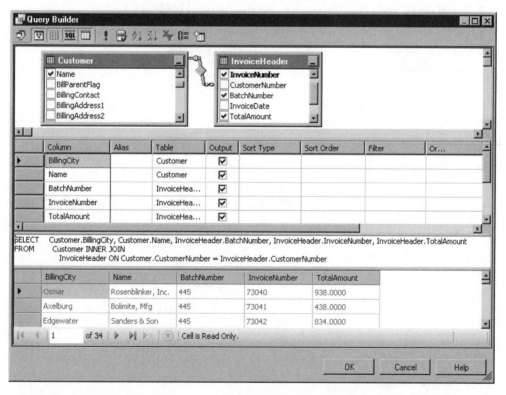

14. Click OK. This returns you to the Design the Query page. Be sure to read the Task Notes for this task found after the Report Builder steps.

RB **Report Builder Steps**

1. If you closed the Report Builder, reopen it. If you have not closed the Report Builder, click the logo button in the upper-left corner, and select New. You will see the New Report or Dataset page.

2. With New Report selected, click Table or Matrix Wizard. The Choose a dataset page of the New Table or Matrix Wizard appears.

3. Ensure the Create a dataset radio button is selected. Click Next. The Choose a connection to a data source page of the New Table or Matrix Wizard appears.

4. The Galactic shared data source should be selected by default. Click Next. The Design a query page of the New Table or Matrix Wizard appears.

5. Expand the Tables folder in the Database view pane.

6. Expand the entry for the Customer table.

7. Check the boxes next to the following fields in the Customer table in this order:
   BillingCity
   Name

8. Scroll down and expand the entry for the InvoiceHeader table.

9. Check the boxes next to the following fields in the InvoiceHeader table in this order:
   BatchNumber
   InvoiceNumber
   TotalAmount

10. Click Run Query. The Design a query page should appear similar to the following illustration.

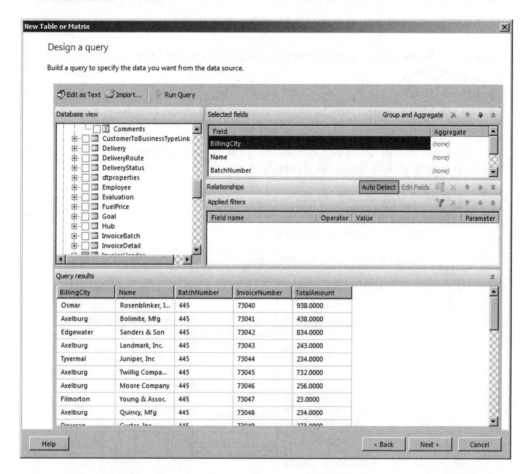

Task Notes   Your dataset contains the columns we need to create the matrix report. Note, we did not specify any sort order for the dataset. The matrix itself takes care of sorting the dataset and displaying things in the correct order. It presents the data in the rows and in the columns in ascending order.

Invoice-Batch Number Report, Task 2: Choose the Report Layout

DT **SSDT and Visual Studio Steps**

   1. Click Next. The Select the Report Type page of the Report Wizard appears.

   2. Select the Matrix radio button.

3. Click Next. The Design the Matrix page of the Report Wizard appears.
4. Use the Columns button to place the following fields in the Displayed fields list:
   BillingCity
   Name
5. Use the Rows button to place the following fields in the Displayed fields list:
   BatchNumber
   InvoiceNumber
6. Use the Details button to place the following field in the Displayed fields list:
   Total Amount
7. Check the Enable drilldown check box at the bottom of the page. The Design the Matrix page should appear as shown.

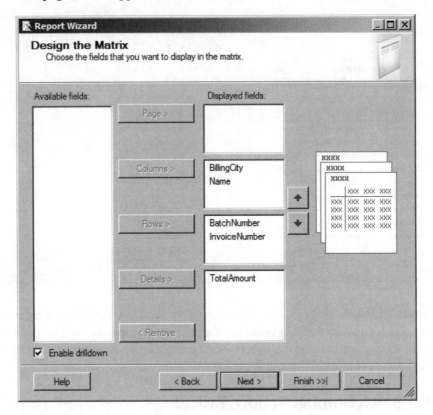

8. Click Next. The Choose the Matrix Style page of the Report Wizard appears.
9. Select Ocean in the style list, and click Next. The Completing the Wizard page appears.

10. Type **Invoice-Batch Number Report** for the report name.

11. Click Finish. The Report Designer window opens.

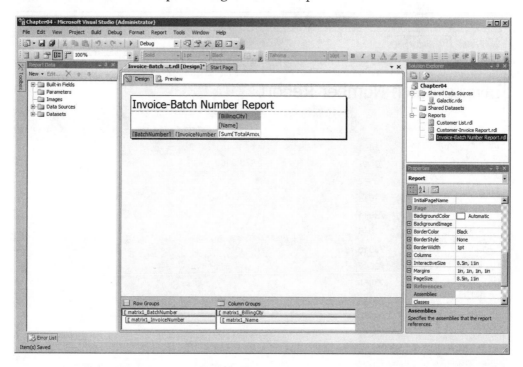

12. Widen the column on the far-right side of the matrix, as shown in the illustration.

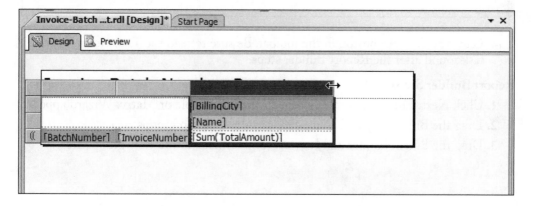

13. Click the Preview tab. A preview of your report appears. Try expanding both rows and columns.

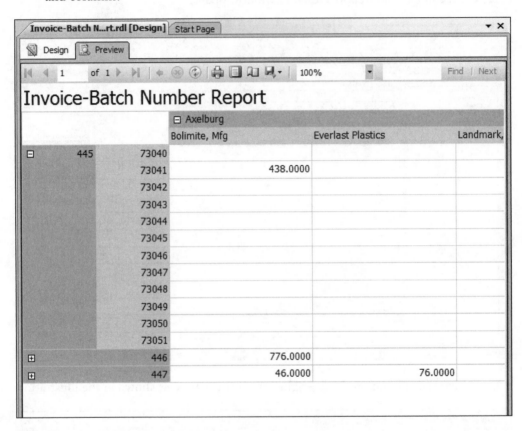

Invoice-Batch N...rt.rdl [Design]	Start Page	▾ ✕

Design | Preview

◀◀ ◀ 1 of 1 ▶ ▶◀ | ◀ ⊗ ⊕ | 🖶 🗐 🗔 🖫▾ | 100% ▾ | Find | Next

Invoice-Batch Number Report

			⊟ Axelburg		
			Bolimite, Mfg	Everlast Plastics	Landmark,
⊟	445	73040			
		73041	438.0000		
		73042			
		73043			
		73044			
		73045			
		73046			
		73047			
		73048			
		73049			
		73050			
		73051			
⊞		446	776.0000		
⊞		447	46.0000	76.0000	

14. Click the Save All button in the toolbar. Be sure to read the Task Notes for this task found after the Report Builder steps.

RB **Report Builder Steps**

1. Click Next. The Arrange fields page of the New Table or Matrix Wizard appears.

2. Drag the BillingCity and Name fields to the Column groups area.

3. Drag the BatchNumber and InvoiceNumber fields to the Row groups area.

4. Drag the Total Amount field to the Values area. The Arrange fields page of the New Table or Matrix Wizard appears as shown.

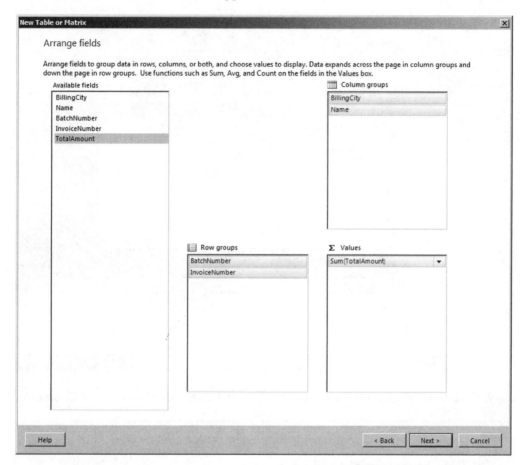

5. Click Next. The Choose the layout page of the New Table or Matrix Wizard appears.

6. Uncheck the Show subtotals and grand totals check box.

7. Click Next. The Choose a style page of the New Table or Matrix Wizard appears.

8. Select the Ocean style, if it is not selected by default. Click Finish. The report design opens in Report Builder.

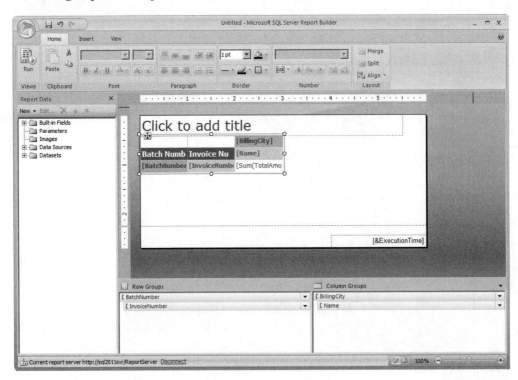

9. Widen the column on the far-right side of the matrix, as shown in the illustration.

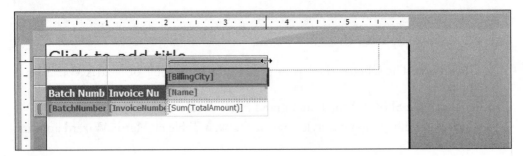

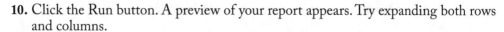

10. Click the Run button. A preview of your report appears. Try expanding both rows and columns.

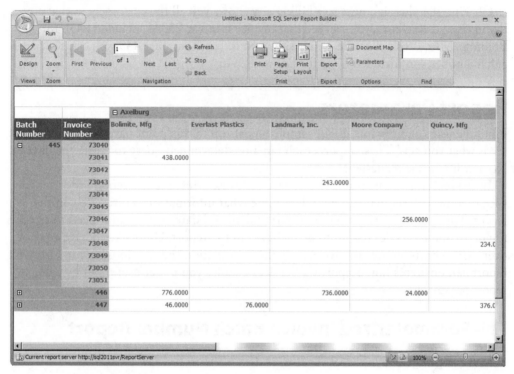

11. Click the Design button.

12. Click the "Click to add title" area, and enter **Invoice-Batch Number Report**.

13. Click the Save button on the toolbar. The Save As Report dialog box appears.

14. Double-click the Galactic Delivery Services folder, and then double-click the Chapter04 folder.

15. Replace Untitled.rdl with **Invoice-Batch Number Report** for the Name.

16. Click Save.

Task Notes   The Invoice-Batch Number Report contains a column for each billing city and a row for each batch number. You need to scroll to the right to see all the columns in the report. The numbers in the matrix are the totals for each batch number in each billing city. For example, $1,903 was invoiced to companies in Axelburg in batch number 445.

The column headings are left-justified, whereas the numeric values are right-justified. This makes the report a bit hard to read. We discuss how to correct these types of formatting issues in Chapter 5.

Clicking the plus sign next to a batch number shows you all the invoices in that batch. If you expand batch number 445, you can see that invoice number 73040 included $938 for companies in Osmar, and invoice number 73041 included $438 for companies in Axelburg.

Clicking the plus sign next to a billing city shows you all the customers in that city. If you expand Axelburg, you can see that invoice number 73041 included $438 for Bolimite, Mfg. If you click the minus sign next to batch number 445, you can see that batch number 446 included $776 for Bolimite, Mfg.

Report Parameters

From the users' standpoint, all our sample reports up to this point have been "what you see is what you get." These reports each ran a predetermined query to create the dataset. No user input was requested.

In the real world, this is not the way things work. Most reports require the user to specify some criteria that can help determine what information is ultimately in the report. The user may need to enter a start and an end date, or they may need to select the department or sales region to be included in the report. Users like to have control over their reports so they receive exactly the information they are looking for. Our next report demonstrates how Reporting Services enables you to get user input by using report parameters.

The Parameterized Invoice-Batch Number Report

Feature Highlighted

▶   Using report parameters

Business Need   The accounting department is pleased with the Invoice-Batch Number Report. Like most users, when they are happy with something, they want to change it. No software or report is ever really completed. It only reaches a resting point until users think of another enhancement.

The accounting department would like to be able to view the Invoice-Batch Number Report for one city at a time. And, they would like to pick the city from a list of all the cities where they have customers. They would also like to specify a start date and an end date, and only view batches that were run between those dates.

We can modify the Invoice-Batch Number Report to include these features. We can add a filter to the dataset. (This will create a WHERE clause in the SELECT statement generated for us.) Then we can send the user's selections for city, start date, and end date to the filter using report parameters.

Task Overview

1. Reopen the Invoice-Batch Number Report, and Add Parameters to the Query in the Original Dataset
2. Create a Second Dataset Containing a List of Cities
3. Customize the Report Parameters

Parameterized Invoice-Batch Number Report, Task 1: Reopen the Invoice-Batch Number Report, and Add Parameters to the Query in the Original Dataset

DT **SSDT and Visual Studio Steps**

1. If you closed the Chapter04 project, reopen it. (If you need assistance with this, see Task 1 of the Customer-Invoice Report.)
2. If the Invoice-Batch Number Report is open, make sure the Design tab, not the Preview tab, is selected. If the Invoice-Batch Number Report is not open, double-click the entry for the Invoice-Batch Number Report in the Solution Explorer on the right side of the screen.
3. Expand the Datasets folder in the Report Data window.
4. Right-click the DataSet1 entry in the Report Data window. You will see the context menu, as shown here.

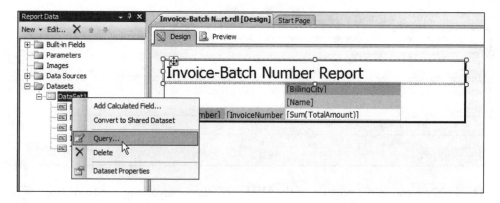

5. Select Query from the context menu. You see the Query Designer screen with the query built for this report while running the Report Wizard.
6. Right-click in the diagram pane, and select Add Table from the context menu.
7. The accounting department wants to specify a date range based on the date each batch was run. This date is stored in the InvoiceBatch table. We need to join this table with the InvoiceHeader table. Double-click InvoiceBatch in the list of tables. The Graphical Query Designer automatically creates the JOIN for us.

8. Click Close to exit the Add Table dialog box.

9. In the InvoiceBatch table, check the check box next to the RunDate field. This adds RunDate to the criteria pane.

10. Now we can create the portion of the WHERE clause involving the billing city. In the criteria pane, click the cell across from BillingCity and under Filter. The cursor moves to that cell. Type **=@BillingCity** and press ENTER. The Graphical Query Designer appears as shown in the following illustration. Notice the SQL statement in the SQL pane now includes a WHERE clause.

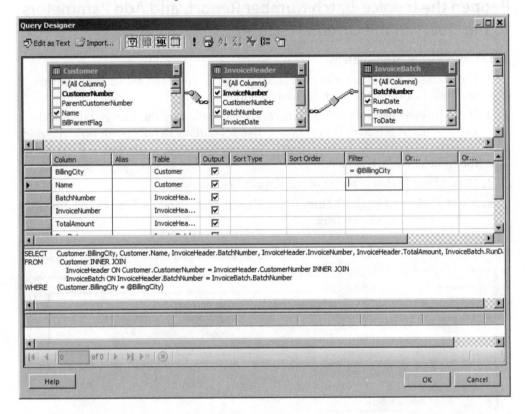

11. Next, we create the portion of the WHERE clause involving the RunDate. Scroll down in the criteria pane until RunDate is visible, if necessary. Click the cell across from RunDate and under Filter. Type **>= @StartDate AND < DATEADD(dd, 1, @EndDate)** and press ENTER. The Query Designer portion of the screen appears as shown in the following illustration. Notice the addition

to the WHERE clause in the SQL pane. We discuss why we are using the DATEADD() function in the task notes.

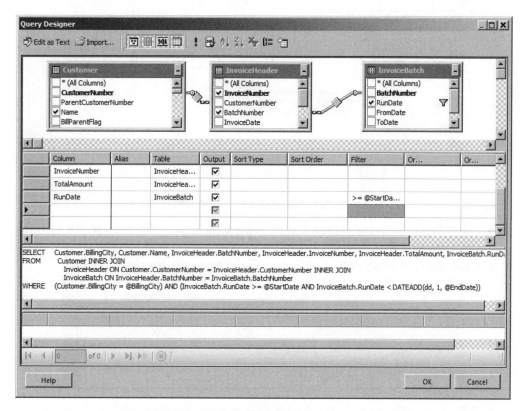

12. We needed to include RunDate in the WHERE clause, but we do not need to include it in the FIELD LIST of the SELECT statement. Click in the cell across from RunDate and under Output to remove the check mark. The RunDate field is no longer in the FIELD LIST for the SELECT statement in the SQL pane.

13. Right-click in the SQL pane, and select Execute SQL from the context menu.

14. The Query Designer requires values for the three parameters you just created to run the query. You see the Define Query Parameters dialog box. Enter **Axelburg** for @BillingCity, **12/01/2012** for @StartDate, and **12/31/2012** for @EndDate. Click OK.

15. After viewing the result set, click OK to exit the Query Designer window. Be sure to read the Task Notes for this task found after the Report Builder steps.

RB   **Report Builder Steps**

1. If you closed the Report Builder, reopen it. On the Getting Started page, select Recent and then select the Invoice-Batch Number Report from the recent reports. If you have not closed the Report Builder, make sure you are in design mode. (The Run button should be visible in the upper-left corner.)

2. Expand the Datasets folder in the Report Data window.

3. Right-click the DataSet1 entry in the Report Data window. You will see the context menu, as shown here.

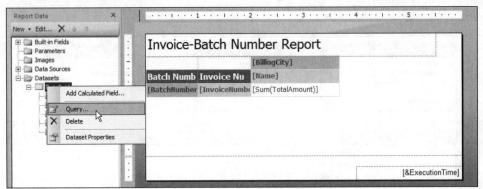

4. Select Query from the context menu. You see the Query Designer screen with the query built for this report by the Report Wizard.

5. Click the Add Filter button in the Applied filters toolbar as shown here.

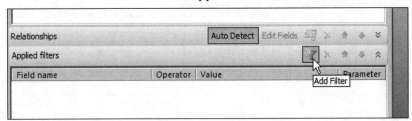

6. A new line will appear in the Applied filters pane. The first field in the list of selected fields appears in this new filter by default. This is the BillingCity field. It just so happens in this case, this is the first field we want to filter on. However, we will change the Operator and Value. Click the area that says "like" in the Operator column. The context menu appears as shown.

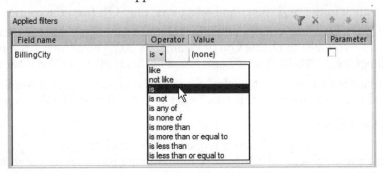

7. Select "is" from the context menu. We will not specify a default value here, so we will leave "(none)" in the Value column.

8. Check the check box in the Parameter column. We have created a parameter that will allow us to select a billing city.

9. Click the Add Filter button again. A new line is added in the Applied filters pane.

10. Click the BillingCity entry in the Field name column for this new line. You will see a pop-up list of the fields in tables in the query with folders for other tables and views in the database.

11. The accounting department wants to specify a date range based on the date each batch was run. This date is stored in the InvoiceBatch table. Expand the Tables folder in the pop-up list.

12. Expand the InvoiceBatch table entry in the pop-up list.

13. Click the RunDate field entry under the InvoiceBatch table in the pop-up list as shown here.

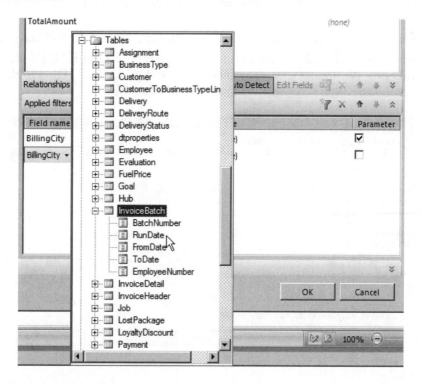

14. Click the area that says "is" in the Operator column across from RunDate. The Context menu appears.

15. Select "is more than or equal to" from the context menu.

16. We will not specify a default value here, so we will leave "(none)" in the Value column. Check the Parameter check box.

17. Click the Add Filter button again. A new line is added in the Applied filters pane.

18. Click the BillingCity entry in the Field name column for this new line.

19. Scroll down and expand the entry for InvoiceBatch. Note that it is now in the Tables in the Current Query area.

20. Select the RunDate field entry.

21. Click the area that says "is" in the Operator column in the third line of the Applied fields pane. The context menu appears.

22. Select "is less than" from the context menu.

23. Check the Parameter check box in the third line of the Applied fields pane.

24. We are going to tweak the query created for us by the Graphical Query Designer. Click the Edit as Text button in the upper-left corner of the Query Designer. You will see the SELECT statement created by the Graphical Query Designer.

25. Drag the query pane (the top portion of the dialog box) wider so you can see the entire query.

26. Replace "@RunDate" in the second-to-last line of the query with **@StartDate**.

27. Replace "@RunDate2" in the last line of the query with **DATEADD(dd, 1, @ EndDate)**. We discuss why we are using the DATEADD() function in the task notes. The SELECT statement should appear as shown.

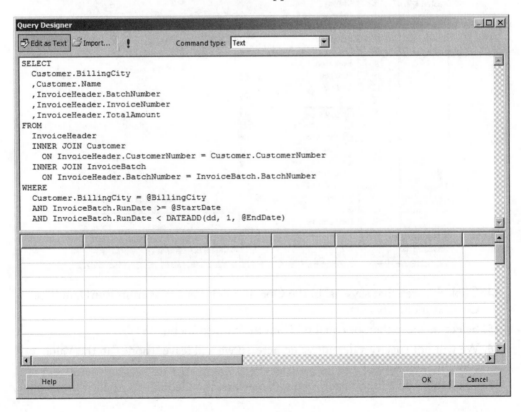

28. Click the red exclamation point to execute the query.

29. The Query Designer requires values for the three parameters you just created to run the query. You see the Define Query Parameters dialog box. In the Parameter Value column, enter **Axelburg** for @BillingCity, **12/01/2012** for @StartDate, and **12/31/2012** for @EndDate. Click OK.

30. After viewing the result set, click OK to exit the Query Designer window.

Task Notes   You have now added three parameters to the WHERE clause of the SELECT statement. Only rows where the City column has a value equal to the value of @BillingCity will be displayed in the result set. When you ran the query in the Query Designer just now, you gave the @BillingCity parameter a value of Axelburg. Therefore, only rows with Axelburg in the City column were included in the result set.

One of the trickiest things about working with datetime data types in SQL Server is remembering that they consist of both a date and a time. The RunDate field we are working with here is a datetime. When the invoice batches are run at GDS, the invoicing program assigns both the date and the time the batch was run. For instance, batch 447 was run on 12/31/2012 at 7:54:49 P.M. It has a value of 12/31/2012 7:54:49 P.M. stored in its RunDate column by the invoicing program.

When a user is asked to enter a date, most of the time, they enter the date without a time. When you were asked for a value for @EndDate, you entered 12/31/2012, without any time specified. Because SQL Server is dealing with a date and a time together, it adds on a time value for you. The default value it uses is 00:00:00 A.M., which is midnight. Remember, midnight is the start of the new day. This means when you're comparing datetime values, midnight is less than any other time occurring on the same day.

Let's think about the comparison created in the WHERE clause involving @EndDate. Assume, for a moment, that instead of using RunDate < DATEADD(dd, 1, @EndDate), we used the more obvious RunDate <= @EndDate. When the user enters 12/31/2012 for the end date, they expect the result set to include batches run on 12/31/2012. However, when SQL Server compares the value of RunDate (12/31/2012 7:54:49 P.M.) with the value of @EndDate (12/31/2012 00:00:00 A.M.), it finds that RunDate is not less than or equal to @EndDate. This is because 7:54:49 P.M., the time portion of RunDate, is greater than 00:00:00 A.M., the time portion of @EndDate. Batch 447 would not be included in this result set.

To include batches that occur on the day specified by @EndDate, you need to use RunDate < DATEADD(dd, 1, @EndDate). What this expression does is add one day to the value of @EndDate and check to see if RunDate is less than this calculated value.

Let's look at our example with Batch 447. This time, SQL Server compares the value of RunDate (12/31/2012 7:54:49 P.M.) with the calculated value (12/31/2012 00:00:00 A.M. + 1 day = 1/1/2013 00:00:00 A.M.). Now it is true that RunDate is less than our calculated value, so Batch 447 is included in the result set.

Parameterized Invoice-Batch Number Report, Task 2: Create a Second Dataset Containing a List of Cities

Steps for SSDT, Visual Studio, and Report Builder

1. The accounting department wants to be able to select a value for the @BillingCity parameter from a list of billing cities. You need to create a second dataset in the report that provides that list for the users. Right-click the Datasets entry in the Report Data window, and select Add Dataset from the context menu.

2. Type **BillingCities** for the name.

> **NOTE**
>
> *Make sure you type BillingCities without a space between the two words. Spaces are not allowed in dataset names.*

3. Check the Use a dataset embedded in my report check box.

4. Select Galactic from the Data source drop-down list.

5. Based on what you learned in Chapter 3, we'll compose the query for this dataset without the Query Designer. We want a list of all the billing cities for GDS customers. It also makes sense that each city name should only show up once in the list. In the Query text box, enter the following SQL statement:

```
SELECT DISTINCT BillingCity FROM Customer
```

6. The Dataset Properties dialog box appears as shown.

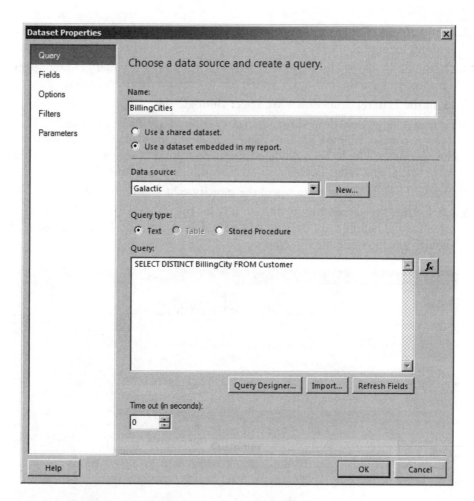

7. Click OK to exit the Dataset Properties dialog box.

Task Notes   Remember, the word DISTINCT means we want SQL Server to remove duplicates for us. To do this, SQL Server automatically sorts the result set. For this reason, you don't need to specify an ORDER BY clause for the SELECT statement.

Parameterized Invoice-Batch Number Report, Task 3: Customize the Report Parameters

Steps for SSDT, Visual Studio, and Report Builder

1. Expand the Parameters entry in the Report Data window.
2. Double-click the BillingCity parameter entry in the Report Data window.

3. Type **Select a City** in the Prompt field. This is the prompt the user sees when running the report.

4. On the Available Values page, select the Get values from a query radio button. This lets you use the BillingCities dataset to create a drop-down list.

5. From the Dataset drop-down list, select BillingCities.

6. From the Value field drop-down list, select BillingCity. From the Label field drop-down list, select BillingCity. The Value field determines what value is assigned to the parameter. The Label field determines what the user sees in the drop-down list when selecting a value. In this case, they are one and the same thing.

7. On the Default Values page, select the Specify values radio button.

8. Click Add. Type **Axelburg** in the text box for the Value. This serves as the default value for the Billing City parameter. The Report Parameter Properties dialog box should now look like the illustration.

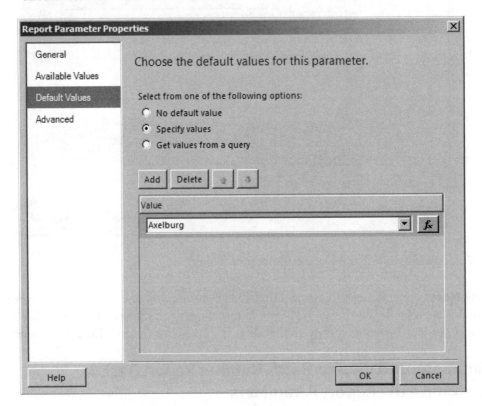

9. Click OK to exit the Report Parameter Properties dialog box.

10. Double-click the StartDate entry in the Report Data window. The Report Parameter Properties dialog box appears.

11. Type **Enter a Start Date** in the Prompt field.

12. Select Date/Time from the Data type drop-down list.

13. Click OK to exit the Report Parameter Properties dialog box.

14. Double-click the EndDate entry in the Report Data window. The Report Parameter Properties dialog box appears.

15. Type **Enter an End Date** in the Prompt field.

16. Select Date/Time from the Data type drop-down list.

17. Click OK to exit the Report Parameter Properties dialog box.

18. If you are using SSDT or Visual Studio, click the Preview tab. If you are using Report Builder, click the Run button.

19. The prompts for the three report parameters appear at the top of the preview area. No report is displayed until a value is entered for each parameter. Axelburg is selected from the Select a City drop-down list because you made this the default. Type or use the date picker to select **12/01/2012** for Enter a Start Date. Type or use the date picker to select **12/31/2012** for Enter an End Date.

20. Click View Report. The report, based on the parameter values you entered, now appears. The report, with all the rows and columns expanded, is shown here.

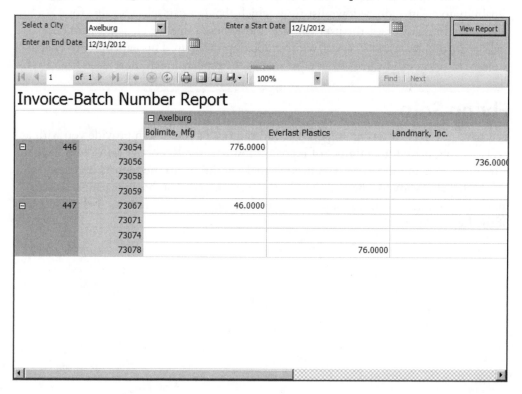

NOTE

In SSDT and Visual Studio, you can change the size of the Solution Explorer window, the Report Data window, and the other windows around the outside of the Report Designer to make more room in the center for your report. Just click the separator between the window and drag in the desired direction.

21. Click the Save button in the toolbar.

Task Notes   When you exited the Query Designer after adding parameters to your query, the Report Designer created a corresponding report parameter for each query parameter. When the report is viewed, the values entered for the report parameters are automatically passed on to the query parameters before the query is executed. In this way, the user can enter information and have it used in the WHERE clause of the SELECT statement to affect the contents of the report.

The Report Parameters dialog box enables you to control the user's interaction with the report parameters. You can change the prompts the user sees. You can specify the data type of a parameter. You can even determine the default value for a parameter.

One of the most powerful features of the Report Parameters dialog box is the capability to create a drop-down list from which the user can select a value for a parameter. In many cases, the user will not know these values, such as department codes, part numbers, and so forth, without looking them up. This capability to enable the user to select valid values from a list makes the reports much more user-friendly.

Flying Solo

You have now seen what the Report Wizard can do for you. It can provide you with a great starting place for a number of reports. However, the Report Wizard does have its limitations and, in most cases, you need to make additions to the reports it generates before they are ready for the end user. In the next chapter, you begin learning how to make those enhancements. In addition, you learn how to create reports without the aid of the Report Wizard.

Chapter 5

Removing the Training Wheels: Building Basic Reports

In This Chapter

- ▶ Riding Down Familiar Roads
- ▶ The Tablix and Data Regions
- ▶ New Territory
- ▶ Getting Graphical

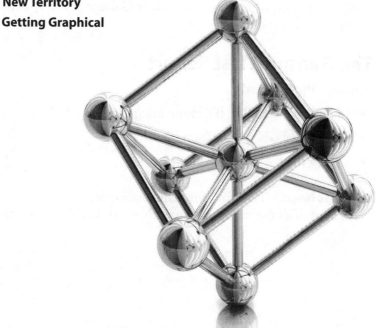

I n Chapter 4, you built your first reports using a wizard. This is like learning to ride your first two-wheeler with the training wheels on. Now it is time for the training wheels to come off so you can see what this baby can really do! We are going to begin building reports from scratch. I hope these next few chapters provide the hand-holding you need, and then you can learn to ride sans training wheels without getting skinned knees.

First, we work with the two types of reports you were introduced to in Chapter 4. We begin by building a table report without the use of a wizard. From there, we do the same with a matrix report. After that, we look at a new report type—the list report. As part of this third report, we work with some of the basic report items that make up each report—namely, the line control, the text box control, and the rectangle control. Along the way, you learn more about the Report Designer or Report Builder that serves as your development platform.

So, the training wheels are off and the wrenches have been put away. Don your helmets; it's time to ride!

Riding Down Familiar Roads

We cover some familiar territory as we begin building reports without a wizard. In Chapter 4, you used a wizard to create table reports (the Customer List Report and the Customer-Invoice Report) and a matrix report (the Invoice-Batch Number Report). We create these types of reports once more, but this time without the aid of the wizard.

Again, we look at the business needs of Galactic Delivery Services (GDS) and create reports to satisfy those business needs.

The Transport List Report

Features Highlighted

▶ Building a GROUP BY clause using the Graphical Query Designer

▶ Creating a table report from scratch

▶ Using the Expression dialog box

Business Need The transport maintenance department at Galactic Delivery Services needs a list of all the transports currently in service. They want this list to be grouped by transport type. The list includes the serial number, the purchase date, and the date the transport was last in for repairs. The list also includes the cargo capacity and range of each transport type.

Task Overview

1. Preparation and Creation of a New Report
2. Create a Dataset
3. Place a Table Item on the Report and Populate It
4. Add Table Grouping and Other Report Formatting

Transport List Report, Task 1: Preparation and Creation of a New Report

`DT` **SSDT and Visual Studio Steps**

1. Run SQL Server Data Tools or Visual Studio 2010. The Start page is displayed (or select File | Close Project from the menu if a solution is already open).

2. Click New Project in the toolbar to create a new project. This displays the New Project dialog box. (Remember, you can create a new project in three different ways: Select File | New | Project from the main menu; click the New Project toolbar button; or click the Create Project link on the Start page. All these actions achieve the same result.)

3. Select Reporting Services under Business Intelligence in the Installed Templates area, if it is not already selected. Click the Report Server Project icon in the center area of the New Project dialog box. (Be sure to click the Report Server Project icon and *not* the Report Server Project Wizard item.)

4. Type **Chapter05** for the project name. This project will contain all the reports you create in this chapter.

5. Click Browse to open the Project Location dialog box.

6. Under My Documents, navigate to the Visual Studio 2010\Projects\MSSQLRS folder.

7. Select the MSSQLRS folder and click OK.

8. Make sure the Create directory for solution check box is unchecked. The New Project dialog box should now look like the illustration.

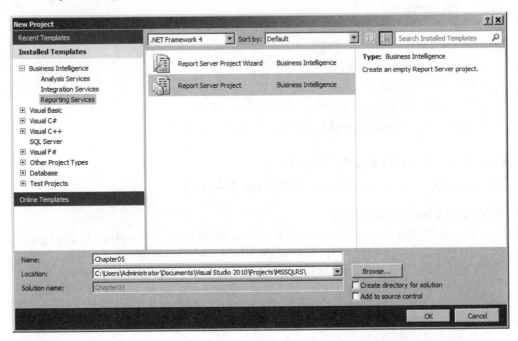

9. Click OK in the New Project dialog box. A new project is created.
10. In the Solution Explorer on the right side of the screen, right-click the Shared Data Sources folder. Select Add New Data Source from the context menu, as shown here.

11. Type **Galactic** for Name. Click Edit. The Connection Properties dialog box appears.

12. Type the name of the Microsoft SQL Server database server hosting the Galactic database in the Server name text box. If the Galactic database is hosted by the computer you are currently working on, you may type **(local)** for the server name.

13. Select the Use SQL Server Authentication radio button.

14. Type **GalacticReporting** for the user name.

15. Type **G@l@ct1c** for the password. (The third character of the password is a lowercase l. The seventh character of the password is the number 1.)

16. Check the Save my password check box.

17. Select Galactic from the Select or enter a database name drop-down list.

18. Click Test Connection. If the message "Test connection succeeded" appears, click OK. If an error message appears, make sure the name of your database server, the user name, the password, and the database are entered properly. If your test connection still does not succeed, make sure you have correctly installed the Galactic database.

19. Click OK to exit the Connection Properties dialog box. Click OK again to exit the Shared Data Source Properties dialog box. A new shared data source called Galactic.rds is created in the Chapter05 project.

20. In the Solution Explorer, right-click the Reports folder.

21. Put your mouse pointer over Add in the context menu, and wait for the submenu to appear. Select the New Item command from the context menu, as shown here.

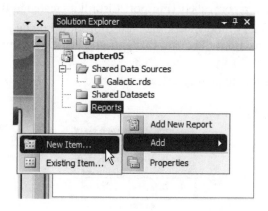

22. The Add New Item - Chapter05 dialog box appears. Make sure the Report item is selected in the center area. Enter **Transport List** for the name. The dialog box appears as shown.

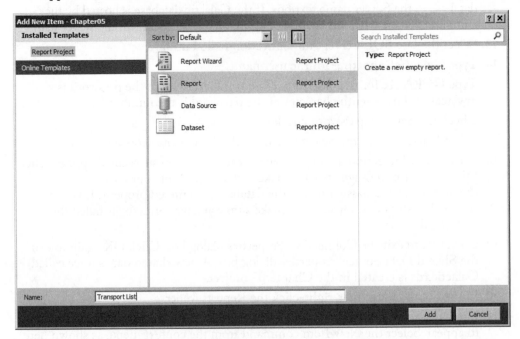

23. Click Add. A new report called Transport List.rdl is created in the Chapter05 project.

24. In the Report Data window, click the New drop-down menu as shown in Figure 5-1. Select Data Source from the menu that appears. The Data Source Properties dialog box appears.

25. Enter **Galactic** for the name.

Figure 5-1 *Creating a new data source*

26. Select the Use shared data source reference radio button, and select Galactic from the drop-down list below it. Click OK. An entry for the Galactic data source appears in the Report Data window.

27. In the Report Data window, right-click the entry for the Galactic data source, and select Add Dataset from the context menu. The Dataset Properties dialog box appears.

28. Enter **TransportList** for the name.

NOTE

The dataset name must not contain any spaces.

29. Click the Query Designer button. The Query Designer window opens, displaying the Graphical Query Designer.

Task Notes for SSDT and Visual Studio   Because we are creating several reports in the Chapter05 project, all of which select data from the Galactic database, we began by creating a shared data source. This saves us time as we create each of the reports. We continue this practice throughout the remaining chapters.

In Step 20 through Step 23, we are adding a report to the project. In Chapter 4, you saw that selecting Add New Report from the context menu causes the new report to be created with the Report Wizard. In this chapter, we are looking to build our reports from scratch, which is why we used Add | New Item in Step 21.

RB **Report Builder Steps**

1. Open a browser and navigate to the Report Manager. (If you need help with this, refer back to Chapter 4.)

2. Navigate to the Galactic Delivery Services folder, and the click the New Folder button. The New Folder page appears.

3. Enter **Chapter05** for Name and click OK. This report server folder will contain all the reports you create in Report Builder for this chapter.

4. Click the Report Builder button to launch Report Builder. The Getting Started page appears.

5. With New Report highlighted in the left column, click Blank Report. The Report Builder shows a new blank report.

6. In the Report Data window, click the New drop-down menu as shown in Figure 5-1 (found in the previous SSDT and Visual Studio steps). Select Data Source from the menu that appears. The Data Source Properties dialog box appears.

7. Enter **Galactic** for the name.

8. Make sure the Use a shared connection or report model radio button is selected.

9. Select the Galactic shared data source as shown here.

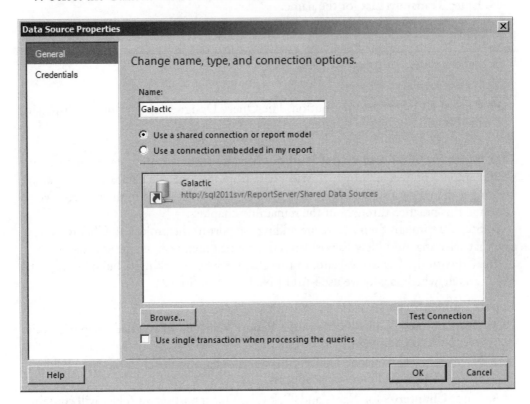

10. Click OK. An entry for the Galactic data source appears in the Report Data window.

11. In the Report Data window, right-click the entry for the Galactic data source, and select Add Dataset from the context menu. The Dataset Properties dialog box appears.

12. Enter **TransportList** for the name.

NOTE

The dataset name must not contain any spaces.

13. Click the Query Designer button. The Graphical Query Designer window appears.

Task Notes for Report Builder   You will notice that we are able to use the same Galactic shared data source for the reports created for this chapter as we did for the reports created for Chapter 4. This is true even though we are going to save the reports for this chapter in a different folder (the Chapter05 folder) than the reports created for Chapter 4. This is one of the advantages of saving items directly to the report server as we have been doing with Report Builder.

Transport List Report, Task 2: Create a Dataset

DT | **SSDT and Visual Studio Steps**

1. Right-click in the diagram pane (the upper area) of the Graphical Query Designer screen. Select Add Table from the context menu.

2. Add the following tables to the query:

Transport
TransportType
Repair

3. Click Close to exit the Add Table dialog box.

4. Right-click the diamond on the connection between the Transport table and the Repair table. You may need to rearrange the TransportType table, the Transport table, and the Repair table to see this diamond. Select the Select All Rows from Transport item from the context menu.

5. Check the following columns in the TransportType table:

Description
CargoCapacity
Range

6. Check the following columns in the Transport table:

SerialNumber
PurchaseDate
RetiredDate

7. Check the following column in the Repair table:

BeginWorkDate

8. In the criteria pane (the second area from the top), type **1** in the Sort Order column across from the Description field, and type **2** in the Sort Order column across from the SerialNumber field.

9. The business need for this report states it is to include only active transports. That means we only want to include transports that do not have a retired date. Type **IS NULL** in the Filter column across from the RetiredDate field. Remove the check mark under the Output column across from the RetiredDate field.

10. Right-click in the SQL pane (the third area from the top), and select Execute SQL from the context menu. In the results pane (the bottom area), notice that several records appear for serial number P-348-23-4532-22A. Your screen should look like the following illustration.

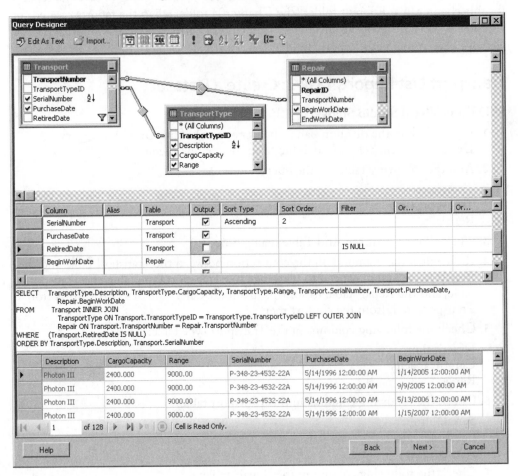

NOTE

You can also run the query by clicking the Run button (the one with a red exclamation point) in the Query Designer window toolbar.

11. Right-click in the diagram pane of the Graphical Query Designer screen. Select Add Group By from the context menu. A new column called Group By is added to the criteria pane.

12. In the criteria pane, click in the Group By column across from BeginWorkDate.

13. Use the drop-down list in this cell to select Max, as shown here.

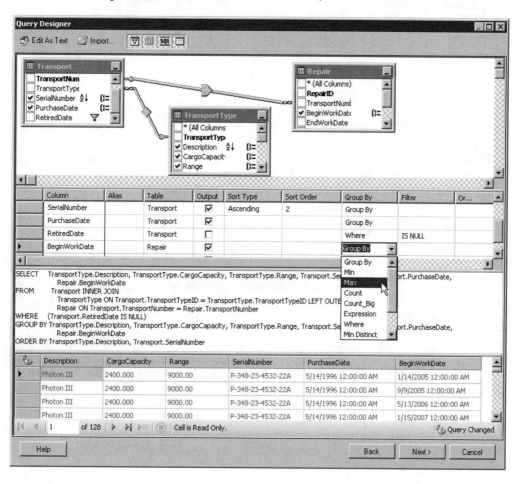

14. When you move your cursor out of the Group By column, Expr 1 will be assigned as the alias for BeginWorkDate. Replace Expr1 with **LatestRepairDate** in the Alias column across from BeginWorkDate.

15. Right-click in the SQL pane, and select Execute SQL from the context menu. Notice that now only one record appears for serial number P-348-23-4532-22A. Be sure to read the Task Notes for this task found after the Report Builder steps.

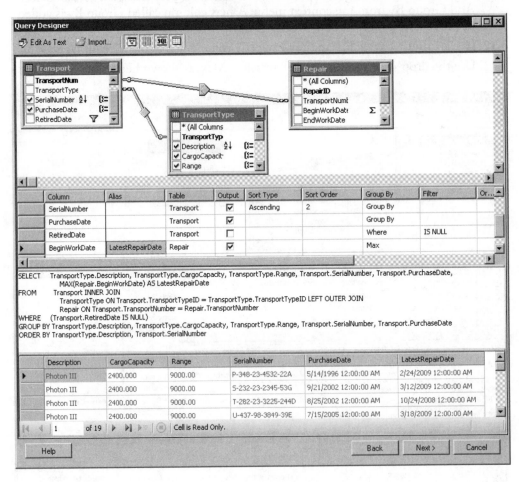

RB   **Report Builder Steps**

1. In the Database view pane, expand the Tables entry.

2. Scroll down and expand the entry for the TransportType table.

3. Check the following fields:

   Description
   CargoCapacity
   Range

4. Expand the entry for the Transport table, and check the following fields:

   SerialNumber
   PurchaseDate

5. Expand the entry for the Repair table, and check the following field:

   BeginWorkDate

6. Expand the Relationships pane.

7. Click the word "Inner" in the Join Type column between the Transport and Repair tables. The Join Type drop-down list appears.

8. Select Left Outer from the drop-down list.

9. The business need for this report states it is to include only active transports. That means we only want to include transports that do not have a retired date. Click the Add Filter button in the Applied filters page.

10. Click the entry for the Description field in the Field Name column in the Applied filters pane. A field selection tree view appears.

11. Expand the entry for the Transport table in the field selection tree view.

12. Click the RetiredDate field to select it.

13. Click "(none)" in the Value column. The Value drop-down list appears.

14. Click "(null)" in the Value drop-down list to select it. Our query will now include only those Transport records where the RetiredDate is null.

15. Click the Run Query button. In the results pane (the bottom area), notice that several records appear for serial number P-348-23-4532-22A. Your screen should appear similar to the following illustration.

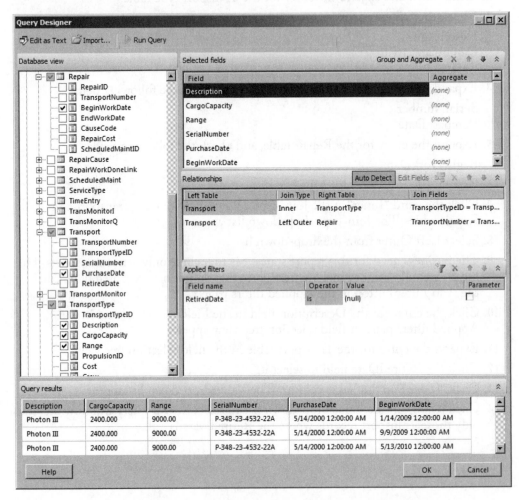

16. In the Selected fields pane click the word "(none)" in the Aggregate column across from the BeginWorkDate field. The Aggregate drop-down list appears.

17. Select "Max" from the Aggregate drop-down list. This will move the BeginWorkDate field to the bottom of the Selected fields pane and change its name to Max_BeginWorkDate. It will also put the phrase "Grouped By" in the Aggregate column for all of the other fields.

18. Click the Run Query button again. Notice that now only one record appears for serial number P-348-23-4532-22A.

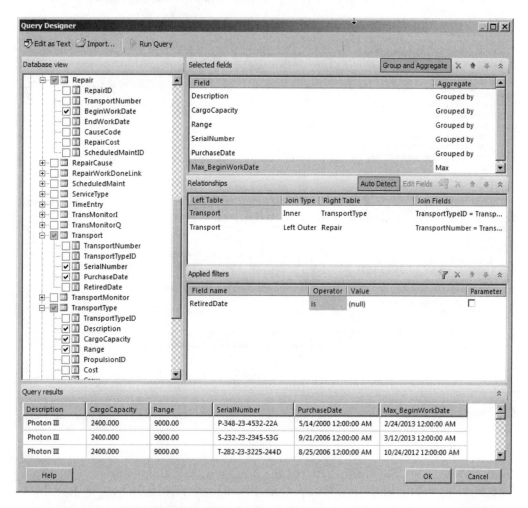

19. We are going to make an adjustment and an addition to the query generated by the Graphical Query Designer. Click the Edit as Text button to switch to viewing the query as text.

20. Expand the query pane (the top part of the window) so you can see the entire query.

21. Replace "Max_BeginWorkDate" with **LatestRepairDate** in the field list portion of the query.

22. Add the following at the end of the query:

```
ORDER BY TransportType.Description, Transport.SerialNumber
```

Your query should now appear as shown.

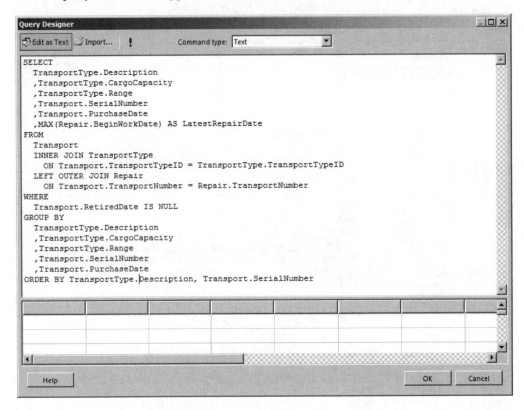

Task Notes The relationship between the Transport table and the Repair table is a one-to-many relationship. One transport may have many repairs. When you join these two tables, you get one record in the result set for each match between records in the Transport table and the Repair table. Because transport P-348-23-4532-22A has been in for repairs ten times, it generates ten records in the result set.

This is not exactly what the business requirements call for. Instead, we want to have one record for transport P-348-23-4532-22A with the latest repair date. To accomplish this, we use the GROUP BY clause. In Step 11 of the SSDT and Visual Studio steps and in Steps 16 and 17 of the Report Builder steps, we instruct the Graphical Query Designer to group together records in the result set that have the same value in all group-by fields.

When you use the GROUP BY clause, all the fields in the FIELD LIST must fit into one of the following two categories:

▶ The field must be included in the GROUP BY clause.

▶ The field must be enclosed in an aggregate function.

Any fields with the words "Grouped By" in the Group By or Aggregate column are included in the GROUP BY clause. These fields also have a special Group By symbol next to them in the diagram pane in SSDT and Visual Studio. By selecting Max under the Group By or Aggregate column, we enclose BeginWorkDate in the MAX() aggregate function. This returns the maximum BeginWorkDate (in other words, the latest repair date) for each transport. Note in SSDT and Visual Studio a special symbol, the Greek letter sigma, next to the BeginWorkDate field in the diagram pane to signify it is enclosed in an aggregate function.

When the BeginWorkDate field is enclosed in the MAX() aggregate function, it becomes a calculated field. It is not simply the value of the BeginWorkDate field that is returned as a column in the result set. Instead, it is a calculation using the value of the BeginWorkDate field that makes up this column of the result set. The Graphical Query Designer needs a name for this calculated column. This is known as the *alias* for the column. To better remember what is in this result set column when the time comes to use it in a report, we changed the default alias to LatestRepairDate.

Transport List Report, Task 3: Place a Table Item on the Report and Populate It

DT | **SSDT and Visual Studio Steps**

  1. Click OK to exit the Query Designer window. Click OK to exit the Dataset Properties dialog box and begin working on the report layout.

NOTE

Your installation of SSDT or Visual Studio may be using a feature called Auto-Hide with the Toolbox. Auto-Hide is used to provide more screen space for your report layout. When Auto-Hide is active for the Toolbox, the Toolbox is only represented on the screen by a tab containing a tool icon and the word "Toolbox" at the extreme left side of the window. To view the actual Toolbox, place your mouse pointer on top of this tab. After a second or two, the Toolbox appears. Once your mouse pointer moves off the Toolbox, it is automatically hidden again.

2. Click the Table report item in the Toolbox. The mouse pointer changes to a table icon and crosshairs when you move your mouse pointer over the report layout area, as shown in the next illustration.

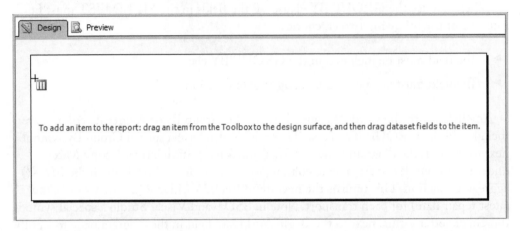

3. Drag the mouse over the lower three-quarters of the design surface, as shown in the following illustration.

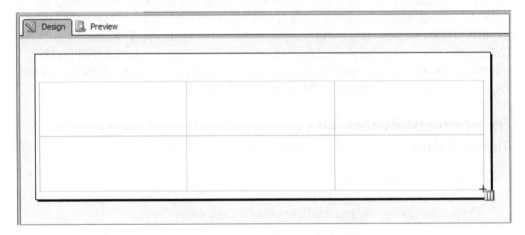

4. When you release the mouse button after dragging, a table is created to occupy the area you just defined. By default, every cell in the table is occupied by an empty text box. Click in each cell of the table, and note the name and type of report item shown at the top of the Properties window.

5. Let's take a few moments to go over the methods for selecting various parts of the table. You have already seen how to select individual cells. When you click the table, gray borders appear on top of and to the left of the table item. These borders provide handles for selecting other parts of the table. Click the table, and then click any of the gray rectangles in the border above the table item. This action selects the corresponding column, as shown in the following illustration.

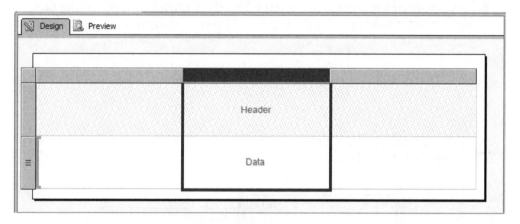

6. Click any of the gray rectangles in the border to the left of the table item. This action selects a row, as shown here.

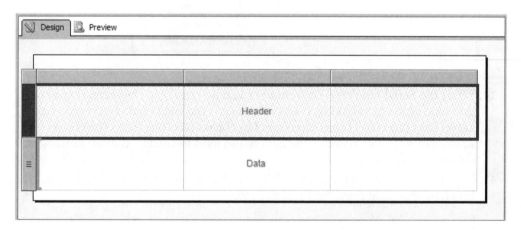

7. Click the gray square in the upper-left corner of the border. This action selects the entire table. When the entire table is selected, the gray border is replaced by the sizing handles (the small white squares) for the table. You must select the entire table before you can move and size the table item. Note in the Properties window the item is called a tablix rather than a table. We will discuss this in the section "The Tablix and Data Regions" later in this chapter.

8. Hover your cursor over the lower-left table cell. A small icon representing the Field Selector will appear in the upper-right corner of the text box, as shown here.

9. Click the icon. The Field Selector, a list of the fields defined in your dataset, is displayed, as shown here.

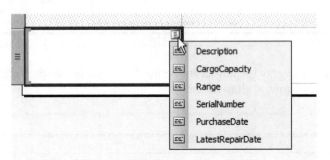

10. Select the SerialNumber field from the Field Selector. An expression that returns the value of the SerialNumber field is placed in the text box that occupies the lower-left table cell. This is represented by the name of the field enclosed in square brackets. The name of the field is also used to create a column heading in the upper-left table cell.

11. Repeat this process in the lower cell in the center column of the table to select the PurchaseDate field from the Field Selector.

12. Repeat the process once more in the lower-right table cell to select the LatestRepairDate field from the Field Selector. The report layout should now appear as shown.

Design Preview		
Serial Number	Purchase Date	Latest Repair Date
[SerialNumber]	[PurchaseDate]	[LatestRepairDate]

13. Select the header row (the top row) by clicking the gray rectangle in the border to the left of the row.

14. Make the following changes in the Properties window:

Property	New Value
FontWeight (expand the Font property to find the FontWeight property)	Bold
TextDecoration (also part of Font property)	Underline

15. In the gray border to the left of the table, click the line between the header row and the data row. Drag it to reduce the height of the header row.

16. In the gray border to the left of the table, click the bottom of the data row rectangle. Drag it to reduce the height of the data row.

17. Click the center cell in the data row. Hold down SHIFT and click the right cell in the data row. Both of these cells are now selected. Make the following changes in the Properties window:

Property	New Value
Format	MM/dd/yyyy
TextAlign	Left

NOTE

Make sure you use uppercase letter M's in the Format property. MM is the placeholder for month in a format string, whereas mm is the placeholder for milliseconds.

18. Click the Preview tab to preview the report. The report should appear as shown here. Be sure to read the Task Notes for this task found after the Report Builder steps.

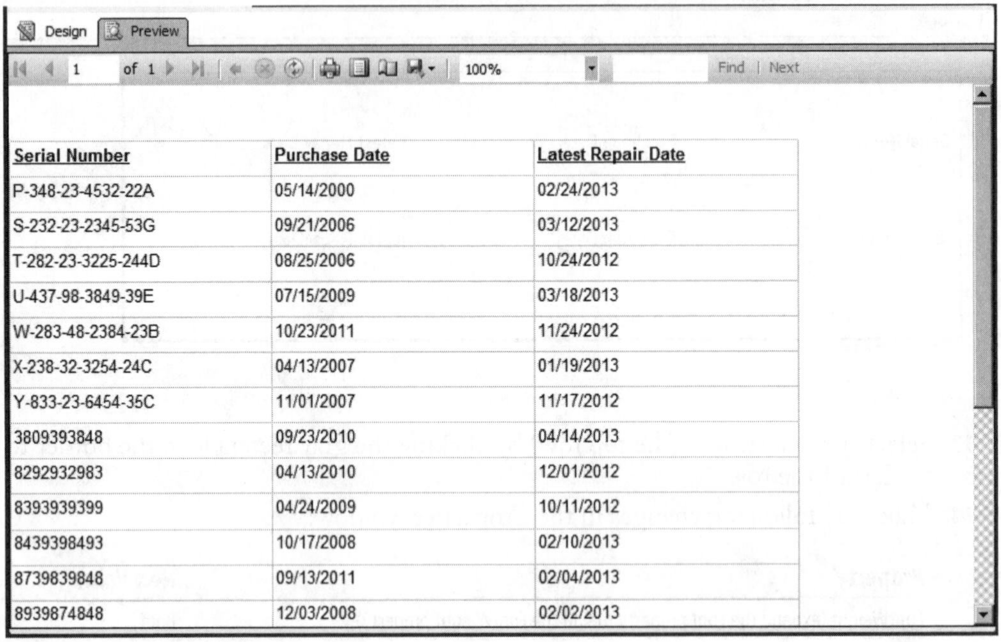

Serial Number	Purchase Date	Latest Repair Date
P-348-23-4532-22A	05/14/2000	02/24/2013
S-232-23-2345-53G	09/21/2006	03/12/2013
T-282-23-3225-244D	08/25/2006	10/24/2012
U-437-98-3849-39E	07/15/2009	03/18/2013
W-283-48-2384-23B	10/23/2011	11/24/2012
X-238-32-3254-24C	04/13/2007	01/19/2013
Y-833-23-6454-35C	11/01/2007	11/17/2012
3809393848	09/23/2010	04/14/2013
8292932983	04/13/2010	12/01/2012
8393939399	04/24/2009	10/11/2012
8439398493	10/17/2008	02/10/2013
8739839848	09/13/2011	02/04/2013
8939874848	12/03/2008	02/02/2013

RB **Report Builder Steps**

1. Click OK to exit the Query Designer window. Click OK to exit the Dataset Properties dialog box and begin working on the report layout.
2. Select the View tab of the ribbon.
3. Check the Properties check box to view the Properties window.
4. Adjust the size of the Report Builder window, if needed, so you can see the entire report layout area.
5. Select the Insert tab of the ribbon. You will use the Insert tab to add items to your report.
6. Click the table item in the ribbon. You will see two options: Table Wizard and Insert Table. We saw the Table Wizard in Chapter 4. Now we will create a table on our own.

7. Click Insert Table. The mouse pointer changes to a table icon and crosshairs when you move your mouse pointer over the report layout area, as shown in the next illustration.

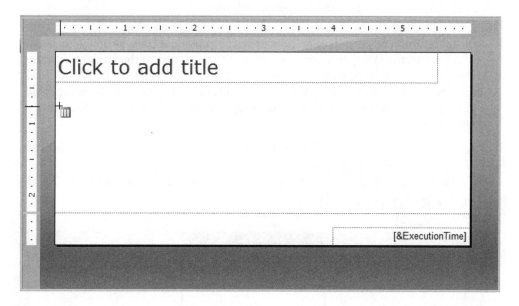

8. Click and drag the mouse over the lower three-quarters of the design surface, as shown in the following illustration.

9. When you release the mouse button after dragging, a table is created to occupy the area you just defined. By default, every cell in the table is occupied by an empty text box. Click in each cell of the table, and note the name of the report item shown at the top of the Properties window.

10. Let's take a few moments to go over the methods for selecting various parts of the table. You have already seen how to select individual cells. When you click anywhere in the table, gray borders appear on top of and to the left of the table item. These borders provide handles for selecting other parts of the table. Click the table, and then click any of the gray rectangles in the border above the table item. This action selects the corresponding column, as shown in the following illustration.

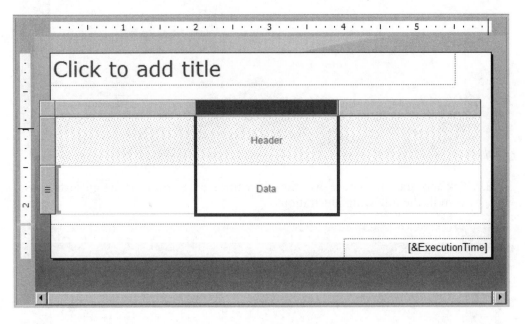

11. Click any of the gray rectangles in the border to the left of the table item. This action selects a row, as shown here.

12. Click the gray square in the upper-left corner of the border. This action selects the entire table. When the entire table is selected, the gray border is replaced by the sizing handles (the small white squares) for the table. You must select the entire table before you can move and size the table item. Note in the Properties window the item is called a tablix rather than a table. We will discuss this in the section "The Tablix and Data Regions" later in this chapter.

13. Hover your cursor over the lower-left table cell. A small icon representing the Field Selector will appear in the upper-right corner of the text box, as shown here.

14. Click the icon. The Field Selector, a list of the fields defined in your dataset, is displayed, as shown here.

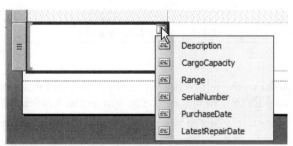

15. Select the SerialNumber field from the Field Selector. An expression that returns the value of the SerialNumber field is placed in the text box that occupies the lower-left table cell. This is represented by the name of the field enclosed in square brackets. The name of the field is also used to create a column heading in the upper-left table cell.

16. Repeat this process in the lower cell in the center column of the table to select the PurchaseDate field from the Field Selector.

17. Repeat the process once more in the lower-right table cell to select the LatestRepairDate field from the Field Selector. The report layout should now appear as shown.

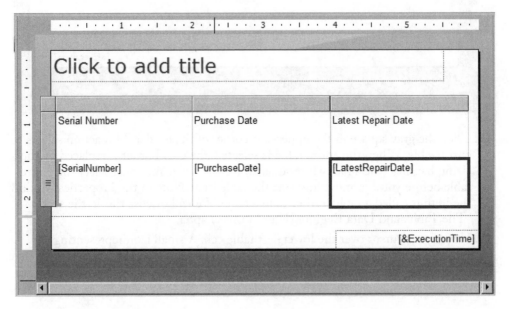

18. Select the header row (the top row) by clicking the gray rectangle in the border to the left of the row.

19. Make the following changes in the Properties window:

Property	New Value
FontWeight (expand the Font property to find the FontWeight property)	Bold
TextDecoration	Underline

20. In the gray border to the left of the table, click the line between the header row and the data row. Drag it to reduce the height of the header row.

21. In the gray border to the left of the table, click the bottom of the data row rectangle. Drag it to reduce the height of the data row.

22. Click the center cell in the data row. Hold down SHIFT and click the right cell in the data row. Both of these cells are now selected. Make the following changes in the Properties window:

Property	New Value
Format	MM/dd/yyyy
TextAlign	Left

NOTE

Make sure you use uppercase letter M's in the Format property. MM is the placeholder for month in a format string, whereas mm is the placeholder for milliseconds.

23. Select the Home tab of the ribbon, and click the Run button to preview the report. The report should appear as shown here.

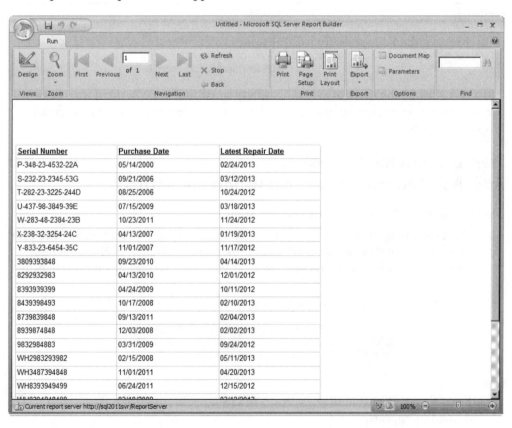

Task Notes In the Properties window are several instances where a group of related properties are combined under a summary property. For instance, the FontFamily, FontSize, FontStyle, FontWeight, and TextDecoration properties are combined under the Font property. The Font property serves as a summary of the other five.

Initially, only the summary property is visible in the Properties window. A plus (+) sign to the left of a property tells you it is a summary property and has several detail properties beneath it. The summary property has a value that concatenates the values of all the detail properties underneath it.

For example, suppose the FontFamily, FontSize, FontStyle, FontWeight, and TextDecoration properties have the following values:

FontFamily:	Arial
FontSize:	10pt
FontStyle:	Normal
FontWeight:	Bold
TextDecoration	Underline

In that case, the Font property has this value:

Font:	Arial, 10pt, Normal, Bold, Underline

You can change the value of a detail property by editing the concatenated values in the summary property, or you can expand the summary property and edit the detail properties directly.

Transport List Report, Task 4: Add Table Grouping and Other Report Formatting

SSDT, Visual Studio, and Report Builder Steps

1. Click the Design tab in SSDT and Visual Studio or the Design button in Report Builder. Notice there is one entry in the Row Groups section of the Grouping pane at the bottom of the Design area. We will add a second row group to display the transport type.

2. Click the drop-down arrow in the Row Groups pane, as shown here.

3. From the menu that appears, select Add Group | Parent Group. The Tablix group dialog box appears.

4. Select [Description] from the Group by drop-down list.

5. Check the Add group header check box.

6. Click OK. A new column and a new row are added to the table. Note that by default the group is named after the grouping column, so this group is named Description. There is now a Description entry in the Row Groups pane. The field we selected as the group expression provides the value in this new column.

7. Select the cell in the upper-left corner of the table. This is the cell containing the word "Description" bold and underlined. Click the cell a second time so the blinking text-edit cursor appears in that cell.

8. Delete "Description" and type the following:

```
Transport Type
```

(Don't worry about the fact that it wraps to a second line.)

9. Select the table cell containing the Description field.

10. Make the following changes in the Properties window:

Property	New Value
FontWeight	Bold

11. Click the empty table cell immediately below the Serial Number heading. Hold down SHIFT, and then click the rightmost cell in the same row. Right-click in any of the selected cells, and select Merge Cells from the Tablix section of the context menu, as shown here.

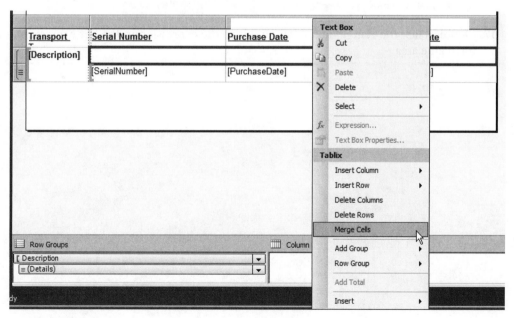

12. Right-click in the newly merged cells, and select Expression from the Textbox section of the context menu. If the Expression item is disabled (grayed out) in the context menu, click on another cell in the tablix, and then right-click the newly merged cells again. The Expression dialog box appears.

13. Type the following after the equal sign (=), including the quotation marks, in the Set expression for: Value area:

```
"Cargo Capacity: " & CStr(
```

14. Select the Fields (TransportList) entry in the tree view in the Category area of the dialog box. Note the fields in the selected dataset appear in the Values area of the dialog box.

15. Double-click the CargoCapacity field to append it to the expression. Note an expression is created, which returns the value of the CargoCapacity field.

CAUTION

If you type the field expression rather than selecting it from the Fields area, it must be typed in the exact case shown in the Fields area. Fields, as well as parameters, are case-sensitive when used in expressions.

16. Type) at the end of the expression in the Set expression for: Value area and press CTRL + ENTER. Type the following:

```
& vbCrLf & "Range: " & CStr(
```

17. Double-click the Range field to append it to the expression in the Set expression for: Value area.

18. Type) at the end of the expression. The Expression dialog box should appear as shown.

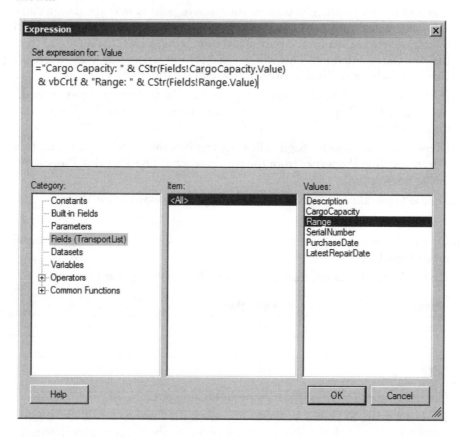

19. Click OK. Note the "<<Expr>>" in the merged cells indicates the value being displayed in this area of the report does not come from a single field, but from an expression.

20. With the merged cells still selected, make the following changes in the Properties window:

Property	New Value
BorderColor:Default (expand the BorderColor property to find the Default property)	Black
BorderWidth:Default	2pt
Font:FontWeight	Bold

21. **(SSDT and Visual Studio only)** If you are using SSDT or Visual Studio, click the Textbox report item in the Toolbox. The mouse pointer changes to a text box icon and crosshairs when you move your mouse pointer over the design surface. Drag the mouse cursor over the entire area above the table on the design surface. When you release the mouse button after dragging, a text box is created to occupy the area you just defined. This will be used for the report title. (If you are using Report Builder, a text box is already provided for the title.)

22. **(SSDT and Visual Studio only)** Right-click the text box you just created. Select Text Box Properties from the context menu. The Text Box Properties dialog box appears.

23. **(Report Builder only)** Right-click the text box that says "Click to add title." Select Text Box Properties from the context menu. The Text Box Properties dialog box appears.

24. On the General page of the dialog box, Type the following for Value:

```
Transport List
```

25. On the Alignment page of the dialog box, select Center from the Horizontal drop-down list.

26. On the Font page of the dialog box, make the following changes:

Property	New Value
Font	Arial
Size	16pt
Style	Bold

27. Click OK to exit the Text Box Properties dialog box.

28. If you are using SSDT or Visual Studio, click the Preview tab. If you are using Report Builder, click the Run button. The report should appear as shown here.

of 1	100%	Find	Next

Transport List

Transport Type	Serial Number	Purchase Date	Latest Repair Date
Photon III	**Cargo Capacity: 2400.000** **Range: 9000.00**		
	P-348-23-4532-22A	05 14/2000	02 24/2013
	S-232-23-2345-53G	09 21/2006	03 12/2013
	T-282-23-3225-244D	08 25/2006	10 24/2012
	U-437-98-3849-39E	07 15/2009	03 18/2013
	W-283-48-2384-23B	10 23/2011	11 24/2012
	X-238-32-3254-24C	04 13/2007	01 19/2013
	Y-833-23-6454-35C	11 01/2007	11 17/2012
Star Lifter	**Cargo Capacity: 5000.000** **Range: 18000.00**		
	3809393848	09 23/2010	04 14/2013
	8292932983	04 13/2010	12 01/2012
	8393939399	04 24/2009	10 11/2012
	8439398493	10 17/2008	02 10/2013
	8739839848	09 13/2011	02 04/2013
	8939874848	12 03/2008	02 02/2013
	9832984883	03 31/2009	09 24/2012
Warp Hauler	**Cargo Capacity: 1000.000**		

29. If you are using SSDT or Visual Studio, click Save All in the toolbar. If you are using Report Builder, save the report under the name "Transport List" in the Chapter05 folder you created on the report server.

Task Notes   When we added the grouping, we selected a field for the group expression in Step 4. The selected field determines when a new group begins in the report. In the Transport List report, we used the Description field from the TransportType table as the group expression. Because our first sort in the dataset was on the Description column in the TransportType table, all the Photon III transports came first in the dataset, followed by the Star Lifter transports, and finally, the Warp Hauler transports. Each time the value of the group expression changes, a new value appears in the group column and a new group header is added to the report.

Be sure you do not confuse the grouping in the report with the GROUP BY clause we used in SQL SELECT statements. The SQL GROUP BY clause takes a number of records and combines them into a single record in the result set. The grouping in the report takes a number of records in the dataset and surrounds them with a group column, along with a possible group header and/or group footer when they are output in the report.

In Steps 12–18, we combined the fields that need to be in the group header into one expression. This was done so we could create a multiline group header, and also to concatenate or combine the labels (Cargo Capacity: and Range:) and the contents of the two fields (CargoCapacity and Range) into one string. The three columns of the group header were merged together to create room for the resulting expression. The Visual Basic concatenation operator (&) is used to combine the values into one long string. The Visual Basic constant vbCrLf is used to put a carriage return and linefeed in the middle of the string. This causes everything following the carriage return and linefeed to be placed on the next line down, giving us a two-line group header. The CStr() function is used to convert the CargoCapacity and Range numeric values to strings so they can be concatenated with the string constants.

Remember, table cells are always occupied by a report item. If no other report item has been placed in a cell, the cell is occupied by a text box. When multiple cells are merged, the report item in the leftmost cell expands to fill the merged table cell. The report items in the other cells involved in the merge are automatically deleted.

We created a border around the text box in the merged cells to set off our group heading. This is easier and more efficient than adding a line or a rectangle report item to the report to get the same result. This is especially true when you are trying to set off something in the middle of a table, such as our group header.

When you typed the text in Step 8, it looked like you were entering the text directly into the text box. However, what you were doing is changing the Value property of the text box. You can change the Value property of a text box by typing directly into the text box in the design surface or by typing in the Value field on the General page of the Text Box Properties dialog box.

In addition, the Expression dialog box can be used to change the Value property of a text box. In Step 12, we used the context menu to bring up the Expression dialog box. The Expression dialog box can also be accessed by clicking the *fx* button in the Text Box Properties dialog box, as the following illustration shows.

You probably noticed a red, jagged line that appears occasionally below the expression as you typed it in the Expression dialog box. If you have ever used Microsoft Word, then you know this means something is wrong with the text you have typed. In Word, this red line indicates a spelling error. In the Expression dialog box, this means a problem exists with the syntax of your expression. Hovering over the red line provides you with a brief description of the problem.

The Tablix and Data Regions

In the report you just completed, you saw when we dragged a table from the Toolbox onto the design surface, we actually ended up with a report item called a tablix. A tablix provides the capabilities of a table and a matrix combined into one. When we selected a table from the toolbox, what we really did was select a template that creates a tablix that functions like a table. When we select a matrix from the toolbox, as we will do in our next report, we really select a template that creates a tablix that functions like a matrix. In the same manner, the list is a template that creates a tablix that functions like a freeform list.

In the previous report, you saw how the tablix, when functioning like a table, starts with a predefined number of columns. It then adds a data row to the resulting report for each record in the dataset. The tablix, when functioning like a matrix, creates both rows and columns based on the contents of the dataset. You see this demonstrated in our next report. The tablix, when functioning like a freeform list, is not limited to rows and columns. It creates a whole section, perhaps a whole page, of layout for each record in the dataset. We create a report using the list template later in this chapter.

These templates help us start work on a particular type of report layout, table, matrix, or list. The templates do not, however, change the functionality of the tablix that appears as part of our report. They just help configure some of the initial settings for the tablix so it looks a certain way. We could start with the table template and end up with a tablix that functions more like a matrix. Or we could start with a matrix template and end up with a tablix that functions more like a table. Underneath it all, a tablix is a tablix is a tablix.

The tablix is one of a number of special report items designed specifically for working with datasets. These special report items are called *data regions*. The other data regions are the chart, the gauge, the map, and the sparkline. (It could also be considered correct to refer to the table, the matrix, and the list as data region items in the Toolbox, even though we now know these are simply templates for creating the tablix data region.)

Data regions are able to work with multiple records from a dataset. The data region reads a record from the dataset, creates a portion of the report using the data found in that record, and then moves on to the next record. It does this until all the records from the dataset have been processed. The tablix creates mainly textual layout for each record in the dataset. The chart, gauge, sparkline, and map data regions create mainly graphical layout for the records in the dataset.

Each data region item has a property called DataSetName. This property contains the name of the dataset used by the data region. In the Transport List report you just created, the DataSetName property of the tablix has the value TransportList (see the following illustration). Each data region always works with one and only one dataset. However, a given dataset can be used by multiple data regions within the same report. For example, you could create a report containing both a tablix data region and a chart data region to present the data from a single dataset in both a textual and a graphical layout.

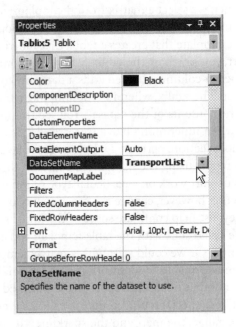

Now let's move down the road a little further and create a matrix report without the wizard.

The Repair Count By Type Report

Features Highlighted

▶ Creating a matrix report from scratch

▶ Using the Property Pages button

Business Need   GDS needs to purchase several new transports to update their delivery fleet. The company must decide which type of transport to purchase. One factor in the decision is the amount of time the new transports will spend in the maintenance hangar for repairs and preventative maintenance.

Upper management has asked the GDS maintenance department to provide a report showing the number of each type of repair required by each type of transport. The report should include statistics from all transports, both active and retired. Also, the report should group the repairs by their cause.

Task Overview

1. Create a New Report, Select the Shared Data Source, and Create a Dataset
2. Place a Matrix Item on the Report and Populate It
3. Add Column Grouping and Other Report Formatting

Repair Count By Type Report, Task 1: Create a New Report, Select the Shared Data Source, and Create a Dataset

DT   **SSDT and Visual Studio Steps**

1. If you closed the Chapter05 project, reopen it.
2. In the Solution Explorer on the right side of the screen, right-click the Reports folder.
3. Put your mouse pointer over Add in the context menu, and wait for the submenu to appear. Select New Item from the context menu. This displays the Add New Item - Chapter05 dialog box.
4. Make sure the Report item is selected in the center area. Enter **RepairCountByType** for the name.
5. Click Add. A new report called RepairCountByType.rdl is created in the Chapter05 project.
6. In the Report Data window, click the New drop-down menu. Select Data Source from the menu that appears. The Data Source Properties dialog box appears.
7. Enter **Galactic** for the name.
8. Select the Use shared data source reference radio button, and select Galactic from the drop-down list below it. Click OK. An entry for the Galactic data source appears in the Report Data window.

9. In the Report Data window, right-click the entry for the Galactic data source, and select Add Dataset from the context menu. The Dataset Properties dialog box appears.

10. Enter **RepairsByType** for the name.

11. Click the Query Designer button. The Query Designer window opens, displaying the Graphical Query Designer.

12. Right-click in the diagram pane of the Graphical Query Designer screen. Select Add Table from the context menu.

13. Add the following tables to the query:

    Repair
    Transport
    TransportType
    RepairWorkDoneLink
    WorkDone
    RepairCause

14. Click Close to exit the Add Table dialog box.

15. Check the following column in the Repair table:

    RepairID

16. Check the following column in the TransportType table:

    Description

17. In the criteria pane, type **TypeOfTransport** in the Alias column in the Description row.

18. Check the following column in the WorkDone table:

    Description

19. In the criteria pane, type **TypeOfWork** in the Alias column in the Description row for the WorkDone table.

20. Check the following column in the RepairCause table:

    Description

21. In the criteria pane, type **RepairCause** in the Alias column in the Description row for the RepairCause table.

22. Type **1** in the Sort Order column for RepairCause. Type **2** in the Sort Order column for TypeOfWork.

23. Right-click in the SQL pane, and select Execute SQL from the context menu. The Graphical Query Designer should appear similar to the illustration.

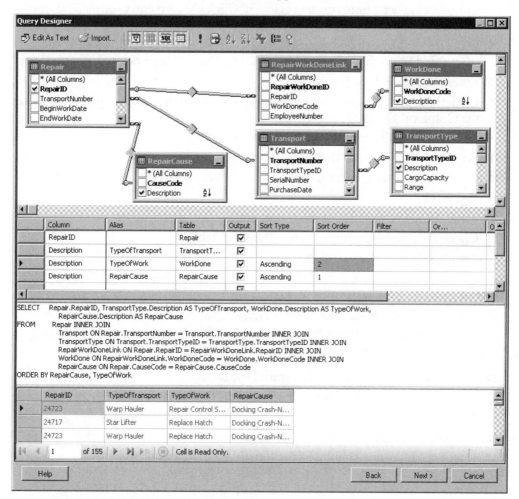

RB   **Report Builder Steps**

1. If you closed the Report Builder, reopen it. Otherwise, click the logo button and select New. The New Report or Dataset dialog box appears.

2. With New Report selected, click Blank Report.

3. In the Report Data window, click the New drop-down menu. Select Data Source from the menu that appears. The Data Source Properties dialog box appears.

4. Enter **Galactic** for the Name.

5. Make sure the Use a shared connection or report model radio button is selected, and select Galactic from the area below it. Click OK. An entry for the Galactic data source appears in the Report Data window.

6. In the Report Data window, right-click the entry for the Galactic data source, and select Add Dataset from the context menu. The Dataset Properties dialog box appears.

7. Enter **RepairsByType** for the name.

8. Click the Query Designer button. The Query Designer window opens, displaying the Graphical Query Designer.

9. Expand the Tables entry in the Database view pane.

10. Scroll down and expand the entry for the Repair table.

11. Check the following column in the Repair table:
    RepairID

12. Scroll down and expand the Transport table.

13. Check the following column in the Transport table:
    TransportNumber

NOTE

We are not going to use the TransportNumber field in the report. However, we are including the TransportNumber field because we need the Transport table included in the query to create a join from the Repair table to the TransportType table.

14. Scroll down and expand the TransportType table.

15. Check the following column in the TransportType table:
    Description

16. Scroll up and expand the RepairWorkDoneLink table.

17. Check the following column in the RepairWorkDoneLink table:
    RepairWorkDoneID

NOTE

Again, we are not going to use the RepairWorkDoneID field in the report. However, we need the RepairWorkDoneLink table included in the query to create a join from the Repair table to the WorkDone table.

18. Scroll down and expand the WorkDone table.

19. Check the following column in the WorkDone table:
    Description

20. Scroll up and expand the RepairCause table.

21. Check the following column in the RepairCause table:

Description

22. Click the Edit as Text button to switch to viewing the query as text.

23. Expand the query pane so you can see the entire query.

24. Replace "[TransportType Description]" with **TypeOfTransport** in the field list portion of the query.

25. Replace "[WorkDone Description]" with **TypeOfWork** in the field list portion of the query.

26. Replace "[RepairCause Description]" with **RepairCause** in the field list portion of the query.

27. Add the following to the end of the query:

```
ORDER BY RepairCause, TypeOfWork
```

28. Click the red exclamation point to execute the query. The Query Designer should appear similar to the illustration.

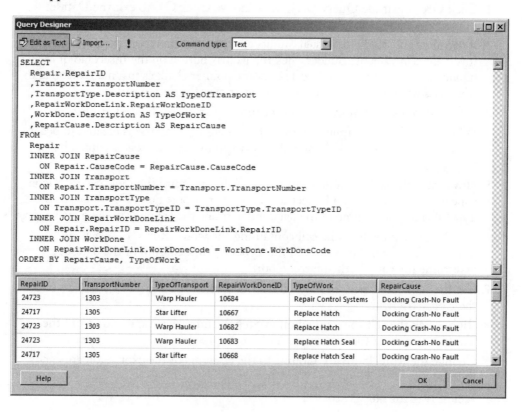

Task Notes   Although this report is a pretty straightforward request, we need to link together a number of tables to collect the necessary data. What we are interested in is repairs, so we start with the Repair table. However, none of the fields we need in the result set are in the Repair table. To find the type of transport being repaired, we need to join the Transport table with the Repair table and then join the TransportType table to the Transport table. To find the type of work done, we need to join the RepairWorkDoneLink table to the Repair table and then join the WorkDone table to the RepairWorkDoneLink table. Finally, to group by the cause of the repair, we need to join the RepairCause table to the Repair table. If you get confused by all of this, refer to Figure 3-23 in Chapter 3.

Repair Count By Type Report, Task 2: Place a Matrix Item on the Report and Populate It

DT
RB   **SSDT, Visual Studio, and Report Builder Steps**

1. Click OK to exit the Query Designer window. Click OK to exit the Dataset Properties dialog box.
2. If you are using SSDT or Visual Studio, click the Matrix report item in the Toolbox. If you are using Report Builder, click the Matrix button on the Insert tab of the ribbon, and select Insert Matrix. The mouse pointer changes to a matrix icon and crosshairs when you move the mouse pointer over the design surface.
3. Drag the mouse cursor over the lower three-quarters of the design surface.
4. When you release the mouse button after dragging, a matrix is created to occupy the area you just defined. By default, every cell in the matrix is occupied by an empty text box.
5. Hover over the cell containing the word "Columns" until the Field Selector icon appears. Click the icon and select the TypeOfTransport field. The values in the TypeOfTransport column of the dataset determine the columns in the matrix report.
6. Use the same process in the cell containing the word "Rows" to select the TypeOfWork field. The values in the TypeOfWork column of the dataset determine the rows in the matrix report.
7. Use the same process once more in the cell containing the word "Data" to select the RepairID field.
8. Right-click the cell you worked on in Step 7, and select Expression from the Textbox section of the context menu. The Expression dialog box appears.
9. Change the word "Sum" to "Count" so the contents of the expression appear as follows:

```
=Count(Fields!RepairID.Value)
```

10. Click OK to exit the Expression dialog box.

11. With this cell still selected, change the following property in the Properties window:

Property	New Value
TextAlign	Center

12. Reduce the width and height of the columns in the matrix. When you finish, your matrix layout should look similar to the illustration.

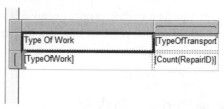

13. Click the Preview tab, if you are using SSDT and Visual Studio; or click the Run button, if you are using Report Builder. Your report should look similar to the following illustration. The rows and columns in your report may appear in a different order from those shown here.

Type Of Work	Photon III	Star Lifter	Warp Hauler
Clean Antimatter Fields	0	32	0
Flush Neutron Emitters	0	0	49
Repair Control Systems	1	0	4
Repair Hatch	1	0	1
Repair Landing Strut	1	1	0
Repair Plating	2	1	0
Replace Fiber Optic Cable	1	0	0
Replace Hatch	0	2	2
Replace Hatch Seal	1	2	2
Replace Landing Strut	1	0	1
Replace Plating	0	2	2
Replace Viewport	0	2	0
Rotate Injector Heads	44	0	0

Task Notes   Because the matrix report always groups a number of records from the dataset to create the entries in the matrix, the field that supplies the data for the matrix must be enclosed in some type of aggregate function. If the field placed in the data cell is a number, the Sum() aggregate function will be used as the default.

The RepairID field, which we placed in the data cell in Step 7, is a number. However, it does not make sense to add up the RepairIDs. Instead, we want to count the number of RepairIDs. For this reason, we changed the Sum() aggregate function to the Count() aggregate function.

We have been referring to this as a matrix report because it was created from the matrix template in the Toolbox. We also refer to this as a matrix report because it will function like a matrix when it is completed. However, we know that the data region being used is actually a tablix.

Repair Count By Type Report, Task 3:
Add Column Grouping and Other Report Formatting

DT

RB

SSDT, Visual Studio, and Report Builder Steps

1. Switch back to design mode.
2. In the Row Groups area of the Grouping pane, click the drop-down arrow, and select Add Group | Parent Group from the menu. The Tablix group dialog box appears.
3. Select [RepairCause] from the Group by drop-down list. Click OK.
4. The matrix layout should appear as shown.

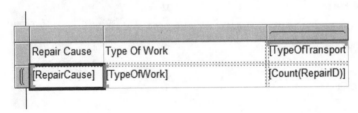

5. Make the Repair Cause group column approximately twice as wide as its default width.
6. Select the text box containing the RepairCause field (*not* the text box with the "Repair Cause" heading).
7. In the Properties window, click the Property Pages button shown in the following illustration. The Text Box Properties dialog box appears.

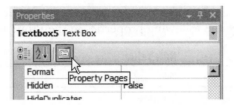

8. Replace the current content of Name with **txtRepairCause**. Click OK. We give this text box an explicit name because we reference it in just a moment.

9. In the Row Groups area, right-click the TypeOfWork entry, and select Group Properties from the context menu. The Group Properties dialog box appears.

10. Select the Visibility page. Set the When the report is initially run radio button to Hide. Check the Display can be toggled by this report item check box, and select txtRepairCause from the associated drop-down list. The Group Properties dialog box should appear as shown.

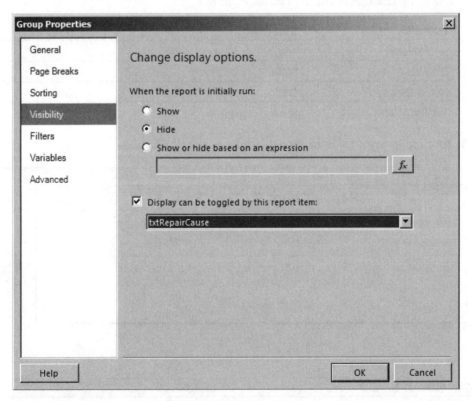

11. Click OK to exit the Group Properties dialog box.

12. Click the gray rectangle to the left of the upper row in the tablix to select this
entire row. Change the following properties in the Properties window:

Property	New Value
Font:FontWeight	Bold
Font:TextDecoration	Underline

13. If you are using SSDT or Visual Studio, click the Textbox report item in the
Toolbox. Drag the mouse cursor over the area above the matrix on the design
surface. When you release the mouse button after dragging, a text box is created
to occupy the area you just defined. If you are using Report Builder, click the text
box that says, "Click to add title." Type the following in the text box:

```
Repair Count By Type Report
```

14. Press ESC to leave text-edit mode. The text box should be selected. Make the
following changes in the Properties window:

Property	New Value
Font:FontFamily	Arial
Font:FontSize	16pt
Font:FontWeight	Bold
TextAlign	Center

15. Your report layout should appear similar to the illustration.

16. Execute the report using the Preview tab or the Run button, as appropriate. Try expanding some of the drilldown sections. The report should appear as shown.

Repair Count By Type Report

Repair Cause	Type Of Work	Photon III	Star Lifter	Warp Hauler
⊟ Docking Crash-No Fault	Repair Control Systems	0	0	1
	Replace Hatch	0	1	1
	Replace Hatch Seal	0	1	1
⊞ Docking Crash-Pilot Fault		3	0	4
⊟ Landing Crash-No Fault	Repair Control Systems	0	0	1
	Repair Landing Strut	0	1	0
	Replace Landing Strut	0	0	1
	Replace Plating	0	1	0
⊞ Landing Crash-Pilot Fault		4	0	0
⊞ Midair Collision-No Fault		1	0	3
⊞ Midair Collision-Pilot Fault		0	6	0
⊞ Scheduled Maintenance		44	32	49

17. If you are using SSDT and Visual Studio, click Save All in the toolbar. If you are using Report Builder, save the report under the name "RepairCountByType" in the Chapter05 folder on the report server.

Task Notes The Property Pages button in the Properties window provides an alternative way to access the properties dialog box for a report item. The properties dialog box can make it much easier to modify the properties of a report item. As we saw in the previous report, you can also access the properties dialog box by right-clicking a report item and selecting Properties from the context menu.

New Territory

Now that you have created the table and matrix reports without the aid of the Report Wizard, it is time to venture into new territory. We will move on to create a list report. List reports are used when you need to repeat a large area of content—perhaps even an entire page—for each record in the dataset. List reports are often used to create forms. They function similarly to a mail merge in a word-processing program, such as Microsoft Word.

The Transport Information Sheet

Feature Highlighted

▶ Creating a list report

Business Need The GDS maintenance department needs an efficient way to look up general information about a particular transport that comes in for repair. The user should be able to select the serial number from a drop-down list and see all the basic information about the transport. This transport information sheet should also include the date of the next scheduled maintenance appointment for this transport.

Task Overview

1. Create a New Report, Select the Shared Data Source, and Create the TransportSNs Dataset
2. Create the TransportDetail Dataset
3. Place a List Item on the Report and Populate It

Transport Information Sheet, Task 1: Create a New Report, Select the Shared Data Source, and Create the TransportSNs Dataset

DT **SSDT and Visual Studio Steps**

1. If you closed the Chapter05 project, reopen it.
2. In the Solution Explorer on the right side of the screen, right-click the Reports folder. Select Add | New Item. This displays the Add New Item-Chapter05 dialog box.
3. Make sure the Report icon is selected in the Templates area. Enter **TransportInfoSheet** for the name. Click Add.
4. In the Report Data window, click the New drop-down menu. Select Data Source from the menu that appears. The Data Source Properties dialog box appears.
5. Enter **Galactic** for the name.
6. Select the Use shared data source reference radio button, and select Galactic from the drop-down list below it. Click OK. An entry for the Galactic data source appears in the Report Data window.
7. In the Report Data window, right-click the entry for the Galactic data source, and select Add Dataset from the context menu. The Dataset Properties dialog box appears.
8. Enter **TransportSNs** for the name.
9. Click the Query Designer button. The Query Designer window opens, displaying the Graphical Query Designer. Click the Edit as Text button to switch to the Generic Query Designer.

10. Enter the following in the upper portion of the Generic Query Designer window:

```
SELECT SerialNumber FROM Transport WHERE RetiredDate IS NULL ORDER BY
SerialNumber
```

11. Click the Run toolbar button (the red exclamation mark). The Generic Query Designer window should appear similar to the illustration.

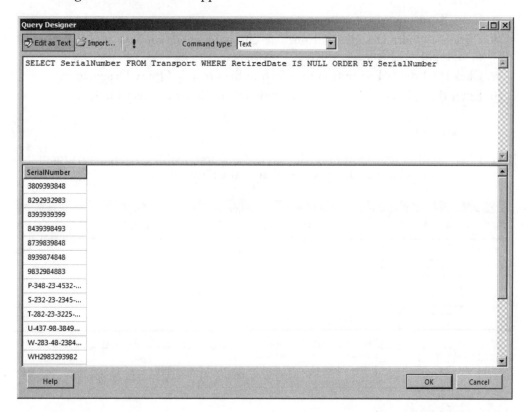

12. Click OK to exit the Query Designer window. Click OK to exit the Dataset Properties dialog box.

RB Report Builder Steps

1. If you closed the Report Builder, reopen it. Otherwise, click the logo button, and select New. The New Report or Dataset dialog box appears.

2. With New Report selected, click Blank Report.

3. In the Report Data window, click the New drop-down menu. Select Data Source from the menu that appears. The Data Source Properties dialog box appears.

4. Enter **Galactic** for the name.

5. Select the Use a shared connection or report model radio button, and select Galactic from the area below it. Click OK. An entry for the Galactic data source appears in the Report Data window.

6. In the Report Data window, right-click the entry for the Galactic data source, and select Add Dataset from the context menu. The Dataset Properties dialog box appears.

7. Enter **TransportSNs** for the name.

8. Click the Query Designer button. The Query Designer window opens, displaying the Graphical Query Designer.

9. Click the Edit as Text button to switch to the Generic Query Designer.

10. Enter the following in the upper portion of the Generic Query Designer window:

```
SELECT SerialNumber FROM Transport WHERE RetiredDate IS NULL ORDER BY
SerialNumber
```

11. Click the Run toolbar button (the red exclamation mark). The Generic Query Designer window should appear similar to the illustration.

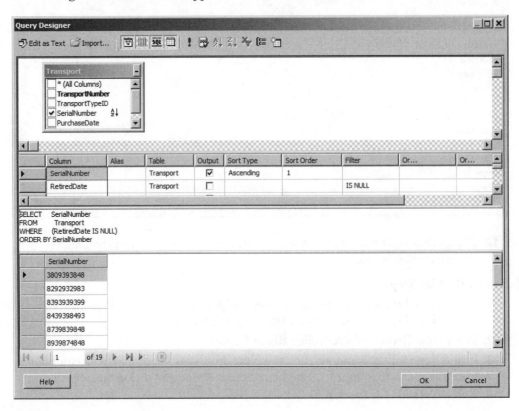

12. Click OK to exit the Query Designer window. Click OK to exit the Dataset Properties dialog box.

Task Notes   The TransportSNs dataset provides a list of the serial numbers for all the active transports at GDS. This dataset is used to populate the drop-down list from which the user selects the transport for which the Transport Information Sheet will be printed. Because the query for this dataset is relatively straightforward, it is faster to type the query string by hand rather than build it using the Graphical Query Designer.

This is not the case with the query string for the second dataset required by this report, as you shall see in the next task.

Transport Information Sheet, Task 2: Create the TransportDetail Dataset

DT   **SSDT and Visual Studio Steps**

1. Right-click the Galactic data source entry in the Report Data window, and select Add Dataset from the context menu. The Dataset Properties dialog box appears.

2. Enter **TransportDetail** for the name.

3. Click the Query Designer button to display the Query Designer window.

4. Right-click in the diagram pane of the Graphical Query Designer screen. Select Add Table from the context menu. Add the following tables to the query:

   Transport
   TransportType
   ScheduledMaint
   Repair

5. Click Close to exit the Add Table dialog box.

6. Right-click the link between the Transport and the Repair tables, and then select Remove from the context menu. (You may have to rearrange the tables in the diagram pane to make this visible.)

7. Right-click the diamond in the middle of the link between the Repair table and the ScheduledMaint table. Choose Select All Rows from ScheduledMaint in the context menu.

8. Find the diamond in the middle of the link between the Transport and ScheduledMaint tables. (You may have to rearrange the tables in the diagram pane to make this visible.) Right-click this diamond and choose Select All Rows

from Transport from the context menu. With a bit of rearranging, your diagram pane should look similar to the illustration.

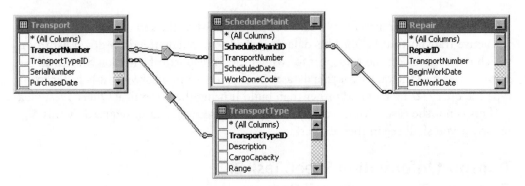

9. Check the following columns in the Transport table:
   SerialNumber
   PurchaseDate

10. Check the following columns in the TransportType table:
    Description
    CargoCapacity
    Range
    Cost
    Crew
    Manufacturer
    ManAddr1
    ManAddr2
    ManCity
    ManState
    ManZipCode
    ManPlanetAbbrv
    ManEmail

11. Check the following column in the ScheduledMaint table:
    ScheduledDate

12. Check the following column in the Repair table:
    RepairID

13. In the criteria pane, type the following in the Filter column for SerialNumber:

    ```
    = @SerialNumber
    ```

14. In the Filter column for RepairID, type this:

    ```
    IS NULL
    ```

15. Right-click in the diagram pane, and select Add Group By from the context menu.

16. In the criteria pane, in the Group By column for ScheduledDate, select Min from the drop-down list.

17. In the Alias column for ScheduledDate, change Expr1 to NextMaintDate.

18. Right-click in the SQL pane, and select Execute SQL from the context menu. Enter **3809393848** for the @SerialNumber parameter, and click OK. The Graphical Query Designer should appear similar to the next illustration.

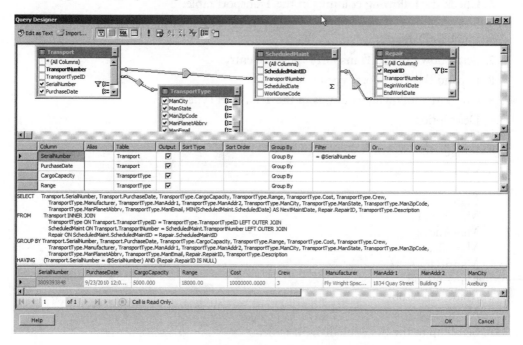

RB **Report Builder Steps**

1. Right-click the Galactic data source entry in the Report Data window, and select Add Dataset from the context menu. The Dataset Properties dialog box appears.
2. Enter **TransportDetail** for the name.
3. Click the Query Designer button to display the Query Designer window.
4. Expand the entry for the Tables in the Database view pane.
5. Scroll down and expand the Transport table entry.
6. Check the following columns in the Transport table:

   SerialNumber
   PurchaseDate

7. Scroll down to the TransportType table entry.
8. Expand the TransportType table entry.
9. Check the following columns in the TransportType table:

   Description
   CargoCapacity
   Range
   Cost
   Crew
   Manufacturer
   ManAddr1
   ManAddr2
   ManCity
   ManState
   ManZipCode
   ManPlanetAbbrv
   ManEmail

10. Scroll up to the ScheduledMaint table.
11. Expand the entry for the ScheduledMaint table.
12. Check the following column in the ScheduledMaint table:

    ScheduledDate

13. Expand the entry for the Repair table.
14. Check the following column in the Repair table:

    RepairID

15. Expand the Relationships pane.

16. Click the Auto Detect button to turn off the auto-detect feature.

17. Click the third entry for Transport in the Left Table column. The word "Transport" in the row containing the Transport table and the Repair table will be selected.

18. Click the red "X" (Delete Relationship) button at the top of the Relationships pane. (Make sure you click the red "X" in the Relationships pane, and not the red "X" in the Selected fields pane.) The direct relationship between the Repair and Transport tables needs to be removed because the Repair table should be related to the Transport table through the ScheduledMaint table.

19. Also in the Relationships pane, click the word "Inner" in the row containing the Transport and ScheduledMaint tables. The Join Type drop-down menu appears.

20. Select "Left Outer" from the Join Type drop-down list.

21. Again in the Relationships pane, click the word "Inner" in the row containing the ScheduledMaint and Repair tables. The Join Type drop-down list appears.

22. Select "Left Outer" from the Join Type drop-down list.

23. In the Applied filters pane, click the Add filter button.

24. In the new row added in the Applied filters pane, click the word "like" in the Operator column. The Operator drop-down list appears.

25. Select "is" from the Operator drop-down list.

26. Check the check box in the Parameter column of this same row in the Applied filters pane.

27. Click the Add filter button in the Applied filters pane again.

28. Click "SerialNumber" in the new row added in the Applied filters pane. (This is the second row in the Applied filters pane.) A field selection tree view appears.

29. Expand the entry for the Repair table.

30. Click the RepairID field to select it.

31. Click the word "(none)" in this same row. (The second row in the Applied filter pane.) The Value drop-down list appears.

32. Select "(null)" from the Value drop-down list.

33. Click the Group and Aggregate button in the top of the Selected fields pane.

34. Scroll down in the Selected fields pane until you can see the ScheduledDate field. Click the words "Grouped by" across from ScheduledDate. The Aggregate drop-down list appears.

35. Select "Min" from the Aggregate drop-down list. The Query Designer should appear as shown.

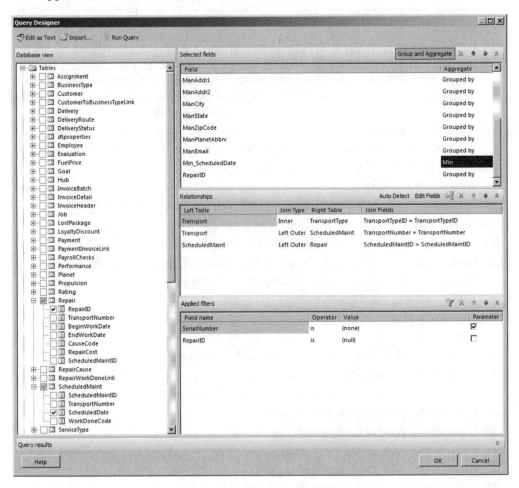

36. Click the Edit as Text button to switch to viewing the query as text.

37. Expand the query pane so you can see the entire field list.

38. Replace "Min_ScheduledDate" with **NextMaintDate** in the field list.

39. Click the Run button (red exclamation point) to execute the query. Enter **3809393848** in the second column for the @SerialNumber parameter, and click OK. The Query Designer should appear similar to the next illustration.

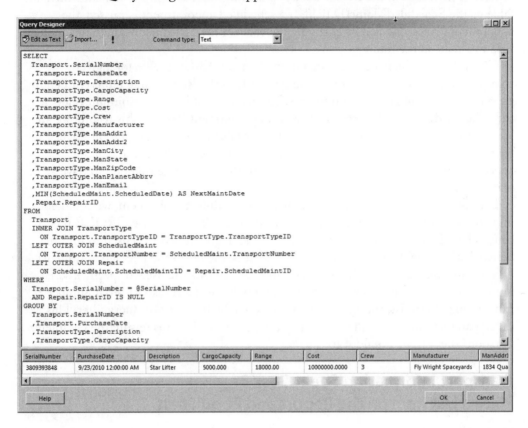

Task Notes   The TransportDetail dataset must include all the information about a selected transport. This is not complicated, except for the last item noted in the business need for this report: the date of the next scheduled maintenance for this transport. You need a little background on the way the Galactic database functions regarding scheduled maintenance to understand this query.

Records are added to the ScheduledMaint table for each time a transport needs to come into a maintenance facility for preventative maintenance. These are considered appointments for preventative maintenance. They are scheduled for dates in the future. Transports may have more than one pending preventative maintenance appointment. The ScheduledMaint table records are linked to a transport by the TransportNumber field.

When a transport comes in for preventative maintenance, a record is added to the Repair table. This indicates an appointment for preventative maintenance has been fulfilled. The record in the Repair table is linked to the record in the ScheduledMaint table by the ScheduledMaintID field. If a scheduled appointment is missed, the appointment is rescheduled by changing the value in the ScheduledMaint.ScheduleDate field to a value in the future.

Given these business rules, records in the ScheduledMaint table for a given transport that do not have corresponding records in the Repair table represent pending preventative maintenance appointments. The record that has the minimum value in the ScheduledDate field represents the next appointment. To find this record, we are joining the ScheduledMaint table to the Repair table using a left outer join. Because we require the RepairID to be NULL, our result set only includes the pending appointments (that is, the records in the ScheduledMaint table that do not have a matching record in the Repair table).

Because a transport may have more than one pending appointment, we could end up with more than one record for a given transport. We need to use GROUP BY to consolidate these into one record. The MIN() aggregate function is used to find the ScheduledDate field with the lowest value (that is, the next scheduled appointment).

The filter we created on the SerialNumber field allows the user to specify a serial number at the time the report is run. The user will select a transport serial number from a drop-down list, and that serial number will be fed into the query filter. This is called parameterizing the query. We next do a bit of work to make sure the parameter functions the way we intend it to.

Transport Information Sheet, Task 3: Place a List Item on the Report and Populate It

DT
RB SSDT, Visual Studio, and Report Server Steps

1. Click OK to exit the Query Designer window. Click OK to exit the Dataset Properties dialog box.
2. In the Report Data window, expand the Parameters folder.
3. Right-click the entry for SerialNumber, and select Parameter Properties from the context menu. The Report Parameter Properties dialog box appears.
4. Select the Available Values page.

5. Select the Get values from a query radio button.

6. Select TransportSNs from the Dataset drop-down list.

7. Select SerialNumber from the Value field drop-down list. Select SerialNumber from the Label field drop-down list as well. The Report Parameter Properties dialog box should appear as shown.

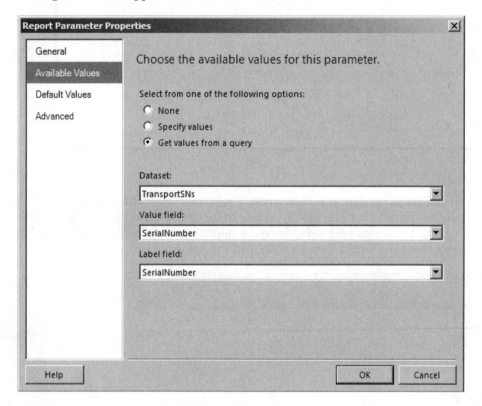

8. Click OK to exit the Report Parameter Properties dialog box.

9. If you are using Report Builder, click the text box that contains the "Click to add title" text. Press DELETE to remove this text box.

10. If you are using SSDT or Visual Studio, move your mouse pointer to the bottom of the white design surface so it changes from the regular mouse pointer to the

double-headed arrow, as shown in the following illustration. The white design surface is the body of the report.

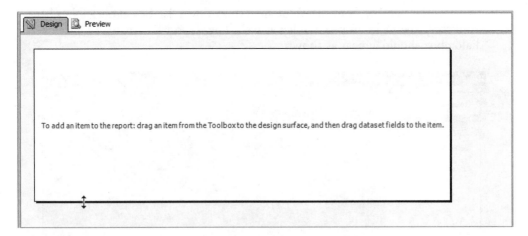

If you are using Report Builder, move your mouse pointer to the dotted line across the bottom of the white design surface so it changes from the regular mouse pointer to the double-headed arrow, as shown in the following illustration. The area above the dotted line is the body of the report.

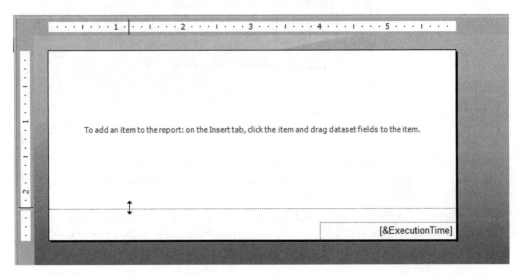

11. Drag the bottom of the report body down to create more room to lay out the list report.
12. If you are using SSDT or Visual Studio, select the Toolbox window, and click the List report item. If you are using Report Builder, select the Insert tab of the

ribbon, and click the List report item. The mouse pointer changes to a list icon and crosshairs when you move your mouse pointer over the design surface.

13. Drag the mouse cursor over the entire available report body.

14. When you release the mouse button after dragging, a list is created to occupy the area you just defined.

15. If you are using SSDT or Visual Studio, select the text box from the Toolbox. If you are using Report Builder, select the text box from the Insert tab of the ribbon. Drag the mouse cursor to create a text box inside the list across the top. This text box will be the title.

16. Click this new text box so the blinking text-edit cursor appears. Type **Transport Information Sheet** in the textbox. Press ESC to leave text-edit mode and select the text box.

17. As an alternative to the Properties window, font and text alignment properties can be set using the toolbar buttons/ribbon buttons similar to working in Microsoft Word or Microsoft Excel. Use the toolbar/ribbon to set the properties of the text box as follows:

Property	Value
FontSize	16pt
FontWeight	Bold
TextAlign	Center

18. Place a second text box under the existing title. Type **Serial Number:** in this text box. Size the text box so it just fits this text. This serves as the label for the Serial Number field.

19. In the Report Data window, expand the TransportDetail dataset, if necessary. Drag the SerialNumber field from the Report Data window, and place it to the right of the text box that was added in Step 18. Click the sizing handle (the small white square) on the right side of this new text box to make it approximately twice its original size.

20. Now use the positioning handle (the square with the four arrow heads) to position the text box relative to the text box containing the "Serial Number:" label. When the two text boxes are aligned, you will see snap lines appear between the two text boxes, as shown here.

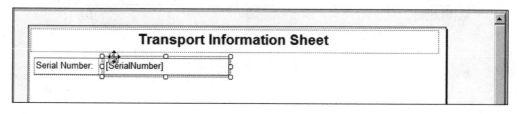

21. Select a line from the Toolbox/ribbon, and place it inside the list below the text box containing the "Serial Number:" label.

22. Drag the end points of the line so it goes across the entire list below the Serial Number text boxes.

23. Repeat Step 18 through Step 20 for each of the following fields, creating a label for the field and then placing the field to the right of the label. (Hint: If you are using SSDT or Visual Studio, you may want to create all the labels first and then add all the fields so you are not switching back and forth between the Toolbox window and the Report Data window.)

Label	Field
Purchase Date:	PurchaseDate
Transport Type:	Description
Cargo Capacity:	CargoCapacity
Range:	Range
Cost:	Cost
Crew:	Crew
Next Maint:	NextMaintDate

24. Use either the Report Formatting toolbar or the Properties window to set the properties for these fields as follows (these properties are for the fields themselves, not the labels):

Field	Property	Value
PurchaseDate	Format	MM/dd/yyyy
PurchaseDate	TextAlign	Left
CargoCapacity	TextAlign	Left
Range	TextAlign	Left
Cost	Format	###,###,##0.00
Cost	TextAlign	Left
Crew	TextAlign	Left
NextMaintDate	Format	MM/dd/yyyy
NextMaintDate	TextAlign	Left

25. Select a rectangle from the Toolbox/ribbon, and place it inside the list below the bottom-most text box. Size the rectangle so it covers the remaining area of the list.

26. Use the Report Borders toolbar, shown here in SSDT and Visual Studio

and shown here in Report Builder

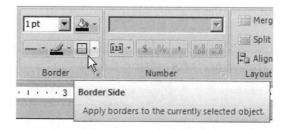

to set the properties for the border of the rectangle. Make sure the toolbar items are set to Solid, 1pt, and Black.

27. Place a text box in the upper-left corner of the rectangle. Type **Manufacturer:** in this text box. This is the manufacturer label.

28. Drag the Manufacturer field from the Report Data window, and place it inside the rectangle to the right of the manufacturer label. Align the Manufacturer field text box with the manufacturer label text box, and size the field text box so it goes almost all the way to the right side of the rectangle. If you drag too far to the right, the Report Designer automatically increases the size of the body of the report. If this happens, simply reduce the width of the body of the report.

29. Place the ManAddr1 and ManAddr2 fields below the Manufacturer field. Make these new fields the same size as the Manufacturer field.

30. Place the ManCity field inside the rectangle, below the ManAddr2 field. Make this new field the same size as the ManAddr2 field.

31. Click on "[ManCity]" in the text box added in Step 30 to select that text, and then right-click on this selected text. Select Expression from the context menu. The Expression dialog box appears.

    Type the following expression in the Set expression for: Value area:

    ```
    =Fields!ManCity.Value & ", " & Fields!ManState.Value & " " &
    Fields!ManZipCode.Value & " " & Fields!ManPlanetAbbrv.Value
    ```

32. Click OK to exit the Expression dialog box.

33. Drag the ManEmail field from the Report Data window, and place it inside the rectangle under the text box added in Step 30. Make this text box as wide as the text boxes above it.

34. Your report layout should appear similar to the illustration.

35. Preview/Run the report.

36. Select the first serial number from the Serial Number drop-down list, and click View Report. Your report should appear similar to the illustration.

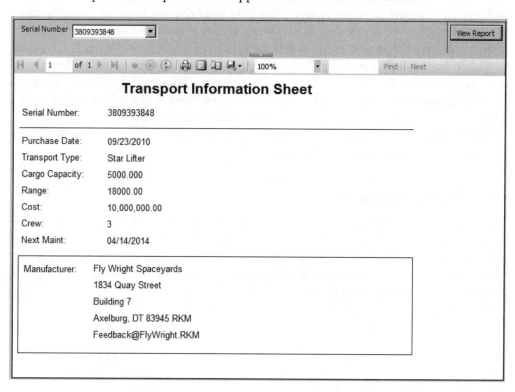

37. If you are using SSDT or Visual Studio, click Save All in the toolbar. If you are using Report Builder, save the report under the name "TransportInfoSheet" in the Chapter05 folder you created on the report server.

Task Notes   As you saw in the Transport Information Sheet report, the List item enables you to place information anywhere. Text boxes, lines, and rectangles can be placed anywhere within the List item to create complex forms. This type of report is good for presenting a large amount of information about a single entity, as we did in this report.

As stated earlier, the contents of the List item are repeated for each record in the dataset. The TransportDetail dataset selects only a single record based on the user's selection of a serial number. Therefore, our report only has one page.

The Line report item is used simply to help format the report. It helps separate information on the report to make it easier for the user to understand. When working with the Table report item, we could use the borders of the text boxes in the table cells to create lines. In the more freeform layout of the List report, the Line report item often works better than using cell borders.

The Rectangle report item serves two purposes. When its border is set to something other than None, it becomes a visible part of the report. Therefore, it can serve to help visibly separate information on the report in the same manner as the Line report item. This is how we are using the Rectangle report item in this report.

The Rectangle report item can also be used to keep together other items in the report. We examine this use of rectangles in Chapter 9.

Getting Graphical

You have now seen the tablix data region, along with its table, matrix, and list templates, in action. In the next chapter, you learn about some of the graphically oriented data regions. We also look at the Image report item and its uses for adding graphics to a report. Finally, in Chapter 6, you learn about ways to control the properties of a report item using Visual Basic expressions.

Chapter 6

Graphic Expression: Using Charts, Images, and Gauges

In This Chapter

- ▶ **Chart Your Course**
- ▶ **Gauging the Results**
- ▶ **Image Is Everything**
- ▶ **From Graphical to Geo-graphical**

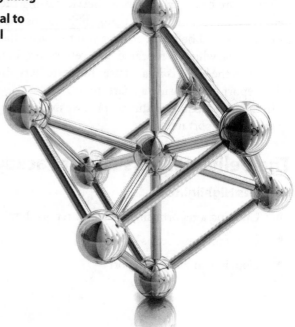

W e live in a world today where image is everything. Color and graphics are used to add interest and convey meaning. This is true not only for TV, newspapers, and magazines, but also for some of the reports you create. Reports going to managers or executives need to provide the quick, concise communication of charts and graphics. Reports shared with customers need the polish provided by a well-placed image or two. Reporting Services has the tools you need to effectively communicate and impress in each of these situations.

In this chapter, we explore the chart and the gauge data regions, and how they can be used to summarize and express data. We also use the image report item to add graphics to our reports. Throughout the chapter, we look at properties that can be used to format the report output and creative ways to control those properties.

Chart Your Course

In many cases, the best way to convey business intelligence is through business graphics. Bar charts, pie charts, and line graphs are useful tools for giving meaning to endless volumes of data. They can quickly reveal trends and patterns to aid in data analysis. They compress lines upon lines of numbers into a format that can be understood in a moment.

In addition, charts can increase the reader's interest in your information. A splash of color excites the reader. Where endless lines of black on white lull people to sleep, bars of red and blue and pie wedges of purple and green wake people up.

You create charts in Reporting Services using the chart report item. The chart report item is a data region like the tablix. This means the chart can process multiple records from a dataset. The tablix enables you to place other report items in a row, a column, or a list area, which is repeated for every record in the dataset. The chart, on the other hand, uses the records in a dataset to create bars, lines, or pie wedges. You cannot place other report items inside a chart item.

In the next sections of this chapter, we explore the many charting possibilities provided by the chart report item.

The Deliveries Versus Lost Packages Chart

Features Highlighted

▶ Creating a report using the chart report item

▶ Using multiple series

▶ Copying an existing report

- ▶ Using scale breaks
- ▶ Using multiple chart areas
- ▶ Using a secondary value axis

Business Need Galactic Delivery Services (GDS) needs to determine if there is a correlation between the number of deliveries in a month and the number of lost packages in that same month. The best way to perform this analysis is by creating a chart of the number of deliveries and the number of lost packages over time.

Task Overview

1. Create a New Report and Two Datasets
2. Place a Chart Item on the Report and Populate It
3. Explore Alternate Ways to Present the Deliveries and Lost Packages Together

Deliveries versus Lost Packages Chart, Task 1: Create a New Report and Two Datasets

`DT` SSDT and Visual Studio Steps

1. Create a new Reporting Services project called Chapter06 in the MSSQLRS folder. (If you need help with this task, see Chapter 5.)
2. Create a shared data source called Galactic for the Galactic database. (Again, if you need help with this task, see Chapter 5.)
3. Add a blank report called DelvLostPkgChart to the Chapter06 project. (Do not use the Report Wizard.)
4. In the Report Data window, click the New drop-down menu. Select Data Source from the menu that appears. The Data Source Properties dialog box appears.
5. Enter **Galactic** for the name.
6. Select the Use shared data source reference radio button, and select Galactic from the drop-down list. Click OK.
7. In the Report Data window, right-click the entry for the Galactic data source, and select Add Dataset from the context menu. The Dataset Properties dialog box appears.
8. Enter **TransportList** for the name.
9. Click the Query Designer button. The Query Designer window opens displaying the Graphical Query Designer.
10. We do not need the aids provided by the Graphical Query Designer, so we will switch to the Generic Query Designer. Click the Edit as Text button to make this switch.

11. Enter the following in the SQL pane of the Generic Query Designer window:

```
SELECT Delivery.DeliveryNumber,
    LostPackage.LostPackageNumber,
    MONTH(PickupDateTime) AS Month
FROM Delivery
LEFT OUTER JOIN LostPackage
    ON Delivery.DeliveryNumber = LostPackage.DeliveryNumber
WHERE YEAR(PickupDateTime) = 2012
ORDER BY MONTH(PickupDateTime)
```

12. Click the Run Query (red exclamation point) button on the Generic Query Designer toolbar to run the query and make sure no errors exist. Correct any typos that may be detected. Click OK to exit the Query Designer window. Click OK to exit the Dataset Properties dialog box.

RB | **Report Builder Steps**

1. Using Report Manager, create a new folder in the Galactic Delivery Services folder. Enter **Chapter06** as the name of this folder. (If you need help with this task, see Chapter 5.)

2. Launch Report Builder from Report Manager.

3. With New Report highlighted in the left column, click Blank Report. The Report Builder shows a new blank report.

4. In the Report Data window, click the New drop-down menu. Select Data Source from the menu that appears. The Data Source Properties dialog box appears.

5. Enter **Galactic** for the name.

6. Make sure the Use a shared connection or report model radio button is selected, and select Galactic from the area below it. Click OK. An entry for the Galactic data source appears in the Report Data window.

7. In the Report Data window, right-click the entry for the Galactic data source, and select Add Dataset from the context menu. The Dataset Properties dialog box appears.

8. Enter **TransportList** for the name.

9. Click the Query Designer button. The Query Designer window opens displaying the Graphical Query Designer.

10. Click the Edit as Text button to switch to the Generic Query Designer.

11. Enter the following in the SQL pane (upper portion) of the Generic Query Designer window:

```
SELECT Delivery.DeliveryNumber,
    LostPackage.LostPackageNumber,
    MONTH(PickupDateTime) AS Month
FROM Delivery
```

```
LEFT OUTER JOIN LostPackage
    ON Delivery.DeliveryNumber = LostPackage.DeliveryNumber
WHERE YEAR(PickupDateTime) = 2012
ORDER BY MONTH(PickupDateTime)
```

12. Click the Run Query button on the Generic Query Designer toolbar to run the query and make sure no errors exist. Correct any typos that may be detected. Click OK to exit the Query Designer window. Click OK to exit the Dataset Properties dialog box.

Task Notes   We created the dataset for this report by typing a query in the SQL pane of the Generic Query Designer. The graphical tools of the Graphical Query Designer are helpful if you are still learning the syntax of SELECT queries, or if you are unfamiliar with the database you are querying. However, it is more efficient to simply type the query into the SQL pane or the Dataset Properties dialog box. In addition, some complex queries must be typed in because they cannot be created through the Graphical Query Designer.

Throughout the remainder of this book, we type our SELECT statements rather than create them using the Graphical Query Designer. This enables us to quickly create the necessary datasets and then concentrate on the aspects of report creation that are new and different in each report. As you create your own reports, use the interface—Graphical Query Designer or Generic Query Designer—with which you are most comfortable.

In the query for this report, we join the Delivery table, which holds one record for each delivery, with the LostPackage table, which holds one record for each package lost during delivery. Because only some Delivery table records have associated LostPackage table records (at least we hope so), we need to use the LEFT OUTER JOIN to get all of the Delivery records joined with their matching LostPackage records. In our chart, we can count the number of DeliveryNumbers and the number of LostPackageNumbers to determine the number of deliveries and the number of lost packages.

Deliveries versus Lost Packages Chart, Task 2: Place a Chart Item on the Report and Populate It

DT
RB
SSDT, Visual Studio, and Report Builder Steps

1. Drag the edges of the design surface to make it larger so the design surface fills the available space on the screen.

2. If you are using Report Builder, select the "Click to add title" text box, and delete it. (The title will be contained within the chart itself.)

3. If you are using SSDT or Visual Studio, select the chart report item in the Toolbox window. If you are using Report Builder, click on Chart in the Insert ribbon, and select Insert Chart. Click and drag to place the chart on the design surface. The chart should cover almost the entire design surface because it will be the only item on the report.

4. After you place the chart on the report, the Select Chart Type dialog box appears. As you can see, the chart report item is extremely flexible. Click the first item in the Line row as shown here. This creates a simple line graph.

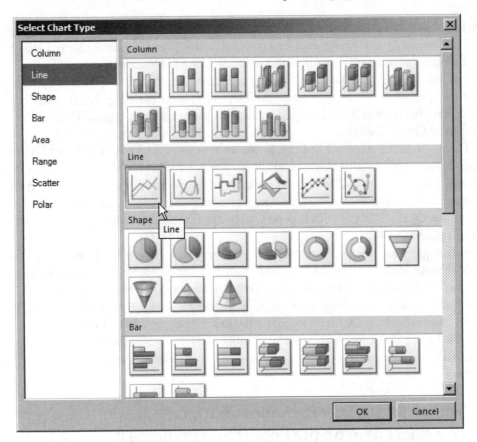

5. Click OK to exit the Select Chart Type dialog box. You will see a representation of the chart on the design surface.

6. Double-click anywhere on the chart. The Chart Data window with three field areas appears to the right of the chart. (You may have to scroll to see it.) The three field areas are Values, Category Groups, and Series Groups.

NOTE

You make the Chart Data window disappear by clicking somewhere on the Design tab that is not covered by the chart. Clicking the chart once will select the chart so you can move and size it. Clicking the chart a second time will cause the Chart Data window to reappear.

7. Click the plus sign next to the Values area. A field selector drop-down list appears. Select DeliveryNumber as shown.

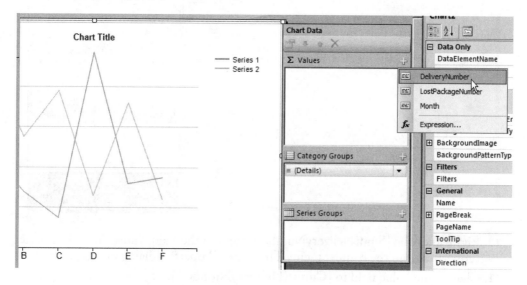

8. Click the plus sign next to the Values area again. A field selector drop-down list appears. Select LostPackageNumber.

9. Click the plus sign next to the Category Groups area. A field selector drop-down list appears. Select Month. The report layout should appear similar to the following illustration.

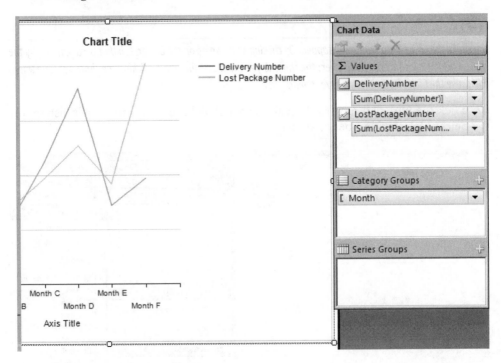

10. Right-click the [Sum(DeliveryNumber)] item in the Values area, and select Series Properties from the context menu. The Series Properties dialog box appears.

11. Change the Value field to **[Count(DeliveryNumber)]**.

12. Select the Legend page of the Series Properties dialog box. Type **Deliveries** in the "Custom legend text" text box.

13. Select the Fill page of the Series Properties dialog box. Select Green from the Color drop-down color picker.

14. Click OK to exit the Select Properties dialog box.

15. Right-click the [Sum(LostPackageNumber)] item in the Values area, and select Series Properties from the context menu. The Series Properties dialog box appears.

16. Change the Value field to **[Count(LostPackageNumber)]**.

17. Select the Legend page of the Series Properties dialog box. Type **Lost Packages** in the "Custom legend text" text box.

18. Select the Fill page of the Series Properties dialog box. Select Red from the Color drop-down color picker.
19. Click OK to exit the Select Properties dialog box.
20. Double-click the words "Chart Title" to edit the text of the chart title. Replace the words "Chart Title" with **Deliveries and Lost Packages**.
21. Double-click the words "Axis Title" below the horizontal axis (the axis with Month A, Month B, etc.). Replace the words "Axis Title" with **Month**.
22. Right-click the words "Axis Title" to the left of the vertical axis (the axis with numeric values). Select Show Axis Title from the context menu to uncheck this item.
23. If you are using SSDT or Visual Studio, click the Preview tab. If you are using Report Builder, click the Run button. Your report appears similar to the illustration.

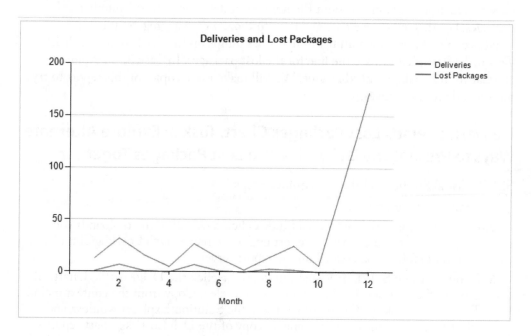

Task Notes   You have now seen how easy it is to create a chart using the chart report item. Simply select the type of chart you want, select the fields from your dataset into the appropriate areas of the Chart Data window, and you have a functioning chart. In the next sections, we explore ways to manipulate the properties of the chart to create more complex results.

The fields you select in the Values area, DeliveryNumber and LostPackageNumber in this report, provide the values for the data points on the chart. Each field creates a series of data points—in this case, a single line—on the graph. The scale for these values is along the vertical axis in this line chart. Therefore, the vertical axis is known as the *value axis.*

The fields you select in the Category Groups area, Month in this report, provide the labels for the horizontal axis of the chart. This axis is called the *category axis.* These category fields also group the rows from the dataset into multiple categories. One data point is created on the category axis for each category in each series.

Because the category fields create groups, we need to use aggregate functions with the values we are charting. Because the DeliveryNumber and LostPackageNumber fields are numeric data types, the Sum() aggregate function was chosen by default. Of course, the sum of the Delivery Numbers or the Lost Package Numbers makes no sense. Instead, we want to count the number of deliveries and the number of lost packages. For this reason, we changed both to the Count() aggregate function.

Notice in our graph the number of deliveries jumps up to over 150 in month 12. This makes it difficult to see the line for the lost packages. In Task 3, we explore three alternatives for dealing with this issue. We will make three copies of this report to try out these three alternatives.

Deliveries versus Lost Packages Chart, Task 3: Explore Alternate Ways to Present the Deliveries and Lost Packages Together

DT
RB   **SSDT, Visual Studio, and Report Builder Steps**

1. Return to design mode.
2. If you are using SSDT or Visual Studio, click Save All in the toolbar. If you are using Report Builder, save the report under the name "DelvLostPkgChart" in the Chapter06 folder you created on the report server.
3. If you are using SSDT or Visual Studio, right-click the DelvLostPkgChart.rdl entry in the Solution Explorer window, and select Copy from the context menu. Then, right-click the Chapter06 entry in the Solution Explorer window, and select Paste from the context menu. A copy of the DelvLostPkgChart report is added to the project. Repeat this twice more so the project contains the original report plus three copies.

4. If you are using SSDT or Visual Studio, close the DelvLostPkgChart report. Double-click the Copy of DelvLostPkgChart.rdl entry in the Solution Explorer window. The Design tab for this report is displayed.

5. Right-click the value axis on this chart, and select Vertical Axis Properties from the context menu. The Vertical Axis Properties dialog box appears, as shown here.

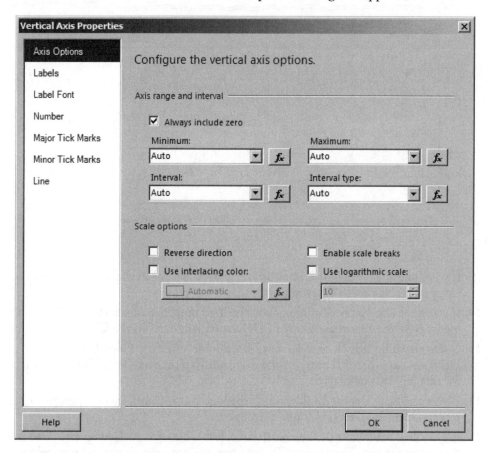

6. Check the Enable scale breaks check box.

7. Click OK to exit the Value Axis Properties dialog box.

8. Preview/Run the report. The value axis now contains two scale breaks, as shown.

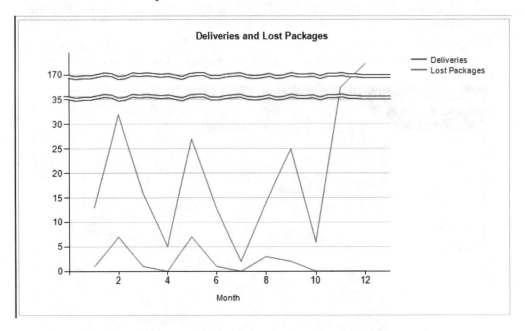

9. If you are using SSDT or Visual Studio, click Save All in the toolbar. Close the Copy of DelvLostPkgChart report.

10. If you are using Report Builder, click the logo button, and select Save As from the menu. Save the report as "Copy of DelvLostPkgChart" in the Chapter06 folder.

11. If you are using SSDT or Visual Studio, double-click the Copy (2) of DelvLostPkgChart.rdl entry in the Solution Explorer window. The Design tab for this report is displayed.

12. If you are using Report Builder, click the logo button, and select Open from the menu. Open the DelvLostPkgChart report.

13. Right-click the center of the chart, and select Chart | Add New Chart Area from the context menu. The chart splits into two regions: one above and one below. The lower portion appears as an empty rectangle, as shown. The upper chart area is known as the Default area, and the lower chart area is given the name Area1.

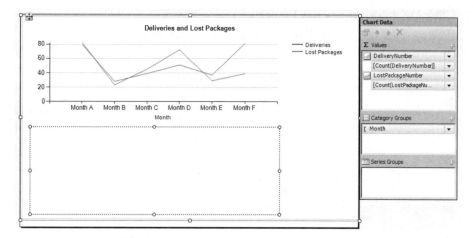

14. Right-click the Count(LostPackageNumber) entry in the Values fields area of the Chart Data window. (It may be cut off so it appears as "Count(LostPackageNu...") Select Series Properties from the context menu. The Series Properties dialog box appears.

15. Select the Axes and Chart Area page of the dialog box.

16. The Chart area drop-down list determines which chart area this series will appear in. Select Area1 from the Chart area drop-down list. This is shown in the following illustration.

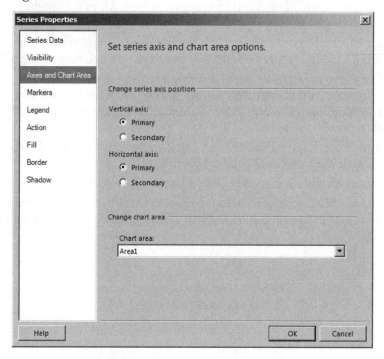

17. Click OK to exit the Series Properties dialog box.

18. Preview/Run the report. The report appears as shown.

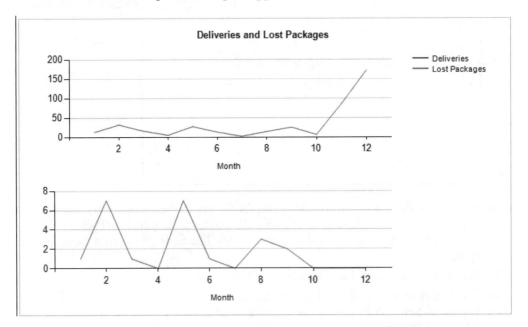

19. If you are using SSDT or Visual Studio, click Save All in the toolbar. Close Copy (2) of DelvLostPkgChart report.

20. If you are using Report Builder, click the logo button, and select Save As from the menu. Save the report as "Copy (2) of DelvLostPkgChart" in the Chapter06 folder.

21. If you are using SSDT or Visual Studio, double-click the Copy (3) of DelvLostPkgChart.rdl entry in the Solution Explorer window. The Design tab for this report is displayed.

22. If you are using Report Builder, click the logo button, and select Open from the menu. Open the DelvLostPkgChart report.

23. Click twice on the chart so the Chart Data window is displayed.

24. Right-click the Count(LostPackageNumber) entry in the Values area. Select Series Properties from the context menu. The Series Properties dialog box appears.

25. Select the Axes and Chart Area page of the dialog box.

26. Select Secondary from the Vertical axis radio buttons.

27. Click OK to exit the Series Properties dialog box. A secondary value axis appears on the right side of the chart, as shown here.

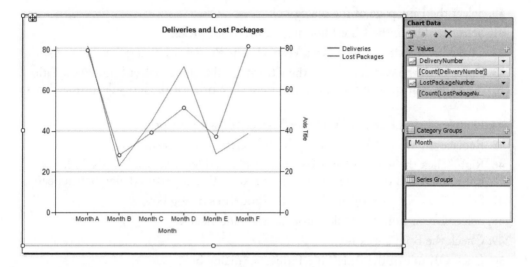

28. Double-click the words "Axis Title" associated with the new, secondary axis.

29. Replace the words "Axis Title" with **Lost Packages**. Press ENTER.

30. Right-click the words "Lost Packages" and select Axis Title Properties from the context menu. The Axis Title Properties dialog box appears.

31. Select the Font page of the Axis Title Properties dialog box.

NOTE

If you ended up with a different default color scheme for your chart and the deliveries line is a color other than green or the lost packages line is a color other than red, simply adapt the following steps to pick the appropriate colors for the two axes.

32. Select Red from the Color drop-down color picker.

33. Check the Bold check box.

34. Click OK to exit the Axis Title Properties dialog box.

35. Right-click the secondary vertical axis itself (the axis on the right side). Select Secondary Vertical Axis Properties from the context menu. The Secondary Vertical Axis Properties dialog box appears.

36. Select the Label Font page of the dialog box.

37. Select Red from the Color drop-down color picker.

38. Select the Major Tick Marks page of the dialog box.

39. Select Red from the Line color drop-down color picker.

40. Select the Line page of the dialog box.

41. Select Red from the Line color drop-down color picker.

42. Click OK to exit the Secondary Vertical Axis Properties dialog box.

43. Right-click the vertical axis on the left side of the chart. Select Show Axis Title from the context menu to check this item. The title for the left side, primary axis appears.

44. Double-click the words "Axis Title" associated with the primary axis.

45. Replace the words "Axis Title" with **Deliveries**. Press ENTER.

46. Right-click the word "Deliveries" that you just added, and select Axis Title Properties from the context menu. The Axis Title Properties dialog box appears.

47. Select the Font page of the Axis Title Properties dialog box.

48. Select Green from the Color drop-down color picker.

49. Check the Bold check box.

50. Click OK to exit the Axis Title Properties dialog box.

51. Right-click the vertical axis next to the Deliveries label (the axis on the left side). Select Vertical Axis Properties from the context menu. The Vertical Axis Properties dialog box appears.

52. Select the Label Font page of the dialog box.

53. Select Green from the Color drop-down color picker.

54. Select the Major Tick Marks page of the dialog box.

55. Select Green from the Line color drop-down color picker.

56. Select the Line page of the dialog box.

57. Select Green from the Line color drop-down color picker.

58. Click OK to exit the Vertical Axis Properties dialog box.

59. Right-click the legend area where "Deliveries" appears next to a green line and "Lost Packages" appears next to a red line. Select Delete Legend from the context menu. The legend disappears.

60. Preview/Run the report. The report appears as shown.

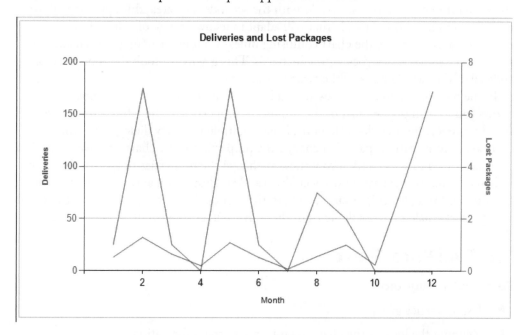

61. If you are using SSDT or Visual Studio, click Save All in the toolbar.

62. If you are using Report Builder, click the logo button, and select Save As from the menu. Save the report as "Copy (3) of DelvLostPkgChart" in the Chapter06 folder.

Task Notes   In this task, we see three methods for analyzing two series with different value ranges on the same chart. In the first copy of the DelvLostPkgChart, we enabled scale breaks. Scale breaks allow portions of the scale that do not contain any values to be skipped over in the chart. On our chart, there are no values between 32 and 86 nor between 86 and 172, so these portions of the scale are eliminated from the chart.

In the second copy of the DelvLostPkgChart, we use a second chart area to display one of the two series. Each chart area has its own vertical axis, so each axis can size itself appropriately. Of course, a similar effect could be achieved by placing two chart items on a single report, one below the other. Using a single chart report item with two chart areas enables us to label both series in a single legend and ensures the category axes of both chart areas will stay aligned.

For the third copy of the DelvLostPkgChart, we use a secondary value axis to display the scale for one of the two series. As with the second chart area, this approach allows each series to have its own scale that will adapt to its own range of values. Using a secondary axis can make the chart confusing unless we provide enough visual cues to tell the user which series goes with which axis. This is why we took the time to color-code all of the various parts of the two vertical axes.

In the previous chapter, you saw the tablix has a single property dialog box that allows you to manipulate most of the important properties of the tablix. Now we see the chart report item works differently. It has multiple property dialog boxes that correspond to its various parts. To change the properties of the chart title, we right-click the chart title and select Title Properties; to change the properties of a vertical axis, we right-click that vertical axis and select Vertical Axis Properties; and so on. When you want to modify a particular item in a chart, right-click that item and odds are there will be a property dialog box available right there that will enable you to make the change.

The Fuel Price Chart

Features Highlighted

▶   Using a series group

▶   Refining the look of the chart to best present the information

Business Need   Galactic Delivery Services needs to analyze the fluctuations in the price of fuel from month to month. The best way to perform this analysis is by creating a chart of the price over time. The user needs to be able to select the year from a drop-down list.

Task Overview

1. Create a New Report and Two Datasets
2. Place a Chart Item on the Report and Populate It
3. Refine the Chart

Fuel Price Chart, Task 1: Create a New Report and Two Datasets

`DT`   SSDT and Visual Studio Steps

1. Add a blank report called FuelPriceChart to the Chapter06 project. (Do not use the Report Wizard.)
2. In the Report Data window, click the New drop-down menu. Select Data Source from the menu that appears. The Data Source Properties dialog box appears.

3. Enter **Galactic** for the name.

4. Select the Use shared data source reference radio button, and select Galactic from the drop-down list. Click OK.

5. In the Report Data window, right-click the entry for the Galactic data source, and select Add Dataset from the context menu. The Dataset Properties dialog box appears.

6. Enter **FuelPrices** for the name.

7. Click the Query Designer button. The Query Designer window opens displaying the Graphical Query Designer. Click the Edit as Text button to switch to the Generic Query Designer.

8. Enter the following in the SQL pane (upper portion) of the Generic Query Designer window:

```
SELECT Description AS FuelType,
     PriceStartDate,
     Price
FROM FuelPrice
INNER JOIN Propulsion
     ON FuelPrice.PropulsionID = Propulsion.PropulsionID
WHERE (YEAR(PriceStartDate) = @Year)
ORDER BY FuelType, PriceStartDate
```

9. Click the Run Query button in the Generic Query Designer toolbar to run the query and make sure no errors exist. Correct any typos that may be detected. When the query is correct, the Define Query Parameters dialog box appears. Enter **2011** as the Parameter Value for the @Year parameter, and click OK.

10. Click OK to exit the Query Designer window. Click OK to exit the Dataset Properties dialog box.

11. The business needs for the report specified the user should select the year from a drop-down list. We need to define a second dataset to populate this drop-down list. In the Report Data window, right-click the entry for the Galactic data source, and select Add Dataset from the context menu. The Dataset Properties dialog box appears.

12. Enter **Years** for the name of the dataset.

13. Galactic is selected for the data source by default. Enter the following in the Query entry area of the Dataset Properties dialog box:

```
SELECT DISTINCT YEAR(PriceStartDate) AS Year FROM FuelPrice
```

14. Click OK to exit the Dataset Properties dialog box. The Years dataset will appear in the Report Data window along with the FuelPrices dataset.

15. We did not have a chance to test the query, so let's see how to go back and do that. In the Report Data window, right-click the Years dataset, and select Query from the context menu. The Query Designer window opens with the Graphical Query Designer containing the dataset query.

16. Run the query to make sure it is correct. You see a list of the distinct years from the FuelPrice table.

17. When the query is working properly, click OK to exit the Query Designer window.

RB **Report Builder Steps**

1. Click the logo button, and select New from the menu. The New Report or Dataset dialog box will appear. With New Report selected on the left, click Blank Report on the right.

2. In the Report Data window, click the New drop-down menu. Select Data Source from the menu that appears. The Data Source Properties dialog box appears.

3. Enter **Galactic** for the name.

4. Make sure the Use a shared connection or report model radio button is selected, and select Galactic from the area below it. Click OK. An entry for the Galactic data source appears in the Report Data window.

5. In the Report Data window, right-click the entry for the Galactic data source, and select Add Dataset from the context menu. The Dataset Properties dialog box appears.

6. Enter **FuelPrices** for the name.

7. Click the Query Designer button. The Query Designer window opens displaying the Graphical Query Designer.

8. Click the Edit as Text button to switch to the Generic Query Designer.

9. Enter the following in the SQL pane (upper portion) of the Generic Query Designer window:

```
SELECT Description AS FuelType,
      PriceStartDate,
      Price
FROM FuelPrice
INNER JOIN Propulsion
      ON FuelPrice.PropulsionID = Propulsion.PropulsionID
WHERE (YEAR(PriceStartDate) = @Year)
ORDER BY FuelType, PriceStartDate
```

10. Run the query to make sure no errors exist. Correct any typos that may be detected. When the query is correct, the Define Query Parameters dialog box appears. Enter **2011** for the @Year parameter, and click OK.

11. Click OK to exit the Query Designer window. Click OK to exit the Dataset Properties dialog box.

12. The business needs for the report specified the user should select the year from a drop-down list. We need to define a second dataset to populate this drop-down list. In the Report Data window, right-click the Galactic entry, and select Add Dataset from the context menu. The Dataset Properties dialog box appears.

13. Enter **Years** for the name of the dataset.

14. Galactic is selected for the data source by default. Enter the following in the Query entry area of the Dataset Properties dialog box:

```
SELECT DISTINCT YEAR(PriceStartDate) AS Year FROM FuelPrice
```

15. Click OK to exit the Dataset Properties dialog box. The Years dataset will appear in the Report Data window along with the FuelPrices dataset.

16. We did not have a chance to test the query, so let's see how to go back and do that. In the Report Data window, right-click the Years dataset, and select Query from the context menu. The Query Designer window opens with the Generic Query Designer containing the dataset query.

17. Run the query to make sure it is correct. You see a list of the distinct years from the FuelPrice table.

18. When the query is working properly, click OK to exit the Query Designer window.

19. Select the "Click to add title" text box, and delete it. (The title will be contained within the chart itself.)

Task Notes   We created two datasets in the FuelPriceChart report—one to populate the Year drop-down list and the other to provide data for the chart. For the previous report, we created our query without the aid of the Graphical Query Designer. Here we are even more daring. We entered our second query right in the Query entry area of the Dataset Properties dialog box. This is the fastest way to enter a straightforward query when creating a dataset.

Fuel Price Chart, Task 2:
Place a Chart Item on the Report and Populate It

DT
RB

SSDT, Visual Studio, and Report Builder Steps

1. Expand the Parameters item in the Report Data window. You see an entry for the Year parameter. This report parameter was created to correspond to the @Year parameter in the FuelPrices dataset.

2. Double-click the Year parameter entry. The Report Parameter Properties dialog box appears.

3. Go to the Available Values page of the dialog box.

4. Select the Get values from a query radio button.

5. In the Dataset drop-down list, select Years. Select Year from both the Value field drop-down list and the Label field drop-down list. Your screen should appear similar to the illustration shown here.

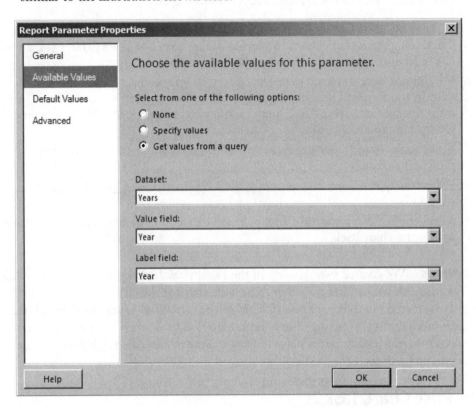

6. Click OK to exit the Report Parameter Properties dialog box.

7. Drag the edges of the design surface so it fills the available space on the screen.

8. Select the chart report item in the Toolbox window/Insert ribbon, and place it on the design surface. The chart should cover almost the entire design surface because it will be the only item on the report. The Select Chart Type dialog box appears.

9. Select the Line with Markers graph, as shown here.

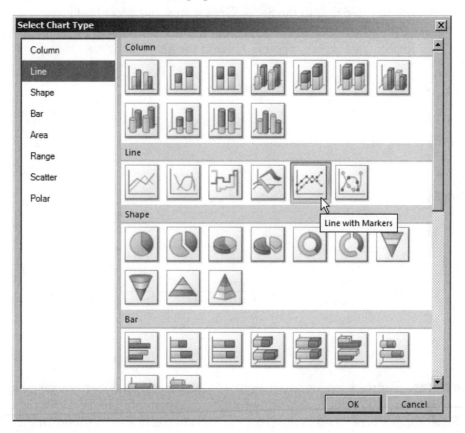

10. Click OK to exit the Select Chart Type dialog box. You will see a representation of the chart on the design surface.

11. Click anywhere on the chart to activate the Chart Data window.

12. Click the plus sign next to the Values area, and select Galactic | FuelPrices | Price as shown.

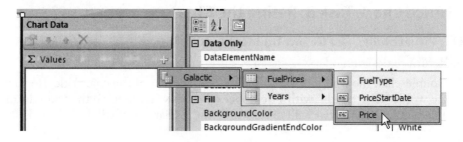

13. Click the plus sign next to the Category Groups area, and select PriceStartDate.

14. Click the plus sign next to the Series Groups area, and select FuelType.

15. Preview/Run the report. Select 2011 from the Year drop-down list, and then click View Report. Your report appears similar to the illustration.

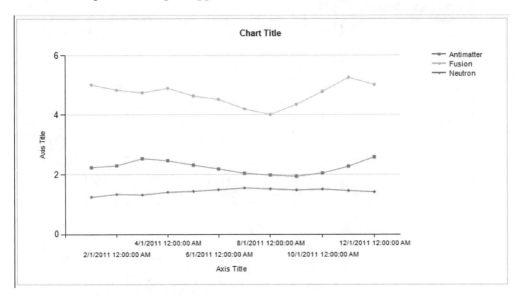

Task Notes   For the previous report, we used multiple series values to create multiple lines on our graph. For this report, we use a different approach. The FuelType field in the Series Groups area serves as the grouping value to create a series group. In the tablix report item, we get one group for each distinct value in the grouping field. Similarly, in the chart we get one series, one line on the graph in this case, for each distinct value in the grouping field. We get one series for the fuel used in the antimatter engines, one series for the fuel used in the fusion engines, and one series for the fuel used in the neutron engines.

Fuel Price Chart, Task 3: Refine the Chart

SSDT, Visual Studio, and Report Builder Steps

1. Return to design mode.

2. Double-click the words "Chart Title" to edit the text of the chart title. Replace the words "Chart Title" with **Fuel Prices**. Press ENTER to leave the text edit mode. The blinking text cursor will disappear and the chart itself will be selected.

3. Right-click the Fuel Prices title, and select Chart | Add New Title from the context menu. A second title line is added to the chart.

4. Click on this new title so the edit cursor appears. Replace "New Title" with **Monthly Fuel Survey**.

5. Right-click the Fuel Prices title, and select Title Properties from the context menu. The Chart Title Properties dialog box appears.

6. Select the Font page of the Chart Title Properties dialog box.

7. Set the following properties:

Property	Value
Size	12pt
Effects	Underline

8. Click OK to exit the Chart Title Properties dialog box.

9. Right-click the title for the horizontal axis, and select Axis Title Properties from the context menu. The Axis Title Properties dialog box appears.

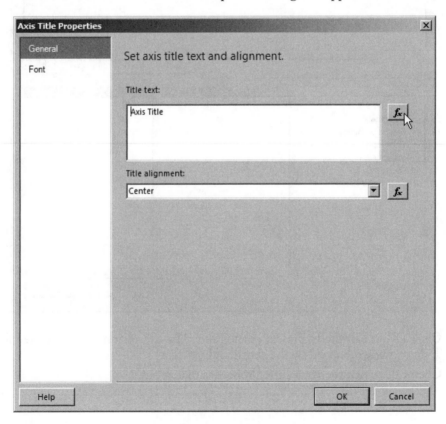

10. Click the *fx* button next to the Title text entry area as shown on the previous illustration. The Expression dialog box appears.

11. Replace the words "Axis Title" in the Set expression for: Caption entry area with the following:

    =

12. Select Parameters in the Category tree view. The report parameters appear in the Values pane of the dialog box. (Year is the only report parameter defined for this report.)

13. Double-click the Year parameter entry in the Values pane of the dialog box. The dialog box should appear as shown.

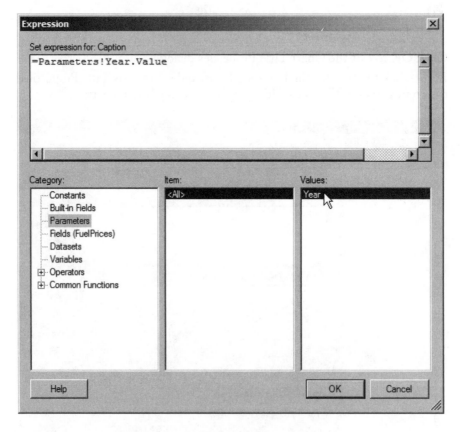

14. Click OK to exit the Expression dialog box. The expression we just created for the Title text is symbolized by the shorthand: [@Year].

15. Click OK to exit the Axis Title Properties dialog box.

16. Select the horizontal axis. When selected, the axis will be surrounded by a dashed rectangle and Chart Axis will be displayed at the top of the Properties window as shown.

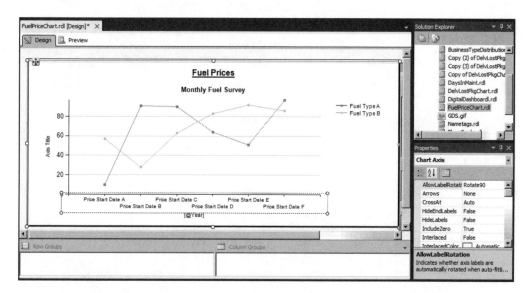

17. In the Properties window, set the following property:

Property	Value
LabelsFormat	MMM

18. Double-click the vertical axis title. Replace the words "Axis Title" with **Price in Dollars** and press ENTER.
19. Right-click the vertical axis, and select Vertical Axis Properties from the context menu. The Vertical Axis Properties dialog box appears.
20. Set the following properties in the Axis range and interval area on the Axis Options page:

Property	Value
Minimum	0
Maximum	6
Interval	1

21. Click OK to exit the Vertical Axis Properties dialog box.

22. Preview/Run the report. Select 2011 from the Year drop-down list, and then click View Report. Your report appears similar to the illustration.

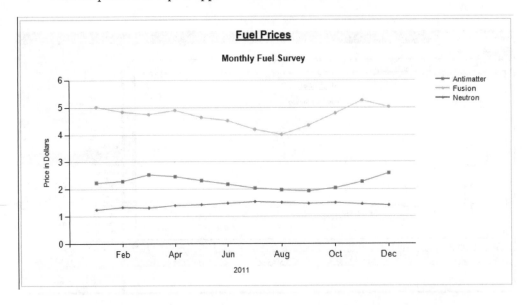

23. If you are using SSDT or Visual Studio, click Save All on the toolbar. If you are using Report Builder, save the report under the name "FuelPriceChart" in the Chapter06 folder on the report server.

Task Notes   The format code MMM is a date-formatting code. It causes the chart to use only the first three characters of the month name for the category axis labels.

The Fuel Price Chart, Version 2

Features Highlighted

▶   Using the union operator in a SELECT statement

▶   Using a WHERE clause to return records of one type or of all types

Business Need   GDS would now like to be able to select a single fuel type or all fuel types from a drop-down list to view in the report.

Task Overview

1. Create a New Dataset for the Second Drop-down List and Revise the FuelPrices Dataset to Allow for Fuel Type Selection

Fuel Price Chart, Version 2, Task 1: Create a New Dataset for the Second Drop-down List and Revise the FuelPrices Dataset to Allow for Fuel Type Selection

DT

RB

SSDT, Visual Studio, and Report Builder Steps

1. Reopen the FuelPriceChart report, if you closed it. If the FuelPriceChart report is open and being previewed/run, return to design mode.

2. Right-click the entry for the Galactic data source in the Report Data window. Select Add Dataset from the context menu. The Dataset Properties dialog box appears.

3. Enter **FuelTypes** for Name.

4. Galactic is selected for the Data source by default. Click the Query Designer button. The Graphical Query Designer appears. Click the Edit as Text button to switch to the Generic Query Designer.

5. Type the following in the SQL pane:

```
SELECT 'All' AS FuelType, '_All' AS SortField
UNION
SELECT Description, Description FROM Propulsion ORDER BY SortField
```

6. Run the query to make sure it is correct. You see a list of the distinct fuel types from the FuelPrice table. There is also a record for "All".

7. Click OK to exit the Query Designer window. Click OK to exit the Dataset Properties dialog box.

8. Right-click the entry for the FuelPrices dataset in the Report Data window. Select Query from the context menu.

9. Change the SELECT statement to the following (the only change is in the second half of the WHERE clause, shown in bold):

```
SELECT Description AS FuelType,
    PriceStartDate,
    Price
FROM FuelPrice
INNER JOIN Propulsion
    ON FuelPrice.PropulsionID = Propulsion.PropulsionID
WHERE (YEAR(PriceStartDate) = @Year)
    AND ((Description = @PropulsionType)
    OR (@PropulsionType = 'All'))
ORDER BY FuelType, PriceStartDate
```

10. Run the query to make sure it is correct. The Define Query Parameters dialog box appears. Enter **2011** for the Parameter Value of the @Year parameter, **All** for Parameter Value of the @PropulsionType parameter, and click OK.

11. Click OK to exit the Query Designer window.

12. Expand the Parameters item in the Report Data window, if it is not expanded already. A report parameter called PropulsionType is created to correspond to the @PropulsionType parameter from the FuelPrices dataset. Double-click the PropulsionType entry in the Report Data window. The Report Parameter Properties dialog box appears.

13. Select the Available Values page.

14. Select the Get values from a query radio button.

15. In the Dataset drop-down list, select FuelTypes. In the Value field drop-down list, select FuelType. In the Label field drop-down list, select FuelType. Click OK to exit the Report Parameter Properties dialog box.

16. Preview/Run the report. Select 2011 from the Year drop-down list, select Antimatter from the Propulsion Type drop-down list, and then click View Report. Your report appears similar to the illustration.

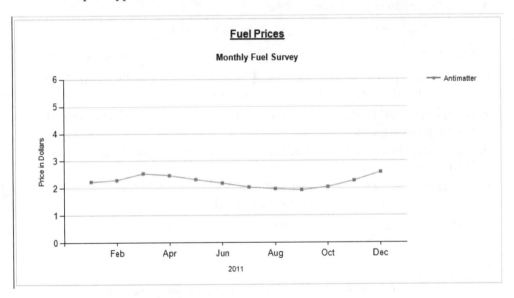

17. Click Save on the toolbar.

Task Notes   The query that creates the FuelTypes dataset is two SELECT statements combined to produce one result set. The first SELECT statement returns a single row with the constant value "All" in the FuelType column and a constant value of "_All" in the SortField. The underscore is placed in front of the word "All" in SortField to make sure it sorts to the top of the list. The second SELECT statement returns a row for each record in the Propulsion table. The two result sets are unified into a single result set by the UNION operator in between the two SELECT statements.

When result sets are *unioned,* the names of the columns in the result set are taken from the first SELECT statement in the union. That is why the FuelTypes dataset has two columns named FuelType and SortField rather than Description. When SELECT statements are unioned, only the last SELECT statement can have an ORDER BY clause. This ORDER BY clause is used to sort the entire result set after it has been unified into a single result set.

The UNION operator can be used with any two SELECT statements as long as the following is true:

▶ The result set from each SELECT statement has the same number of columns.

▶ The corresponding columns in each result set have the same data type.

In fact, the UNION can be used to combine any number of SELECT statements into a unified result set as long as these two conditions hold true for all the SELECT statements in the UNION.

The Business Type Distribution Chart

Features Highlighted

▶ Creating a report using a pie chart

▶ Using the Data Label property

▶ Changing the chart palette

▶ Using the 3-D effect

Business Need The Galactic Delivery Services marketing department needs to analyze what types of businesses are using GDS for their delivery services. This information should be presented as a pie chart.

Task Overview

1. Create a New Report and a Dataset
2. Place a Chart Item on the Report and Populate It

Business Type Distribution Chart, Task 1: Create a New Report and a Dataset

DT   **SSDT and Visual Studio Steps**

1. Reopen the Chapter06 project, if it was closed. Close the FuelPriceChart report.

2. Add a blank report called BusinessTypeDistribution to the Chapter06 project. (Do not use the Report Wizard.)

3. In the Report Data window, click the New drop-down menu. Select Data Source from the menu that appears. The Data Source Properties dialog box appears.

4. Enter **Galactic** for the name.

5. Select the Use shared data source reference radio button, and select Galactic from the drop-down list. Click OK.

6. In the Report Data window, right-click the entry for the Galactic data source, and select Add Dataset from the context menu. The Dataset Properties dialog box appears.

7. Enter **CustomerBusinessTypes** for the name.

8. Click the Query Designer button. The Query Designer window opens displaying the Graphical Query Designer. Click the Edit as Text button to switch to the Generic Query Designer.

9. Enter the following in the SQL pane (upper portion) of the Generic Query Designer window:

```
SELECT Name AS CustomerName,
    Description AS BusinessType
FROM Customer
INNER JOIN CustomerToBusinessTypeLink
    ON Customer.CustomerNumber
        = CustomerToBusinessTypeLink.CustomerNumber
INNER JOIN BusinessType
    ON CustomerToBusinessTypeLink.BusinessTypeCode
        = BusinessType.BusinessTypeCode
```

10. Run the query to make sure no errors exist. Correct any typos that may be detected.

11. Click OK to exit the Query Designer window. Click OK to exit the Dataset Properties dialog box.

RB   **Report Builder Steps**

1. Click the logo button, and select New from the menu. The New Report or Dataset dialog box will appear. With New Report selected on the left, click Blank Report on the right.

2. In the Report Data window, click the New drop-down menu. Select Data Source from the menu that appears. The Data Source Properties dialog box appears.

3. Enter **Galactic** for the name.

4. Make sure the Use a shared connection or report model radio button is selected, and select Galactic from the area below it. Click OK. An entry for the Galactic data source appears in the Report Data window.

5. In the Report Data window, right-click the entry for the Galactic data source, and select Add Dataset from the context menu..The Dataset Properties dialog box appears.

6. Enter **CustomerBusinessTypes** for the name.

7. Click the Query Designer button. The Query Designer window opens displaying the Graphical Query Designer.

8. Click the Edit as Text button to switch to the Generic Query Designer.

9. Enter the following in the SQL pane (upper portion) of the Generic Query Designer window:

```
SELECT Name AS CustomerName,
      Description AS BusinessType
FROM Customer
INNER JOIN CustomerToBusinessTypeLink
      ON Customer.CustomerNumber
         = CustomerToBusinessTypeLink.CustomerNumber
INNER JOIN BusinessType
      ON CustomerToBusinessTypeLink.BusinessTypeCode
         = BusinessType.BusinessTypeCode
```

10. Run the query to make sure no errors exist. Correct any typos that may be detected.

11. Click OK to exit the Query Designer window. Click OK to exit the Dataset Properties dialog box.

12. Select the "Click to add title" text box, and delete it. (The title will be contained within the chart itself.)

Task Notes   The CustomerBusinessTypes dataset simply contains a list of customer names and their corresponding business type. Remember, some customers are linked to more than one business type. That means some of the customers appear in the list more than once.

This dataset is used to populate a pie chart in the next task. The BusinessType field is used to create the categories for the pie chart. The items in the CustomerName field are counted to determine how many customers are in each category.

Business Type Distribution Chart, Task 2:
Place a Chart Item on the Report and Populate It

DT

RB

SSDT, Visual Studio, and Report Builder Steps

1. Drag the edges of the design surface larger so it fills the available space on the screen.

2. Select the chart report item in the Toolbox window/Insert ribbon, and place it on the design surface. The chart should cover almost the entire design surface because it will be the only item on the report. The Select Chart Type dialog box appears.

3. Select the pie chart from the Shape area.

4. Click OK to exit the Select Chart Type dialog box. You will see a representation of the pie chart on the design surface.

5. Click anywhere on the chart to activate the Chart Data window.

6. Click the plus sign next to the Values area, and select CustomerName.

7. Click the plus sign next to the Category Groups area, and select BusinessType.

8. Right-click BusinessType in the Category Groups area of the Chart Data window, and select Category Group Properties from the context menu. The Category Group Properties dialog box appears.

9. Click the *fx* button next to the Label drop-down list. The Expression dialog box appears.

10. Enter the following in the Set expression for: Label entry area:

```
=Fields!BusinessType.Value & vbcrlf &
"(" & CStr(Count(Fields!CustomerName.Value)) & ")"
```

    Remember you can select the fields using the Fields(CustomerBusinessType) entry in the Category pane along with the Field list in the lower-right pane of the dialog box.

11. Click OK to exit the Expression dialog box.

12. Click OK to exit the Category Group Properties dialog box.

13. Change the Chart Title to **Customer Business Types**.

14. Right-click the pie chart itself, and select 3D Effects from the context menu. The Chart Area Properties dialog box appears.

15. Check the Enable 3D check box.

16. Set Rotation to **50**.

17. Set Inclination to **50**.

18. Click OK to exit the Chart Area Properties dialog box.

19. Preview/Run the report. Your report appears similar to the illustration.

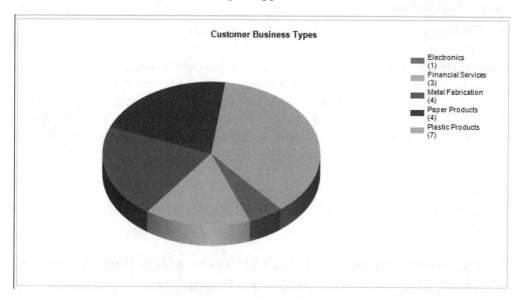

20. If you are using SSDT or Visual Studio, click Save All on the toolbar. If you are using Report Builder, save the report as "BusinessTypeDistribution" in the Chapter06 folder on the report server.

Task Notes   By default, the pie chart uses a legend, located to the side of the chart, to provide labels for each wedge in the pie. The Label item in the Category Group Properties dialog box determines what is displayed as the legend for each category group (pie wedge). In the Business Type Distribution chart, we added to the label expression so it not only showed the name of the category, the business type, but also the number of customers in that category. The expression concatenates the business type and the count of the number of customers with a carriage return/linefeed (vbcrlf) in between. The carriage return/linefeed causes the business type and the count to each appear on its own line.

In this chart, we are also using the 3-D effect. The 3-D effect can help to add interest to a chart by taking a flat graphic and lifting it off the page.

Now let's try one more chart before looking at the items that make up a digital dashboard.

The Days in Maintenance Chart

Feature Highlighted

▶ Creating a report using a 3-D stacked column chart

Business Need   The Galactic Delivery Services transport maintenance department is looking to compare the total maintenance downtime for each year. They would also like to know how that maintenance time is distributed among the different transport types. They would like a graph showing the number of days that each type of transport spent "in for repairs." This information should be presented as a 3-D stacked column chart. The underlying data should be displayed as a label on each column in the chart.

Task Overview

1. Create a New Report, Create a Dataset, Place a Chart Item on the Report, and Populate It

Days in Maintenance Chart, Task 1: Create a New Report, Create a Dataset, Place a Chart Item on the Report, and Populate It

DT
RB
SSDT, Visual Studio, and Report Builder Steps

1. If you are using SSDT or Visual Studio, reopen the Chapter06 project, if it was closed. Close the BusinessTypeDistribution report, and add a blank report called DaysInMaint to the Chapter06 project. (Do not use the Report Wizard.)
2. If you are using Report Builder, create a new blank report, and delete the "Click to add title" text box.
3. In the Report Data window, click the New drop-down menu. Select Data Source from the menu that appears. The Data Source Properties dialog box appears.
4. As we have done previously, create a new data source named **Galactic** that references the Galactic shared data source. Click OK to exit the Data Source Properties dialog box.
5. In the Report Data window, right-click the entry for the Galactic data source, and select Add Dataset from the context menu. The Dataset Properties dialog box appears.
6. Enter **DaysInMaint** for the name.
7. Click the Query Designer button. The Query Designer window opens.
8. Click the Edit as Text button to switch to the Generic Query Designer.

9. Enter the following in the SQL pane (upper portion) of the Generic Query Designer window:

```
SELECT Description AS PropulsionType,
    YEAR(BeginWorkDate) AS Year,
    DATEDIFF(dd, BeginWorkDate, EndWorkDate) AS DaysInMaint
FROM Repair
INNER JOIN Transport
    ON Repair.TransportNumber = Transport.TransportNumber
INNER JOIN TransportType
    ON Transport.TransportTypeID = TransportType.TransportTypeID
ORDER BY PropulsionType, Year
```

10. Run the query to make sure there are no errors. Correct any typos that may be detected.

11. Click OK to exit the Query Designer window. Click OK to exit the Dataset Properties dialog box.

12. Click the design surface. The body of the report will be selected in the Properties window. Set the following properties of the body in the Properties window:

Property	Value
Size: Width	7.5in
Size: Height	4.375in

13. Select the chart report item in the Toolbox window/Insert ribbon, and place it on the report layout. Resize the chart so it almost covers the entire report layout because it is the only item on the report. The Select Chart Type dialog box appears.

14. Select the 3-D Stacked Column chart from the Column area.

15. Click OK to exit the Select Chart Type dialog box. You will see a representation of the 3-D stacked column chart on the design surface.

16. Click anywhere on the chart to activate the Chart Data window. You may need to scroll right to see it.

17. Click the plus sign next to the Values area, and select DaysInMaint.

18. Click the plus sign next to the Category Groups area, and select Year.

19. Click the plus sign next to the Series Groups area, and select PropulsionType.

20. Change the chart title to **Days In Maintenance**.

21. Right-click the PropulsionType entry in the Series Groups area. Select Series Group Properties from the context menu. The Series Group Properties dialog box appears.

22. Click the *fx* button next to the Label drop-down list. The Expression dialog box appears.

23. Enter the following in the Set expression for: Label entry area:

```
=Fields!PropulsionType.Value & " (All Yrs) - "
   & CStr(Sum(Fields!DaysInMaint.Value))
```

24. Click OK to exit the Expression dialog box. Click OK to exit the Series Group Properties dialog box.

25. Right-click the Year entry in the Category Groups area. Select Category Group Properties from the context menu. The Category Group Properties dialog box appears.

26. Click the *fx* button next to the Label drop-down list. The Expression dialog box appears.

27. Enter the following in the Set expression for: Label entry area:

```
="Total Maint. Days - " & CStr(Sum(Fields!DaysInMaint.Value))
   & vbcrlf & Fields!Year.Value
```

28. Click OK to exit the Expression dialog box. Click OK to exit the Category Group Properties dialog box.

29. Right-click one of the bars in the chart area. Select Show Data Labels from the context menu. Numbers will appear on the columns.

30. Right-click the chart legend. Select Legend Properties as shown here.

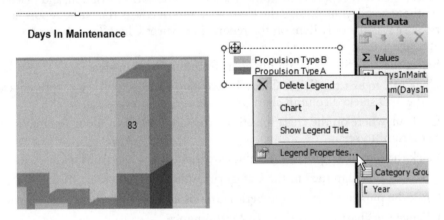

31. In the Legend Properties dialog box, select Tall table from the Layout drop-down box.

32. Select the legend position in the center-bottom of the Legend position circle as shown.

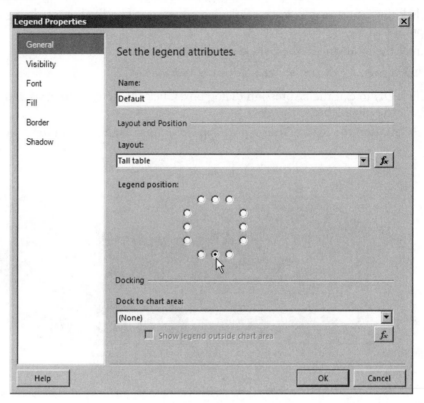

NOTE

You can also change the position of the legend by selecting it and using the positioning handle to drag it to the desired location.

33. Select the Border page of the dialog box.

34. Select Solid from the Line style drop-down box.

35. Select the Shadow page of the dialog box.

36. Click the up arrow of the Shadow offset entry area until the shadow offset is set to 1 pt.

37. Select Silver from the Shadow color drop-down color picker.

38. Click OK to exit the Legend Properties dialog box.

39. Change the horizontal axis title to **Year**.

40. Right-click the vertical axis title, and select Axis Title Properties from the context menu. The Axis Title Properties dialog box appears.

41. Click the *fx* button next to the Title text entry area. The Expression dialog box appears.

42. Enter the following in the Set expression for: Title area:

```
="Days in" & vbcrlf & "Maintenance Hanger"
```

43. Click OK to exit the Expression dialog box. Click OK to exit the Axis Title Properties dialog box.

44. Preview/Run the report. Your report appears similar to the illustration.

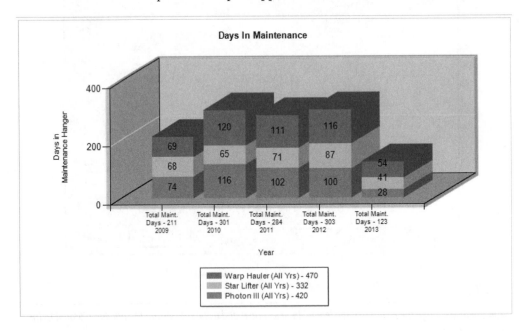

45. If you are using SSDT or Visual Studio, click Save All on the toolbar. If you are using Report Builder, save the report as "DaysInMaint" in the Chapter06 folder on the report server.

Task Notes The stacked column chart is a good choice to fulfill the business needs for this report, because it can graphically illustrate two different pieces of information at the same time. Each colored section of the graph shows the number of maintenance days for a given propulsion type. In addition, the combined height of the three sections of the column shows the fluctuations in the total maintenance days from year to year.

Above and beyond the graphical information provided in the chart, several additional pieces of information are provided numerically. This includes the category labels along the horizontal axis, the legend at the bottom of the graph, and the detail data displayed right on the column sections themselves. The values on the columns are the result of the expression being charted, which is SUM(DaysInMaint).

This expression uses the SUM() aggregate function to add up the values from the DaysInMaint field. It may seem this sum should give us the total for the DaysInMaint field for the entire dataset. After all, there is nothing in this expression that references the category or series groups. The reason this does not occur is because of the scope in which this expression is evaluated. The *scope* sets boundaries on which rows from the dataset are used with a given expression.

The data label expression operates at the innermost scope in the chart. This means expressions in the data label are evaluated using only those rows that come from both the current category group and the current series group. For example, let's look at the column section for Star Lifters for the year 2009. This column section is part of the Star Lifter series group. It is also part of the year 2009 category group. When the report is evaluating the data label expression to put a label on the Star Lifter/year 2009 column section, it uses only those rows in the result set for the Star Lifters in the year 2009. Using this scope, the report calculates the sum of DaysInMaint for Star Lifters in the year 2009 as 68 days.

Next, let's consider the summary data that appears in the labels along the horizontal axis. These entries are the result of the expression entered for the label in the category groups. This expression also uses the SUM() function to add up the values from the DaysInMaint column. However, it calculates different totals because it is operating in a different scope.

In this case, the calculations are being done in the category scope, which means the expression for the label in the category group is evaluated using all the records from the current category group. For example, let's look at the category label for the year 2009 column. This column is part of the year 2009 category group. When the report is evaluating the label expression to put a label below this column, it uses all the rows in the result set for the year 2009. The propulsion type of each row does not make a difference because it is not part of this scope. Using the year 2009 category scope, the report calculates the sum of DaysInMaint for the year 2009 as 211 days.

Finally, we come to the summary data that appears in the legend below the chart. These entries are the result of the expression entered for the label in the series groups. Yet again, this expression uses the SUM() function to add up the values from the DaysInMaint column. And yet again, we get different numbers because it is working in a different scope. Here, the calculations are being done in the series scope. That means the expressions are evaluated using all the records from the current series group. For example, let's look at the entry in the legend for the Star Lifter series. When the report is evaluating the series group label expression, it uses all the rows in the result set for Star Lifters. The year of each row does not make a difference because it is not part of this scope. Using the Star Lifter series scope, the report calculates the sum of DaysInMaint for the Star Lifters as 332 days.

In several expressions used in this chart, we are concatenating several strings to create the labels we need. This is done using the Visual Basic string concatenation operator (&). You may notice several of the fields being concatenated are numeric rather than string fields. The reason these concatenations work is the & operator automatically converts numeric values to strings. In this way, we can take "Total Maint. Days -" and concatenate it with 211 to get the first lines of the year 2009 column label. The 211 is converted to "211" and then concatenated with the rest of the string.

The final noteworthy item on this report is the expression used to create the label on the vertical axis. To have this label fit nicely along the vertical axis, we used our old friend the carriage return/linefeed to split the label on to two lines. Because the text is rotated 90 degrees, the first line of the label is farthest from the vertical axis and the second line is to the right of the first line.

Gauging the Results

One of the current trends in business intelligence is the digital dashboard. The dashboard on a car tells the driver the current state of the car's operations: current speed, current amount of gas in the tank, and so on. The gauges and displays on the dashboard allow the driver to take in this current information at a glance.

In the same manner, the digital dashboard tells a decision maker the current state of the organization's operations. This digital dashboard also uses gauges and other easy-to-understand displays. The digital dashboard makes it easy for the decision maker to get current information at a glance.

Reporting Services provides the gauge data region for building reports that serve as digital dashboards.

The Digital Dashboard

Feature Highlighted

▶ Using the gauge data region

Business Need Three key indicators of the health of Galactic Delivery Services are the number of deliveries in the past four weeks, the number of lost packages in the past four weeks, and the number of transport repairs in the past four weeks. The GDS executives would like a digital dashboard showing these three key performance indicators using easy-to-read gauges.

Task Overview

1. Create a New Report along with a Dataset and Present the Data on a Gauge
2. Refine the Appearance of the Gauge
3. Modify the Dataset and Add a Second Gauge

Digital Dashboard, Task 1: Create a New Report along with a Dataset and Present the Data on a Gauge

DT
RB

SSDT, Visual Studio, and Report Builder Steps

1. If you are using SSDT or Visual Studio, reopen the Chapter06 project, if it was closed. Close the DaysInMaint report, and add a blank report called DigitalDashboard to the Chapter06 project.

2. If you are using Report Builder, create a new blank report, and delete the "Click to add title" text box.

3. In the Report Data window, click the New drop-down menu. Select Data Source from the menu that appears. The Data Source Properties dialog box appears.

4. As we have done previously, create a new data source named **Galactic** that references the Galactic shared data source. Click OK to exit the Data Source Properties dialog box.

5. In the Report Data window, right-click the entry for the Galactic data source, and select Add Dataset from the context menu. The Dataset Properties dialog box appears.

6. Enter **PickupsAndLost** for the name.

7. Click the Query Designer button. The Query Designer window opens.

8. Click the Edit as Text button to switch to the Generic Query Designer.

9. Enter the following in the SQL pane (upper portion) of the Generic Query Designer window:

```
SELECT COUNT(Delivery.DeliveryNumber) AS NumOfPickups,
    COUNT(LostPackage.LostPackageNumber) AS NumLost
FROM Delivery
LEFT OUTER JOIN LostPackage
    ON Delivery.DeliveryNumber = LostPackage.DeliveryNumber
WHERE PickupDateTime BETWEEN DATEADD(d, -28, @GaugeDate)
                            AND @GaugeDate
```

10. Click the Run Query button on the Generic Query Designer toolbar to run the query and make sure no errors exist. Correct any typos that may be detected. When the query is correct, the Define Query Parameters dialog box appears. Enter **3/1/2012** for the Parameter Value of the @GaugeDate parameter, and click OK.

11. Click OK to exit the Query Designer window. Click OK to exit the Dataset Properties dialog box.

NOTE

The following uses a more abbreviated format for specifying which properties need to be changed in a given dialog box. A table is provided for each dialog box with the page names and properties along with the desired property values. Simply select the appropriate page of the dialog box and change the items specified.

12. Click the design surface. The body of the report will be selected in the Properties window. Set the following properties of the body in the Properties window:

Property	Value
Size: Width	8.5in
Size: Height	5in

13. Select the gauge report item in the Toolbox window/Insert ribbon, and place it on the report layout. The gauge should cover almost the entire report layout because it is the only item on the report. The Select Gauge Type dialog box appears.

14. Select the Radial-Two Scales gauge as shown here.

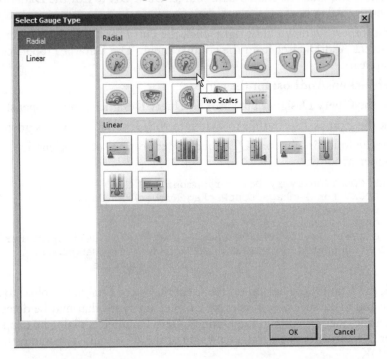

15. Click OK to exit the Select Gauge Type dialog box. You will see a representation of the gauge on the design surface.

16. Click anywhere on the gauge to activate The Gauge Data window. You may have to scroll right to see it.

17. There is an item in the Values area labeled RadialPointer1. This item allows you to associate a dataset field with the large pointer on the gauge. Below the RadialPointer1 item is a second item labeled (Unspecified). A field has yet to be specified for this association. Click the drop-down arrow to the right of the (Unspecified) entry. A field list appears as shown.

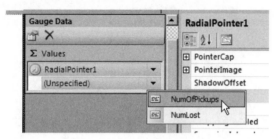

18. Select the NumOfPickups field.

19. Right-click on the outer rim of the gauge, and select Add Pointer For | RadialScale2, as shown.

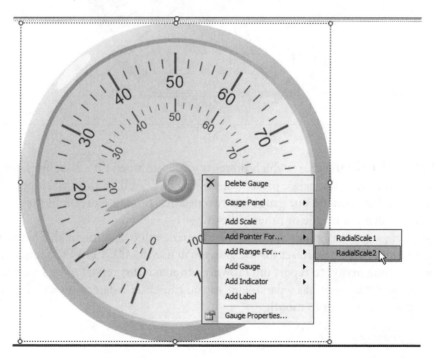

20. A second item, labeled RadialPointer2, appears in the Gauge Data area with an item labeled (Unspecified) underneath it. Click the drop-down arrow to the right of this new (Unspecified) item, and select NumLost. This field will be associated with the small pointer on the gauge.

21. Preview/Run the report. Type **3/1/2012** for Gauge Date, and click View Report. Your report should appear as shown here.

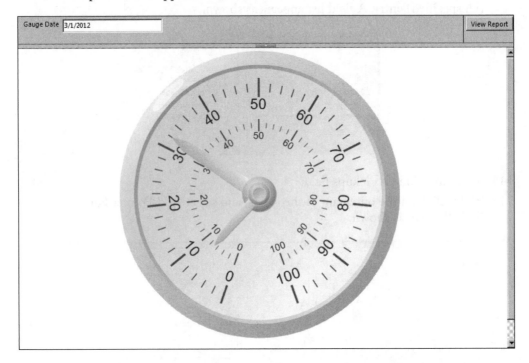

Task Notes   Unlike the chart, which presents values grouped into categories, often days, months, or years, the gauge presents a single value. Well, in this task, it actually presents two values because our gauge has two needles. So, more precisely, the gauge presents one value per needle or other indicator.

Most often, a gauge is going to present the current value of some field. Therefore, the query that creates the dataset for the gauge will use the GETDATE() function to calculate the time period to report on. However, to make this report more interesting with our static database, it has a parameter so you can enter a date and view the gauge as it changes from month to month.

Digital Dashboard, Task 2: Refine the Appearance of the Gauge

DT
RB
SSDT, Visual Studio, and Report Builder Steps

1. Return to design mode.
2. Right-click the large outer scale, and select Scale Properties from the context menu. The Radial Scale Properties dialog box appears.
3. Set the following properties of the dialog box:

Property	Value
General page:	
Maximum value	200
Interval	20
Layout page:	
Scale radius	31
Labels page:	
Rotate labels with scale	Unchecked
Placement (Relative to scale)	Outside
Minor Tick Marks page:	
Interval	5

4. Click OK to exit the Radial Scale Properties dialog box.
5. Right-click the small inner scale, and select Scale Properties from the context menu. The Radial Scale Properties dialog box appears.
6. Set the following properties of the dialog box:

Property	Value
General page:	
Maximum value	30
Interval	2
Layout page:	
Scale bar width (percent)	6
Labels page:	
Rotate labels with scale	Unchecked

Property	Value
Label Font page:	
Color	Red
Minor Tick Marks page:	
Interval	1
Fill page:	
Fill style	Gradient
Color	Yellow
Secondary color	Red
Gradient style	Left right

7. Click OK to exit the Radial Scale Properties dialog box.

8. Click the large pointer to select it.

9. Right-click the large pointer, and select Pointer Properties from the context menu. The Radial Pointer Properties dialog box appears.

10. Set the following properties of the dialog box:

Property	Value
Pointer Options page:	
Needle style	Tapered with tail
Shadow page:	
Shadow offset	3pt

11. Click OK to exit the Radial Pointer Properties dialog box.

12. Right-click the small pointer, and select Pointer Properties from the context menu. The Radial Pointer Properties dialog box appears.

13. Set the following properties of the dialog box:

Property	Value
Pointer Fill page:	
Secondary color	Red
Shadow page:	
Shadow offset	6pt

14. Click OK to exit the Radial Pointer Properties dialog box.

15. Right-click the outer edge of the gauge, and select Add Range For | RadialScale1 from the context menu. A range appears on the gauge as shown.

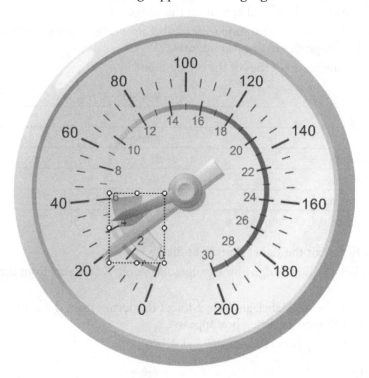

16. Right-click the range and select Range Properties from the context menu. The Radial Scale Range Properties dialog box appears.

17. Set the following properties in the dialog box:

Property	Value
General page:	
Start range at scale value	0
End range at scale value	20
Placement relative to scale	Outside
Fill page:	
Color	Red
Secondary color	White
Border page:	
Line style	None

18. Click OK to exit the Radial Scale Range Properties dialog box.

19. Right-click the outer edge of the gauge, and select Add Label from the context menu. The word "Text" will appear on the gauge.

20. Right-click the word "Text" and select Label Properties from the context menu. The Label Properties dialog box appears.

21. Set the following properties of the dialog box:

Property	Value
General page:	
Text	Deliveries
Top (percent)	80
Left (percent)	40
Width (percent)	19
Height (percent)	9

22. Click OK to exit the Label Properties dialog box.

23. Right-click the outer edge of the gauge, and select Add Label from the context menu.

24. Right-click the new label, and select Label Properties from the context menu. The Label Properties dialog box appears.

25. Set the following properties of the dialog box:

Property	Value
General page:	
Text	Lost
Top (percent)	71
Left (percent)	45
Width (percent)	21
Height (percent)	6
Font page:	
Color	Red

26. Click OK to exit the Label Properties dialog box.

27. Preview/Run the report.

28. Enter **3/1/2012** for Gauge Date, and click View Report. Your report should appear as shown.

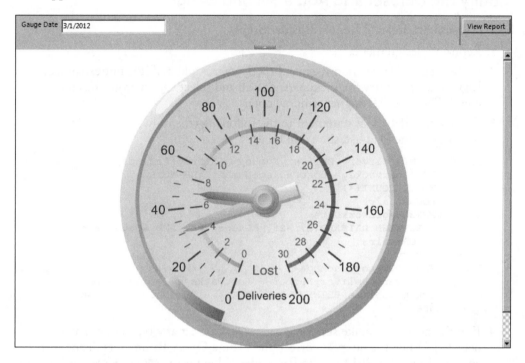

Task Notes   As with the chart report item, the gauge uses several properties dialog boxes, which enable you to change its configuration. There are properties dialog boxes to configure each pointer, each scale, each range, and one for the gauge itself. The chart and the gauge are also similar in that we can add new items to build a rich data presentation for the user. On the chart, we can add titles and legends, and even new chart areas. On the gauge, we can add scales, pointers, ranges, labels, and, as we will see in the next task, even new gauges.

On a gauge, it is often helpful to provide the user with visual clues for interpreting the data. We do this in two ways on our gauge. First, we use the range with the outer scale to indicate when deliveries are getting to be too few and far between. Second, the gradient shading from yellow to red—the bar with the inner scale—aids the user in determining when the number of lost packages approaches an unacceptable level.

Digital Dashboard, Task 3:
Modify the Dataset and Add a Second Gauge

`DT`
`RB`

SSDT, Visual Studio, and Report Builder Steps

1. Return to design mode.

2. In the Report Data window, expand the Datasets folder, if it is not expanded. Right-click the entry for PickupsAndLost, and select Query from the context menu. The Query Designer window opens.

3. Change the SELECT statement to the following (the only change is the subquery in the field list, shown in bold):

```
SELECT COUNT(Delivery.DeliveryNumber) AS NumOfPickups,
       COUNT(LostPackage.LostPackageNumber) AS NumLost,
       (SELECT COUNT(*)
        FROM Repair
        WHERE BeginWorkDate
           BETWEEN DATEADD(d, -28, @GaugeDate) AND @GaugeDate)
       AS NumRepairs
FROM Delivery
LEFT OUTER JOIN LostPackage
       ON Delivery.DeliveryNumber = LostPackage.DeliveryNumber
WHERE PickupDateTime BETWEEN DATEADD(d, -28, @GaugeDate) AND
@GaugeDate
```

4. Run the query and make sure no errors exist. Correct any typos that may be detected. When the query is correct, the Define Query Parameters dialog box appears. Enter **3/1/2012** for the Parameter Value for the @GaugeDate parameter, and click OK.

5. Click OK to exit the Query Designer window.

6. Right-click the edge of the gauge, and select Add Gauge | Adjacent from the context menu. The Select Gauge Type dialog box appears.

7. Select the Three Color Range gauge from the Linear list as shown here.

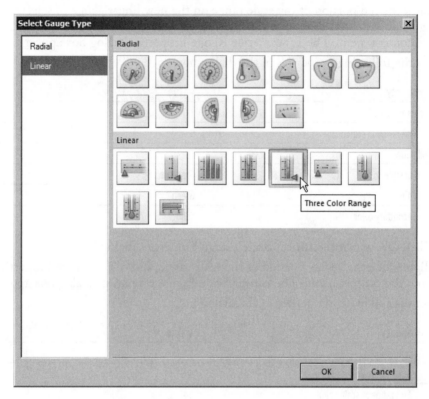

8. Click OK to exit the Select Gauge Type dialog box.
9. Right-click the new gauge, and select Gauge Properties from the context menu. The Linear Gauge Properties dialog box appears.
10. Set the following properties of the dialog box:

Property	Value
General page:	
Auto-fit all gauges in panel	Unchecked
X position (percent)	71
Y position (percent)	0
Width (percent)	20
Height (percent)	100
Aspect ratio (defined as width over height)	0.3

11. Click OK to exit the Linear Gauge Properties dialog box.

12. Click the red portion of the scale range on the new linear gauge to select it. Now right-click the red portion of the scale range, and select Range Properties from the context menu. The Linear Scale Range Properties dialog box appears.

13. Set the following properties in the dialog box:

Property	Value
General page:	
End range at scale value	6
Fill page:	
Fill style	Gradient
Color	Green
Secondary color	Yellow

14. Click OK to exit the Linear Scale Range Properties dialog box.

15. Right-click the yellow portion of the scale range, and select Range Properties from the context menu. The Linear Scale Range Properties dialog box appears.

16. Set the following properties in the dialog box:

Property	Value
General page:	
Start range at scale value	6
End range at scale value	14
Fill page:	
Fill style	Gradient
Color	Yellow
Secondary color	Orange

17. Click OK to exit the Linear Scale Range Properties dialog box.

18. Right-click the green portion of the scale range, and select Range Properties from the context menu. The Linear Scale Range Properties dialog box appears.

19. Set the following properties in the dialog box:

Property	Value
General page:	
Start range at scale value	14
End range at scale value	20

Property	Value
Fill page:	
Fill style	Gradient
Color	Orange
Secondary color	Red

20. Click OK to exit the Linear Scale Range Properties dialog box.
21. Right-click the scale, and select Scale Properties from the context menu. The Linear Scale Properties dialog box appears.
22. Set the following property in the dialog box:

Property	Value
General page:	
Maximum	20

23. Click OK to exit the Linear Scale Properties dialog box.
24. Right-click the outer rim of the gauge, and select Add Label from the context menu. The word "Text" is added to the gauge.
25. Right-click the word "Text" and select Label Properties from the context menu. The Label Properties dialog box appears.
26. Set the following properties in the dialog box:

Property	Value
General page:	
Text	Repairs
Text alignment	Center
Vertical alignment	Middle
Top (percent)	27
Left (percent)	47
Width (percent)	63
Height (percent)	45
Angle (degree)	270

27. Click OK to exit the Label Properties dialog box.
28. In the Gauge Data window there is a new entry for LinearPointer1 and a new (Unspecified) item below it. Click the drop-down arrow to the right of the (Unspecified) entry, and select the NumRepairs field.
29. Preview/Run the report.

30. Enter **3/1/2012** for Gauge Date, and click View Report. Your report should appear as shown.

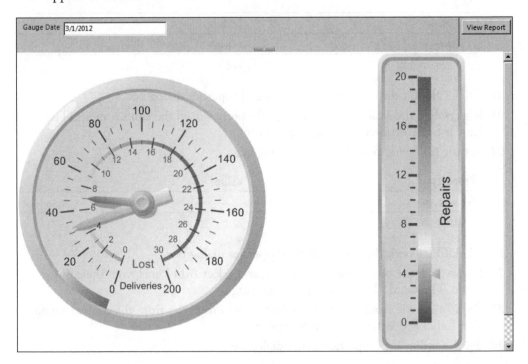

31. If you are using SSDT or Visual Studio, click Save All on the toolbar. If you are using Report Builder, save the report as "DigitalDashboard" in the Chapter06 folder on the report server.

Task Notes   The modification we made to the SELECT statement may look a bit strange. We are adding the count of repairs to the result set. However, repairs are not related to deliveries. The only thing they have in common is the fact that we are using the same date range. Therefore, we add the count of repairs by simply adding a subquery in the field list. This works in this case because we are only expecting a single row in the result set.

Image Is Everything

You have seen in the previous sections that charts and gauges allow us to create some pretty flashy output in a short time. Now it is time to turn our attention to two other methods for adding color to a report. One way is through the use of borders and background colors. Almost all report items have properties you can use to specify borders and background colors.

The other way to add color to your reports is through the use of images. Images can be placed on a report using the image report item. They can serve as a background for other report items. They can even serve as the background to the main body of the report itself.

In addition to determining where an image is placed on the report, you have to determine where the image will come from. Images can be stored in the report project, embedded in the report itself, pulled from a binary field in a database, or obtained from the Web using a Uniform Resource Locator (URL). Each image location has its own benefits and drawbacks.

Images stored in the report project are, of course, saved as separate files. They are not stored as part of the report definition. This means when the report is rendered, the renderer must find each of these image files to render the report correctly.

Images stored in the report project are easier to update if they have to be changed in the future. You can simply modify the image file because it is not embedded in a report definition file. These images can also be shared among several reports. However, because the report and its required images exist as separate files, some care has to be taken to ensure that the renderer can always locate the images when it is rendering the report.

Embedded images are stored right in the report definition file. With embedded images, only one file is required for rendering the report. There is no risk of the renderer being unable to find a required image. The downside of embedded images is it is more difficult to update an image. To change an embedded image, you need to modify the source image, re-embed the modified image, and redeploy the report. Also, it is impossible to share an embedded image between reports. The image can only be used by the report in which it is embedded.

Images stored in a database file can be shared among reports and are easy to track down when a report is rendered. In addition, when images are stored with the data in the database, it is possible to use a different image in your report for each row in the dataset. This is more difficult to do with project or embedded images.

Images in the database do pose two concerns. First, retrieving images from the database puts an additional load on your database server. Care must be taken to make sure your server can handle this additional load without degradation in response time. Second, managing large binary objects, such as images, in database records is not always a trivial task.

Images obtained through the Internet have a number of advantages. They can be easily shared among tens or even hundreds of reports; all the reports simply reference the same URL. They can be updated easily; just post a new image to the web server, and all the reports will reference this new version. In addition, web servers are designed for serving images, so there should not be an issue with additional load on the web server, unless it is extremely busy already.

The downside to obtaining images from a web server is this: the renderer must take the time to make a Hypertext Transfer Protocol (HTTP) request for each image it needs to put in the report. If the image's URL points to the report server itself or if it points to another server on the same internal network, this may not be a big deal. If, on the other hand, the URL points to a server across the Internet from the report server, the time required for rendering will increase. You also need to ensure that the report server can always connect to the web server hosting the image.

As a rule of thumb, images to be shared among many reports, such as company logos, should be kept either in the report project or accessed through a URL. These shared images should be put in one central location so they can be accessed by the reports when they are needed. Images that have a strong association with data in a particular record in a database table should be stored in the database itself. For example, a picture of a particular employee has a strong association with that employee's record in the Employee table. We are only interested in displaying the picture of a particular employee when the row in the dataset for that employee is being processed. Any images that do not fall into these two categories should be embedded in the report to ease deployment issues.

Conference Nametags

Features Highlighted

► Using background colors on report items

► Using borders on report items

► Placing an image on a report

Business Need   Galactic Delivery Services is preparing for its annual customer conference. The billing contact for each customer has been invited to the conference. As part of the preparations, the GDS art department must create nametags for the conference attendees. Because the names of all the billing contacts are available in the Galactic database and this database can be accessed easily from Reporting Services, the art department has decided to use Reporting Services to create the nametags.

The conference nametags should include the name of the attendee and the name of the company they work for. The art department would like the nametags to be bright and colorful. They should include the GDS logo.

NOTE

The image files used in the reports in this chapter are available on the website for this book. If you have not done so already, go to www.mhprofessional.com. Search for the book's webpage using the ISBN, which is 0071760474, and then use the "Sample Code" link to download the zip file containing the book's material. Follow the instructions to unzip the image files.

Task Overview

1. Place the GDS.gif File in the Appropriate Location
2. Create a New Report, Create a Dataset, and Place the Report Items on the Report

Conference Nametags, Task 1: Place the GDS.gif File in the Appropriate Location

DT **SSDT and Visual Studio Steps**

1. Find the GDS.gif file in the materials downloaded for this book. (It is in ImagesFiles.Zip inside of the main zip file.) Copy this to a location on your computer.
2. Reopen the Chapter06 project, if it was closed. Close the DigitalDashboard report.
3. Right-click the Reports entry in the Solution Explorer window, and select Add | Existing Item from the context menu. The Add Existing Item - Chapter06 dialog box appears.
4. Select All Files (*.*) from the drop-down list right above the Add and Cancel buttons.
5. Browse to the copy of the GDS.gif file you just saved. Select the GDS.gif file, and click Add. The GDS.gif file is added to the Chapter06 project.
6. Add a blank report called Nametags to the Chapter06 project.

RB **Report Builder Steps**

1. Find the GDS.gif file in the materials downloaded for this book. (It is in ImagesFiles. Zip inside of the main zip file.) Copy this to a location on your computer.
2. Using Report Manager, navigate to the Chapter06 folder.
3. Click Upload File. The Upload File page appears.
4. Click Browse. The Choose File to Upload dialog box appears.
5. Browse to the copy of the GDS.gif file you just saved. Select the GDS.gif file, and click Open.

6. Click OK to upload the file. You will see the GDS.gif file in the Chapter06 folder along with all of the reports you have created for this chapter.

7. Create a new blank report.

8. Delete the "Click to add title" text box.

9. Right-click in the page footer area of the report (the area below the dashed line), and select Remove Page Footer from the context menu.

Task Notes We will use the GDS.gif image as an external image in the following steps. If you are using SSDT or Visual Studio, this means we just added the image to the project. If you are using Report Builder, this means we just uploaded the image to the report server.

Conference Nametags, Task 2: Create a New Report, Create a Dataset, and Place the Report Items on the Report

| DT |
| RB |

SSDT, Visual Studio, and Report Builder Steps

1. In the Report Data window, click the New drop-down menu. Select Data Source from the menu that appears. The Data Source Properties dialog box appears.

2. As we have done previously, create a new data source named **Galactic** that references the Galactic shared data source. Click OK to exit the Data Source Properties dialog box.

3. In the Report Data window, right-click the entry for the Galactic data source, and select Add Dataset from the context menu. The Dataset Properties dialog box appears.

4. Enter **BillingContacts** for the name.

5. Click the Query Designer button. The Query Designer window opens.

6. Click the Edit as Text button to switch to the Generic Query Designer.

7. Enter the following in the SQL pane (upper portion) of the Generic Query Designer window:

```
SELECT BillingContact, Name
FROM Customer
ORDER BY BillingContact
```

8. Run the query to make sure no errors exist. Correct any typos that may be detected.

9. Click OK to exit the Query Designer window. Click OK to exit the Dataset Properties dialog box.

10. Select the list report item in the Toolbox window/Insert ribbon, and place it on the design surface. This will create a tablix report item using the list template. Modify the following properties of the tablix in the Properties window:

Property	Value
BackgroundColor	DarkOrange (Either type **DarkOrange** in place of "No Color" in the Properties window or use the color picker drop-down list in the Properties window and select the More colors link.)
Location: Left	0.125in
Location: Top	0.125in
Size: Width	4.75in
Size: Height	2.125in

We are using the list template to create the tablix for this report because it is going to have a freeform layout rather than the rows and columns of a table or matrix.

11. In the Report Data window, drag the BillingContact field onto the tablix. Click the BillingContact text box to select it, and use the Properties window to modify the following properties:

Property	Value
BackgroundColor	Gold
BorderColor: Default	DarkBlue
BorderStyle: Default	Solid
BorderWidth: Default	4pt
Color	DarkBlue
Font: FontSize	20pt
Font: FontWeight	Bold
Location: Left	0.125in
Location: Top	0.125in
Size: Width	4.5in
Size: Height	0.5in
TextAlign	Center
VerticalAlign	Middle

12. Drag the Name field from the Report Data window onto the tablix. Click the Name text box to select it, and using the Properties window, modify the following properties:

Property	Value
BackgroundColor	Gold
BorderColor: Default	DarkBlue
BorderStyle: Default	Solid
BorderWidth: Default	4pt
Color	DarkBlue
Font: FontSize	16pt
Font: FontWeight	Bold
Location: Left	0.125in
Location: Top	0.875in
Size: Width	4.5in
Size: Height	0.375in
TextAlign	Center
VerticalAlign	Middle

13. Place a text box from the Toolbox/Insert ribbon onto the tablix. Click the resulting text box to select it, and modify the following properties:

Property	Value
Font: FontSize	23pt
Location: Left	1in
Location: Top	1.375in
Size: Width	3.625in
Size: Height	0.625in
TextAlign	Center
VerticalAlign	Middle

14. Click this text box again so the blinking edit cursor appears. Type **GDS Conference 2013**.

15. Place a line from the Toolbox/Insert ribbon onto the tablix. Click the resulting line to select it, and modify the following properties of the line *in this order*:

Property	Value
Location: Left	0in
Location: Top	2.125in
EndPoint: Horizontal	4.75in
EndPoint: Vertical	2.125in
LineColor	DarkBlue
LineWidth	10pt

16. Place an image report item from the Toolbox/Insert ribbon onto the list. The Image Properties dialog box appears.

17. In the Select the image source drop-down list, select External.

18. If you are using SSDT or Visual Studio, in the Use this image drop-down list, select GDS.gif. This is the image file you added to the project in the previous task.

19. If you are using Report Builder, click the Browse button. Navigate to the GDS.gif image you uploaded to the report server in the previous task. Select GDS.gif and click Open.

20. Click OK to exit the Image Properties dialog box.

21. Click the image to select it, if it is not selected already, and modify the following properties using the Properties window:

Property	Value
Location: Left	0.125in
Location: Top	1.375in
Sizing	AutoSize

22. Check to make sure the tablix is still the correct size. Select the tablix, and then use the Properties window to change the dimensions to match the following, if necessary:

Property	Value
Size: Width	4.75in
Size: Height	2.125in

NOTE

Clicking the orange background will select the rectangle in the tablix cell, not the tablix itself. To select the tablix, click the gray square in the upper-left corner of the tablix.

23. Click in the design surface outside of the tablix. This causes the report body to be selected in the Properties window. Modify the following properties of the report body:

Property	Value
BackgroundColor	DarkBlue
Size: Width	5in
Size: Height	2.25in

24. Preview/Run the report. The nametags are ready to be printed, cut apart, and placed in nametag holders, as shown here.

25. If you are using SSDT or Visual Studio, click Save All on the toolbar. If you are using Report Builder, save the report as "Nametags" in the Chapter06 folder on the report server.

Task Notes We used several properties of the report items in our Conference Nametags report to add color. The BackgroundColor property controls the color in the background of the report item. This defaults to Transparent, meaning that whatever is behind the item shows through. When the BackgroundColor property is set to a color rather than Transparent, that color fills in and covers up everything behind the item.

The BorderColor property controls the color of the border around the outside of the report item. BorderColor works in cooperation with two other properties: BorderStyle and BorderWidth. The BorderStyle property defaults to None. When BorderStyle is None, the border is invisible. No matter what color you set for BorderColor, it does not show up when the BorderStyle is set to None.

To have a visible border around an item, you must change the BorderStyle property to a solid line (Solid), a dotted line (Dotted), a dashed line (Dashed), a double line (Double), or one of the other settings in the BorderStyle drop-down list. Once you select one of these visible settings for the BorderStyle property, you can set the color of the border using the BorderColor property and the thickness of the border using the BorderWidth property.

The border settings for each side of a report item can be controlled separately or altogether. If you expand any of the three border properties, you can see they have separate entries for Default, Left, Right, Top, and Bottom. The Default property is, as it says, the default value for all four sides of the report item. When the Left, Right, Top, or Bottom property is blank, the setting for that particular side is taken from the Default property. For example, if the BorderStyle: Default property is set to None and BorderStyle: Left, BorderStyle: Right, BorderStyle: Top, and BorderStyle: Bottom are all blank, then there is no border around the report item. If the BorderStyle: Bottom property is set to Double, this overrides the default setting and a double line appears across the bottom of the item. The borders on the other three sides of the item (left, right, and top) continue to use the default setting.

The Color property controls the color of the text created by a report item. There is a Color property for each text box, which is expected, because the main purpose of a text box is to create text. You also find a Color property for the tablix data region. The tablix can create a text message when no rows are in the dataset attached to it. The Color property specifies the color of the text in this special "no rows" message when it is displayed. (We discuss the "no rows" message more in Chapter 8.)

The final color property we used in the Conference Nametags report is the LineColor property. This property exists only for line report items. It should come as no surprise that this property controls the color of the line.

We used the TextAlign property to adjust the way text is placed horizontally inside a text box (left, center, or right). In this report, we also used the VerticalAlign property to adjust the way text is placed vertically inside a text box (top, middle, or bottom). The vertical alignment of text in a text box is not usually an issue unless the border of the text box is visible and you can see where the text is being placed relative to the top and bottom of the text box.

Conference Place Cards

Features Highlighted

▶ Using background images on report items

▶ Using an embedded image

▶ Using the WritingMode property of a text box

Business Need   Galactic Delivery Services is continuing its preparations for the annual customer conference. In addition to the nametags, the GDS art department must create place cards for the conference attendees. The place cards are going to be put on the table in front of each attendee during roundtable discussions. As with the nametags, place cards should be created for all the billing contacts.

The conference place cards should include the name of the attendee and the name of the company they work for. The art department would like the place cards to continue the color scheme set by the nametags, but with a more intricate pattern. They should include the GDS logo.

Task Overview

1. Create a New Report, Create a Dataset, and Place the Report Items on the Report

Conference Place Cards, Task 1: Create a New Report, Create a Dataset, and Place the Report Items on the Report

`DT`
`RB`
SSDT, Visual Studio, and Report Builder Steps

1. Find the GDSBackOval.gif, GDSBackRect.gif, and GDSBig.gif files in the materials downloaded for this book. (They are in ImagesFiles.Zip inside of the main zip file.) Copy these files to a location on your computer.

2. If you are using SSDT or Visual Studio, reopen the Chapter06 project, if it was closed. Close the Nametags report, and add a blank report called PlaceCards to the Chapter06 project.

3. If you are using Report Builder, create a new blank report, delete the "Click to add title" text box, and remove the page footer.

4. In the Report Data window, click the New drop-down menu. Select Data Source from the menu that appears. The Data Source Properties dialog box appears.

5. As we have done previously, create a new data source named **Galactic** that references the Galactic shared data source. Click OK to exit the Data Source Properties dialog box.

6. In the Report Data window, right-click the entry for the Galactic data source, and select Add Dataset from the context menu. The Dataset Properties dialog box appears.

7. Enter **BillingContacts** for the name.

8. Click the Query Designer button. The Query Designer window opens.

9. Click the Edit as Text button to switch to the Generic Query Designer.

10. Enter the following in the SQL pane (upper portion) of the Generic Query Designer window:

```
SELECT BillingContact, Name
FROM Customer
ORDER BY BillingContact
```

11. Run the query to make sure no errors exist. Correct any typos that may be detected.

12. Click OK to exit the Query Designer window. Click OK to exit the Dataset Properties dialog box.

13. In the Report Data window, right-click the Images entry, and select Add Image from the context menu. The Open dialog box appears.

14. Select GIF files from the drop-down list above the Open and Cancel buttons. Navigate to the location where you stored the images in Step 1. Select the GDSBackOval.gif file, and click Open. This image is now embedded in the report. It will be encoded as part of the Report Definition Language (RDL) file.

15. In the Report Data window, right-click the Images entry again, and select Add Image from the context menu. The Open dialog box appears.

16. Select GIF files from the Files of type drop-down list. Navigate to the location where you stored the images in Step 1. Select the GDSBackRect.gif image file, and click Open. This image is also embedded in the report.

17. In the Report Data window, right-click the Images entry again, and select Add Image from the context menu. The Open dialog box appears.

18. Select GIF files from the Files of type drop-down list. Navigate to the location where you stored the images in Step 1. Select the GDSBig.gif image file, and click Open. This image is also embedded in the report.

19. Click the design surface. This causes the report body to be selected in the Properties window. Modify the following properties of the report body:

Property	Value
BackgroundColor	DarkOrange
BackgroundImage: Source	Embedded
BackgroundImage: Value	GDSBackRect (The drop-down list shows all the images embedded in the report.)
Size: Width	8.875in
Size: Height	3.2in

20. Place a list from the Toolbox window/Insert ribbon onto the report layout. Modify the following properties of the resulting tablix:

Property	Value
Location: Left	0in
Location: Top	0in
Size: Width	8.75in
Size: Height	3.2in

21. In the Report Data window, drag the BillingContact field onto the tablix. Click the BillingContact text box to select it, and use the Properties window to modify the following properties:

Property	Value
BackgroundImage: Source	Embedded
BackgroundImage: Value	GDSBackOval
Font: FontSize	30pt
Font: FontWeight	Bold
Location: Left	2.5in
Location: Top	1.75in
Size: Width	6.125in
Size: Height	0.625in
TextAlign	Center
VerticalAlign	Middle

22. Drag the Name field from the Report Data window onto the tablix. Click the Name text box to select it, and, using the Properties window, modify the following properties:

Property	Value
BackgroundImage: Source	Embedded
BackgroundImage: Value	GDSBackOval
Color	DarkBlue
Font: FontSize	30pt
Font: FontWeight	Bold
Location: Left	2.5in
Location: Top	2.5in

Property	Value
Size: Width	6.125in
Size: Height	0.625in
TextAlign	Center
VerticalAlign	Middle

23. In the Report Data window, select the entry for the GDSBig image. Drag this item onto the tablix near the top. The Image Properties dialog box appears.

24. Click OK to exit the Image Properties dialog box.

25. Click the image to select it, and modify the following properties of the image in the Properties window:

Property	Value
BorderStyle: Default	Double
BorderWidth: Default	3pt
Location: Left	0.3in
Location: Top	1.715in
Size: Width	1.625in
Size: Height	1.375in
Sizing	Fit

26. Make sure the rectangle in the tablix is selected, and then place a text box from the Toolbox window/Insert ribbon onto the tablix.

27. Double-click the text box so the blinking edit cursor appears. Type **GDS Conference 2013**, and then press ESC.

28. The text box should be selected. Modify the following properties of this text box:

Property	Value
Font: FontSize	9pt
Font: FontWeight	Bold
Location: Left	0.05in
Location: Top	1.715in
Size: Width	0.25in
Size: Height	1.375in
TextAlign	Center
WritingMode	Vertical

29. Make sure the rectangle in the tablix is selected, and then place a second text box from the Toolbox window/Insert ribbon onto the tablix.

30. Double-click this text box so the blinking edit cursor appears. Type **GDS Conference 2013**, and then press ESC.

31. The text box should be selected. Modify the following properties of this text box:

Property	Value
Font: FontSize	9pt
Font: FontWeight	Bold
Location: Left	1.925in
Location: Top	1.715in
Size: Width	0.25in
Size: Height	1.375in
TextAlign	Center
VerticalAlign	Bottom
WritingMode	Rotate270

32. Preview/Run the report. The place cards are ready to be printed, cut apart, folded, and placed on the tables, as shown here.

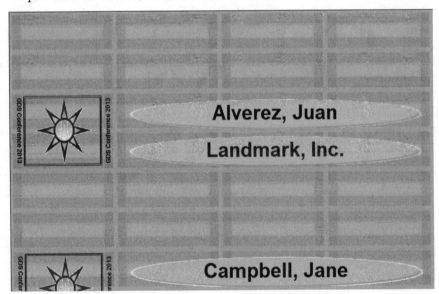

33. If you are using SSDT or Visual Studio, click Save All on the toolbar. If you are using Report Builder, save the report as "PlaceCards" in the Chapter06 folder on the report server.

Task Notes In this report, we used embedded images instead of external images, as we did in the previous report. Remember, the method of storing the image has nothing to do with the way the image is used in the report. External images can be used as background images. Embedded images can be used in image report items.

The Images entry in the Report Data window enables you to manage the images embedded in the report. Remember, an embedded image remains in the report even if no report item is referencing it. The only way to remove an embedded image from a report is to delete it from the Report Data window. Always remove embedded images from the report if they are not being used. This way, the report definition does not become any larger than it needs to be.

In this report, we also used the WritingMode property to rotate the content of one text box by 90 degrees and the content of another text box by 270 degrees. The normal writing mode for English text in a text box is horizontal. We changed this default writing mode and told these two text boxes to output our text vertically. The WritingMode property was implemented to allow Reporting Services to work with languages written from top to bottom and right to left, a vertical writing format rather than the horizontal format that is used for English. However, that does not prevent us from using the WritingMode property to produce a fancy effect with our English text.

The Rate Sheet Report

Features Highlighted

- ▶ Using database images
- ▶ Using rectangle report items within table cells

Business Need The Galactic Delivery Services marketing department needs to produce a new rate sheet. The rate sheet needs to include a description of each type of delivery service provided by GDS. Each type has its own image to help customers remember the three types of service. The rate sheet also includes the name of each service type with a longer description below it and the cost of each service type off to the right side of the page.

Because all the information on the three types of service is available in the database, the marketing department wants to produce the rate sheet from a report rather than creating or updating a document each time the rates change.

Task Overview

1. Create a New Report, Create a Dataset, and Place the Report Items on the Report
2. Refine the Report Layout

Rate Sheet Report, Task 1: Create a New Report, Create a Dataset, and Place the Report Items on the Report Layout

DT

RB

SSDT, Visual Studio, and Report Builder Steps

1. If you are using SSDT or Visual Studio, reopen the Chapter06 project, if it was closed. Close the PlaceCards report, and add a blank report called RateSheet to the Chapter06 project.

2. If you are using Report Builder, create a new blank report.

3. In the Report Data window, click the New drop-down menu. Select Data Source from the menu that appears. The Data Source Properties dialog box appears.

4. As we have done previously, create a new data source named **Galactic** that references the Galactic shared data source. Click OK to exit the Data Source Properties dialog box.

5. In the Report Data window, right-click the entry for the Galactic data source, and select Add Dataset from the context menu. The Dataset Properties dialog box appears.

6. Enter **ServiceTypes** for the name.

7. Click the Query Designer button. The Query Designer window opens.

8. Click the Edit as Text button to switch to the Generic Query Designer.

9. Enter the following in the SQL pane (upper portion) of the Generic Query Designer window:

```
SELECT Description, LongDescription, Cost, PriceSheetImage
FROM ServiceType
ORDER BY Cost
```

10. Run the query to make sure no errors exist. Correct any typos that may be detected.

11. Click OK to exit the Query Designer window. Click OK to exit the Dataset Properties dialog box.

12. Make the design surface larger, and then place an image report item from the Toolbox window/Insert ribbon onto the report layout. The Image Properties dialog box appears.

13. In the Select the image source drop-down list, select External.

14. If you are using SSDT or Visual Studio, select GDS.gif from the Use this image drop-down list.

15. If you are using Report Builder, click Browse. Navigate to the Chapter06 folder. Select the GDS.gif image file, and click Open.

16. Click OK to exit the Image Properties dialog box.

17. Modify the following properties of the image:

Property	Value
Location: Left	0in
Location: Top	0in
Sizing	AutoSize

18. If you are using SSDT or Visual Studio, drag a text box from the Toolbox onto the report layout. If you are using Report Builder, select the "Click to add title" text box.

19. Modify the following properties of this text box:

Property	Value
Color	DarkBlue
Font: FontFamily	Arial
Font: FontSize	30pt
Font: FontWeight	Bold
Location: Left	0.875in
Location: Top	0in
Size: Width	6in
Size: Height	0.625in
VerticalAlign	Middle

20. Click this text box again so the blinking edit cursor appears. Type **Galactic Delivery Services**.

21. Place a text box from the Toolbox window/Insert ribbon onto the report layout. Modify the following properties of this text box:

Property	Value
Color	DarkOrange
Font: FontSize	25pt
Font: FontWeight	Bold
Location: Left	0.875in
Location: Top	0.625in
Size: Width	6in
Size: Height	0.5in
VerticalAlign	Middle

22. Click this text box again so the blinking edit cursor appears. Type **Type of Service**.

23. Place a text box from the Toolbox window/Insert ribbon onto the report layout. Modify the following properties of this text box:

Property	Value
Color	Gold
Font: FontSize	20pt
Font: FontWeight	Bold
Format	MMMM d, yyyy
Location: Left	0.875in
Location: Top	1.125in
Size: Width	6in
Size: Height	0.5in
TextAlign	Left
VerticalAlign	Middle

24. Right-click the last text box added to the report, and select Expression from the context menu. The Expression dialog box appears.

25. Click Built-in Fields in the Category pane.

26. Double-click ExecutionTime in the Item pane.

27. Click OK to exit the Expression dialog box.

28. Place a table from the Toolbox window/Insert ribbon onto the report layout to create a tablix.

29. Click the tablix to activate the gray sizing rectangles.

30. Right-click in the gray rectangle to the left of the header row. Select Delete Rows from the context menu. This removes the header row.

31. Click the gray square in the upper-left corner of the tablix. This selects the tablix. Modify the following properties of the tablix:

Property	Value
DataSetName	ServiceTypes
Location: Left	0.875in
Location: Top	1.75in
Size: Width	6.25in
Size: Height	2.125in

32. Place an image report item from the Toolbox window/Insert ribbon in the leftmost table cell. The Image Properties dialog box appears.
33. In the Select the image source drop-down list, select Database.
34. In the Use this field drop-down list, select [PriceSheetImage].
35. In the Use this MIME type drop-down list, select image/gif.
36. Click OK to exit the Image Properties dialog box.
37. Click the center table cell, and then select the Description field from the Field Selector. Modify the following properties of the text box in this cell:

Property	Values
BorderStyle: Default	None
Color	DarkBlue
Font: FontSize	14pt
Font: FontWeight	Bold
Size: Width	2.45in

38. Click the rightmost table cell, and then select the Cost field from the Field Selector. Modify the following properties of the text box in this cell:

Property	Values
BorderStyle	None
Font: FontSize	14pt
Format	$###,##0.00
VerticalAlign	Middle

39. Preview/Run the report. Your report appears similar to the illustration.

 Galactic Delivery Services

Type of Service

June 12, 2011

 Next Day Delivery

$14.75

 Same Day Delivery

$22.50

 Previous Day Delivery

$74.95

Task Notes   In the Rate Sheet Report, we used image data stored in a database table. As we discussed earlier in the chapter, this allows the report to have a different image for each row in the table report object. The Next Day Delivery row, the Same Day Delivery row, and the Previous Day Delivery row each have their own unique image on the report.

We have one requirement left to fulfill. The business needs specified that the long description of the service type should come below the name of that service type. Let's reformat our report to include the long description in the report.

Rate Sheet Report, Task 2: Refine the Report Layout

1. Return to design mode.
2. Click the center table cell. This selects the text box in the cell.
3. Press DELETE to remove the text box.
4. Place a rectangle from the Toolbox window/Insert ribbon in the center table cell. A rectangle report item is now in the center table cell.
5. Drag the Description field from the Report Data window onto the rectangle you just created.
6. Click the resulting text box to select it and modify the following properties:

Property	Value
Color	DarkBlue
Font: FontSize	14pt
Font: FontWeight	Bold
Location: Left	0.125in
Location: Top	0.125in
Size: Width	2.3in
Size: Height	0.375in

7. Drag the LongDescription field from the Report Data window onto the same rectangle that contains the text box for the Description field. Click the resulting text box to select it, and modify the following properties:

Property	Value
Location: Left	0.125in
Location: Top	0.625in
Size: Width	2.3in
Size: Height	0.875in

8. Preview/Run the report. Your report appears similar to the illustration.

9. If you are using SSDT or Visual Studio, click Save All on the toolbar. If you are using Report Builder, save the report as "RateSheet" in the Chapter06 folder on the report server.

Task Notes   In reviewing this task, you can see the rectangle allowed us to do some creative formatting within a table cell. The business needs specified the long description of the service type should appear below the name of the service type. We could accomplish this by putting a rectangle in the center table cell and then putting two text boxes inside the rectangle.

This is similar to what happens when we use the list template to create a tablix. The tablix has a single cell, which is filled with a rectangle. This rectangle then enables the freeform layout we expect from a list.

The Rate Sheet report is ready to go.

From Graphical to Geo-graphical

In this chapter we looked at adding charts and graphics to our reports to let the data better tell its own story. In the next chapter, we look at another way for our reports to present data through a visual representation—that is, by using maps.

So, let's move on and study some geography.

Chapter 7

Geography Lesson: Using Maps and Spatial Data Types

In This Chapter

- ► **Colors and Bubbles: Representing Quantities on Maps**
- ► **Building Higher**

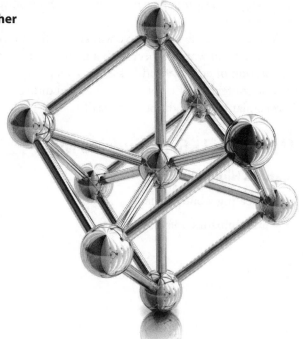

S ome of the data we seek to present to our users is geographical in nature. What are the sales for each territory? How are our customers distributed throughout the region? What does worldwide production of a given product or commodity look like? Being able to represent these facts and figures on a map gives the data instant context. The map data visualization lets you do just that.

Using the map data visualization, we can add instant meaning to data that has a geographic component. We can see that a trend correlates to population centers. It is easy to note that a particular opinion breaks down along regional lines. Conclusions that are not at all obvious from columns of location names and statistics jump off the page when data is plotted on a map.

Even if you can't tell Colorado from Wyoming in the United States or couldn't find Sweden, Switzerland, or Swaziland on a globe, you can use the map data visualization in Reporting Services. So grab your GPS and let's navigate the world of maps.

Colors and Bubbles: Representing Quantities on Maps

We are going to begin by associating quantities with regions on a map. This is done through two different techniques. First we look at putting a "bubble" over each geographic region. On this type of map, called a *bubble map*, the size of the bubble shows the relative size of the quantity being mapped. The second technique we examine involves changing the color or shading of the geographic region to represent relative quantities. This is known as a *color analytical map*.

At the end of the chapter, we will switch from representing quantities on a map to doing what you would expect with a map—namely, representing locations. We will plot the location of employee addresses on a map. In this example, we will use Bing maps to provide context for the points we plot. You didn't know Bing maps included the planet Noxicomian? You might be surprised!

The Earth U.S. Deliveries Map

Features Highlighted

▶ Creating a bubble map

▶ Manipulating map layout

Business Need   Galactic Delivery Services (GDS) is considering expanding its operations to include the planet Earth. While Earth is not a big participant in interplanetary commerce, it is believed that Earthlings' strong tendency toward procrastination will make the previous-day delivery service quite popular, even for packages going from one place to another on Earth. In order to determine where to establish shipping hubs, the GDS planning department needs a geographic representation of the volume of shipping by existing carriers in the United States of America. (My apologies to non-American readers. Please know that this exercise is not so much a manifestation of American ego as it is a reflection of the fact that SQL Server Reporting Services ships with only U.S. maps in its default map gallery.)

Task Overview

1. Create a New Report and a New Dataset
2. Place a Map Item on the Report and Populate It

Earth U.S. Deliveries Map, Task 1: Create a New Report and a New Dataset

DT   **SSDT and Visual Studio Steps**

1. Create a new Reporting Services project called **Chapter07** in the MSSQLRS folder. (If you need help with this task, see Chapter 5.)
2. Create a shared data source called **Galactic** for the Galactic database. (Again, if you need help with this task, see Chapter 5.)
3. Add a blank report called **Earth US Deliveries** to the Chapter07 project. (Do not use the Report Wizard.)
4. In the Report Data window, click the New drop-down menu. Select Data Source from the menu that appears. The Data Source Properties dialog box appears.
5. As we have done previously, create a new data source named **Galactic** that references the Galactic shared data source. Click OK to exit the Data Source Properties dialog box.
6. In the Report Data window, right-click the entry for the Galactic data source, and select Add Dataset from the context menu. The Dataset Properties dialog box appears.
7. Enter **EarthUSDeliveries** for the name.
8. Click the Query Designer button. The Query Designer window opens displaying the Graphical Query Designer. Click the Edit as Text button to switch to the Generic Query Designer.

9. Enter the following in the SQL pane (upper portion) of the Generic Query Designer window:

```
SELECT
   State,
   DeliveryCount
FROM
   EarthUSDelivery
```

10. Click the Run Query button on the Generic Query Designer toolbar to run the query and make sure no errors exist. Correct any typos that may be detected. Click OK to exit the Query Designer window. Click OK to exit the Dataset Properties dialog box.

`RB` **Report Builder Steps**

1. Using Report Manager, create a new folder in the Galactic Delivery Services folder. Enter **Chapter07** as the name of this folder. (If you need help with this task, see Chapter 5.)

2. Launch Report Builder from Report Manager.

3. With New Report highlighted in the left column, click Blank Report. The Report Builder shows a new blank report.

4. In the Report Data window, click the New drop-down menu. Select Data Source from the menu that appears. The Data Source Properties dialog box appears.

5. As we have done previously, create a new data source named **Galactic** that references the Galactic shared data source. Click OK to exit the Data Source Properties dialog box.

6. In the Report Data window, right-click the entry for the Galactic data source, and select Add Dataset from the context menu. The Dataset Properties dialog box appears.

7. Enter **EarthUSDeliveries** for the name.

8. Click the Query Designer button. The Query Designer window opens displaying the Graphical Query Designer.

9. Click the Edit as Text button to switch to the Generic Query Designer.

10. Enter the following in the SQL pane (upper portion) of the Generic Query Designer window:

```
SELECT
   State,
   DeliveryCount
FROM
   EarthUSDelivery
```

11. Click the Run Query button on the Generic Query Designer toolbar to run the query and make sure no errors exist. Correct any typos that may be detected. Click OK to exit the Query Designer window. Click OK to exit the Dataset Properties dialog box.

Task Notes   To put data on a map, we only need two columns in our result set. One column contains the label we will use to tie records to regions on our map. In this case, it is the state abbreviation in the State column. A second column contains the quantities to represent on the map. This is, of course, the DeliveryCount column.

Earth U.S. Deliveries Map, Task 2: Place a Map Item on the Report and Populate It

DT

RB

SSDT, Visual Studio, and Report Builder Steps

1. Drag the edges of the design surface to make it larger so the design surface fills the available space on the screen.

2. If you are using Report Builder, select the "Click to add title" text box, and delete it. (The title will be contained within the map itself.)

3. If you are using SSDT or Visual Studio, select the map report item in the Toolbox window. Click and drag to place the map on the design surface. The map should cover almost the entire design surface because it will be the only item on the report. The Choose a source of spatial data page of the Map Wizard appears.

4. If you are using Report Builder, click on Map in the Insert ribbon, and select Map Wizard. The Choose a source of spatial data page of the Map Wizard appears.

NOTE

In SSDT and Visual Studio, the Map Wizard dialog box is entitled "New Map Layer." In Report Builder, it is entitled "New Map." The wizard functions the same for all three. The images will come from SSDT, but apply to all three environments.

5. The Map gallery radio button should be selected to allow us to choose a map from the Map gallery.

6. Click on each of the three USA map options in the Map gallery and note the differences in the Map preview.

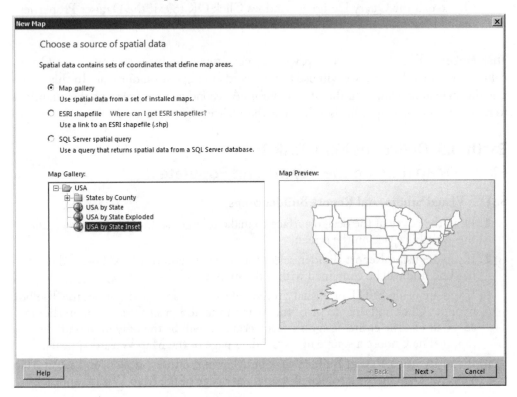

7. For this report, we will use the USA by State Inset map. Select this map and click Next. The Choose spatial data and map view options page of the wizard appears.

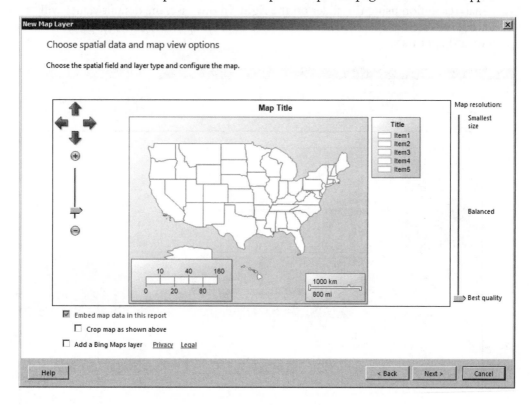

8. This page of the wizard allows you to adjust the size of the map using the slider on the left and to move the map using the four arrows. You can also adjust the map resolution using the slider on the right. In our case, the default values will work well for our map. Click Next. The Choose map visualization page of the wizard appears.

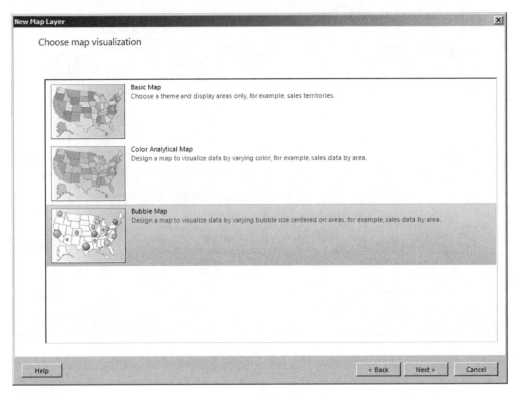

9. Click the Bubble Map item, and click Next. The Choose the analytical dataset page of the wizard appears.

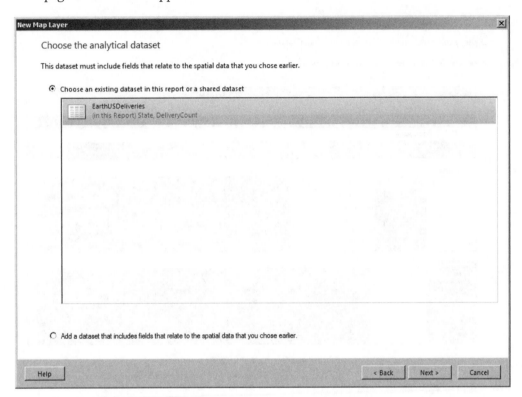

10. The Choose an existing dataset in this report or a shared dataset radio button should be selected by default. Select the entry for the EarthUSDeliveries dataset.

11. Click Next. The Specify the match fields for spatial and analytical data page of the wizard appears.

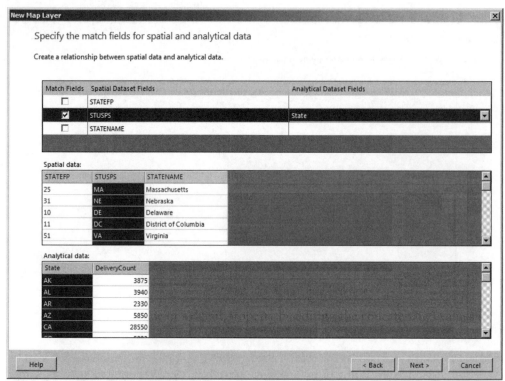

NOTE

The Spatial data (middle section) of the page shows content of the spatial data fields that go with the USA by State Inset map we selected earlier. These fields identify each region on the map—in this case, each state on the map. The Analytical data (bottom section) of the page shows the content of the EarthUSDeliveries dataset we created earlier and selected as our analytical dataset.

12. Our task on this page is to identify one spatial data field and one analytical data field that will tie analytical data to regions on the map. In the top section of the page, check the check box in the Match Fields column next to STUSPS. (STUSPS is the U.S. Postal Service state abbreviation.) A drop-down list will appear in the STUSPS row in the Analytical dataset fields column.

13. Select State from this drop-down list.

NOTE

This matching process between spatial data and analytical data is case-sensitive.

14. Click Next. The Choose color theme and data visualization page of the wizard appears.

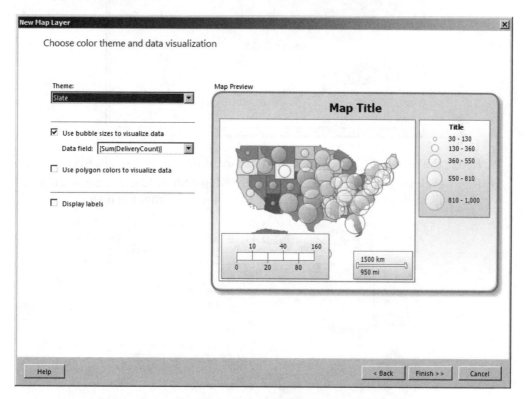

15. Select Slate from the Theme drop-down list.
16. The Use bubble sizes to visualize data check box should be checked. Select [Sum(DeliveryCount)] from the drop-down list right below this check box.

17. Click Finish. The map is created on the design surface as shown.

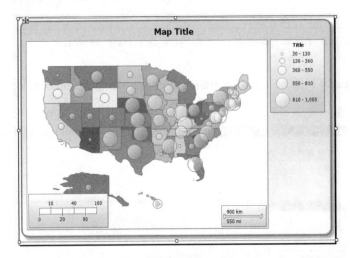

18. Resize the map to fill the entire design surface, if does not do so already.

19. Right-click anywhere in the map, and select Map | Show Color Scale as shown. This will uncheck this item and remove the color scale from the map.

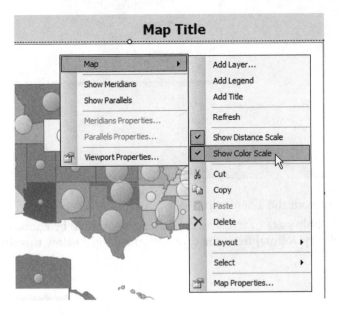

20. Double-click the Map Title, and replace "Map Title" with **Earth – US**, and then press ENTER.

21. Double-click the Title in the map legend showing the bubble size scale. Replace "Title" with **Deliveries**, and then press ENTER.

22. Preview/Run the report. The report should appear as shown.

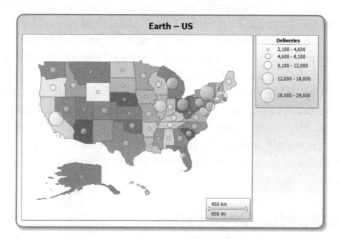

23. If you are using SSDT or Visual Studio, click Save All on the toolbar. If you are using Report Builder, save the report as **Earth US Deliveries** in the Chapter07 folder on the report server.

Task Notes   The size of the bubbles on our map is proportional to the number of deliveries made in each state. The scale on the right side of the map gives us an idea of the quantities associated with each size bubble. More important, however, is the relative size of the bubbles. This lets us quickly determine areas of the country that have higher concentrations of deliveries.

In Steps 12 and 13, we instructed the map as to how it should tie analytical data from the EarthUSDeliveries dataset we created with the spatial data inherent in the map. For this particular set of data, we used the two-letter state abbreviations standardized by the U.S. Postal Service. If, instead of two-letter abbreviations, our analytical data had contained state names, then we could have used the STATENAME field to make this association. The spatial data also includes the Federal Information Processing Standard (FIPS) state code in the STATEFP field.

Of course, different maps have different spatial data associated with them. In addition to the maps of the United States, Reporting Services includes a map of each U.S. state showing its constituent counties. Rather than state abbreviations, names, and codes, these maps will have county identifiers instead. (Technically, the state of Louisiana is divided into parishes and the state of Alaska is divided into boroughs, but these divisions are still referred to as counties in the Reporting Services maps.)

When making the tie between your own analytical dataset and the spatial data inherent in a map, make sure you are selecting the appropriate fields from both so you achieve a match. In the previous example, our data contains a field called "State." Because our data contains addresses, this State field actually contains the two-letter state abbreviation. It is tempting to link the State field to the STATENAME field rather than to a field with the cryptic name of STUSPS. Be sure to use the sample spatial data and sample analytical data displayed on the "Specify the match fields for spatial and analytical data" page of the wizard to determine the proper fields to link.

Reporting Services is not limited to creating maps of the United States of America. (It can even create maps of planetary systems, as we will see in our next example!) For a number of reasons, Microsoft chose to ship only U.S. maps with the product. The ESRI shapefile standard is widely accepted and will provide access to a large variety of maps for your use. In addition, we can create our own maps using the SQL Server spatial data types. First, a little background.

SQL Server Spatial Data Types

Beginning with the 2008 release, SQL Server has provided data types for storing the definition of items from two-dimensional geometry. These are known as the spatial data types. The *spatial data types* let us represent the following items:

▶ Points

▶ Lines

▶ Polygons (multisided closed figures)

Spatial Functions

We use various functions to define these items. For instance:

```
geography::STPointFromText('POINT(-122.3308333 47.6063889)', 4326)
```

defines the point signifying the center of Seattle, Washington, USA. In this case, we are using the coordinate system utilized by GPS devices. The first parameter is a string representing a point with a given longitude (−122.3308333) and latitude (47.6063889). The second parameter identifies the geography instance or coordinate system we are using.

Here is another example. This example defines a line that roughly approximates Interstate Highway 5 as it goes north from downtown Seattle:

```
geography::STLineFromText('LINESTRING(-122.3308333 47.6063889,
                                      -122.327852 47.690012)', 4326)
```

Again, the 4326 in the second parameter shows we are using the coordinate system utilized by GPS systems.

Spatial Data Types

The functions described in the previous section encode the point, line, or polygon into a binary representation of the spatial entity. This binary representation can then be efficiently stored in a SQL Server table. This allows us to do things like store the exact geographic location of any address in a database.

SQL Server has two spatial data types: geography and geometry. The *geography* data type is designed to store data in a curved two-dimensional space. This would apply to mapping of points on the surface of the earth, which is curved.

If you are creating a spatial representation of something on a much smaller scale, such as an office floor plan, or if you believe in a flat earth, then you can use the geometry data type. The *geometry* data type is designed to store data in a flat two-dimensional space.

In addition to representing spatial data objects on a map in Reporting Services, you can do things like calculate the distance between two points, determine whether a point lies inside a given polygon, determine whether two polygons intersect, and so on. These uses of spatial data types are beyond the scope of this book. What we will do is use spatial data types to assist us with the creation of maps in Reporting Services.

Putting Polygons to Use

It may surprise you to discover that it is a bit tough to track down a map of the planetary systems where Galactic Delivery Services completes its deliveries. So, rather than having you hunt all day for an ESRI map of Noxicomian, we are going to make use of the polygon feature of the geometry spatial data type and build our own map. (We are going to discount the curvature of space for this exercise and plot our planets in a flat coordinate system.)

The Planet table in the Galactic database contains a field called PlanetGeometry. This field has a data type of geometry and contains a polygon representing each planet. We will use this data to create a map of these planets.

Now, polygons by definition have straight sides, while circles (planets) are curved. This presents a bit of a challenge. The polygons in the Planet table fields are 16-sided figures. If you squint a bit at the map we create from these polygons, they look circular—good enough for our purposes at any rate.

The Deliveries per Planet Map

Features Highlighted

▶ Creating a color analytical map

▶ Using spatial data types to define map polygons

Business Need Galactic Delivery Services (GDS) has a board of directors meeting coming up. The CEO would like to show the distribution of deliveries among the planets served by GDS, but would like to show that information in a manner that really captures the board members' attention. After some thought, the CEO has decided he wants a map showing the planets in this part of the galaxy with the shading of each planet representing the number of deliveries for that planet.

Task Overview

1. Create a New Report and Two New Datasets
2. Place a Map Item on the Report and Populate It

Deliveries per Planet Map, Task 1: Create a New Report and Two New Datasets

DT
RB

SSDT, Visual Studio, and Report Builder Steps

1. If you are using SSDT or Visual Studio, reopen the Chapter07 project, if it was closed. Close the Earth US Deliveries report and add a blank report called **Deliveries Per Planet** to the Chapter07 project.
2. If you are using Report Builder, create a new blank report.
3. In the Report Data window, click the New drop-down menu. Select Data Source from the menu that appears. The Data Source Properties dialog box appears.
4. As we have done previously, create a new data source named **Galactic** that references the Galactic shared data source. Click OK to exit the Data Source Properties dialog box.
5. In the Report Data window, right-click the entry for the Galactic data source, and select Add Dataset from the context menu. The Dataset Properties dialog box appears.
6. Enter **SpatialData** for the name.
7. Click the Query Designer button. The Query Designer window opens.
8. Click the Edit as Text button to switch to the Generic Query Designer.

9. Enter the following in the SQL pane (upper portion) of the Generic Query Designer window:

```
SELECT PlanetAbbrv, PlanetGeometry
FROM Planet
```

10. Run the query to make sure no errors exist. Correct any typos that may be detected. You'll see a result set similar to the following illustration.

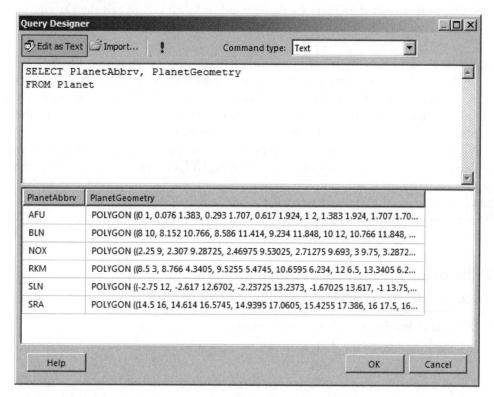

11. Click OK to exit the Query Designer window. Click OK to exit the Dataset Properties dialog box.
12. In the Report Data window, right-click the entry for the Galactic data source, and select Add Dataset to create a second dataset. The Dataset Properties dialog box appears.
13. Enter **DeliveryData** for the name.
14. Click the Query Designer button. The Query Designer window opens.
15. Click the Edit as Text button to switch to the Generic Query Designer.

16. Enter the following in the SQL pane (upper portion) of the Generic Query Designer window:

```
SELECT DeliveryPlanetAbbrv, DeliveryNumber
FROM Delivery
```

17. Run the query to make sure no errors exist. Correct any typos that may be detected.

18. Click OK to exit the Query Designer window. Click OK to exit the Dataset Properties dialog box.

Task Notes   This time we created two queries to use in our map report. That's because one of the queries is going to create the regions on the map for us. The SpatialData query will use the polygons in the PlanetGeometry field of the Planet table to create the planets on the map. The PlanetAbbrv field in that dataset will be used to associate the quantities in the DeliveryData dataset with the different regions.

When you executed the spatial query, the content of each PlanetGeometry field was displayed as a text string. This string shows the POLYGON function that was used to create each polygon. This is only a representation of the actual data in each field that the Generic Query Builder is displaying for our benefit. The actual content of each PlanetGeometry field is a binary representation of the polygon that is much more efficient for storage and calculation.

Deliveries per Planet Map, Task 2: Place a Map Item on the Report and Populate It

SSDT, Visual Studio, and Report Builder Steps

1. Drag the edges of the design surface to make it larger so the design surface fills the available space on the screen.

2. If you are using Report Builder, select the "Click to add title" text box, and delete it.

3. If you are using SSDT or Visual Studio, select the map report item in the Toolbox window. Click and drag to place the map on the design surface. The map should cover almost the entire design surface because it will be the only item on the report. The Choose a source of spatial data page of the Map Wizard appears.

4. If you are using Report Builder, click on Map in the Insert ribbon, and select Map Wizard. The Choose a source of spatial data page of the Map Wizard appears.

5. Select the SQL Server spatial query radio button.

6. Click Next. The Choose a dataset with SQL Server spatial data page of the Map Wizard appears.

7. Click the entry for the SpatialData dataset to select it.

8. Click Next. The Choose spatial data and map view options page of the Map Wizard appears. The field containing the spatial data is selected using the Spatial field drop-down list. The Map Wizard found the spatial data in the PlanetGeometry field, selected it, and has plotted it as a number of circles in the map layout as shown.

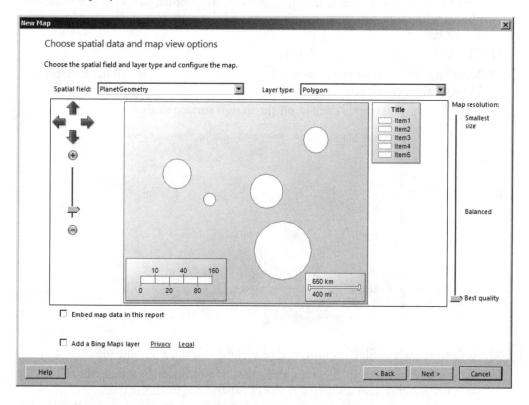

9. Click Next. The Choose map visualization page of the Map Wizard appears.

10. Select Color Analytical Map.

11. Click Next. The Choose the analytical dataset page of the Map Wizard appears.

12. Click the entry for the DeliveryData database to select it.

13. Click Next. The Specify the match fields for spatial and analytical data page of the Map Wizard appears.

14. Check the check box in the Match Fields column next to PlanetAbbrv. A drop-down list will appear in the Analytical Dataset Fields column.

15. Select DeliveryPlanetAbbrv from this drop-down list.

16. Click Next. The Choose color theme and data visualization page of the Map Wizard appears.

17. Select [Count(DeliveryNumber)] from the Field to visualize list. This will cause the color of each spatial region to vary, depending on the number of deliveries.

18. Select Red-Yellow-Green from the Color rule drop-down list. This will make the planets with more deliveries appear green and the planets with fewer deliveries appear red.

19. Check the Display labels check box.

20. Make sure #PlanetAbbrv is selected in the Data field drop-down list under the Display labels check box.

21. Click Finish. The map is created on the design surface as shown.

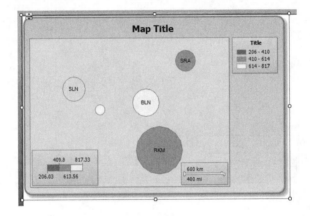

22. Resize the map to fill the entire design surface, if it does not already.

23. Right-click anywhere in the map, and select Map | Show Distance Scale. This will uncheck this item and remove the distance scale from the map.

24. Double-click the Map Title, replace "Map Title" with **Deliveries per Planet**, and then press ENTER.

25. Right-click in the lower part of the map legend, and select Delete Legend from the context menu. This will remove the legend from the map.

26. Click the inner rectangle area of the map (the area where the actual map appears) until it is selected. This is the *map viewport*. The Properties window will say "MapViewport" at the top.

27. Set the BackgroundColor property to Black and the BackgroundGradientType to None.

28. When you selected the map viewport, a new window appeared to the right of the map. This is the Map Layers window. (You may need to scroll right to see this window.) Use the four arrows and the slider at the bottom of the Map Layers window to position the circles in the map viewport. They should occupy the entire viewport without any of the planets being obscured by the color scale in the lower-left corner of the map.

29. At the top of the Map Layers window is an entry for PolygonLayer1. (Its label will probably say, "PolygonL…" Right-click the entry for PolygonLayer1 in the Map Layers window, and select Polygon Color Rule from the context menu as shown.

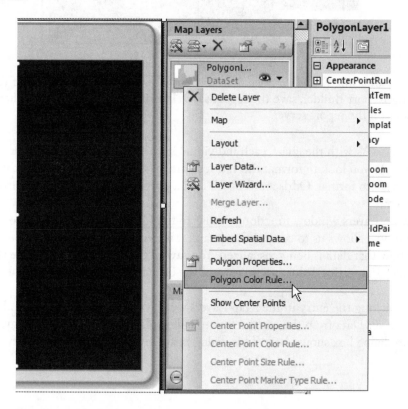

30. The Map Color Rules Properties dialog box appears. Go to the Distribution page of this dialog box.

31. In the Change distribution options to divide data into subranges drop-down box, select Equal Distribution.

32. Click OK to exit the Map Color Rules Properties dialog box.
33. Preview/Run the report. The report should appear as shown.

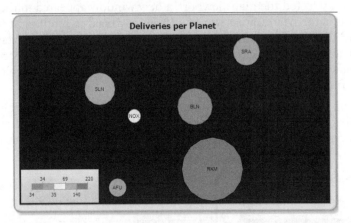

34. If you are using SSDT or Visual Studio, click Save All on the toolbar. If you are using Report Builder, save the report as **Deliveries per Planet** in the Chapter07 folder on the report server.

Task Notes   As with the chart, each individual item on a map has its own properties dialog box. As you look to format the various parts of the map, try right-clicking the item you wish to format. Odds are you will find a properties entry in the resulting context menu.

The Map Layers window functions similar to the Chart Data window. The Map Layers window allows us to control the data that is being displayed on the map. It also controls how that data is being visualized. You saw in this example how to use the Map Color Rules Properties dialog box to control the distribution on our color analytical scale.

Right-clicking the entry in the Map Layers window of a particular layer and then selecting Layer Data from the context menu will display the Map Polygon Layer Properties dialog box shown here. This dialog box allows you to control which datasets and which fields within those datasets are being used as a source for spatial information and which are being used for analytical data.

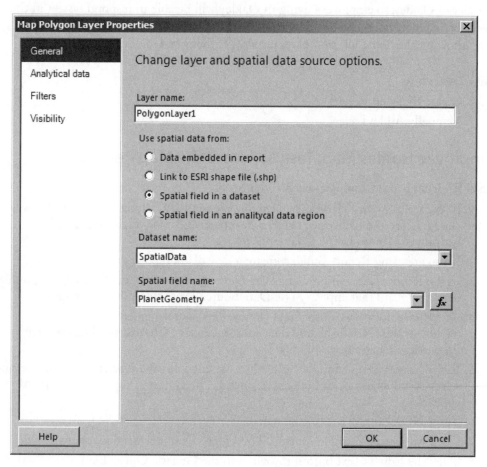

Thus far, we have created maps with only one layer. In our next example, we create a map with two layers.

The Employee Homes Map

Features Highlighted

▶ Creating a Basic Marker map

▶ Using a Bing Maps layer

Business Need GDS is doing business continuation planning. They are starting with the delivery hub on the planet Noxicomian. The Noxicomian delivery hub is located in the city of Oakley, so employees living in Oakley will be able to respond fastest in the event of an emergency. The business continuation planning committee has asked for a map showing the home location of all employees living in Oakley.

Task Overview
1. Create the Map Report
2. Manually Add a Layer

Employee Homes Map, Task 1: Create the Map Report

`DT`
`RB` **SSDT, Visual Studio, and Report Builder Steps**

1. If you are using SSDT or Visual Studio, reopen the Chapter07 project, if it was closed. Close the Deliveries Per Planet report, and add a blank report called **Employee Homes** to the Chapter07 project.
2. If you are using Report Builder, create a new blank report.
3. In the Report Data window, click the New drop-down menu. Select Data Source from the menu that appears. The Data Source Properties dialog box appears.
4. As we have done previously, create a new data source named **Galactic** that references the Galactic shared data source. Click OK to exit the Data Source Properties dialog box.
5. In the Report Data window, right-click the entry for the Galactic data source, and select Add Dataset from the context menu. The Dataset Properties dialog box appears.
6. Enter **NOXEmployees** for the name.
7. Click the Query Designer button. The Query Designer window opens.
8. Click the Edit as Text button to switch to the Generic Query Designer.
9. Enter the following in the SQL pane (upper portion) of the Generic Query Designer window:

```
SELECT EmployeeNumber, FirstName, LastName, GeoPoint
FROM Employee
WHERE City = 'Oakley'
```

10. Run the query to make sure no errors exist. Correct any typos that may be detected. You'll see a result set similar to the following illustration.

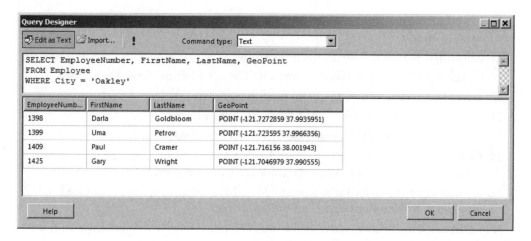

11. Click OK to exit the Query Designer window. Click OK to exit the Dataset Properties dialog box.

12. Drag the edges of the design surface to make it larger so the design surface fills the available space on the screen.

13. If you are using Report Builder, select the "Click to add title" text box, and delete it.

14. If you are using SSDT or Visual Studio, select the map report item in the Toolbox window. Click and drag to place the map on the design surface. The map should cover almost the entire design surface because it will be the only item on the report. The Choose a source of spatial data page of the Map Wizard appears.

15. If you are using Report Builder, click on Map in the Insert ribbon, and select Map Wizard. The Choose a source of spatial data page of the Map Wizard appears.

16. Select the SQL Server spatial query radio button.

17. Click Next. The Choose a dataset with SQL Server spatial data page of the Map Wizard appears.

18. Click the entry for the NOXEmployees dataset to select it.

19. Click Next. The Choose spatial data and map view options page of the Map Wizard appears. The Map Wizard found spatial data in the GeoPoint field, selected it, and has plotted it as a number of points in the map layout area.

20. Check the Add a Bing Maps layer check box. The Tile type drop-down list appears and, after a moment, a Bing map appears in the map layout area if you have access to the Internet.

21. Select Hybrid from the Tile type drop-down list. The Bing map changes to a hybrid map in the map layout area.

22. Click Next. The Choose map visualization page of the Map Wizard appears.

23. Select Basic Marker Map, if it is not already selected.

24. Click Next. The Choose color theme and data visualization page of the Map Wizard appears.

25. Select Star from the Marker drop-down list.

26. Check the Display labels check box. The Data field drop-down list appears.

27. Select [LastName] from the Data field drop-down list.

28. Click Finish. The map is created on the design surface.

29. Resize the map to fill the entire design surface, if it does not already.

30. Right-click anywhere in the map, and select Map | Show Color Scale. This will uncheck this item and remove the color scale from the map.

31. Double-click the Map Title, replace "Map Title" with **Employees in Oakley, UZ on Planet Noxicomian,** and then press ENTER.

32. Right-click in the lower part of the map legend, and select Delete Legend from the context menu. This will remove the legend from the map.

33. Scroll right so you can see the Map Layers window.

34. Right-click the entry for PointLayer1, and select Point Properties from the context menu. The Map Point Properties dialog box appears.

35. Click the *fx* button next to the Tooltip text box. The Expression dialog box appears.

36. Enter the following in the Set expression for: Tooltip text box:

```
= "Employee Number: " & Fields!EmployeeNumber.Value & vbcrlf &
Fields!FirstName.Value & " " & Fields!LastName.Value
```

37. Click OK to exit the Expression dialog box.

38. Set the following properties in the Map Point Properties dialog box:

Property	Value
General page:	
Marker size	20pt
Font page:	
Size	22pt
Style	Bold
Color	White
Fill page:	
Color	Red
Border page:	
Line width	4pt

39. Click OK to exit the Map Point Properties dialog box.

40. Right-click the entry for PointLayer1, and select Point Color Rule from the context menu. The Map Color Rules Properties dialog box appears.

41. Select the Apply template style radio button, if it is not already selected.

42. Click OK to exit the Map Color Rules Properties dialog box.

43. Use the four arrows and the slider at the bottom of the Map Layers window to position the points in the map viewport. Make sure all the Last Name labels fit in the map viewport and that none are obscured by the distance scale.

44. Preview/Run the report. The report should appear as shown.

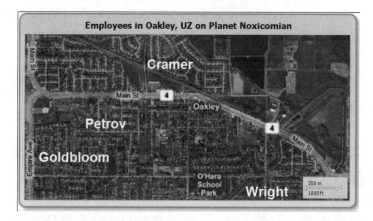

45. Hover the mouse pointer over one of the point markers to see the tooltip text.

Task Notes   In this task, you were introduced to the concept of layers on the map. One layer is added over the top of another layer to deliver more information on the map. In the map you just created, there are two layers: the point layer that contains the stars indicating employee homes and the tile layer that contains the Bing map. Maps may also contain a polygon layer and/or a line layer.

The properties of the items in each layer are controlled by a number of dialog boxes. These dialog boxes are launched by the context menu for each layer shown in the Map Layers window. The Layer Data dialog box controls which dataset, if any, provides spatial data for the layer and which dataset, if any, provides analytical data for the layer.

In the tile layer, there is a dialog box to control the type of Bing map used as a background of the map item. This can be a road map, an aerial map (satellite image), or a hybrid of the two. We saw this layer for the first time in our current example.

In the point layer, there are dialog boxes to control the color of each point, the size of each point, and the marker used for each point. Each of these characteristics can change to correspond to the data being presented, if desired. We saw this in the Earth US Deliveries report, our bubble map. To create a bubble map, the Map Wizard uses a circular marker that is colored a semitransparent white for each point. The size of these point markers varies in proportion to the data.

In the polygon layer, there is a dialog box to control the color of each polygon region. The color can change to correspond to the data being presented, if desired. We saw this in the Deliveries per Planet report, our color analytical map.

In the line layer, there are dialog boxes to control the color and the size of each line. Each of these characteristics can change to correspond to the data being presented, if desired.

NOTE

As you have no doubt figured out, this is not a map of Oakley, UZ on the Planet Noxicomian. See if you can figure out what terrestrial Oakley I have playing the role for us in this map.

Building Higher

We have now covered all the basic aspects of creating reports in Reporting Services. In the next two chapters, we continue to look at report creation, but we move to the intermediate and advanced levels. Building on what you have learned so far, we create more complex reports with more interactivity.

With each new feature you encounter, you gain new tools for turning data into business intelligence.

Chapter 8

Kicking It Up a Notch: Intermediate Reporting

In This Chapter

- ► Never Having to Say "I'm Sorry"
- ► Putting the Report Template to Use
- ► Data Caching During Preview
- ► Under the Hood
- ► Advance, Never Retreat

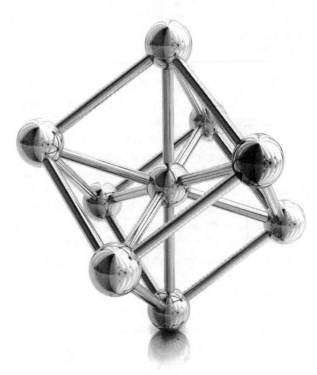

B asic training is at an end. Boot camp is over. You now know the basics of building reports in Reporting Services. You should be able to create reports, both with the Report Wizard and from scratch. When needed, you can spice up your reports with color, images, charts, and gauges—even maps.

In the last two chapters, you learned how to add punch to your reports with color and graphics. In this chapter, you learn how to add value to your reports through summarizing and totaling, and added interactivity. All this enhances the users' experience and allows them to more readily turn information into business intelligence.

We begin the chapter, however, by looking for a way to enhance your experience as a report developer. In the first section, we create a report template that can be used to standardize the look of your reports. The report template can also take care of some of the basic formatting tasks so they do not need to be repeated for each report.

Never Having to Say "I'm Sorry"

Users can be particular about the way their reports are laid out. In many cases, you will be creating new reports to replace existing ones. It may be that the user was getting a report from a legacy system, from an Access report or a spreadsheet, or from a ledger book. Whatever the case, the user is used to seeing the data presented in a certain way, with everything arranged just so.

Now you come along with Microsoft SQL Server 2012 Reporting Services, telling the user that the new reporting system is infinitely better than the old way—more efficient, more timely, and with more delivery options. That is all well and good with the user, but, invariably, the question will arise, "Can you make the report look the same as what I have now?" No matter how antiquated or inefficient the current reporting system might be, it is familiar, perhaps even comforting, to your users. Change is difficult. The irony of the human race is this: on a large scale, we like change, but on an individual level, we mainly want things to stay the same.

Even if Reporting Services is well established and you are not converting reports from an existing system, users still have preconceived notions. They have a vision for the way a new report should be laid out. These visions need to be respected. After all, the report developer is not the one who has to look at the report every day, week, or month—the user is! The user is the one who probably knows how to best turn the data into something useful.

What the users don't want to hear is, "I'm sorry, but we can't do it that way in Reporting Services." You will be miles ahead if you spend your time fulfilling your users' vision, rather than trying to convince them that Reporting Services is a great tool, despite the fact that it cannot do what they want it to. The techniques in this section, and also in parts of Chapter 9, can help you to make Reporting Services reports do exactly what your users want them to. After all, if your users ain't happy, ain't nobody happy!

Successful report development means never having to say, "I'm sorry."

The Report Template

Features Highlighted

▶ Creating a reusable template for reports

▶ Using values from the Built-in Fields collection

Business Need   Galactic Delivery Services (GDS) is looking to increase the efficiency of its report developers. GDS would like a template that can be used for each new report created. The report template is to include the GDS logo and the company name in a header across the top of each page. The template is also to include a footer across the bottom of each page showing the date and time the report was printed, who printed the report, the current page number, and the total number of pages in the report.

Task Overview

1. Create a Template Report with a Page Header
2. Create the Page Footer on the Template Report
3. Copy the Template to the Appropriate Location

Report Template, Task 1: Create a Template Report with a Page Header

| DT | **SSDT and Visual Studio Steps**

1. Create a new Reporting Services project called Template in the MSSQLRS folder. (If you need help with this task, see Chapter 5.)
2. Add a blank report called GDSReport to the Template project.
3. From the main menu, select Report | Add Page Header. A space for the page header layout appears at the top part of the design surface. (If the Report menu is not visible, click anywhere on the design surface.)
4. From the Toolbox, place an image item in the layout area for the page header. The Image Properties dialog box appears.
5. Click the Import button. The Open dialog box appears.
6. Select "GIF files (*.gif)" from the file type drop-down list just above the Open button.
7. Navigate to the GDS.gif image file, and select it. (This is the same image file you used in Chapter 6.) Click Open.
8. Click OK to exit the Image Properties dialog box. The image is embedded in the report and used by the image report item you placed in the page header.

NOTE

From this point on, the book will not give specific instructions for setting the values of object properties. You can set the properties in the Properties window or in the properties dialog box specific to that object, whatever you are most comfortable with.

9. Modify the following properties of the image:

Property	Value
Location: Left	0in
Location: Top	0in
Size: Width	0.75in
Size: Height	0.625in
Sizing	Fit

10. Place a text box in the layout area for the page header. Modify the following properties of the text box:

Property	Value
Color	DarkBlue
Font: FontSize	30pt
Font: FontWeight	Bold
Location: Left	0.75in
Location: Top	0in
Size: Width	5.75in
Size: Height	0.625in
Value (See the following note.)	Galactic Delivery Services
VerticalAlign	Middle

NOTE

The Value property is not found in the Properties window. It can be set by entering the text directly into the text box, using the Text Box Properties dialog box, or using the Expression dialog box.

11. Click in the page header layout area outside the text box and image. Page Header is selected in the drop-down list at the top of the Properties window.

12. Modify the following property for the page header:

Property	Value
Height	0.75in

RB Report Builder Steps

1. Using Report Manager, create a new folder in the Galactic Delivery Services folder. Enter **Template** as the name of this folder. (If you need help with this task, see Chapter 5.)

2. Launch Report Builder from Report Manager.

3. With New Report highlighted in the left column, click Blank Report. The Report Builder shows a new blank report.

4. In the Insert tab, select Header | Add Header. A space for the page header layout appears at the top part of the design surface.

5. From the Insert tab, place an image item in the layout area for the page header. The Image Properties dialog box appears.

6. Click the Import button. The Open dialog box appears.

7. Select "GIF files (*.gif)" from the file type drop-down list just above the Open button.

8. Navigate to the GDS.gif image file, and select it. (This is the same image file you used in Chapter 6.) Click Open.

9. Click OK to exit the Image Properties dialog box. The image is embedded in the report and used by the image report item you placed in the page header.

NOTE

From this point on, the book will not give specific instructions for setting the values of object properties. You can set the properties in the Properties window or in the properties dialog box specific to that object, whatever you are most comfortable with.

10. Modify the following properties of the image:

Property	Value
Location: Left	0in
Location: Top	0in
Size: Width	0.75in
Size: Height	0.625in
Sizing	Fit

11. Place a text box in the layout area for the page header. Modify the following properties of the text box:

Property	Value
Color	DarkBlue
Font: FontSize	30pt
Font: FontWeight	Bold
Location: Left	0.75in
Location: Top	0in
Size: Width	5.75in
Size: Height	0.625in
Value (See the following note.)	Galactic Delivery Services
VerticalAlign	Middle

NOTE

The Value property is not found in the Properties window. It can be set by entering the text directly into the text box, using the Text Box Properties dialog box, or using the Expression dialog box.

12. Click in the page header layout area outside the text box and image. Page Header is selected in the drop-down list at the top of the Properties window.

13. Modify the following property for the page header:

Property	Value
Height	0.75in

Task Notes Reporting Services reports have a page header layout area that can be used to create a page heading for the report. The page header has properties, so it can be turned off on the first page or the last page of the report. Aside from these options, if the page header is turned on in the Report menu, it appears on each report page.

The page header can be populated with images, text boxes, lines, and rectangles. You cannot, however, place any data regions, tables, matrixes, lists, or charts in a page header. You can place a text box that references a field from a dataset in the page header. As with any other field expression placed outside of a data region, the value will not change from page to page.

In the previous task, you made the logo image in the report header an embedded image. This was done for reasons of convenience for these exercises. In an actual template created for your company, retrieving images from an Internet or intranet site is probably a good idea. As discussed previously, this allows for the image to be used in a multitude of reports while being stored in a single location. This also makes it easy to update the image the next time the marketing department gives it a makeover.

Report Template, Task 2: Create the Page Footer on the Template Report

DT **SSDT and Visual Studio Steps**

1. Click anywhere on the design surface.
2. From the main menu, select Report | Add Page Footer. A space for the page footer layout appears below the layout area for the body of the report.
3. In the Report Data window, expand the Built-in Fields entry. Select ReportName and drag it onto the page footer layout area.
4. Modify the following properties of the text box that results:

Property	Value
Font: FontSize	8pt
Location: Left	0in
Location: Top	0.125in
Size: Width	2.25in
Size: Height	0.25in

5. Place a text box in the layout area for the page footer. Modify the following properties of the text box:

Property	Value
Font: FontSize	8pt
Location: Left	2.75in
Location: Top	0.125in
Size: Width	1in
Size: Height	0.25in

6. Right-click this text box and select Expression from the context menu. The Expression dialog box appears.
7. Type the following in the Set expression for: Value area after the equal (=) sign:

```
"Page " &
```

A space should be typed both before and after the ampersand character (&).

8. Select Built-in Fields in the Category pane.

9. Double-click PageNumber in the Item pane to append it to the expression. The expression to return PageNumber from the Globals collection is added to the Expression area.

NOTE

Globals and Built-in Fields are two different names for the same group of items.

10. After the PageNumber expression, type the following:

```
& " of " &
```

A space should be typed both before and after each ampersand.

11. Double-click TotalPages in the Item pane. The expression to return TotalPages from the Globals collection is added to the Expression area.

12. Click OK to exit the Expression dialog box.

13. In the Report Data window, select ExecutionTime and drag it onto the page footer layout area.

14. Modify the following properties of the text box that results:

Property	Value
Font: FontSize	8pt
Location: Left	4.25in
Location: Top	0.125in
Size: Width	2.25in
Size: Height	0.25in
TextAlign	Right

15. Click in the page footer layout area outside of the three text boxes so Page Footer is selected in the Properties window. Modify the following property of the page footer:

Property	Value
Height	0.375in

Your report layout should appear similar to Figure 8-1.

16. Click the Preview tab. Your report should appear similar to Figure 8-2.

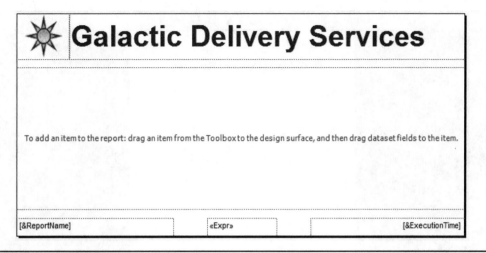

Figure 8-1   *The report template layout*

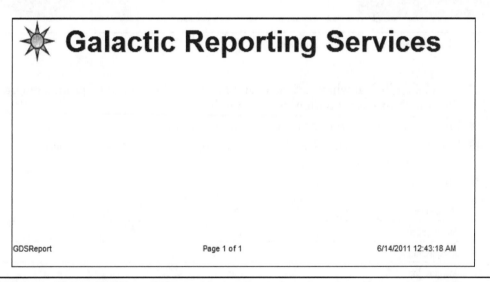

Figure 8-2   *The report template on the Preview tab*

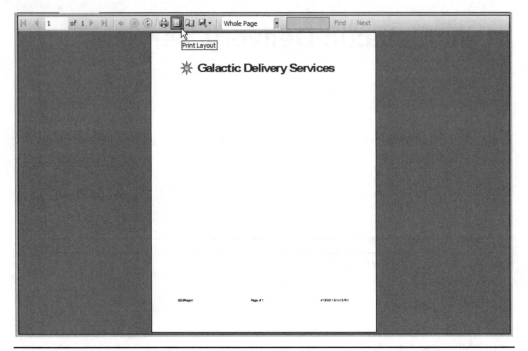

Figure 8-3   *The report template in print layout mode*

17. For a better look at what the header and footer will look like on a printed report, click the Print Layout button, as shown in Figure 8-3.

18. Finally, let's set the margins for the report. Click the Design tab.

19. In the main menu, select Report | Report Properties. The Report Properties dialog box appears.

20. Modify the following values:

Property	Value
Margins: Left	1in
Margins: Right	1in
Margins: Top	0.5in
Margins: Bottom	0.5in

21. Click OK to exit the Report Properties dialog box.

22. Click the Preview tab. The header and footer should appear to be positioned better on the page.

23. Click the Print Layout button to exit the print layout mode.
24. Click Save All on the toolbar.

RB **Report Builder Steps**

1. Select the "Click to add title" text box, and delete it.
2. In the Report Data window, expand the Built-in Fields entry. Select Report Name and drag it onto the page footer layout area.
3. Modify the following properties of the text box that results:

Property	Value
Font: FontSize	8pt
Location: Left	0in
Location: Top	0.125in
Size: Width	2.25in
Size: Height	0.25in

4. Place a text box in the layout area for the page footer. Modify the following properties of the text box:

Property	Value
Font: FontSize	8pt
Location: Left	2.75in
Location: Top	0.125in
Size: Width	1in
Size: Height	0.25in

5. Right-click this text box and select Expression from the context menu. The Expression dialog box appears.
6. Type the following in the Set expression for: Value area after the equal (=) sign:

```
"Page " &
```

A space should be typed both before and after the ampersand character (&).

7. Select Built-in Fields in the Category pane.
8. Double-click PageNumber in the Item pane to append it to the expression. The expression to return PageNumber from the Globals collection is added to the Expression area.

NOTE

Globals and Built-in Fields are two different names for the same group of items.

9. After the PageNumber expression, type the following:

   `& " of " &`

   A space should be typed both before and after each ampersand.

10. Double-click TotalPages in the Item pane. The expression to return TotalPages from the Globals collection is added to the Expression area.

11. Click OK to exit the Expression dialog box.

12. Select the text box containing "[&ExecutionTime]" in the layout area for the page footer.

13. Modify the following properties of this text box:

Property	Value
Font: FontSize	8pt
Location: Left	4.25in
Location: Top	0.125in
Size: Width	2.25in
Size: Height	0.25in
TextAlign	Right

14. Click in the page footer layout area outside of the three text boxes so Page Footer is selected in the Properties window. Modify the following property of the page footer:

Property	Value
Height	0.375in

   Your report layout should appear similar to Figure 8-1, which is found earlier in the book with the SSDT and Visual Studio steps for this task.

15. Click Save. Save the report as "GDSReport" in the Template folder on the report server.

16. Click Run. Your report should appear similar to Figure 8-2. (The content of the footer many differ.)

17. For a better look at what the header and footer will look like on a printed report, click the Print Layout button, as shown in Figure 8-4.

18. Finally, let's set the margins for the report. Click Design.

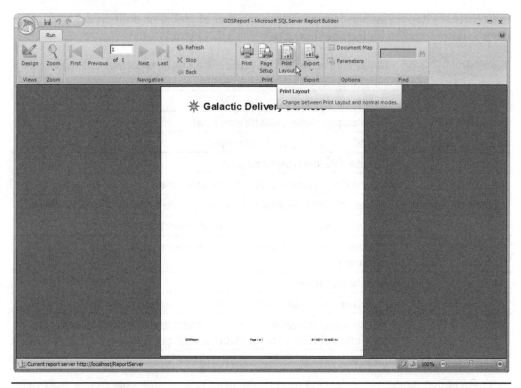

Figure 8-4   *The report template in print layout mode in the Report Builder*

19. Right-click in the blue area immediately outside the report layout area. Select Report Properties from the context menu. The Report Properties dialog box appears.

20. Modify the following values:

Property	Value
Margins: Left	1in
Margins: Right	1in
Margins: Top	0.5in
Margins: Bottom	0.5in

21. Click OK to exit the Report Properties dialog box.

22. Click Run. The header and footer should appear to be positioned better on the page.

23. Click the Print Layout button to exit the print layout mode.

24. Click Save and close Report Builder.

Task Notes Reporting Services provides a number of global or built-in fields you can use in your reports, including the following:

ExecutionTime	The date and time the report was executed. (This is not the time it takes for the report to run, but rather, the time at which the report was run.)
Language	The language the report is output in.
OverallPageNumber	The current page number within the entire report.
OverallTotalPages	The total number of pages in the entire report.
PageName	The name of the current page in the report.
PageNumber	The current page number since the last page number reset.
RenderFormat.IsInteractive	Indicates whether the rendering format requested by the user supports interactive features.
RenderFormat.Name	The name of the rendering format requested by the user to render the report.
ReportFolder	The report server folder the report resides in. ReportFolder is blank in the development environment.
ReportName	The name of the report.
ReportServerUrl	The Uniform Resource Locator (URL) of the Internet server hosting the report.
TotalPages	The total number of pages until the next page number reset. If there are no page number resets in the report, this will be equal to OverallTotalPages.
UserID	The network user name of the person executing the report.

These global fields are commonly used in the page header and page footer areas of the report. It is possible, however, to use most of them anywhere in the report.

The report has its own properties that can be modified. You are most likely to use the Report Properties dialog box to modify the orientation, page size, and the margins. In Chapter 9, however, we explore some of the other properties available in this dialog box.

Report Template, Task 3:
Copy the Template to the Appropriate Location

DT | **SSDT and Visual Studio Steps**

1. From the main menu, select File | Close Project to close the project and its associated solution.
2. Open Windows Explorer and navigate to the folder you created for the Template project. From the My Documents folder, the path should be the following:

```
Visual Studio 2010\Projects\MSSQLRS\Template
```

3. In the Template folder, highlight the file GDSReport.rdl. This is the template report we just created.
4. Press CTRL-C to copy this file.

5. Navigate to the directory where the Report Designer stores its templates. In a default installation on 32-bit Windows, this is

```
C:\Program Files\Microsoft Visual Studio 10.0\Common7\IDE\
                         PrivateAssemblies\ProjectItems\
                         ReportProject
```

If you are using 64-bit Windows, replace "Program Files" with "Program Files (x86)" in the above path.

NOTE

In a 64-bit environment, the path will be:
C:\Program Files (x86) \Microsoft Visual Studio 9.0\Common7\IDE\PrivateAssemblies\ProjectItems\ReportProject

6. Select the ReportProject folder.
7. Press CTRL-V to paste the copied file into this directory.
8. Close Windows Explorer.

Task Notes for SSDT and Visual Studio When we add a new item to a report project, the Report Designer looks in the ProjectItems\ReportProject folder. Any report files (.rdl) it finds in this folder are included in the Templates area of the Add New Item dialog box. This is shown in Figure 8-5.

In the remainder of this chapter, we use our new template to create reports.

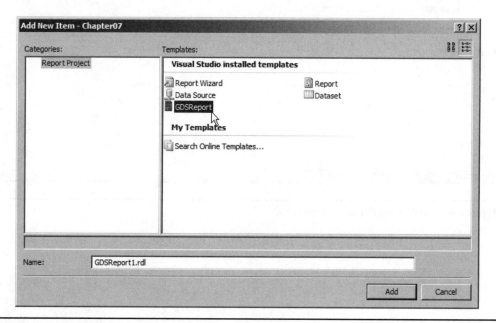

Figure 8-5   *The Add New Item dialog box with a custom template*

RB   **Report Builder Steps**

1. In Report Manager, hover over the Template folder to activate the drop-down list.

2. From the drop-down list for the Template folder, select Security as shown in Figure 8-6.

3. The Security page for the Template folder appears in the browser. Click the Edit Item Security button.

4. The Message from webpage dialog box appears. Click OK.

5. Click the Edit link next to the first item in the security entry list as shown in Figure 8-7.

6. The Edit Role Assignment page appears.

7. Check the Browser role and the Report Builder role on this page. Uncheck any other roles that might be checked.

8. Click Apply. This will return you to the Security page for the Template folder.

9. Repeat Step 5 through Step 8 for all entries on the Security page, if there are any.

10. Click the Galactic Delivery Services link in the upper-left corner of the page.

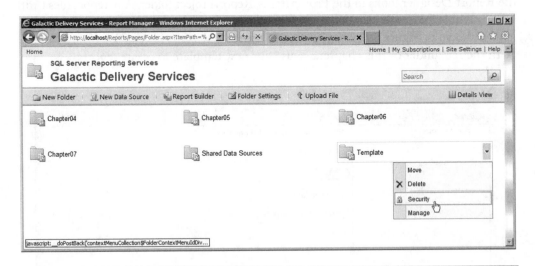

Figure 8-6   *The drop-down list for the Template folder*

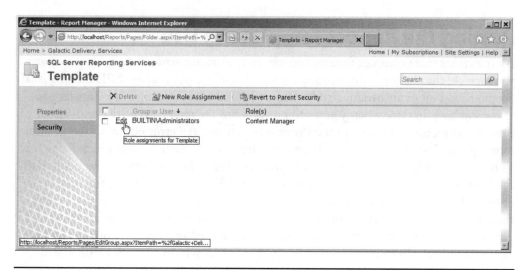

Figure 8-7   *The Edit link on the Security page*

Task Notes for Report Builder   Our changes to the Template folder have made it read-only. When we want to create a report using our GDSReport template, we will open this report in Report Builder and then save the modified version under another name. If you forget and try to save a modified version of the template back in the Template folder, you will receive an error similar to that shown in Figure 8-8. This is your cue to use Save As rather than Save in Report Builder.

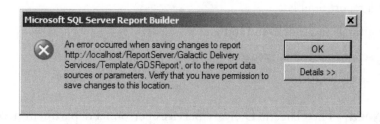

Figure 8-8   *The save error appears if you try to save to a read-only folder on the report server.*

Putting the Report Template to Use

As you create more complex reports and use more intricate expressions in those reports, you increase the chance of introducing errors. This is one place where SSDT and Visual Studio have a bit of an advantage over Report Builder. All three environments let you know you have an error when you try to preview/run the report. In SSDT and Visual Studio, you receive a message in the Preview tab saying, "An error occurred during local report processing." In Report Builder, you receive a similar error message in a dialog box.

In addition, SSDT and Visual Studio provide a list of detailed error messages in both the Build section of the Output window and in the Error List window. (You may need to select Error List from the View menu to see the Error List window.) In most cases, these error messages provide a pretty good description of the problem. In many cases, the problem is a syntax error in an expression you constructed in a property of a report item.

If you double-click an error entry in the Error List window in SSDT or Visual Studio, you return to the Design tab (if you are not already there) and the report item that contains the offending expression is selected. You can then use the error message to determine which property contains the error and fix the problem. In some cases, if you open the Properties dialog box for the report item, the property containing the error has an exclamation mark surrounded by a red circle placed next to it.

Once you make changes to remedy each error listed in the Error List window, you can click the Preview tab to run the report. If all the errors have been corrected, the Build section of the Output window shows zero errors and all the entries are cleared out of the Error List window. If you still have errors, continue the debugging process by double-clicking an Error List window entry and trying again to correct the error.

The Employee Time Report

Features Highlighted

▶ Using a report template

▶ Putting totals in headers and footers

▶ Using scope to affect aggregate function results

▶ Toggling visibility

Business Need   The Galactic Delivery Services personnel department needs a report showing the amount of time entered by its employees on their weekly timesheets. The report should group the time by job, employee, and week, with totals presented for each grouping. The groups should be collapsed initially, and the user should be able to drill down into the desired group. Group totals should be visible even when the group is collapsed.

Task Overview

1. Create a New Report and a New Dataset
2. Populate the Report Layout
3. Add Drilldown Capability
4. Add Totaling

Employee Time Report, Task 1: Create a New Report and a New Dataset

DT | **SSDT and Visual Studio Steps**

1. Create a new Reporting Services project called Chapter08 in the MSSQLRS folder. (If you need help with this task, see Chapter 5.)
2. Create a shared data source called Galactic for the Galactic database. (Again, if you need help with this task, see Chapter 5.)
3. Right-click Reports in the Solution Explorer. Select Add | New Item from the context menu. The Add New Item – Chapter08 dialog box appears.
4. Single-click GDSReport in the center area to select it. Change the Name to EmployeeTime and click Add.
5. Create a data source called "Galactic" in this new report. This new data source should reference the Galactic shared data source. (If you need help with this task, see Chapter 5.)
6. Create a dataset called "EmployeeTime" with the following query:

```
SELECT Description AS Job,
       Employee.EmployeeNumber,
       FirstName,
       LastName,
       CONVERT(char(4),DATEPART(yy, WorkDate))+'-'+
           CONVERT(char(2),DATEPART(wk, WorkDate)) AS Week,
       WorkDate,
       HoursWorked
FROM TimeEntry
INNER JOIN Assignment
       ON TimeEntry.AssignmentID = Assignment.AssignmentID
INNER JOIN Employee
       ON Assignment.EmployeeNumber = Employee.EmployeeNumber
INNER JOIN Job
       ON Assignment.JobID = Job.JobID
ORDER BY Job, Employee.EmployeeNumber, Week, WorkDate
```

RB **Report Builder Steps**

1. Using Report Manager, create a new folder in the Galactic Delivery Services folder. Enter **Chapter08** as the name of this folder. (If you need help with this task, see Chapter 5.)

2. Launch Report Builder from Report Manager.

3. Click Open. The Open Report dialog box appears.

4. Navigate to the Template folder.

5. Double-click the GDSReport item to open it.

6. Click the logo button, and select Save As from the menu. The Save As Report dialog box appears.

7. Click the "Up One Level" button as shown in the upper-right corner of Figure 8-9 to navigate from the Template folder to the Galactic Delivery Services folder.

8. Navigate to the Chapter08 folder.

9. Enter **EmployeeTime** for Name, and click Save.

10. Create a data source called "Galactic" in this new report. This new data source should reference the Galactic shared data source. (If you need help with this task, see Chapter 5.)

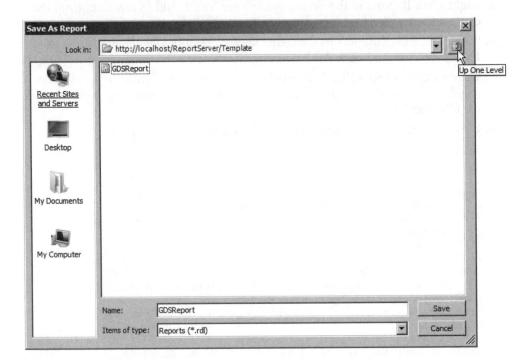

Figure 8-9   *The Up One Level button*

11. Create a dataset called "EmployeeTime" with the following query:

```
SELECT Description AS Job,
    Employee.EmployeeNumber,
    FirstName,
    LastName,
    CONVERT(char(4),DATEPART(yy, WorkDate))+'-'+
        CONVERT(char(2),DATEPART(wk, WorkDate)) AS Week,
    WorkDate,
    HoursWorked
FROM TimeEntry
INNER JOIN Assignment
    ON TimeEntry.AssignmentID = Assignment.AssignmentID
INNER JOIN Employee
    ON Assignment.EmployeeNumber = Employee.EmployeeNumber
INNER JOIN Job
    ON Assignment.JobID = Job.JobID
ORDER BY Job, Employee.EmployeeNumber, Week, WorkDate
```

Task Notes   If you need to, refer to the database diagram for the personnel department in Chapter 3 to see how the TimeEntry, Assignment, Employee, and Job tables are related. Our query joins these four tables to determine what work hours were entered for each employee and what job they held.

We are using a combination of the CONVERT() and DATEPART() functions to create a string containing the year and the week number for each time entry. This enables us to group the time into work weeks. Note, the year comes first in this string so it sorts correctly across years.

When you created the new report, content was already in the page header and page footer. This, of course, is because we used our new GDSReport template to create the report. By using our report template, we have a consistent header and footer on our reports without having to work at it.

Employee Time Report, Task 2: Populate the Report Layout

DT
RB   **SSDT, Visual Studio, and Report Builder Steps**

1. Place a text box onto the body of the report. Modify the following properties of this text box:

Property	Value
Font: FontSize	25pt
Font: FontWeight	Bold
Location: Left	0in
Location: Top	0in
Size: Width	2.875in
Size: Height	0.5in
Value	Employee Time

2. Use the table template to place a tablix onto the body of the report immediately below the text box you just added. (If you are using Report Builder, do not use the Table Wizard.)

3. In the Report Data window, drag the WorkDate field into the data row in the center column of the tablix.

4. Drag the HoursWorked field into the data row in the right-hand column of the table.

5. Select the entire header row in the tablix. Modify the following property:

Property	Value
Font: TextDecoration	Underline

6. Right-click anywhere in the lower row of the tablix, and hover over the Add Group item in the Tablix area of the context menu. Select the Parent Group item from the Row Group area of the submenu. The Tablix group dialog box appears.

7. Select [Week] from the Group by drop-down list.

8. Check the Add group header check box and the Add group footer check box.

9. Click OK to exit the Tablix group dialog box.

10. Right-click the cell containing the [Week] field, and select Tablix: Add Group | Row Group: Parent Group from the context menu. The Tablix group dialog box appears.

11. Select [EmployeeNumber] from the Group by drop-down list.

12. Check the Add group header check box and the Add group footer check box.

13. Click OK to exit the Tablix group dialog box.

14. Right-click the cell containing the [EmployeeNumber] field, and select Tablix: Add Group | Row Group: Parent Group from the context menu. The Tablix group dialog box appears.

15. Select [Job] from the Group by drop-down list.

16. Check the Add group header check box and the Add group footer check box.

17. Click OK to exit the Tablix group dialog box. The report layout should appear as shown in Figure 8-10.

18. In addition to the header and footer rows for each group, we have a header column for each group. These are the columns to the left of the double dashed line. We saw this form of group headings in the TransportList report in Chapter 5. For this report, we are going to try a different format. Click the gray rectangle above the Job column, and hold down the left mouse button. Drag the mouse pointer to the gray rectangle above the Week column, and release the mouse button. All three group columns to the left of the double dashed lines should be selected.

19. Right-click in the gray rectangle above the Week column, and select Delete Columns from the context menu. This deletes the grouping columns, but it does not delete the groups or the group header and footer rows.

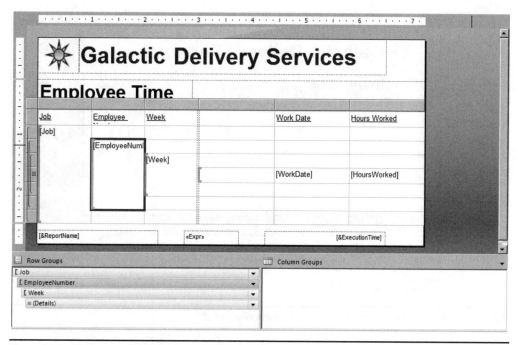

Figure 8-10   *Three groups added to the Employee Time report layout*

20. The symbols in the gray boxes to the left of the tablix identify the three groupings and the detail row. The detail row has the gray box with the three horizontal lines. Immediately above the detail row is the header for the innermost group. Immediately below the detail row is the footer for the innermost group. The innermost group is the Week group. This is surrounded by the header and footer for the middle group, which is the EmployeeNumber group. The middle group is surrounded by the header and footer for the outermost group, which is the Job group. At the very top of the tablix is a tablix header row for column headings (see Figure 8-11). Hover over the leftmost cell in the top group header row. (This is the second row from the top.) Select the Job field from the Field Selector.

21. Modify the following property of this cell:

Property	Value
Font: FontWeight	Bold

22. Right-click anywhere in the leftmost column in the table. Select Tablix: Insert Column | Right from the context menu.

23. Hover over the cell in the middle group header row in the column you just created. Select the EmployeeNumber field from the Field Selector.

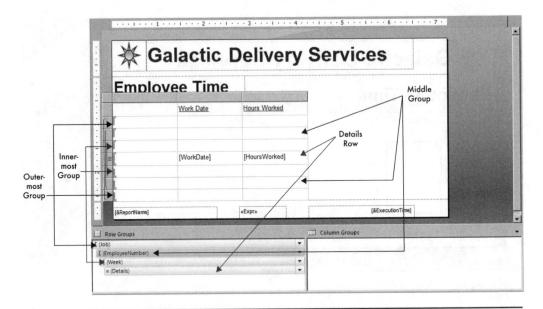

Figure 8-11 *The group header and footer rows in the EmployeeTime report*

24. Modify the following property of this cell:

Property	Value
Font: FontWeight	Bold

25. Drag the width of the leftmost column in the table until the column is just wide enough for the word "Job" in the table header cell.

26. Select the two leftmost cells in the row for the outermost group header, right-click and select Tablix: Merge Cells from the context menu. (Click and drag or hold down SHIFT while clicking to select multiple cells at the same time.)

27. Right-click anywhere in the second-from-the-left column in the table. Select Tablix: Insert Column | Right from the context menu.

28. Hover over the cell in the column you just created in the innermost group header row. Select the Week field from the Field Selector.

29. Modify the following property of this cell:

Property	Value
Font: FontWeight	Bold

30. Drag the width of the second column from the left until it is just wide enough for the words "Employee Number" in the tablix header cell.

31. Drag the width of the third column from the left until it is about twice as wide as the word "Week" in the tablix header cell.

32. Drag the width of the fourth column from the left until it is about twice as wide as the words "Work Date" in the tablix header cell.

33. Select the cell containing "[Sum(EmployeeNumber)]" (you may not be able to see all of this expression on the screen). In addition, select the two cells to the right of this cell. Right-click this group of cells and select Tablix: Merge Cells from the context menu.

NOTE

If you are using SQL Server Data Tools or Visual Studio, the Expression and Text Box Properties items in the context menu may be disabled after you merge cells. To re-activate these context menu items, click elsewhere on the report to unselect the newly merged cell and then try right-clicking the merged cell again.

34. Modify the value of the merged cell that results from Step 33. Select Expression from the drop-down list to make editing easier. (You can select the field expressions from the Fields area and use Append to add them to the Expression area. Remember, the Globals, Parameters, and Fields expressions are case-sensitive!) Set the value to the following:

```
=Fields!EmployeeNumber.Value & "-" &
Fields!FirstName.Value & " " & Fields!LastName.Value
```

35. Click OK to exit the Expression dialog box. Your report layout should appear similar to Figure 8-12. (Adjust the row heights to match Figure 8-12, if necessary.)

36. Preview/Run the report. Your report should appear similar to Figure 8-13.

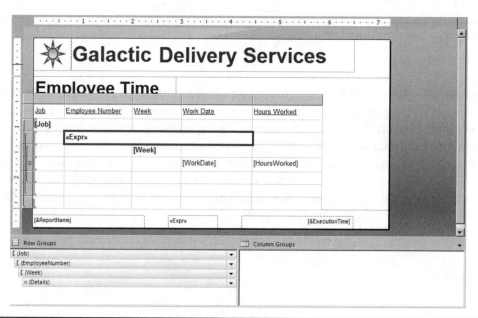

Figure 8-12   *Employee Time Report layout after Task 2*

Galactic Delivery Services

Employee Time

Job	Employee Number	Week	Work Date	Hours Worked
Mechanic I				
	1387-Lia Wong			
		2013-10		
			3/3/2013 12:00:00 AM	9.00
			3/4/2013 12:00:00 AM	8.00
			3/5/2013 12:00:00 AM	9.00
			3/6/2013 12:00:00 AM	9.00
			3/9/2013 12:00:00 AM	8.00
		2013-11		
			3/10/2013 12:00:00 AM	8.00
			3/11/2013 12:00:00 AM	9.00
			3/12/2013 12:00:00 AM	8.00
			3/13/2013 12:00:00 AM	9.00

Figure 8-13   *Employee Time Report preview after Task 2*

Task Notes   We placed a table on our report to contain the employee time information. We created three groups within the table to contain the groups required by the business needs for this report. The detail information is grouped into weeks. The week groups are grouped into employees. The employee groups are grouped into jobs. By merging cells in the grouping rows, we can give the report a stepped look, the same as we had in the TransportList report in Chapter 5. However, this approach, along with the merged cells, allows each group heading to flow across the top of the information below it. This provides more room for the detail information.

Employee Time Report, Task 3: Add Drilldown Capability

DT
RB

SSDT, Visual Studio, and Report Builder Steps

1. Return to Design mode.
2. Using the drop-down menu for EmployeeNumber group in the Row Groups pane, select Group Properties, as shown in Figure 8-14. The Group Properties dialog box appears.
3. Select the Visibility page.
4. Select the Hide radio button under the When the report is initially run: prompt.
5. Check the Display can be toggled by this report item check box.
6. Select Job from the drop-down list immediately below this check box.
7. Click OK to exit the Group Properties dialog box.
8. Using the drop-down menu for the Week group in the Row Groups pane, select Group Properties. The Group Properties dialog box appears.

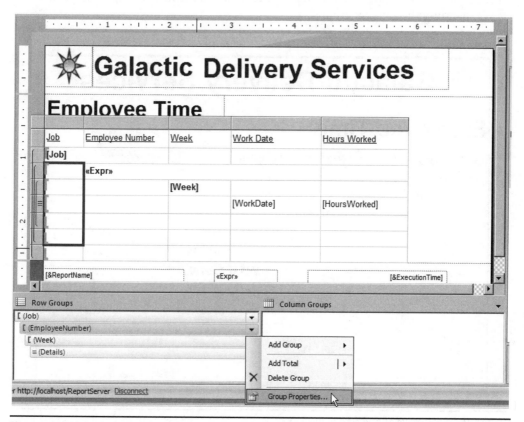

Figure 8-14 *Selecting Group Properties from the drop-down menu in the Row Groups pane*

9. Select the Visibility page.
10. Select the Hide radio button under the When the report is initially run: prompt.
11. Check the Display can be toggled by this report item check box.
12. Select EmployeeNumber from the drop-down list immediately below this check box.
13. Click OK to exit the Group Properties dialog box.
14. Using the drop-down menu for the Details group in the Row Groups pane, select Group Properties. The Group Properties dialog box appears.
15. Select the Visibility page.
16. Select the Hide radio button under the When the report is initially run: prompt.
17. Check the Display can be toggled by this report item check box.
18. Select Week from the drop-down list immediately below this check box.
19. Click OK to exit the Group Properties dialog box.
20. Preview/Run the report. Your report should appear similar to Figure 8-15 after expanding the top few groups.

Figure 8-15 *Employee Time Report preview after Task 3*

Task Notes   We now have the drilldown capability working as required for this report. This was done using the visibility and toggling properties of the groupings in the tablix. The visibility of each group is set to be toggled by a report item in the group above it. Therefore, the EmployeeNumber group is set to be toggled by the Job report item and the Week group is set to be toggled by the EmployeeNumber report item. The detail row of the table is treated as a group and is called the Details group. The details group is set to be toggled by the Week report item.

The Employee Number group, the Week group, and the Details group all have their initial visibility set to Hide. This means when you run the report in the Preview tab, you do not see any of these groups. Only the top group, the Job group, is visible.

Remember, in data regions, the items are repeated according to the rows in the dataset. Therefore, the report contains a number of Job group rows, one for each distinct job contained in the dataset. Each Job group contains sets of EmployeeNumber group rows, Week group rows, and the Details group rows.

The first Job group contains a Job report item (text box) with a value of Mechanic I. There is a small plus (+) sign in front of Mechanic I because it controls the visibility of the EmployeeNumber group rows in the Mechanic I Job group. Clicking the plus sign changes the visibility of all the EmployeeNumber group rows in the Mechanic I Job group from Hide to Show. The EmployeeNumber group rows in the Mechanic I Job group now show up on the report.

When the EmployeeNumber group rows are visible in the Mechanic I Job group, the plus sign next to Mechanic I changes to a minus sign. Clicking the minus (–) sign will again change the visibility of all the EmployeeNumber group rows in the Mechanic I Job group, this time from Show to Hide. The EmployeeNumber group rows in the Mechanic I Job group now disappear from the report.

Click the plus and minus signs to change the visibility of various groups and detail rows in the report. Make sure you have a good understanding of how visibility and toggling are working in the report. We make it a bit more complicated in Task 4.

Employee Time Report, Task 4: Add Totaling

DT
RB
SSDT, Visual Studio, and Report Builder Steps

1. Return to Design mode.
2. Right-click the rightmost cell in the header row for the outermost group (the Job group), and select Textbox: Text Box Properties from the context menu. The Text Box Properties dialog box appears.
3. Type the following for Value:

   ```
   =Sum(Fields!HoursWorked.Value)
   ```

4. Select the Visibility page of the dialog box.

5. Check the Display can be toggled by this report item check box.

6. Select Job from the drop-down list immediately below this check box. (We are leaving the Show radio button selected.)

7. Click OK to exit the Text Box Properties dialog box.

8. Right-click the rightmost cell in the header row for the middle group (the EmployeeNumber group), and select Textbox: Text Box Properties from the context menu. The Text Box Properties dialog box appears.

9. Type the following for Value:

```
=Sum(Fields!HoursWorked.Value)
```

10. Select the Visibility page of the dialog box.

11. Check the Display can be toggled by this report item check box.

12. Select EmployeeNumber from the drop-down list immediately below this check box. (We are leaving the Show radio button selected.)

13. Click OK to exit the Text Box Properties dialog box.

14. Right-click the rightmost cell in the header row for the innermost group (the Week group), and select Textbox: Text Box Properties from the context menu. The Text Box Properties dialog box appears.

15. Type the following for Value:

```
=Sum(Fields!HoursWorked.Value)
```

16. Select the Visibility page of the dialog box.

17. Check the Display can be toggled by this report item check box.

18. Select Week from the drop-down list immediately below this check box. (We are leaving the Show radio button selected.)

19. Click OK to exit the Text Box Properties dialog box.

20. Click the gray square for the footer row of the outermost group. Modify the following properties for this footer row using the Properties window:

Property	Value
Hidden	True
ToggleItem	Job

21. Click the gray square for the footer row of the middle group. Modify the following properties for this footer row using the Properties window:

Property	Value
Hidden	True
ToggleItem	EmployeeNumber

22. Click the gray square for the footer row of the innermost group. Modify the following properties for this footer row using the Properties window:

Property	Value
Hidden	True
ToggleItem	Week

23. Select the rightmost cell in the footer row of the innermost group. Modify the following properties for this text box using the Properties window:

Property	Value
BorderColor: Top	Black
BorderStyle: Top	Solid
Font: FontWeight	Bold
Value (Right-click the text box and select Expression from the drop-down list to make it easier to enter this value.)	=Sum(Fields!HoursWorked.Value)

24. Repeat Step 23 for the rightmost cell in the footer row of the middle group.

25. Repeat Step 23 for the rightmost cell in the footer row of the outermost group.

26. Right-click anywhere in the last row of the tablix, and select Tablix: Insert Row | Outside Group - Below from the context menu. A row that will serve as a tablix footer row is added.

27. Select the rightmost cell in this new tablix footer row. Modify the following properties for this text box using the Properties window:

Property	Value
BorderColor: Top	Black
BorderStyle: Top	Double
BorderWidth: Top	3pt
Font: FontWeight	Bold
Value (Right-click the text box and select Expression from the drop-down list to make it easier to enter this value.)	=Sum(Fields!HoursWorked.Value)

28. Your report layout should appear similar to Figure 8-16.

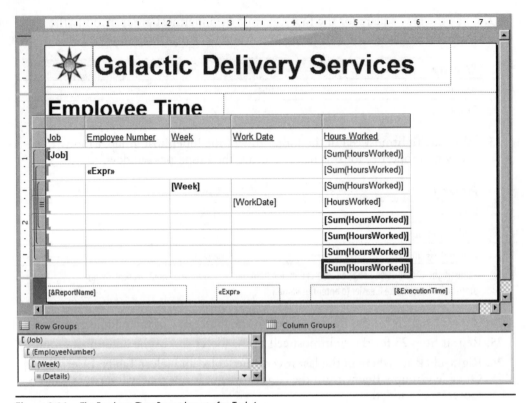

Figure 8-16   *The Employee Time Report layout after Task 4*

29. Preview/Run the report. Your report should appear similar to Figure 8-17 when the top few groups are expanded.
30. Save the report.

Task Notes   Now we not only have a report with group totals, we have a report that keeps its group totals where they ought to be. When the group is collapsed, the group total is on the same line with the group header. When the group is expanded, the group total moves from the group header to the group footer.

When you think about it, this is how you would expect things to work. When the group is collapsed, we expect it to collapse down to one line. Therefore, the group total should be on the line with the group header. When the group is expanded, we see a column of numbers in the group. We would naturally expect the total for that column of numbers to be below it. Therefore, the group total should move to the group footer.

Galactic Delivery Services

Employee Time

Job	Employee Number	Week	Work Date	Hours Worked
⊟ Mechanic I				
	⊟ 1387-Lia Wong			
		⊟ 2013-10		
			3/3/2013 12:00:00 AM	9.00
			3/4/2013 12:00:00 AM	8.00
			3/5/2013 12:00:00 AM	9.00
			3/6/2013 12:00:00 AM	9.00
			3/9/2013 12:00:00 AM	8.00
				43.00
		⊞ 2013-11		42.00
		⊞ 2013-12		44.00
		⊞ 2013-13		42.00
		⊞ 2013-14		44.00

Figure 8-17   *The Employee Time Report preview after Task 4*

We achieved this functionality by using our toggle items to control the visibility of three other items at the same time. In the previous section, we discussed the fact that Mechanic I controls the visibility of the EmployeeNumber group rows in the Mechanic I Job group. Now, Mechanic I also controls the visibility of the Hours Worked total in the group header and the Hours Worked total in the group footer. The Hours Worked total in the group header is initially set to Visible. The Hours Worked total in the group footer is initially set to Hidden.

When the plus sign next to Mechanic I is clicked, three things occur:

▶ The EmployeeNumber group rows are set to Visible.

▶ The Hours Worked total in the group header is set to Hidden.

▶ The Hours Worked total in the group footer is set to Visible.

When the minus sign next to Mechanic I is clicked, the reverse takes place. This same behavior occurs at each level. Again, you can click the plus and minus signs to change the visibility of various groups and detail rows in the report. Make sure you understand how the visibility and toggle items interrelate.

The other feature of note used in this task is the Sum( ) aggregate function. If you were paying attention, you noticed we used the following expression in a number of different locations:

```
= Sum(Fields!HoursWorked.Value)
```

If you were paying close attention, you also noticed this expression yields a number of different results. How does this happen? It happens through the magic of scope.

Scope is the data grouping in which the aggregate function is placed. For example, the Sum() function placed in the Job group header row (the outermost header row) uses the current Job group as its scope. It sums hours worked only for those records in the current Job group data grouping. The Sum() function placed in the EmployeeNumber group header row (the middle header row) uses the current EmployeeNumber group as its scope. It sums the hours worked only for those records in the current EmployeeNumber group data grouping. The Sum() function placed in the footer row at the bottom of the tablix is not within any data grouping, so it sums the hours worked in the entire dataset.

As you have seen in this report, it does not make a difference whether the aggregate function is placed in the group header or the group footer—either way, the aggregate function acts on all the values in the current data grouping. At first, this may seem a bit counterintuitive. It is easy to think of the report being processed sequentially, from the top of the page to the bottom. In this scenario, the total for a group would only be available in the group footer after the contents of that group are processed. Fortunately, this is not the way Reporting Services works. The calculation of aggregates is separate from the rendering of the report. Therefore, aggregates can be placed anywhere in the report.

Finally, it is important not to confuse the aggregate functions within Reporting Services with the aggregate functions that exist within the environs of SQL Server. Many of the Reporting Services aggregate functions have the same names as SQL Server aggregate functions. Despite this, Reporting Services aggregate functions and SQL Server aggregate functions work in different locations.

SQL Server aggregate functions work within a SQL Server query. They are executed by SQL Server as the dataset is being created by the database server. SQL Server aggregate functions do not have a concept of scope. They simply act on all the data that satisfies the WHERE clause of the query. As just discussed, Reporting Services aggregate functions are executed after the dataset is created, as the report is executing, and are dependent on scope.

Here is a list of the Reporting Services aggregate functions:

Avg()	Calculates the average of the values in a scope.
Count()	Counts the number of values in a scope.
CountDistinct()	Counts the number of unique values in a scope.
CountRows()	Counts the number of rows in a scope.
First()	Returns the first value in the scope.
Last()	Returns the last value in the scope.
Max()	Returns the maximum value in the scope.
Min()	Returns the minimum value in the scope.
StDev()	Calculates the standard deviation of the values in the scope.
StDevP()	Calculates the population standard deviation of the values in the scope.
Sum()	Calculates the sum of the values in the scope.
Var()	Calculates the variance of the values in the scope.
VarP()	Calculates the population variance of the values in the scope.

Each of the aggregate functions in the previous table returns a single result for the entire scope. The following two functions are known as running aggregates. The *running aggregates* return a result for each record in the scope. That result is based on a value in the current row and all of the previous rows in the scope.

The running aggregate functions are:

RowNumber()	Returns the number of the current row, starting at 1 and counting upward. (Found under Common Functions | Miscellaneous.)
RunningValue()	Returns the running sum of the values.

Data Caching During Preview

You switched between layout and preview a number of times during the development of the Employee Time report. If you were to look on your SQL Server, however, you would find the rather complex query that provides the data for this report was only executed once. This is because the data returned for the dataset the first time the report was run is stored in cache. Any time after that, when the same report is run in the authoring environment with the same query, same parameters, and same data access credentials, the cached data is used.

This data caching helps to make your report development sessions more efficient. Even if you have a report based on a query that takes a fair amount of time to run,

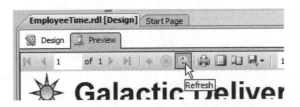

Figure 8-18   *The Refresh toolbar button in SSDT and Visual Studio*

you only have to wait for it once. Any time you preview/run the report after that, the data is pulled from the cache file with no delay. This caching process also substantially decreases the load on your SQL server. This can be important if you are following the frowned-upon practice of developing reports against a production database server.

The drawback to the data-caching process comes when you are making changes to the data at the same time you are developing a report. If you insert new records or update existing records after the first time you preview the report and then expect to see those changes in your report the next time you preview it, you are going to be confused, disappointed, or perhaps both. The report is rendered from the cached data that does not include the changes.

To remedy this situation, click the Refresh toolbar button, shown in Figure 8-18 in SSDT and Visual Studio, and in Figure 8-19 in Report Builder. This will cause the authoring environment to rerun the queries in the report and create a new cache. SSDT and Visual Studio store this cached data in a file in the same folder as the report definition file that has the same name, with a .data extension on the end. For example, MyReport.rdl has a cache file located in the same folder called MyReport.rdl.data.

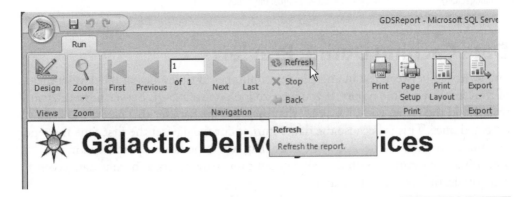

Figure 8-19   *The Refresh ribbon button in Report Builder*

Remember, this data-caching process is only used by the authoring environment during report development. A different data-caching scheme operates on the report server after the report has been put into production. We discuss that caching scheme in Chapter 11.

The Employee List Report

Features Highlighted

▶ Implementing user-selectable grouping

▶ Implementing interactive sorting

▶ Using explicit page breaks

▶ Using a floating header

Business Need   The Galactic Delivery Services personnel department wants a flexible report for listing employee information. Rather than having a number of reports for each of their separate grouping and sorting needs, they want a single report where they can choose the grouping and sort order each time the report is run. The report should be able to group on job, hub, or city of residence. The report should be able to sort by employee number, last name, or hire date. Also, each new group should start on a new page. The header information should remain visible even when the user scrolls down the report page.

Task Overview

1. Create a New Report and a Dataset
2. Create the Report Layout
3. Add Interactive Sorting and a Floating Header

Employee List Report, Task 1: Create a New Report and a Dataset

DT   **SSDT and Visual Studio Steps**

1. Reopen the Chapter08 project, if it was closed. Close the EmployeeTime report, if it is still open.
2. Right-click Reports in the Solution Explorer, and select Add | New Item from the context menu. The Add New Item - Chapter08 dialog box appears.
3. Single-click GDSReport in the Templates area to select it. Change the name to EmployeeList, and click Add.

4. Create a data source called "Galactic" in this new report. This new data source should reference the Galactic shared data source.

5. Create a dataset called "Employees" with the following query:

```
SELECT Job.Description AS Job,
       Hub.Description AS Hub,
       Employee.EmployeeNumber,
       FirstName,
       LastName,
       Address1,
       City,
       State,
       ZipCode,
       HireDate,
       HighestLevelOfEducation,
       UnionMembership
FROM Employee
INNER JOIN Assignment
       ON Employee.EmployeeNumber = Assignment.EmployeeNumber
INNER JOIN Job
       ON Assignment.JobID = Job.JobID
INNER JOIN Hub
       ON Assignment.HubCode = Hub.HubCode
```

`RB`   **Report Builder Steps**

1. Click the logo button, and select Open from the menu. The Open Report dialog box appears.

2. Navigate to the Template folder.

3. Double-click the GDSReport item to open it.

4. Click the logo button, and select Save As from the menu. The Save As Report dialog box appears.

5. Navigate to the Chapter08 folder.

6. Enter **EmployeeList** for Name, and click Save.

7. Create a data source called "Galactic" in this new report. This new data source should reference the Galactic shared data source.

8. Create a dataset called "Employees" with the following query:

```
SELECT Job.Description AS Job,
       Hub.Description AS Hub,
       Employee.EmployeeNumber,
       FirstName,
       LastName,
       Address1,
       City,
       State,
       ZipCode,
       HireDate,
```

```
        HighestLevelOfEducation,
        UnionMembership
FROM Employee
INNER JOIN Assignment
        ON Employee.EmployeeNumber = Assignment.EmployeeNumber
INNER JOIN Job
        ON Assignment.JobID = Job.JobID
INNER JOIN Hub
        ON Assignment.HubCode = Hub.HubCode
```

Task Notes   Notice no ORDER BY clause is in our SELECT statement. In most cases, this would cause a problem. Users like to have their information show up in something other than a random sort order. In this case it is fine, because we are sorting the data within the report itself according to what the user selects as report parameters.

Employee List Report, Task 2: Create the Report Layout

DT   **SSDT, Visual Studio, and Report Builder Steps**

RB
1. Place a text box onto the body of the report. Modify the following properties of this text box:

Property	Value
Font: FontSize	25pt
Font: FontWeight	Bold
Location: Left	0in
Location: Top	0in
Size: Width	2.875in
Size: Height	0.5in
Value	Employee List

2. Use the table template to place a tablix onto the body of the report immediately below the text box you just added.
3. Hover over the leftmost field in the data row of the tablix, and select the EmployeeNumber field from the Field Selector.

NOTE

From this point on, the steps will simply instruct you to select a given field in a given cell. You should use the Field Selector to make these selections.

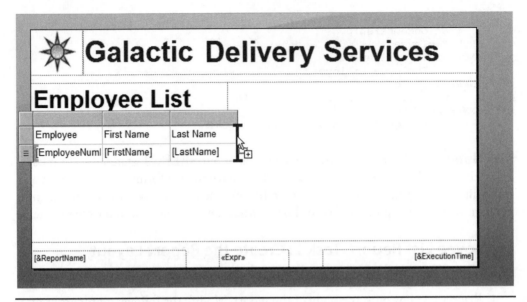

Figure 8-20   *Dragging a field to add a new column to a tablix*

4. Select the FirstName field in the middle cell in the data row of the tablix.

5. Select the LastName field in the rightmost cell in the data row of the tablix.

6. Drag the Address1 field from the Report Data window onto the right edge of the tablix, as shown in Figure 8-20. This will create a new column in the tablix.

7. Repeat Step 6 for the City, State, ZipCode, HireDate, HighestLevelOfEducation, and UnionMembership fields. As the tablix grows wider, the report body will also grow wider to accommodate it.

8. Right-click the cell in the detail row containing the HireDate, and select Textbox: Text Box Properties from the context menu. The Text Box Properties dialog box appears.

9. Modify the following properties:

Property	Value
Number page:	
Category	Date
Type	January 31, 2000
Alignment page:	
Horizontal	Left

10. Click OK to exit the Text Box Properties dialog box.
11. Size each column and row appropriately. Preview/Run the report to check your work. Continue switching between Design and Preview/Run until you have the table columns sized correctly.
12. Drag the right edge of the report body layout area until it is just touching the right side of the tablix.
13. Click the gray square for the table header row to select the entire row. Modify the following property:

Property	Value
Font: TextDecoration	Underline

14. In the Report Data window, right-click the Parameters entry, and select Add Parameter from the context menu. The Report Parameter Properties dialog box appears.
15. Type **GroupOrder** for Name and **Group By** for Prompt.
16. Select the Available Values page.
17. Select the Specify values radio button.
18. Add the following items to the list. (Click Add to create each new entry.)

Label	Value
Job	Job
Hub	Hub
City	City

19. Select the Default Values page.
20. Select the Specify values radio button.
21. Add the following item to the list. (Click Add to create a new entry.)

Value
Job

22. Click OK to exit the Report Parameter Properties dialog box.
23. Right-click in the gray square in the upper-left corner of the tablix, and select Tablix Properties from the context menu. The Tablix Properties dialog box appears.

24. In the Column Headers section of the General page, check the Repeat header columns on each page check box. (Make sure you are in the Column Headers section and not the Row Headers section of the General page.)

25. Click OK to exit the Tablix Properties dialog box.

26. Right-click anywhere in the detail row of the tablix, and select Tablix: Add Group | Row Group: Parent Group. The Tablix group dialog box appears.

27. Click the *fx* button. The Expression dialog box appears.

28. Type the following in the Set expression for: GroupExpression area:

```
= IIF(Parameters!GroupOrder.Value = "Job", Fields!Job.Value,
    IIF(Parameters!GroupOrder.Value = "Hub", Fields!Hub.Value,
        Fields!City.Value))
```

NOTE

Use the Parameters and Fields entries in the Expression dialog box to help build expressions, such as the previous one. Double-click the desired parameter or field to add it to the expression you are building.

29. Highlight the entire expression you just entered, and press CTRL-C to copy this text.

30. Click OK to exit the Expression dialog box.

31. Check the Add group header check box.

32. Click OK to exit the Tablix group dialog box.

33. In the Row Groups pane, use the drop-down menu for Group1 to select Group Properties. The Group Properties dialog box appears.

34. Select the Page Breaks page.

35. Check the Between each instance of a group check box.

36. Select the Sorting page.

37. Click the *fx* button. The Expression dialog box appears. Note the tablix is automatically set to sort by our grouping expression.

38. Click OK to exit the Expression dialog box.

39. Leave the Order set to "A to Z." Click OK to exit the Group Properties dialog box.

40. In the Row Groups pane, use the drop-down menu for Details to select Group Properties. The Group Properties dialog box appears.

41. Select the Sorting page.

42. Click Add to create a new sorting entry.

43. Select [EmployeeNumber] from the Sort by drop-down list.

44. Leave the Oorder set to "A to Z." Click OK to exit the Group Properties dialog box.

45. Click the cell in the tablix containing the "<<Expr>>" expression placeholder. Press DELETE to remove the text box in this cell. Repeat this with the cell containing the "Group1" heading. Size the leftmost column so it is as narrow as possible.

46. Right-click the cell containing the [EmployeeNumber] placeholder, and select Tablix: Insert Column | Left.

47. Right-click the detail row of this new column, and select Tablix: Add Group | Column Group: Parent Group. The Tablix group dialog box appears.

48. Enter **=1** for Group by, and check the Add group header check box. Click OK to exit the Tablix group dialog box.

49. Click the cell in the tablix containing the "<<Expr>>" expression placeholder. Press DELETE to remove the text box in this cell. Size the two leftmost columns so they are as narrow as possible.

50. Select the three cells in the group header row under EmployeeNumber, FirstName, and LastName. (This is the third row from the top in the tablix.) Right-click these cells, and select Tablix: Merge Cells from the context menu.

51. Right-click these cells again, and select Textbox: Expression from the context menu. The Expression dialog box appears.

52. Delete the equal sign from the Set expression for: Value area, and press CTRL-V to paste the expression into the Expression area. This should be the same expression you entered in Step 28.

53. Click OK to exit the Expression dialog box.

54. Modify the following property of the merged cells:

Property	Value
Font: Weight	Bold

55. Click the text box containing the Employee Number header (only the "Employee" portion may be visible). Hold down SHIFT and click the text box containing the Union Membership header (again, only the "Union" portion may be visible). This will select all of the header text boxes.

56. Press CTRL-X to cut these text boxes.

57. Press UP ARROW to select a text box in the top row of the tablix.

58. Press CTRL-V to paste the header text boxes in the top row of the tablix.

59. Right-click the gray box to the left of the empty row (the row from which we just removed the header text boxes), and select Delete Rows from the context menu. Your report layout should appear similar to Figure 8-21.

Figure 8-21   *The Employee List report layout after Task 2*

60. Preview/Run the report. Your report should appear similar to Figure 8-22. Experiment with changing the grouping. Remember to click View Report each time to refresh the report and to page through the report to view the pagination.

61. Save the report.

Task Notes   In this report, the report parameter is used to control properties within the report rather than as a parameter to a SQL query. Because of this, we needed to create this report parameter manually, rather than having it created automatically from

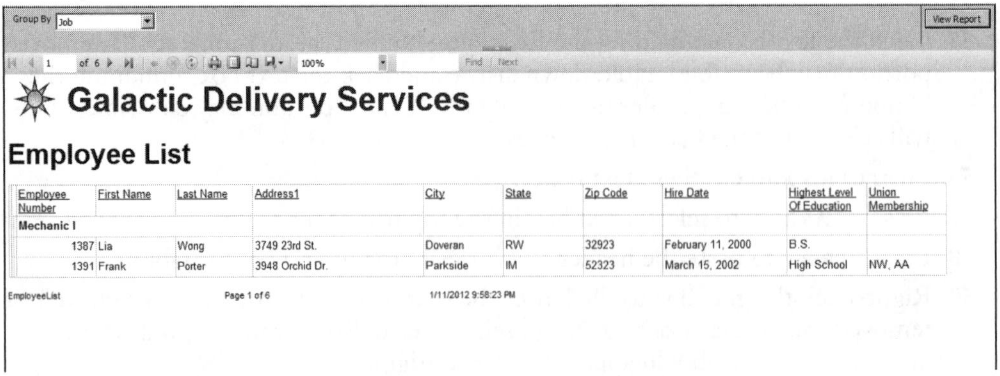

Figure 8-22   *The Employee List report preview after Task 2*

the dataset query. We also manually constructed a list of valid values and provided a default value. We were then able to use the value selected for this parameter to change the grouping and the group sorting of the tablix in the report.

We are able to change the grouping and group sorting of the tablix because of the IIF() function. This function has three parameters. The first parameter is a Boolean expression (in other words, an expression that results in either a true or false value). The second parameter is the value returned if the Boolean expression is true. The third parameter is the value returned if the Boolean expression is false.

Let's take a look at our expressions using the IIF() function:

```
= IIF( Parameters!GroupOrder.Value = "Job", Fields!Job.Value,
      IIF(Parameters!GroupOrder.Value = "Hub", Fields!Hub.Value,
          Fields!City.Value))
```

This expression uses two IIF() functions, one nested inside the other. The first parameter of the outer IIF() function is

```
Parameters!GroupOrder.Value = "Job"
```

If Job is selected for the grouping, the value of the second parameter is returned by the function. In this case, the second parameter is

```
Fields!Job.Value
```

Therefore, if Job is selected for the grouping, the value of the Job field is used.

If Job is not selected for the grouping, the value of the third parameter is returned. The value of this third parameter is another complete IIF() function:

```
IIF(Parameters!GroupOrder.Value = "Hub", Fields!Hub.Value,
            Fields!City.Value)
```

In this second IIF() function, if Hub is selected for the grouping, the second parameter of this IIF() function is returned. Here, the second parameter is

```
Fields!Hub.Value
```

Therefore, if Hub is selected for the grouping, the value of the Hub field is used.

Finally, if Hub is not selected for the grouping, the value of the third parameter of this IIF() function is returned. Here, the third parameter is

```
Fields!City.Value
```

Therefore, if Hub is not selected for the grouping, the value of the City field is used.

We used the same expression for both the grouping and the group sorting. The group sorting property sorts the groups themselves so they come out in the proper order. We also set the sorting for the Details Group. This provided a default sort order for the rows within each group. In other words, it provided a sorting at the detail level.

In many cases, a report needs to start each new group on a new page. We used the Between each instance of a group page break option in the Tablix Group Properties dialog box to force the report to start a new page between each grouping. Additional page break options can be set to force a page break before the first grouping or after the last grouping. Page breaks can also be set for other report items. For instance, you can force a page break before the beginning of a tablix or after the end of a tablix. We created what amounts to a dummy column group in the tablix. This dummy group uses a grouping expression of "=1" that will have a value of 1 for every record in the data set. Therefore, all of the records will be in the same group. This dummy group allows us to create a set of column headers that will be repeated on each page and will also remain visible while scrolling down a page (see Step 3 in the next section). In Figure 8-21, notice the double-dashed line separating the top row from the rest of the tablix. The rows above the double-dashed line are recognized as column header rows. The repeat header rows and headers remain visible properties only apply to these special column header rows. The same is true with the equivalent settings for row header columns.

Employee List Report, Task 3: Add Interactive Sorting and a Floating Header

SSDT, Visual Studio, and Report Builder Steps

1. Return to Design mode.
2. Bring up the Tablix Properties dialog box.
3. In the Column Headers section of the General page, check the Keep header visible while scrolling check box. (Make sure you are in the Column Headers section and not the Row Headers section of the General page.)
4. Click OK to exit the Tablix Properties dialog box.
5. Click anywhere on the tablix. Click the gray square for the tablix header row. (The row containing the column headings.) Modify the following property:

Property	Value
BackgroundColor	White

6. Right-click the Employee Number text box in the tablix header row, and select Text Box Properties from the context menu. The Text Box Properties dialog box appears.

7. Select the Interactive Sorting page.

8. Check the Enable interactive sorting on this text box check box.

9. Make sure the Detail rows radio button is selected.

10. Select [EmployeeNumber] from the Sort by drop-down list.

11. Click OK to exit the Text Box Properties dialog box.

12. Right-click the Last Name text box in the tablix header row, and select Text Box Properties from the context menu. The Text Box Properties dialog box appears.

13. Select the Interactive Sorting page.

14. Check the Enable interactive sorting on this text box check box.

15. Make sure the Detail rows radio button is selected.

16. Click the Expression button (the button with *fx* on it) next to the Sort by drop-down list. The Expression dialog box appears.

17. Type the following in the Set expression for: SortExpression area:

```
=Fields!LastName.Value & " " & Fields!FirstName.Value
```

18. Click OK to exit the Expression dialog box.

19. Click OK to exit the Text Box Properties dialog box.

20. Right-click the Hire Date text box in the tablix header row, and select Text Box Properties from the context menu. The Text Box Properties dialog box appears.

21. Select the Interactive Sorting page.

22. Check the Enable interactive sorting on this text box check box.

23. Make sure the Detail rows radio button is selected.

24. Select [HireDate] from the Sort by drop-down list.

25. Click OK to exit the Text Box Properties dialog box.

26. Preview/Run the report.

27. Click the Interactive Sort button next to the Last Name column, as shown in Figure 8-23.

28. Page through the report and note that, within each group, the rows are now sorted by last name in ascending order.

29. Click the Interactive Sort button next to the Last Name column again. You return to the first page of the report. Again, page through the report and note that the rows are now sorted by last name in descending order.

30. Click the Interactive Sort button next to the Hire Date column heading. You return to the first page of the report.

31. Page through the report once more. The rows are now sorted by hire date in ascending order.

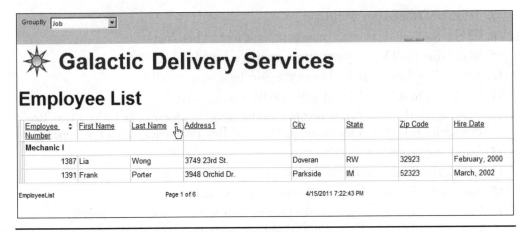

Figure 8-23 *The Employee List Report with interactive sorting*

32. Go to Page 5 of the report.

33. Scroll up and down through the page, and notice the table headers always remain visible at the top of the page.

34. Save the report.

Task Notes   The interactive sort feature enables the user viewing the report to choose the sort order they would like to see. This could also be done using a report parameter passed as part of the query that creates the dataset. This scheme requires the query to be rerun every time the sort order is changed. Interactive sorting, on the other hand, redisplays the report in the newly selected sort order without rerunning the dataset query. The sorting is all done within the report renderer, using the data already collected from the data source.

The Interactive Sorting page of the Text Box Properties dialog box, shown in Figure 8-24, gives us a number of options for the interactive sort. In our report, we chose to have the interactive sort work on the detail rows of the tablix. This option changes the order of the detail records within each of the groups in the tablix. There is also a radio button that enables the sorting of groups themselves within the tablix. In addition, there is an option to enable the sorting of other groups and data regions based on this interactive sort selection.

The floating header does, indeed, seem to float over the columns of the report as you scroll down the page. For this reason, the background of a floating header row should be set to something other than transparent. If this is not done, the column data shows right through the header, making it rather difficult to read.

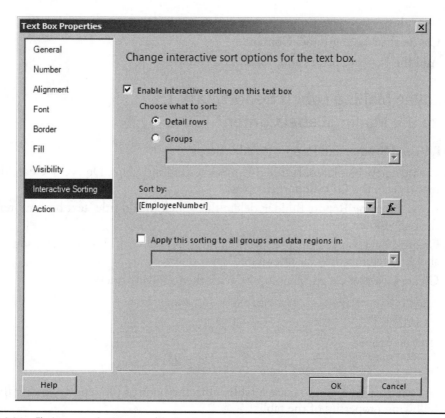

Figure 8-24   *The Interactive Sorting page of the Text Box Properties dialog box*

The Employee Mailing Labels Report

Features Highlighted

▶   Enable multiple columns

▶   Put information from the database into the report header

Business Need   The Galactic Delivery Services personnel department has a new version of the employee manual. The personnel department needs mailing labels to send the new manual out to each employee. The mailing labels are to be printed on a 2½-inches wide by 1-inch high label. The label sheet has three labels across the sheet and ten labels down the sheet, with no margin between each label.

The labels should be sorted by ZIP code and then last name. It would also be helpful if the total number of labels is printed in the top margin of the first page printed. Finally, a sequence number should be printed in the lower-right corner of each label.

Task Overview

1. Create the Mailing Label Content
2. Add the Report Header and Multiple Columns

Employee Mailing Labels Report, Task 1: Create the Mailing Label Content

 SSDT, Visual Studio, and Report Builder Steps

1. Create a new blank report called EmployeeMailingLabels. Do NOT create this report from the GDSReport template.
2. If you are using Report Builder, delete the "Click to add title" text box and remove the page footer.
3. Create a data source called "Galactic" in this new report. This new data source should reference the Galactic shared data source.
4. Create a dataset called "Employees" with the following query:

```
SELECT FirstName + ' ' + LastName AS Name,
     Address1,
     City + ', ' + State + ' ' + ZipCode AS CSZ
FROM Employee
WHERE TerminationDate IS NULL
ORDER BY ZipCode, LastName, FirstName
```

5. Use the List template to place a tablix onto the body of the report. Modify the following properties of the tablix:

Property	Value
Location: Left	0in
Location: Top	0in
Size:Width	2.5in
Size:Height	1in

6. In the Report Data window, select the Name field and drag it onto the tablix. Select the resulting text box, and set the following properties:

Property	Value
Location: Left	0in
Location: Top	0in
Size:Width	2.25in
Size:Height	0.25in

7. Drag the Address1 field onto the tablix, and set the following properties of the resulting text box:

Property	Value
Location: Left	0in
Location: Top	0.25in
Size:Width	2.25in
Size:Height	0.25in

8. Drag the CSZ field onto the tablix, and set the following properties of the resulting text box:

Property	Value
Location: Left	0in
Location: Top	0.5in
Size:Width	2.25in
Size:Height	0.25in

9. Place a text box onto the list, and set the following properties of the text box:

Property	Value
Font: FontSize	8 pt
Location: Left	1.125in
Location: Top	0.75in
Size:Width	1.375in
Size:Height	0.25in
TextAlign	Right
VerticalAlign	Bottom

10. Right-click the text box you just added, and select Expression from the context menu. The Expression dialog box appears.

11. Expand the Common Functions item in the Category pane, and select Miscellaneous. The Item list in the center contains the miscellaneous functions available in Reporting Services.

12. Double-click RowNumber in the Item list to add the RowNumber aggregate to the expression.

13. To complete the expression, type **"Tablix1")** after the (.

14. Click OK to exit the Expression dialog box.

15. Adjust the size of the tablix if it grew during the creation of the layout.

Property	Value
Size:Width	2.5in
Size:Height	1in

16. Adjust the report body so it is exactly the same size as the tablix report item.
17. Preview/Run the report. Your report should appear similar to Figure 8-25.
18. Save the report.

Task Notes   The Expression dialog box provides assistance in building expressions. Earlier, we talked about the syntax checking done as you type an expression and the jagged red line that indicates an error. The Expression dialog box enables you to add global variables, parameters, fields, and even common functions to an expression with a double-click.

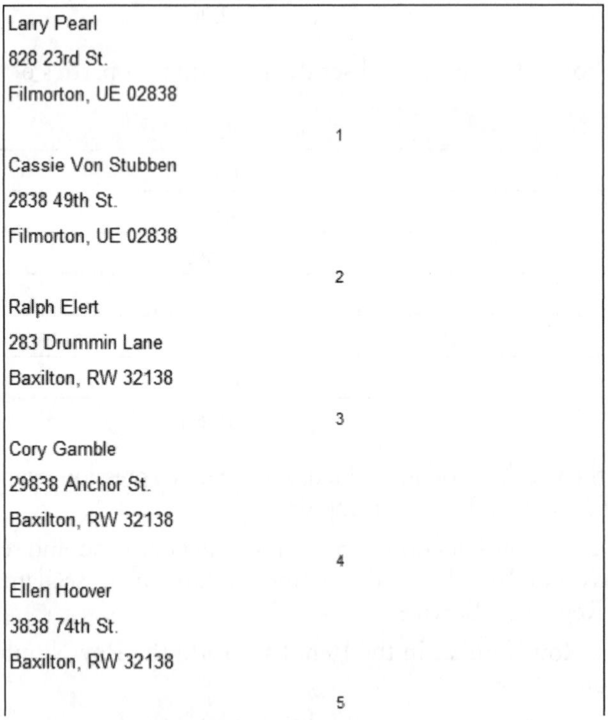

```
Larry Pearl
828 23rd St.
Filmorton, UE 02838
                                    1

Cassie Von Stubben
2838 49th St.
Filmorton, UE 02838
                                    2

Ralph Elert
283 Drummin Lane
Baxilton, RW 32138
                                    3

Cory Gamble
29838 Anchor St.
Baxilton, RW 32138
                                    4

Ellen Hoover
3838 74th St.
Baxilton, RW 32138
                                    5
```

Figure 8-25   *The Employee Mailing Labels Report preview after Task 1*

The business requirements call for a sequence number on each label. To do this, we look to the functions available in Reporting Services. The RowNumber function provides just what is needed.

In the next section, you finalize the formatting of the mailing labels. One of the business requirements was for the count of the number of employees at the top of the first page of labels. The Employees dataset returns the employee count, so we have the information we need. The only place we can put this employee count without messing up the label layout is in the page header.

Employee Mailing Labels Report, Task 2: Add the Report Header and Multiple Columns

DT
RB
SSDT, Visual Studio, and Report Builder Steps

1. Return to Design mode.

2. If you are using SSDT or Visual Studio, select Report | Add Page Header from the main menu. If you are using Report Builder, select Header | Add Header on the Insert tab of the ribbon.

3. Drag the Name field from the Report Data window, and drop it in the page header layout area.

4. Position the text box created in Step 3 in the upper-left corner of the page header. Make the text box as wide as the Name, Address1, and CSZ fields in the report body. A blue alignment line will appear when these text boxes are the same width.

5. Drag the page header so it is only as tall as the text box you just created. This is done by clicking the dotted line between the page header and the report body and dragging upward.

6. Right-click the text box in the page header, and select Expression from the context menu. The Expression dialog box appears.

NOTE

The Name field was placed on the report layout outside of a data region. Therefore, the Report Builder must place the field inside an aggregate function to get a single value. By default, a numeric field is placed inside a Sum() aggregate and a non-numeric field is placed inside a First() aggregate.

7. Replace the word "First" with **Count** to get a count of the number of records in the dataset.

8. Modify the expression so it appears as follows:

```
="Total Employees: " & CStr(Count(Fields!Name.Value, "Employees"))
```

9. Click OK to exit the Expression dialog box.

10. Right-click the text box in the page header, and select Text Box Properties from the context menu. The Text Box Properties dialog box appears.

11. Select the Visibility page.

12. Select the Show or hide based on an expression radio button under the When the report is initially run prompt.

13. Click the *fx* button below and to the right of the radio button you just selected. The Expression dialog box appears.

14. Expand Common Functions in the Category pane, and select Program Flow in the list on the left.

15. Double-click IIf in the Item pane.

16. Select Built-in Fields in the Category pane.

17. Double-click PageNumber in the Item pane.

18. Type > **1, true, false)** at the end of the expression.

19. Click OK to exit the Expression dialog box.

20. Click OK to exit the Text Box Properties dialog box.

21. Click in the design window someplace outside of the report body. In the Properties window, Report will be selected at the top of the window.

22. Modify the following properties of the report:

Property	Value
Columns: Columns	3
Columns: ColumnSpacing	0in

23. Right-click anywhere in the design window outside of the report body, and select Report Properties from the context menu. The Report Properties dialog box appears.

24. Modify the following properties:

Property	Value
Margins: Left	0.5in
Margins: Right	0.5in
Margins: Top	0.25in
Margins: Bottom	0.5in

25. Click OK to exit the Report Properties dialog box. Your report layout should appear similar to Figure 8-26.

26. Preview/Run the report. Click the Print Layout toolbar button. The report appears similar to Figure 8-27 when viewed at 50 %.

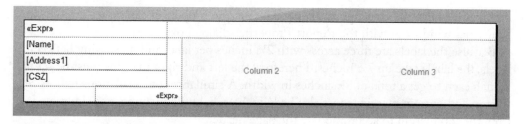

Figure 8-26   *The Employee Mailing Labels Report layout after Task 2*

27. Click the Print Layout toolbar button to exit print layout mode.

28. Save the report.

Task Notes   The business requirements specify that the employee count should only be displayed on the first page. The page header has properties that hide it on the first page or the last page. There is no option to have it display only on the first page. To accomplish this, you created an expression to control the visibility of the text box in the page header. If the page number is less than or equal to 1, the employee count is visible. If the page number is greater than 1, the employee count is hidden.

In addition, you need to set up the report layout to match the label sheet. This is done using properties of the report itself. The Columns property, of course, specifies the number of columns in the report. The Spacing property specifies the amount of space in between each column. These must be set using the Properties window. In addition,

Total Employees: 56

Larry Pearl	Ramona Carson	Walter Hederson
828 23rd St.	2384 Juniper Ln.	135 Small Street
Filmorton, UE 02838	Doveran, RW 32923	Axion, RE 37487
1	11	21
Cassie Von Stubben	Stanley Roosevelt	Greg Perkins
2838 49th St.	2839 32nd Ave.	8283 58th Ave.
Filmorton, UE 02838	Doveran, RW 32923	Axion, RE 37487
2	12	22
Ralph Elert	Winifred Stanton	Daniel Taylor
283 Drummin Lane	2839 Overton Dr.	8232 Baker Ave.
Baxilton, RW 32138	Doveran, RW 32923	Axion, RE 37487
3	13	23

Figure 8-27   *The Employee Mailing Labels Report print layout preview after Task 2*

the margins need to be set appropriately. The margin properties can be set through the Properties window or with the Report Properties dialog box.

Because the labels are three across with 2½ inches per label and no spacing between labels, the labels take up 7½ inches. Therefore, the left and right margins must be set to ½ inch each to get a total of 8½ inches in width. A similar set of calculations tells us that the top and bottom margins must also be ½ inch each, but ¼ inch must be subtracted from the top margin to accommodate the page header.

The Overtime Report

Features Highlighted

▶ Implementing cascading parameters

▶ Using SQL stored procedures

▶ Using table filters

▶ Using the NoRows property

Business Need   The Galactic Delivery Services personnel department needs to monitor the amount of overtime put in at each of its repair and distribution hubs to determine when additional personnel must be hired. The personnel department needs a report that lists the employees with more than 45 hours worked in a given week at a given hub. The report should have two sections. The first section should list employees with more than 45 hours and less than 55 hours worked for the selected week. The second section should list employees with more than 55 hours worked for the selected week.

The user should be able to select a work week from a drop-down list and then see a second drop-down list, showing the hubs that have one or more employees with more than 45 hours for the selected week. The user selects a hub from this second list and then sees the report for that hub.

Two stored procedures in the Galactic database should be used for retrieving data. The stp_HubsOver45 stored procedure returns a list of hubs with one or more employees who have more than 45 hours worked for the selected week. The stp_EmployeesOver45 stored procedure returns a list of employees who have more than 45 hours worked for the selected week at the selected hub. We discuss stored procedures in the Task Notes.

Task Overview

1. Create a New Report and Three Datasets
2. Create the Report Layout
3. Add Data Bars to the Report

Overtime Report, Task 1: Create a New Report and Three Datasets

`DT` `RB` **SSDT, Visual Studio, and Report Builder Steps**

1. Create a new report from the GDSReport template. Name the new report **Overtime** in the Chapter08 folder.

2. Create a data source called "Galactic" in this new report. This new data source should reference the Galactic shared data source.

3. Create a dataset called "Weeks" with the following query:

```
SELECT DISTINCT CONVERT(char(4), DATEPART(yy,WorkDate))+'-'+
    RIGHT('0'+CONVERT(varchar(2), DATEPART(wk,WorkDate)),2) as Week
FROM TimeEntry
ORDER BY Week
```

4. Right-click the Galactic entry in the Report Data window. Select Add Dataset from the context menu. The Dataset Properties dialog box appears.

5. Enter **HubsOver45** for the name in the Dataset Properties dialog box.

6. Select the Stored Procedure radio button under the Query type prompt.

7. Select stp_HubsOver45 from the Select or enter stored procedure name drop-down list.

8. Click OK to exit the Dataset Properties dialog box. An entry for the HubsOver45 dataset appears in the Report Data window.

9. Right-click the Galactic entry in the Report Data window. Select Add Dataset from the context menu. The Dataset Properties dialog box appears.

10. Enter **EmployeesOver45** for the name in the Dataset Properties dialog box.

11. Select the Stored Procedure radio button under the Query type prompt.

12. Select stp_EmployeesOver45 from the Select or enter stored procedure name drop-down list.

13. Click OK to exit the Dataset Properties dialog box. An entry for the EmployeesOver45 dataset appears in the Report Data window.

Task Notes   For two of our three datasets, we used stored procedures rather than queries. A stored procedure is a query or a set of queries given a name and stored in the database itself. You can think of a stored procedure as a data-manipulation program created and kept right inside the database.

Stored procedures have several advantages over queries:

► **Speed**   A certain amount of preprocessing must be done on any query before it can be run in the database. This preprocessing creates an execution plan. Essentially, SQL Server selects the approach it will use to actually execute the query. Stored procedures are preprocessed when they are created, and the resulting query plan is saved with the stored procedure. This means when you execute a stored procedure, you do not need to wait for the preprocessing. The result is faster execution time.

▶ **Simplicity**   A developer or database administrator can create a stored procedure that uses a number of intricate queries. When you execute the stored procedure, you do not need to understand, or even see, this complexity. All you need to do is execute the stored procedure to get the result set you need.

▶ **Security**   When you query a set of tables, you must be given rights to see any and all data in each of the tables. However, when a stored procedure is used, you only need rights to execute the stored procedure. You do not need rights to any of the tables being queried by the stored procedure. The stored procedure can then control which rows and columns can be seen by each user.

▶ **Reusability**   A single stored procedure can be used by a number of reports. Therefore, complex queries do not have to be created over and over again when a number of reports need to use the same data.

▶ **Maintainability**   When changes are made to the database structure, the developer or database administrator can make the corresponding changes in the stored procedure so the stored procedure continues to return the same result set. Without stored procedures, a change in the database structure could result in a number of reports needing to be edited.

For these reasons, it is often advantageous to use stored procedures rather than queries for your datasets.

NOTE

Querying against database views has a number of the same benefits as stored procedures and is also a good choice as the source for your datasets. Because querying views is much the same as querying tables (they present fields to the Query Builder just as tables do), we will not spend time discussing views.

When you are using a stored procedure for your dataset, all you need to do is set Query Type to Stored Procedure and select the name of the stored procedure. The Report Designer can figure out the parameters required by the stored procedure and add them to the report. Can't get much simpler than that!

Overtime Report, Task 2: Create the Report Layout

DT
RB

SSDT, Visual Studio, and Report Builder Steps

1. Expand the Parameters entry in the Report Data window. Notice two parameters, Week and HubCode, were created automatically for us based on the parameters required by the stored procedures we selected.

2. Right-click the entry for the Week parameter in the Report Data window, and select Parameter Properties from the context menu. The Report Parameter Properties dialog box appears.

3. Select the Available Values page.

4. Select the Get values from a query radio button.

5. Select Weeks from the Dataset drop-down list. Select Week from the Value field drop-down list. Select Week from the Label field drop-down list.

6. Click OK to exit the Report Parameter Properties dialog box.

7. Right-click the entry for the HubCode parameter in the Report Data window, and select Parameter Properties from the context menu. The Report Parameter Properties dialog box appears.

8. Change Prompt to **Hub**.

9. Select the Available Values page.

10. Select the Get values from a query radio button.

11. Select HubsOver45 from the Dataset drop-down list. Select HubCode from the Value field drop-down list. Select Hub from the Label field drop-down list.

12. Click OK to exit the Report Parameter Properties dialog box.

13. Place a text box onto the body of the report. Modify the following properties of this text box:

Property	Value
Font: FontSize	25pt
Font: FontWeight	Bold
Location: Left	0in
Location: Top	0in
Size: Width	2in
Size: Height	0.5in
Value	Overtime

14. Place a second text box onto the body of the report. Modify the following properties of this text box:

Property	Value
Font: FontSize	16pt
Location: Left	0in
Location: Top	0.5in
Size: Width	5.25in
Size: Height	0.375in

15. Right-click this text box, and select Expression from the context menu.

16. Type the following in the Set expression for: Value area:

```
= "Week: " &  Parameters!Week.Value &
"       Hub: " &  Parameters!HubCode.Value
```

17. Click OK to exit the Expression dialog box.

18. Place a third text box onto the body of the report. Modify the following properties of this text box:

Property	Value
Font: FontSize	16pt
Font: FontWeight	Bold
Location: Left	0in
Location: Top	1.125in
Size: Width	5.25in
Size: Height	0.375in
Value	Employees with 45 to 55 hours for this week

19. Use the table template to a tablix onto the body of the report immediately below the third text box.

20. Place the EmployeeNumber field from the EmployeesOver45 dataset in the leftmost cell in the detail row of the tablix.

21. Place the FirstName field from the EmployeesOver45 dataset in the center cell in the detail row of the tablix.

22. Place the LastName field from the EmployeesOver45 dataset in the rightmost cell in the detail row of the tablix.

23. Drag the HoursWorked field from the EmployeesOver45 dataset, and use the field to add a new column on the right side of the tablix.

24. Select the tablix header row. Modify the following property:

Property	Value
TextDecoration	Underline

25. Select the leftmost table column. Modify the following property:

Property	Value
TextAlign	Left

NOTE

Remember, you can use the items in the Report Formatting toolbar or Report Builder ribbon to do things such as turning on underlining and changing the text alignment.

26. Right-click the gray box in the upper-left corner of the tablix, and select Tablix Properties from the context menu. The Tablix Properties dialog box appears.
27. Select the Filters page.
28. Click Add to create a new filter entry.
29. Select [HoursWorked] from the Expression drop-down list.
30. Select <= from the Operator drop-down list.
31. Type =**55** for Value.
32. Click OK to exit the Tablix Properties dialog box.
33. Modify the following property of the tablix using the Properties window:

Property	Value
NoRowsMessage	No Employees

34. Select both the tablix and the text box containing the string "Employees with 45 to 55 hours for this week." Press CTRL-C to copy these two report items. We are going to paste a copy of these two items and use it to create the layout for the Employees over 55 Hours portion of the report.
35. Drag the report body larger. Do this by dragging the dashed line between the report body and the page footer.
36. Press CTRL-V to paste a copy of the two report items. Drag the two new items so they are below the originals.
37. Select the new text box by itself. Change the value of the text box to **Employees with over 55 hours for this week**.

38. Click anywhere in the new tablix, right-click the gray box in the upper-left corner of the tablix, and select Tablix Properties from the context menu. The Tablix Properties dialog box appears.
39. Select the Filters page.
40. Select > from the Operator drop-down list.
41. Click OK to exit the Tablix Properties dialog box. Your report layout should appear similar to Figure 8-28.
42. Preview/Run the report.
43. Notice the Week drop-down list is enabled but the Hub drop-down list is disabled. Select 2013–15 from the Week drop-down list.
44. Once a week is selected, the Hub drop-down list is enabled. Select Borlaron Repair Base from the Hub drop-down list. Click the View Report button. Your report should appear similar to Figure 8-29.

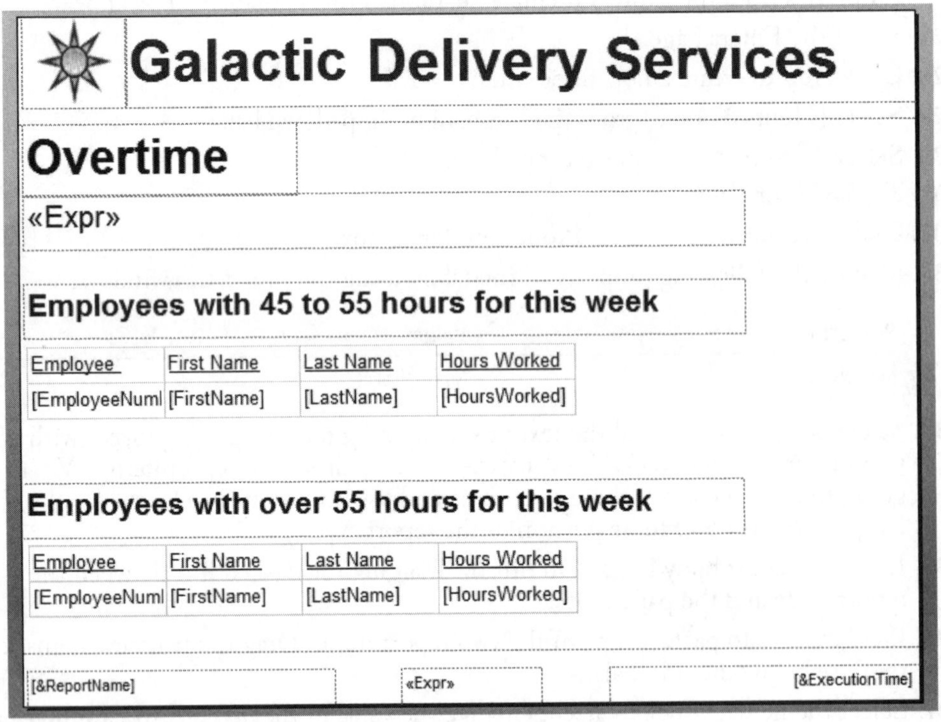

Figure 8-28   *The Overtime Report layout*

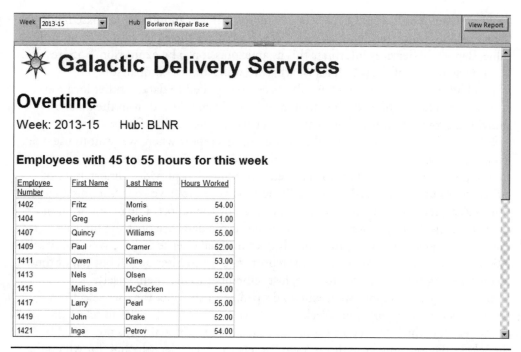

Week 2013-15 ▼   Hub Borlaron Repair Base ▼   View Report

☀ Galactic Delivery Services

Overtime
Week: 2013-15   Hub: BLNR

Employees with 45 to 55 hours for this week

Employee Number	First Name	Last Name	Hours Worked
1402	Fritz	Morris	54.00
1404	Greg	Perkins	51.00
1407	Quincy	Williams	55.00
1409	Paul	Cramer	52.00
1411	Owen	Kline	53.00
1413	Nels	Olsen	52.00
1415	Melissa	McCracken	54.00
1417	Larry	Pearl	55.00
1419	John	Drake	52.00
1421	Inga	Petrov	54.00

Figure 8-29   *The Overtime Report preview*

45. Select 2013–10 from the Week drop-down list. Borlaron Repair Base is still selected in the Hub drop-down list. Click the View Report button. Note the text under the "Employees with over 55 hours for this week" heading.

46. Save the report.

Task Notes   In this report, we used the same dataset to populate two tablixes. We got different information in the two tablixes by applying different filters on each. The filter for the upper table on the report says we only want records in this tablix where the number of hours worked is less than or equal to 55. The filter for the lower tablix on the report says we only want records in this tablix where the number of hours worked is greater than 55. In this way, we can divide the data in the dataset to fulfill the business requirements of the report.

You may have noted that we used an equal sign in front of the number 55 in the Value field for our filter expressions. This is due to the fact that the Value, without an equal sign in front of it, is interpreted as a string constant. In other words, without the equal sign, the report would have been trying to compare an integer database field with the string "55" which results in an error. When we place the equal sign in front of the value, Reporting Services interprets this as an expression. The expression "=55" results in an integer value of 55, which is just what we want for our comparison.

In addition to what you saw here, filters can be applied to data in other locations. A dataset can have a filter applied to it after it has been selected from the database. Individual groups within a table, matrix, or chart can also utilize filters.

Filters work well in situations like the one in this report where we want to use one dataset to provide a slightly different set of records to multiple data regions. They can also be useful for taking data from a stored procedure that provides almost, but not quite, the result set you need. It is usually best, however, to have your filtering done by your select query or stored procedure rather than by the report. The reason is, in most cases it is considerably faster and more efficient if the database does the filtering as it executes the query or stored procedure. It does not make sense to have your query select 1,000 records from the database if your report is going to filter out all but ten of these records. Filters are a good tool to have; just remember to use them wisely.

In the Overtime Report, we used two drop-down lists to let the user select the parameters for our report. The Week drop-down list enables the user to select the week of the year for which the report should be run. This drop-down list is populated by the Weeks dataset. The Hub drop-down list lets the user select the hub for which the report should be run. This drop-down list is populated by the HubsOver45 dataset. The HubsOver45 dataset requires a value from the Week drop-down list before it can return a list of the hubs with employees working over 45 hours for that week. In this way, the data that populates the Hub drop-down list is dependent on the value selected in the Week drop-down list.

Reporting Services is smart enough to recognize this dependency and act accordingly. If no value is selected in the Week drop-down list, the Hub drop-down list cannot be populated, so it is disabled. Every time the selected value in the Week drop-down list changes, the Hub drop-down list is repopulated.

Finally, in this report we used the NoRowsMessage property of each of the tablixes. This property enables you to define a string that is output when there are no rows to populate the tablix. When the filter on either tablix in the report filters out all the rows in the dataset, the content of the NoRowsMessage property is displayed. This is more helpful to the user than simply having a blank space where a tablix should be. The NoRowsMessage property is available on any of the data region report items.

Overtime Report, Task 3: Add Data Bars to the Report

DT
RB

SSDT, Visual Studio, and Report Builder Steps

1. Return to Design mode.
2. Click the Data Bar entry in the Toolbox, if you are using SSDT or Visual Studio, or on the Insert ribbon tab, if you are using Report Builder. (Just click. Do not click and drag.)
3. Move the mouse pointer over the design area; you will see the data bar insert cursor.
4. Click the cell containing "[HoursWorked]" in the detail row of the upper tablix. The Select Data Bar Type dialog box appears.
5. Select the Bar type style as shown in Figure 8-30.
6. Click OK. The text box is replaced by a data bar in this cell of the tablix.

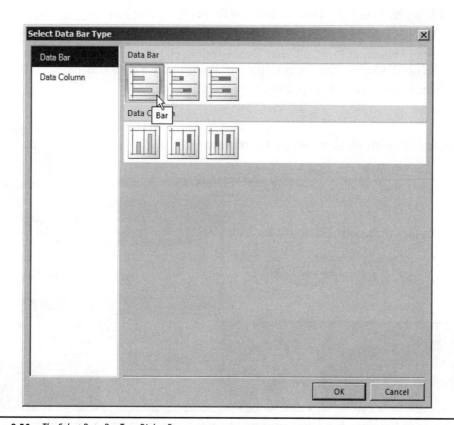

Figure 8-30   *The Select Data Bar Type Dialog Box*

7. Repeat Step 2 through Step 6 for the cell containing "[Hours Worked]" in the detail row of the lower tablix.

8. Double-click the data bar in the upper tablix. The Chart Data window appears.

9. In the Values pane of the Chart Data window, click the drop-down arrow next to "HoursWorked"—the upper of the two items in the Values pane.

10. Select "Show Data Labels" from the menu as shown in Figure 8-31.

11. Click the same drop-down arrow, and select "Horizontal Axis Properties" from the menu. The Horizontal Axis Properties dialog box appears.

12. Modify the following properties of the Horizontal Axis using the dialog box:

Property	Value
Minimum	45
Maximum	55

13. Click OK to exit the Horizontal Axis Properties dialog box.

14. Double-click the data bar in the lower tablix. The Chart Data window appears.

15. In the Values pane of the Chart Data window, click the drop-down arrow next to "HoursWorked"—the upper of the two items in the Values pane.

16. Select "Show Data Labels" from the menu.

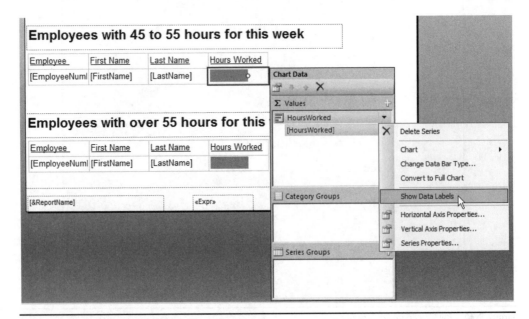

Figure 8-31 *The menu for Values in the Chart Data window*

17. Click the same drop-down arrow, and select "Horizontal Axis Properties" from the menu. The Horizontal Axis Properties dialog box appears.

18. Modify the following properties of the Horizontal Axis using the dialog box:

Property	Value
Minimum	55
Maximum	70

19. Click OK to exit the Horizontal Axis Properties dialog box.

20. Preview/Run the report.

21. Select 2013–15 from the Week drop-down list.

22. Select Borlaron Repair Base from the Hub drop-down list. Click the View Report button. Your report should appear similar to Figure 8-32.

23. Save the report.

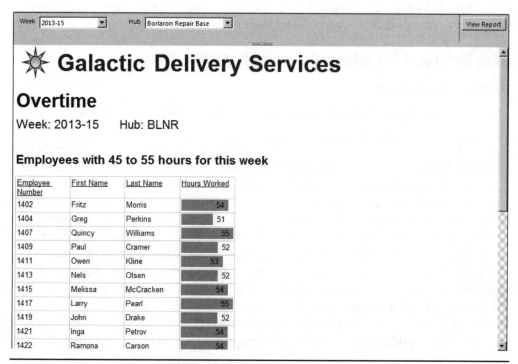

Figure 8-32　*The Overtime Report with data bar preview*

Task Notes The *data bar* provides a way to easily visualize relative quantities. It enables us to add a touch of color and interest to a tablix report. The *sparkline* and the *indicator* perform a similar function, allowing us to provide a compact graphical interpretation of a quantity or series of quantities. We will use the sparkline and the indicator in examples later in this book.

The data bar is essentially a regular chart spread across a number of rows or columns of a tablix. It is possible to make a chart behave exactly like a data bar, but it requires the manipulation of a number of chart parameters. The data bar item gives us an efficient way to get this behavior. Just as we can make a chart behave as a data bar, we can convert a data bar to a regular chart item. This is done by right-clicking on a data bar and selecting "Convert to Full Chart" from the context menu.

In the previous task, we got a little help formatting our data bar item because we placed it in a tablix cell that was already displaying a field from the dataset. The report authoring environment was smart enough to recognize this situation and to associate that dataset field with the data bar item it created. That is why, when we displayed the Chart Data window, it already showed the HoursWorked field. If this prepopulation had not been done for us, we would have had to use the green plus sign to associate a field with the data bar as we did with the chart item in Chapter 6.

The Revised Employee Time Report

Features Highlighted

▶ Implementing fixed and dynamic columns and rows in the same tablix

▶ Using the Switch() function

Business Need The Galactic Delivery Services personnel department is finding the Employee Time Report to be useful. To make the report even more useful, they would like to add summary information to the report. To the right of the current report, they would like to summarize the hours worked by the day of the week—in other words, how many hours were put in on Mondays, Tuesdays, Wednesdays, and so on. They would like a summary of the hours worked at each delivery hub specified by hub code.

Finally, at the bottom of the report, they would like a summary of the hours worked by job type. Our database does not contain a definition of job type. Job type is an ad hoc classification that the personnel department uses for some analysis. All levels of mechanics, both I and II, form one job type. All levels of sorters, both I and II, form a second job type, while transport pilots and transport copilots make up the third job type.

Task Overview

1. Copy and Rename the Existing Report
2. Modify the Dataset and the Layout

Revised Employee Time Report, Task 1: Copy and Rename the Existing Report

`DT` **SSDT, and Visual Studio Steps**

1. Reopen the Chapter08 project, if it was closed. Close the Overtime Report, if it is open.
2. Right-click the EmployeeTime Report in the Solution Explorer, and select Copy from the context menu.
3. Right-click the Chapter08 project in the Solution Explorer, and select Paste from the context menu. A copy of the report appears in the Solution Explorer.
4. Right-click this new copy, and select Rename from the context menu. Rename the report **RevisedEmployeeTime.rdl**.
5. Double-click the entry for the RevisedEmployeeTime report to open this report for editing.

`RB` **Report Builder Steps**

1. Click the logo button, and select Open from the menu.
2. Double-click the entry for the EmployeeTime report to open it.
3. Click the logo button, and select Save As from the menu. The Save As Report dialog box appears.
4. Enter **RevisedEmployeeTime** for Name.
5. Click Save.

Task Notes   We have kept a copy of the original report layout in case you want to refer back to it. We have a second copy of the report ready for us to modify to satisfy the new user requirements. Saving a copy of a report layout that your users really like before making modifications is a good idea, even if it is the users themselves asking for the modifications. Users have been known to change their minds and utter the words, "I think I liked it better the way it was."

Revised Employee Time Report, Task 2: Modify the Dataset and the Layout

`DT`
`RB` **SSDT, Visual Studio, and Report Builder Steps**

1. In the Report Data window, expand the Datasets folder.
2. Right-click EmployeeTime and select Query from the context menu. The Query Designer window opens.

3. Add the HubCode field to the end of the field list, as shown here in bold:

```
SELECT Description AS Job,
       Employee.EmployeeNumber,
       FirstName,
       LastName,
       CONVERT(char(4),DATEPART(yy, WorkDate))+'-'+
           CONVERT(char(2),DATEPART(wk, WorkDate)) AS Week,
       WorkDate,
       HoursWorked,
           HubCode
FROM TimeEntry
INNER JOIN Assignment
       ON TimeEntry.AssignmentID = Assignment.AssignmentID
INNER JOIN Employee
       ON Assignment.EmployeeNumber = Employee.EmployeeNumber
INNER JOIN Job
       ON Assignment.JobID = Job.JobID
ORDER BY Job, Employee.EmployeeNumber, Week, WorkDate
```

4. Run the query to make sure no errors exist. Correct any typos that may be detected.
5. Click OK to exit the Query Designer window.
6. Right-click in the bottom row of the tablix. Select Tablix: Insert Row | Below from the context menu. A new static row is added at the bottom of the tablix.
7. Right-click in the row you just added, and select Tablix: Add Group | Row Group: Adjacent Below from the context menu. The Tablix group dialog box appears.
8. Select [HubCode] from the Group by drop-down list.
9. Click OK to exit the Tablix group dialog box. A new row group is added at the bottom of the tablix.
10. Merge the leftmost three cells in the bottom row of the tablix.
11. Select the HubCode field in the newly merged cells.
12. Merge all of the cells in the second-from-the-bottom row in the tablix.
13. Set the following properties of this newly merged cell:

Property	Value
BorderColor: Top	Black
BorderWidth: Top	4pt
Font: TextDecoration	Underline

14. In the cell in the lower-right corner of the tablix, select the HoursWorked field. This field will automatically be enclosed in a Sum() aggregate function.

15. Set the following property of this cell:

Property	Value
BorderStyle: Top	None

16. Preview/Run the report. The bottom of your report should appear as shown in Figure 8-33.

17. Return to design mode.

18. Right-click in the bottom row of the tablix. Select Tablix: Insert Row | Outside Group - Below from the context menu. A new static row is added at the bottom of the tablix.

19. Right-click in the row you just added, and select Tablix: Add Group | Row Group: Adjacent Below from the context menu. The Tablix group dialog box appears.

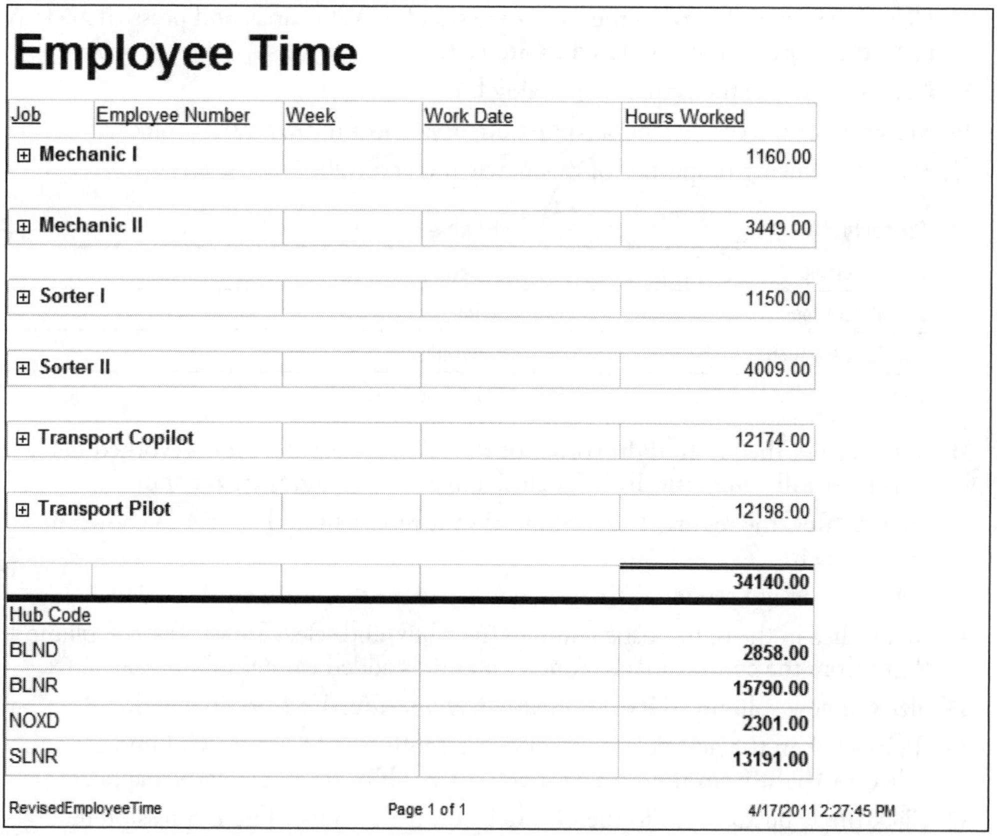

Employee Time

Job	Employee Number	Week	Work Date	Hours Worked
⊞ Mechanic I				1160.00
⊞ Mechanic II				3449.00
⊞ Sorter I				1150.00
⊞ Sorter II				4009.00
⊞ Transport Copilot				12174.00
⊞ Transport Pilot				12198.00
				34140.00
Hub Code				
BLND				**2858.00**
BLNR				**15790.00**
NOXD				**2301.00**
SLNR				**13191.00**
RevisedEmployeeTime		Page 1 of 1		4/17/2011 2:27:45 PM

Figure 8-33   *The Revised Employee Time Report with Hub Code summary*

20. Click the *fx* button next to the Group by drop-down list. The Expression dialog box appears.

21. Enter the following in the Set expression for: GroupExpression area:

```
=Switch(LEFT(Fields!Job.Value, 8) = "Mechanic", "Mechanics",
    LEFT(Fields!Job.Value, 6) = "Sorter", "Sorters",
    LEFT(Fields!Job.Value, 9) = "Transport", "Pilots")
```

22. Highlight the entire expression you just entered, and press CTRL-C to copy this text.

23. Click OK to exit the Expression dialog box.

24. Click OK to exit the Tablix group dialog box. A new row group is added at the bottom of the tablix.

25. Merge the leftmost three cells in the bottom row of the tablix.

26. Right-click in the newly merged cells, and select Text Box: Expression from the context menu. The Expression dialog box appears.

27. Delete the equal sign from the Set expression for: Value area, and press CTRL-V to paste the expression you entered in Step 21.

28. Click OK to exit the Expression dialog box.

29. Merge all of the cells in the second-from-the-bottom row in the tablix.

30. Set the following properties of this newly merged cell:

Property	Value
BorderColor: Top	Black
BorderWidth: Top	4pt
Font: TextDecoration	Underline
Value	Job Type

31. In the cell in the lower-right corner of the tablix, select the HoursWorked field. This field will automatically be enclosed in a Sum() aggregate function.

32. Preview/Run the report. The bottom of your report should appear as shown in Figure 8-34.

33. Return to design mode.

34. Right-click in the rightmost column in the tablix, and select Tablix: Insert Column | Right from the context menu. A new column is added to the right of the tablix.

35. Size the new column so it is approximately one-fourth its original width.

36. Right-click in the new column, and select Tablix: Add Group | Column Group: Adjacent Right from the context menu. The Tablix group dialog box appears.

37. Click the *fx* button next to the Group by drop-down list. The Expression dialog box appears.

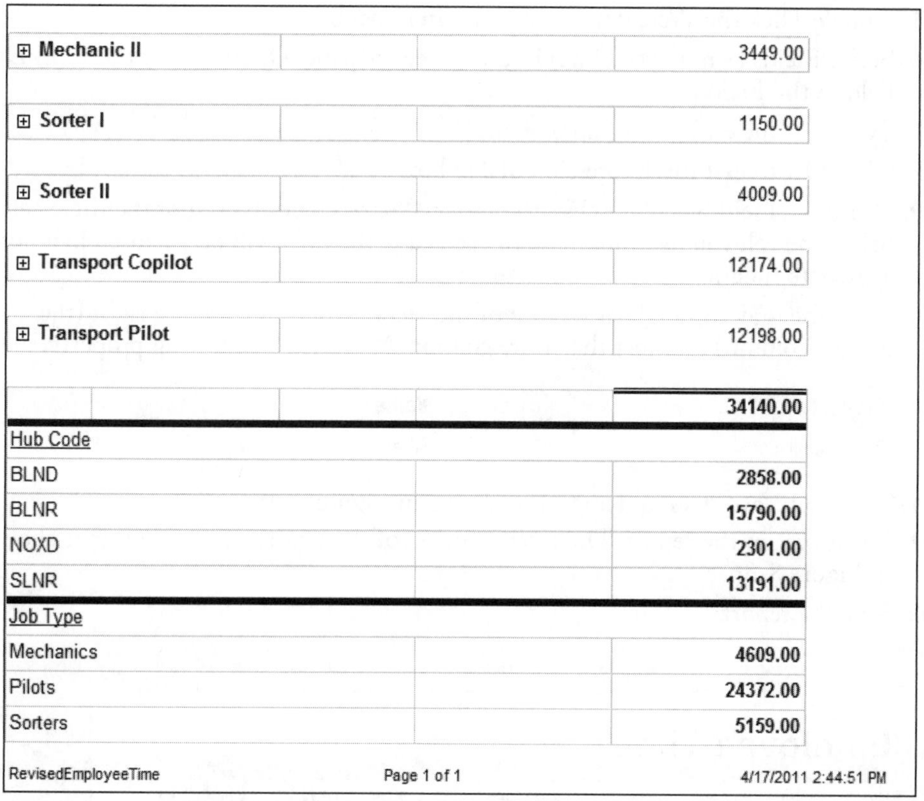

⊞ Mechanic II			3449.00
⊞ Sorter I			1150.00
⊞ Sorter II			4009.00
⊞ Transport Copilot			12174.00
⊞ Transport Pilot			12198.00
			34140.00
Hub Code			
BLND			2858.00
BLNR			15790.00
NOXD			2301.00
SLNR			13191.00
Job Type			
Mechanics			4609.00
Pilots			24372.00
Sorters			5159.00
RevisedEmployeeTime	Page 1 of 1		4/17/2011 2:44:51 PM

Figure 8-34   *The Revised Employee Time Report with Job Type summary*

38. Expand the Common Functions entry in the Category pane. Select the Date & Time entry in the Category pane. Double-click the Weekday entry in the Item pane.

39. Select Fields (EmployeeTime) in the Category pane. Double-click the WorkDate field in the Field pane.

40. Type **)** at the end of the expression.

41. Click OK to exit the Expression dialog box.

42. Click OK to exit the Tablix group dialog box. A new column group is added at the right of the tablix.

43. Right-click the upper cell in the new column, and select Textbox: Expression from the context menu. The Expression dialog box appears.

44. Expand the Common Functions entry in the Category pane. Select the Date & Time entry in the Category pane. Double-click the WeekdayName entry in the Item pane.

45. Double-click the Weekday entry in the Item pane.

46. Select Fields (EmployeeTime) in the Category pane. Double-click the WorkDate field in the Field pane.

47. Type **))** at the end of the expression.

48. Click OK to exit the Expression dialog box.

49. Using the Field Selector, select the HoursWorked field in each of the three cells below the cell you just modified. In each case, the field will be enclosed in a Sum() aggregate function.

50. Click the gray rectangle at the top of the second column from the right (the narrow column) to select the entire column. Modify the following property:

Property	Value
BackgroundColor	Silver

51. The tablix layout should appear as shown in Figure 8-35.

52. Preview/Run the report. The tablix portion of the report should appear as shown in Figure 8-36.

53. Save the report.

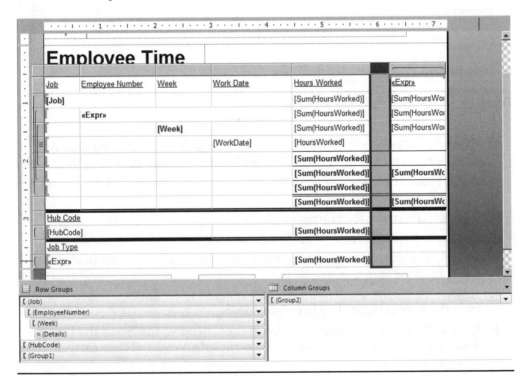

Figure 8-35   *The Revised Employee Time Report final layout*

Job	Employee Number	Week	Work Date	Hours Worked		Sunday	Monday	Tuesday	Wednesday	Saturday
⊞ Mechanic I				1160.00		228.00	226.00	227.00	230.00	249.00
⊞ Mechanic II				3449.00		677.00	684.00	680.00	682.00	726.00
⊞ Sorter I				1150.00		228.00	226.00	229.00	220.00	247.00
⊞ Sorter II				4009.00		786.00	794.00	789.00	789.00	851.00
⊞ Transport Copilot				12174.00		2438.00	2432.00	2434.00	2441.00	2429.00
⊞ Transport Pilot				12198.00		2444.00	2437.00	2442.00	2436.00	2439.00
				34140.00		6801.00	6799.00	6801.00	6798.00	6941.00
Hub Code										
BLND				2858.00						
BLNR				15790.00						
NOXD				2301.00						
SLNR				13191.00						
Job Type										
Mechanics				4609.00						
Pilots				24372.00						
Sorters				5159.00						

Figure 8-36   *The Revised Employee Time Report final preview*

Task Notes   The types of additional summary information requested in the business need for this report are the reason the tablix came along. Without the tablix, this kind of formatting was difficult, if not impossible. With the tablix, however, the report is straightforward to create, if perhaps a bit confusing at first. The key is to look at the symbols in the gray boxes across the top and down the left side of the tablix, along with the entries in the Row Groups and Column Groups areas. As was discussed previously, these symbols in the gray boxes tell you which columns and rows are static and which are dynamic. The entries in the Row Groups and Column Groups areas allow you to edit the properties of each dynamic grouping.

Static rows and static columns appear once in the tablix. The first row in the tablix containing the column headings is an example of a static row. The narrow column containing the gray background is an example of a static column. Each appears only once in the rendered report.

Dynamic rows and columns repeat, depending on the data in the dataset used to populate the tablix. The group header rows are examples of dynamic rows. The rightmost day of the week group column is an example of a dynamic column. We don't know how many of these rows or columns will appear in the report until it is actually rendered.

Dynamic groups can be nested one inside the other. This is the case with the original version of the Employee Time Report, where we had Job, Employee, Week, and Detail groupings nested one inside the other. Dynamic groups can also be adjacent to one another, as our hub code and job type groups were in the revised version of the report.

To create the job type group, we used the Switch() function. The Switch() function is similar to the IIF() function. The IIF() function enables us to test a single Boolean (true/false) statement and return one value if it is true and another if it is false. The Switch() function allows us to test multiple Boolean statements in a specific order. The function will return the value associated with the first Boolean statement that turns out to be true.

Here is the expression we used in the report:

```
=Switch(LEFT(Fields!Job.Value, 8) = "Mechanic", "Mechanics",
     LEFT(Fields!Job.Value, 6) = "Sorter", "Sorters",
     LEFT(Fields!Job.Value, 9) = "Transport", "Pilots")
```

The Switch() function first tests to see if the left eight characters of the Job field are equal to the word Mechanic. If so, the string "Mechanics" is returned by the function. If it is not, the function tests to see if the left six characters of the Job field are equal to the word Sorter. If so, the string "Sorters" is returned by the function. Finally, the function tests to see if the left nine characters of the Job field are equal to the word Transport. If so, the string "Pilots" is returned by the function.

The Revised Employee List Report

Features Highlighted

- ▶ Using the Lookup function
- ▶ Using the LookupSet function
- ▶ Using the MultiLookup function
- ▶ Using the Join function
- ▶ Using the Split function

Business Need As with the Employee Time Report, the Galactic Delivery Services personnel department likes the Employee List Report. To add to its functionality, they would like to add information about the total hours worked by each employee. They would also like to see the levels of education for other employees at the hub where the employee works and the highest level of education for each union the employee is a member of.

We could modify our existing query for this report or create a complex stored procedure to gather and return all of these items. Instead, we are going to make use of some existing stored procedures that return the data required. These additional stored procedures will each have their own dataset in the report. It is not possible to join data between two datasets in a report. What we can do instead is use the Lookup functions in Reporting Services to look up a value from one dataset and find related information in another dataset.

Task Overview

1. Copy and Rename the Existing Report, Add Datasets, and Utilize the Lookup Functions

Revised Employee List Report, Task 1: Copy and Rename the Existing Report, Add Datasets, and Utilize the Lookup Functions

DT

RB

SSDT, Visual Studio, and Report Builder Steps

1. Copy the EmployeeList Report the same way you copied the EmployeeTime Report in the previous exercise. Name the copy of the report **RevisedEmployeeList.rdl**. Double-click the RevisedEmployeeList report to edit it.
2. In the Report Data window, expand the Data Sources folder.
3. Right-click the entry for the Galactic data source, and select Add Dataset from the context menu. The Dataset Properties dialog box appears.
4. Enter **TotalHours** for Name.
5. Select the Stored procedure radio button.
6. Select stp_TotalHoursWorked from the Select or enter stored procedure name drop-down list.
7. Click OK to exit the Dataset Properties dialog box.
8. Right-click the entry for the Galactic data source, and select Add Dataset from the context menu. The Dataset Properties dialog box appears.
9. Enter **EdByHub** for Name.
10. Select the Stored procedure radio button.
11. Select stp_EducationByHub from the Select or enter stored procedure name drop-down list.
12. Click OK to exit the Dataset Properties dialog box.
13. Right-click the entry for the Galactic data source, and select Add Dataset from the context menu. The Dataset Properties dialog box appears.
14. Enter **EdByUnion** for Name.
15. Select the Stored procedure radio button.
16. Select stp_HighestEdByUnion from the Select or enter stored procedure name drop-down list.
17. Click OK to exit the Dataset Properties dialog box.

18. Scroll through the Design area to the right side of the table.

19. Right-click anywhere in the rightmost column of the table, and select Tablix | Insert Column | Right from the context menu.

20. Enter **Total Hours** in the topmost cell of this new column.

21. Right-click the bottom-most cell of this new column, and select Expression from the context menu. The Expression dialog box appears.

22. Enter the following in the Set expression for: Value area:

```
=Lookup(Fields!EmployeeNumber.Value, Fields!EmployeeNumber.Value,
                Fields!TotalHoursWorked.Value, "TotalHours")
```

23. Click OK to exit the Expression dialog box.

24. Right-click anywhere in the rightmost column of the table, and select Tablix | Insert Column | Right from the context menu.

25. Enter **Educ. for Hub** in the topmost cell of this new column.

26. Right-click the bottom-most cell of this new column, and select Expression from the context menu. The Expression dialog box appears.

27. Enter the following in the Set expression for: Value area:

```
=Join(LookupSet(Fields!Hub.Value, Fields!Hub.Value,
        Fields!HighestLevelOfEducation.Value, "EdByHub"), ", ")
```

Be sure to include a space after each comma, including the comma in quotes.

28. Click OK to exit the Expression dialog box.

29. Right-click anywhere in the rightmost column of the table, and select Tablix | Insert Column | Right from the context menu.

30. Enter **Educ. for Union** in the topmost cell of this new column.

31. Right-click the bottom-most cell of this new column, and select Expression from the context menu. The Expression dialog box appears.

32. Enter the following in the Set expression for: Value area:

```
=Join(MultiLookup(Split(Fields!UnionMembership.Value, ", "),
    Fields!UnionMembership.Value, Fields!HighestLevelOfEducation.Value,
    "EdByUnion"), ", ")
```

Be sure to include a space after each comma, including the commas in quotes.

33. Click OK to exit the Expression dialog box.

34. Preview/Run the report. The report should appear as shown in Figure 8-37.

35. Save the report.

Task Notes   As stated in the business need for this report revision, Reporting Services does not allow us to directly join the records from two datasets. The three functions used here, Lookup, LookupSet, and MultisetLookup, allow us to take a value from one

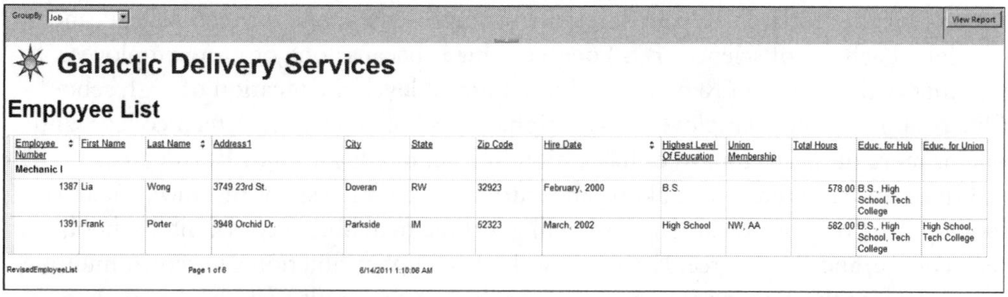

Figure 8-37 *The Revised Employee List Report*

dataset and use it to look up one or more values from a second dataset. This enables us to get behavior that comes very close to this join behavior.

In our first requirement for this revision, we were asked to find the total hours worked for each employee in the report. The stp_TotalHours stored procedure returns a dataset that includes two columns. The first is the Employee Number, and the second is the total hours worked for that employee. To get the results we want, we need to look up each Employee Number and put the associated total hours worked in the report column.

The *Lookup function* does this for us. It works with two datasets: the current dataset and the lookup dataset. The current dataset is the dataset tied to the data region that is displaying the result of the lookup. In this exercise, the current dataset is the Employees dataset. The lookup dataset is the dataset where the result of the Lookup function is coming from. In this exercise, the lookup dataset is the TotalHours dataset.

The parameters of the Lookup function are shown in Table 8-1.

In our second requirement for this revision, we were asked to find the levels of education completed by employees at this employee's hub. The stored procedure used to return this data provides a hub name and a level of education completed by one or more employees working at that hub. The stored procedure result set includes three

Parameter	Description
Current Lookup Expression	The expression for the value from the current data that is searched for in the lookup dataset.
Lookup Matching Expression	The expression for the value from the lookup data that is to be searched.
Lookup Return Value Expression	The expression for the value that is to be returned from the matching record in the lookup dataset.
Lookup Dataset Name	The name of the dataset that is to be searched.

Table 8-1 *Parameters of the Lookup and LookupSet Functions*

records for the Borlaron Repair Base: one for high school, one for tech college, and one for a bachelor of science (B.S.) degree. This is because one or more employees working at the Borlaron Repair Base has a highest level of education of high school. One or more of these employees has a highest level of education of tech college, and one or more of these employees has a highest level of education of B.S. degree.

Given this structure, our lookup can return multiple values. For instance, when we look up the Borlaron Repair Base, we will get three matching records: high school, tech college, and B.S. degree. Fortunately, the LookupSet function can return multiple values. It does this by returning an array of values as the result of each lookup operation.

The *LookupSet function* works with two datasets: the current dataset and the lookup dataset, just like the Lookup function. It also has the same parameters as the Lookup function. The only difference is the LookupSet function returns an array of values rather than a single value. It is up to us to take that array and turn it into something we can display in a report text box. We use another function, the Join function, for this purpose.

The *Join function* takes two parameters. The first parameter is an array. The second parameter is a separator. The Join function takes all of the values in the array and puts them together in a string. It puts the separator text between each value. If we call the Join function with an array containing three values: High School, Tech College, and B.S. degree. along with a separator of ", ", then we get the string "High School, Tech College, B.S. degree."

In our third requirement for this revision, we were asked to find the highest level of education for members of each union that a given employee is a member of. The stp_HighestEdByUnion stored procedure returns only one record for each union. However, an employee can be a member of more than one union. Therefore, we may need to look up the highest education value for more than one union. The MultiLookup function does this for us.

The *MultiLookup function* works with two datasets: the current dataset and the lookup dataset, just like the Lookup and LookupSet functions. It returns an array of values just like the LookupSet function. It differs in that its first parameter is an array rather than a single value. See Table 8-2.

Parameter	Description
Array of Current Lookup Values	An array of values that is searched for in the lookup dataset.
Lookup Matching Expression	The expression for the value from the lookup data that is to be searched.
Lookup Return Value Expression	The expression for the value that is to be returned from the matching record in the lookup dataset.
Lookup Dataset Name	The name of the dataset that is to be searched.

Table 8-2   *Parameters of the MultiLookup Function*

It is up to us to create an array to pass as the first parameter. We use one more function, the Split function, for this purpose.

The *Split function* takes two parameters. The first parameter is a string of values that are separated by a set of characters—for example, a comma and a space. The second parameter is the separator. The Split function looks at the string of values until it finds the first occurrence of the separator. Everything up to the point of the separator is placed in the first element of an array. Everything between the first and second occurrences of the separator is placed in the second element of the array, and so on. After all of the separators have been found in the string, the array is returned as the result of the function. The split function enables us to turn a comma-separated list of union memberships into an array that can be used as the first parameter of the MultiLookup function.

The Lookup, LookupSet, and MultiLookup functions give us the flexibility we need to perform just about any type of lookup that might be required.

Under the Hood

In Chapter 1, we talked about the fact that the report definitions are stored using the Report Definition Language (RDL). RDL was created by Microsoft specifically for Reporting Services. It was one of the first published Extensible Markup Language (XML) document standards created by Microsoft.

Microsoft has gone public with the specifications for RDL. Third parties can create their own authoring environments for creating report definitions. If the RDL from these third-party tools conforms to the RDL standard, the reports created by these tools can be managed and distributed by Reporting Services.

Because RDL is an XML document, you can look at a report definition in its raw form. If you were so inclined, you could use Notepad to open an RDL file and look at its contents. In fact, you don't even need Notepad. You can look at the contents of an RDL file right in SSDT or Visual Studio.

NOTE

This ability to view the contents of an RDL file is not available in Report Builder.

Viewing the RDL

If you are using SSDT or Visual Studio, right-click the entry for Overtime.rdl in the Solution Explorer, and then select View Code from the context menu. You see a new tab in the layout area called Overtime.rdl. This tab contains the actual RDL of the report, as shown in Figure 8-38.

```
Overtime.rdl ×
              <Textbox Name="Textbox2">
                <CanGrow>true</CanGrow>
                <KeepTogether>true</KeepTogether>
                <Paragraphs>
                  <Paragraph>
                    <TextRuns>
                      <TextRun>
                        <Value>Overtime</Value>
                        <Style>
                          <FontSize>25pt</FontSize>
                          <FontWeight>Bold</FontWeight>
                        </Style>
                      </TextRun>
                    </TextRuns>
                    <Style />
                  </Paragraph>
                </Paragraphs>
                <rd:DefaultName>Textbox2</rd:DefaultName>
                <Height>0.5in</Height>
                <Width>2in</Width>
                <Style>
                  <Border>
                    <Style>None</Style>
                  </Border>
                  <PaddingLeft>2pt</PaddingLeft>
                  <PaddingRight>2pt</PaddingRight>
                  <PaddingTop>2pt</PaddingTop>
                  <PaddingBottom>2pt</PaddingBottom>
                </Style>
              </Textbox>
100 %
```

Figure 8-38   *The RDL for the Overtime Report*

XML Structure

Because the RDL is an XML document, it is made up of pairs of tags. A begin tag is at the beginning of an item, and an end tag is at the end of the item. A *begin tag* is simply a string of text, the tag name, with < at the front and > at the back. An *end tag* is the same string of text with </ at the front and > at the back. This pair of tags creates an XML element. The information in between the two tags is the value for that element. In the following example, the Height element has a value of 0.625in:

```
<Height>0.625in</Height>
```

There can never be a begin tag without an end tag, and vice versa. In fact, it can be said that XML is the Noah's Ark of data structures, because everything must go two by two.

In addition to simple strings of text, XML elements can contain other elements. In fact, a number of elements can nest one inside the other to form complex structures. Here's an example:

```
<Textbox>
  <Style>
    <Color>DarkBlue</Color>
  </Style>
</Textbox>
```

In some cases, begin tags contain additional information as attributes. An *attribute* comes in the form of an attribute name, immediately following the tag name, followed by an equal sign (=) and the value of the attribute. In this example, the Textbox element has an attribute called Name with a value of "Textbox1":

```
<Textbox Name="Textbox1">...</Textbox>
```

The RDL contains several sections: the page header, the body, the data sources, the datasets, the embedded images, the page footer, and the report parameters. Each section starts with a begin tag and is terminated by an end tag. For example, the page header section of the RDL starts with <PageHeader> and is terminated by </PageHeader>.

In Figure 8-38, you can see the entire XML structure for the Textbox2. The begin tag of the data source includes a Name attribute. This corresponds to the Name property of the text box. In between the begin and end tags of the text box element are additional elements, such as the FontSize. These elements correspond to the other properties of this text box. Only those properties that have been changed from their default values are stored in the RDL.

Editing the RDL

One other interesting thing about viewing the RDL is you can make changes to the RDL and have them affect the report design. Use the text find capabilities of this RDL editor to find the "ReportParameters" section of the RDL. Find the Prompt element within the Week report parameter element, as shown in Figure 8-39. Replace "Week" with "Work Week" and click Save All on the toolbar. Right-click the entry for Overtime.rdl in the Solution Explorer, and then select View Designer from the context menu. Click the Preview tab. You notice the prompt has been changed to Work Week.

If you do find a reason to make modifications directly to the RDL, do so with care. If you break up a begin/end pair or enter an invalid value for a property element (such as puce for a color), you can end up with a report that will not load in the Report Designer. Save your work immediately before making changes directly to the RDL. In just about

Figure 8-39   *The Prompt element of the Week report parameter*

every case, however, the designer works better for making changes to a report layout, so do your editing there.

Advance, Never Retreat

In this chapter, we continued to unlock additional features of Reporting Services. We're always working toward the goal of giving you the tools you need to meet your reporting needs. You should now be well on your way to being able to say, "Yes, I can do that!"

In the next chapter, we look at some of the advanced features of Reporting Services. After that, we take a look at working with reports on the report server.

Chapter 9

Beyond Wow: Advanced Reporting

In This Chapter

► **Speaking in Code**

► **Reports Within Reports**

► **Interacting with Reports**

► **What's Next**

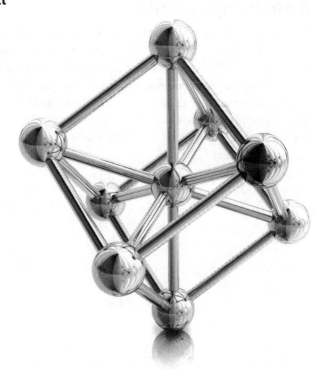

In this chapter, we explore some of the flashy features of Reporting Services. These are the features that get us techies excited. If you do not say "Wow!" after seeing at least one of these features in the reports created in this chapter, then we (the developers at Microsoft and I) are not doing our jobs. Just to clarify, the "Wow!" does not need to be said out loud. Simply thinking "Wow!" in your head counts just as much.

Getting you to say, or think, "Wow!" is not ultimately the goal of the Microsoft developers who created Reporting Services or the goal of this author as he writes this chapter. The developers who create games for Microsoft can be satisfied with eliciting a "Wow!" from their clientele and consider it a job well done. The developers who create business intelligence tools for Microsoft have to aim a bit higher.

If you develop business intelligence tools, you need to go beyond the "Wow!" to the "Ah-ha!" The "Wow!" comes when you see a feature of a software product and think, "Wow! That is really cool!" The "Ah-ha!" comes when you see a feature of a software product and say, "Ah-ha! That is how we can make that report work just the way we need it to," or "Ah-ha! That is how we can turn that bit of data into meaningful business intelligence." Only when we hear the "Ah-ha!" can we be satisfied.

So, don't be shy when that moment comes along. When you get to that "Ah-ha!" feature you have been searching for, say it nice and loud. I want to hear it so I can go home happy.

Speaking in Code

One of the features of Reporting Services that gives it a tremendous amount of power and flexibility is its capability to speak in code—Visual Basic .NET code, that is. Valid Visual Basic .NET expressions can be used to control many of the properties of report items. They can even be used to control the query you are using to create your dataset.

For more complex tasks, you can embed whole Visual Basic .NET functions in your report. If that isn't enough, you can access methods from .NET assemblies. These assemblies are not limited to Visual Basic .NET. They can be written in any .NET language, such as C#.

Let's write some

-.-. --- -.. .

and have some

..-. ..- -.

NOTE

For those of you who may not be familiar with it, the previous sentence contains two words in Morse code. If you want to know what it says, do what I did: Look it up on the Internet.

The Delivery Status Report

Features Highlighted

▶ Using the label property of a parameter

▶ Using multiline headers and footers

▶ Using Visual Basic .NET expressions to control properties

▶ Specifying scope in aggregate functions

Business Need   The customer service department at Galactic Delivery Services (GDS) would like a report to check on the status of deliveries for a customer. The customer service representative should be able to select a customer and a year, and then see all the deliveries for that customer in that year. The hubs each package went through as it was in transit should be listed as well.

The status for packages that have been delivered should show up in green. The status for packages still en route should be blue. The status for packages that have been lost should be red. In case of a problem, the name and e-mail address of the person to be contacted at that customer site should appear below the entry for each lost package.

Task Overview

1. Create a New Report and Two Datasets
2. Set Up the Report Parameters and Place the Titles on the Report Layout
3. Add a Tablix to the Report
4. Add the Expressions

Delivery Status Report, Task 1:
Create a New Report and Two Datasets

`DT` SSDT and Visual Studio Steps

1. Create a new Reporting Services project called Chapter09 in the MSSQLRS folder.
2. Create a shared data source called Galactic for the Galactic database.
3. Create a new report called DeliveryStatus using the GDSReport template.

4. Create a new data source called Galactic that references the Galactic shared data source.

5. Create a new dataset called DeliveryStatus that calls the stp_DeliveryStatus stored procedure.

6. Create a second dataset called Customers that uses the following query:

```
SELECT CustomerNumber, Name FROM Customer ORDER BY Name
```

RB   **Report Builder Steps**

1. Create a new folder in the Galactic Delivery Services folder. Enter **Chapter09** as the name of this folder.

2. Launch Report Builder and create a new report from the GDSReport template. Call this report DeliveryStatus and save it in the Chapter09 folder.

3. Create a data source called Galactic that references the Galactic shared data source.

4. Create a new dataset called DeliveryStatus that calls the stp_DeliveryStatus stored procedure.

5. Create a second dataset called Customers that uses the following query:

```
SELECT CustomerNumber, Name FROM Customer ORDER BY Name
```

Task Notes   You probably noticed the instructions are a bit sketchy here. Now that you have reached the level of advanced report authoring, you can handle these basic tasks on your own. If you have any trouble with these steps, refer to the previous chapters for a refresher.

Delivery Status Report, Task 2: Set Up the Report Parameters and Place the Titles on the Report Layout

DT   **SSDT, Visual Studio, and Report Builder Steps**

RB

1. The stored procedure triggered the creation of two report parameters. Configure the properties of the CustomerNumber parameter as follows:

Property	Value
General page:	
Prompt	Customer
Available Values page:	
Select from one of the following options	Get values from a query
Dataset	Customers
Value field	CustomerNumber
Label field	Name

2. Configure the properties of the Year parameter as follows:

Property	Value
Available Values page:	
Select from one of the following options	Specify values
(Enter the values from the Available Values table that follows)	
Default Values page:	
Select from one of the following options	Specify values
(Enter the value from the Default Values table that follows)	

On the Available Values page, add the following rows to the grid at the bottom of the dialog box:

Label	Value
2011	2011
2012	2012
2013	2013

On the Default Values page, add the following row to the grid at the bottom of the dialog box:

Value
2012

3. Place a text box onto the body of the report. Modify the following properties of this text box:

Property	Value
Font: FontSize	16pt
Font: FontWeight	Bold
Location: Left	0in
Location: Top	0in
Size: Width	3.5in
Size: Height	0.375in
Value	="Delivery Status for " & Parameters!Year.Value

4. Place a second text box onto the body of the report. Modify the following properties of this text box:

Property	Value
Font: FontSize	16pt
Font: FontWeight	Bold
Location: Left	0in
Location: Top	0.375in
Size: Width	4.75in
Size: Height	0.375in

5. Right-click this text box and select Expression from the context menu. The Expression dialog box appears.

6. Select Parameters in the Category pane, and double-click CustomerNumber in the Parameter pane.

7. Use the BACKSPACE key to remove the word "Value" at the end of the expression. (Do not delete the period.) If you are using SSDT or Visual Studio, you see a context menu showing you the available properties of the CustomerNumber parameter.

8. If you are using SSDT or Visual Studio, double-click Label in the context menu. If you are using Report Builder, type **Label**.

9. Click OK to exit the Expression dialog box.

Task Notes   We have two parameters for this report. The CustomerNumber parameter is selected from a drop-down list created by a dataset. The customer names are displayed in the drop-down list because Name was chosen as the Label field. However, the customer number is the value assigned to this parameter because CustomerNumber is chosen as the Value field. The Year parameter is selected from a drop-down list created by a static list of values we entered. The Label and Value are the same for each entry in this list.

The items placed on the report thus far were put there to provide a heading for the report and to indicate which parameters were selected to create the report. This is pretty straightforward for the Year parameter. All we need is a text box that displays the value of this parameter, with a little explanatory text thrown in for good measure.

The CustomerNumber parameter presents a bit of a problem, though. When we select a parameter in an expression, the value property of the parameter is selected by default. The value property of the CustomerNumber parameter contains the customer number of the selected customer. However, it makes more sense to the user if the customer's name is displayed at the top of the report. To accomplish this, we use the label property rather than the value property. The label property contains the text that appears in the parameter drop-down list for the selected item. In this case, the label property contains the customer's name.

Delivery Status Report, Task 3: Add a Tablix to the Report

DT

RB

SSDT, Visual Studio, and Report Builder Steps

1. Use the table template to add a tablix to the body of the report immediately below the text boxes.

2. In the leftmost cell in the data row of the tablix, select the Hub field from the DeliveryStatus dataset.

3. In each of the two remaining cells in the data row of the tablix, select the TimeIn and TimeOut fields.

4. Right-click anywhere in the data row, and select Tablix: Add Group | Row Group: Parent Group from the context menu. The Tablix group dialog box appears.

5. Select [DeliveryNumber] from the Group by drop-down list. We are now grouping the information in the table by the values in the DeliveryNumber field.

6. Check the Add group header and Add group footer check boxes.

7. Click OK to exit the Tablix group dialog box.

8. A group header cell is added along the left side of the tablix. This cell contains a text box, which, in turn, contains the DeliveryNumber field. (Don't confuse this with the group header row across the top of the tablix.) Modify the following properties of the text box containing the DeliveryNumber field:

Property	Value
Font: FontWeight	Bold
TextAlign	Left

Remember, you can set these text box properties using the Properties window or the ribbon/toolbar buttons.

9. We need to move some of the labels in the table header row to the group header row. Select the text box that contains the word "Hub" (not the text box containing the field reference "[Hub]"). Do this by clicking once in this text box. If you can see a text-editing cursor blinking in this cell, you clicked too many times. If you see the blinking cursor, click elsewhere, and then try again.

10. Press CTRL-X to cut the text box from this table header cell. Click in the group header cell immediately below it, and press CTRL-V to paste the text box there.

11. Repeat this for the text boxes containing Time In and Time Out.

12. Right-click the gray square to the left of the table header row. (This row now only contains the text "Delivery Number." Only "Delivery" may be showing if the column is too narrow for the entire header text.) Select Delete Rows from the context menu. This removes the table header row from this table.

13. Right-click anywhere in the group header row, and select Tablix: Insert Row | Inside Group - Above from the context menu. An additional group header row appears. This is not a new grouping, but rather an additional row for the current grouping.

14. Select the ServiceType field in the leftmost cell in the new group header row.

15. Select the StatusName field in the next cell in the new group header row.

16. Right-click anywhere in the new group header row, and select Tablix: Insert Row | Inside Group - Above from the context menu. Another new group header row appears.

17. Double-click the leftmost cell in the new group header row and type **Pickup:**.

18. Select the PickupPlanet field in the next cell to the right in the new group header row.

19. Select the PickupDateTime field in the rightmost cell in the new group header row.

20. Double-click in the group footer cell below the [Hub] field, and type **Delivery:**.

21. Select the DeliveryPlanet field in the next cell to the right in the group footer row.

22. Select the DeliveryDateTime field in the rightmost cell in the group footer row.

23. Right-click anywhere in the group footer row, and select Tablix: Insert Row | Inside Group - Below from the context menu. A new group footer row appears.

24. Double-click in the group footer cell below "Delivery:" and type **Problem Contact:**.

25. Select the ProblemContact field in the next cell to the right in the new group footer row.

26. Select the ProblemEMail field in the rightmost cell in the new group footer row.

27. Right-click anywhere in the new group footer row, and select Tablix: Insert Row | Inside Group - Below from the context menu. A new group footer row appears. This row is left blank.

28. Click the cell in the second column of the top group header row. Hold down the SHIFT key and click the rightmost cell of the bottom group header row. You have selected the nine cells in the three group header rows.

29. Modify the following property for these cells:

Property	Value
Font: FontWeight	Bold

30. Repeat Steps 28 and 29 for the six cells in the two group footer rows.

31. Click in the cell containing the [DeliveryNumber] field. Hold down the SHIFT key and click the cell in the lower-right corner of the tablix. You have selected all of the cells in the tablix.

32. Modify the following properties for these cells:

Property	Value
BorderColor: Default	Black
BorderStyle: Default	None

33. Click the gray box in the upper-left corner of the tablix to select the entire tablix. Use the sizing handle on the right side of the tablix to make it as wide as the design surface. Your report layout should appear similar to Figure 9-1.

34. Preview/Run the report. Select Bolimite, Mfg from the Customer drop-down list. Confirm that 2012 is selected in the Year drop-down list. (The year 2012 should be selected because you set it up as the default value for the Year parameter.) Click View Report.

Figure 9-1   *The Delivery Status Report layout after Task 3*

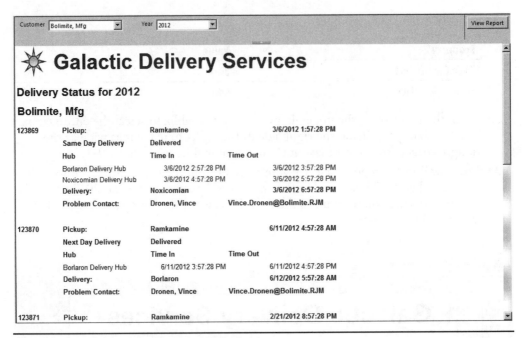

Figure 9-2   *The Delivery Status Report preview after Task 3*

35. You may want to return to the Design tab and adjust the size of some of the columns so the data does not wrap within text boxes. Hint: The DeliveryNumber column can be made narrow in order to gain space for some of the other columns. After making size adjustments, your report should appear similar to Figure 9-2.

Task Notes   The default behavior for the tablix is to create a light gray border around all of the cells. In our previous reports, we have stuck with that behavior. For this report, however, we are going to deviate from that approach and not have any border around most cells. The approach you use for your report authoring depends on the preference of you and your report users. What is appropriate and looks the best will probably vary from report to report.

We were able to add rows to both the group header and footer. This let us create more complex group header and footer layouts. In the same fashion, you can add rows to the table header, table footer, or data lines, as needed.

We now have the proper layout for our report, but we do not have the proper behavior of some of the report items. The delivery status is supposed to appear in color. The problem contact information is only supposed to be displayed with lost deliveries. Some additional formatting lines would also make the report more readable. All of this is accomplished in the next task with the aid of expressions.

Delivery Status Report, Task 4: Add the Expressions

SSDT, Visual Studio, and Report Builder Steps

1. Return to Design mode.

2. Select the entire tablix, if it is not selected already. Modify the following properties of the tablix:

Property	Value
BorderStyle: Top	Double
BorderStyle: Bottom	Double
BorderWidth	6pt

3. Enter the following expression for the Color property of the cell containing the StatusName field:

```
= IIF(Fields!StatusName.Value = "Delivered", "Green",
        IIF(Fields!StatusName.Value = "In Route", "Blue", "Red"))
```

NOTE

When entering each of the expressions, you probably want to select <Expression…> from the drop-down list for the property and enter this expression in the Expression dialog box. Also, remember the Expression dialog box offers help for finding the correct function and for inserting fields and parameters. Expressions involving the Built-in Fields, Parameters, and Fields collections are case-sensitive.

4. Click the gray square to the left of the top group header row so the entire row is selected. Modify the following properties for these cells:

Property	Value
BorderStyle: Top	=IIF(Fields!DeliveryNumber.Value = First(Fields!DeliveryNumber.Value, "DeliveryStatus"), "None", "Solid")
BorderWidth: Top	4pt

5. Click the cell containing the word "Hub." Hold down the SHIFT key and click the Time Out cell. Three cells should now be selected. Modify the following property for these cells:

Property	Value
BorderStyle: Bottom	Solid

6. Select the following three cells using the same method as in Step 5: "Delivery:", "[DeliveryPlanet]", and "[DeliveryDateTime]". Modify the following properties for these cells:

Property	Value
BorderStyle: Top	Solid
BorderStyle: Bottom	= IIF(Fields!StatusName.Value = "Lost", "None", "Solid")
BorderWidth: Bottom	2pt

NOTE

"StatusName" is case-sensitive in this expression.

7. Select the following three cells: "Problem Contact:", "[ProblemContact]", and "[ProblemEmail]". Modify the following properties for these cells:

Property	Value
BorderStyle: Bottom	= IIF(Fields!StatusName.Value <> "Lost", "None", "Solid")
BorderWidth: Bottom	2pt
Hidden	= IIF(Fields!StatusName.Value = "Lost", false, true)

8. Preview/Run the report. Select Bolimite, Mfg from the Customer drop-down list and 2012 from the Year drop-down list, if they are not already selected. Click View Report. Your report should appear similar to Figure 9-3.

9. Save the report.

Task Notes   If you scroll through the pages of the report, you see the report now meets the business needs specified. Let's look at what each expression is doing. The expression entered in Step 3 returns green when the status is Delivered, and blue when the status is In Route. Otherwise, it returns red.

The expression in Step 4 is a bit more complex. It checks whether the current value of the DeliveryNumber field is equal to the first value of the DeliveryNumber field in the DeliveryStatus dataset. As you saw in Chapter 8, aggregate functions act within a scope. By default, the First() aggregate function would return the value for the first

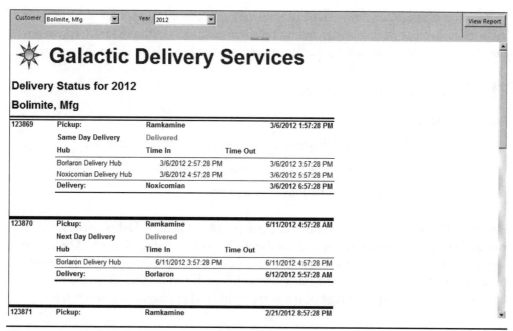

Figure 9-3   *The Delivery Status Report preview after Task 4*

record in the current scope. Because this expression is in the group header, by default, it would return the value for the first record in each group.

However, in this expression, the First() aggregate function includes a second parameter that specifies the scope it should use. This parameter specifies that the First() aggregate function should use the scope of the entire DeliveryStatus dataset rather than just the current group. Therefore, it returns the first record in the dataset. When the current delivery number is equal to the first delivery number in the dataset, no border is created across the top of these text boxes. This prevents the border across the top of the text boxes from interfering with the border across the top of the tablix. When the current delivery number is not equal to the first delivery number in the dataset, a border is created across the top of the text boxes.

The expression in Step 6 and the first expression in Step 7 use the value of the StatusName field to control the border across the bottom of each grouping. If the problem contact text boxes are displayed, the border should appear across the bottom of these text boxes. However, if the problem contact text boxes are not displayed, the border should appear across the bottom of the text boxes in the row above. The second expression in Step 7 controls whether the text boxes containing the problem contact are displayed. This is also based on the value of the StatusName field.

As you can see, expressions can be useful when the formatting, or even the visibility, of a report item needs to change depending on some condition in the report. Expressions can also be used to calculate the values to appear in a text box, as you see in the next report.

The Lost Delivery Report

Features Highlighted

▶ Using Visual Basic .NET expressions to calculate values in a text box

▶ Adding static columns to a tablix functioning as a matrix

▶ Adding totals to a tablix functioning as a matrix

Business Need   The quality assurance department at Galactic Delivery Services would like a report to help them analyze the packages lost during delivery. The report should show the number of packages lost each year at each processing hub. It should break down these numbers by the cause for each loss. It should also show the number of losses by cause as a percentage of the total number of packages lost for each hub.

Task Overview

1. Create a New Report, Create a Dataset, and Add a Tablix to the Report
2. Add a Calculated Column to the Tablix
3. Add an Indicator and Totals to the Tablix

Lost Delivery Report, Task 1: Create a New Report, Create a Dataset, and Add a Tablix to the Report

DT
RB   SSDT, Visual Studio, and Report Builder Steps

1. Create a new report called LostDelivery using the GDSReport template.
2. Create a new data source called Galactic that references the Galactic shared data source.
3. Create a new dataset called LostDelivery that calls the stp_LostDeliveries stored procedure.
4. Use the matrix template to place a tablix onto the body of the report.
5. Select the Cause field in the Rows cell. Select the Hub field in the Columns cell.
6. Select the DeliveryNumber field in the Data cell. Use the Expression dialog box to edit the aggregate function in the resulting expression by changing it from Sum to Count.

7. Click in the upper-left cell of the tablix. Hold down the SHIFT key and click the lower-right cell. All four cells in the tablix should be selected.

8. Modify the following properties of the selected cells:

Property	Value
BorderColor: Default	Black
BorderStyle: Default	None

9. Click outside of the tablix to unselect the cells.

10. Right-click the Hub cell and select Tablix: Add Group | Column Group | Parent Group. The Tablix group dialog box appears.

11. Click the Expression (*fx*) button. The Expression dialog box appears.

12. Type the following in the Set expression for: GroupExpression area to group the values by year:

```
=Year(Fields!PickupDateTime.Value)
```

13. Click OK to exit the Expression dialog box.

14. Click OK to exit the Tablix group dialog box.

15. Select the empty cell in the upper-left corner of the tablix. Hold down the SHIFT key and click the cell immediately below it. Right-click in this same cell and select Tablix: Merge Cells from the context menu.

16. Modify the following properties of the text box in the merged cell you just created:

Property	Value
BackgroundColor	LightGrey
Font: FontSize	18pt
Font: FontWeight	Bold
Size: Width	2in
Size: Height	0.75in
Value	Lost Deliveries by Cause

NOTE

You may need to click elsewhere to unselect the newly merged cells and then reselect the newly merged cells to get some of the properties to function properly.

17. Modify the following property of the text box in the lower-left corner of the tablix:

Property	Value
BackgroundColor	LightGrey

18. Modify the following properties of the text box in the upper-right corner of the tablix:

Property	Value
BackgroundColor	LightGrey
BorderStyle: Left	Solid
Font: FontSize	14pt
Font: FontWeight	Bold
TextAlign	Center

19. Modify the following properties of the text box in the center of the right-hand column of the tablix:

Property	Value
BackgroundColor	LightGrey
BorderStyle: Left	Solid
BorderStyle: Bottom	Solid
Font: FontWeight	Bold
TextAlign	Center

20. Modify the following property of the text box in the lower-right corner of the matrix:

Property	Value
BorderStyle: Left	Solid

Task Notes   So far, we have a fairly straightforward matrix report. Let's see what happens when we add another column and totals to the matrix.

Lost Delivery Report, Task 2: Add a Calculated Column to the Tablix

DT

RB

SSDT, Visual Studio, and Report Builder Steps

1. Right-click the text box in the lower-right corner of the matrix, and select Tablix: Insert Column | Inside Group - Right from the context menu. A new column is created inside of the Hub group.

2. Right-click the same text box, and select Tablix: Insert Row | Outside Group - Above from the context menu. A new row appears above the Cause group.

3. Modify the following properties of the new text box in the lower-right corner of the tablix:

Property	Value
BorderStyle: Left	Solid
Format	##0.00%
TextAlign	Right
Value	=Count(Fields!DeliveryNumber.Value)/ Count(Fields!DeliveryNumber.Value, "Hub")

4. Modify the following properties of the text box immediately above the text box modified in Step 3:

Property	Value
BorderStyle: Left	Solid
Font: TextDecoration	Underline
TextAlign	Right
Value	% of Column

5. Modify the following properties of the text box immediately to the left of the text box modified in Step 4:

Property	Value
BorderStyle: Left	Solid
Font: TextDecoration	Underline
TextAlign	Right
Value	# Lost

6. After adjusting row heights and column widths, your report layout should appear similar to Figure 9-4.

7. Preview/Run the report. Your report should appear similar to Figure 9-5.

Task Notes   In the previous report, we created a multirow group header and a multirow group footer. In this report, we created a multicolumn detail section. We did this by adding a second column inside of the column groupings. We also created headings for our columns by adding a new row outside of the row grouping. We want one set of columns for each column grouping. However, we only want one set of headings at the top of each row group.

The row containing the column headings is a static row in the tablix. We took our first look at static rows and columns in Chapter 8. Here they are, back again, to help

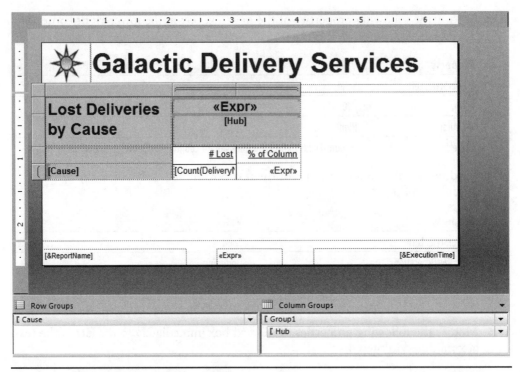

Figure 9-4 *The Lost Delivery Report layout after Task 2*

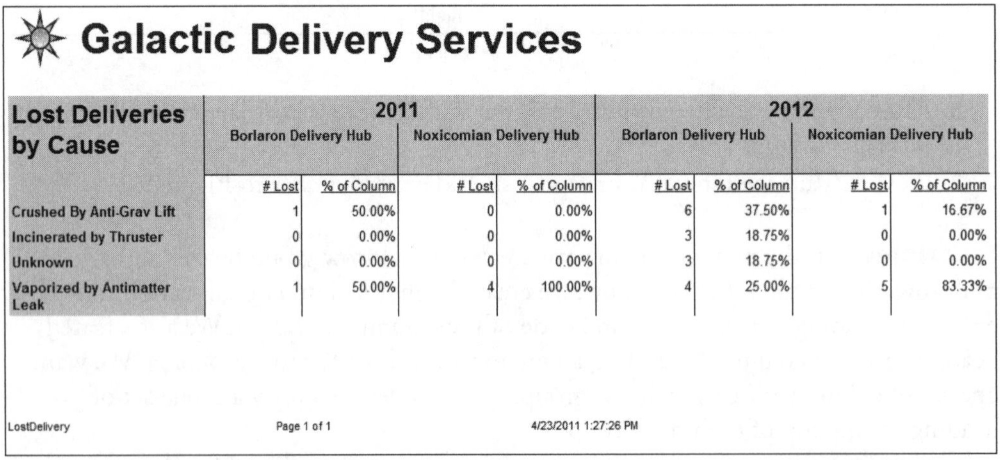

Galactic Delivery Services

Lost Deliveries by Cause	2011				2012			
	Borlaron Delivery Hub		Noxicomian Delivery Hub		Borlaron Delivery Hub		Noxicomian Delivery Hub	
	# Lost	% of Column	# Lost	% of Column	# Lost	% of Column	# Lost	% of Column
Crushed By Anti-Grav Lift	1	50.00%	0	0.00%	6	37.50%	1	16.67%
Incinerated by Thruster	0	0.00%	0	0.00%	3	18.75%	0	0.00%
Unknown	0	0.00%	0	0.00%	3	18.75%	0	0.00%
Vaporized by Antimatter Leak	1	50.00%	4	100.00%	4	25.00%	5	83.33%

LostDelivery   Page 1 of 1   4/23/2011 1:27:26 PM

Figure 9-5 *The Lost Delivery Report preview after Task 2*

us do more creative formatting within our tablix. In Task 3 of this report, we will use additional static rows and columns to include an indicator and to provide totals.

Our new column takes the count from the current row and calculates it as a percentage of the total for the column. This is done, once again, through the magic of scope. The first Count() aggregate function does not have a scope parameter, so it defaults to the scope of the current cell. In other words, it counts the number of lost deliveries in the current cell.

The second Count() aggregate function has a scope parameter of Hub. This is the name of the column group that creates the column for each hub. Therefore, this aggregate function counts the number of lost deliveries in the entire column. We then divide and use the ###.00% format string to create a percentage.

Lost Delivery Report, Task 3:
Add an Indicator and Totals to the Tablix

`DT`
`RB` SSDT, Visual Studio, and Report Builder Steps

1. Return to Design mode.
2. Right-click the text box containing "# Lost" and select Tablix: Insert Column | Inside Group – Right.
3. Select an Indicator from the Toolbox or Insert tab and place it in the lower of the two new cells you just created.
4. The Select Indicator Type dialog box appears.
5. Select "3 Signs" as shown in Figure 9-6.
6. Click OK to exit the Select Indicator Type dialog box.
7. Modify the following properties of the indicator you just created using the Indicator Properties dialog box:

Property	Value
Value and States page:	
Value	=Count(Fields!DeliveryNumber.Value)
States Measurement Unit	Numeric
Red Diamond Icon: Start	6
Red Diamond Icon: End	20
Yellow Triangle Icon: Start	3
Yellow Triangle Icon: End	5
Green Circle Icon: Start	0
Green Circle Icon: End	2

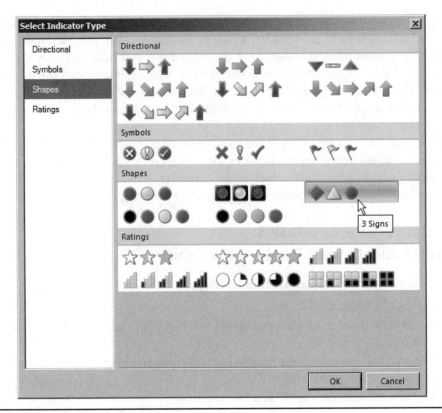

Figure 9-6 *The Select Indicator Type dialog box*

8. Narrow the column containing the indicator so it is just wide enough for the indictor itself.

9. Right-click the text box in the lower-left corner of the matrix, and select Tablix: Add Total | After from the context menu. A total row is added at the bottom of the tablix.

10. Modify the following properties of the text box containing the word "Total":

Property	Value
BorderStyle: Top	Solid
BorderWidth	2pt

11. Modify the following properties of the text box at the bottom of the column containing "# Lost":

Property	Value
BorderStyle: Top	Solid
BorderWidth: Top	2pt

12. Modify the following properties of the text box at the bottom of the column containing the indicator:

Property	Value
BorderColor: Top	Black
BorderStyle: Top	Solid
BorderWidth: Top	2pt

13. Modify the following properties of the text box at the bottom of the column containing "% of Column":

Property	Value
BorderStyle: Top	Solid
BorderWidth: Top	2pt

14. Right-click the text box in the upper-right corner of the matrix. Select Tablix: Add Total | After from the context menu. A set of three columns is added at the right of the tablix.

15. Right-click the gray rectangle above the middle of the three new columns. Select Delete Columns from the context menu.

16. Right-click the cell in the lower-right corner of the tablix. Select Expression from the context menu. The Expression dialog box appears.

17. Modify the expression to match the following:

```
=Count(Fields!DeliveryNumber.Value)/ Count(Fields!DeliveryNumber.Value,
                        "LostDelivery")
```

The change is the scope parameter in the second Count() aggregate function.

18. Click OK to exit the Expression dialog box.

19. Right-click the cell immediately above the cell you modified in Steps 16–18. Select Expression from the context menu. The Expression dialog box appears.

20. Modify the expression to match the following:

```
=Count(Fields!DeliveryNumber.Value)/ Count(Fields!DeliveryNumber.Value,
                                        "LostDelivery")
```

The change is the scope parameter in the second Count() aggregate function.

21. Click OK to exit the Expression dialog box.

22. Enter **% of Column** in the text box immediately above the text box you modified in Steps 19–21.

23. Enter **# Lost** in the text box to the left of the text box you modified in Step 22.

24. When completed, your report layout should appear similar to Figure 9-7.

25. Preview/Run the report. Your report should appear similar to Figure 9-8.

26. Save the report.

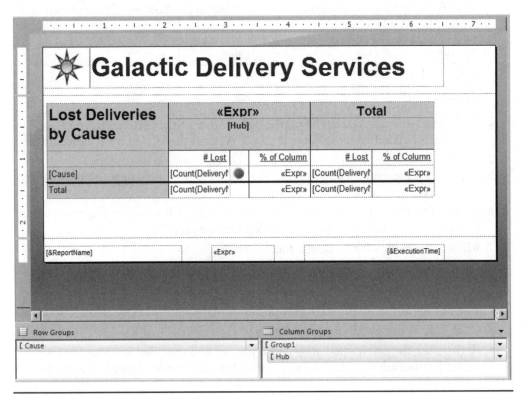

Figure 9-7   *The Lost Delivery Report layout after Task 3*

☀ Galactic Delivery Services

Lost Deliveries by Cause	2011				2012				Total	
	Borlaron Delivery Hub		Noxicomian Delivery Hub		Borlaron Delivery Hub		Noxicomian Delivery Hub			
	# Lost	% of Column	# Lost	% of Column	# Lost	% of Column	# Lost	% of Column	# Lost	% of Column
Crushed By Anti-Grav Lift	1 ●	50.00%	0 ●	0.00%	6 ◆	37.50%	1 ●	16.67%	8	28.57%
Incinerated by Thruster	0 ●	0.00%	0 ●	0.00%	3 △	18.75%	0 ●	0.00%	3	10.71%
Unknown	0 ●	0.00%	0 ●	0.00%	3 △	18.75%	0 ●	0.00%	3	10.71%
Vaporized by Antimatter Leak	1 ●	50.00%	4 △	100.00%	4 △	25.00%	5 △	83.33%	14	50.00%
Total	2	100.00%	4	100.00%	16	100.00%	6	100.00%	28	100.00%

LostDelivery   Page 1 of 1   6/19/2011 5:17:59 PM

Figure 9-8   *The Lost Delivery Report preview after Task 3*

Task Notes   This is the first use of the indicator item in a report. An *indicator* enables us to graphically show the state of a particular value. If it is in the range that we want it to be in, then the "good" indicator is shown. If it is in the range where we should start to show some concern, then the "caution" indicator is shown. If it is in the range where we need to really address the factors behind this number, then the "bad" indicator is shown.

The Select Indicator Type dialog box and the Indicator Properties dialog box allow us to pick the symbols that will be used for good, caution, and bad. They also allow us to set the range of values for good, caution, and bad. While the three-level indicator symbols are most often used, you should note that there are sets of indicators on the Select Indicator Type dialog box that can represent four and even five states.

Adding totals to our report involves creating additional static rows and columns in our tablix. We first added a total row at the bottom of the tablix. The cells in this total row are inside of the column groupings on year and hub but outside of the row grouping on repair cause. Therefore, these cells give us the totals for each hub across all of the repair causes as we expect. The second set of totals we added are inside of the row grouping on repair cause but outside of the column groupings on hub and year. These cells give us the totals for a repair cause across all hubs and years. The two cells in the lower-right corner of the tablix are outside of all column and row groupings, so they provide totals for the entire tablix.

We had to use a different scope for the totals in the rightmost columns because, as we just said, these columns are outside of the hub grouping. An aggregate function must be inside of a scope in order for it to be used as the scope parameter. Instead of using the hub grouping, we use the scope of the entire LostDelivery dataset to create these totals.

The Customer List Report—Revisited

Features Highlighted

▶ Copying a report between projects/launching Report Builder from a report

▶ Using Visual Basic .NET expressions to specify a dataset query

Business Need   The Customer List Report you developed for the Galactic Delivery Services accounting department in Chapter 4 has proved to be popular. Several other departments would like similar reports to help them track their own lists of e-mail contacts. Rather than create separate reports for each department, which would be hard to maintain, the IT manager has asked for one report that enables the user to select which type of contact they want to view.

Task Overview

1. Copy the Report from Chapter04 for Use in Chapter09
2. Add a Report Parameter and Modify the Dataset to Use the Report Parameter

Customer List Report—Revisited, Task 1: Copy the Report from Chapter04 for Use in Chapter09

DT SSDT and Visual Studio Steps

1. Use Windows Explorer to copy the report definition file for the Customer List Report (Customer List.rdl) from the Chapter04 project folder and paste it in the Chapter09 project folder. Both of these folders should be found under My Documents in the Visual Studio 2010\Projects\MSSQLRS folder.

2. In Report Designer, reopen the Chapter09 project, if it was closed.

3. Right-click the Reports folder in the Solution Explorer, and select Add | Existing Item from the context menu. The Add Existing Item–Chapter09 dialog box appears.

4. Make sure you are looking at the Chapter09 folder in the dialog box, and select the Customer List.rdl file. Click Add to exit the Add Existing Item–Chapter09 dialog box.

5. Double-click the Customer List.rdl entry in the Solution Explorer to open the report definition.

6. Click the Preview tab to show this report is functioning properly in the Chapter09 project.

Task Notes for SSDT and Visual Studio   Because the entire definition of a report is contained within a single Report Definition Language (RDL) file, it is easy to copy reports to different locations. As you saw here, we can even add them to a project other than the project within which they were originally created. The Customer List Report uses a shared data source called Galactic. We did not need to copy the shared data source because we already have a shared data source with the same name and the same properties in the Chapter09 project. If this was not the case, we could have copied the shared data source file (Galactic.rds), along with the report file, and added that to our new project as well.

RB | **Report Builder Steps**
1. Close Report Builder, if it is open.
2. In Report Manager, navigate to the Chapter04 folder.
3. Hover over the Customer List report to activate the drop-down list.
4. From the drop-down list for the Customer List report, select Edit in Report Builder. The Report Builder application will start up and load the Customer List report definition.
5. Click the logo button and select Save As from the menu. The Save As Report dialog box appears.
6. Navigate to the Chapter09 folder on the report server.
7. Click Save to exit the Save As Report dialog box.
8. Run the report to show it is functioning properly in the Chapter09 folder.

Task Notes for Report Builder   The Edit in Report Builder menu option in the Report Manager allows us to both launch the Report Builder application and open a report definition for editing with a single click. As we have seen before, the Save As menu choice allows us to save a report definition in a different location—effectively making a copy of that report. The report can still access the Galactic shared data source from the new location in the Chapter09 folder, so there is no need to make any changes to the report definition to have it run properly.

Customer List Report—Revisited, Task 2: Add a Report Parameter and Modify the Dataset to Use the Report Parameter

DT | **SSDT, Visual Studio, and Report Builder Steps**
RB |
1. Return to design mode.
2. Right-click the Parameters item in the Report Data window. Select Add Parameter from the context menu. The Report Parameter Properties dialog box appears.

3. Modify the properties for this new report parameter as follows:

Property	Value
General page:	
Name	ListType
Prompt	Select a List
Available Values page:	
Select from one of the following options:	Specify values
(Enter the values from the Available Values table that follows)	

On the Available Values page, add the following rows to the grid at the bottom of the dialog box:

Label	Value
Billing Contacts	B
Manufacturer Contacts	M
Problem Contacts	P

4. Click OK to exit the Report Parameter Properties dialog box.

5. In the Report Data window, right-click the entry for DataSet1 and select Dataset Properties from the context menu. The Dataset Properties dialog box appears.

6. Click the Expression (*fx*) button next to the Query area. The Expression dialog box appears.

7. Replace the entire select statement with the following expression:

```
=IIF(Parameters!ListType.Value="B", "EXEC stp_BillingContacts",
     IIF(Parameters!ListType.Value="M",
         "EXEC stp_ManufacturerContacts",
         "EXEC stp_ProblemContacts"))
```

CAUTION

If you use this method to build a SQL statement by concatenating parameter values into the query text, you must take care to guard against query injection attacks on your SQL server.

8. Click OK to exit the Expression dialog box.

NOTE

In the Dataset Properties dialog box, the only way to edit our query expression now is to click the Expression (fx) button next to the Query area on this dialog box.

9. Select the Fields page.

10. Change the table on the Fields page to match the following:

Field Name	Field Source
Name	Name
Contact	Contact
Email	Email

11. Click OK to exit the Dataset Properties dialog box.

12. In the text box that currently says "[BillingContact]," select the Contact field using the Field Selector.

13. Double-click the table header cell directly above the text box from Step 12, and change the text to **Contact**.

14. In the text box that currently says "[BillingEmail]," select the Email field using the Field Selector.

15. Double-click the table header cell directly above the text box from Step 14, and change the text to **Email**.

16. Save the report.

17. Preview/Run the report. Try selecting each of the list types. Remember to click View Report each time after changing your parameter selection.

NOTE

The database does not contain a contact name for each manufacturer, so no contact names are in the manufacturer list.

Task Notes   Rather than specifying a query to be executed, we used an expression to choose among three possible queries (in this case, three stored procedure calls). This is known as a dynamic query. The name comes from the fact that the query that is run depends on input from the user at the time the report is run.

Because the content of the query is not known until run time, the Report Designer cannot "pre-run" the query to determine the fields that will result. Instead, we need to manually specify the fields that will result from our dynamic query. All the possible queries that could be run must return result sets with the same field names for your report to work properly.

At this point, you may be ready to suggest two or three alternative approaches to creating this report. It is certainly not unusual to come up with a number of possible ways to meet the business needs of a report. When this happens, use the following criteria to evaluate the possible solutions:

▶ Efficiency of operation

▶ Your comfort with implementing and debugging a given solution in a reasonable amount of time

▶ Maintainability

▶ Your need to illustrate a certain point in a book chapter

Well, maybe that last point won't apply to you, but it was, in fact, the overriding reason for choosing this approach for this particular report.

The Delivery Trend Report

Features Highlighted

▶ Using the Sparkline report item

Business Need   The marketing department at Galactic Delivery Services would like a compact report showing customer delivery trends. The report should show the total number of deliveries for each customer along with a chart showing deliveries by month for each customer. The report should be as small as possible so it can be used as part of a company intranet page.

Task Overview

1. Create a New Report, Create a Dataset, and Create a Report Layout

Delivery Trend Report, Task 1: Create a New Report, Create a Dataset, and Create a Report Layout

SSDT, Visual Studio, and Report Builder Steps

1. Create a new report called DeliveryTrend. Do *not* use the GDSReport template. (If you are using Report Builder, remove the "Click to add title" text box and the page footer.)

2. Create a new data source called Galactic that references the Galactic shared data source.

3. Create a new dataset called DeliveryTrend that calls the stp_DeliveryTrend stored procedure.

4. Use the table template to place a tablix onto the body of the report.

5. Modify the following properties of the tablix in the Properties window:

Property	Value
Location: Left	0in
Location: Top	0in
Size: Width	5.5in
Size: Height	0.5in

6. Change the size of the report body so it is the same size as the tablix.
7. Select the Name field in the left-hand Data cell.
8. Use the Details drop-down button in the Row Groups area to select Group Properties. The Group Properties dialog box appears.
9. Click the Add button in the Group Expressions area.
10. Select Name from the Group on drop-down list.
11. Click OK to exit the Group Properties dialog box.
12. Select the DeliveryCount field in the center Data cell.
13. Change the heading for this center column to **Total Deliveries**.
14. Place a sparkline in the right-hand data cell. The Select Sparkline Type dialog box appears.
15. Select Area as shown in Figure 9-9.
16. Click OK to exit the Select Sparkline Type dialog box.
17. Click the sparkline item to activate the Chart Data window.
18. Click the green plus sign next to the Values area, and select DeliveryCount.
19. Click the green plus sign next to the Category Groups area, and select YearMonth.
20. Enter **Delivery Trend Over Time** in the text box above the sparkline.
21. Click the gray rectangle to the left of the tablix header row.
22. Modify the following property in the Properties window:

Property	Value
Font: FontWeight	Bold

23. Select the gray rectangle above the center column.
24. Modify the following property in the Properties window:

Property	Value
TextAlign	Center

25. Preview/Run the report. Your report will appear similar to Figure 9-10.
26. Save the report.

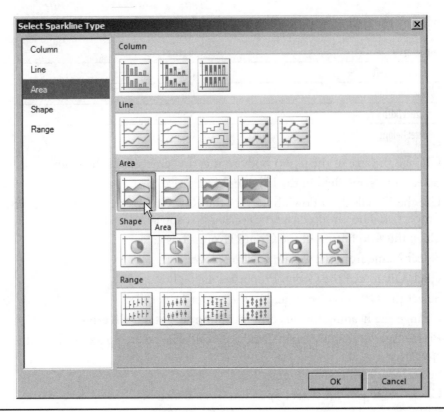

Figure 9-9   *The Select Sparkline Type dialog box*

Name	Total Deliveries	Delivery Trend Over Time
Bolimite, Mfg	48	
Custer, Inc.	36	
Everlast Plastics	12	
Juniper, Inc	36	
Landmark, Inc.	24	
Moore Company	24	
Phillips Mfg, Inc.	36	
Quincy, Mfg	24	
Rhinehardt Companies	36	
Rosenblinker, Inc.	60	
Sanders & Son	48	
Twillig Companies	36	
Young & Assoc.	36	

Figure 9-10   *The Delivery Trend Report*

Task Notes   As we saw with the data bar in Chapter 8 and the indicator earlier in this chapter, the *sparkline* is a way to provide a compact data visualization within a tablix. Essentially, it is a line or area chart without any axis labels. Similar to the data bar, the sparkline can be converted to a regular chart item, if desired.

Where the data bar and the indicator graphically represent a single value in their tablix scope, the sparkline represents a series of values. For this reason, a sparkline can only be used in an area of the tablix where grouping is taking place. A sparkline cannot be used in the detail row of a tablix, unless grouping is set up at the detail level, which is the case in the Delivery Trend report.

Payroll Checks

Features Highlighted

- ▶ Using Visual Basic .NET functions embedded in the report to create reusable code

- ▶ Using a stored procedure that updates data

- ▶ Grouping in the details row of a data region

- ▶ Using nested data regions

- ▶ Resetting the page number

Business Need   The Galactic Delivery Services accounting department needs a report to print payroll checks for its hourly employees. The checks should have the check portion in the top one-third of the page and the check register in the bottom two-thirds of the page. The check register should list the work hours included in this check. The user should be able to select a week for which unpaid time is entered and receive the payroll checks for that week. The planetary system tax amount (25 percent) and state tax amount (5 percent) must be deducted from the amount being paid.

Task Overview

1. Create a New Report, Create Two Datasets, Add a Tablix to the Report Layout, and Populate It
2. Add a Second Tablix to the Report Layout and Populate It
3. Configure the Report Parameter and Add Embedded Code to the Report

Payroll Checks, Task 1: Create a New Report, Create Two Datasets, Add a Tablix to the Report Layout, and Populate It

DT

RB

SSDT, Visual Studio, and Report Builder Steps

1. Create a new report called PayrollChecks. Do *not* use the GDSReport template. (If you are using Report Builder, remove the "Click to add title" text box and the page footer.)

2. Create a new data source called Galactic that references the Galactic shared data source.

3. Create a new dataset called PayrollChecks that calls the stp_PayrollChecks stored procedure.

4. Create a new dataset called WeekNumbers that calls the stp_WeekNumbers stored procedure.

5. Use the list template to place a tablix onto the body of the report. Modify the following properties of this tablix in the Properties window:

Property	Value
BackgroundColor	LightGreen
BorderStyle: Default	Solid
DataSetName	PayrollChecks
Location: Left	0in
Location: Top	0in
PageBreak: BreakLocation	Start

6. In the Row Group pane, select Group Properties from the (Details) drop-down menu. The Group Properties dialog box appears.

7. On the General page, click Add to add an item to the group expression.

8. Select [PayrollCheckNumber] from the Group on drop-down list.

9. Click OK to exit the Group Properties dialog box.

10. Add text boxes to the list to get the layout shown in Figure 9-11. Make sure the rectangle in the tablix is selected each time before you drag a field or text box onto it. Remember, the square brackets around an item indicate that a field is being displayed in that text box. You can create text boxes containing fields by dragging the fields from the Report Data window. Enlarge the report body and the tablix, if necessary.

11. Click the text box containing the PayrollCheckNumber field to select it. Right-click the text box and select Expression from the context menu. The Expression dialog box appears.

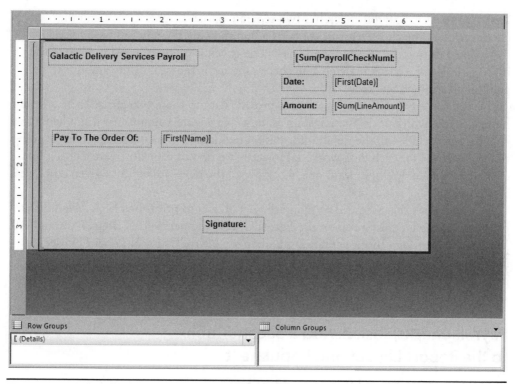

Figure 9-11   *The Payroll Check layout after Step 10*

12. Remove the Sum() aggregate function so the expression is as follows:

```
=Fields!PayrollCheckNumber.Value
```

13. Click OK to exit the Expression dialog box.

14. Right-click the text box containing the LineAmount field, and select Textbox Properties from the context menu. The Text Box Properties dialog box appears.

15. Modify the following properties of this text box:

Property	Value
Number page:	
Category	Currency
Use 1000 separator check box	checked

16. Click OK to exit the Text Box Properties dialog box.

Task Notes   Our payroll check has two separate parts: the check itself and the check register. The check register contains a line showing the amount paid for each day worked during the selected workweek. The check is essentially a summary of the information in the check register. The check amount is the sum of the amount to be paid for all the days worked.

We could use two different datasets to provide data to these two areas. To be a little more efficient with our database resources, however, we are going to use a single dataset. The dataset includes all the detail information required by the check register. It is going to have one row for each date worked. However, we do not want to create a check for each date worked. We only want one check for all the days worked by a given employee in the week.

To accomplish this, we need to group the detail data to print the check. We did this by grouping the DetailsGroup on the PayrollCheckNumber field in Steps 7 through 10. Because we want one check per check number, the PayrollCheckNumber field seems an obvious choice for grouping. (The number in the PayrollCheckNumber field is generated by the stored procedure.) With this details grouping, our tablix receives one record for each check number; therefore, we get one check per check number.

Payroll Checks, Task 2: Add a Second Tablix to the Report Layout and Populate It

DT

RB

SSDT, Visual Studio, and Report Builder Steps

1. Increase the height of the report body and the tablix. For the remainder of the report, we will refer to this tablix as the "list tablix."

2. Use the table template to place a tablix *inside* the list tablix. The new tablix should be below the signature text box. We will refer to this new tablix as the "table tablix."

3. Make the table tablix almost as wide as the list tablix.

4. Select the WorkDate, HoursWorked, and LineAmount fields in the cells in the data row of the table tablix.

5. Right-click anywhere in the lower row of the table tablix, and select Tablix: Insert Row | Outside Group - Below from the context menu. This new row will serve as a total row.

6. Select the LineAmount field in the rightmost cell of the row we just added to the table tablix. Set the following properties for the text box in this cell:

Property	Value
BorderColor: Top	Black
Format	C

7. Set the following property for the text box in the cell immediately above the cell modified in Step 6:

Property	Value
Format	C

NOTE

Entering C for the Format property is the same as selecting Currency in the Text Box Properties dialog box.

8. Set the following properties for the table tablix:

Property	Value
BackgroundColor	White
PageBreak: BreakLocation	End
PageBreak: ResetPageNumber	True

9. Drag the bottom of the list tablix and the bottom of the report body up so they are the same as the bottom of the table tablix.
10. Right-click anywhere outside the report body but inside the design area. Select Add Page Footer from the context menu.
11. Place a text box in the center of the page footer.
12. Right-click the text box and select Expression from the context menu. The Expression text box appears.
13. Select Built-in Fields in the Category area. (Take note of the OverallPageNumber and OverallTotalPages fields in the Item area. These will be discussed in the Task Notes.)
14. Double-click Page Number.
15. Click OK to exit the Expression dialog box.
16. Your report layout appears similar to Figure 9-12.

Task Notes In Task 1, we created a tablix from a list template with a detail grouping to create the check portion of our payroll checks. In Task 2, we created a tablix from a table template to provide the detail information for the check register. The table tablix data region must be nested inside of the list tablix data region so that we get one set of detail information for each check. If the table was placed below the list, we would get all the checks first and then all the check register information at the end.

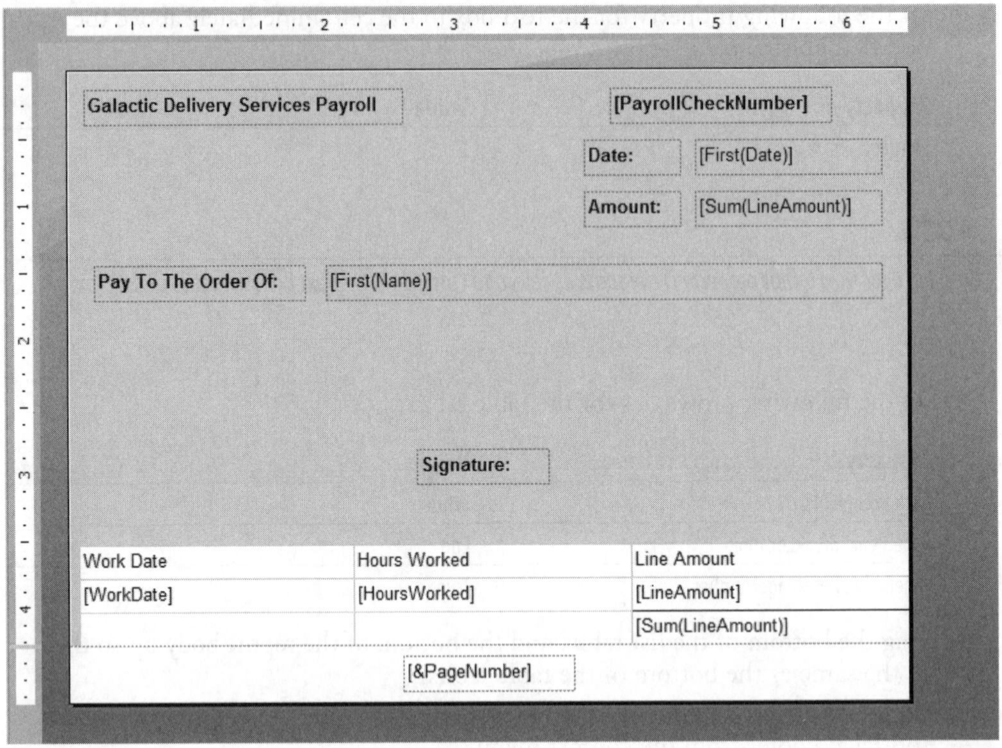

Figure 9-12 *The Payroll Check layout after Task 2*

The PageBreak: BreakLocation property was set to End on the table tablix, so there is a page break immediately after the table. This starts each check on a new page. It is possible, however, that a long check register section could cause an employee's check to wrap to a second page. For this reason, we want to put a page number in the footer of the report and we want to reset the page number as we start each new employee. The PageBreak: PageNumberReset enables us to do that.

When the PageNumberReset property is set to true, the page number returned by Globals!PageNumber and the total pages returned by Globals!PageNumber is reset. If, for some reason, you also want to show page number and/or the total pages for the entire report, you can use Globals!OverallPageNumber and Globals!OverallTotalPages.

Payroll Checks, Task 3: Configure the Report Parameter and Add Embedded Code to the Report

`DT`
`RB`
SSDT, Visual Studio, and Report Builder Steps

1. Expand the Parameters entry in the Report Data window.
2. Right-click the WeekNumber entry and select Parameter Properties from the context menu. The Report Parameter Properties dialog box appears.
3. Modify the following properties for the WeekNumber parameter:

Property	Value
Available Values page:	
Select from one of the following options:	Get values from a query
Dataset	WeekNumbers
Value field	WeekNumber
Label field	WeekNumber

4. Click OK to exit the Report Parameter Properties dialog box.
5. Right-click anywhere outside the report body but in the layout area. Select Report Properties from the context menu. The Report Properties dialog box appears.
6. Select the Code page.
7. Enter the following in the Custom code area:

```
' State and Planetary System Tax Deductions
Public Function TaxDeductions(ByVal Amount As Double) As Double
        ' Planetary System Tax = 25%
        ' State Tax = 5%
        TaxDeductions = Amount * .25 + Amount * .05
End Function
```

8. Click OK to exit the Report Properties dialog box.
9. Right-click the text box in the list tablix (but not in the table tablix) containing the [Sum(LineAmount)] value, and select Expression from the context menu. The Expression dialog box appears.
10. Replace the contents of the Set expression for: Value area with the following:

```
=Sum(Fields!LineAmount.Value) -
        Code.TaxDeductions(Sum(Fields!LineAmount.Value))
```

Ignore the red line under "TaxDeductions" if one appears.

11. Click OK to exit the Expression dialog box.
12. Repeat Steps 9 through 11, with the text box in the table tablix containing the sum of the LineAmount values.

13. Right-click the text box in the details row of the table tablix containing the LineAmount field, and select Expression from the context menu. The Expression dialog box appears.
14. Replace the contents of the Set expression for: Value area with the following:

```
=Fields!LineAmount.Value - Code.TaxDeductions(Fields!LineAmount.Value)
```

15. Click OK to exit the Expression dialog box.
16. Preview/Run the report.
17. Select 10-2013 from the Week Number drop-down list, and click View Report. Your report should appear similar to Figure 9-13. Remember, once checks have been run for a given week, you cannot produce checks for that week again. Each time you run the report, the Week Number drop-down list only contains entries for weeks that have not been run. (The check number you see on the first page in your preview may be different from the check number shown in the figure. This is normal.)
18. Save the report.

Task Notes Payroll tax calculations are straightforward on the planets where Galactic Delivery Services operates. Everyone pays 25 percent of their pay to the planetary system government and 5 percent of their pay to the state government. Even though

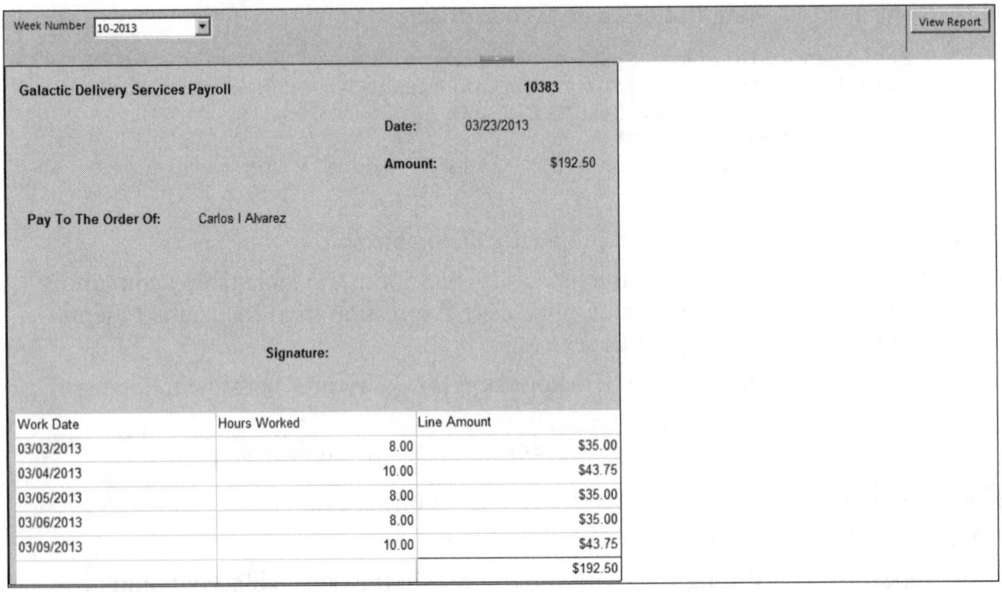
Week Number
10-2013
View Report
Galactic Delivery Services Payroll
10383
Date:
03/23/2013
Amount:
$192.50
Pay To The Order Of:
Carlos I Alvarez
Signature:
Work Date
Hours Worked
Line Amount
03/03/2013
8.00
$35.00
03/04/2013
10.00
$43.75
03/05/2013
8.00
$35.00
03/06/2013
8.00
$35.00
03/09/2013
10.00
$43.75
$192.50

Figure 9-13 *The Payroll Check preview*

this is a simple formula, we need to use it in three different places. Using the embedded code feature of Reporting Services, we are able to put this formula in one location and use it in several locations. This also makes things easier to change when one or the other of these tax rates is increased.

We created a function called TaxDeductions on the Code page in the Report Properties dialog box. This is simply a valid Visual Basic .NET function definition. We access this function by using the key word "Code" followed by a period and the name of the function. You can see this in the expression we entered in Step 10.

The Weather Report

Features Highlighted

▶   Referencing .NET assemblies in the report

▶   Using a multivalued parameter

Business Need   The Galactic Delivery Services flight control department needs a way to quickly list the current weather conditions at selected planets served by GDS. (After all, space transports have to go through the atmosphere to take off and land.) One of the GDS programmers has created a .NET assembly that uses a web service to get the weather from various locations. The user should be able to select one or more planets from a list and see the weather for all selected planets. A call must be made to a method of the .NET assembly for each of the selected planets and the results must be incorporated into the report.

Task Overview

1. Copy the .NET Assembly into the Appropriate Location, Create a New Report, and Create a Reference to the Assembly
2. Create a Dataset, Add a Tablix to the Report Layout, and Populate It

Weather Report, Task 1: Copy the .NET Assembly into the Appropriate Location, Create a New Report, and Create a Reference to the Assembly

`DT` SSDT and Visual Studio Steps

1. If you have not already done so, download the WeatherInfo.dll assembly from the website for this book.

2. Copy this file to both the PrivateAssemblies folder and the PublicAssemblies folder of the Report Designer. If you are using a 32-bit version of Windows, the default path for these folders is

```
C:\Program Files\Microsoft Visual Studio 10.0\Common7\IDE
```

Or if you are using a 64-bit version of Windows, the default path for these folders is

```
C:\Program Files (x86)\Microsoft Visual Studio 10.0\Common7\IDE\
PublicAssemblies
```

3. We need to make some additions to the authoring environment's security configuration to provide our custom assembly with the rights it needs to execute. The security configuration for the authoring environment is in the RSPreviewPolicy.config file. The default path for this file is

```
C:\Program Files\Microsoft Visual Studio 10.0\Common7\IDE\
PrivateAssemblies
```

or

```
C:\Program Files (x86)\Microsoft Visual Studio 10.0\Common7\IDE\
PrivateAssemblies
```

This file contains the code-access security information in an Extensible Markup Language (XML) structure. We will talk more about code-access security in Chapter 10.

CAUTION

Make a backup copy of the RSPreviewPolicy.config file before making any modifications to it. If you accidentally create an invalid XML structure or otherwise cause a problem with the security configuration, the report server cannot execute any reports.

4. Open the RSPreviewPolicy.config file in Notepad or another text editor.
5. The XML structure in the RSPreviewPolicy.config file can be divided into three sections: Security Classes, Named Permission Sets, and Code Groups. We only need to make changes to the Code Groups section of the document. Scroll down until you locate the Code Group portion of the document. The Code Group portion of the document starts on the line after the closing XML tag for the named permission sets:

```
</NamedPermissionSets>
```

6. The first code group is the parent code group, which makes use of the AllMembershipCondition to assign the Nothing permission to all .NET assemblies and web services. We add a new child code group right beneath this. Insert this new code group as shown. (Add the lines shown in bold.) Alternatively, you can copy the

text to be inserted from the "First Code-Access Security Insert.txt" file in the Code Access Modifications folder included with the download materials for this book.

```
  .
  .
  .
<CodeGroup
        class="FirstMatchCodeGroup"
        version="1"
        PermissionSetName="Nothing">
    <IMembershipCondition
            class="AllMembershipCondition"
            version="1"
    />
    <CodeGroup
            class="UnionCodeGroup"
            version="1"
            PermissionSetName="Execution"
            Name="WeatherWebServiceCodeGroup"
            Description="Code group for the Weather Web Service">
        <IMembershipCondition class="UrlMembershipCondition"
                version="1"
                Url="http://live.capescience.com/*"
        />
    </CodeGroup>
    <CodeGroup
        class="UnionCodeGroup"
        version="1"
        PermissionSetName="Execution"
        Name="Report_Expressions_Default_Permissions"
        Description="This code group grants default permissions for
                    code in report expressions and Code element. ">
  .
  .
  .
```

7. Another parent code group uses ZoneMembershipCondition to assign Execution permissions to all .NET assemblies and web services in the MyComputer zone. We add a new child code group right beneath this. Insert this new code group as shown. (Add the lines shown in bold.) Note, the Description and PublicKeyBlob should each be entered on one line. Alternatively, you can copy the text to be inserted from the "Second Code-Access Security Insert.txt" file included with the download materials for this book.

```
  .
  .
  .
    <CodeGroup
        class="FirstMatchCodeGroup"
        version="1"
        PermissionSetName="Execution"
```

```
                    Description="This code group grants MyComputer code
                    Execution permission. ">
      <IMembershipCondition
                  class="ZoneMembershipCondition"
                  version="1"
                  Zone="MyComputer"/>
      <CodeGroup
                  class="UnionCodeGroup"
                  version="1"
                  PermissionSetName="FullTrust"
                  Name="MSSQLRSCodeGroup"
                  Description="Code group for the MS SQL RS Book Custom
                                                  Assemblies">

          <IMembershipCondition
                      class="StrongNameMembershipCondition"
                      version="1"
                      PublicKeyBlob="00240000004800000940000000602000000
                                24000052534131000400000100010 0B9F7
                                4F2D5B0AAD33AA619B00D7BB8B0F767839
                                3A0F4CD586C9036D72455F8D1E85BF635C
                                9FB1DA9817DD0F751DCEE77D9A47959E87
                                28028B9B6CC7C25EB1E59CB3DE01BB516D
                                46FC6AC6AF27AA6E71B65F6AB91B957688
                                6F2EF39417F17B567AD200E151FC744C6D
                                A72FF5882461E6CA786EB2997FA968302B
                                7B2F24BDBFF7A5"
                      />

      </CodeGroup>
      <CodeGroup
                  class="UnionCodeGroup"
                  version="1"
                  PermissionSetName="FullTrust"
                  Name="Microsoft_Strong_Name"
                  Description="This code group grants code signed with the
                                      Microsoft strong name full trust. ">
          <IMembershipCondition
                      class="StrongNameMembershipCondition"
                      version="1"
                      PublicKeyBlob="00240000004800000940000000602000000
                                2400005253413100040000010 0010007D1
                                FA57C4AED9F0A32E84AA0FAEFD0DE9E8FD
                                6AEC8F87FB03766C834C99921EB23BE79A
                                D9D5DCC1DD9AD236132102900B723CF980
                                957FC4E177108FC607774F29E8320E92EA
                                05ECE4E821C0A5EFE8F1645C4C0C93C1AB
                                99285D622CAA652C1DFAD63D745D6F2DE5
                                F17E5EAF0FC4963D261C8A12436518206D
                                C093344D5AD293"
                      />
      </CodeGroup>
                  .
                  .
                  .
```

8. Save the modified file and exit your text editor.

9. Reopen the Chapter09 project in the Report Designer, if it was closed. Create a new report called WeatherReport using the GDSReport template.

10. Open the Report Properties dialog box, and select the References page.

11. Click Add under the Add or remove assemblies heading. Click the ... button that appears. The Add Reference dialog box appears.

12. Scroll down to the entry for the WeatherInfo assembly and select it. Click OK to exit the Add Reference dialog box. Click OK to exit the Report Properties dialog box.

RB **Report Builder Steps**

1. If you have not already done so, download the WeatherInfo.dll assembly from the website for this book.

2. Copy this file to the Report Server\bin folder. The default path for the Report Server\bin folder is

```
C:\Program Files\Microsoft SQL Server\MSRS11.MSSQLSERVER\
                           Reporting Services\ReportServer\bin
```

3. We need to make some additions to the report server's security configuration to provide our custom assembly with the rights it needs to execute. The security configuration for the report server is in the rssrvpolicy.config file. The default path for this file is

```
C:\Program Files\Microsoft SQL Server\MSRS11.MSSQLSERVER\
                           Reporting Services\ReportServer
```

This file contains the code-access security information in an Extensible Markup Language (XML) structure. We will talk more about code-access security in Chapter 10.

CAUTION

Make a backup copy of the rssrvpolicy.config file before making any modifications to it. If you accidentally create an invalid XML structure or otherwise cause a problem with the security configuration, the report server cannot execute any reports.

4. Open the rssrvpolicy.config file in Notepad or another text editor.

5. The XML structure in the rssvrpolicy.config file can be divided into three sections: Security Classes, Named Permission Sets, and Code Groups. We only need to make changes to the Code Groups section of the document. Scroll down until you locate the Code Group portion of the document. The Code Group portion of the document starts on the line after the closing XML tag for the named permission sets:

```
</NamedPermissionSets>
```

6. The first code group is the parent code group, which makes use of the AllMembershipCondition to assign the Nothing permission to all .NET assemblies and web services. We add a new child code group right beneath this. Insert this new code group as shown. (Add the lines shown in bold.) Alternatively, you can copy the text to be inserted from the "First Code-Access Security Insert. txt" file in the Code Access Modifications folder included with the download materials for this book.

```
    .
    .
    .
<CodeGroup
        class="FirstMatchCodeGroup"
        version="1"
        PermissionSetName="Nothing">
    <IMembershipCondition
            class="AllMembershipCondition"
            version="1"
    />
    <CodeGroup
            class="UnionCodeGroup"
            version="1"
            PermissionSetName="Execution"
            Name="WeatherWebServiceCodeGroup"
            Description="Code group for the Weather Web Service">
        <IMembershipCondition class="UrlMembershipCondition"
                version="1"
                Url="http://live.capescience.com/*"
        />
    </CodeGroup>
    <CodeGroup
        class="UnionCodeGroup"
        version="1"
        PermissionSetName="Execution"
        Name="Report_Expressions_Default_Permissions"
        Description="This code group grants default permissions for
                    code in report expressions and Code element. ">
    .
    .
    .
```

7. Another parent code group uses ZoneMembershipCondition to assign Execution permissions to all .NET assemblies and web services in the MyComputer zone. We add a new child code group right beneath this. Insert this new code group as shown. (Add the lines shown in bold.) Note, the Description and PublicKeyBlob should each be entered on one line. Alternatively, you can copy the text to be

inserted from the "Second Code-Access Security Insert.txt" file included with the download materials for this book.

```
.
.
.

<CodeGroup
      class="FirstMatchCodeGroup"
      version="1"
      PermissionSetName="Execution"
      Description="This code group grants MyComputer code
      Execution permission. ">
   <IMembershipCondition
         class="ZoneMembershipCondition"
         version="1"
         Zone="MyComputer"/>
   <CodeGroup
         class="UnionCodeGroup"
         version="1"
         PermissionSetName="FullTrust"
         Name="MSSQLRSCodeGroup"
         Description="Code group for the MS SQL RS Book Custom
                                             Assemblies">
      <IMembershipCondition
            class="StrongNameMembershipCondition"
            version="1"
            PublicKeyBlob="00240000048000009400000006020000000
                     24000052534131000400000100010000B9F7
                     4F2D5B0AAD33AA619B00D7BB8B0F767839
                     3A0F4CD586C9036D72455F8D1E85BF635C
                     9FB1DA9817DD0F751DCEE77D9A47959E87
                     28028B9B6CC7C25EB1E59CB3DE01BB516D
                     46FC6AC6AF27AA6E71B65F6AB91B957688
                     6F2EF39417F17B567AD200E151FC744C6D
                     A72FF5882461E6CA786EB2997FA968302B
                     7B2F24BDBFF7A5"
                        />
   </CodeGroup>
   <CodeGroup
         class="UnionCodeGroup"
         version="1"
         PermissionSetName="FullTrust"
         Name="Microsoft_Strong_Name"
         Description="This code group grants code signed with the
                        Microsoft strong name full trust. ">
      <IMembershipCondition
            class="StrongNameMembershipCondition"
            version="1"
```

```
PublicKeyBlob="002400000480000094000000602000000
               2400005253413100040000010001007D1
               FA57C4AED9F0A32E84AA0FAEFD0DE9E8FD
               6AEC8F87FB03766C834C99921EB23BE79A
               D9D5DCC1DD9AD236132102900B723CF980
               957FC4E177108FC607774F29E8320E92EA
               05ECE4E821C0A5EFE8F1645C4C0C93C1AB
               99285D622CAA652C1DFAD63D745D6F2DE5
               F17E5EAF0FC4963D261C8A12436518206D
               C093344D5AD293"
```

```
            />
        </CodeGroup>
```

.
.
.

8. Save the modified file and exit your text editor.

9. Create a new report called WeatherReport using the GDSReport template.

10. Open the Report Properties dialog box, and select the References page.

11. Click Add under the Add or remove assemblies heading. Click the … button that appears. The Open dialog box appears.

12. Navigate to the Report Server\bin folder. This is the folder where you copied the WeatherInfo.dll assembly in Step 2. Select the WeatherInfo.dll assembly. Click Open to exit the Open dialog box. Click OK to exit the Report Properties dialog box.

Task Notes For a custom assembly to be used in our reports, it must be in a location where it can be found by the Report Designer. When you are designing reports, the assembly must be either in the Public Assemblies folder or in the Global Assembly Cache for SSDT and Visual Studio, or in the ReportServer\bin folder or Global Assembly Cache for Report Builder. In these steps, we placed the WeatherInfo.dll assembly in one of these folders. Consult your .NET documentation for information on placing an assembly in the Global Assembly Cache.

We are using a class from the WeatherInfo assembly called PlanetaryWeather and a method from that class called GetWeather. The GetWeather method is a shared method. This means you do not need to create an instance of the PlanetaryWeather class to use the GetWeather method.

To use a method that is not a shared method, you need to use the Classes area of the References page of the Report Properties dialog box. First, create a reference in the References area, as we did in Steps 10 through 12. Then, under Class name, specify the name of the class within that assembly you want to instantiate. Finally, provide a name for the instance of that class. Reporting Services creates an instance of the class with the name you provide when the report is run.

Once the assembly is in the correct location and you have created a reference to that assembly, you can use the methods of this assembly in your reports. When referencing a shared method in an assembly, use the following syntax:

```
Namespace.ClassName.MethodName(Parameters...)
```

For the WeatherInfo assembly, the syntax is

```
WeatherInfo.PlanetaryWeather.GetWeather(PlanetAbbrv)
```

To use a nonshared method from a class you instantiated, use the syntax

```
Code.InstanceName.MethodName(Parameters...)
```

Weather Report, Task 2: Create a Dataset, Add a Tablix to the Report Layout, and Populate It

DT
RB

SSDT, Visual Studio, and Report Builder Steps

1. Create a new data source called Galactic that references the Galactic shared data source.

2. Create a new dataset called Planets. Use the following for the query string:

   ```
   SELECT Name, PlanetAbbrv FROM Planet ORDER BY Name
   ```

3. In the Report Data window, right-click the Parameters entry and select Add Parameter from the context menu. The Report Parameter Properties dialog box appears.

4. Set the properties of this new parameter as follows:

Property	Value
General page:	
Name	Planets
Prompt	Select Planets
Allow multiple values	Checked
Available Values page:	
Select from one of the following options:	Get values from a query
Dataset	Planets
Value field	PlanetAbbrv
Label field	Name

Click OK to exit the Report Parameter Properties dialog box.

5. Place two text boxes onto the body of the report. Then use the table template to place a tablix onto the body of the report. The expression in the second text box should be:

```
="Here is the current weather for the " & Parameters!Planets.Count &
                                " planet(s) you selected"
```

6. Complete your report layout so it is similar to Figure 9-14. The expression in the right-hand detail cell should be:

```
=WeatherInfo.PlanetaryWeather.GetWeather(Fields!PlanetAbbrv.Value)
```

7. Open the Tablix Properties dialog box. Select the Filters page.

8. Click Add.

9. Enter the following for Expression:

```
=Array.IndexOf(Parameters!Planets.Value, Fields!PlanetAbbrv.Value)
```

10. Select >= from the Operator drop-down list.

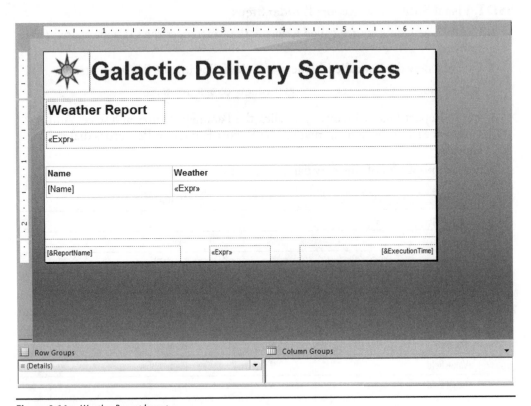

Figure 9-14   *Weather Report layout*

11. Enter the following expression for Value:

   = 0

12. Click OK to exit the Tablix Properties dialog box.

13. Preview/Run the report.

14. Use the Select Planets drop-down list to check Borlaron and Stilation. Click View Report. Your report should appear similar to Figure 9-15.

NOTE

Remember, the GetWeather method is going out to the Internet and retrieving weather conditions when you run the report. Because of this, you must be connected to the Internet when you run this report. This process may take some time if you are using a slow Internet connection and have selected a number of planets to report on. Also, the weather conditions you see in your report vary from those shown in Figure 9-15. Finally, some locations may show "null" for a certain condition if that condition has not been reported in the past hour.

15. Save the report.

Task Notes   The Weather Report makes use of a special type of parameter that allows for more than one value to be selected. Rather than requiring the user to select a single value from the Available Values drop-down list, a multivalued parameter enables the user to check off a number of values to be used when creating the report. Then, it is up to the Report Designer to figure out how to use those multiple values to return a report with the desired information.

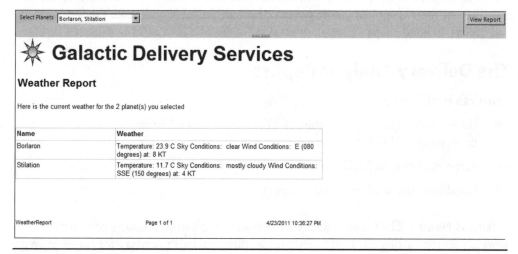

Figure 9-15   *Weather Report preview*

The properties of the report parameter change when that parameter becomes multivalued. Instead of containing single values, the Value and Label properties become arrays. The arrays have one element for each of the items selected by the user. If the user checks three items in the drop-down list, the Value and Label arrays each have three elements. (These are zero-based arrays, so they are elements 0, 1, and 2 in this case.) The Length property of each array contains the number of elements in that array.

In this report, we used the multivalue parameter in a table filter to determine which records would be output. (Later in this chapter, we use a multivalue parameter in the Transport Monitor report to create a WHERE clause in a query.) We are using a shared method of the Array class called IndexOf, which searches an array for a value. In this case, the IndexOf method is searching for each planet abbreviation in the Parameters!Planets.Value array. If the abbreviation is found, the index of the element that contains the abbreviation is returned by the IndexOf method; otherwise, it returns -1. Therefore, we want only those records where the IndexOf method returns a value greater than or equal to 0 to be included in the table.

When you first encountered filters in Chapter 8, you were cautioned to use them wisely. The filter makes sense here for three reasons. First, the dataset we are filtering is small. Selecting just two or three records versus selecting all six is not a significant time savings. Second, as with the example in Chapter 8, the filter enables us to use the same dataset to populate the drop-down list and the table in the report body. It would be inefficient to run two database queries, one without a WHERE clause to get the list of planets for the drop-down list and one with a WHERE clause to get the planets selected for the table in the report. Finally, the most time-consuming part of the report is not the database interaction, but the calls to the web service over the Internet. Because our filter is applied before we step through the table and make the web service call, we are in good shape.

The Delivery Analysis Report

Features Highlighted

▶ Using an Analysis Services cube as a data source via a Multidimensional Expression (MDX) query

▶ Parameterizing an MDX query

▶ Localizing the label strings in a report

Business Need   The Galactic Delivery Services long-range planning committee is working on forecasting the equipment and workforce needs necessary for future growth. They need a report showing the number of deliveries and the average weight of those deliveries grouped by customer by quarter. They would also like to select whether the data includes next day deliveries, same day deliveries, previous day deliveries, or some combination of the three. The data for this report should come from the GalacticDeliveriesDataMart cube hosted by Microsoft SQL Server Analysis Services.

There are committee members from a number of planets. Most speak English, but the committee does include several Spanish-speaking members. (I know it is rather strange that people in a galaxy far, far away should speak English and Spanish, but work with me here!)

Task Overview

1. Copy the .NET Assembly into the Appropriate Location, Create a New Report, Create a Reference to the Assembly, and Create a Dataset Using the MDX Query Designer
2. Add a Tablix to the Report Layout, Populate It, and Localize the Report Strings

Delivery Analysis Report, Task 1: Copy the .NET Assembly into the Appropriate Location, Create a New Report, Create a Reference to the Assembly, and Create a Dataset Using the MDX Query Designer

NOTE

You need to download the GalacticOLAP project from the website for this book and deploy it to a SQL Server Analysis Services server before you can complete this report. If you do not have access to Analysis Services, skip this report and continue with the "Reports Within Reports" section of this chapter.

DT **SSDT and Visual Studio Steps**

1. If you have not already done so, download the ReportUtil.dll assembly and the accompanying ES folder from the website for this book.
2. Copy the file and the folder to the Report Designer folder. The default path for the Report Designer folder is

```
C:\Program Files\Microsoft Visual Studio 10.0\Common7\IDE\
PublicAssemblies
```

or

```
C:\Program Files (x86)\Microsoft Visual Studio 10.0\Common7\IDE\
PublicAssemblies
```

3. Create a new report called DeliveryAnalysis using the GDSReport template.

4. Open the Report Properties dialog box, and select the References page.

5. Click Add under the Add or remove assemblies heading. Click the … button that appears. The Add Reference dialog box appears.

6. Scroll down to the entry for ReportUtil Assembly and select it. Click OK to exit the Add Reference dialog box. Click OK to exit the Report Properties dialog box.

7. In the Report Data window, select New | Data Source from the menu. The Data Source Properties dialog box appears.

8. Enter **GalacticDM** for the Name. Select Microsoft SQL Server Analysis Services from the Type drop-down list.

9. Click Edit next to the Connection String text box. The Connection Properties dialog box appears.

10. Enter the name of the SQL Server Analysis Services server for Server name.

11. Select GalacticOLAP from the Select or enter a database name drop-down list. You can test the connection if you like, but if GalacticOLAP shows up in the drop-down list, the connection has already been tested.

12. Click OK to exit the Connection Properties dialog box. Click OK to exit the Data Source Properties dialog box.

13. Right-click the GalacticDM entry in the Report Data window, and select Add Dataset from the context menu. The Dataset Properties dialog box appears.

14. Enter **DeliveryInfo** for the Name.

15. Click the Query Designer button. The MDX Query Designer appears as shown in Figure 9-16.

16. Expand the Measures entry in the Metadata pane. Expand the Delivery measure group, and then expand the Delivery entry within it.

17. Drag the Delivery Count measure onto the Results pane (the pane with the words "Drag levels or measures here to add to the query" in the center). The total count of all deliveries currently in the GalacticDeliveriesDataMart cube is shown in the Results pane.

18. Expand the Customer dimension in the Metadata pane. Drag the CustomerName attribute onto the Results pane to the left of the Delivery Count. The Results pane now shows the total count of all deliveries for each customer.

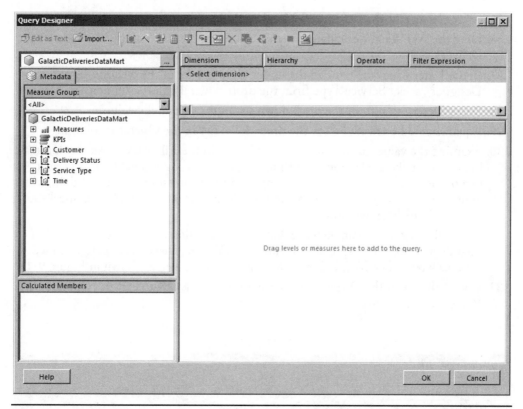

Figure 9-16 *The MDX Query Designer*

19. Expand the Time dimension in the Metadata pane. Drag the DeliveryQuarter attribute onto the Results pane to the left of the CustomerName column. The Results pane now shows the total count of all deliveries for each customer for each quarter.

20. Right-click in the Calculated Members pane, and select New Calculated Member from the context menu. The Calculated Member Builder dialog box appears.

21. Enter **AvgWeight** for the Name.

22. In the Expression area, enter **ROUND(**. Expand the Measures in the Metadata area, expand the Delivery measure group, and then expand the Delivery entry within it. Double-click Package Weight to add it to the expression.

23. Enter / at the end of the expression. Double-click Delivery Count to add it to the expression.

24. Enter **,2)** at the end of the expression, and click Check to check the syntax of the expression. Click OK to close the Check Syntax dialog box. Make any corrections to the expression if a syntax error is encountered.

25. Click OK to exit the Calculated Member Builder dialog box.

26. Drag the AvgWeight calculated member onto the Results pane to the right of the Delivery Count.

27. In the Filter pane (the pane in the upper-right corner of the MDX Query Designer), select Service Type from the drop-down list in the Dimension column.

28. Select Description from the drop-down list in the Hierarchy column.

29. Equal should be selected from the drop-down list in the Operator column.

30. Examine the values in the drop-down window in the Filter Expression column, but do not make a selection. The Filter Expression column enables us to select one or more values for the right side of our filter expression. Instead of doing this at design time, we let our users make the selection at run time. Click Cancel to exit the drop-down window.

31. Check the box in the Parameters column. This selection enables the user to select the values of the filter expression at run time. (You may have to scroll right to see the check box.) The MDX Query Designer should appear as shown in Figure 9-17.

32. Click OK to exit the Query Designer window. Click OK to exit the Dataset Properties dialog box.

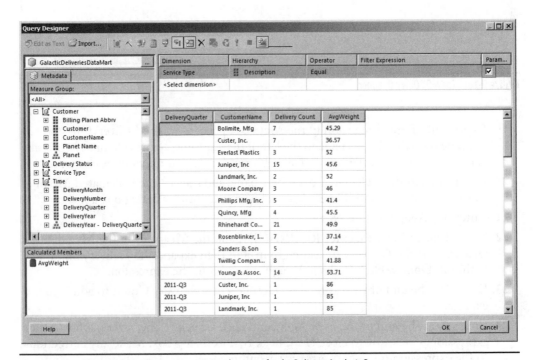

Figure 9-17 *The MDX Query Designer containing the query for the Delivery Analysis Report*

RB   **Report Builder Steps**

1. If you have not already done so, download the ReportUtil.dll assembly and the accompanying ES folder from the website for this book.

2. Copy the file and folder to the Report Server\bin folder. Merge the new and existing folders. The default path for the Report Server\bin folder is

```
C:\Program Files\Microsoft SQL Server\MSRS11.MSSQLSERVER\
                          Reporting Services\ReportServer\bin
```

NOTE

No security changes are necessary for the ReportUtil.dll assembly.

3. Create a new report called DeliveryAnalysis using the GDSReport template.

4. Open the Report Properties dialog box, and select the References page.

5. Click Add under the Add or remove assemblies heading. Click the ... button that appears.

6. The Open dialog box appears. Navigate to the Report Server\bin folder. This is the folder where you copied the ReportUtil.dll assembly in Step 2. Select the ReportUtil.dll assembly. Click Open to exit the Open dialog box. Click OK to exit the Report Properties dialog box.

7. In the Report Data window, select New | Data Source from the menu. The Data Source Properties dialog box appears.

8. Enter **GalacticDM** for the Name.

9. Select the Use a connection embedded in my report radio button.

10. Select Microsoft SQL Server Analysis Services from the Select connection type drop-down list.

11. Click Build next to the Connection String text box. The Connection Properties dialog box appears.

12. Enter the name of the SQL Server Analysis Services server for Server name.

13. Select GalacticOLAP from the Select or enter a database name drop-down list. You can test the connection if you like, but if GalacticOLAP shows up in the drop-down list, the connection has already been tested.

14. Click OK to exit the Connection Properties dialog box. Click OK to exit the Data Source Properties dialog box.

15. Right-click the GalacticDM entry in the Report Data window, and select Add Dataset from the context menu. The Dataset Properties dialog box appears.

16. Enter **DeliveryInfo** for the Name.

17. Click the Query Designer button. The MDX Query Designer appears as shown in Figure 9-16 (found in the SSDT and Visual Studio steps section for this task).

18. Expand the Measures entry in the Metadata pane. Expand the Delivery measure group, and then expand the Delivery entry within it.

19. Drag the Delivery Count measure onto the Results pane (the pane with the words "Drag levels or measures here to add to the query" in the center). The total count of all deliveries currently in the GalacticDeliveriesDataMart cube is shown in the Results pane.

20. Expand the Customer dimension in the Metadata pane. Drag the CustomerName attribute onto the Results pane to the left of the Delivery Count. The Results pane now shows the total count of all deliveries for each customer.

21. Expand the Time dimension in the Metadata pane. Drag the DeliveryQuarter attribute onto the Results pane to the left of the CustomerName column. The Results pane now shows the total count of all deliveries for each customer for each quarter.

22. Right-click in the Calculated Members pane, and select New Calculated Member from the context menu. The Calculated Member Builder dialog box appears.

23. Enter **AvgWeight** for the Name.

24. In the Expression area, enter **ROUND(**. Expand the Measures in the Metadata area, expand the Delivery measure group, and then expand the Delivery entry within it. Double-click Package Weight to add it to the expression.

25. Enter **/** at the end of the expression. Double-click Delivery Count to add it to the expression.

26. Enter **,2)** at the end of the expression.

27. Click OK to exit the Calculated Member Builder dialog box.

28. Drag the AvgWeight calculated member onto the Results pane to the right of the Delivery Count.

29. In the Filter pane (the pane in the upper-right corner of the MDX Query Designer), select Service Type from the drop-down list in the Dimension column.

30. Select Description from the drop-down list in the Hierarchy column.

31. Equal should be selected from the drop-down list in the Operator column.

32. Examine the values in the drop-down window in the Filter Expression column, but do not make a selection. The Filter Expression column enables us to select one or more values for the right side of our filter expression. Instead of doing this at design time, we let our users make the selection at run time. Click Cancel to exit the drop-down window.

33. Check the box in the Parameters column. (You may have to enlarge the window to see it.) This selection enables the user to select the values of the filter expression at run time. The MDX Query Designer should appear as shown in Figure 9-17.

34. Click OK to exit the Query Designer window. Click OK to exit the Dataset Properties dialog box.

Task Notes   The assembly we are using for this report does not try to venture outside of its sandbox. Therefore, we do not need to make any code-access security changes in order for it to function. We will talk more about what this assembly actually does in the next set of Task Notes.

The MDX Query Designer works almost entirely through drag-and-drop. We drag measures, dimensions, and hierarchies from the Metadata Browser pane and drop them in the Results pane to create our query. We can define calculated members and add them to the Results pane as well.

At the top of the Metadata pane is the name of the cube being queried. To select a different cube, click the . . . button and make a selection from the Cube Selection dialog box that appears.

In SSDT and Visual Studio, the toolbar button with the pickaxe icon switches from the MDX Query Designer to the Data Mining Expression (DMX) Query Designer. (This is not available in Report Builder.) The toolbar button with the X and Y axes switches back to the MDX Query Designer. Where the MDX Query Designer is used to query cubes in an Analysis Services database, the DMX Query Designer is used to query data mining models in an Analysis Services database. Because the same Analysis Services database may contain both cubes and data mining models, the Report Designer may not be able to tell which query designer you need simply by examining the database. Therefore, it is necessary to have a way to switch between the two.

The Show Empty Cells toolbar button toggles between showing and hiding empty cells in the Results pane. An empty cell is a combination of dimension and hierarchy members that have a null value for every measure, calculated or otherwise, in the Results pane. If empty cells are hidden in the Results pane, they are also hidden in the final report query. The Design Mode toolbar button enables you to toggle between the design view and the query view of the MDX query. If you are comfortable with MDX query syntax, you may want to type your queries into the query view rather than creating them through the drag-and-drop programming method of the design view. The Auto Execute toolbar button toggles autoexecute mode in the Query Designer. When autoexecute mode is on, the cube is requeried and the Results pane is updated every time an item is added or removed.

The Filter pane enables us either to hardcode filter expressions at design time or use report parameters for the user to make selections at run time. When the Parameters check box is checked, a parameterized filter is created. Several things happen when we exit the MDX Query Designer dialog box for the first time after a parameterized filter has been added to the query. When this occurs, the authoring environment creates a new dataset for each item being used in a parameterized filter. This dataset includes all the valid members of that item.

In addition to the datasets, new report parameters are created for each parameterized filter. The datasets are used to populate the available values for these report parameters. The report parameters are multivalued. Using this mechanism, the user is allowed to select one or more valid members to be used in the parameterized filters at the time the report is executed.

Delivery Analysis Report, Task 2: Add a Tablix to the Report Layout, Populate It, and Localize the Report Strings

DT
RB

SSDT, Visual Studio, and Report Builder Steps

1. Place a text box onto the body of the report and set its properties as follows:

Property	Value
Font:FontSize	20pt
Font: FontWeight	Bold
Location: Left	0in
Location: Top	0in
Size: Width	5.875in
Size: Height	0.375in

2. Set the content of the text box to the following expression:

```
=ReportUtil.Localization.LocalizedString("DeliveryReportTitle",
User!Language)
```

3. Use the matrix template to place a tablix onto the report body.

4. Select the DeliveryQuarter field from the DeliveryInfo dataset in the Columns cell. Click the Bold button and the Center button on the toolbar.

5. Select the CustomerName field in the Rows cell. Click the Bold button on the toolbar.

6. Select the Delivery_Count field in the Data cell.

7. In the Report Data window, drag the AvgWeight field into the same cell where Delivery_Count was placed. Drag to the right side of the cell. This creates a second data column to the right of the first.

8. Right-click the cell that was just created, and select Tablix: Insert Row | Outside Group - Above from the context menu.

9. Enter the following expression in the text box above the cell containing the DeliveryCount field:

```
=ReportUtil.Localization.LocalizedString("DeliveryCountColHead",
User!Language)
```

10. Enter the following expression in the text box above the cell containing the AvgWeight field:

```
=ReportUtil.Localization.LocalizedString("AvgWeightColHead",
User!Language)
```

11. Select the cell in the upper-left corner of the tablix, and press DELETE to remove the heading created here.
12. Expand the Parameters entry in the Report Data window.
13. Right-click the ServiceTypeDescription entry in the Report Data window, and select Parameter Properties from the context menu.
14. Enter **Select Service Types** for the Prompt.
15. Click OK to exit the Report Parameter Properties dialog box.
16. Preview/Run the report. Check All in the Select Service Types drop-down list, and click View Report.
17. Save the report.

Task Notes   You may have noticed we did not type text strings for the report title and the two column headings on the report. Instead, we used expressions that call the LocalizedString method of the Localization class in the ReportUtil assembly. (Localization refers to the process of making a report or computer program appear in the language of a certain location.) This method requires two parameters: the name of the string to localize and the language it should be localized into. The string name is hardcoded in each expression. The language comes from the User!Language global variable. This global variable is populated with the language of the client application requesting the report.

The ReportUtil assembly uses multiple resource files to manage the localization. There is one resource file for each language it must support. In the demonstration code supplied for this example, the ReportUtil assembly only has two resource files: one for English and one for Spanish. To support another language, you simply need to add another resource file and rebuild the project.

We used the LocalizedString method to get localized versions of the report title and the two column headers. The remainder of the report content is either proper names or numeric. Neither of these needs to be translated. If you are sharp, you will notice the report parameter prompt and the items in the report parameter drop-down list have not been localized. We cannot use expressions for either of these items, so we cannot use our nifty LocalizedString method.

The drop-down list content is selected from the Analysis Services cube, so some localization of the data could be done in the cube itself. That, unfortunately, is beyond the scope of this book. The report parameter prompt is a bigger problem. In fact, the current version of Reporting Services does not have a nice way to deal with this.

We will look at what the Spanish localization looks like when we work with the report on the report server in Chapter 10.

Reports Within Reports

Thus far, we have placed report items within report items and data regions within data regions. In this section, we look at putting whole reports inside one another. This is done using the subreport report item.

The *subreport item* is simply a placeholder in a report. It sits in the parent report and shows the space to be occupied by another report when the parent report is run. Nothing is special about a report placed in a subreport item. Any report can be used as a subreport.

The report placed in the subreport can even contain parameters. These parameter values can be passed from the parent report to the subreport. Any field value, parameter value, or expression in the parent report can be used as a parameter in the subreport.

Subreports are used for many reasons. They can provide an easy way to reuse a complex report layout within a parent report. They can also be used to implement a more complex form of drilldown.

The following subreports are anything but subpar!

The Employee Evaluation Report

Features Highlighted

▶ Using a subreport as reusable code

▶ Creating a landscape report

▶ Using a rectangle for grouping

▶ Using rich formatting

Business Need   The Galactic Delivery Services personnel department has created an application for employees to conduct peer reviews as part of each employee's annual review process. They are also collecting a review and comments from each employee's manager. They need a report that can be used to present the results of the peer review at the employee's meeting with their supervisor.

The manager's review and comments should be noted as coming from the manager. The peer reviews, however, should be presented anonymously.

Task Overview

1. Create a New Report, Create a Dataset, Add a Tablix to the Report Layout, and Populate It
2. Create a New Report, Create a Dataset, and Populate the Report Layout
3. Add a Rectangle
4. Add Rich Formatting

Employee Evaluation Report, Task 1: Create a New Report, Create a Dataset, Add a Tablix to the Report Layout, and Populate It

DT
RB
SSDT, Visual Studio, and Report Builder Steps

1. Create a new report called EvalDetail. Do *not* use the GDSReport template. (If you are using Report Builder, remove the "Click to add title" text box and the page footer.)
2. Create a new data source called Galactic that references the Galactic shared data source.
3. Create a new dataset called EvalRatings that calls the stp_EvalRatings stored procedure.
4. Use the table template to place a tablix onto the body of the report.
5. Select the Goal, Rating, and GoalComment fields in the data row of the table.
6. Add a parent row group to the table that groups by EvaluatorEmployeeNumber. The group should have a group header and a group footer.
7. Complete your report layout so it is similar to Figure 9-18. The top row has the BorderColor: Top property set to Black. The bottom row has the BorderColor: Bottom property set to Black and the BorderWidth: Bottom property set to 5pt. Also note that the table header row was deleted.
8. Save the report.

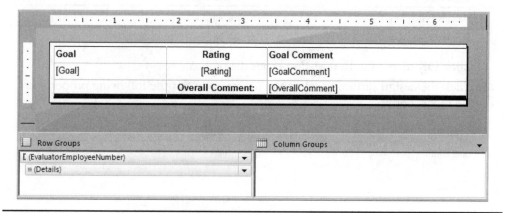

Figure 9-18   *The Employee Evaluation Detail Report layout*

Task Notes   The EvalDetail report is going to be used in two subreports in our parent report. It is going to be used in one location to display the peer reviews and in another location to display the manager review. We can create this layout for displaying review information and then use it in multiple places.

Subreports have several uses. One use is to serve as reusable layout, as we are doing here. Second, subreports can create nested reports from multiple data sources. Finally, subreports can be used to display multiple one-to-many relationships.

Subreports, however, can be inefficient if overused. Every time a subreport executes, its dataset queries must be run. When a subreport is embedded in a data region, it can be executed many times, perhaps once for each record in the parent report. This can result in a long-running report that puts a good deal of stress on your database server. So use those subreports, but use them wisely.

Employee Evaluation Report, Task 2: Create a New Report, Create a Dataset, and Populate the Report Layout

DT
RB
SSDT, Visual Studio, and Report Builder Steps

1. Create a new report called EmployeeEval using the GDSReport template.
2. Create a new data source called Galactic that references the Galactic shared data source.
3. Create a new dataset called EvalPerformance that calls the stp_EvalPerformance stored procedure.
4. Open the Report Properties dialog box.
5. Modify the following properties of the report:

Property	Value
Orientation	Landscape
Margins: Left	0.5in
Margins: Right	0.5in

6. Click OK to exit the Report Properties dialog box.
7. Click the design surface to select the report body. Set the following property of the report body:

Property	Value
Size: Width	10in

8. Drag the EmployeeName field onto the report body. Modify the following properties of the text box that results:

Property	Value
Font: FontSize	20pt
Font: FontWeight	Bold
Location: Left	0in
Location: Top	0in
Size: Width	6.875in
Size: Height	0.5in

9. Place a text box onto the report body. Modify the following properties of this text box:

Property	Value
Font: FontSize	20pt
Font: FontWeight	Bold
Location: Left	8.25in
Location: Top	0in
Size: Width	1.625in
Size: Height	0.5in
Value	=Parameters!Year.Value

10. Place a text box onto the report body. Modify the following properties of this text box:

Property	Value
Font: FontSize	16pt
Font: FontWeight	Bold
Location: Left	0in
Location: Top	0.625in
Size: Width	2.75in
Size: Height	0.375in
Value	Peer Evaluations

11. Place a subreport onto the report body immediately below the text box. Modify the following properties of this subreport:

Property	Value
Location: Left	0in
Location: Top	1in
Size: Width	6.875in
Size: Height	1.125in

12. Right-click the subreport and select Subreport Properties from the context menu. The Subreport Properties dialog box appears.

13. If you are using SSDT or Visual Studio, select EvalDetail from the Use this report as a subreport drop-down list. If you are using Report Builder, click Browse, and then double-click EvalDetail in the Select Report dialog box.

14. Select the Parameters page.

15. Click Add to add parameters to the grid. Configure the parameters as shown here:

Name	Value
EmpNum	=Parameters!EmpNum.Value
Year	=Parameters!Year.Value
MgrFlag	=0

You can use the drop-down list to select the parameter names. You can use the Expression dialog box to select the parameter values.

16. Click OK to exit the Subreport Properties dialog box.

17. Select the Peer Evaluations text box and the subreport. Press CTRL-C to copy these two items. Press CTRL-V to paste a copy of these items on the report body. Drag the two copied items so they are immediately below the original subreport.

18. Modify the new text box to read "Manager Evaluations." Adjust the width of the text box as needed.

19. Open the Subreport Properties dialog box for the new subreport, and select the Parameters page.

20. Change the parameter value for MgrFlag from = 0 to = 1. This causes the second subreport to contain the manager's evaluation rather than the peer evaluations.

21. Click OK to exit the Subreport Properties dialog box.

22. Place a text box onto the report body. Modify the following properties of this text box:

Property	Value
Font: FontWeight	Bold
Location: Left	7.125in
Location: Top	1in
Size: Width	2in
Size: Height	0.25in
Value	Areas of Excellence

23. Drag the AreasOfExcellence field onto the report body. Modify the following properties of the text box that results:

Property	Value
Location: Left	7.125in
Location: Top	1.375in
Size: Width	2.75in
Size: Height	0.25in

24. Place a text box onto the report body. Modify the following properties of this text box:

Property	Value
Font: FontWeight	Bold
Location: Left	7.125in
Location: Top	1.875in
Size: Width	2in
Size: Height	0.25in
Value	Areas for Improvement

25. Drag the AreasForImprovement field onto the report body. Modify the following properties of the text box that results:

Property	Value
Location: Left	7.125in
Location: Top	2.25in
Size: Width	2.75in
Size: Height	0.25in

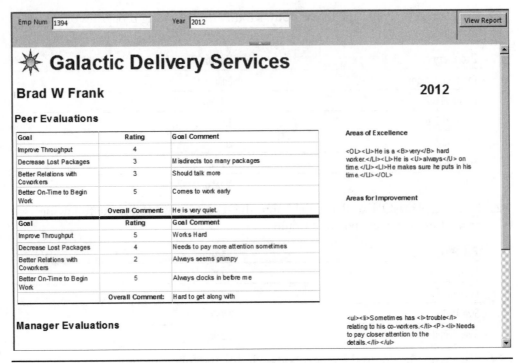

Figure 9-19   *The Employee Evaluations Report preview after Task 2*

26. Preview/Run the report. Enter **1394** for EmpNum and **2012** for Year, and then click View Report. Your report should appear similar to Figure 9-19.

Task Notes   We used the Report Properties dialog box to change this report's orientation from portrait to landscape. When you are creating your report templates, you may want to create one template for portrait reports and another template for landscape reports.

Two steps are required to get each subreport item ready to use. First, you have to specify which report is going to be used within the subreport item. Once this is done, you need to specify a value for each of the parameters in the selected report. With these two tasks completed, your subreports are ready to go.

In this report, we are using several fields outside of a data region: the EmployeeName field, the AreasOfExcellence field, and the AreasForImprovement field. Remember, data regions are set up to repeat a portion of their content for each record in the result set. When a field value occurs outside of a data region, it is not repeated; it occurs only once. Therefore, one record must be selected by the authoring environment for display in these fields. It happens that the first record in the dataset is selected in these situations.

In this particular report, the EvalPerformance dataset has only one record. Of course, the authoring environment does not know at design time how many records the dataset will have at run time. (Even if the dataset has only 1 record at design time, it could have 100 records at run time.) Therefore, the authoring environment always uses the first record for references outside of a data region.

Finally, you may have noticed a little problem with the text box that contains the contents of the AreasForImprovement field. (Not the HTML formatting tags—we will deal with those in Task 4.) It seems to be sliding down the page. In actuality, it was pushed down the page when the subreport grew.

The text boxes that contain the Areas of Excellence title, the AreasOfExcellence field value, and the Areas for Improvement title are all even with the first subreport. However, the text box containing the value of the AreasForImprovement field starts below the bottom of the first subreport. When the subreport grows because of its content, the text box is pushed farther down the report, so it remains below the bottom of the subreport.

In Task 3, you see a way to prevent this problem.

Employee Evaluation Report, Task 3: Add a Rectangle

DT

RB

SSDT, Visual Studio, and Report Builder Steps

1. Return to Design mode.
2. Select the Areas of Excellence text box, the AreasOfExcellence field value text box, the Areas for Improvement text box, and the AreasForImprovement field value text box. Press CTRL-X to cut these four text boxes.
3. Place a rectangle on the report in the area just vacated by these four text boxes.
4. With the rectangle still selected, press CTRL-V to paste the four text boxes into the rectangle.
5. Arrange the rectangle and the four text boxes as needed. Your layout should appear similar to Figure 9-20.
6. Preview/Run the report. Enter **1394** for EmpNum and **2012** for Year, and then click View Report. Your report should appear similar to Figure 9-21.
7. Save the report.

Task Notes   The rectangle report item comes to your rescue here. Once the four text boxes are inside the rectangle, they remain together no matter how much the subreport grows. As your report designs become more complex, rectangles are often necessary to keep things right where you want them.

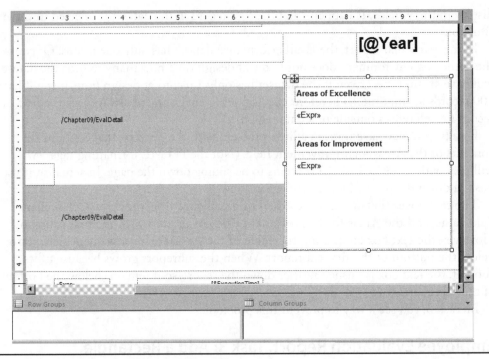

Figure 9-20 *The Employee Evaluation Report layout with a rectangle*

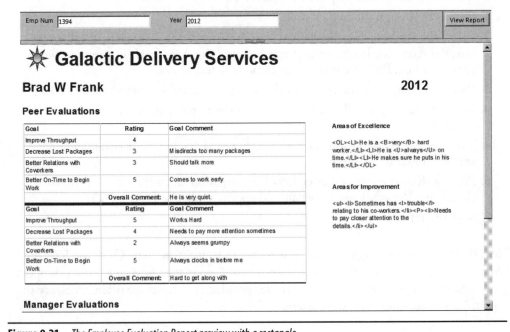

Figure 9-21 *The Employee Evaluation Report preview with a rectangle*

Figure 9-22   *Adding text to the Employee field text box*

Employee Evaluation Report, Task 4: Add Rich Formatting

DT
RB
SSDT, Visual Studio, and Report Builder Steps

  1. Return to Design mode.
  2. Double-click the text box containing the expression for the employee name (the large text box right below the Galactic Delivery Services logo and heading). The text edit cursor will be to the left of the "<<Expr>>" placeholder in the text box.
  3. Type **Employee:** as shown in Figure 9-22.
  4. Highlight the text just entered in Step 3.
  5. Click the bold button on the ribbon/toolbar to unbold the selected text.
  6. Select "12pt" from the font size drop-down list in the ribbon/toolbar (see Figure 9-23).
  7. Double-click the text box containing the Year parameter. The text edit cursor will be to the left of the "[@Year]" placeholder.
  8. Type **Year:** and press ENTER.
  9. Highlight the text entered in Step 8.
  10. Click the bold button on the toolbar to unbold the selected text.

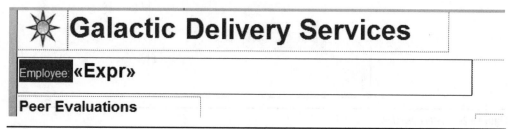

Figure 9-23   *Adding rich formatting to text*

11. Select "12pt" from the font size drop-down list in the toolbar.

12. Click outside of the Year parameter text box to unselect it. Single-click the Year parameter text box to select the text box.

13. Modify the following property of this text box:

Property	Value
TextAlign	Center

14. Double-click the text box for the AreasOfExcellence field.

15. Click "<<Expr>>" to highlight it.

16. Right-click the highlighted text and select Placeholder Properties from the context menu as shown in Figure 9-24. The Placeholder Properties dialog box appears.

17. On the General page, select the HTML - Interpret HTML tags as styles radio button.

18. Click OK to exit the Placeholder Properties dialog box.

19. Repeat Step 14 through Step 18 for the AreasForImprovement field text box.

20. Preview/Run the report. Enter **1394** for EmpNum and **2012** for Year, and then click View Report. Your report should appear similar to Figure 9-25.

21. Save the report.

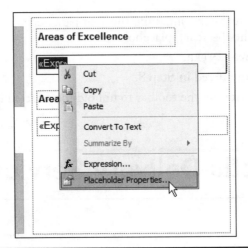

Figure 9-24 *Setting placeholder properties*

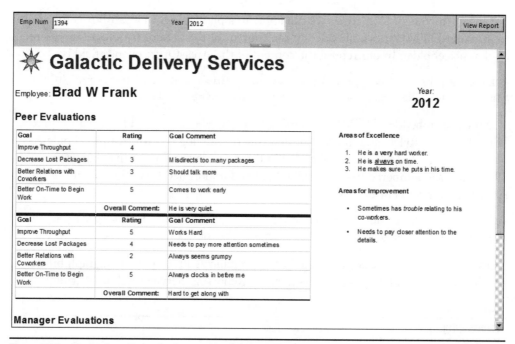

Figure 9-25   *The Employee Evaluation Report with rich formatting*

Task Notes   In previous reports, we have used Visual Basic expressions to combine static text, such as labels, with dynamic text from fields and parameters. As an alternative, we can type text into the text box before or after the field, parameter, or expression placeholder. In fact, we can combine several placeholders in a single text box, just as we have sometimes combined several fields in a Visual Basic expression. To manually add a placeholder to a text box, right-click while editing text in the text box, and select Create Placeholder from the context menu.

Use the Visual Basic expressions or the combination of static text and placeholders. Either method works just fine. Note, however, once you use a placeholder/static text combination in a text box, you can no longer view the expression for that text box, only for an individual placeholder.

In addition to combining static text and placeholders in a single text box, we combined different formatting within a single text box. This is called *rich formatting*. Rich formatting enables us to treat different parts of the contents of a text box as distinct items and allows us to apply different formatting to each of these items.

One of the bits of formatting we can apply to a placeholder in a text box is the ability to interpret HTML tags embedded in the content of the field or parameter represented by that placeholder. In our report, the content of the AreasOfExcellence field is:

```
<OL><LI>He is a <B>very</B> hard worker.</LI><LI>He is <U>always</U> on
time.</LI><LI>He makes sure he puts in his time.</LI></OL>
```

Note the embedded HTML formatting tags. By selecting the HTML - Interpret HTML tags as styles radio button in the Properties dialog box for this placeholder, we can have the HTML tags embedded in this text used as formatting characters. The result is a numbered list containing bold and underlined text. The content of the AreasForImprovement field is:

```
<ul><li>Sometimes has <I>trouble</I> relating to his co-workers.</li>
<P><li>Needs to pay closer attention to the details.</li></ul>
```

These HTML tags produce a bulleted list with italicized text and a paragraph break.

The following HTML tags are handled by Reporting Services rich formatting:

<A href></A>	Hyperlink
<FONT></FONT>	Font
<H*n*></H*n*>	Header
<DIV></DIV>	Division
<SPAN></SPAN>	Inline Element Grouping
<P></P>	Paragraph
<B></B>	Bold
<I></I>	Italics
<U></U>	Underline
<S></S>	Strikethrough
<OL></OL>	Numbered List
<UL></UL>	Bulleted List
<LI></LI>	List Item

The Invoice Report

Features Highlighted

▶ Using a subreport in a table

▶ Using a subreport to facilitate drilldown

▶ Using RenderFormat.Name

▶ Exporting to PDF

Business Need   The Galactic Delivery Services accounting department wants an interactive Invoice Report. The Invoice Report needs to show the invoice header and invoice detail information. The user can then expand an invoice detail entry to view information on the delivery that created that invoice detail.

Task Overview

1. Create a New Report, Create a Dataset, and Copy the Layout from the DeliveryStatus Report
2. Create a New Report, Create a Dataset, and Populate the Report Layout
3. Improve PDF Export

Invoice Report, Task 1: Create a New Report, Create a Dataset, and Copy the Layout from the DeliveryStatus Report

`DT`
`RB`
SSDT, Visual Studio, and Report Builder Steps

1. Open the DeliveryStatus report.
2. Select the tablix in the DeliveryStatus report, and press CTRL-C to copy it. (Make sure you have the entire tablix selected and not just a single cell in the tablix.)
3. Close the DeliveryStatus report.
4. Create a new report called DeliveryDetail. Do *not* use the GDSReport template.
5. Create a new data source called Galactic that references the Galactic shared data source.
6. Create a new dataset called DeliveryStatus that calls the stp_DeliveryDetail stored procedure.
7. If you are using Report Builder, delete the "Click to add title" text box and remove the page footer.
8. Press CTRL-V to paste the tablix into the report body.
9. Move the tablix to the upper-left corner of the report body. Size the report body so it exactly contains the table.
10. Save the report.

Task Notes   Instead of re-creating a layout for the delivery detail, we borrowed a layout created previously in another report. This works because the stp_DeliveryDetail stored procedure returns the same columns as the stp_DeliveryStatus stored procedure used for the previous report. The other requirement needed to make this cut-and-paste operation successful was to use the same name for the dataset in both reports.

When you have a layout that is nice and clean, reusing it whenever possible is always a good idea. In Chapter 11, we look at another way to share layout items using published report parts. This method allows us to share layout among multiple authors. Something to look forward to in a future chapter!

Invoice Report, Task 2: Create a New Report, Create a Dataset, and Populate the Report Layout

DT

RB

SSDT, Visual Studio, and Report Builder Steps

1. Create a new report called Invoice using the GDSReport template.
2. Create a new data source called Galactic that references the Galactic shared data source.
3. Create a new dataset called InvoiceHeader that calls the stp_InvoiceHeader stored procedure.
4. Create a second dataset called InvoiceDetail that calls the stp_InvoiceDetail stored procedure.
5. Use the list template to place a tablix onto the report body.
6. Size the tablix and add fields to create the layout shown in Figure 9-26. The fields come from the InvoiceHeader dataset. The black line across the bottom is a solid bottom border on the tablix with a border width of 10 points.
7. Drag the report body to make it larger.

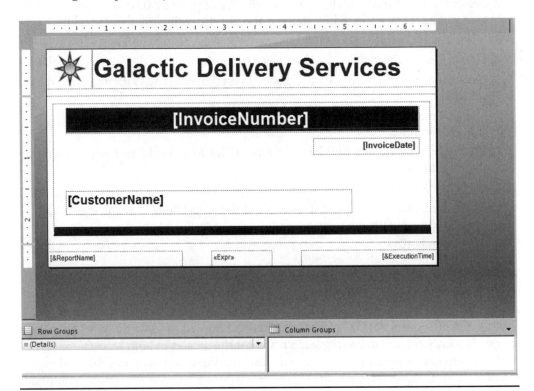

Figure 9-26 *The Invoice Report layout with an invoice header*

8. Use the table template to place a tablix onto the report body immediately below the existing tablix.

9. Select the LineNumber, Description, and Amount fields from the InvoiceDetail dataset in the data row of the tablix.

10. Size the table columns appropriately, but ensure the tablix has a Location: Left of 0in and a Size: Width of 6.5in exactly. Type the letter **C** for the Format property of the text box containing the Amount field value.

11. Delete the table header row.

12. Select all three of the remaining cells in the tablix and set the following property:

Name	Value
BorderStyle	None

13. Add a second details row below the existing data row. (In other words, insert a second row inside the details group.)

14. Merge the three cells in this new details row.

15. Place a subreport in the merged cell.

16. Open the Subreport Properties dialog box. Set the subreport to use the DeliveryDetail report.

17. Select the Parameters page and configure it as follows:

Name	Value
DeliveryNumber	[DeliveryNumber]

18. Click OK to exit the Subreport Parameters dialog box.

19. Click the gray box to the left of the row containing the subreport. Modify the following properties for this table row using the Properties window:

Property	Value
Hidden	True
ToggleItem	LineNumber

20. Preview/Run the report. Type **73054** for InvoiceNumber, and click View Report.

21. Expand one of the invoice detail entries and observe how the subreport appears. Your report should appear as shown in Figure 9-27.

Task Notes In the Invoice Report, we placed our subreport right in a table cell. A field from the table's dataset is used as the parameter for the subreport. Because of this, the subreport is different for each detail row in the table.

Figure 9-27   *The Invoice Report*

We chose to have the subreport initially hidden in our report. The reason for this is the subreport contains a large amount of detail information. This detail would overwhelm the users if it were displayed all at once. Instead, the users can selectively drill down to the detail they need.

In our next report, you look at another way to manage large amounts of detail by using the drillthrough feature of Reporting Services.

Invoice Report, Task 3: Improve PDF Export

`DT`

`RB`

SSDT, Visual Studio, and Report Builder Steps

1. Click the Export drop-down button, as shown in Figure 9-28 for SSDT and Visual Studio, or as shown in Figure 9-29 for Report Builder. Select PDF from the drop-down menu.

2. Save the resulting PDF file, and open it with Adobe Reader. The PDF format does not support the drilldown activity, so we are not able to view the detail of any of the invoices. It would be helpful to have the invoice detail expanded when the report is exported to a PDF file.

3. Close Adobe Reader and delete the PDF file.

4. Back in the report authoring environment, return to Design mode.

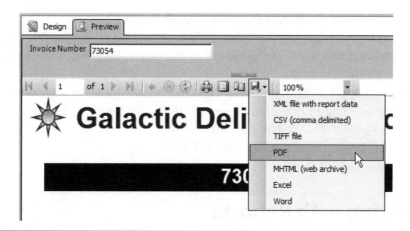

Figure 9-28   *The Export drop-down button in SSDT and Visual Studio*

5. Click anywhere in the table tablix on the report.
6. Click the gray box to the left of the row containing the subreport. Replace the value for the Hidden property with the following expression:

```
=IIF(Globals!RenderFormat.Name="PDF", False, True)
```

7. Right-click outside the report body but inside the layout area. Select Report Properties from the context menu. The Report Properties dialog box appears.

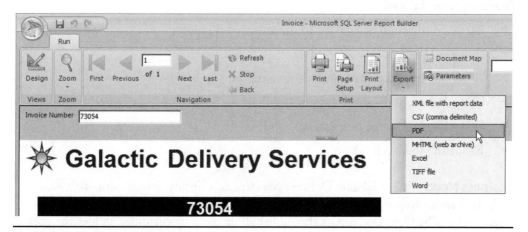

Figure 9-29   *The Export drop-down button in Report Builder*

8. Click OK to exit the Report Properties dialog box.

9. Preview/Run the report. Type **73054** for InvoiceNumber, and click View Report. The invoice detail is initially hidden when the report is viewed in the authoring environment.

10. Click the Export drop-down button, and select PDF from the drop-down menu.

11. Save the resulting PDF file, and open it with Adobe Reader. The invoice detail is not hidden when the rendering format is PDF.

12. Close Adobe Reader and delete the PDF file.

13. Save the report.

Interacting with Reports

In many cases, your reports can be much more effective when users can view them electronically. Reporting Services offers a number of options for enabling the user to interact with the reports when viewed in this way. You have already seen several examples of drilldown interactivity. This type of interactivity hides detail information until the user needs it.

In this section, you learn additional methods for navigating within reports and even moving between reports. You also see how to link a report to Internet content. Finally, you look at a way for your report to interact with you by always keeping its data current.

So don't be shy: interact!

The Invoice Front-End Report

Features Highlighted

▶   Using drillthrough navigation to move between reports

▶   Using the document map to navigate within a report

▶   Using bookmarks to navigate within a report

▶   Using links to navigate to Internet content

▶   Using the page name property and built-in field

▶   Exporting to Excel

Business Need   The Galactic Delivery Services accounting department is pleased with the Invoice Report. They would now like a front end to make the Invoice Report easier to use. The front-end report should list all invoices by customer and let the user click an invoice to see the complete Invoice Report. The front end should have each customer start on a new page. In addition, the front end should provide a quick way to navigate to the page for a particular customer and a way to move from a customer to the page for its parent company. Finally, the front end should include a link to the customer's website for further information.

Task Overview

1. Create a New Report, Create a Dataset, and Populate the Report Layout
2. Add the Navigation
3. Improve Excel Export

Invoice Front-End Report, Task 1: Create a New Report, Create a Dataset, and Populate the Report Layout

`DT`
`RB`

SSDT, Visual Studio, and Report Builder Steps

1. Create a new report called FrontEnd using the GDSReport template.
2. Create a new data source called Galactic that references the Galactic shared data source.
3. Create a new dataset called CustomerInvoices that calls the stp_CustomerInvoices stored procedure.
4. Use the table template to place a tablix onto the report body.
5. Select the InvoiceNumber, InvoiceDate, and TotalAmount fields in the Data row of the table.
6. Type the letter **C** for the Format property for the text box containing the TotalAmount field value.
7. Delete the table header row.
8. Add a parent row group to the table using the CustomerName as the group expression. The group should have a group header, but not a group footer. Use the Page Breaks page of the Group Properties dialog box to set a page break between each instance of a group.
9. Drag the cell containing the CustomerName field wide enough to contain the customer name without wrapping. Set the FontWeight property of this cell to Bold.
10. Merge the left and center cells in the group header row. Select the ParentName field in the newly merged cells.

Task Notes   We have the layout for the Invoice Front-End Report. However, it is not really a front end because it does not lead anywhere yet. Let's continue to the good stuff.

Invoice Front-End Report, Task 2: Add the Navigation

DT

RB **SSDT, Visual Studio, and Report Builder Steps**

1. Right-click the cell containing the Invoice Number field, and select Textbox: Text Box Properties from the context menu. The Text Box Properties dialog box appears.
2. Select the Action page.
3. Select the Go to report option under the Enable as an action prompt.
4. Select the Invoice report for the Specify a report prompt.
5. Click Add in the parameters area and configure the parameter as follows:

Name	Value
InvoiceNumber	[InvoiceNumber]

6. Click OK to exit the Text Box Properties dialog box.
7. In the Row Groups pane, use the CustomerName drop-down menu to select Group Properties. The Group Properties dialog box appears.
8. Select the Advanced page.
9. Select [CustomerName] from the Document map drop-down list.
10. Click OK to exit the Group Properties dialog box.
11. Select the cell containing the CustomerName field. Set the following property in the Properties window:

Name	Value
Bookmark	=Fields!CustomerName.Value

12. Right-click the cell containing the ParentName field, and select Textbox: Text Box Properties from the context menu. The Text Box Properties dialog box appears.
13. Select the Action page.
14. Select the Go to bookmark option under the Enable as an action prompt.
15. Select [ParentName] from the Select bookmark drop-down list.
16. Click OK to exit the Text Box Properties dialog box.
17. Right-click the rightmost cell in the group header row, and select Textbox: Text Box Properties from the context menu. The Text Box Properties dialog box appears.
18. Type **Website Link** for Value.
19. Select the Action page.
20. Select the Go to URL option under the Enable as an action prompt.

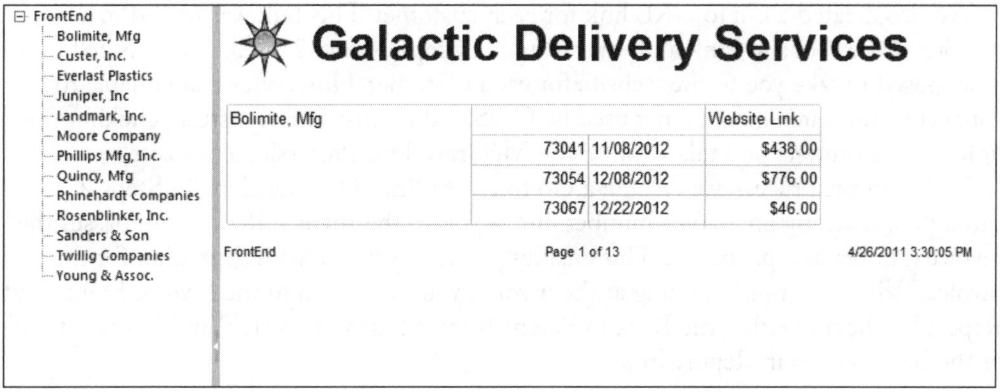

Figure 9-30   *The Front-End Report*

21. Select [CustomerWebsite] from the Select URL drop-down list.
22. Click OK to exit the Text Box Properties dialog box.
23. Preview/Run the report. Your report should appear similar to Figure 9-30.

Task Notes   When you look at the report preview, you notice a new feature to the left of the report. This is the document map, which functions like a table of contents for your report. We created entries in the document map when we selected a field from the Document map drop-down list in Step 9.

Because you used CustomerName as the document map field, you see a list of all the customer names in the document map. When you click a customer name in the document map, you are taken directly to the page for that customer.

If you are not using the document map, you can hide it. This is done by clicking the small white arrow in the middle of the bar separating the document map from the report. In Report Builder, you also have the option of clicking the Document Map button, which is in the Options section of the ribbon. Clicking either of these items a second time causes the document map to return.

In addition to creating document map entries for each customer name, we created bookmarks for each customer name. This was done in Step 11. We are using these bookmarks to link child companies to their parent company. We are creating a Go to bookmark link using the value of the ParentName field. This was done in Steps 14 and 15.

When a customer has a value in the ParentName field, a Go to bookmark link is created on that parent name. The bookmark link jumps to the page for the customer with the matching name. To try this out, use the document map to jump to the page for Everlast Plastics. Everlast's parent company is Young & Assoc. Click the link for Young & Assoc., and you will jump to the page for Young & Assoc.

We also created a Go to URL link for each customer. This link was placed in the cell that reads Website Link and was created in Steps 20 and 21. Clicking this cell is supposed to take you to the website for each customer. However, we are unable to connect to the Inter-galactic-net used by GDS and its customers. Instead, clicking this link opens a browser and takes you to the McGraw-Hill Professional website.

Earlier in the process, we created a Go to report link. This was done in Steps 2 through 6. Clicking an invoice number jumps you to the Invoice Report and passes the invoice number as a parameter. This enables you to see the detail information for the invoice. When you finish looking at the invoice, you can return to the Invoice Front-End Report by clicking either the Back to Parent Report button in SSDT and Visual Studio or the Back button in Report Builder.

Invoice Front-End Report, Task 3: Improve Excel Export

 SSDT, Visual Studio, and Report Builder Steps

1. Click the Export drop-down button. Select Excel from the drop-down menu.

2. Save the resulting Excel workbook file and open it in Excel 2007 or Excel 2010. Each page of the report appears as a separate spreadsheet tab. The first spreadsheet functions as the document map and the name on the tab says "Document map." The other tabs have generic names: Sheet2, Sheet3, and so on. What would make this even better is to have each tab show the name of the customer whose information it displays.

3. Close Excel and delete the workbook file.

4. Back in the report authoring environment, return to Design mode.

5. Click the CustomerName item in the Row Groups area to select it. The Properties window says "Tablix Member" at the top.

6. Set the following property:

Property	Value
Group: PageName	=Fields!CustomerName.Value

This will name each page after the Customer Name.

7. Right-click the text box containing "[&ReportName]" in the lower-left corner of the report, and select Expression from the context menu. The Expression dialog box appears.

8. Add to the expression in the Set expression for: Value so it matches the following:

```
=Globals!ReportName & "-" & Globals!PageName
```

9. Click OK to exit the Expression dialog box.

10. Preview/Run the report.

11. Page through the report and note the page name is now shown with the report name in the report footer.

12. Export the report to Excel and save the worksheet file as you did before.

13. Open the Excel workbook file. Note the names on the tabs now reflect the value of the PageName property.

14. Close Excel and delete the worksheet file.

15. Save the report.

Task Notes   Our FrontEnd Report works well when it is exported as an Excel workbook file. Excel provides features that allow all of the interactivity to be preserved. As we look at our initial worksheet export, it is obvious that the one thing missing is better naming of the spreadsheet tabs. This is especially true once you navigate away from the Document map tab. You really can't navigate directly to another customer's tab without first going back to the Document map.

The PageName property allows us to associate a name with each page of the report. We can use the PageName built-in field (Globals!PageName) to display that page name anywhere on the report, including the page header or page footer. When the report is exported in the Excel format, we get the added bonus of having the page names show up on the spreadsheet tabs.

The Transport Monitor Report

Features Highlighted

- ▶ Using a chart as the data section of a tablix

- ▶ Indicating values over a set maximum on a chart

- ▶ Using the autorefresh report property

- ▶ Using a multivalued parameter with a WHERE clause

Business Need   The Galactic Delivery Services maintenance department needs a report to assist in monitoring transport operations. Each transport feeds real-time sensor data back to the central database. The maintenance department needs a report to display this information for a selected set of transports. Because the sensor data is updated every minute, the report should refresh every minute. The sensor data should be displayed in a graphical form, with a highlight of any values that are above the normal maximums.

Task Overview

1. Create a New Report, Create a Dataset, Populate the Report Layout, and Set Report Properties

Transport Monitor Report, Task 1: Create a New Report, Create a Dataset, Populate the Report Layout, and Set Report Properties

DT

RB

SSDT, Visual Studio, and Report Builder Steps

1. Create a new report called TransportMonitor. Do *not* use the GDSReport template.
2. Create a new data source called Galactic that references the Galactic shared data source.
3. Create a new dataset called TransportMonitor that calls the stp_TransportMonitor stored procedure.
4. Create a second dataset called TransportList that calls the stp_TransportList stored procedure.
5. Configure the TransportNumber Report Parameter as follows:

Property	Value
General page:	
Prompt	Transports
Allow multiple values	Checked
Available Values page:	
Select from one of the following options	Get values from a query
Dataset	TransportList
Value field	TransportNumber
Label field	TransportNumber

6. Click OK to exit the Report Parameter Properties dialog box.
7. If you are using Report Builder, delete the "Click to add title" text box and remove the page footer.
8. Place a text box on the report body, and set its properties as follows:

Property	Value
Font: FontSize	20pt
Font: FontWeight	Bold
Location: Left	0in
Location: Top	0in

Property	Value
Size: Width	3in
Size: Height	0.375in
Value	Transport Monitor

9. Use the matrix template to place a tablix onto the report body. Set the properties of the tablix as follows:

Property	Value
Location: Left	0in
Location: Top	0.5in

10. Select the TransportNumber field from the TransportMonitor dataset in the Rows cell. Set the following properties of the text box created in that cell:

Property	Value
BackgroundColor	White
Font: FontWeight	Bold
VerticalAlign	Middle

11. Select the Item field in the Columns cell. Set the following properties of the text box created in that cell:

Property	Value
BackgroundColor	White
Font: FontWeight	Bold
TextAlign	Center

12. Open the Tablix Properties dialog box. Set the following properties:

Property	Value
Row Headers: Keep header visible while scrolling	checked
Column Headers: Keep header visible while scrolling	checked

13. Click OK to exit the Tablix Properties dialog box.

14. Select the Data cell of the tablix, and set the following properties:

Property	Value
Size: Width	2.25in
Size: Height	1.625in

15. Place a chart in the Data cell. The Select Chart Type dialog box appears.

16. Select the stacked column chart, and click OK.

17. Click the chart to view the Chart Data window. Use the green plus sign next to the Values area to select the Value field.

18. Use the green plus sign next to the Category Groups area to select the Reading field. Use the green plus sign next to the Series Groups area to select the ReadingPortion field.

19. In the Chart Properties dialog box, set the following property:

Property	Value
Color palette	Excel

20. In the Vertical Axis Properties dialog box, set the following property:

Property	Value
Maximum	100

21. Right-click the chart title, and select Delete Title from the context menu.

22. Right-click the legend area of the chart, and select Delete Legend from the context menu.

23. Right-click the horizontal axis title, and select Show Axis Title from the context menu. This will uncheck this option and hide the axis title.

24. Right-click the vertical axis title, and select Show Axis Title from the context menu. This will uncheck this option and hide the axis title.

25. Click anywhere outside the report body to bring up the report properties in the Properties window. Set the following property in the Properties window:

Property	Value
Autorefresh	60

26. Preview/Run the report.

27. Select several transport numbers from the drop-down list, and click View Report. Your report appears similar to Figure 9-31.

28. Save the report.

Task Notes A number of interesting things are going on in this report. First, a multivalued parameter is being sent to SQL Server for use in a stored procedure. The stored procedure uses the contents of this multivalued parameter to build a query string on the fly. The SELECT statement in the stored procedure is a bit complicated because

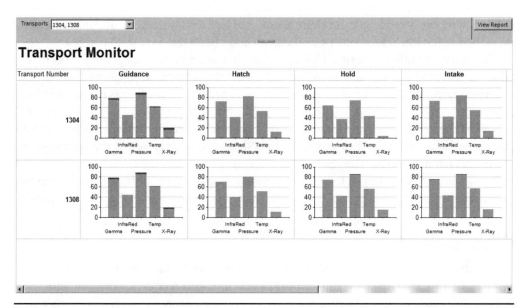

Figure 9-31   *The Transport Monitor Report preview*

it is using some random number generation to simulate the Transport telemetry. Here is a more straightforward version of the content of the stored procedure:

```
DECLARE @DynamicQuery varchar(8000)
SET @DynamicQuery = 'SELECT TransportNumber, Item, Reading, Value '
SET @DynamicQuery = @DynamicQuery + 'FROM transMonitor '
SET @DynamicQuery = @DynamicQuery + 'WHERE TransportNumber IN
                                    ('+@TransportNumber+') '
EXEC (@DynamicQuery)
```

This stored procedure code builds the SELECT statement in the @DynamicQuery variable. It uses the IN operator to look for the content of the TransportNumber field in a list of values. The values must be comma-separated and enclosed in parentheses to be used with the IN operator. The values in the multivalued parameter are being passed to the @TransportNumber stored procedure parameter. Because these values are already comma-separated, all we have to do is place them inside the parentheses to use them with the IN operator.

We placed a chart in the data portion of the matrix data region. Because the data portion of a matrix is an aggregate, the chart has a set of values to use for charting.

When the report is rendered, the chart is repeated in each data cell in the matrix. Each chart then acts within the scope of its data cell and charts the data in that scope.

The chart contains two series. The first series is a value up to the maximum normal value for that reading. The second series is the amount of the reading above the maximum normal value. The second series value is zero if the reading is below or at its maximum normal value. The stacked column chart puts these two series one on top of the other. The result is any readings that are above their maximum normal value have a maroon section at the top of the column. This should be enough to get the attention of any technician monitoring the readings.

Finally, we used autorefresh to meet the business requirements of the report. When the AutoRefresh property is set, the report is automatically rerun on the schedule you specify.

What's Next

We have now touched on almost all the report-authoring features for Reporting Services. It is time to move on from report development to report deployment and delivery. We move on to managing reports.

Part III

Report Serving

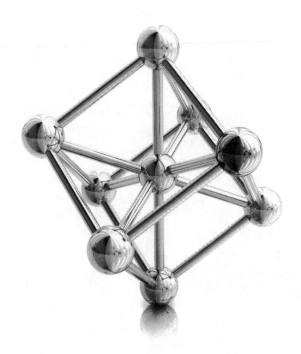

Chapter 10

How Did We Ever Manage Without You? The Report Manager

In This Chapter

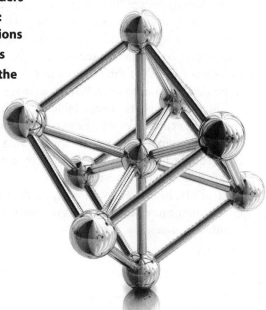

I n Part II of this book, we focused on report authoring. You learned fancy techniques for creating whiz-bang reports. However, the fact is, even the whiz-bangiest of reports are not much good if you cannot easily share them with end users.

In this chapter, you learn how to do just that. We move from authoring to managing reports and delivering them to the end users. This is done through the report server and its Report Manager web interface.

> **NOTE**
>
> *If you are using SharePoint integration for hosting Reporting Services, these management tasks can be performed through the SharePoint user interface. See the section "Reporting Services in SharePoint Integrated Mode" later in this chapter.*

We took a brief look at the report server and the Report Manager in Chapter 1. Now, we take a more detailed look. Much of our examination focuses on the Report Manager and how it is used to access and control the report server.

The first step is to move your report definitions and supporting files from the development environment to the Report Catalog. Recall that the Report Catalog is the SQL Server database where the report server keeps all its information, which includes the definitions of the reports it is managing. We look at several ways to accomplish this report deployment.

If you used Report Builder to create your reports, you have saved those reports and the shared data source directly to the Report Manager, so Report Builder users will not need to go through the process of deploying reports described in this chapter. For the most part, you can skip the section entitled "Moving Reports and Supporting Files to the Report Server." You may want to take note of the technique for hiding items in the "Hiding an Item" subsection, along with the difference between the tile view and detail view covered in this subsection. You may also want to look at the "Uploading Supporting Materials" subsection and the "A Look at Localization" subsection. Be sure to look at the rest of the material in this chapter beginning with the "Managing Items in Folders" section to learn how to manage the reports you already have on the server.

Once your reports are available through the report server, you need to control how they are executed. We use the report server's security features to control who can access each report, and we use the caching and report history to control how a report is executed each time it is requested by a user. Finally, we control all these report server features using the Report Manager.

In short, in this chapter, we take your reports from a single-user development environment to a secure, managed environment where they can be executed by a number of users.

Folders

Before you deploy reports to the report server, you need to have an understanding of the way the report server organizes reports in the Report Catalog. In the Report Catalog, reports are arranged into a system of folders similar to the Windows or Mac file system. Folders can contain reports, supporting files (such as external images and shared data sources), and even other folders. The easiest way to create, view, and maintain these folders is through the Report Manager.

Although the Report Catalog folders look and act like Windows file system folders, they are not actual file system folders. You cannot find them anywhere in the file system on the computer running the report server. *Report Catalog folders* are screen representations of records in the Report Catalog database.

Each folder is assigned a name. Folder names can include just about any character, including spaces. However, folder names cannot include any of the following characters:

```
; ? : @ & = + $ , \ * < > | " /
```

Also, a folder name cannot consist exclusively of dots or spaces.

In addition to a name, folders can be assigned a description. The description can contain a long explanation of the contents of the folder. It also can help users determine what types of reports are in a folder without having to open that folder and look at the contents. Both the folder name and the description can be searched by a user to help them find a report.

The Report Manager

The Report Manager web application provides a straightforward method for creating and navigating folders in the Report Catalog. When you initially install Reporting Services, the Home folder is created by default. This is the only folder that exists at first.

The default Uniform Resource Locator (URL) for accessing the Report Manager site on the computer running Reporting Services is:

```
http://ComputerName/reports
```

In this case, ComputerName is the name of the computer where Reporting Services was installed. If you are using a secure connection to access the Report Manager site, replace http: with https:. If you are on the same computer where Reporting Services is running, you can use the following URL:

```
http://localhost/reports
```

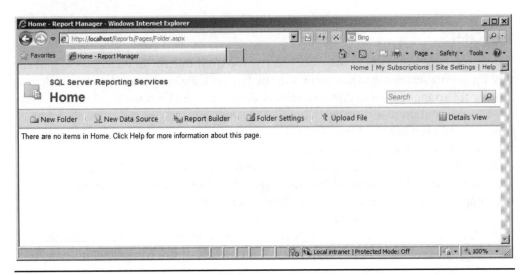

Figure 10-1   *The Report Manager with no folders defined*

No matter how you get there, when you initially access the Report Manager, it appears similar to Figure 10-1.

Notice the URL shown in Figure 10-1 is a bit different from the URLs given previously. This is because the Report Manager web application redirects you to the Pages/Folder.aspx web page. The Folder.aspx page is used to display folder contents.

NOTE

Figure 10-1 shows the Report Manager as it appears for a user with content manager privileges. If you do not see the New Folder, New Data Source, Report Builder, Folder Settings, and Upload File buttons in the toolbar on the Contents tab, you do not have content manager privileges and will be unable to complete the exercises in this section of the chapter. If possible, log out and log in with a Windows login that has local administration privileges on the computer running the report server.

To use the Report Manager, you must be using Microsoft Internet Explorer 6.0 with Service Pack 1 (SP1) or higher. You must also have scripting enabled.

Adding a New Folder Using the Report Manager

Let's create a new folder into which we will deploy some of the Galactic Delivery Services reports from the previous chapters. Here are the steps to follow:

NOTE

Examples showing report deployment throughout this chapter assume the Galactic Delivery Services folder is created in the Home folder. If you already have other folders created in your Report Catalog, be sure you are in the Home folder when you complete the following steps.

1. Click the New Folder button in the toolbar. The New Folder page appears, as shown in Figure 10-2.
2. Type **Galactic Delivery Services** for Name and **Reports created while learning to use Reporting Services** for Description.
3. Click OK to create the new folder and return to the Home folder.

You see an entry for your new folder with its name and description in the Home folder.

If you were observant, you noticed one item on the New Folder page we did not use. (If you missed it, look at Figure 10-2.) This is the Hide in tile view check box. When the Hide in tile view check box is checked, the new folder does not appear in the Home folder. This is useful when you want to make the reports in a folder available through a custom interface but unavailable through the Report Manager. We discuss this in detail in Chapter 12.

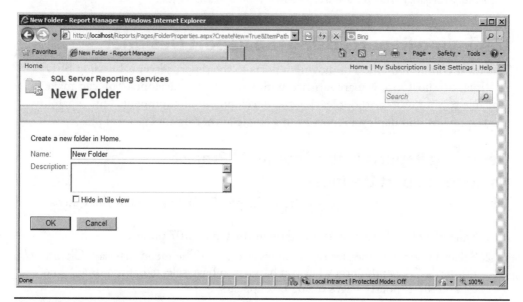

Figure 10-2 *The New Folder page*

To view the contents of the new folder, click the folder name. The name of the current folder appears in bold text near the top of the page. Above the name of the current folder is the path from the Home folder to the current folder. Because the Galactic Delivery Services folder is in the Home folder, the path only contains "Home." You can return to any folder in the current path by clicking that folder name in the path shown near the top of the page. You can return to the Home folder by clicking Home at the beginning of the current path or by clicking Home in the upper-right corner of the page.

Moving Reports and Supporting Files to the Report Server

Now that you know how to create folders, it is time to put some content in those folders. You do this by moving reports and their supporting files from the development environment to the report server. This can be done using a number of different methods. We look at two of those methods now: using the Report Designer and using the Report Manager.

NOTE

The following sections are for reports created with SSDT or Visual Studio. If you created your reports with Report Builder, they are already saved to the report server and do not need to be deployed. If you authored your reports using Report Builder, you can skip ahead to the section entitled "Hiding an Item."

Deploying Reports Using the Report Designer

The most common method of moving reports to the report server is by using SSDT or Visual Studio. Once you are satisfied with a report you developed, you can make it available to your users without leaving the development environment. This capability to create, preview, and deploy a report from a single authoring tool is a real plus.

Deploying Reports in the Chapter07 Project Using the Report Designer

Let's try deploying the report project from Chapter 7. To do so, follow these steps:

1. Start SSDT or Visual Studio, and open the Chapter07 project.
2. Select Project | Properties from the main menu. (The menu may say "Chapter07 Properties" depending on what you happen to have selected at the time.) The Chapter07 Property Pages dialog box appears.
3. Type **Galactic Delivery Services/Data Sources** for TargetDataSourceFolder.

4. Type **Galactic Delivery Services/Chapter07** for TargetReportFolder. This is the folder into which the report is going to be deployed.

5. Type **http://ComputerName/ReportServer** for TargetServerURL, where ComputerName is the name of the computer where the report server is installed. You should replace http: with https: if you are using a secure connection. You can use localhost in place of the computer name if the report server is installed on the same computer you are using to run Visual Studio (see Figure 10-3).

NOTE

If your report server does not have the Reporting Services web service configured in its default location, you will need to modify the URL in Step 5 appropriately.

6. Click OK to exit the Chapter07 Property Pages dialog box.

7. Right-click the Chapter07 project entry in the Solution Explorer, and select Deploy from the context menu.

8. The authoring environment builds all the reports in the project and then deploys all the reports, along with their supporting files, to the report server. (During the

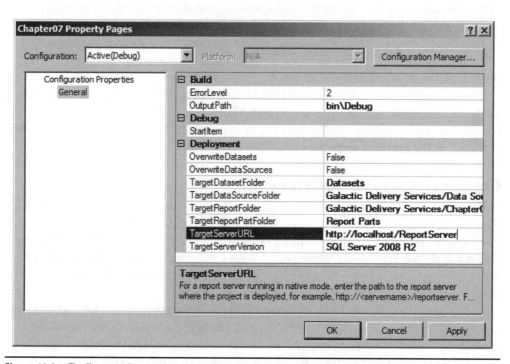

Figure 10-3 *The Chapter07 Property Pages dialog box*

build process, the authoring environment checks each report for any errors that would prevent it from executing properly on the report server.) The results of the build and deploy are shown in the Output window.

9. Open the Report Manager in your browser. Click the Galactic Delivery Services folder to view its contents. You see that the authoring environment created two new folders in the Galactic Delivery Services folder: one called Chapter07 and one called Data Sources.

10. Click the Chapter07 folder to view its contents. All of the reports in the Chapter07 project were deployed.

11. Click the Earth US Deliveries report. You see the rendered report.

NOTE

You can also deploy the contents of a project by selecting Build | Deploy Project Name from the main menu.

Working Through the Web Service

When the authoring environment deploys reports, it works through the Reporting Services web service. The Report Manager web application provides a human interface to Reporting Services. The web service provides an interface for other programs to communicate with Reporting Services. Because the authoring environment falls into the latter of these two categories, it uses the web service to deploy reports.

The web service has a different URL from the Report Manager. You must enter the URL for the web service and not the Report Manager in the Properties Pages dialog box for the deployment to work properly. The default URL for the web service is shown in Step 5 in the previous section.

Creating Folders While Deploying

In Steps 2 through 6, you entered information into properties of the Chapter07 project. These values tell the authoring environment where to put the reports and supporting items when the project is deployed. In this case, you instructed the authoring environment to put our shared data source in the Data Sources folder within the Galactic Delivery Services folder and our reports in the Chapter07 folder within the Galactic Delivery Services folder.

We created the Galactic Delivery Services folder in the previous section. We did not create the Data Sources and Chapter07 folders. Instead, the authoring environment created those folders for us as it deployed the items in the project. In fact, the authoring environment creates folders for any path we specify.

Deploying a Single Report

In Step 7, you used the project's context menu to deploy all the items in the project. Alternatively, you could have right-clicked a report and selected Deploy from the report's context menu. However, this would have deployed only this report, not the entire project.

On some occasions, you might want to deploy a single report rather than the entire project. At times, one report is going to be completed and ready for deployment, while the other reports in the project are still under construction. At other times, one report will be revised after the entire project has already been deployed. In these situations, it is only necessary to redeploy the single revised report.

Deploying Shared Data Sources

Even when a single report is deployed, any shared data sources used by that report are automatically deployed along with it. This only makes sense. A report that requires shared data sources does not do much if those shared data sources are not present.

If you look back at Figure 10-3, you notice an OverwriteDataSources item in the dialog box. This controls whether a shared data source that has been deployed to the report server is overwritten by subsequent deployments. In most cases, shared data sources do not change, so they do not need to be overwritten. For this reason, OverwriteDataSources is set to False, meaning do not overwrite existing data sources.

Aside from saving unnecessary effort, not overwriting data sources also helps out in another way. Consider the environment shown in Figure 10-4. In this environment,

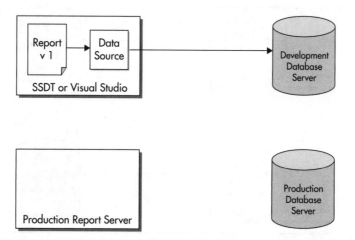

Figure 10-4   *A report and a shared data source ready to deploy*

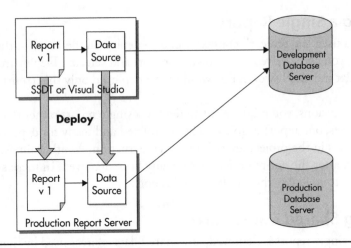

Figure 10-5 *Deploying the report and the shared data source*

reports are developed in the authoring environment using a shared data source that points to a development database server. Once the first version of the report is completed, it is deployed to a production report server, as shown in Figure 10-5. As soon as the deployment is complete, the shared data source on the production report server needs to be changed to point to the production database server. This is shown in Figure 10-6.

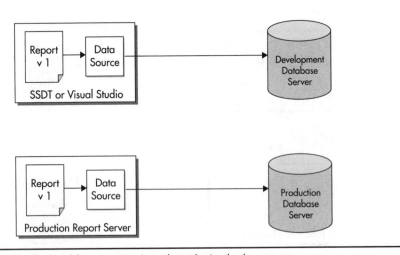

Figure 10-6 *Modifying the shared data source to point to the production database server*

Now, as time has passed, a new version of the report (version 2) is created in the development environment. This time, when version 2 of the report is deployed to the production report server, the shared data source already exists there.

If OverwriteDataSources is set to True, the data source from the development environment would overwrite the data source in the production environment, and we would be back to the situation in Figure 10-5. With this setting, we would have to redirect the shared data source each time a report is deployed.

To avoid this, OverwriteDataSources is set to False. Now, when version 2 of the report (and subsequent versions) is deployed to the production report server, the shared data source is not overwritten. It remains pointing to the production database server. This is shown in Figure 10-7. We have saved a bit of extra effort with each deployment.

As you will see throughout this chapter, folders are used to organize reports on the report server and help manage security for those reports. If you are managing your report server properly, you can have reports deployed in a number of different folders. A number of these reports use the same database as the source for their data. Rather than having a number of shared data sources scattered throughout the folders on your report server, it makes more sense to have the reports all reference a single data source or a set of data sources stored in one central folder. This is accomplished through the use of the TargetDataSourceFolder.

Just as the TargetReportFolder property enables you to specify the path where a report is to be deployed, the TargetDataSourceFolder property lets you specify the path where the shared data source should be deployed or found, if it already exists on the report server. If no folder path is specified, the TargetDataSourceFolder defaults to the

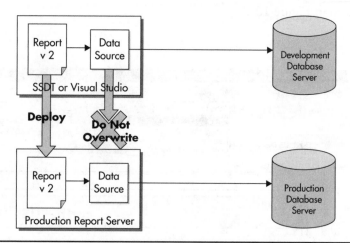

Figure 10-7 *A subsequent deployment with OverwriteDataSources set to False*

TargetReportFolder. The OverwriteDataSources flag applies, whether the shared data source is being deployed to the TargetReportFolder or the TargetDataSourceFolder.

Additional Properties in the Property Pages Dialog Box

If you look back at Figure 10-3, you can see a few additional items in the Property Pages dialog box that we have not discussed. We look at those two items now.

Maintaining Multiple Configurations   At the top of the dialog box is the Configuration drop-down list. This drop-down list enables you to maintain several different deployment configurations for the same project. Each configuration has its own values for TargetDataSourceFolder, TargetReportFolder, TargetServerURL, and the other settings in the dialog box.

This is useful if you need to deploy the reports in a project to more than one report server. Perhaps you have the report server loaded on your PC for your own testing, a development report server where the report undergoes quality assurance testing, and a production report server where the report is to be made available to the end users. You can enter the properties for deploying to the report server on your PC in the DebugLocal configuration, the properties for deploying to the development report server in the Debug configuration, and the properties for deploying to the production report server in the Release configuration.

You can then easily switch between deploying to each of these report servers as new versions of your reports go from your own testing to quality assurance testing and are then made available to the users. You can change the configuration you are using for deployment through the Solution Configuration drop-down list in the Report Designer toolbar, as shown in Figure 10-8.

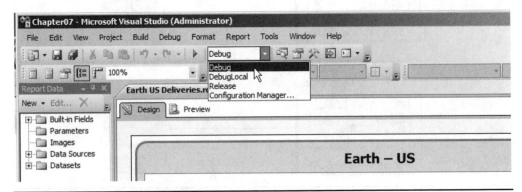

Figure 10-8   *The Solution Configuration drop-down list*

> **NOTE**
>
> *Active(Debug) in the Configuration drop-down list of the Property Pages dialog box simply refers to the Debug configuration that is currently the selected or active configuration.*

Target Server Version   The Project Property Pages dialog box also enables you to specify the version of the report server to which you are deploying the report. This is because the Reporting Services web service interface varies slightly between different versions of SQL Server. This option will allow you to deploy reports to report servers running older versions of SQL Server, as well as those running the current version.

Running a Report Project   The final item we will look at in the Project Property Pages dialog box is StartItem, which is used when running your report project. Use the StartItem drop-down list to select which report from your project should be executed when you run the project. The report selected as the start item is displayed in a browser window.

When you run a report project, you deploy all the reports, shared data sources, and other supporting information in the project to the target server and target folders in your active configuration. Once the deployment is complete, the report specified as the start item is executed in a browser window. You can then debug this report, making sure it looks correct and functions properly. You can run the project by clicking the Start Debugging button on the toolbar (to the left of the Solution Configuration drop-down list) or by selecting any of the following items from the Debug menu (or by pressing any of the shortcut keys that correspond to these menu items):

▶ Start Debugging

▶ Start Without Debugging

▶ Step Over

There is no such thing as stepping over a report. These menu items pertain to other types of SQL Server Data Tools and Visual Studio projects. Here they simply run the project. The report selected as the start item is executed in a browser window from start to finish.

Uploading Reports Using Report Manager

Another common method of moving a report to the report server is by using the Report Manager. This is known as *uploading* the report. Deploying reports from SSDT or Visual Studio can be thought of as pushing the reports from the authoring environment to the report server, whereas uploading reports from the Report Manager can be thought of as pulling the reports from the authoring environment to the report server.

You may need to use the Report Manager upload feature in situations where your report authors do not have rights to deploy reports on the report server. The report authors create their reports and test them within the authoring environment. When a report is completed, the report author can place the Report Definition Language (RDL) file for the report in a shared directory or send it as an e-mail attachment to the report server administrator. The report server administrator can upload the RDL file to a quality assurance report server and test the report for clarity, accuracy, and proper use of database resources. Once the report has passed this review, the report server administrator can upload the report to the production report server.

Uploading Reports in the Chapter06 Project Using the Report Manager

Let's try uploading some of the reports from the Chapter06 report project.

1. Open the Report Manager in your browser. Click the Galactic Delivery Services folder to view its contents.
2. Create a new folder called **Chapter06**.
3. Select the new folder to view its contents.
4. Click the Upload File button in the Report Manager toolbar. The Upload File page appears, as shown in Figure 10-9.
5. Click Browse. The Choose File to Upload dialog box appears.
6. Navigate to the folder where you created your solution for Chapter 6. If this folder is in the default location, you can find it under the following path:

   `My Documents\Visual Studio 2010\Projects\MSSQLRS\Chapter06`

7. Select the Nametags report (Nametags.rdl), and click Open to exit the Choose File to Upload dialog box.
8. Click OK to upload the file. The Nametags report has been uploaded to the Chapter06 folder.
9. Click the Nametags report to execute it. You see an error similar to the one in Figure 10-10. You received this because, unlike the deployment from the Report Designer, the upload in Report Manager did not bring the shared data source along with the report.
10. Click the link to the Chapter06 folder at the top of the page.

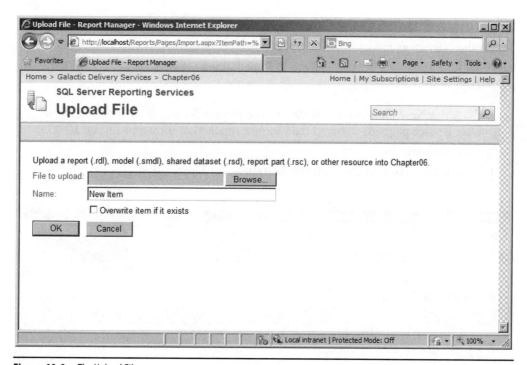

Figure 10-9   *The Upload File page*

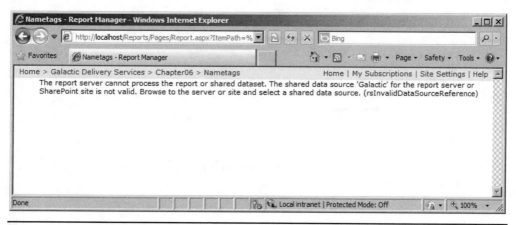

Figure 10-10   *The Reporting Services error page*

Creating a Shared Data Source in the Report Manager

To get the Nametags report functioning, you need to provide it with a shared data source. One way to do this is to create a new shared data source using the Report Manager. Follow these steps:

1. Click the New Data Source button in the Report Manager toolbar. The New Data Source page for a shared data source appears, as shown in Figure 10-11.
2. Type **Galactic** for Name.
3. Type **Connection to the Galactic Database** for Description.

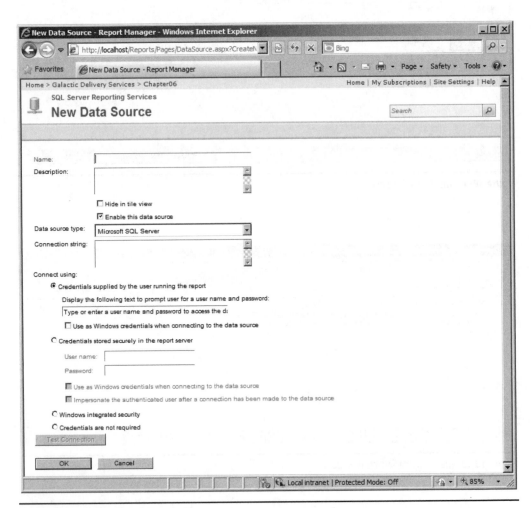

Figure 10-11 *The New Data Source page*

4. Make sure Microsoft SQL Server is selected in the Data Source Type drop-down list. Other options here include OLE DB, Microsoft SQL Server Analysis Services, Oracle, ODBC, and XML.

5. Type **data source=(local); initial catalog=Galactic** for Connection String. If the Galactic database is not on the report server, but is on a different computer, put the name of that computer in place of (local) in the connection string.

NOTE

Do not include the parentheses if you use a computer name in place of (local).

6. Select the Credentials stored securely in the report server option.

7. Type **GalacticReporting** for User Name.

8. Type **G@l@ct1c** for Password.

9. Click Test Connection. Fix any errors if the connection is not successful.

10. Click OK to save the data source and return to the Chapter06 folder.

11. Click the Nametags report to execute it. You receive the same error message page because we have not yet told the report to use our new data source.

12. Click the Nametags link in the upper-left corner of the page. The Properties page for the Nametags report appears.

13. Click the Data Sources link on the left side of the screen. The Data Sources page for the Nametags report appears.

14. A shared data source should be selected. Click Browse. The Select a Shared Data Source page appears.

15. Expand each folder in the tree view under Location until you can see the Galactic shared data source in the Chapter06 folder. Click the Galactic shared data source. The path to the Galactic shared data source is filled in Location. (You can also type this path into the Location text box if you do not want to use the tree view.)

16. Click OK to exit the Select a Shared Data Source page.

17. Click Apply at the bottom of the page.

NOTE

It is easy to forget to click Apply when making changes to a report's data sources. If you do not click Apply, none of your changes are saved. This can lead to confusion, frustration, and wasted troubleshooting time. At least, that is what I have been told.

18. Click the large "Nametags" heading at the top of the page to view the report. The report now generates using the new shared data source. (An image placeholder is where the GDS logo should be. We deal with this in the section "Uploading External Report Images.")

19. Once the report has completed generating, click the Chapter06 link at the top of the page.

Hiding an Item

Figure 10-12 shows the tile view of the Chapter06 folder. The Galactic shared data source appears in the left column. Shared data sources have a cylinder icon. The Nametags report appears in the right column. Reports have an icon showing a piece of paper with columns of data and a bar chart along with a drafting triangle and ruler.

> **NOTE**
>
> *If you used Report Builder to complete the exercises earlier in the book, your Chapter 6 folder looks very different. You can follow the same steps to hide the GDS .gif image*

When users are browsing through folders to find a report, you may not want other items, such as shared data sources, cluttering things up. It makes more sense to have the shared data sources where the reports can use them, but out of sight of the users. Fortunately, Report Manager provides a way to do just that.

1. Hover over the Galactic data source and select Manage from the drop-down menu. The Properties page appears.
2. Check the Hide in tile view check box.
3. Click Apply to save this change.
4. Click the Chapter06 link at the top of the page.

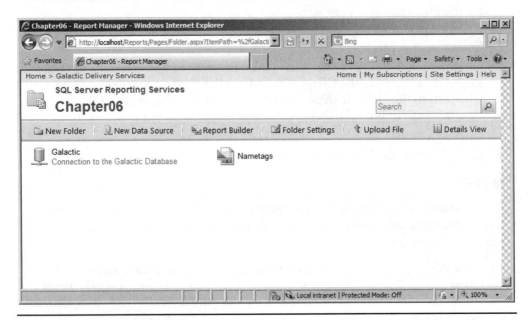

Figure 10-12   *The Chapter06 folder tile view*

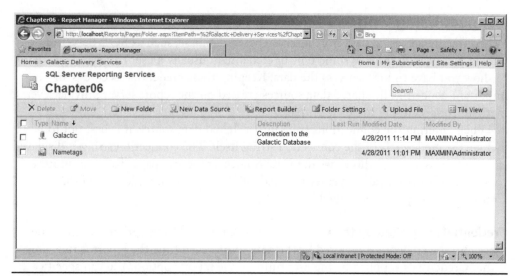

Figure 10-13 *The Chapter06 folder detail view*

The Galactic data source is no longer visible in the tile view. You can use this same technique to hide reports you do not want to have generally available to users browsing through the folders.

If you do need to edit the Galactic data source, you can view it by using the detail view of the folder. Follow these steps:

1. Click the Details View button in the toolbar. The Galactic data source is now visible in this detail view, as shown in Figure 10-13. By default, the detail view is in alphabetical order by name.

2. Click the Type column heading. The detail view is now sorted by type in ascending order. (In an ascending sort by type, the reports are at the top of the list, with supporting items, such as shared data sources, at the bottom.) Note the downward-pointing arrow is now next to the Type column heading on your screen.

3. Click the Type column heading again. The detail view is now sorted by type in descending order. Now the arrow is pointing upward next to the column heading.

NOTE

The name of the sort order (ascending or descending) and the direction of the arrow may seem opposite to one another. Remember this: In an ascending sort, you move from smaller values (A, B, C . . .) to larger values (. . . X, Y, Z). When you move through the list in the direction of the arrow, you also move from smaller values to larger values.

4. Click the Modified Date column heading. The detail view is sorted by modified date in ascending order. You can sort the detail view by Type, Name, Description, Last Run, Modified Date, or Modified By, in either ascending or descending order.

5. Click the Tile View button in the toolbar. You are back to the tile view.

Connect Using Options

When you are accessing data from a server-based database, such as SQL Server or Oracle, you need to provide some type of credentials, usually a user name and password, to show you have rights to access the data. Keeping these credentials secure is an important concern. The shared data sources created on the report server provide several methods for specifying these credentials.

When entering the connection string into a shared data source, it is best not to include the credentials in the connection string itself. The connection string is displayed as plain text to anyone who views the Data Source Properties page. To better protect password information, always enter the credential information under one of the Connect Using options described here.

Credentials Supplied by the User   The first Connect Using option is to have the user enter the credentials required by the data source each time the report is run. This is the "Credentials supplied by the user running the report" option. You can specify the prompt to be presented each time the user must enter these credentials. If the "Use as Windows credentials when connecting to the data source" check box is checked, the user name and password entered by the user are treated as a Windows login. This means the user name and password provide database access using Windows integrated security. If this check box is not checked, the user name and password are treated as a database login.

Having the user enter the credentials each time the report is run is the most secure option. No login information is stored with the data source, but most users are not pleased with a system where they must enter login information each time they run a report. This option may be appropriate when your organization's security policy forbids storing login information in any way. In most other cases, the other Connect Using options provide a better solution.

Credentials Stored in the Report Server   The next option enables you to have the user name and password stored in the Report Catalog on the report server. This is the "Credentials stored securely in the report server" option. The user name and password entered with this option are encrypted when they are stored in the Report Catalog. Also, the password is not displayed to the user on the Data Source Properties page.

This Connect Using option is convenient for the user because they do not need to remember and enter credentials to run reports using this data source. It also provides the required security for most situations through the measures noted in the previous paragraph.

As with the first Connect Using option, there is a "Use as Windows credentials when connecting to the data source" check box here as well. If this check box is checked, the user name and password stored in the Report Catalog are treated as a Windows login. If this check box is not checked, the user name and password are treated as a database login.

The second check box under this Connect Using option is "Impersonate the authenticated user after a connection has been made to the data source." If this check box is checked, the data source can use these credentials to impersonate this user. This feature is supported by the SQL Server relational database engine and SQL Server Analysis Services.

Integrated Security   If you are not comfortable storing credentials in the Report Catalog, but you do not want your users entering credentials every time a report is run, integrated security may be the solution for you. The "Windows integrated security" option does not require the user to enter credentials. Instead, it takes the Windows login credentials that let the user access the Report Manager and passes them along to the database server. Your database server, of course, needs to be set up to accept these credentials.

Integrated security always works when the data source exists on the same server as the report server. It may run into problems, however, if the data source is on another server. The problems are caused by the way integrated security works between servers.

For a better understanding of the problems with integrated security, let's look at an example of the way integrated security works. The user logs in to their computer. This computer knows everything about this user because the original authentication occurred here.

When the user accesses the Report Manager application, the user's credentials are passed from the original computer to the computer hosting the report server. However, using standard Windows security, not everything about this login is passed to the report server computer—only enough information to authenticate the user. Some sensitive information does not make this hop across the network.

When the user runs a report with a data source using integrated security, the report server must pass on the credentials to the database server. However, the report server does not have the complete credentials to pass along. In fact, it does not know enough about the user to successfully authenticate them on the database server. The authentication on the database server fails. Using standard Windows security, integrated security only works across one hop, from the original authenticating computer to a second computer. In the case of the Report Manager, this is the hop from the user's computer to the report server.

To get integrated security to work across more than one hop, your Windows domain must use a special kind of security known as Kerberos, which allows authentication across multiple hops. Using Kerberos security, integrated security works across any number of servers in the network.

Credentials Not Required   The final Connect Using option is for data sources that do not require any authentication. This option would be used for connection to some Access databases, FoxPro databases, and others that do not require any login or password. This option could also be used if you insist, despite prior warnings here, on putting your credentials right in the connection string.

Uploading Other Items Using Report Manager

In addition to reports and shared data sources, other items can be uploaded to report server folders. External images needed as part of the reports can be uploaded, for example, as well as documentation and other supporting materials.

Uploading External Report Images

If you look closely at the Nametags report when it comes up in Report Manager, you notice this report has a problem. The GDS logo that should appear in the lower-left corner of each nametag is missing. You see the broken-link *X* symbol instead of the GDS logo.

This image was stored as an external image in the Chapter06 project. We need to upload this image to the report server. Once the image is uploaded into the same folder as the report, the report can find it. Here are the steps to do this:

1. Return to the Chapter06 folder in the Report Manager.
2. Click Upload File in the toolbar. The Upload File page appears.
3. Click Browse. The Choose File to Upload dialog box appears.
4. Navigate to the folder containing the Chapter06 project. Select the GDS.gif file, and click Open to exit the Choose File dialog box.
5. Leave the name as GDS.gif. The image needs to keep this name so it can be found by the report. Click OK to upload this file.
6. Click the Nametags report to execute it. If the image placeholder is still visible, click the Refresh button in the Report Viewer toolbar, as shown in Figure 10-14.

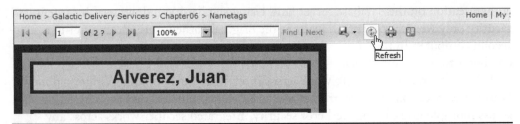

Figure 10-14 *The Refresh button in the Report Viewer toolbar*

NOTE

When you need to have Report Manager refresh a report, always use the Refresh button in the Report Viewer toolbar. Do not use the browser's Refresh button. The browser's Refresh button causes the page to be refreshed, but it does not cause the report to be reexecuted.

7. Click the link for the Chapter06 folder.
8. The entry for the GDS.gif image shows in the tile view of the Chapter06 folder. As with the Galactic shared data source, you probably don't want entries for supporting resources cluttering up your list view. Hover over the entry for GDS.gif.
9. Click the drop-down arrow, and select Manage from the menu. The Properties page appears.
10. Check the Hide in tile view check box.
11. Click Apply.
12. Click the link for the Chapter06 folder.

Uploading Supporting Materials

In some cases, you need to provide your users with documentation on one or more reports in the form of either a text file or a Word or HTML document. Supporting materials may also be created in other applications. For example, you may have a PowerPoint presentation or a Visio diagram that aids in the interpretation and understanding of a set of reports. These materials can be uploaded as folder items just like report files.

A text file or an HTML document can be displayed right in the browser without any additional software. For other types of documents, if the appropriate application is installed on the user's computer, the documents can be viewed right in the browser as well. These documents can also be downloaded and saved to the user's computer, if desired.

Now, we'll create a simple text document and then upload it to the Chapter06 folder.

1. Open Notepad or another text editor.
2. Type the following in the text editor:

```
The items in this folder are for the GDS Conference.
```

3. Save this as ReportReadMe.txt in a temporary location on your computer.
4. Return to your browser with the Report Manager viewing the Chapter06 folder. Click Upload File in the toolbar. The Upload File page appears.
5. Click Browse. The Choose File to Upload dialog box appears.
6. Navigate to the ReportReadMe.txt file, select it, and click Open to exit the Choose File to Upload dialog box.
7. Click OK to upload this file.

8. Select the ReportReadMe.txt entry in the Chapter06 folder. You see the contents of the text file displayed within the Report Manager.

9. Click the link for the Chapter06 folder.

10. Let's add a second line to our text file. Open the ReportReadMe.txt file in your text editor, and add the following as a second line:

```
These items were created for the GDS Art Department.
```

11. Save the changes and close your text editor.

12. Return to your browser with the Report Manager viewing the Chapter06 folder. Click Upload File in the toolbar. The Upload File page appears.

13. Click Browse. The Choose File to Upload dialog box appears.

14. Navigate to the ReportReadMe.txt file, select it, and click Open to exit the Choose File to Upload dialog box.

15. Check the Overwrite item if it exists check box. If you fail to check this check box, the new version of the text file does not overwrite the older version on the report server.

16. Click OK to upload this file.

17. Select the ReportReadMe.txt entry in the Chapter06 folder. You see the new version of the text file.

18. Click the ReportReadMe.txt link at the top of the web page. The Properties page appears.

19. Type **The purpose of these reports ...** for the description.

20. Click Apply to save your changes.

21. Click the link for the Chapter06 folder. The description shows up under the entry for ReportReadMe.txt.

22. Let's make another change to our text file and look at another way to overwrite an entry on the report server. Open the ReportReadMe.txt file in your text editor, and add the following as a third line:

```
These items were created for all billing contacts.
```

23. Save the changes and close your text editor.

24. Return to your browser with the Report Manager viewing the Chapter06 folder. Hover over the entry for ReportReadMe.txt.

25. Click the drop-down arrow, and select Manage from the menu. The Properties page appears.

26. Click Replace. The Import Resource page appears.

27. Click Browse. The Choose File to Upload dialog box appears.

28. Navigate to the ReportReadMe.txt file, select it, and click Open to exit the Choose File to Upload dialog box.

29. Click OK to upload this file.
30. Click the link for the Chapter06 folder at the top of the page.
31. Click the link for ReportReadMe.txt. You see the latest version of the text file.
32. Click the link for the Chapter06 folder.
33. Delete the ReportReadMe.txt file on your computer.

Uploading Reports Using .NET Assemblies

In addition to external images, reports can reference .NET assemblies. You saw this in the Weather Report and the Delivery Analysis Report created in Chapter 9. Let's look at the steps necessary to move these reports to the report server.

Copying the .NET Assembly to the Report Server

For a report to access a .NET assembly, the assembly must be in the application folder of the report server. No fancy deployment, upload, or installation routine is required here. Simply copy the assembly's DLL file to the appropriate directory. We can give this a try using the Weather Report and its .NET assembly, WeatherInfo.dll, as well as the Delivery Analysis Report and its .NET assembly, ReportUtil.dll. Here are the steps to follow:

1. Locate the WeatherInfo.dll and ReportUtil.dll files. You also need the ES folder that contains the Spanish version of the ReportUtil.dll. This Spanish version is called ReportUtil.resources.dll. (The folder name, ES, is the two-letter code for Español.) If you do not have them anywhere else, they should be in the Public Assemblies folder on your development computer. The default path for the Public Assemblies folder is

```
C:\Program Files\Microsoft Visual Studio 10.0\Common7\IDE\
PublicAssemblies
```

or

```
C:\Program Files (x86)\Microsoft Visual Studio 10.0
                              \Common7\IDE\PublicAssemblies
```

2. Copy these files and the ES folder.
3. Paste the files and the ES folder into the report server application folder on the computer acting as your report server computer. You may receive a warning because a folder called ES already exists. Click Yes to continue. The default path for the report server application folder is

```
C:\Program Files\Microsoft SQL Server\MSRS11.MSSQLSERVER\
                          Reporting Services\ReportServer\bin
```

Code Access Security

Because Reporting Services is a .NET application, it uses *code access security* to determine what execution permissions each assembly possesses. A *code access group* associates assemblies with specific permissions. The criteria for membership in a code access group are determined by a *security class,* and the permissions are determined by *named permission sets.*

Figure 10-15 provides an illustration of code access security. A .NET assembly or web service can gain entry into a code access group only if it matches the criteria specified by the security class. Once the .NET assembly or web service is allowed into a code access group, it can use the named permission set associated with that code access group to gain rights. These rights allow the .NET assembly or web service to perform tasks on a computer. Full trust rights and execution rights are the two types of rights we use with the Weather Report. A number of different types of rights, however, can be included in a named permission set.

Code access groups can be nested inside one another. A .NET assembly or web service can be allowed into a parent group and gain its permissions; then it can try to gain membership in child code access groups to accumulate additional rights. A code access group can be a *first match code group,* where a .NET assembly or web service can only gain membership in one code access group—the first one it matches. Or, a code access group can be a *union code group,* where a .NET assembly or web service is

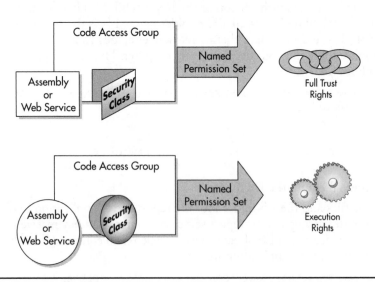

Figure 10-15 *Code access security*

allowed to gain membership in a number of code access groups, joining together the permissions from each group.

For our Weather Report to execute properly, we will have to create a code access group that provides permissions to the WeatherInfo.dll assembly. Also, we will have to create a second code access group to provide permissions to the web service that we are using to get our weather information. Even though this web service is not executing on our server, our WeatherInfo.dll assembly is executing some of its methods, so it needs to have permission to execute.

Security Classes   A security class describes the conditions a .NET assembly or web service needs to meet to get into a code access group. We use two different types of security classes with the Weather Report. The UrlMembershipCondition security class is used with the web service, and the StrongNameMembershipCondition security class is used with the WeatherInfo.dll and ReportUtil.dll assemblies.

The UrlMembershipCondition security class says that any assembly or web service being executed from a specified URL is to be included in a particular code access group. The URL that must be matched is listed in each code access group using the UrlMembershipCondition security class. For example, the GDSServer code access group may use UrlMembershipCondition and give http://GDSServer/* as the URL that must be matched. Any web service running on the GDSServer would be included in this code access group.

The StrongNameMembershipCondition security class uses the strong name associated with an assembly to identify it. The *strong name,* which is a long string of hexadecimal digits that uniquely identifies an assembly, is assigned to the assembly when it is created. The StrongNameMembershipCondition security class is a good way to ensure that only the intended assembly is allowed into your code access group.

You see a couple of other security classes in the report server security configuration. The AllMembershipCondition security class allows in all .NET assemblies and web services. The ZoneMembershipCondition security class allows in .NET assemblies and web services that originate in a particular zone. Some of the different zones are MyComputer, intranet, and Internet.

Named Permission Sets   Named permission sets group together the permissions to be assigned by code access groups. The security configuration used by the report server contains three named permission sets. The *Nothing permission,* which grants no rights, is used to initially take away all rights from a .NET assembly or web service before specific rights are added back by subsequent code access groups. This ensures each .NET assembly or web service has only the rights it should have.

The *Execution permission* grants execution rights to a .NET assembly or web service. This means the .NET assembly or web service can be run. The .NET assembly or web service does not, however, have rights to access any protected resources, such as the file system, the registry, or the Internet.

The *FullTrust permission* grants the .NET assembly or web service access to everything. This includes access to all the protected resources. FullTrust permission should only be granted to .NET assemblies and web services that you trust not to mess up your computer!

Modifying the Report Server's Security Configuration

Now that you have a basic understanding of code access security, we can modify the report server's security configuration to allow the WeatherInfo.dll and the ReportUtil .dll to run.

CAUTION

Consult with your Reporting Services or network administrator before making any changes to server security.

We need to make some additions to the report server's security configuration to provide our custom assemblies with the rights they need to execute. The security configuration for the report server is in the rssrvpolicy.config file. The default path for this file is

```
C:\Program Files\Microsoft SQL Server\MSRS11.MSSQLSERVER\
                              Reporting Services\ReportServer
```

This file contains the code access security information in an Extensible Markup Language (XML) structure.

CAUTION

Make a backup copy of the rssrvpolicy.config file before making any modifications to it. If you accidentally create an invalid XML structure or otherwise cause a problem with the security configuration, the report server cannot execute any reports.

The XML structure in the rssrvpolicy.config file can be divided into three sections: Security Classes, Named Permission Sets, and Code Groups. We only need to make changes to the Code Groups section of the document. Here are the steps to follow:

1. Open the rssrvpolicy.config file in Notepad or another text editor.

2. Scroll down until you locate the Code Group portion of the document. The Code Group portion starts on the line after the closing XML tag for the named permission sets:

```
</NamedPermissionSets>
```

3. The first code group is the parent code group, which makes use of the AllMembershipCondition to assign the Nothing permission to all .NET assemblies and web services. We need to add a new child code group right beneath this. Insert this new code group as shown. (Add the lines shown in bold.) Alternatively, you can copy the text to be inserted from the "First Code-Access Security Insert.txt" file included with the download materials for this book.

```
.
.
.
<CodeGroup
        class="FirstMatchCodeGroup"
        version="1"
        PermissionSetName="Nothing">
    <IMembershipCondition
            class="AllMembershipCondition"
            version="1"
    />
    <CodeGroup
            class="UnionCodeGroup"
            version="1"
            PermissionSetName="Execution"
            Name="WeatherWebServiceCodeGroup"
            Description="Code group for the Weather Web Service">
        <IMembershipCondition class="UrlMembershipCondition"
                version="1"
                Url="http://live.capescience.com/*"
        />
    </CodeGroup>
    <CodeGroup
        class="UnionCodeGroup"
        version="1"
        PermissionSetName="Execution"
        Name="Report_Expressions_Default_Permissions"
        Description="This code group grants default permissions for
                    code in report expressions and Code element. ">
.
.
.
.
```

4. Another parent code group uses ZoneMembershipCondition to assign Execution permissions to all .NET assemblies and web services in the MyComputer zone. We will add a new child code group right beneath this. Insert this new code group as

shown here (add the lines shown in bold). Note the Description and PublicKeyBlob should each be entered on one line. Alternatively, you can copy the text to be inserted from the "Second Code-Access Security Insert.txt" file included with the download materials for this book.

.
.
.

```
<CodeGroup
      class="FirstMatchCodeGroup"
      version="1"
      PermissionSetName="Execution"
      Description="This code group grants MyComputer code
      Execution permission. ">
  <IMembershipCondition
        class="ZoneMembershipCondition"
        version="1"
        Zone="MyComputer"/>
  <CodeGroup
        class="UnionCodeGroup"
        version="1"
        PermissionSetName="FullTrust"
        Name="MSSQLRSCodeGroup"
        Description="Code group for the MS SQL RS Book Custom
                                          Assemblies">
    <IMembershipCondition
            class="StrongNameMembershipCondition"
            version="1"
            PublicKeyBlob="002400000480000094000000060200000
                    240000525341310004000001000100B9F7
                    4F2D5B0AAD33AA619B00D7BB8B0F767839
                    3A0F4CD586C9036D72455F8D1E85BF635C
                    9FB1DA9817DD0F751DCEE77D9A47959E87
                    28028B9B6CC7C25EB1E59CB3DE01BB516D
                    46FC6AC6AF27AA6E71B65F6AB91B957688
                    6F2EF39417F17B567AD200E151FC744C6D
                    A72FF5882461E6CA786EB2997FA968302B
                    7B2F24BDBFF7A5"
                    />
  </CodeGroup>
  <CodeGroup
        class="UnionCodeGroup"
        version="1"
        PermissionSetName="FullTrust"
        Name="Microsoft_Strong_Name"
        Description="This code group grants code signed with the
                        Microsoft strong name full trust. ">
      <IMembershipCondition
            class="StrongNameMembershipCondition"
            version="1"
```

```
PublicKeyBlob="0024000004800000940000000602000000
               2400005253413100040000010001007D1
               FA57C4AED9F0A32E84AA0FAEFD0DE9E8FD
               6AEC8F87FB03766C834C99921EB23BE79A
               D9D5DCC1DD9AD236132102900B723CF980
               957FC4E177108FC607774F29E8320E92EA
               05ECE4E821C0A5EFE8F1645C4C0C93C1AB
               99285D622CAA652C1DFAD63D745D6F2DE5
               F17E5EAF0FC4963D261C8A12436518206D
               C093344D5AD293"
```

```
        />
     </CodeGroup>
```

5. Save the modified file, and exit your text editor.

NOTE

Looking at the rssrvpolicy.config file, you can see that expressions written within a report are granted Execute permissions. Because the WeatherInfo.GetWeather method is called from a report expression, by default, it should only be able to get Execute permissions. .NET Security says a process cannot get rights that exceed the rights granted to processes farther up the stack. The GetWeather method needs FullTrust rights to make the web service call. The GetWeather method uses a special process to assert that it needs to exceed the rights of the calling process and gain FullTrust rights. If you downloaded the source code for the WeatherInfo.dll, you can look to see how the assert is accomplished.

Uploading the Report

You are now ready to upload the Weather Report. Complete the following steps using the Report Manager:

1. Create a folder called **Chapter09** in the Galactic Delivery Services folder.
2. Open the Chapter09 folder, and upload the WeatherInfo.rdl file from the Chapter09 project folder.
3. Click the report WeatherReport to execute it. The report produces an error because the shared data source does not exist.
4. Click the WeatherReport link at the top of the page. The Properties page for WeatherReport appears.
5. Click the Data Sources link on the left side of the screen. The Data Sources page for an individual report appears.
6. A shared data source should be selected. Click Browse. The Select a Shared Data Source page appears.

7. Rather than create another shared data source, we are going to use the existing shared data source in the Galactic Delivery Services/Data Sources folder. Expand each folder in the tree view under Location until you can see the Galactic shared data source. Click the Galactic shared data source.

8. Click OK to exit the Select a Shared Data Source page.

9. Click Apply at the bottom of the page.

10. Click the WeatherReport title at the top of the page. Select one or more planets, and click View Report. The report now generates. (Remember, the .NET assembly calls a web service, so it requires an Internet connection.)

Try the Deploy One More Time

This last report upload required us to manually point the report to a shared data source in a different folder. This is because we do not want to have a shared data source in every report folder. If we had numerous shared data sources spread across a number of report folders, this would defeat much of the purpose of having shared data sources. When the database server name changes or the login credentials need to be updated, we would still have a major headache.

Instead, we want to have just one shared data source for each unique connection needed by our reports. This small group of shared data sources should be placed in one central location. That still leaves us with the task of manually pointing each report at the central group of shared data sources after each report upload.

You may recall there was a property on the report project's Property Pages dialog box specifying the folder path where the shared data source is to be deployed. Let's try deploying the Delivery Analysis Report from the authoring environment and see if this property can help us avoid all of the manual updating. Try the following:

1. Open the Chapter09 project in SSDT or Visual Studio.

2. From the main menu, select Project | Properties. (The menu may say "Chapter09 Properties" depending on what you happen to have selected at the time.) The Chapter09 Property Pages dialog box appears.

3. Enter **Galactic Delivery Services/Data Sources** for TargetDataSourceFolder.

4. Enter **Galactic Delivery Services/Chapter09/** for TargetReportFolder.

5. Enter **http://ComputerName/ReportServer** for TargetServerURL. Substitute the appropriate value for ComputerName as you did earlier in this chapter.

6. Click OK to close the Chapter09 Property Pages dialog box.

7. Select Save All from the toolbar.

8. Right-click the entry for the DeliveryAnalysis report in the Solution Explorer window, and select Deploy from the context menu.

9. Switch to the browser, and navigate to the Chapter09 folder.
10. Execute the DeliveryAnalysis report.
11. Select a number of service types from the drop-down list, and click View Report. The report displays using the shared data source found in the Data Sources folder.

A Look at Localization

You may recall we used the ReportUtil.dll assembly to present the report labels in both English and Spanish. (If you do not recall this, look at the instructions for this report in Chapter 9.) We passed the User!Language parameter to the LocalizedString method to retrieve a report label in the appropriate language. The User!Language parameter contains the language setting for the application requesting the report. When we are using the Report Manager, the browser is that application.

Let's try changing the language setting of the browser and see if our localization works the way it should. (The following directions apply to Internet Explorer.)

1. Select Tools | Internet Options from Internet Explorer's main menu. The Internet Options dialog box appears.
2. Click Languages. The Language Preference dialog box appears.
3. If an entry for Spanish (Mexico) [es-MX] is not in the Language list, click Add. The Add Language dialog box appears.
4. Highlight Spanish (Mexico) [es-MX] in the Language list, and click OK to exit the Add Language dialog box.
5. Highlight Spanish (Mexico) [es-MX] in the Language list, and click Move Up as many times as necessary to move the Spanish entry to the top of the list.
6. Click OK to exit the Language Preference dialog box. Click OK to exit the Internet Options dialog box.
7. Click the link for the Chapter09 folder, and then reexecute the Delivery Analysis report. The User!Language parameter now has a value of es-MX because you set the primary language of your browser to Spanish (Mexico). Because of this, the title of the report and the column headings are now in Spanish.
8. Use the Language Preference dialog box to remove the Spanish entry, if you created it in Steps 3 and 4. Make sure you return the correct language to the top of the Language list.

The ReportUtil.dll assembly has resource files for English and Spanish. English is the default language. If the parameter passed to the LocalizedString method is any of the cultural variations of Spanish, the method uses the Spanish resource file to look up the text for the report title or a column heading. If anything else is passed to the LocalizedString method, the English resource file is used.

Modifying Reports from the Report Server

In addition to uploading a report definition to the report server, it is possible to download a report definition, modify it, and send your modifications back to the report server as an update. You only need to do this if you do not have a copy of the RDL file for a report that is on the report server and needs to be modified. If you already have the report in a report project, you can edit that report using the Report Designer and then redeploy it.

Downloading a Report Definition

For this example, imagine we do not have the RDL file for the DeliveryAnalysis report and need to make a change to the report. The first task we need to complete is to download this report's RDL file from the report server to our local computer. Follow these steps:

1. Open the Report Manager in your browser, and navigate to the Chapter09 folder.
2. Hover over the entry for the DeliveryAnalysis report so the drop-down arrow appears.
3. Click the drop-down arrow, and select Download from the menu. The File Download dialog box or the File Download bar appears, depending on your version of Internet Explorer.
4. If the dialog box appears, click Save. If the bar appears across the bottom of the window, click the down arrow next to the Save button and select Save as. The Save As dialog box appears.
5. Browse to an appropriate temporary location on your computer. Leave the filename as DeliveryAnalysis.rdl. Click Save to exit the Save As dialog box. The file is downloaded and saved in the specified location.
6. Close the Download dialog box or the Download bar when the download is complete.

NOTE

If you have logon credentials stored in one or more data source definitions in the report, for security purposes, these are not saved in the resulting report definition file.

Editing the Report Definition

We now have the report definition file for the DeliveryAnalysis report copied from the report server to our local computer. However, an RDL file by itself is not useful. To edit it, we have to place it in a report project. Again, remember, for this example, we are imagining we do not already have the DeliveryAnalysis report in a report project. Here are the steps to follow:

1. Start SSDT or Visual Studio.
2. Create a new report project in the MSSQLRS folder called **EditDeliveryAnalysis**. (Do not use the Report Wizard.)

3. Right-click the Reports entry in the Solution Explorer, and select Add | Add Existing Item from the context menu. The Add Existing Item dialog box appears.

4. Navigate to the location where you stored the DeliveryAnalysis.rdl file in the previous section. Select the DeliveryAnalysis.rdl file, and click Add to exit the Add Existing Item dialog box.

5. Double-click the DeliveryAnalysis report to open it for editing. (If you encounter an error while trying to edit this report, save the project, close the Report Designer, restart it again, and reopen the EditDeliveryAnalysis project.)

6. Add a text box at the bottom of the report body saying, "This report is available in English and Spanish."

7. Click Save All in the toolbar.

8. Close the authoring environment.

Uploading the Modified Report Definition

Now that the report definition changes are completed, we are ready to upload the modified report.

1. Return to the Report Manager. Go to the Properties page for the DeliveryAnalysis report.

2. Click the Replace link in the toolbar. The Upload Report page appears.

3. Click Browse. The Choose File to Upload dialog box appears.

4. Navigate to the EditDeliveryAnalysis folder to find the updated version of the DeliveryAnalysis.rdl file.

NOTE

Do not select the copy of DeliveryAnalysis.rdl you originally downloaded. The modified version is in the folder with the EditDeliveryAnalysis report project.

5. Select DeliveryAnalysis.rdl, and click Open to exit the Choose File to Upload dialog box.

6. Click OK to upload the file.

7. Click the DeliveryAnalysis title at the top of the page to view the report.

8. Select several service types, and click View Report. The added text is now at the bottom of the page.

Managing Items in Folders

You now know how to load items into folders on the report server. Of course, we live in a dynamic world, so things seldom stay where they are originally put. We need to be able to move items around as we come up with better ways of organizing them. We also need to be able to delete items as they are replaced by something better or are simply not needed anymore. Fortunately, the Report Manager provides ways for us to do this housekeeping in an efficient manner.

Moving Items Between Folders

As an example, let's create a more descriptive folder for our Nametags Report and its supporting items. We begin by moving a single item to this new folder. Then, we look at a method for moving multiple items at the same time.

Moving a Single Item

Here are the steps to follow to move a single item:

1. Open the Report Manager in your browser, and navigate to the Galactic Delivery Services folder.
2. Click New Folder. The New Folder page appears.
3. Type **2013 Conference** for Name, and type **Materials for the 2013 User Conference** for Description.
4. Click OK to create the new folder.
5. Click Chapter06 to view the contents of this folder.
6. Hover over the entry for the Nametags report. Click the drop-down arrow, and select Move from the menu. The Move Item page appears.
7. Select the 2013 Conference folder in the tree view.
8. Click OK to move the report to this folder.
9. Navigate to 2013 Conference to view the contents of this folder.

Moving Multiple Items

You can see the Nametags report has been moved to the 2013 Conference folder. However, the report cannot function until the supporting items are also moved to this folder. Moving each item individually, as we did with the report, is rather time-consuming. Fortunately, there is another way.

1. Click the Galactic Delivery Services link at the top of the page.
2. Click Chapter06 to view the contents of this folder.

3. Click Details View to return to the details view. In the detail view, you see check boxes next to each item in the folder. These check boxes work with the Delete and Move buttons in the toolbar. When you click Delete, any checked items are deleted. Likewise, when you click Move, any checked items are moved.

4. Check the uppermost check box (the check box to the left of the word "Type"). Checking this check box selects all items in the folder. Unchecking this check box deselects all items in the folder. Because we are moving all the items in the folder, we want all the items to be selected.

5. Click Move in the Contents tab toolbar. The Move Multiple Items page appears.

6. Select the 2013 Conference folder in the tree view.

7. Click OK to move these items to this folder.

This method works for moving a single item, multiple items, or the entire contents of a folder. Just check the items you want to move and click the Move button. Remember, you need to be in the detail view when using this method.

This section demonstrated moving reports and supporting items. You can also move whole folders using the same techniques.

Deleting a Folder

The Chapter06 folder is now empty and ready to be deleted. As with the Move function, you can accomplish this in two ways. The first way is to view the Properties tab for the folder you want to delete and then click the Delete button. Just for fun, we'll try the second method.

Deleting a Folder Using the Check Boxes and Toolbar

1. Click the Galactic Delivery Services link at the top of the page to view the contents of this folder.

2. Check the Chapter06 folder.

3. Click Delete. The confirmation dialog box appears.

4. Click OK to confirm your deletion. The Chapter06 folder is deleted.

Folders do not need to be emptied before they are deleted. If the Chapter06 folder had contained reports, supporting items, or even other folders, these would have been deleted along with the folder.

Renaming a Folder

In addition to moving and deleting items, we may want to rename items. Let's give the Chapter07 folder a more descriptive name.

1. Hover over the Chapter07 entry. Click the drop-down arrow, and select Manage from the menu. The Chapter07 Properties tab appears.
2. Replace the contents of Name by typing **Map Reports**. Then type **Reports for analyzing geographic information** for Description.
3. Click Apply.
4. Click the Galactic Delivery Services link at the top of the page.
5. Click Tile View.

This same technique makes it just as easy to change the names and descriptions for reports and other items. However, just because it is easy to make these changes does not mean you should do it often. Once users become familiar with a folder name, a report name, or a report's location within the folder structure, you should change it only if you have a good reason to do so.

You may have noted that we could have changed the name of the Chapter06 folder rather than going through the move and delete processes of the previous sections. This is true; we could have simply changed the folder name. If we had done that, though, you would not know how to do moves and deletes!

Seek and Ye Shall Find: Search and Find Functions

The Report Manager provides two features to help users find information. The Search function helps the user locate a report within the report server folder structure, and the Find function enables the user to jump to a certain piece of information while viewing a report.

Searching for a Report

First, we look at the Search function. This function lets the user enter a portion of a word, a complete word, or a phrase. The Report Manager then searches the names and descriptions of items in the report server folder structure for occurrences of this text. The Report Manager does not search the contents of a report or supporting files.

For example, searching for "GDS Report" would find "The GDS Report" and "GDS Reporting." It would not find "Report GDS Income" or "GDS Accounting Report." This is strictly a search for the text exactly as it is entered—no Boolean logic, proximity searching, or other features you find in Internet search engines. Also, the search is not case-sensitive.

Follow these steps to use the Search function:

1. Open the Report Manager in your browser, and navigate to the Home folder.
2. Type **report** in the Search box in the upper-right corner of the screen, and then click the magnifying glass. The Search page is displayed with the search results.
3. The Report Manager lists several items of various types. No weighting or relevance is assigned to each result. Click an item to see its contents.
4. Click your browser's Back button to return to the search results.

Finding Text Within a Report

Next, we look at the Find function. This function also enables the user to enter a portion of a word, a complete word, or a phrase. The Report Manager then searches the contents of the current report for occurrences of this text. Next, it highlights the first occurrence that it finds. The user can use the Next button to move to the next occurrence.

As with the Search function, Find locates text just as it is entered—no Boolean logic or proximity searching. Also, Find is not case-sensitive. Find will, however, find occurrences of the string on pages beyond the page being viewed, all the way to the end of the report.

We use the DeliveryAnalysis report to demonstrate the Find function. Navigate to this report in the Chapter09 folder, and run the report. Select All for the Select Service Types parameter. The DeliveryAnalysis report looks at the delivery statistics for each Galactic customer. Suppose we want to look at just the manufacturing companies sprinkled throughout the report. Rather than skimming through the report, looking for what we are interested in, here is a better way:

1. Type **mfg** in the entry area to the left of the words "Find | Next" in the Report Viewer toolbar.
2. Click Find. The first manufacturing company is found: Bolimite, Mfg. The "Mfg" is highlighted.
3. Click Next. (Make sure you do not click Find. Clicking Find simply starts the find operation again from the top of the page.) The next manufacturing company is found: Phillips Mfg, Inc.
4. Click Next. Quincy, Mfg is found. You many need to scroll down to see this.

Report Output Formats

Up to this point, we have been viewing reports in the preview format in SSDT, Visual Studio, or Report Builder. In the Report Manager, we have viewed reports in HTML format in the browser. Both the report authoring environments and Report Manager offer a number of other options for report output.

Exporting Reports in Other Formats

To export a report in another format from Report Manager, use the Export drop-down list as shown in Figure 10-16. Select your desired format from the menu. Then, follow the instructions in the resulting dialog box to either save the exported report or view it on the screen in the appropriate viewer.

Presentation Rendering Formats

A number of formats can be presented to a user. These *presentation rendering formats* retain the layout, fonts, colors, and graphics of the report. A complete list of the presentation rendering formats is as follows:

▶ Preview

▶ HTML

▶ TIFF Image

▶ Adobe PDF

▶ MHTML (web archive)

▶ Excel

▶ Word

▶ Print

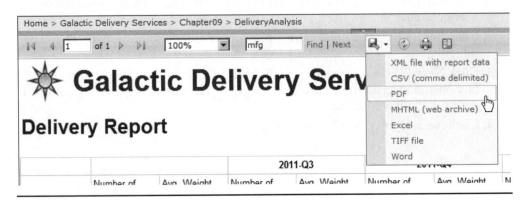

Figure 10-16 *The Export drop-down list*

The presentation rendering formats can be further divided into three groups. The *interactive presentation rendering formats,* preview and Hypertext Markup Language (HTML), support all of the interactive features of Reporting Services. The *physical page presentation formats,* TIFF Image, Adobe PDF, Word, and Print, are primarily concerned with fitting content on a specific page size that can become a printout on a physical piece of paper. The *logical page presentation formats,* MHTML (web archive) and Excel, are primarily concerned with formatting the content for viewing on a screen.

NOTE

By default, the Excel export is the Open XML format compatible with Excel 2007 and Excel 2010. In the RSReportServer.config file, this is called the EXCELOPENXML rendering extension. There is also an EXCEL rendering extension, which creates files compatible with Excel 2003 and earlier. To use this EXCEL rendering format, you must set the Visible property to True for this rendering format in the RSReportServer.config file. (See the RSReportServer.config File section of Chapter 12 for information on locating and modifying the RSReportServer .config file.)

Data Exchange Rendering Formats

Reporting Services also lets you export your report to two additional formats, which are used primarily for rendering report data into a form that can be used by other computer programs. These *data exchange rendering formats* contain the data portion of the report, along with a minimal amount of formatting. Here are the data exchange rendering formats:

▶ Comma-Separated Values (CSV)

▶ Extensible Markup Language (XML)

The XML Export Format

Unlike the other export formats, Reporting Services includes several report properties that allow you to customize the output of the XML export format. By default, XML exports include the data contained within tablixes and charts in your report. All the data from the tablix or chart is included in the XML export, even if a column or a row is hidden. XML exports do not contain values from text boxes that are not within a tablix.

Because each item in the XML export is labeled with an XML tag, reports to be exported using the XML format can be more complex than those exported using the CSV format. Thus, reports to be exported using the XML format may have more than one tablix or chart.

The following is a section of an XML file that results from a report:

```xml
<Report xsi:schemaLocation=... >
 <matrix1>
  <matrix1_CustomerName_Collection>
   <matrix1_CustomerName CustomerName="Bolimite, Mfg">
    <matrix1_RowGroup2_Collection>
     <matrix1_RowGroup2 textbox6="Previous Day Delivery">
      <matrix1_Year_Collection>
       <matrix1_Year Year="2007">
        <matrix1_ColumnGroup2_Collection>
         <matrix1_ColumnGroup2 textbox5="Sep" DeliveryNumber="0" />
         <matrix1_ColumnGroup2 textbox5="Oct" DeliveryNumber="0" />
         <matrix1_ColumnGroup2 textbox5="Nov" DeliveryNumber="2" />
         <matrix1_ColumnGroup2 textbox5="Dec" DeliveryNumber="1" />
        </matrix1_ColumnGroup2_Collection>
       </matrix1_Year>
```

You can quickly see how the XML structure follows the report layout. The Report tag provides information about the report as a whole. After that tag is a series of tags containing the data in a tablix.

Customizing the XML Data Exchange Format You can customize the XML export to fit your needs. Each item on the report contains three properties that control whether or not the item appears in an XML export and, if it does, how it is formatted.

▶ **DataElementName** The DataElementName property controls the element name used in the XML structure for a particular item. If this is not specified for an item, the name of the item in the report definition is used as the data element name in any XML export.

▶ **DataElementOutput** The DataElementOutput property controls whether or not a particular item is included in any XML export. By default, only those items in a tablix or chart are included.

▶ **DataElementStyle** The DataElementStyle property controls how an item's output is formatted in any XML export. By default, an item's data is presented as attributes. This property enables us to present an item's data in an element format.

The Atom Data Feed

In addition to the two data exchange rendering formats, it is possible to make report content available for use by PowerPivot for Excel. Specifically, you can make the

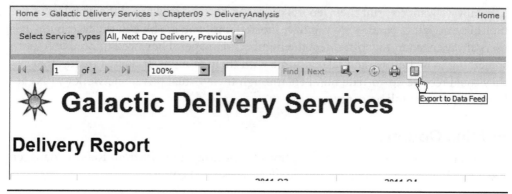

Figure 10-17 *The Export to Data Feed button*

content of the data regions in a report available as an atom data feed. An *atom data feed* allows PowerPivot to execute the report using the Atom rendering format and then import the report data for further analysis.

To accomplish this, PowerPivot must know the appropriate URL to use to execute your report and have it rendered in the Atom format. Report Manager offers a way to automatically generate this URL and make it available to PowerPivot. This is the Export to Data Feed button in the toolbar shown in Figure 10-17.

When you click the Export to Data Feed button, Report Manager generates an XML document known as a data service document. The data service document contains, among other things, the URL needed by PowerPivot. The data service document is sent to your browser causing a File Download dialog box to display. You have the option to open, save, or cancel. If you have Excel 2010 and PowerPivot for Excel installed on the computer where the browser is running, you can click the Open button. This causes PowerPivot to open and import the data from the report.

If you do not have PowerPivot for Excel installed on the computer where the browser is running, or if you wish to launch PowerPivot at a later time, you can click the Save button. This brings up a Save As dialog box allowing you to save the data service document to a file with an .atomsvc extension. When you use PowerPivot to open a data service document, it reads the URL from the document and then uses the URL to execute the report, rendering it in the Atom format, and importing the resulting report data. Obviously, PowerPivot must have a path to the report server in order for the data service document to be utilized successfully.

Printing from Report Manager

No matter how convenient you make it for your users to access reports in a browser, and no matter how many interactive drilldown and drillthrough features you provide, your users always want to print their reports on paper. You can explain all the wonders of the multiple, cascading parameters you have created until you are blue in the face, but some users always need to touch and feel the numbers on paper. They need to be able to put something in a briefcase and take it home with them at night. It doesn't matter that they could receive up-to-date numbers through their virtual private network (VPN) at home. They want ink on paper.

Printing Options

Reporting Services provides several options for printing a report from Report Manager. Each provides some advantages and disadvantages for the user.

HTML Printing   These users could just print from their browser and get whatever type of printout HTML printing provides. As you are probably aware, HTML printing is not a good choice when formatting is important, as it usually is for reports. Lines of text can wrap in unusual ways or simply be cut off. A line of text at the bottom of the page can even be cut right in half, with the top half on one page and the bottom half on the next page.

Fortunately, the Report Manager provides a couple of alternatives to HTML printing.

Printing from a PDF Document or TIFF File   A Portable Document Format (PDF) document or a Tagged Image File Format (TIFF) file does an excellent job of maintaining report format when a report is printed. Therefore, when users want to have a high-quality report printout, they can export the report to a PDF document or a TIFF file. Once this is complete, they can view the exported report using the appropriate viewer: Adobe Acrobat Reader for the PDF document or the Windows Picture and Fax Viewer for a TIFF file. The report can then be printed using the viewer.

This process provides the user with a quality printout. However, not all users are comfortable with saving a file to a local disk, finding that file and opening it in the appropriate viewer, and then printing the report. There is another printing alternative, which is even more straightforward.

Client-Side Printing   You may have noticed a button with a printer icon on the Report Manager toolbar. This button is for the client-side printing feature of Reporting Services. *Client-side printing* works through an ActiveX object downloaded to the user's computer. From then on, whenever the Client-Side Printing button is clicked, this ActiveX object provides the user interface and controls the printing.

The first time a user activates the client-side printing feature, they may be prompted with a security warning about the ActiveX download. After taking the appropriate precautions, such as making sure the ActiveX object is signed by Microsoft, the user should approve the download to enable client-side printing. Once the ActiveX object has been downloaded by this first use, it does not need to be downloaded again.

If a user has trouble downloading the ActiveX control, they may need to set the Report Manager as a trusted site in their browser. This is done on the Security tab of the Internet Options dialog box. The user should not lower their security setting for all sites in general to accomplish the ActiveX download.

Once downloaded, client-slide printing enables users to set various report attributes. These include margins, page size, and even page orientation. Users can also preview a report before putting it on paper.

Managing Reports on the Report Server

With reports in place on the report server, you may be thinking your job is about done, but it is just beginning. At this point you need to manage the reports and supporting materials to ensure the reports can be utilized properly by your users.

Two of the biggest concerns when it comes to managing reports are security and performance. Reports containing sensitive data must be secured so they are only accessible by the appropriate people. Reports must return information to users in a reasonable amount of time without putting undo stress on database resources. Fortunately, Reporting Services provides tools for managing both of these concerns. Security roles and item-level security give you extremely fine control over just who has access to each report and resource. Caching, snapshots, and history let you control how and when reports are executed.

Security

In Reporting Services, security was designed with both flexibility and ease of management in mind. Flexibility is provided by the fact that individual access rights can be assigned to each folder and to each item within a folder. An item is either a report or a resource. You can specify exactly who has rights to each item and exactly what those rights are. Ease of management is provided by security inheritance, security roles, and integration with Windows security. We begin our discussion with the last entry in this list.

NOTE

Remember, although we are creating and maintaining these role assignments using the Report Manager, the security rights apply to Reporting Services as a whole. No matter how you access folders and items—through the Report Manager or through the web service—these security rights are enforced.

Integration with Windows Security

Reporting Services does not maintain its own list of users and passwords. Instead, in its default configuration, it depends entirely on integration with Windows security. When a user accesses either the Report Manager web application or the web service, that user must authenticate with the report server. In other words, the user must have either a valid domain user name and password or a local user name and password to log on to the report server. Both the Report Manager web application and the web service are set up requiring integrated Windows authentication to ensure this logon takes place.

> **NOTE**
>
> *If it is impossible for each report user to have their own credentials on the report server, it is possible to configure Reporting Services to use forms-based security through a custom security extension.*

Once this logon occurs, Reporting Services utilizes the user name and the user's group memberships to determine what rights the user possesses. The user can access only those folders and items they have rights to. In the Report Manager, users do not even see the folders they cannot browse and reports they cannot run. There is no temptation for the user to try and figure out how to get into places they are not supposed to go, because they do not even know these places exist.

Local Administrator Privileges

In most cases, rights must be explicitly assigned to folders and items. There is, however, one security assignment that is created by default. Any user who is a member of the local administrators group on the computer hosting the report server has content manager rights to all folders and all items. This is done through the BUILTIN\ Administrators designation on the report server.

Let's look at the Security page.

1. Open the Report Manager in your browser, and navigate to the Home folder.
2. Click the Folder Settings toolbar button. You see the Security page for the Home folder, as shown in Figure 10-18.

The report server maintains a Security page for each item in the Report Catalog— every folder, every report, and every supporting item. The Security page lists all the role assignments for an item. Each role assignment is made up of two things: a Windows user or group and a security role. The rights associated with the security role are assigned to the Windows user or group.

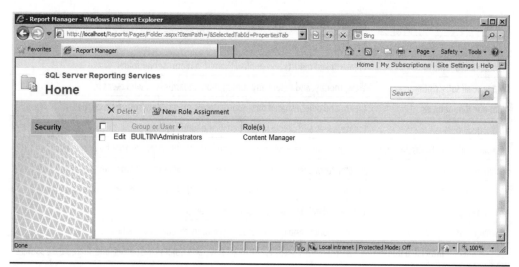

Figure 10-18 *The Security page for the Home folder*

Initially, one role assignment is on the Security page for each item. This entry assigns the Content Manager security role to the BUILTIN\Administrators group. This entry is the default entry that grants any user who is a member of the local administrators group rights to manage the contents of this folder.

Tasks and Rights

You can perform a number of tasks in Reporting Services, each with its corresponding right. For example, you can view reports. Therefore, a corresponding right exists to view reports. The tasks within Reporting Services are shown in Table 10-1.

You may not be familiar with some of these tasks. We discuss linked reports in the section "Linked Reports," and we discuss report history snapshots and subscriptions in Chapter 11. For now, you simply need to know these are tasks with associated rights within Reporting Services.

In addition to the tasks listed in Table 10-1, there are system-wide tasks with associated rights. These system-wide tasks deal with the management and operation of Reporting Services as a whole. The system-wide tasks within Reporting Services are shown in Table 10-2.

Again, you may not be familiar with all the tasks in this list. We discuss jobs and shared schedules in Chapter 11.

Task	Description
Consume reports	Read report definitions.
Create linked reports	Create linked reports and publish them to a report server folder.
Manage all subscriptions	View, modify, and delete any subscription, regardless of who owns it.
Manage data sources	Create and delete shared data source items; modify data source properties.
Manage folders	Create, view, and delete folders; view and modify folder properties.
Manage individual subscriptions	Each user can create, view, modify, and delete subscriptions that he or she owns.
Manage models	Create, view, and delete models; view and modify model properties.
Manage report history	Create, view, and delete report history snapshots; modify report history properties.
Manage reports	Create and delete reports; modify report properties.
Manage resources	Create, modify, and delete resources; modify resource properties.
Set security for individual items	View and modify security settings for reports, folders, resources, and shared data sources.
View data sources	View shared data source items in the folder hierarchy; view data source properties.
View folders	View folder items in the folder hierarchy; view folder properties.
View models	View models in the folder hierarchy, use models as data sources for a report, and run queries against the model to retrieve data.
View reports	View reports and linked reports in the folder hierarchy; view report history snapshots and report properties.
View resources	View resources in the folder hierarchy; view resource properties.

Table 10-1   *Security Tasks Within Reporting Services*

Task	Description
Execute report definitions	Start execution from report definition without publishing it to the report server.
Generate events	Provides an application with the ability to generate events within the report server namespace.
Manage jobs	View and cancel running jobs.
Manage report server properties	View and modify properties that apply to the report server and to items managed by the report server.
Manage report server security	View and modify system-wide role assignments.
Manage roles	Create, view, modify, and delete role definitions.
Manage shared schedules	Create, view, modify, and delete shared schedules used to run reports or refresh a report.
View report server properties	View properties that apply to the report server.
View shared schedules	View a predefined schedule that has been made available to general use.

Table 10-2   *System-Wide Security Tasks Within Reporting Services*

Roles

The rights to perform tasks are grouped together to create *roles*. Reporting Services includes several predefined roles to help you with security management. In addition, you can create your own custom roles, grouping together any combination of rights that you like. The predefined roles and their corresponding rights are discussed here.

The Browser Role   The Browser role is the basic role assigned to users who are going to view reports but who are not going to create folders or upload new reports. The Browser role has rights to perform the following tasks:

▶ Manage individual subscriptions

▶ View folders

▶ View models

▶ View reports

▶ View resources

The Publisher Role   The Publisher role is assigned to users who are going to create folders and upload reports. The Publisher role does not have rights to change security settings or manage subscriptions and report history. The Publisher role has rights to perform the following tasks:

▶ Create linked reports

▶ Manage data sources

▶ Manage folders

▶ Manage models

▶ Manage reports

▶ Manage resources

The My Reports Role   The My Reports role is designed to be used only with a special folder called the My Reports folder. Within this folder, the My Reports role gives the user rights to do everything except change security settings. The My Reports role has rights to perform the following tasks:

▶ Create linked reports

▶ Manage data sources

- ▶ Manage folders
- ▶ Manage individual subscriptions
- ▶ Manage report history
- ▶ Manage reports
- ▶ Manage resources
- ▶ View data sources
- ▶ View folders
- ▶ View reports
- ▶ View resources

The Content Manager Role   The Content Manager role is assigned to users who are managing the folders, reports, and resources. The Content Manager role has rights to perform all tasks, excluding system-wide tasks.

The Report Builder Role   The Report Builder role gives users the right to create and edit reports using Report Builder. The Report Builder role has rights to perform the following tasks:

- ▶ Consume reports
- ▶ Manage individual subscriptions
- ▶ View folders
- ▶ View models
- ▶ View report definitions
- ▶ View reports
- ▶ View resources

The System User Role   The system-wide security tasks have two predefined roles. The System User role has rights to perform the following system-wide tasks:

- ▶ Execute report definitions
- ▶ View report server properties
- ▶ View shared schedules

NOTE

If a user is not a member of the System User role, they will not see the toolbar button to launch Report Builder.

The System Administrator Role   The System Administrator role provides the user with rights to complete any of the tasks necessary to manage the report server. This role has rights to perform the following system-wide tasks:

► Execute report definitions

► Manage jobs

► Manage report server properties

► Manage report server security

► Manage roles

► Manage shared schedules

Creating Role Assignments

As stated previously, role assignments are created when a Windows user or a Windows group is assigned a role for a folder, a report, or a resource. Role assignments are created on the Security page for the folder, report, or resource. These role assignments control what the user can see within a folder and what tasks the user can perform on the folder, report, or resource.

Let's try creating role assignments for some of our folders and reports.

NOTE

To complete the next set of procedures, you need a user who has rights to log on to the report server, but who is not a member of the local administrators group on that computer. You should know the password for this user so you can log on as that user and view the results of your security settings.

Creating a Role Assignment for a Folder   Let's try creating a new role assignment for the Home folder.

1. Open the Report Manager in your browser. Navigate to the Home folder, if not already there.
2. Click Folder Settings in the toolbar. You see the Security page for this folder.
3. Click New Role Assignment. The New Role Assignment page appears, as shown in Figure 10-19.
4. Type the name of a valid user for Group or User Name. If you are using a domain user or domain group, this must be in the format DomainName\UserName or DomainName\GroupName. If you are using a local user or local group, this must be in the format ComputerName\UserName or ComputerName\GroupName.

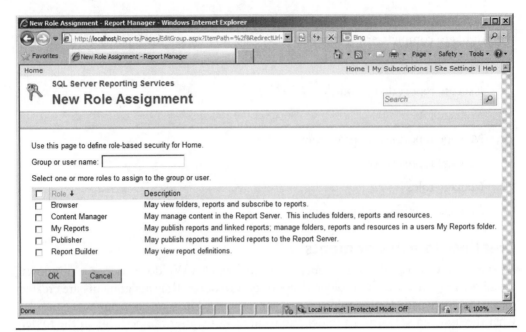

Figure 10-19 *The New Role Assignment page*

5. Check the check box for the Browser role.

6. Click OK to save your role assignment and return to the Security page. Reporting Services makes sure you entered a valid user or group for the role assignment. If this is not a valid user or group, you receive an error message and your role assignment is not saved.

NOTE

A user needs to have at least viewing rights in the Home folder to view other folders and navigate to them.

Inherited Role Assignments   By default, folders (other than the Home folder), reports, and resources inherit their role assignments from the folder that contains them. You can think of the nested folders as branches of a tree, with the reports and resources as the leaves. Inherited security means you can make security changes to one folder and have those changes take effect for all the branches and leaves further along the tree.

This makes managing security easy. You can maintain security for all the reports and resources within a folder simply by modifying the role assignments for the folder itself. You can maintain security for an entire branch of the tree structure by modifying the role assignments for the folder that forms the base of that branch. Let's look at the security for the Galactic Delivery Services folder.

1. Click the Home link at the top of the page.
2. Select the Galactic Delivery Services folder to view its contents.
3. Click Folder Settings. You see the Properties page for this folder.
4. Select Security on the left side of the page. You see the Security page for this folder.

The Galactic Delivery Services folder is inheriting its role assignments from the Home folder. You did not add a role assignment giving Browser rights to your user in this folder and, yet, there it is! As soon as you added the role assignment to the Home folder, it appeared for all the items within the Home folder.

You gave your user Browser rights in the Home folder so they could view the contents of the Home folder and then navigate into other folders to find the reports they need. You may want to give this user additional rights in folders further along in the tree. Perhaps the user can manage the content of certain folders that belong to their department, but can only browse when in the Home folder.

To accomplish this task, you must first break the inherited security for the Galactic Delivery Services folder.

1. Click Edit Item Security. A dialog box with an inherited security message appears. The Report Manager is confirming you want to break that inheritance by creating your own role assignments for this folder.
2. Click OK to confirm you want to break the inherited security.

Now that you have broken the inherited security, you have new buttons on the toolbar for adding a new role assignment, deleting existing role assignments, and reverting to inherited security.

Now you can edit the role assignment for your user.

1. Click the Edit link next to the role assignment giving your user Browser rights. The Edit Role Assignment page appears.
2. Uncheck the check box for the Browser role.
3. Check the check box for the Content Manager role.
4. Click Apply to save the changes to your role assignment and return to the Security page. The user now has Content Manager rights in the Galactic Delivery Services folder.

5. Click the Home link at the top of the page, and then navigate to the Galactic Delivery Services folder.

6. Select the Map Reports folder (formerly the Chapter07 folder) to view its contents.

7. Click Folder Settings. You see the Properties page for this folder.

8. Select Security on the left side of the page. You see the Security page for this folder.

You can see the folder is inheriting its role assignments from the Galactic Delivery Services folder.

NOTE

Although we do not do so in these exercises, you can check more than one role when creating or editing a role assignment. The user's rights are then the sum of the rights granted by each role.

Managing Role Assignments for Reports   Now, let's try managing role assignments for reports.

1. Click the Galactic Delivery Services link at the top of the page, and then navigate to the Map Reports folder.

2. Hover over the Deliveries Per Planet Report, and select Security from the drop-down menu. The Security page for this report appears.

Again, you can see this report is inheriting its role assignments from the folder that contains it. Because the user has Content Manager rights for the folder, the user also has Content Manager rights for the report. This means the user can change any and all properties of this report and even delete the report altogether.

To continue our security example, we are going to suppose it is all right for the user to have Content Manager rights for the Map Reports folder, but not for the Deliveries Per Planet Report. We need to edit the role assignment for your user. However, before we can do this, we must break the inheritance, as explained in the following steps:

1. Click Edit Item Security. The confirmation dialog box appears.

2. Click OK to confirm.

3. Click the Edit link next to the role assignment giving your user Content Manager rights. The Edit Role Assignment page appears.

4. Uncheck the check box for the Content Manager role.

5. Check the check box for the Browser role.

6. Click Apply to save the changes to your role assignment and return to the Security page.

Now we modify the rights granted to this user for the Earth US Deliveries Report. In our example, we assume the user should have limited rights to this report. In fact, they should only be able to view the report. In this case, the predefined Browser role has too many rights. We have to define our own custom role.

To do this, we need to use the SQL Server Management Studio. Follow these steps:

1. In the Windows Start menu, select All Programs | Microsoft SQL Server 2012 | SQL Server Management Studio. The SQL Server Management Studio will start up, and the Connect to Server dialog box will appear.

2. Select Reporting Services from the Server type drop-down list, as shown in Figure 10-20.

3. Enter the name of the report server for Server name.

4. Click Connect. The SQL Server Management Studio will connect to the report server.

5. Expand the Security entry in the Object Explorer window. Next, expand the Roles entry in the Object Explorer window. You will see the five default security roles, as shown in Figure 10-21.

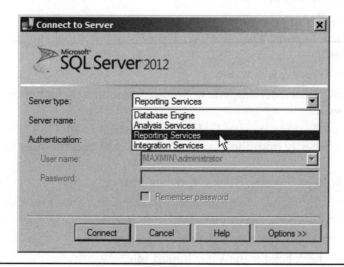

Figure 10-20 *The SQL Server Management Studio Connect to Server dialog box*

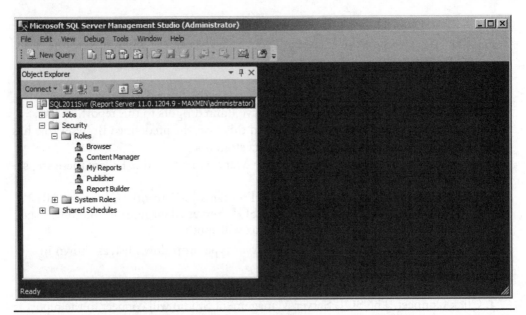

Figure 10-21   *The default Reporting Services security roles*

6. Right-click the Roles entry in the Object Explorer window, and select New Role from the context menu. The New User Role dialog box appears.

7. Type **View Report** for Name.

8. Type **View Report Only** for Description.

9. Check View Reports. The New User Role dialog box should appear as shown in Figure 10-22.

10. Click OK to save this new role.

11. Exit the SQL Server Management Studio, and return to the Report Manager in your browser.

12. Navigate to the Map Reports folder, hover over the Earth US Deliveries Report, and select Security from the drop-down menu. The Security page for this report appears.

13. Click Edit Item Security. Click OK to confirm.

14. Click the Edit link next to the role assignment giving your user Content Manager rights. The Edit Role Assignment page appears.

15. Uncheck the check box for the Content Manager role.

16. Check the check box for the View Report role.

17. Click Apply to save the changes to your role assignment and return to the Security page. The user has rights to view the Earth US Deliveries Report, but no other rights with that report.

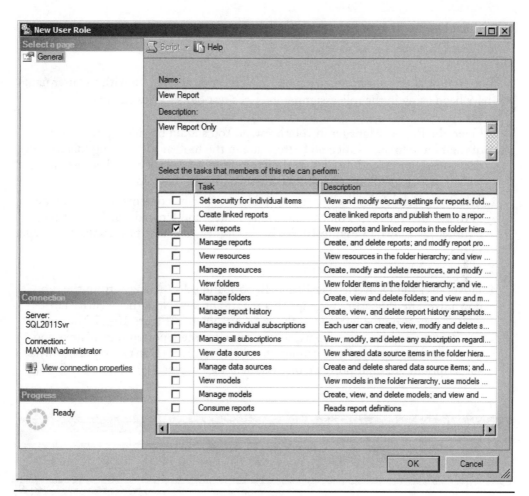

Figure 10-22 *The View Report role in the New User Role dialog box*

We make one more change to test security. We remove all rights assigned to this user for the Employee Homes report.

1. Click the Map Reports link at the top of the page.
2. Hover over the Employee Homes Report, and select Security from the drop-down menu. The Security page for this report appears.
3. Click Edit Item Security. Click OK to confirm.
4. Check the check box next to the role assignment giving your user Content Manager rights.

5. Click Delete. The confirmation dialog box appears.
6. Click OK to confirm the deletion.

You can now close your browser, log out of Windows, and log on with the user name you have been using in the role assignments. Let's test our security changes.

1. Open the Report Manager in your browser. You should be viewing the contents of the Home folder. Notice no buttons are in the toolbar for creating folders and data sources or uploading files, as shown in Figure 10-23. That is because the user you are now logged on as has only Browser rights in this folder.
2. Select the Galactic Delivery Services folder to view its contents. When you are in this folder, the New Folder, New Data Source, and Upload File buttons have returned, as shown in Figure 10-24. In this folder, your user has Content Manager rights.
3. Select the Map Reports folder to view its contents.
4. Hover over the Deliveries Per Planet Report, and select Manage from the drop-down list. The Properties page for this report appears. Note the Security tab doesn't appear on the left side of the page, as shown in Figure 10-25. Your user has Browser rights to this report, so you can view the report and its history and create subscriptions, but you cannot change its security. (Don't worry about what subscriptions are right now; we discuss them in Chapter 11.)

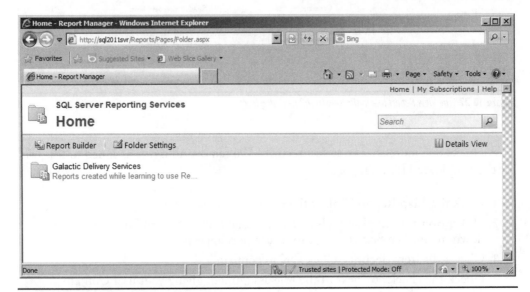

Figure 10-23 *Browser rights in the Home folder*

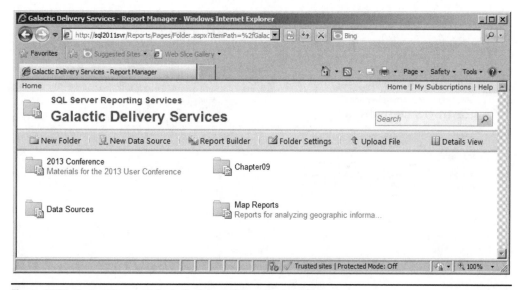

Figure 10-24 *Content Manager rights in the Galactic Delivery Services folder*

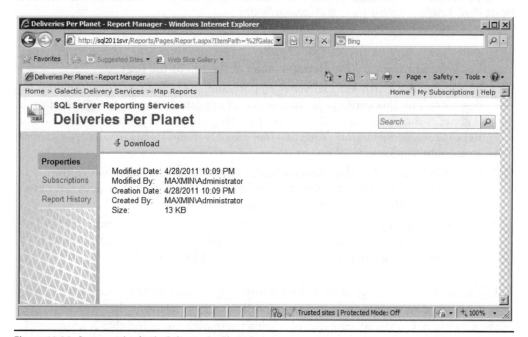

Figure 10-25 *Browser rights for the Deliveries Per Planet Report*

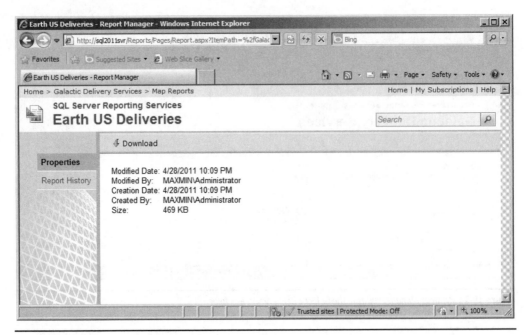

Figure 10-26 *View Report rights for the Earth US Deliveries Report*

5. Click the link for the Map Reports folder at the top of the page.

6. Hover over the Earth US Deliveries Report, and select Manage from the drop-down list. The Properties page for this report appears. Now, the Subscriptions tab is gone, as shown in Figure 10-26. Your user has the rights from our custom View Report role for this report. You can view the report and its history, but you cannot create subscriptions.

7. Click the link for the Map Reports folder at the top of the page. Notice the Employee Homes Report is nowhere to be seen because your user does not have any rights for this report, not even the rights to view it.

8. Hover over the Deliveries Per Planet Report, and select Security from the drop-down list. Your user does not have rights to modify the security settings of this report, so they will receive an error page as shown in Figure 10-27.

Giving users only the rights they need is important. This prevents users from viewing data they should not see or from making modifications or deletions they should not be allowed to make. On the other hand, providing users with enough rights is important so their reports function properly.

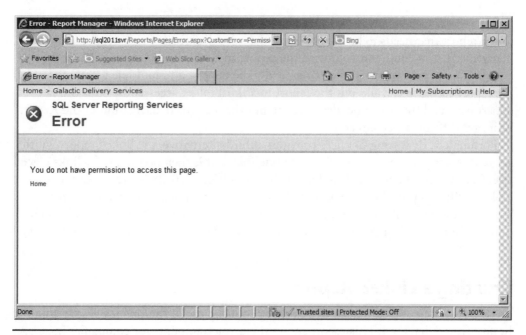

Figure 10-27 *Permissions error message*

Role Assignments Using Windows Groups

As mentioned previously, role assignments can be made to Windows users or to Windows groups. If you create your role assignments using Windows users, you need to create a new set of role assignments every time a new user needs to access Reporting Services. This can be extremely tedious if you have a complex set of role assignments for various folders, reports, and resources.

In most cases, creating role assignments using Windows groups is better. Then, as new users come along, you simply need to add them to the Windows group that has the appropriate rights in Reporting Services. This is much easier!

Linked Reports

In many cases, the security set up within Reporting Services restricts the folders a user can access. The sales department may be allowed to access one set of folders. The personnel department may be allowed to access another set of folders. The personnel department doesn't want to see sales reports and, certainly, some personnel reports should not be seen by everyone in the sales department.

This works well—a place for everything and everything in its place—until you come to the report that needs to be used by both the sales department and the personnel department. You could put a copy of the report in both places, but this gets to be a nightmare as new versions of reports need to be deployed to multiple locations on the report server. You could put the report in a third folder accessed by both the sales department and the personnel department, but that can make navigation in the Report Manager difficult and confusing.

Fortunately, Reporting Services provides a third alternative: the linked report. With a *linked report,* your report is deployed to one folder. It is then pointed to by links placed elsewhere within the Report Catalog, as shown in Figure 10-28. To the user, the links look just like a report. Because of these links, the report appears to be in many places. The sales department sees it in their folder. The personnel department sees it in their folder. The fact of the matter is the report is only deployed to one location, so it is easy to administer and maintain.

Creating a Linked Report

To demonstrate a linked report, we are going to make use of the Invoice-Batch Number Report from Chapter 4. This report shows the invoice amounts for companies in various cities. Galactic Delivery Services has sales offices in each of these cities, and each sales office has its own folder within the GDS Report Catalog.

A sales office should be able to access the Invoice-Batch Number Report in their own folder and see the invoices for customers in their city.

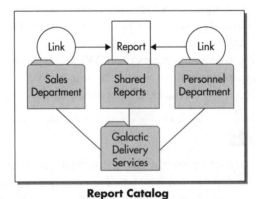

Report Catalog

Figure 10-28 *A linked report*

Deploying the Report to a Common Folder

We begin by deploying the report to a common folder. Here are the steps to follow:

1. Log in with a user name and password that has Content Manager rights in Reporting Services.

NOTE

If you created the reports for Chapter 4 using the Report Builder, then manually create the Shared Reports folder in the Galactic Delivery Services folder and move the Invoice-Batch Number Report into this new folder.

2. Start SSDT or Visual Studio, and open the Chapter04 project.
3. Modify the properties of the Chapter04 project as follows:

Property	Value
TargetDataSourceFolder	Galactic Delivery Services/Data Sources
TargetReportFolder	Galactic Delivery Services/Shared Reports
TargetServerURL	http://ServerName/ReportServer

4. Replace ServerName with the appropriate server name or with localhost.
5. Deploy the Invoice-Batch Number Report.
6. Close the development environment.

Creating Linked Reports

Now that the report is in the Shared Reports folder, it is time to create our linked reports.

1. Open the Report Manager in your browser, and navigate to the Galactic Delivery Services folder.
2. Create a new folder. Type **Axelburg** for Name and **Axelburg Sales Office** for Description.
3. Create another new folder. Type **Utonal** for Name and **Utonal Sales Office** for Description.
4. Navigate to the Shared Reports folder.
5. Hover over the Invoice-Batch Number Report, and select Manage from the drop-down menu.
6. Click Create Linked Report. The Create Linked Report page appears.
7. Type **Invoice-Batch Number Report** for Name and **Axelburg invoices in each batch** for Description.

8. Click Change Location. The Folder Location page appears.

9. Select the Axelburg folder, and click OK to return to the Create Linked Report page.

10. Click OK to create and execute this linked report in the Axelburg folder.

11. Type **01/01/2012** for Enter a Start Date and **12/31/2012** for Enter an End Date. Click View Report.

12. Click the link for the Axelburg folder at the top of the page. You can see the linked report we just created looks like a regular report.

13. Navigate back to the Shared Reports folder.

14. Hover over the Invoice-Batch Number Report, and select Manage from the drop-down menu.

15. Click Create Linked Report. The Create Linked Report page appears.

16. Type **Invoice-Batch Number Report** for Name and **Utonal invoices in each batch** for Description.

17. Click Change Location. The Folder Location page appears.

18. Select the Utonal folder, and click OK to return to the Create Linked Report page.

19. Click OK to create and execute this linked report in the Utonal folder.

20. Select Utonal from the Select a City drop-down list. Type **01/01/2012** for Enter a Start Date and **12/31/2012** for Enter an End Date. Click View Report.

We have now successfully created and tested our two linked reports.

Managing Report Parameters in Report Manager

We have our linked reports, but we have not quite fulfilled all the business needs stated for these linked reports. The Axelburg sales office is supposed to be able to see only their own invoice data. The same is true for the Utonal sales office. We can meet these business needs by managing the report parameters right in the Report Manager. Here are the steps to follow:

1. Navigate to the Axelburg folder. Note the small chain links on the icon for the Invoice-Batch Number Report. This indicates it is a linked report.

2. Hover over the Invoice-Batch Number Report, and select Manage from the drop-down menu.

3. Click Parameters on the left side of the screen. The Parameter Management page appears. Note that the City parameter has a default of Axelburg. Because this is the Axelburg folder, we leave that default alone. What we modify is the user's ability to change this default value.

4. Uncheck the Prompt User check box in the City row. The user is no longer prompted for a city. Instead, the report always uses the default value. As you may have guessed, you can have a default value, you can prompt the user for the value, or you can do both. You must do at least one of these.

5. Check the Has Default check box in the StartDate row. Type **01/01/2012** for the default value for this row.

6. Check the Has Default check box in the EndDate row. Type **12/31/2012** for the default value for this row.

7. Click Apply to save your changes.

8. Click the large Invoice-Batch Number Report title at the top of the page to run the report.

9. Notice you can no longer select a city. It is always Axelburg. Also, notice we now have default values for the date. Also worth noting is these default values are much easier to modify than the default values that are part of the report, because we can make changes without having to redeploy the report.

10. Navigate to the Utonal folder.

11. Hover over the Invoice-Batch Number Report, and select Manage from the drop-down menu.

12. Click Parameters on the left side of the screen.

13. Change the City field's default parameter to Utonal.

14. Uncheck the Prompt User check box in the City row.

15. Check the Has Default check box in the StartDate row. Type **01/01/2012** for the default value for this row.

16. Check the Has Default check box in the EndDate row. Type **12/31/2012** for the default value for this row.

17. Click Apply to save your changes.

18. Click the large Invoice-Batch Number Report title at the top of the page to run the report.

Now we have the linked reports working just the way we need them. Not only did we simplify things by not deploying the report in multiple places, but we also were able to hardcode parameter values for each linked report.

Reporting Services in SharePoint Integrated Mode

As we saw in Chapter 2, it is possible to install Reporting Services to run in SharePoint Integrated mode. When Reporting Services is installed in this manner, the SharePoint user interface replaces the Report Manager. This has the advantage of allowing reports to be managed by the same tool that manages documents in the organization. In fact, reports appear to the end user as if they are just another document type like a Word document or an Excel spreadsheet.

For organizations where SharePoint is already being used, this has the advantage of providing the user with a familiar interface for locating and viewing reports. Likewise, it provides the administrator with an interface they are familiar with for deploying and managing reports. SharePoint Integrated mode operation also allows many of the SharePoint document management features, such as version control and routing and approval, to be applied to our reports.

After installing Reporting Services in SharePoint integrated mode, as described in Chapter 2, we need to prepare SharePoint by creating a document library that knows how to deal with Reporting Services objects. We also need to use the appropriate URLs for deploying reports from SSDT and Visual Studio, if we use that report authoring environment.

Creating a Document Library

One of the features of SharePoint is that it knows what applications to use for viewing and editing the different types of documents that are stored in its document libraries. When working with Reporting Services reports, we want SharePoint to have that same knowledge so our users can seamlessly run and modify reports. To facilitate this, we need to create a document library with knowledge of the Reporting Services document types.

Follow these steps to create a document library ready to work with Reporting Services reports:

1. Open the SharePoint site where Reporting Services was set up. (This is the regular SharePoint site, not the Central Administration site.)
2. Click the Site Actions drop-down menu in the upper-left corner of the page.
3. Select New Document Library from the drop-down menu.
4. The Create dialog box appears. Enter a name and a description, if desired.
5. Set the Navigation and Document Version History settings as desired.
6. If you are managing a number of different document types in this library, set the Document Template appropriately. If you are managing only Reporting Services reports in this document library, set Document Template to None. The completed Create dialog box should appear similar to Figure 10-29.
7. Click Create to exit the Create dialog box. After a bit of processing, you will be taken to your new document library.

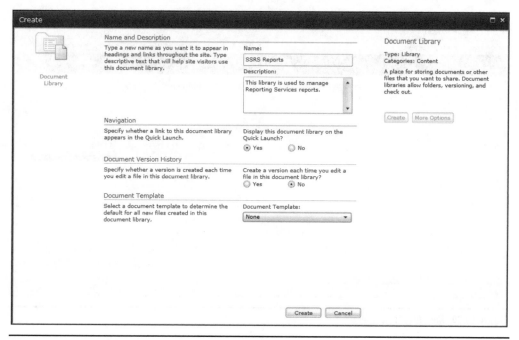

Figure 10-29 *The document library Create dialog box*

 8. On the right side of the document library ribbon, select Library Settings. The Document Library Settings page appears.

 9. In the General Settings area, click Advanced settings. The Advanced Settings page appears.

10. In the Content Types area, select yes to allow the management of content types.

11. Scroll down and click OK. You will return to the Document Library Settings page.

12. Scroll down to the Content Types area, and click the "Add from existing site content types" link. The Add Content Types page appears.

13. In the Select site content types from: drop-down list, select SQL Server Reporting Services Content Types. Three content types are now available for you to select: Report Builder Model, Report Builder Report, and Report Data Source.

14. Double-click Report Builder Report to move it to the Content types to add: list.

15. Double-click Report Data Source to move it to the Content types to add: list. The Add Content Types page should appear as shown in Figure 10-30.

16. Click OK. You will return to the Document Library Settings page.

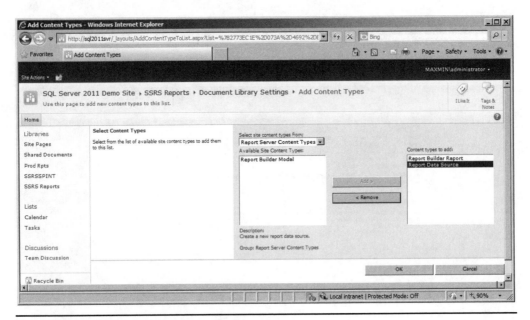

Figure 10-30 *The Add Content Types page*

17. Scroll down to the Content Types area, and click the "Change new button order and default content type" link. The Change New Button Order and Default Content Type page appears.

18. If you intend to manage only Reporting Services reports in this document library, uncheck the Document check box.

19. Set the Position from Top drop-down list for Report Builder Report to 1.

20. Set the Position from Top drop-down list for Report Data Source to 2. The Change New Button Order and Default Content Type page should appear as shown in Figure 10-31.

21. Click OK. You will return to the Document Library Settings page.

22. Navigate to your new document library.

23. Go to the Documents tab of the ribbon.

24. Click the New Document drop-down menu in the ribbon. Note the two choices are Report Builder Report and Report Data Source, just as we configured. This is shown in Figure 10-32.

You can select Report Builder Report from the New Document drop-down menu to launch Report Builder and create a new report. You can select Report Data Source from the New Document drop-down menu to be taken to the page for defining a new data source. As an alternative to creating items from within SharePoint, we can also

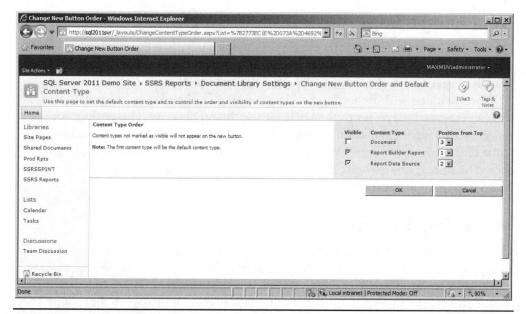

Figure 10-31 *The Change New Button Order and Default Content Type page*

upload our data sources and reports from SSDT or Visual Studio. We look at this in the following section.

NOTE

To copy a report saved on a native mode report server to a SharePoint Integrated mode report server, use the report manager to download the report definition to a file as discussed early in this chapter. Then, use the upload document button in SharePoint to upload the document. Any shared data sources in the uploaded report will need to be pointed to shared data sources in the SharePoint library.

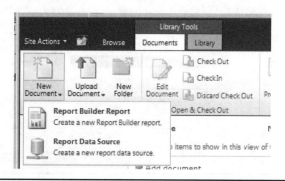

Figure 10-32 *The New Document drop-down menu on the Documents tab of the ribbon*

Deploying a Report to a Document Library

Reports can be uploaded to a SharePoint document library in a manner similar to the way they are uploaded to a report server running in native mode. The only difference is the URLs specified in the Project Properties dialog box.

When working with Reporting Services running in SharePoint Integrated mode, the TargetServerURL is set to the URL for the SharePoint site. The settings for the reports, data sources, and so on are the URL for the SharePoint site followed by the name of the document library within the SharePoint site where each type of item should be stored. The example in Figure 10-33 shows all item types going to the same SSRS Reports document library.

Managing Reports

Once reports are in place in the SharePoint document library, they are managed in much the same manner as they would be in Report Manager. To manage the various aspects of a report, hover over the report entry in the document library and click the drop-down button to display the list of options available for managing the report. This is shown in Figure 10-34.

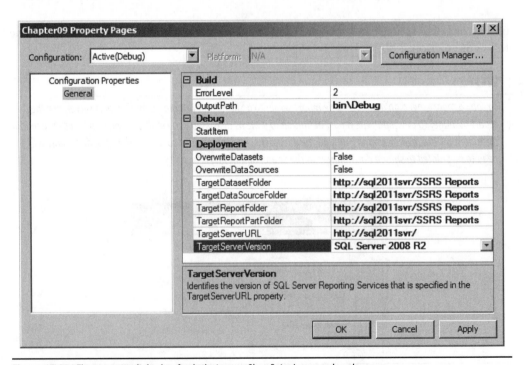

Figure 10-33 *The properties dialog box for deploying to a SharePoint Integrated mode server*

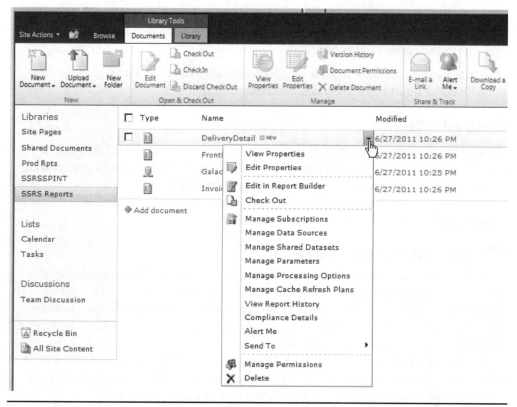

Figure 10-34 *The report management menu in SharePoint*

Security Roles

As with other documents in SharePoint, you can control access to a report using the Manage Permissions option available on the report management menu. Users are assigned to a SharePoint group to gain rights to an item. SharePoint offers three built-in groups that function similarly to the built-in groups in Reporting Services native mode.

▶ Site Owners have full control over reports and other items (similar to Content Manager rights in native mode). Site Owners can create, modify, and delete content, as well as control who has rights to that content.

▶ Site Members can create reports and other items (similar to Publisher rights in native mode). Site Members can create, modify, and delete content, but cannot control the access rights of others.

▶ Site Visitors can view reports (similar to Browser rights in native mode). Site Visitors cannot modify any site content.

Data Alerts

Data Alerts are a new feature of SQL Server Reporting Services 2012 running in SharePoint Integrated mode. A *data alert* enables Reporting Services to generate an e-mail whenever the data in a report meets a certain set of criteria. This feature allows a user to be notified of a certain situation reflected in the data, rather than constantly monitoring a report to look for that situation to occur.

The Data Alert Architecture

Data alert definitions are created within SharePoint using the Data Alert Designer. This definition includes one or more rules that must be met in order to trigger the data alert. Once created, these definitions are stored in the SQL Server alerting database. The SQL Server alerting database is automatically created when Reporting Services is installed in SharePoint Integrated mode.

A SQL Agent job is created for each alert definition. The recurrence pattern defined for the data alert determines the execution schedule for the SQL Agent job. The job causes the following steps to be executed each time it runs:

1. The report is executed to generate the data in the data feeds.
2. The rules are applied to the specified data feed.
3. If one or more rules are satisfied, the alert e-mail is sent.

If a data alert is being specified for a report that requires parameters, those parameter values must be provided at the time the data alert definition is created. These parameter values are stored with the data alert definition. They are used each time the report is subsequently executed to generate the data in the data feeds.

If an error should occur during the processing of a data alert definition, an e-mail detailing the error is sent to the normal recipients of the data alert.

Requirements for Creating a Data Alert on a Report

A Reporting Services report must meet certain requirements before data alerts can be defined for that report. Those requirements are

▶ The report must be deployed to a SharePoint Library with Reporting Services operating in SharePoint Integrated mode.

- ▶ All of the data sources used by the report must use stored credentials or must require no credentials. Windows integrated security and the prompt for credentials data source security options are not supported by data alerts.

- ▶ The report must contain at least one data region. The data regions create the data feeds for the report. It is the data feeds that make data alerts possible.

- ▶ The data in the report must change over time, even when the same set of parameters is entered.

This last item is important to understand. If the report always returns the same data for a given set of parameters, then either an alert is always generated with each recurrence because the rules are always satisfied or an alert is never generated because the rules are never satisfied. Instead, we need a report whose data will change over time, even when the same parameters are passed to it. This type of report will yield interesting results when data alerts are applied.

Creating a Data Alert

Once you have a report meeting for the specified requirements deployed to a SharePoint Library, you can create a data alert definition using the following steps:

1. Click the report to execute it.
2. Provide values for the parameters, if there are any.
3. Once you have executed the report, select New Data Alert from the Actions menu in the upper-left corner as shown in Figure 10-35.

The New Data Alert dialog box appears. The upper-left corner of the dialog box contains the Report data name drop-down list. This drop-down list enables you to select the data feed whose data will be used by the rules in this data alert definition.

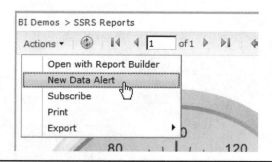

Figure 10-35 *Creating a new data alert*

The data feeds are named for the data regions in the report that created each of them. This is one case where taking the time to give meaningful names to a data region and its constituent parts might be a good idea.

Below the Report data name drop-down list is a grid showing the data in the selected data feed. The first 100 rows in the data feed are displayed. This provides you with some context as you create the rules for the data alert definition.

1. Select the desired data feed using the Report data name drop-down list.
2. On the right side of the New Data Alert dialog box, specify a meaningful name for the alert in Alert name. This will be used to identify this alert as it is managed in the future.
3. You can have the data alert send an alert e-mail when any of the data in the data feed has met the rules or if no data in the data feed has met the rules. Click the "Alert me if any data has" item to toggle between these two options.
4. Click Add rule to begin adding rules to the data alert definition. A list of all of the columns in the data feed appears.
5. Select the desired column for this rule. (In the example shown in Figure 10-36, we are using the value being represented on a linear gauge on a dashboard.)
6. Click the "is" comparison operator and select the comparison operator you wish to use for this rule.

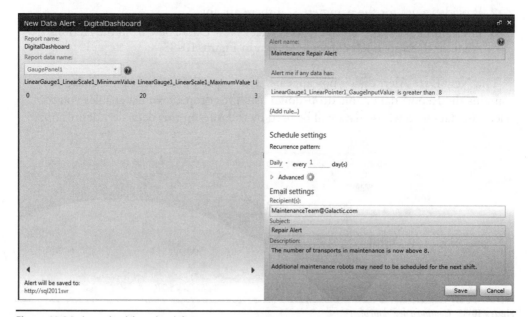

Figure 10-36 *A completed data alert definition*

7. To the right of the comparison operator, enter a constant value or select another column from the data feed to complete the rule. Depending on which comparison operator you are using, you can specify multiple values using the ellipsis (…) button.

8. Click Add rule to define additional rules for this data alert definition, if desired.

9. Use the Recurrence pattern area to define the frequency with which this data alert definition should be executed.

10. You can use the Advanced area to set a start and/or a stop date for the execution of this data alert definition. The Advanced area also lets you specify whether the alert e-mail should be sent every time the data alert is executed and the rules are met or only when the rules are met and the data has changed since the previous execution.

11. Use the Email settings area to specify the recipients of the alert e-mail, along with the subject and any content you would like to appear in the body of the e-mail.

12. Click Save when your data alert definition is complete.

To manage existing data alerts, hover over the report in the SharePoint Library and select Manage Data Alerts from the drop-down menu.

Delivering the Goods

In this chapter, you learned how to put the reports where your users could come and get them. Your users were set up to pull the reports off the report server. In the next chapter, you learn how to deliver the goods right to the users. In Chapter 11, the report server pushes the reports out to the users. The pull and push capabilities combine to give Reporting Services some powerful tools for putting information in the hands of the users, right where it needs to be.

Chapter 11

Delivering the Goods: Report Delivery

In This Chapter

- ▶ The Joy of Sharing
- ▶ Caching In
- ▶ Report Snapshots
- ▶ Cache Refresh Options
- ▶ Report History

- ▶ Subscriptions
- ▶ Site Settings
- ▶ A Sense of Style
- ▶ Building On

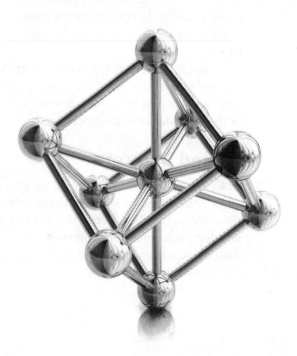

In the previous chapter, we moved from the development environment to the report server. The report server enables us to make our reports available to end users. We reviewed the various ways reports and their supporting resources can be moved from the development environment to the report server. We also reviewed the security features the report server provides.

In addition to all this, we looked at the Report Manager interface, which provides users with one method of accessing reports on the report server. In this chapter, you learn about additional ways to take reports from the report server to the users. You also learn ways to manage how and when reports are executed. These features can be used to level out server load and to increase user response time.

But first, we look at something you should have learned in kindergarten—how to share. We take some of the parts and pieces of reports we created earlier in the book and see how to share those items with other report authors. This allows others to take advantage of queries that are already proven to be correct and use bits of complex report layout in their own reports.

The Joy of Sharing

Reporting Services, and especially the Report Builder authoring tool, are designed to allow business people (also known as subject matter experts) to create their own reports without having to depend on the IT department for every view into the data. All report authors, but especially these more inexperienced users, benefit from being able to leverage and build upon the work done by others. To facilitate this, Reporting Services supports two types of sharing through the report server: shared datasets and report parts.

A *shared dataset* is simply a query that can be used to provide data in multiple reports. A *report part* is a combination of query and layout from one report that can be utilized in other reports. The report server provides a convenient and secure method for managing both shared datasets and report parts.

Shared Datasets

In Chapters 8 and 9 of this book, we used stored procedures as a way to share queries. I created the queries and shared them with you. I'm sure you noticed you spent much less time working in the Query Designer in Chapters 8 and 9. We discussed the advantages of using stored procedures, including the ability to share complex query code among multiple reports. So, if stored procedures give us this sharing capability, why do we even need shared datasets?

I was able to create stored procedures because I have rights to do so in the Galactic database. This is a privilege that should not be granted to every user. Shared datasets provide a way to share queries without having to open up big holes in our database security. In order to create a shared dataset, the user must have rights to select data from tables in the database, but does not need any database rights beyond that. The user does need to have rights to manage shared datasets in one or more folders on the report server. I'm sure this is a right our administrators will grant much more readily.

Creating a Shared Dataset from Scratch

Creating a shared data source is similar to creating a dataset within a report. The only real difference is where the result is stored—inside a report or on its own. Shared datasets can be created in SSDT, Visual Studio, and Report Builder. So, fire up your favorite authoring environment and let's give it a try.

DT **SSDT and Visual Studio Steps**

1. Start SSDT or Visual Studio, and open the Chapter08 project.
2. Select Project | Properties from the main menu. The Chapter08 Property Pages dialog box appears.
3. Type **Galactic Delivery Services/Datasets** for TargetDatasetFolder.
4. Type **Galactic Delivery Services/Data Sources** for TargetDataSourceFolder.
5. Type **Galactic Delivery Services/Chapter08** for TargetReportFolder.
6. Type **http://ComputerName/ReportServer** for TargetServerURL, where ComputerName is the name of the computer where the report server is installed. You should replace http: with https: if you are using a secure connection. You can use localhost in place of the computer name if the report server is installed on the same computer you are using to run Visual Studio (see Figure 11-1).

NOTE

If your report server does not have the Reporting Services web service configured in its default location, you will need to modify the URL in Step 6 accordingly.

7. Click OK to exit the Chapter08 Property Pages dialog box.
8. In the Solution Explorer, right-click the Share Datasets folder, and select Add New Dataset from the context menu. The Shared Dataset Properties dialog box appears.
9. This should look familiar. It is, in fact, the same as the Dataset Properties dialog box you have seen many times before. You know how to build queries using this dialog box, so we will keep things simple. Enter **CustomerInfo** for Name.
10. Enter the following for Query:

```
SELECT * FROM Customer
```

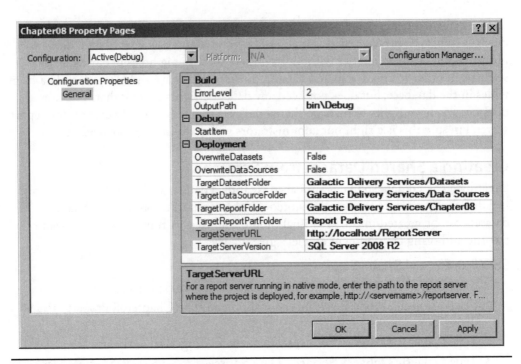

Figure 11-1 *The Chapter08 Property Pages dialog box*

11. Click OK to exit the Shared Dataset Properties dialog box. You will see the entry for your new shared dataset in the Solution Explorer window with .rsd extension.

12. Right-click the CustomerInfo.rsd item in the Solution Explorer window, and select Deploy from the context menu. The shared dataset will be deployed to the Galactic Delivery Services/Shared Datasets folder on the report server.

RB   Report Builder Steps

1. Open Report Manager in a browser window.

2. Create a new folder in the Galactic Delivery Services folder called **Datasets**.

3. Launch Report Builder. The Getting Started dialog box appears.

4. Select New Dataset from the left side of the dialog box. The right side of the screen will show shared data sources that are available.

5. Select the Galactic shared data source you have been using for the report authoring exercises.

6. Click the Create button.

7. The Report Builder window will become a large version of the graphical query designer window that you have seen many times before. You know how to build queries using this tool, so we will keep things simple. Expand the Tables item in the Database view pane.

8. Check the entry for the Customer table.

9. Click the Save toolbar item in the upper-left corner of the window. The Save As Dataset dialog box appears.

10. Navigate to the Datasets folder you created in Step 2.

11. Enter **CustomerInfo.rsd** for Name.

12. Click OK.

Creating a Shared Dataset from an Existing Dataset

In addition to creating shared datasets from scratch, we can convert a dataset that exists in a report into a shared dataset. Here's how:

`DT` **SSDT and Visual Studio Steps**

1. In SSDT or Visual Studio, open the Chapter08 solution, if it is not already open.

2. Open the EmployeeTime report.

3. In the Report Data window, expand the Datasets folder.

4. Right-click the entry for the EmployeeTime dataset, and select Convert to Shared Dataset from the context menu.

5. You'll see there is now an entry for the EmployeeTime dataset in the Solution Explorer window under Shared Datasets. In the Report Data window, the entry for EmployeeTime now includes a shortcut icon indicating it is a pointer to the new EmployeeTime shared dataset. In the Report Data window, right-click the entry for the EmployeeTime dataset. Select Dataset Properties from the context menu. The Dataset Properties dialog box appears.

6. Note the Dataset Properties dialog box now shows the two shared datasets in our project, CustomerInfo and EmployeeTime, with the EmployeeTime shared dataset selected. Click Cancel to exit the Dataset Properties dialog box.

7. Click Save All.

8. Right-click the entry for the EmployeeTime shared dataset in the Solution Explorer window, and select Deploy from the context menu. The shared dataset is deployed to the server.

9. Right-click the entry for the EmployeeTime report in the Solution Explorer window, and select Deploy from the context menu.

10. Navigate to the Galactic Delivery Services/Chapter08 folder on the report server. Click EmployeeTime to execute the report. The report runs using the EmployeeTime shared dataset.

11. Navigate to the Galactic Delivery Services/Datasets folder.

12. Hover over the entry for the EmployeeTime shared dataset, and select View Dependent Items from the menu. You will see a list of items dependent on the EmployeeTime shared dataset. This list shows the EmployeeTime report is dependent on the EmployeeTime shared dataset.

RB **Report Builder Steps**

1. If the CustomerInfo shared dataset is displayed in the Report Builder, click the logo button and select Open from the menu. Otherwise, start Report Builder and select Open in the Getting Started dialog box. The Open Report dialog box appears.

2. Navigate to the Chapter08 folder, and open the EmployeeTime report.

3. Click the logo button, and select Publish Report Parts from the menu. The Publish Report Parts dialog box appears.

4. Click Review and modify report parts before publishing. A second version of the Publish Report Parts dialog box appears.

5. Uncheck Report parts. (We'll get to those later in this chapter.)

6. Check Datasets.

7. Click the arrow next to EmployeeTime as shown in Figure 11-2.

8. Click Browse to select where the EmployeeTime dataset should be stored. The Select Folder dialog box appears.

9. Navigate to the Datasets folder in the Galactic Delivery Services folder.

10. Click OK to exit the Select Folder dialog box.

11. Click Publish. You should see a green check mark across from the EmployeeTime entry in the dialog box.

12. Click Close to exit the Publish Report Parts dialog box.

13. Click Save to save the EmployeeTime report.

14. Navigate to the Chapter08 folder on the report server. Click EmployeeTime to execute the report. The report runs using the EmployeeTime shared dataset.

15. Navigate to the Datasets folder.

16. Hover over the entry for the EmployeeTime shared dataset and select View Dependent Items from the menu. You will see a list of items dependent on the EmployeeTime shared dataset. This list shows the EmployeeTime report is dependent on the EmployeeTime shared dataset.

Modifying Shared Datasets

Modifying a shared dataset is straightforward. When using SSDT or Visual Studio, simply open the project containing the shared dataset and double-click the entry for that dataset in the Solution Explorer window. This will open the Shared Dataset

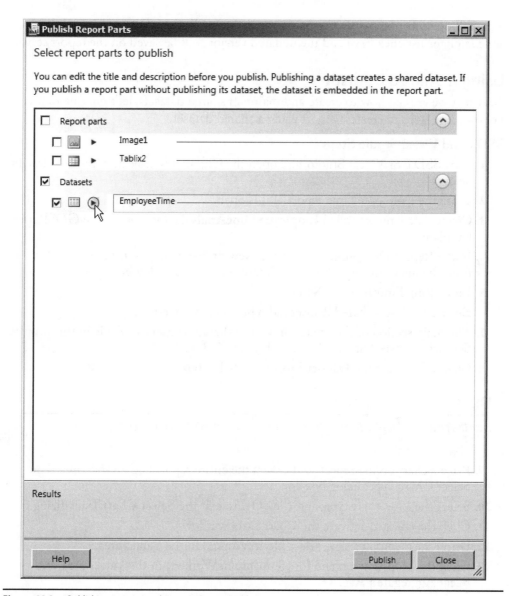

Figure 11-2 *Publishing an existing dataset in Report Builder*

Properties dialog box. You can modify the shared dataset as needed, and then redeploy it to the report server.

When using Report Builder, navigate to the shared dataset on the report server, hover over the entry for that dataset, and select Edit in Report Builder from the menu.

This will open the dataset for modification in Report Builder. When the modifications are complete, just click Save and the updated version will be saved on the report server.

Using a Shared Dataset

Now that we've seen how to create and maintain shared datasets, let's put one to use. Follow these steps to create a report using a shared dataset.

DT **SSDT and Visual Studio Steps**

1. Start SSDT or Visual Studio, and open the Chapter08 project, if it is not already open.

2. Close the EmployeeTime report, if it is open.

3. Create a new report called **EmployeeTimeAnalysis**. Do not use the GDSReport template.

4. In the Report Data window, click the New drop-down menu, and select Dataset from the menu that appears. The Dataset Properties dialog box appears.

5. Enter **EmpTimeInfo** for Name.

6. Ensure the Use a shared dataset radio button is selected.

7. The main section of the screen shows the shared datasets available in this project. Select EmployeeTime as shown in Figure 11-3.

8. Click OK to exit the Dataset Properties dialog box.

NOTE

From this point, the shared dataset is used just like a dataset embedded in your report.

9. Place a chart on the report so it covers the entire report body layout area. The Select Chart Type dialog box appears.

10. Select the Line chart type, and click OK to exit the Select Chart Type dialog box.

11. Click the chart to activate the Chart Data window.

12. Using the green plus sign, select HoursWorked in the Values area.

13. Click the drop-down menu for [Sum(HoursWorked)] in the Values area, and select Aggregate | Avg.

14. Using the green plus signs, select Work Date in the Category Groups area and Job in the Series Groups area.

15. Preview the report.

16. Save the report.

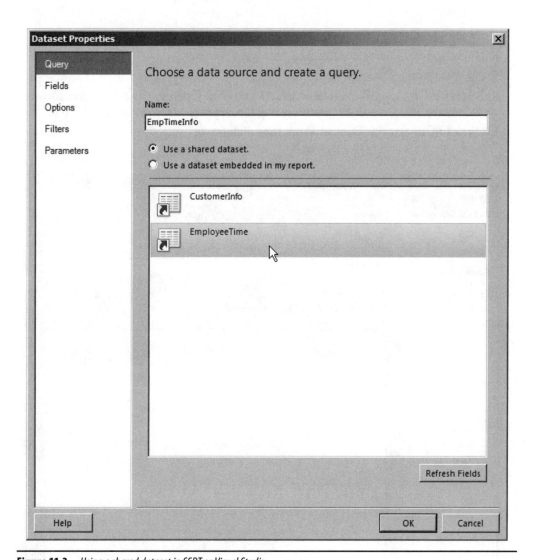

Figure 11-3 *Using a shared dataset in SSDT or Visual Studio*

RB **Report Builder Steps**

1. Start Report Builder, if it is not already open.
2. Create a new, blank report.
3. In the Report Data window, click the New drop-down menu and select Dataset. The Dataset Properties dialog box appears.
4. Enter **EmpTimeInfo** for Name.

5. Ensure the Use a shared dataset radio button is selected.

6. Click Browse. The Select Dataset dialog box appears.

7. Navigate to the Datasets folder.

8. Select the EmployeeTime shared dataset, and click Open to close the Select Dataset dialog box. The Dataset Properties dialog box appears as shown in Figure 11-4.

9. Click OK to exit the Dataset Properties dialog box.

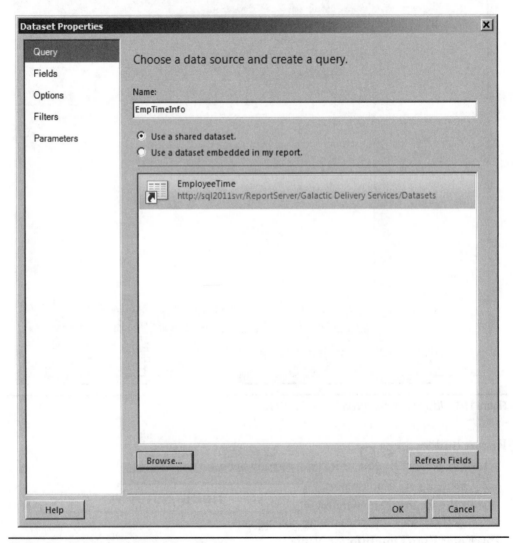

Figure 11-4   *Using a shared dataset in Report Builder*

NOTE

From this point, the shared dataset is used just like a dataset embedded in your report.

10. Place a chart on the report so it covers the entire report body layout area. The Select Chart Type dialog box appears.
11. Select the Line chart type, and click OK to exit the Select Chart Type dialog box.
12. Click the chart to activate the Chart Data window.
13. Using the green plus sign, select HoursWorked in the Values area.
14. Click the drop-down menu for [Sum(HoursWorked] in the Values area, and select Aggregate | Avg.
15. Using the green plus signs, select Work Date in the Category Groups area and Job in the Series Groups area.
16. Run the report.
17. Save the report as **EmployeeTimeAnalysis** in the Chapter08 folder.

As you can see, using a shared dataset can make report development quick and easy. It is possible, however, to make things even easier. We do that by taking further advantage of previous efforts through report parts.

Report Parts

Report parts work similar to shared datasets. The difference is a report part includes a report layout component in addition to the dataset. Report parts are created by taking the individual layout components and parameters of an existing report and saving them to the report server. These bits of report definition can then be incorporated into other reports.

Report parts can be saved to the server from SSDT, Visual Studio, and Report Builder. However, only Report Builder can make use of report parts in the reports it creates. This is one of the few places where SSDT, Visual Studio, and Report Builder do not have the same capabilities.

Saving Report Parts on the Report Server

Saving report parts to the report server is as easy as saving existing datasets as shared datasets. Let's give it a try.

DT **SSDT and Visual Studio Steps**

1. In SSDT or Visual Studio, open the Chapter08 solution, if it is not already open.
2. Close any open reports, and then open the Overtime Report.
3. In the Report menu, select Publish Report Parts. The Publish Report Parts dialog box appears. This dialog box lists the layout items and parameters in the Overtime Report.
4. Check the box for Hubcode.
5. Click the arrow next to HubCode as shown in Figure 11-5.

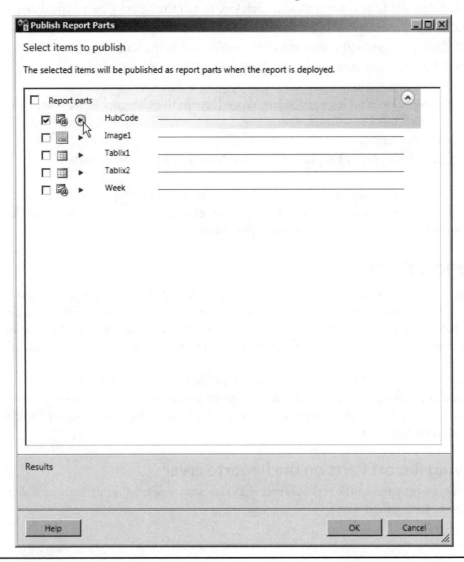

Figure 11-5 *Adding detail to report parts before publishing*

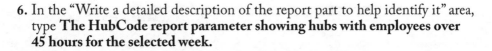

6. In the "Write a detailed description of the report part to help identify it" area, type **The HubCode report parameter showing hubs with employees over 45 hours for the selected week.**

NOTE

As your Report Part Gallery grows, it is important to have detailed descriptions of each report part. Otherwise, it will be impossible to tell one report part from another when trying to find the appropriate bit for incorporation into a new report.

7. Check the box for Tablix1.
8. Click Tablix1, and replace this text with **Employees 45–55 Hours Worked.**
9. Click the arrow next to this item, and type the following in the detailed description area: **A tablix showing employees for a selected week at a selected hub with 45–55 hours worked.**
10. Check the box for Tablix2.
11. Click Tablix2, and replace this text with **Employees Over 55 Hours Worked.**
12. Click the arrow next to this item, and type the following in the detailed description area: **A tablix showing employees for a selected week at a selected hub with over 55 hours worked.**
13. Check the box for Week.
14. Click the arrow next to Week, and type the following in the detailed description area: **The Week report parameter showing weeks for which employee time has been entered.**
15. Click OK to publish the report parts.
16. Right-click the entry for the Overtime Report in the Solution Explorer, and select Deploy from the context menu. The report and the report parts will be deployed to the report server.
17. In Report Manager, navigate to the Report Parts folder. You should see the four report parts in the folder as shown in Figure 11-6.

NOTE

Report parts are published to the report server and the report server folder specified in the project properties dialog box. See the "Creating a Shared Dataset from Scratch" section earlier in this chapter.

RB   **Report Builder Steps**

1. Start Report Builder, if it is not already running, and open the Overtime Report from the Chapter08 folder.
2. Click the logo button, and select Publish Report Parts from the menu. The Publish Report Parts dialog box appears.

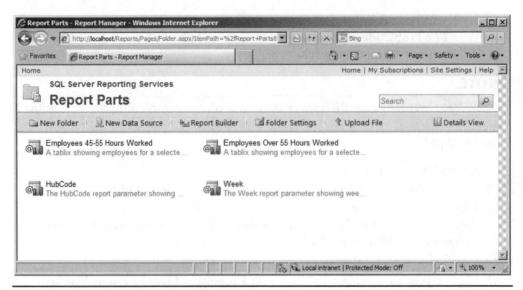

Figure 11-6 *The published report parts on the report server*

3. Click "Review and modify report parts before publishing." A second version of the Publish Report Parts dialog box appears listing all layout items, parameters, and datasets in the report.

4. Click the arrow next to HubCode.

5. In the "Write a detailed description of the report part to help identify it" area, type **The HubCode report parameter showing hubs with employees over 45 hours for the selected week**.

NOTE

As your Report Part Gallery grows, it is important to have detailed descriptions of each report part. Otherwise, it will be impossible to tell one report part from another when trying to find the appropriate bit for incorporation into a new report.

6. Click Browse. The Select Folder dialog box appears. Make sure this has defaulted to the Report Parts folder in the Home folder, and then click OK to exit the dialog box.

7. Uncheck the box for Image1.

8. Click Tablix1, and replace this text with **Employees 45–55 Hours Worked**.

9. Click the arrow next to this item, and type the following in the detailed description area: **A tablix showing employees for a selected week at a selected hub with 45–55 hours worked**.

10. Click Tablix2, and replace this text with **Employees Over 55 Hours Worked**.

11. Click the arrow next to this item, and type the following in the detailed description area: **A tablix showing employees for a selected week at a selected hub with over 55 hours worked.**

12. Click the arrow next to Week, and type the following in the detailed description area: **The Week report parameter showing weeks for which employee time has been entered.**

13. Click Publish. The results message should indicate four parts published successfully and there should be a green check mark next to the four items we chose to publish.

14. Click Close.

15. Save the report.

16. In Report Manager, navigate to the Report Parts folder. You should see the four report parts in the folder as shown in Figure 11-6.

Using Report Parts in a Report

Once the report parts are published to the report server, we can take advantage of them in new reports. Remember, only Report Builder can utilize report parts in a new report. We use the following steps to add the Employees Over 55 Hours Worked tablix to our EmployeeTimeAnalysis report.

RB | **Report Builder Steps**

1. In Report Builder, open the EmployeeTimeAnalysis report found in the Chapter08 folder.

2. Make the report body longer so there is ample room below the chart.

3. On the Insert tab, select Report Parts. The Report Part Gallery window appears.

4. If no items are displayed in the Report Part Gallery window, click the magnifying glass icon in the search area.

5. Click the Employees Over 55 Hours Worked item to view the detail at the bottom of the Report Part Gallery window. The Report Part Gallery window appears as shown in Figure 11-7.

6. Drag the Employees Over 55 Hours Worked item from the Report Part Gallery, and drop it on the report layout below the chart. The tablix appears on the report.

7. In the Report Data window, expand the Parameters folder. Note the Week and HubCode parameters were automatically added to the report along with the tablix.

8. In the Report Data window, expand the Datasets folder. Note the Weeks, HubsOver45, and EmployeesOver45 datasets were automatically added to the report along with the tablix.

9. Run the report.

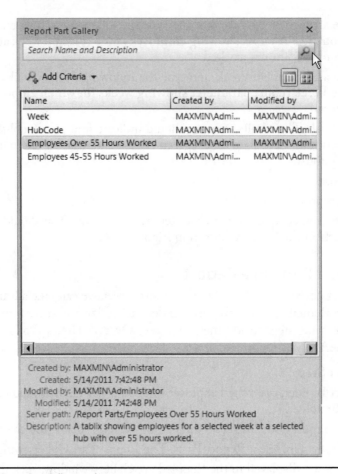

Figure 11-7 *The Report Part Gallery window*

10. Select "2013-13" for Week and "Borlaron Repair Base" for Hub, and then click
    View Report. The report should appear similar to Figure 11-8.

11. Save the report.

Updating Report Parts

It is possible for a report part on a server to be modified from time to time. When
this happens, the report author who has utilized that report part has the option to
incorporate the changes into his or her own report. Alternately, the report author can
choose to ignore the update and continue to use the current version of the report part.

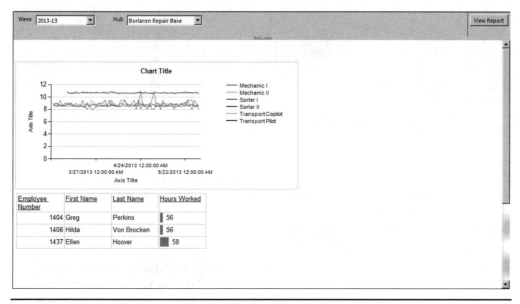

Figure 11-8 *The EmployeeTimeAnalysis report with a report part added*

Let's see how this works. Again, because only Report Builder can consume report parts, this example is limited to Report Builder.

RB **Report Builder Steps**

1. In Report Builder, open the Overtime Report.
2. In the tablix for employees with over 55 hours for this week (the tablix near the bottom of the report), select the cell containing the databar. (It has a background of bright blue.)
3. In the Properties window, change the Palette property to **Fire**. The databar background will change to yellow.
4. Save the report.
5. Click the logo button, and select Publish Report Parts from the menu. The Publish Report Parts dialog box appears.
6. Select "Review and modify report parts before publishing." The Publish Report Parts dialog box changes to show all report parts and datasets.
7. Uncheck all items except for Employees Over 55 Hours Worked.
8. Click Publish.
9. Click Close.
10. Save the report.

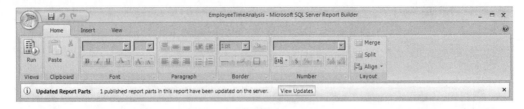

Figure 11-9 *The updated report parts notification bar*

11. Open the EmployeeTimeAnalysis report. You will see a bar right under the ribbon indicating that a published report part has been updated on the server as shown in Figure 11-9.

12. Click the View Updates button in this bar. The Updated Report Parts dialog box appears as shown in Figure 11-10.

13. If you do not wish to incorporate this change into the EmployeeTimeAnalysis report, you can simply click Close. However, in this case, we will incorporate the change. Click the check box for Tablix2.

NOTE

You have the option to turn off further notifications of changes to this report part by unchecking the Notify me when this report part is updated on the server check box.

14. Click Update.

15. Click Close.

16. Run the report.

17. Select "2013-13" for Week and "Borlaron Repair Base" for Hub, and then click View Report. The databar now appears in yellow on this report, too.

18. Save the report.

Using Shared Datasets and Report Parts Wisely

Shared datasets and report parts bring with them tremendous benefits. Once a robust set of shared datasets and report parts is collected on the server, a number of report authoring tasks can be completed quickly by building on items created previously. Even if there isn't a dataset or a report part that provides precisely what is needed, there may be something that will serve with only slight modifications rather than having to start from scratch.

However, some care must be taken to prevent the report server from becoming a dumping ground so cluttered that it is hard to find anything useful. Not every dataset

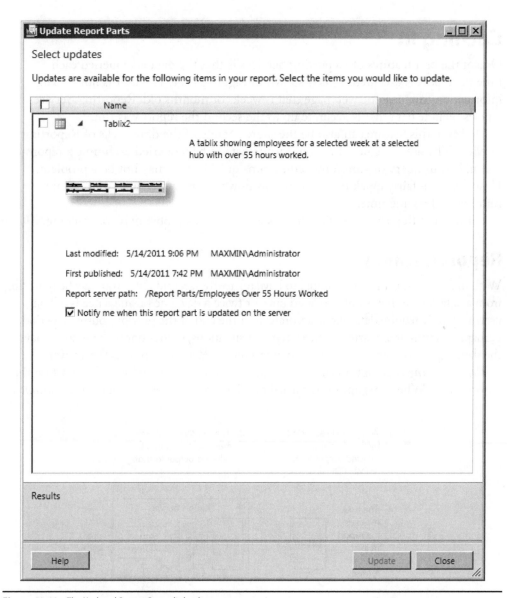

Figure 11-10 *The Updated Report Parts dialog box*

and bit of report layout is worthy of being placed in these server repositories. Some discretion must be used to determine what is likely to be reused and what is so unique or so unpolished that it does not deserve publication.

With some care and management, these repositories can become invaluable libraries for both novice and experienced report authors within an organization.

Caching In

One of the best features of Reporting Services is that the data is requeried each time the report is executed. This is shown in Figure 11-11. The user is not viewing information from a static web page that is weeks or months old. Reporting Services reports include data that is accurate up to the second the report was run.

However, this feature can also be the source of one of the drawbacks of Reporting Services. The user is required to wait for the data to be requeried each time a report is run. If your query or stored procedure runs quickly, this may not be a problem. However, even fairly quick queries can slow down a server if enough of them are running at the same time.

Fortunately, Reporting Services has a solution to this problem: report caching.

Report Caching

With many reports, it is not essential to have up-to-the-second data. You may be reporting from a data source that is only updated once or twice a day. The business needs of your users may only require data that is accurate as of the end of the previous business period, perhaps a month or a quarter. In these types of situations, it does not make sense to have the data requeried every time a user requests a report. Report caching is the answer.

Report caching is an option that can be turned on individually for each report on the report server. When this option is turned on, the report server saves a copy, or *instance,*

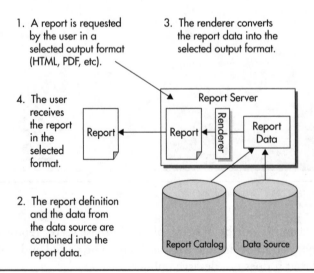

Figure 11-11 *Serving a report without caching*

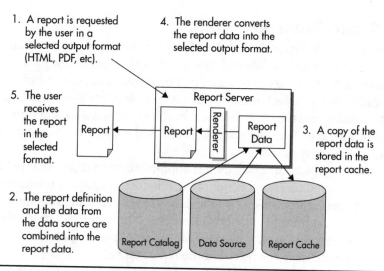

Figure 11-12 *Serving a report with caching, the first time*

of the report in a temporary location the first time the report is executed, as shown in Figure 11-12.

On subsequent executions, with the same parameter values chosen, the report server pulls the information necessary to render the report from the report cache, rather than requerying data from the database, as shown in Figure 11-13. Because these subsequent executions do not need to requery data, they are, in most cases, faster than the report execution without caching.

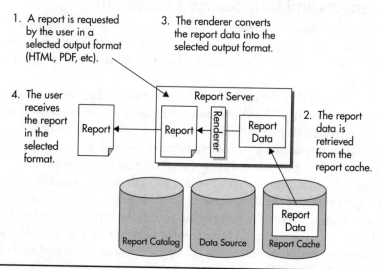

Figure 11-13 *Serving a report with caching, subsequent times*

Cached Report Expiration

Once an instance of the report is stored in the report cache, it is assigned an expiration date and time. The expiration date and time can be calculated in one of two ways. The expiration date and time can be calculated based on a certain number of minutes after the creation of the cached instance. For example, the cached instance of the report exists for 30 minutes, and then it is deleted. Or, the expiration date and time can be determined by a set schedule. For example, the cached instance of the report is deleted at 2:00 A.M. every Sunday morning.

The first type of expiration calculation is appropriate for a report that requires a large amount of database resources and is run often, but does not require up-to-the-second data. We can decrease the workload on the database server by fulfilling most of the requests for the report from the report cache. Every 30 minutes, we throw the cached report away. The next person who requests the report causes a new instance of the report, with updated data, to be placed in the report cache.

The second type of expiration calculation is appropriate for reports run against data that changes on a scheduled basis. Perhaps you have a report being run from your data warehouse. The data warehouse is updated from your transactional database each Sunday at 12:30 A.M. The data in the warehouse remains static in between these loads. The cached report is scheduled to expire right after the data load is completed. The next time the user requests the report after the expiration, a new instance of the report with the updated data is placed in the cache. This cached report contains up-to-date data until the next data load.

Cached Reports and Data Source Credentials

To create a cached instance of a report, the report must be using stored credentials. These can be credentials for either a Windows logon or a database logon, but they must be stored with the data source. If you think about this from a security standpoint, this is how it has to be.

Suppose for a minute that Reporting Services allowed a cached report to be created with Windows integrated security. The Windows credentials of the first person to run the report would be used to create a cached instance of the report. Subsequent users who request this report would receive this cached instance. However, this would mean the subsequent users are receiving data in the report created using the credentials from another user.

If the results of the database query or stored procedure that populates this report vary, based on the rights of the database login, we have the potential for a big problem. If the vice president of sales is the first person to run the report and create the cached instance, all subsequent users would receive information meant only for the VP! Conversely, if a sales representative is the first person to run the report and create the cached instance, when the VP comes along later and requests the report, he will not receive all the information he needs.

The same problem exists if the report prompts for credentials. The first person who runs the report and creates the cached instance is the one who supplies the credentials. Everyone who views the cached instance is essentially using someone else's logon to see this data.

The only way that caching works without creating the potential for a security problem is with credentials stored with the report. In this situation, the same credentials are used to access the database—whether it is the VP or a lowly sales representative running the report. There is no risk that the cached instance of the report will create a breach in database security.

Caching and Report Formats

As you can see in Figure 11-12, the report data, not the final format of the report, is stored in the report cache. The report data is a combination of the report definition and the data from the datasets. It is not formatted as a Hypertext Markup Language (HTML) page, a Portable Document Format (PDF) document, or other type of rendering format. It is an internal format ready for rendering.

Because the report data is stored in the report cache, the cached report can be delivered in any rendering format. The user who first requested the report, and thus caused the cache instance to be created, may have received the report as an HTML document. The next user may receive the cached instance of the report and export it to a PDF document. A third user may receive the cached instance of the report and export it to an Excel file. Caching the report data gives the report cache the maximum amount of flexibility.

Enabling Report Caching

Let's try enabling caching for one of our deployed reports. We have a report that is a good candidate for caching. The WeatherInfo report takes a long time to execute because of the calls to the web service. Also, the weather conditions returned by the web service are not going to change from minute to minute, so it is not essential to retrieve new information every time the report is executed. The WeatherInfo report works just fine if it is retrieved from the cache, as long as we expire the cached instance fairly often, say, every 45 minutes.

Enabling Report Caching for the Weather Report

Let's try enabling caching for the Weather Report.

1. Open the Report Manager, and navigate to the Chapter09 folder.
2. Hover over the WeatherReport, and select Manage from the drop-down menu. The Properties page for the WeatherReport appears.

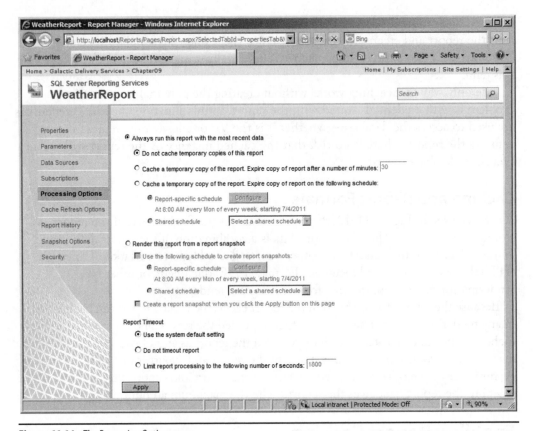

Figure 11-14   *The Processing Options page*

3. Select Processing Options from the left side of the screen. The Processing Options page appears, as shown in Figure 11-14.

4. Select the "Cache a temporary copy of the report. Expire copy of report after a number of minutes" option.

5. Set the number of minutes to 45.

6. Click Apply.

7. Click the large WeatherReport title at the top of the page to run the report. Select (Select All) in the Select Planets drop-down list, and click View Report. The WeatherReport runs.

The first time the Weather Report runs after caching is turned on, the report needs to perform its regular execution process to gather the data for the intermediate format. This intermediate format is then copied to the report cache before it is rendered for you in the browser. Because the report goes through its regular execution process, it still takes a while to appear.

Viewing the Report from the Report Cache

Now let's run the report again. Because a cached copy of the report has not expired, the report is rendered from the cached copy.

1. Click the Refresh Report button in the toolbar. The report appears almost immediately. That happened so fast, I bet you don't even believe it retrieved the report. Let's try it again another way.
2. Click the Chapter09 link at the top of the page.
3. Click the WeatherReport link to run this report.
4. Select (Select All) in the Select Planets drop-down list, and click View Report.

NOTE

Be sure to make the same parameter selection each time you run this test. We discuss how report parameters affect caching in the section "Report Caching and Report Parameters."

Pretty slick! The report server doesn't need to retrieve any data, execute any expressions, call any assemblies, or create the intermediate format. All it needs to do is convert the intermediate format into the rendered format (in this case, HTML).

What happens if we ask for a different rendering format?

1. Select PDF file from Export drop-down list.
2. If a File Download dialog box appears, click Open.
3. Close the Adobe Acrobat Reader when you finish viewing the report.

A brief delay occurs as the PDF document is created and your Acrobat Reader is opened, but there is no delay to retrieve the information using the web service. Instead, the intermediate format comes from the report cache and is rendered into a PDF document.

If you wait 45 minutes, the cached copy will have expired and the report is again executed to create the intermediate format. If you want to try this, you can put the book down, go have lunch, and then come back and run the report. It's okay. You go right ahead. I'll be here waiting when you get back.

Cache Expiration on a Schedule

You have just learned the weather web service we are using for our Weather Report is updated every hour, on the hour. It makes sense for us to set our cached copy of this report to expire on this same schedule. The cached copy should expire at five minutes past the hour so a new copy of the weather information shows up the next time the report is run after the web service information is updated.

1. Navigate to the Chapter09 folder in the Report Manager, if you are not already there.
2. Hover over the WeatherReport, and select Manage from the drop-down menu. The Properties page appears.
3. Select Processing Options from the left side of the screen. The Processing Options page appears.
4. Select the "Cache a temporary copy of the report. Expire copy of report on the following schedule" option.
5. Report-specific schedule is selected by default. Click Configure next to Report-specific schedule. The Schedule page appears, as shown in Figure 11-15.

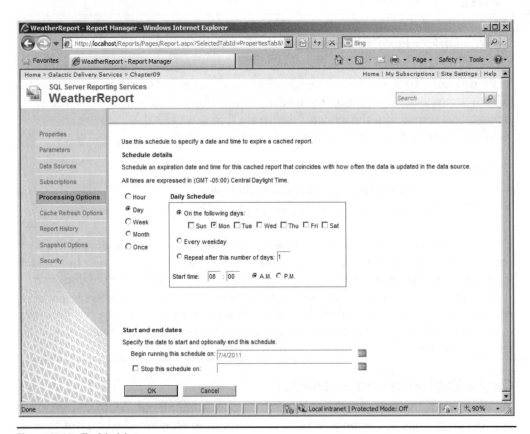

Figure 11-15 *The Schedule page*

6. You can specify hourly, daily, weekly, monthly, or one-time schedules. Select Hour.

7. Leave the Hourly Schedule set to run every 1 hours 00 minutes. Set Start Time to five minutes after the next hour. (If it is 2:30 P.M. now, set Start Time to 3:05 P.M.)

8. Today's date should be selected for Begin running this schedule on. Leave the Stop this schedule on blank. (You change these dates by clicking the calendar icon to the right of the entry area. You cannot type in the date directly.)

9. Click OK to return to the Processing Options page. Note the description of the schedule you just created under Report-specific schedule.

10. Click Apply to save your changes to the report cache settings.

NOTE

The SQL Server Agent must be running for this and other scheduled items to function properly. If you receive an error message, ensure that the SQL Server Agent service is running on the report server.

11. Click the large WeatherReport title at the top of the page to run the report. Check (Select All) in the Select Planets drop-down list, and click View Report. The Weather Report runs.

Again, the report takes longer to execute the first time as the intermediate format is created and put into the report cache. This cached instance of the report remains there until five minutes past the hour.

Report Cache and Deploying

When a cached report instance expires, either because of a schedule or because it has existed for its maximum length of time, it is removed from the report cache. One other circumstance can cause a cached report instance to be removed from the report cache. If a new copy of a report is deployed from the authoring environment or uploaded using the Report Manager, any cached instances of that report are removed from the report cache.

Report Caching and Report Parameters

What happens with our report caching if different users enter different parameters when the report is executed? Suppose one user runs the Weather Report and only selects Borlaron from the Select Planets drop-down list. The Weather Report is cached with only the Borlaron information. Now a second user runs the report, selecting only Stilation. Because a nonexpired instance of this report is in the report cache, it seems the report should come from the report cache. If this were to happen, though, the second user would receive the Borlaron data instead of the Stilation data.

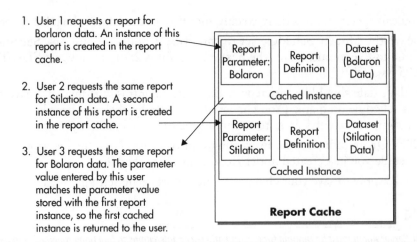

1. User 1 requests a report for Borlaron data. An instance of this report is created in the report cache.

2. User 2 requests the same report for Stilation data. A second instance of this report is created in the report cache.

3. User 3 requests the same report for Bolaron data. The parameter value entered by this user matches the parameter value stored with the first report instance, so the first cached instance is returned to the user.

Figure 11-16 *Report caching with parameters*

Fortunately, the report server is smart enough to handle this situation. As part of the instance of the report in the report cache, the report server stores any parameter values used to create that cached instance, as shown in Figure 11-16. The cached instance is used to satisfy requests made by a subsequent user only if all the parameters used to create the cached instance match the parameters entered by the subsequent user.

Report Caching and Security

Not all users can change report caching properties. To change the report caching properties for a report, you must have rights to the Manage Reports task. Of the five predefined security roles, the Content Manager, My Reports, and Publisher roles have rights to this task.

Report Snapshots

Report caching is a great tool for improving the performance of reports with long execution times, but one problem still exists. The first user who requests the report after the cached instance has expired must wait for the report to be created from the underlying data. It would be nice if there were a way to have cached report instances created automatically so no user has to endure these wait times. Fortunately, Reporting Services can do this as well.

A *report snapshot* is another way to create a cached report instance. Up to this point, we have discussed situations where cached report instances are created as the result of a user action. A user requests a report, and a copy of that report's intermediate format is placed in the report cache. With report snapshots, a cached report instance is created automatically.

Report snapshots can create cached report instances on a scheduled basis, or they can be created as soon as this feature is turned on for a particular report. If a schedule is used, each time the schedule is run, it replaces the current cached instance with a new one. Cached report instances created by a report snapshot are used to satisfy user report requests the same as any other cached report instance.

Enabling Report Snapshots

You can enable the creation of report snapshots using two methods. Let's look at the manual method first.

Manually Creating a Report Snapshot

Let's try enabling report snapshots for the Weather Report.

1. Navigate to the Chapter09 folder in the Report Manager, if you are not already there.
2. Hover over the WeatherReport, and select Manage from the drop-down menu. The Properties page appears.
3. Select Processing Options from the left side of the screen. The Processing Options page appears.
4. Select the Render this report from a report snapshot option.
5. Make sure the "Check the Create a report snapshot when you click the Apply button on this page" check box is checked.
6. Click Apply. Note the error message that appears next to the report snapshot option. When a report snapshot is created, it is done as a background process, so no one will be available to select a value for the report parameter. Because this parameter has no default value, the report server does not know what value to use for the report parameter when the report is run by the schedule. Let's provide a default value for the parameter so we can proceed.
7. Select Parameters from the left side of the screen. The Parameters page appears.
8. Check the check box in the Has Default column.
9. Enter the following in the Default Value drop-down edit area:
   AFU
   BLN
   NOX
   RKM
   SLN
   SRA

(We need to enter the values passed to the parameter—in this case, the planet abbreviations, not the planet names that are displayed in the drop-down list. Each value should be entered on a separate line.)

10. Click Apply to save the default value.
11. Let's try to set up snapshot execution again. Select Processing Options from the left side of the screen. The Processing Options page appears.
12. Select the Render this report from a report snapshot option.
13. Check the Create a report snapshot when you click the Apply button on this page check box, if it is not already checked.
14. Click Apply. As soon as you click Apply, the report server executes the report and places an instance of the report in the report cache. Allow time for this process to complete.
15. Click the large WeatherReport title at the top of the page to run the report.

The report is rendered from the cached report instance created by the report snapshot.

Creating Report Snapshots on a Schedule
Now let's try the scheduled approach to creating report snapshots.

1. Click the WeatherReport link at the top of the page. The Processing Options page should appear. If not, select Processing Options from the left side of the page.
2. Check the Use the following schedule to create report snapshots check box.
3. Report-specific schedule is selected by default. Click Configure next to Report-specific schedule. The Schedule page appears.
4. You can specify hourly, daily, weekly, monthly, or one-time schedules. The Day option should be selected by default. Leave this option selected.
5. Select the On the following days option, if it is not already selected.
6. Uncheck all the days except for today. (If you are reading this on Monday, for example, leave only Monday checked.)
7. Set the start time to five minutes from now.
8. Select today's date for Begin running this schedule on.
9. Check the Stop this schedule on check box, and then select tomorrow's date.

NOTE

I know this schedule does not fit the stated business requirements of refreshing the report at five minutes past the hour. However, you probably don't want to waste computer resources generating a report snapshot of the Weather Report hour after hour, day after day, so we use this schedule for the demonstration.

10. Click OK to return to the Processing Options page. Note the description of the schedule you just created under Report-specific schedule.
11. Click Apply to save your changes to the report snapshot settings. After five minutes, the scheduled report snapshot will create a cached instance of the report.
12. Click the large WeatherReport title at the top of the page to execute the report. (Go grab some caffeine while you are waiting. You wouldn't want to fall asleep while you are working through all this good stuff!) The Weather Report runs and is rendered from the cached report instance created by your scheduled report snapshot.

This type of report snapshot schedule would be appropriate for a report whose underlying data is changed only periodically (again, think of a data warehouse updated from a transactional system). The report snapshot would be scheduled to create a new cached instance of the report right after the new data is available in the warehouse.

Report Snapshots and Security

Not all users can change report snapshots. To change the report snapshot properties for a report, you must have rights to the Manage Reports task. Of the five predefined security roles, the Content Manager, My Reports, and Publisher roles have rights to this task.

Cache Refresh Options

There are limitations to each of the two processing options just discussed: caching and report snapshots. Caching does not create a cached copy of a report until the report is actually executed by a user. If a report has a number of parameters, then a cached copy of the report suitable to satisfy requests for a given combination of parameters is not created until a user first executes the report with that combination of parameters.

Report snapshots allow for a "preexecuted" version of a report to be created in advance, but that preexecuted version can only be created for the default parameters assigned to that report. Given these limitations, it is clear we need a more flexible form of caching. Fortunately, Reporting Services has cache refresh options to fill this need.

Cache Refresh Plans

The cache refresh options available in Reporting Services give us a more powerful way to control the content of our report cache. *Cache Refresh Plans* give us the ability to schedule the execution of a report with any given combination of parameters we desire. When this scheduled execution occurs for a report that has caching enabled, the resulting intermediate format is placed in the report cache. As long as we can create cache refresh plans for all possible parameter combinations, or more realistically, all common or likely parameter combinations, we can ensure that our users get all the benefits of receiving reports from cache even when the report is highly parameterized.

Creating a Cache Refresh Plan

Let's return to our Weather Report one more time and create a cache refresh plan. We first need to change the processing options for the report from using the report snapshot back to using caching.

1. Navigate to the Chapter09 folder in the Report Manager, if you are not already there.
2. Hover over the WeatherReport, and select Manage from the drop-down menu. The Properties page appears.
3. Select Processing Options from the left side of the screen. The Processing Options page appears.
4. Select Always run this report with the most recent data.
5. Select the "Cache a temporary copy of the report. Expire copy of report on the following schedule" option.
6. Report-specific schedule is selected by default. Click Configure next to Report-specific schedule.
7. Leave Day selected, and select Every weekday in the Daily Schedule area.
8. Set Start Time to 1:00 A.M.
9. Click OK to return to the Processing Options page.
10. Click Apply to save your changes to the report cache settings.
11. Click Cache Refresh Options on the left side of the page. This will take you to the Cache Refresh Options page.
12. Click New Cache Refresh Plan at the top of the page.

NOTE

If caching is not enabled for the report, you will receive an error message when trying to create a cache refresh plan. If this occurs, click OK to turn on caching.

13. Enter **Borlaron Only** for Description.
14. Click the Configure button to create an item-specific schedule. The Schedule page appears.

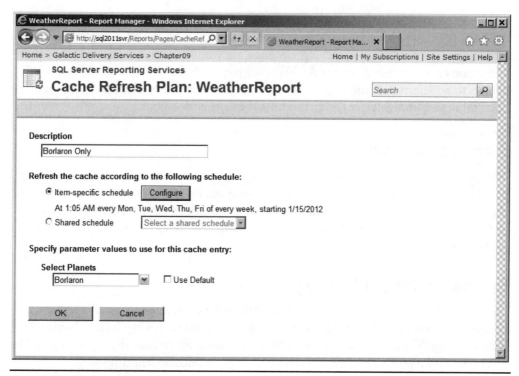

Figure 11-17   *The Cache Refresh Plan page*

15. Leave Day selected, and select Every weekday in the Daily Schedule area.
16. Set Start Time to 1:05 A.M.
17. Click OK to return to the Cache Refresh Plan page.
18. From the Select Planets drop-down list, uncheck all planet names except for Borlaron. The Cache Refresh Plan page will appear as shown in Figure 11-17.
19. Click OK to exit the Cache Refresh Plan page.

NOTE

The settings in this example have created scheduled processes that will run each night on your report server at 1:00 A.M. and 1:05 A.M. If you do not want these processes to run each night, you may want to delete the cache refresh plan and turn off report caching.

The Weather Report is now set to expire its cache every weekday at 1:00 A.M. and then at 1:05 A.M. create a cached copy of the report run with the Planets parameter set to Borlaron. To get adequate caching coverage, we would need to continue this process and create cache refresh plans for the Weather Report for each likely combination of planets to be selected. If you want to go through that exercise, you are welcome to do so, but I think you probably get the gist of how it works at this point.

Report History

The *report history* feature of the Report Manager enables you to keep copies of a report's past execution. This lets you save the state of your data without having to save copies of the data itself. You can keep documentation of inventory levels, production schedules, or financial records. You can look back in time, using the report history, to do trend analysis or to verify past information.

Enabling Report History

To demonstrate the report history feature of Reporting Services, we need a report whose results change often. It just so happens we created such a report in Chapter 9. The TransportMonitor report provides different values every time the report is run. We can move that report to the report server and then enable the report history.

1. If you composed your reports with SSDT or Visual Studio, upload the TransportMonitor report from the Chapter09 project.
2. Navigate to the Chapter09 folder, hover over the TransportMonitor report, and select Manage from the drop-down menu. The Properties page appears.
3. Click Parameters on the left side of the page.
4. Select the Has Default check box, and type **1304** for Default Value.
5. Click Apply.
6. Click Snapshot Options on the left side of the page. The Snapshot Options page appears, as shown in Figure 11-18.
7. Make sure the Allow report history to be created manually check box is checked. If it is not, check it and click Apply.
8. Click the large TransportMonitor title at the top of the page to execute the report. Remember, this report has autorefresh set. After about a minute, the report refreshes and new data is displayed.

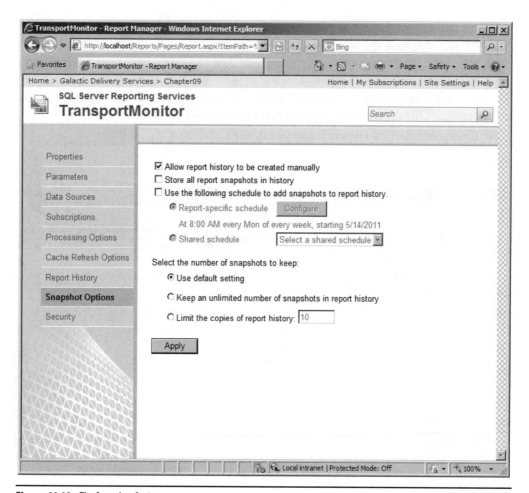

Figure 11-18 *The Snapshot Options page*

Manually Creating a Report History Snapshot

One way to create a report history is to do so manually. We can give this a try in the following example.

1. Click the TransportMonitor link at the top of the page.
2. Click Report History on the left side of the page.

3. Click the New Snapshot button in the report viewer toolbar. An entry for a report history snapshot appears.

4. Click the New Snapshot button two more times to create two more report history snapshots, as shown in Figure 11-19.

5. Click the link in the Last Run column to the first report history snapshot you created. This report should appear in a new browser window.

6. Open the other two report history snapshots, and compare all three.

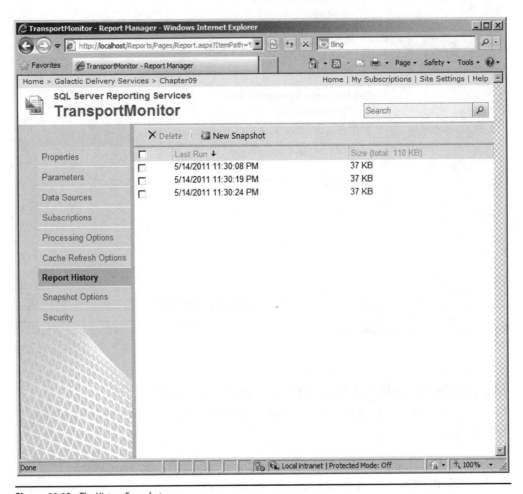

Figure 11-19 *The History Snapshot page*

As with the cached report instances, the report history snapshots store the intermediate format of the report. Because of this, you can export this report to any of the rendering formats.

1. Select one of your browser windows containing a report history snapshot.
2. Export the snapshot to the PDF file format, and open it in Adobe Acrobat Reader.
3. Close Acrobat Reader and the browser windows containing your report history snapshots.

Report History Snapshots and Report Parameters

To make our TransportMonitor report work with report history snapshots, we had to provide a default value for the transport number parameter. These parameters cannot be changed when each snapshot is created. (They can be changed, however, if the report is run normally through the Report Manager.)

Essentially, we are saving report history snapshots for only one transport. To save report history snapshots for other transports, we need to create linked reports with parameters defaulted to the other transport numbers.

1. Click Properties on the left side of the page.
2. Click Create Linked Report.
3. Type **Transport 1305 Monitor** for Name and **The Transport Monitor Report for Transport 1305** for Description.
4. Click OK. The linked report executes.
5. Click the Transport 1305 Monitor link at the top of the page. This takes us to the Properties page for the report.
6. Click Parameters on the left side of the page.
7. Change Default Value to **1305**.
8. Click Apply.
9. Click Report History on the left side of the page.
10. Click New Snapshot.
11. Click the entry for the new snapshot to view it. You can see this is a snapshot for transport number 1305.
12. Close the browser window containing your report history snapshot.

We can create as many linked reports as we need to collect report history snapshots for the different possible parameter values. Remember, linked reports all point back to a single report definition. If the TransportMonitor report is ever updated, it only needs to be deployed to one location, and all the linked reports will have the updated report definition.

Additional Methods for Creating Report History Snapshots

You can create report history snapshots in two other ways in addition to the manual method just described. You can instruct the report server to create a report history snapshot each time it creates a report snapshot. With this setting turned on, any time the report server creates a report snapshot—either manually or on a scheduled basis—a copy of that report snapshot is saved as a history snapshot.

You can also set up a schedule to create report history snapshots. Let's give that a try.

1. Click the Chapter09 link at the top of the page.
2. Hover over the TransportMonitor report (the original report, not the linked copy), and select Manage from the drop-down menu. The Properties page appears.
3. Click Snapshot Options on the left side of the page.
4. Check the Use the following schedule to add snapshots to report history check box.
5. The Report-specific schedule option is selected by default. Click Configure next to Report-specific schedule. The Schedule page appears.
6. Select Hour.
7. Change the Hourly Schedule to run every 0 hours 1 minutes. Set Start Time to five minutes from now.
8. Today's date should be selected for Begin running this schedule on.
9. Check the Stop This Schedule On check box, and set it to tomorrow's date.
10. Click OK to return to the Snapshot Options page. Note the description of the schedule you just created under Report-specific schedule.
11. Click Apply to save your changes to the history snapshot settings.
12. Click Report History on the left side of the page.

As each minute passes beyond the time you chose for the schedule to start, a new report history snapshot is created. You need to refresh your browser to see the new history snapshots in the list.

Report History Snapshots and Security

Not all users can change report history snapshot properties. To change the report history snapshot properties for a report, you must have rights to the Manage Report History task. Of the five predefined security roles, the Content Manager and My Reports roles have rights to this task.

Managing Report History Snapshots

You will not usually have a report that requires a new report history snapshot every minute of the day, as we set up in our example. Even so, report history snapshots can start to pile up if you let them. Making business decisions about the number of history snapshots to save for each report is important. Even more important, then, is to implement those business decisions and manage the number of history snapshots being saved on the report server.

Setting Limits on the Number of Report History Snapshots

Reporting Services provides a way to limit the number of history snapshots saved for any given report. Let's take a look and put a limit on our TransportMonitor report snapshots at the same time.

1. Click Snapshot Options on the left side of the page.
2. In the Select the number of snapshots to keep section of the page, select the Limit the copies of report history option.
3. Set the limit to 5.
4. Click Apply to save your changes to the history snapshot settings.
5. Click OK in response to the warning dialog box.
6. Click Report History.

If you waited long enough to accumulate more than five report history snapshots, you see the list was reduced to the five most recent history snapshots. The older history snapshots were automatically deleted. As each new history snapshot is created, the oldest history snapshot is deleted, so the total always remains at five. Again, remember you need to refresh your browser to see these changes as each minute passes.

We chose to set a limit on the number of history snapshots saved for this report. In addition to this option, you have two others to choose from (see Figure 11-18). You can keep an unlimited number of history snapshots, or you can use the default setting for history snapshot retention. You see how to change this default setting in the section "The General Site Settings Page."

Manually Deleting Report History Snapshots

In addition to using the history snapshot limit on the Snapshot Options page, you can manually delete unwanted history snapshots.

1. Refresh your browser.

CAUTION

If you reached the limit of five history snapshots, the report server is automatically deleting old history snapshots as new ones are created. If your Report History page is not current, you could try to delete a history snapshot that has already been removed by the report server. This results in an error.

2. Check the check box in the Delete column for three of the history snapshot entries.
3. Click Delete in the History tab toolbar.
4. Click OK to confirm the deletion.

The report server again accumulates history snapshots for this report until it has reached our five-snapshot limit. At that point, it again deletes the oldest history snapshot as each new one is created.

Disabling Report History Snapshot Creation

We can now disable the creation of report history snapshots for this report so we are not wasting valuable execution cycles.

1. Click Snapshot Options on the left side of the screen.
2. Uncheck the Use the following schedule to add snapshots to report history check box.
3. Click Apply.
4. Click Report History.

New history snapshots are no longer created for this report on a scheduled basis. Note, however, that the existing history snapshots were not deleted. These history snapshots are still available for viewing, even though the schedule that created them was disabled.

Updating Report Definitions and Report History Snapshots

One of the best features of report history snapshots is this: they are not lost if the definition of the underlying report is changed. Let's see this in action.

1. Open the TransportMonitor report in your report authoring environment of choice.
2. In the Report Data window, right-click the entry for the TransportMonitor dataset, and select Dataset Properties from the context menu. The Dataset Properties dialog box appears.
3. Select the Filters page.

4. Click the Add button to add a filter.

5. Select [Item] from the Expression drop-down list. Select <> from the Operator drop-down list. Enter **Thruster** for the Value. This filter removes the thruster data from the report.

6. Click OK to exit the Dataset Properties dialog box.

7. Preview/Run the report. Check 1304 in the Transports drop-down list, and click View Report. Note the Thruster graph is missing.

8. Save the report.

9. If you are using SSDT or Visual Studio, deploy the report.

10. Close your development environment.

11. Return to the Report Manager in your browser.

12. If you are using Report Builder, you need to reset the parameter default. Go to the Parameters page to select the Has Default check box, type **1304** for Default Value, and click Apply.

13. Click the large TransportMonitor title to run the report. Note the report now includes our change, eliminating the thruster data from the report.

14. Click the TransportMonitor link at the top of the page. This should return you to the Report History page. We still have some report history snapshots based on the old report definition.

15. Click New Snapshot to manually create a report history snapshot based on the new report definition. Our five-history-snapshot limit is still in effect, so one of the old history snapshots may have to be deleted to make room for the new one.

16. Click the most recent history snapshot to view it. It does not contain thruster data because it is based on the new report definition.

17. Close this browser window.

18. Click the oldest history snapshot to view it. It does contain thruster data because it is based on the old report definition.

19. Close this browser window.

Just like the cached report instance, the history snapshot contains both the report definition and the dataset. Therefore, it is unaffected by subsequent changes to the report definition.

Subscriptions

Up to this point, we have discussed only one way for users to receive reports. They log on to the Report Manager site, find the report they want, and execute it, which is known as *pull* technology. The user pulls the information out of Reporting Services by initiating the execution of the report.

Reporting Services also supports push technology for delivering reports. In a *push* technology scenario, Reporting Services initiates the execution of the report and then sends the report to the user. This is done through the report subscription.

Standard Subscriptions

Reporting Services supports several types of *subscriptions*. The first is the *standard* subscription, which is a request to execute a report once and push the result to a particular user or set of users. The standard subscription is usually a self-serve operation. A user logs on to the Report Manager site and finds the report they want. The user then creates the subscription by specifying the schedule for the push delivery and the delivery options.

Standard subscriptions have two delivery options: e-mail and file share. The *e-mail delivery* option, of course, sends an e-mail to the specified e-mail addresses with a link to the report or with the report itself either embedded as HTML or as an attached document. The *file share* option creates a file containing the report in a specified folder on a file share. The file share option can be used to place the report into a document store managed and/or indexed by another application, such as Microsoft's Office SharePoint Server.

Creating a Standard E-mail Subscription with an Embedded Report

You have been hired as the traffic manager for Galactic Delivery Services and are responsible for routing transport traffic. As part of your job, it is important to know what the weather is like at all the hubs. Rather than taking the time to go look at the Weather Report on the Report Manager website, you want to have the report e-mailed to you hourly.

1. Open the Report Manager, and navigate to the Chapter09 folder.
2. Hover over the WeatherReport, and select Manage from the drop-down menu. Click Subscriptions on the left side of the page.
3. Click New Subscription. The Subscription Properties page appears, as shown in Figure 11-20.

NOTE

You can go directly to the Subscription Properties page to create a new subscription by hovering over the report name and selecting Subscribe from the drop-down menu.

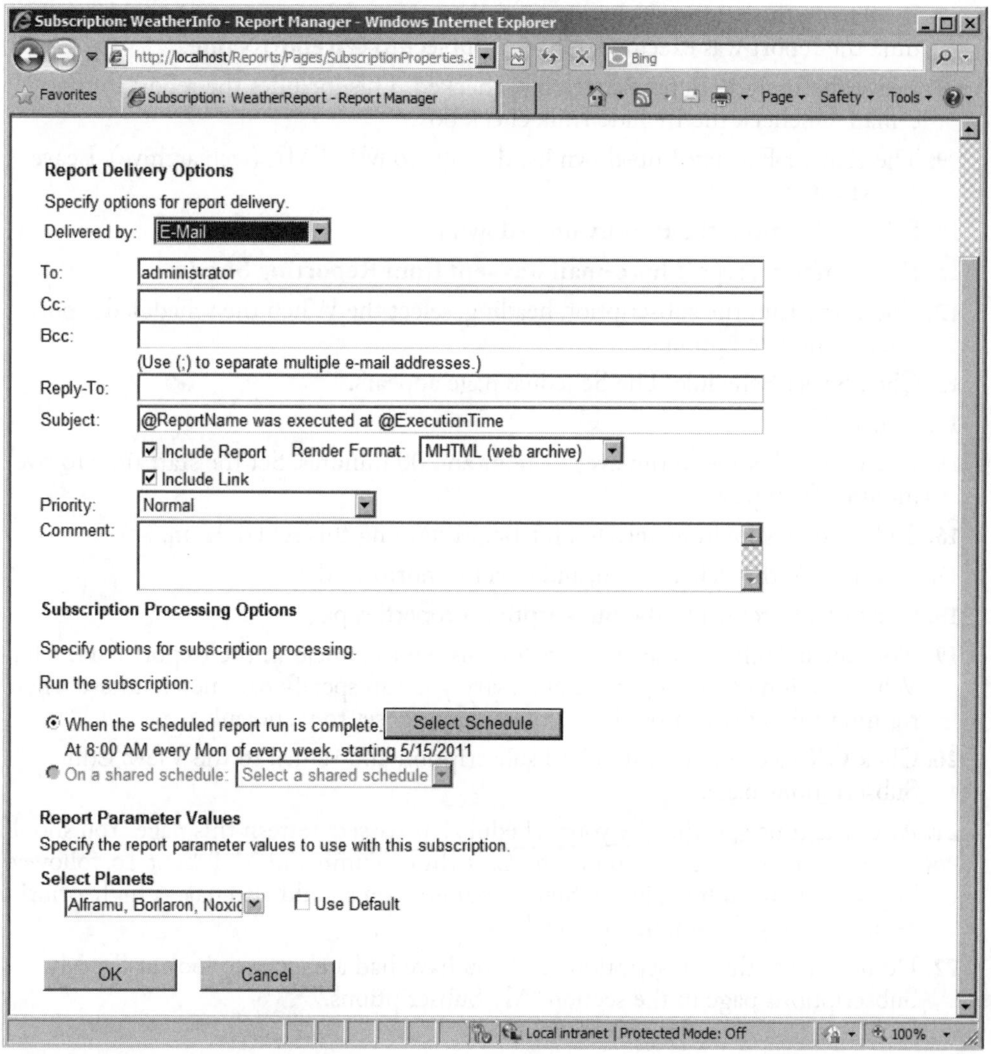

Figure 11-20 *The Subscription Properties page*

4. The Delivered by drop-down list defaults to E-Mail. Leave this set to the default setting.

5. Type your e-mail address for To. Note that you can enter multiple e-mail addresses, separated by a semicolon (;), and you can also enter e-mail addresses for Cc and Bcc.

6. Enter an e-mail address for Reply-To. This can be your own e-mail address, someone else's, or a dummy e-mail address that does not exist.

7. By default, the subject of the e-mail is the name of the report, followed by the time the report was executed. Change Subject to **@ReportName**.

8. Leave the Include Report check box checked. This includes the report in the e-mail. Uncheck the Include Link check box.

9. The Render Format drop-down list defaults to MHTML (web archive). Leave this selected.

10. Select High from the Priority drop-down list.

11. For Comment, type **This e-mail was sent from Reporting Services**.

12. Under the Run the subscription heading, select the When the scheduled report run is complete option.

13. Click Select Schedule. The Schedule page appears.

14. Select Hour.

15. Leave the schedule to run every 1 hour and 00 minutes. Set the start time to five minutes from now.

16. Today's date should be selected for Begin running this schedule on.

17. Check Stop this schedule on, and select tomorrow's date.

18. Click OK to return to the Subscription Properties page.

19. Note the default parameter values for this report appear in the Report Parameter Values section of this report. If necessary, you can specify parameters to use when running this subscription. Leave the parameter set to its default.

20. Click OK to create this standard subscription and return to the View/Edit Subscriptions page.

21. After the time specified by your schedule has passed, refresh this page. You should see the time of the execution in the Last Run column and Mail Sent To, followed by your e-mail address, in the Status column. You should also have a high-priority e-mail waiting for you in your mailbox.

22. Do not delete this subscription until you have had a chance to look at the My Subscriptions page in the section "My Subscriptions."

Creating a Standard E-mail Subscription with a Report Link

You have just been promoted to sales manager for the Axelburg office of Galactic Delivery Services. Congratulations! Being a good manager, you want to keep tabs on how your salespeople are doing. To do this, you want to view the Invoice-Batch Number Report each week to see how much you are invoicing your clients. As a memory aid, you want to receive an e-mail each week with a link to this report.

1. Open the Report Manager, and navigate to the Axelburg folder.

2. Hover over the Invoice-Batch Number Report, and select Subscribe from the drop-down menu. The Subscription Properties page appears.

3. The Delivered by setting defaults to E-Mail. Leave this as the default setting.

4. Type your e-mail address for To.

5. Enter an e-mail address for Reply-To.

6. Change Subject to **@ReportName**.

7. Uncheck the Include Report check box. Leave the Include Link check box checked.

8. Render Format is not used because we are just embedding a link to the report.

9. Select High from the Priority drop-down list.

10. For Comment, type **Remember to check the invoice amounts**.

11. Under the Run the subscription heading, select the When the scheduled report run is complete option.

12. Click Select Schedule. The Schedule page appears.

13. Select Week.

14. Leave Repeat after this number of weeks set to 1.

15. Check today for On day(s). For example, check Mon if today is Monday. Uncheck all the other days.

16. Set the start time to five minutes from now.

17. Today's date should be selected for Begin running this schedule on.

18. Check Stop this schedule on, and select tomorrow's date.

19. Click OK to return to the Subscription Properties page.

20. At the bottom of the Schedule Properties page, you see a list of the parameters for the selected report. Leave the default values for the parameters.

21. Click OK to create this standard subscription and return to the Report Viewer page.

When the scheduled time has passed, you will receive an e-mail with a link to this report.

Standard Subscriptions and Report Snapshots

In addition to creating your own schedules for your standard subscriptions, you can synchronize your subscriptions with scheduled report snapshots. For example, if the Weather Report is set to create a report snapshot every hour, you can receive an e-mail with the new version of the report after each new report snapshot has been created.

One way to do this is to keep the schedule for the report snapshot synchronized with the schedule for the subscription. The report snapshot runs, and then the subscription runs one minute later. This can cause problems if the report snapshot occasionally takes more than one minute to create or if one of the schedules is edited.

A better solution is to let the creation of the report snapshot drive the delivery of the subscription. The When the Report Content Is Refreshed option does just that. When this option is selected for a subscription, the subscription is sent out every time a new report snapshot is created. Of course, this option is only available for reports that have report snapshots enabled; otherwise, it does not show up on the screen.

Multiple Subscriptions for One Report

Nothing prevents a user from creating more than one subscription for the same report. Perhaps you want a report delivered every Friday and on the last day of the month. You can't do this with one subscription, but you can certainly do it with two—a weekly subscription for the Friday delivery and a monthly subscription for delivery on the last day of the month.

Another reason for multiple subscriptions is to receive a report run for multiple sets of parameters. You saw it is possible to specify parameter values as part of the subscription properties. Using this feature, you could have one subscription send you a report with one set of parameters and another subscription send you the same report with a different set of parameters.

Embedded Report Versus Attached Report

When you choose to include the report along with the subscription e-mail, the report can show up either embedded in an HTML e-mail or as an attached document. If you select the MHTML Web Archive format, the report is embedded. If you select any of the other render formats, the report is sent as an attached document.

Having the report embedded in the e-mail makes it convenient for the user to view the report: it is simply part of the body of your e-mail. However, not all e-mail packages support HTML e-mail, so some users might be unable to view an embedded report. If a user is unsure of the capabilities of their e-mail package, they should choose the PDF file format. This format is sent as an attachment and can be viewed by just about anyone.

Standard Subscriptions and Security

Not all users can create standard subscriptions. In fact, it is possible to view a report but not be able to subscribe to it. To subscribe to a report or create a subscription for delivery to others, you must have rights to the Manage Individual Subscriptions task. Of the five predefined security roles, the Browser, Content Manager, and My Reports roles have rights to manage individual subscriptions.

Managing Your Subscriptions

An active user may subscribe to a number of reports scattered throughout a number of folders. Just remembering all the reports you subscribed to can be a big challenge. Managing all those subscriptions can be even tougher. Fortunately, the Report Manager provides a way to view all your subscriptions in one place.

My Subscriptions

The My Subscriptions page consolidates all your standard subscriptions in one place.

1. Click the My Subscriptions link at the top of the page. The My Subscriptions page appears, as shown in Figure 11-21.
2. You can click any heading to sort your list of subscriptions.
3. Click the Edit link next to WeatherReport. The Subscription Properties page appears.

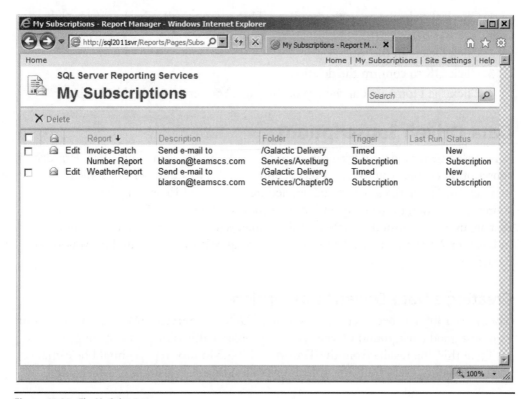

Figure 11-21 *The My Subscriptions page*

4. You can make changes to this subscription, if you desire. Click Cancel to return to the My Subscriptions page.

5. Click the WeatherReport link in the Report column. You jump to the Weather Report.

6. Click your browser's Back button.

7. Click the text in the Folder column for the Invoice-Batch Number Report. You jump to the Axelburg folder.

8. Click your browser's Back button.

The My Subscriptions page lists all the standard subscriptions you created on this report server. This makes the subscriptions much easier to manage. You can sort the list several different ways to help you find and manage the subscriptions. You can also use the My Subscriptions page to delete unwanted subscriptions.

Let's delete these subscriptions so you do not waste computing power e-mailing reports.

1. Check the check box in the headings. This automatically checks the check box next to each subscription.

2. Click Delete in the toolbar.

3. Click OK to confirm the deletion.

4. Click the Home link at the top of the page. You return to the Home folder.

Data-Driven Subscriptions

A better name for a data-driven subscription might be "mass mailing." The data-driven subscription enables you to take a report and e-mail it to a number of people on a mailing list. The mailing list can be queried from any valid Reporting Services data source. In addition to the recipient's e-mail address, the mailing list can contain fields that are used to control the content of the e-mail sent to each recipient. As mentioned in Chapter 2, the Enterprise Edition of Reporting Services is required for you to use data-driven subscriptions.

Creating a Data-Driven Subscription

Transport 1305 has been acting up. Galactic Delivery Services wants all its mechanics to have a good background on the types of problems this transport is having. To facilitate this, the results from the Transport 1305 Monitor report should be e-mailed to all mechanics every four hours. Employees holding the position of Mechanic I should receive the report as a high-priority e-mail. Employees holding the position of Mechanic II should receive the report as a normal-priority e-mail.

1. Open the Report Manager, and navigate to the Chapter09 folder.
2. Hover over the Transport 1305 Monitor report, and select Manage from the drop-down menu.
3. Click Subscriptions on the left side of the page.
4. Click the New Data-driven Subscription button. The first page of the data-driven subscription process appears, as shown in Figure 11-22.

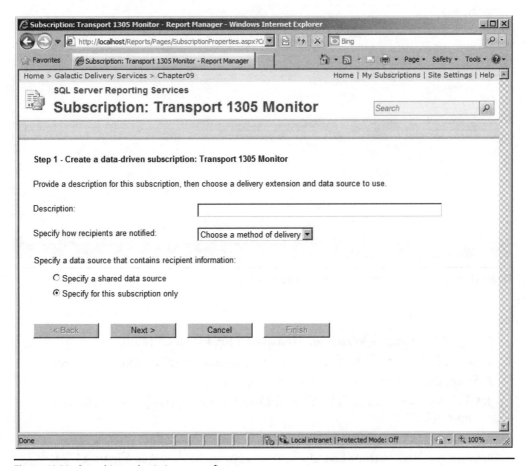

Figure 11-22 *Data-driven subscription process, first page*

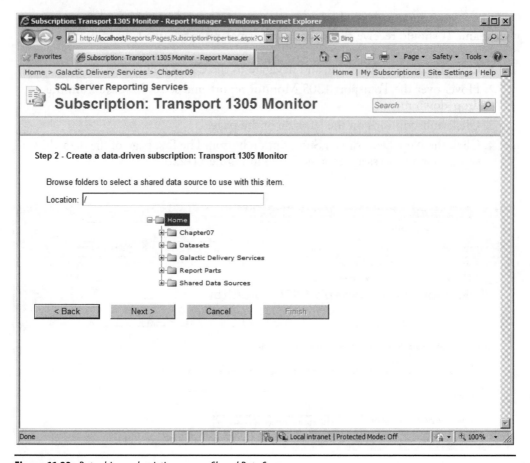

Figure 11-23 *Data-driven subscription process, Shared Data Source page*

5. Type **Maintenance Watch on Transport 1305** for Description.
6. Select E-Mail from the Specify how recipients are notified drop-down list.
7. Select the Specify a shared data source option.
8. Click the Next button. The Shared Data Source page appears, as shown in Figure 11-23.
9. Use the tree view to find and select the Galactic shared data source.
10. Click the Next button. The Query page appears, as shown in Figure 11-24.

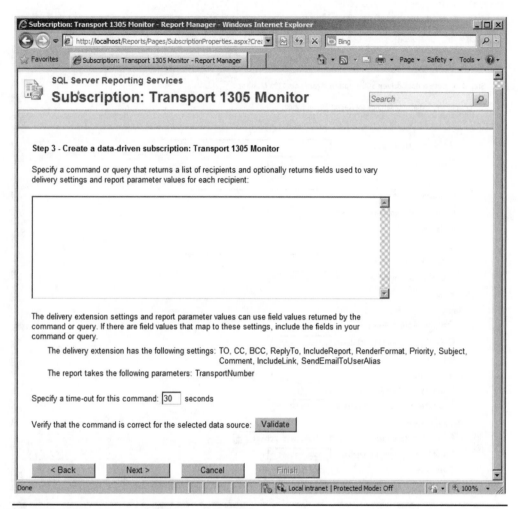

Figure 11-24 *Data-driven subscription process, Query page*

11. Type the following for the query:

```
EXEC stp_MechanicMailingList
```

12. Click Validate to make sure you don't have any typos or other problems.

13. If the query does not validate successfully, look for the error in the query you typed. Otherwise, click Next. The Data Association page appears, as shown in Figure 11-25. Here, you can associate columns in the result set with fields in the subscription e-mail.

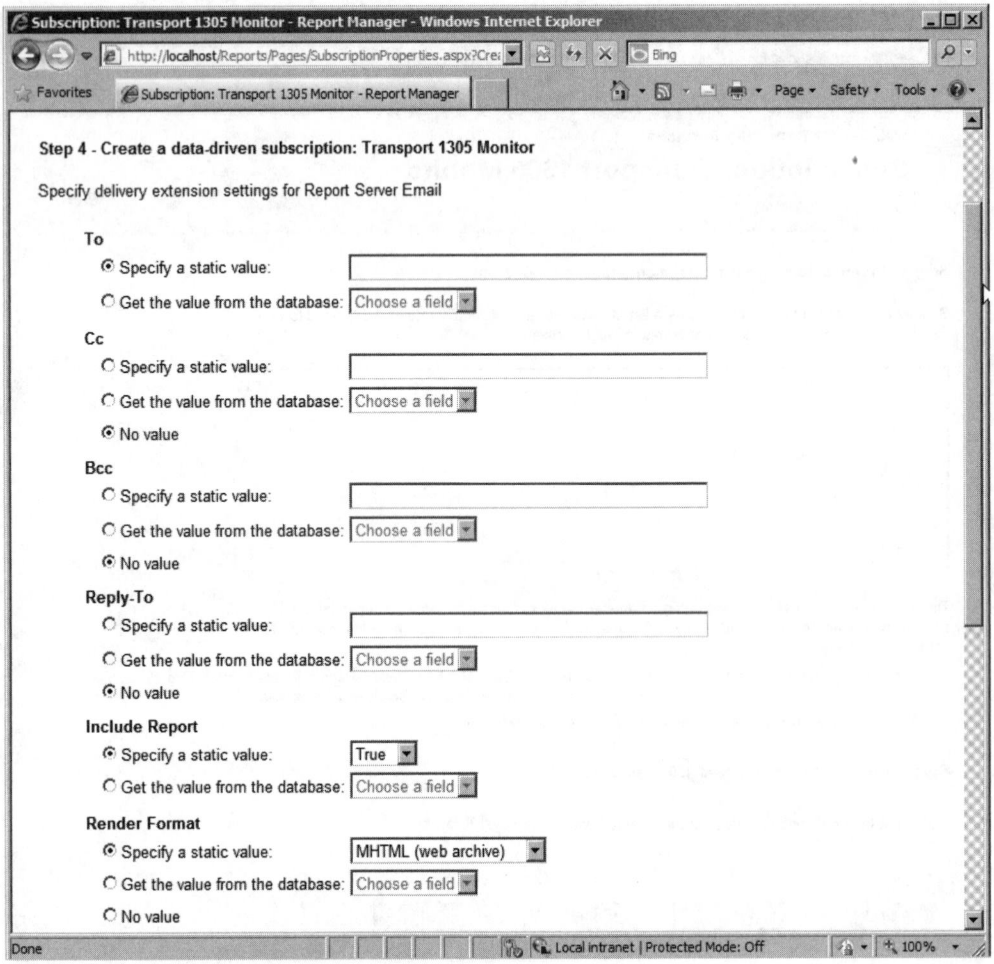

Figure 11-25 *Data-driven subscription process, Data Association page*

14. Set the following properties on this page:

Property	Value
To	Specify a static value.
Specify a static value (For To)	(Type your e-mail address here. Normally, you would select the e-mail address from a database field, but we want to have a valid e-mail address for our example. Because your system cannot send interplanetary e-mail, we have to use your e-mail address.)

Property	Value
Reply-To	Specify a static value.
Specify a static value (Reply-To)	Reports@Galactic.SRA
Render Format	Specify a static value.
Specify a static value (Render Format)	PDF
Priority	Get the value from the database.
Get the value from the database (Priority)	Priority
Subject	Get the value from the database.
Get the value from the database (Subject)	Subject
Include Link	Specify a static value.
Specify a static value (Include Link)	False

15. Click the Next button. The Parameter Values page appears, as shown in Figure 11-26.

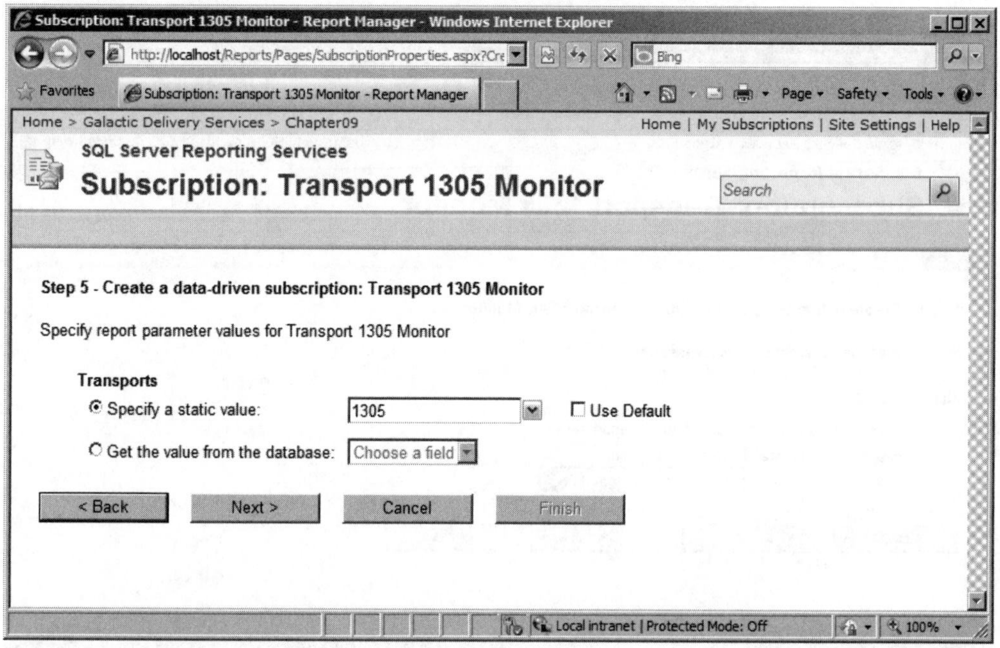

Figure 11-26 *Data-driven subscription process, Parameter Values page*

NOTE

Because we do not allow the user to change the TransportNumber parameter, the subscription does not allow us to change that default parameter value here. For a report that does include user-enterable parameters, the parameter values would be specified here. As with other items, parameter values can be static values or can come from the database.

16. Click the Next button. The Notify Recipients page appears, as shown in Figure 11-27.
17. Select the On a schedule created for this subscription option.
18. Click the Next button. The Schedule page appears.
19. Select the Hour option.
20. Change the schedule to run every 4 hours 00 minutes.
21. Set the start time to five minutes from now.
22. Today's date should be selected for Begin running this schedule on.
23. Check Stop this schedule on, and select tomorrow's date.

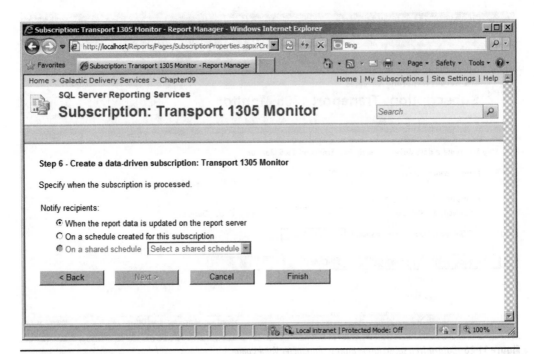

Figure 11-27 *Data-driven subscription process, Notify Recipients page*

24. Click Finish.

25. Once the scheduled time for your subscription has passed, refresh this page. You should see the time of the execution in the Last Run column and Done: 8 processed of 8 total; 0 errors in the Status column. You should also receive eight e-mails (eight mechanics are in the database, and we sent an e-mail to each one) with the Transport 1305 Monitor report attached.

26. If you do not want to receive eight e-mails every four hours for the next day, you can delete this subscription.

Data-Driven Subscriptions and Security

Not all users can create data-driven subscriptions. To create a data-driven subscription for a report, you must have rights to the Manage All Subscriptions task. Of the five predefined security roles, only the Content Manager role has rights to this task.

Data-Driven Subscriptions and Event-Driven Behavior

You can do a couple of tricks with data-driven subscriptions that make them even more powerful. For instance, at times, you might not want a subscription sent out until after a certain event has occurred. For instance, you may want to e-mail a report to a number of recipients after a specific data update process has completed. While a data-driven subscription is a scheduled process, rather than triggered by a particular event, we can make it behave almost as if it were event-driven.

You need a field in a status table that contains the completion date and time of the last data load. You also need a field in a status table that contains the date and time when the report was last distributed. With these two flag fields in place, you can simulate event-driven behavior for your data-driven subscription.

First, you need to build a stored procedure that returns the mailing list for the report distribution. To this stored procedure, add logic that checks the date and time of the last data load against the date and time of the last report distribution. If the data load is complete and the report has not yet been distributed today, the stored procedure returns the mailing list result set. If the data load is incomplete, or if the report has already been distributed today, the stored procedure returns an empty result set.

Now you create a series of data-driven subscriptions based on this stored procedure. If the data load completes sometime between 1:00 A.M. and 3:00 A.M., you might schedule one data-driven subscription to execute at 1:00 A.M., another at 1:30 A.M., another at 2:00 A.M., and so on. When each data-driven subscription executes, the stored procedure determines whether the data load is complete and whether the report was already distributed. If the stored procedure returns a result set, the data-driven subscription e-mails the report to the mailing list. If the stored procedure returns an empty result set, the data-driven subscription terminates without sending any e-mails.

This same approach can be used to e-mail reports only when the report data has changed. You create a stored procedure that only returns a mailing list result set if the data has changed since the last time the report was e-mailed. This stored procedure is used to create a data-driven subscription. Now the data-driven subscription only sends out reports when the data has changed; otherwise, it sends nothing.

Data-Driven Subscriptions and Report Caching

If you looked closely, you may have noticed that the Specify how recipients are notified drop-down list on the first page of the data-driven subscription process included the entry Null Delivery Provider. This doesn't seem to make much sense—why would you create a subscription and then not send it anywhere? This Null Delivery Provider is used to support report caching.

The Null Delivery Provider allows us to use a data-driven subscription as a data-driven cache refresh plan. Rather than creating a number of cache refresh plans to account for all of the possible parameter combinations we want to cache, we could create one data-driven subscription that ran the report for all of those possible parameter combinations. In that case, we don't really want the resulting reports to go anywhere except into cache, so we can use the Null Delivery Provider.

The first step to implement this scheme is to create a query that returns all the possible report parameter combinations (or at least the most popular ones) for this report. You then use this query to create a data-driven subscription to execute the report with each of these parameter combinations. If report caching is enabled, the data-driven subscription would cause a copy of the report to be cached with each of these parameter combinations. This is true even if the Null Delivery Provider is used and the report is never delivered anywhere by the subscription. Because the subscription created all these cached copies with the various parameter value combinations, no matter what combination of parameters a user enters the following day, the report is rendered from a cached copy.

Site Settings

When setting the limit for the number of history snapshots kept for a given report, we encountered a setting that referred to using a default value. Each time you have the opportunity to specify a schedule for an execution snapshot, a subscription, or other feature, you have an option to select a shared schedule. The report history snapshot default value, the shared schedules, and several other site-wide settings are managed on the Site Settings page.

The General Site Settings Page

The main Site Settings page enables you to set several default values and configuration options. This page also acts as a front end for other configuration screens. You can access the Site Settings page by clicking the Site Settings link at the top of the page. The General Site Settings page is shown in Figure 11-28.

We begin our examination of the site settings by looking at the configuration items and default values on the General Site Settings page.

Name

The value in the Name field appears at the top of each page in the Report Manager. You can change this to the name of your company or some other phrase that can help users identify this report server.

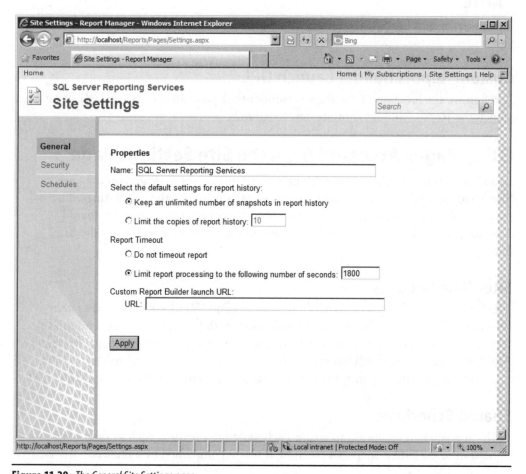

Figure 11-28 *The General Site Settings page*

Report History Default

The report history default setting lets you specify a default value for the maximum number of history snapshots to keep. This can be set to a specific number or set to allow an unlimited number of snapshots. Each report utilizing report history snapshots can either specify its own maximum number or use this default value.

Report Timeout

The default for Report Timeout enables you to specify a default value for the maximum amount of time a report may run before it times out. This can be a specific number of seconds or set to no timeout (unlimited execution time). Each report can either specify its own timeout value or use this default value.

NOTE

The report timeout is specified on the Processing Options page for each report.

Custom Report Builder Launch URL

If you move the location of the Report Builder tool, you can specify the URL used to launch the Report Builder from its new location.

Other Pages Accessed from the Site Settings Page

In addition to the configuration options and default values managed on the General Site Settings page, there are two other pages available under the site settings. These pages enable you to manage the site-wide security configuration and the shared schedules. The following is a brief discussion of each area managed from the Site Settings pages.

Site-Wide Security

The Security page lets you assign Windows users and Windows groups to system-level roles. These system-level roles provide users with the rights to view and modify settings for the report server, such as those found on the Site Settings page. System Administrator and System User are the two predefined system-level roles.

For more information on system-level roles and system-level tasks, see Chapter 10.

Shared Schedules

Each time you had an option to create a schedule for a feature, such as report cache expiration or execution snapshot creation, it was accompanied by a choice to use a shared schedule. A *shared schedule* lets you use a single schedule definition in multiple places. A shared schedule is created through the same user interface used to create all the other schedules we have been looking at in this chapter.

Shared schedules are beneficial for situations where a number of events should use the same timing. For example, suppose you have ten reports that utilize report snapshots, all pulling data from a data warehouse. That data warehouse is updated once a week. It makes sense to create one shared schedule that can be used to run the report snapshots for all these reports.

Not only does this save the time that would otherwise be necessary to create the schedule ten times, but it also makes it easier if the timing of the data warehouse update is changed and the report snapshot schedule must be changed. If you are using a shared schedule, you only need to make this change once in the shared location. Without the shared schedule, you would be forced to make this change ten times.

Managing Reporting Services Through the SQL Server Management Studio

In Chapter 10, we used the SQL Server Management Studio to help manage security on the report server. We created a new security role. We did this in the SQL Server Management Studio because this activity could not be done through the Report Manager. Let's look at a couple of other aspects of report server management that require the SQL Server Management Studio.

The Server Properties Dialog Box

Follow these steps to view the Server Properties dialog box in SQL Server Management Studio:

1. Start SQL Server Management Studio, and connect to the report server as we did in Chapter 10.
2. Right-click the report server in the Object Explorer window, and select Properties from the context menu. The Server Properties dialog box appears, as shown in Figure 11-29.

As you can see, a number of the characteristics of the report server that can be managed through the Report Manager can also be controlled here. We will not discuss this ground that has already been covered; instead, we will cover the items that are unique to the Server Properties dialog box.

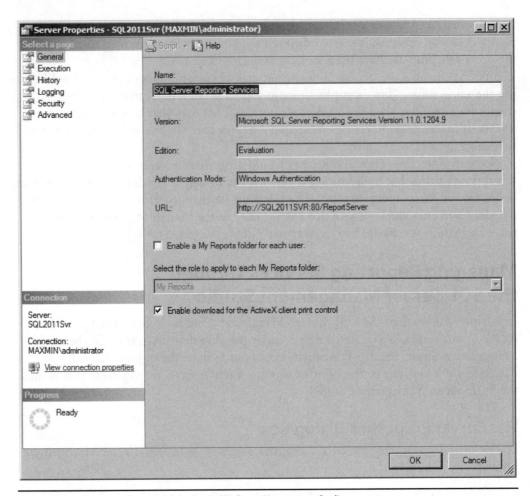

Figure 11-29   *The Server Properties dialog box in SQL Server Management Studio*

My Reports

The Enable a My Reports folder for each user option, on the General page of the
Server Properties dialog box, turns on a feature giving each user their own private folder
on the report server. When this option is enabled, a special folder called Users Folders is
created in the Home folder. Only users assigned the System Administrator role can see
this folder.

CAUTION

You should enable the My Reports option only if you intend to use it. Getting rid of the Users Folders folder and its content once it is created is a bit tricky. If you do create the folder and then need to delete it, turn off the My Reports option, go into each folder in the Users Folders folder, and give yourself Content Manager rights. Now you can delete the folders.

As each user logs on for the first time after the My Reports option is enabled, a new folder is created in the Users Folders folder. This new folder has the same name as the domain and logon name of the user signing in. The new folder is mapped to a folder called My Reports.

Let's discuss an example to make this clearer. Sally and José are two users in the Galactic domain. Shortly after the My Reports option is enabled, Sally accesses the report server using the Report Manager. A new folder is created in the Users Folders folder called Galactic Sally.

Sally is not assigned the System Administrator role, so she cannot see the Users Folders folder or the Galactic Sally folder inside of it. Instead, when Sally views her Home folder, she sees a folder called My Reports. Sally's My Reports folder is a mapping to the Galactic Sally folder.

When José accesses the report server using the Report Manager, a new folder is created in the Users Folders folder called Galactic José. José sees a folder called My Reports in his Home folder. José's My Reports folder is a mapping to the Galactic José folder.

José is assigned the System Administrator role. In addition to the My Reports folder, José can view the Users Folders folder. When José opens the Users Folders folder, he can see both the Galactic Sally and the Galactic José folders. In fact, José can open the Galactic Sally folder and view its contents.

Security and My Reports

Because the My Reports folder is for each user's personal reports, the users are granted more rights in the My Reports folder than they might be granted anywhere else on the site. On the General Settings page of the Site Settings, you decide which security role to assign to the user in their own My Reports folder. By default, users are assigned the My Reports role in their own My Reports folder.

A user can be granted broader rights in the My Reports folder because they are the only one using the reports in this folder. No one else is going to set up caching and report history snapshots, for example, because no one else is going to use these reports. You want to be sure to assign the user to a role that has rights to publish reports; otherwise, each user will be unable to put reports in their own My Reports folder.

When to Enable the My Reports Option

The My Reports option can be useful in two situations. First, if you have a number of individuals creating ad hoc reports for their own personal use, the My Reports folder provides a convenient spot for this to take place. If you do use the My Reports folder in this manner, you want to have some policies in place to ensure that each user's My Reports folder does not become an ad hoc dumping ground.

The second viable use of the My Reports folder is as a quality assurance (QA) testing area for report developers. The report developers can use their individual My Reports folders as a place to test a report in the server environment before it is deployed to a folder available to the users. This is convenient, because the system administrator can navigate through the Users Folders folder to access the report after it has passed QA testing and move it to its production location. Of course, having a dedicated quality assurance server for this purpose is far better, but in situations where this is not feasible, the My Reports folder can be considered as an option.

Report Execution Logging

The Enable Report Execution Logging option, on the Logging page of the Server Properties dialog box, determines whether information about each report execution is placed in the execution log. The execution log this option refers to is the ExecutionLogStorage table in the ReportServer database. This is not referring to any of the log text files created by the report server application. Along with turning logging off and on, you can specify how long the report server should keep these log entries.

The ExecutionLogStorage table uses cryptic globally unique identifier (GUID) strings to identify the reports being run. This is not going to be helpful when trying to figure out who has run the Invoice-Batch Number Report in the past month. Instead of querying the ExecutionLogStorage table directly, use the ExecutionLog2 view in the ReportServer database. This view decodes the GUID strings into the report paths and report names, making it much easier to work with.

Additional Settings

In addition to the configuration items on the Report Manager Site Settings page and the SQL Server Management Studio Server Properties dialog box, you can modify the functionality of the report server in other ways. In Chapter 12, we look at settings that can be changed using system properties. The system properties can be set through the Reporting Services Configuration Tool and through the SetSystemProperties method of the Reporting Services web service. See Chapter 12 for more details.

A Sense of Style

We do not have access to the source code of the Report Manager pages, so we cannot make changes to the way they function. However, because these pages are ultimately HTML pages sent to a browser, we can make changes to the way the pages look. This is done through a cascading style sheet (CSS).

The Reporting Services Style Sheet

The look of the Report Manager is controlled by the ReportingServices.css cascading style sheet. The default location for this file is

```
C:\Program Files\Microsoft SQL Server\MSRS11.MSSQLSERVER\Reporting Services\
                        ReportManager\Styles\ReportingServices.css
```

(There is also a cascading style sheet in this folder that controls the look of the web parts used to display reports in SharePoint.)

Let's take a look at the steps necessary to make a change to the cascading style sheet.

Modifying the Reporting Services Style Sheet

The following procedure changes the fonts for both the name displayed at the top of the Report Manager pages and the text showing the current folder.

1. Make a backup copy of the ReportingServices.css file.
2. Open the ReportingServices.css file in Notepad.
3. Locate the entry for msrs-lowertitle.
4. Change the font-size entry from 16px to 10px to decrease the size of the current folder text.
5. Locate the entry for msrs-uppertitle.
6. Change the font-size entry from x-small to large to increase the size of the name.
7. Add the following text immediately to the right of the semicolon after the font-size entry:

```
font-weight:bold;
```

8. Save your changes to the ReportingServices.css file, and exit Notepad.

NOTE

You need to remove any cached copies of the ReportingServices.css file from your browser before the changes to this style sheet can take effect.

9. Open the Report Manager in your browser, if it is not already open. If it is already open, navigate to a different folder in the Report Manager. You see the name at the top of the page now appears in large, bold text and the text showing the current folder is smaller.

Building On

In this chapter, you learned ways to deliver reports and control their execution from within the Report Manager. In the next chapter, we look at ways to customize report delivery by building onto Reporting Services. These techniques enable you to integrate Reporting Services reports with your own websites and custom applications.

Chapter 12

Teamwork: Integrating Reporting Services

In This Chapter

▶ **Using Reporting Services Without the Report Manager**

▶ **Best Foot Forward**

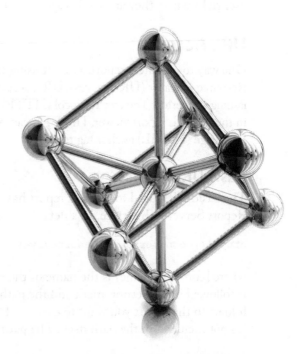

Up to this point, we have been using Reporting Services just as it comes out of the box (or off the installation disc, if you want to get technical). All our management of Reporting Services features and all our report execution have been through the Report Manager or the SQL Server Management Studio. Reporting Services, the Report Manager, and the SQL Server Management Studio do, after all, provide a feature-rich environment in their default configuration.

One of the best features of Reporting Services, however, is the capability to extend it beyond its basic operation. In this chapter, we do just that. You learn ways to execute reports without using the Report Manager interface. You also look at ways to manage Reporting Services without using the Report Manager or the SQL Server Management Studio.

All of this provides us ways to team up Reporting Services with other applications. Through this integration we can create great, full-featured solutions.

Using Reporting Services Without the Report Manager

The Report Manager provides a nice interface for finding and executing reports. However, the Report Manager is not always the best way to deliver a report to your users. Perhaps the user is browsing your website or using a custom application and needs to view a report. In these situations, it does not make sense to force the user to jump to the Report Manager and begin navigating folders. We want to deliver the report to the user right where they are. In this section, we explore several ways to do just that.

URL Access

One way to execute a report without using the Report Manager is through Uniform Resource Locator (URL) access. URL access allows a browser or a program capable of issuing Hypertext Transfer Protocol (HTTP) requests to specify a URL and receive a report in the HTML report viewer. This URL can be built into a standard Hypertext Markup Language (HTML) anchor tag to allow a report to be displayed with one mouse click.

Basic URL Access

The basic URL used to access a report has two parts. The first part is the URL of the Report Server web service. In a default installation, this is

```
http://{computername}/ReportServer
```

where {computername} is the name of the computer hosting the report server. This is followed by a question mark and the path through the Reporting Services virtual folders to the report you want to execute. The Home folder is the root of this path, but it's not included in the path itself. The path must begin with a forward slash (/).

Let's try an example. We can execute the Invoice-Batch Number Report for the Axelburg office. This report is in the Axelburg folder inside the Galactic Delivery Services folder.

> **NOTE**
>
> *In the examples used throughout the rest of this chapter, we assume Reporting Services is installed on your computer. The localhost name is used to access the report server on this computer. If you have Reporting Services installed on a different computer, substitute the name of that computer in place of localhost in the following examples.*

1. Start Internet Explorer.
2. Enter the following URL in the address bar:

```
http://localhost/ReportServer?/Galactic Delivery Services/Axelburg/
                                Invoice-Batch Number Report
```

3. Press ENTER. The Invoice-Batch Number Report appears in the browser inside the HTML report viewer.

> **NOTE**
>
> *When your URL is submitted, it is URL-encoded. Some of the characters in your URL may be replaced by other characters or by hexadecimal strings, such as %20. This ensures the URL can be interpreted correctly when it is sent to the web server.*

As with Report Manager, Windows integrated security is being used when a user executes a report through URL access. The user must have rights to execute the report; otherwise, an error results. However, because the user is not browsing through the folder structure to get to the report, the user does not need to have any rights to the folder containing the report. You can use this fact to hide a report from nonadministrative users who are browsing through folders in the Report Manager, while still making the report accessible to someone using URL access.

In addition to executing reports, you can view the contents of folders, resources, and shared data sources. Try the following:

1. Enter this URL in the address bar:

```
http://localhost/ReportServer?/Galactic Delivery Services
```

2. Press ENTER. The contents of the Galactic Delivery Services folder appear.
3. Click the link for the 2013 Conference folder. The contents of the 2013 Conference folder appear, as shown in Figure 12-1.

Command Parameters

Look at the URL in the address bar. You see something has been added to the URL, namely &rs:Command=ListChildren. This is called a *command parameter*. It tells

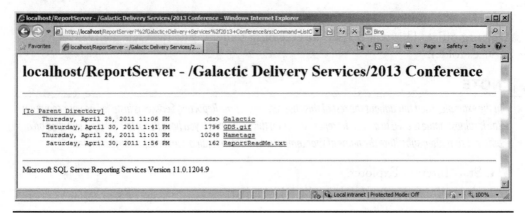

Figure 12-1   *Browsing folder contents using URL access*

Reporting Services what to do with the item pointed to by the URL. The four possible values for the command parameter are listed in Table 12-1.

Looking at this table, you quickly realize that only one command parameter value applies to each type of item you can encounter in the Reporting Services virtual folders. Attempting to use a command parameter with the wrong type of item results in an error. If you do not include the command parameter, Reporting Services simply performs the one and only command that applies to the type of item you are targeting in your URL. Because specifying the command parameter is completely unnecessary, one can only assume this was put in place to allow for future growth.

Passing Parameters

When you executed the Invoice-Batch Number Report through URL access, you received the default values for the start date and end date. You can change these dates in the Report Viewer, but only after waiting for the report to execute with the default values. It would be much better to get exactly what you want the first time around.

Command Parameter	Applies To	Result
GetDataSourceContents	Data Source	Displays the data source definition as an Extensible Markup Language (XML) structure.
GetResourceContents	Resource Item	Displays the contents of the resource item in the browser.
ListChildren	Folder	Lists the contents of the folder with links to each content item.
Render	Report	Displays the report in the Report Viewer.

Table 12-1   *Values for the Command Parameter*

Fortunately, you have a way to do just that. You can pass the values for report parameters as part of the URL. On the URL, include an ampersand (&) followed by the name of the report parameter, an equal sign, and the parameter value.

Try the following:

1. Enter the following URL in the address bar:

```
http://localhost/ReportServer?/Galactic Delivery Services/Axelburg/
    Invoice-Batch Number Report&StartDate=11/1/2012&EndDate=11/30/2012
```

2. Press ENTER. The Invoice-Batch Number Report appears with data for November 2012.

It is possible to hide parameters from interactive report users while still allowing values to be passed to those parameters through the URL or web service access. This is done through the Hide option for each parameter. Let's try the following:

1. Open the Report Manager, and navigate to the /Galactic Delivery Services/ Axelburg folder.
2. Hover over the Invoice-Batch Number Report item, and select Manage from the drop-down menu.
3. Click Parameters on the left side of the page.
4. Check the Hide check box in the StartDate row. (Notice the default value for the StartDate parameter is 1/1/2012.)
5. Click Apply.
6. Click the large report title at the top of the page to execute the report. Notice the Start Date prompt no longer appears in the parameter area.
7. Enter the following URL in the address bar:

```
http://localhost/ReportServer?/Galactic Delivery Services/Axelburg/
    Invoice-Batch Number Report&StartDate=12/1/2012&EndDate=12/31/2012
```

8. Press ENTER. The Invoice-Batch Number Report appears with data for December 2012.

Even though the StartDate parameter does not appear in the parameters area, we can still specify a value for it other than the default value. The Hide check box is not checked for the City parameter. Instead, the Prompt User check box is unchecked. In this situation, you cannot specify a value for this parameter in the URL. The following URL is going to fail:

```
http://localhost/ReportServer?/Galactic Delivery Services/Axelburg/
        Invoice-Batch Number Report&City=Utonal&EndDate=12/31/2012
```

Controlling the Report Viewer

In addition to specifying report parameters in the URL, you can include parameters to control the format of the response from Reporting Services. You can specify which rendering format should be used for the report. Rather than using the Export drop-down list in the Report Viewer to export the report to a particular format, you can have it delivered in that format straight from Reporting Services.

Give this a try:

1. Enter the following URL in the address bar:

```
http://localhost/ReportServer?/Galactic Delivery Services/
                        2013 Conference/Nametags&rs:Format=PDF
```

2. Press ENTER.
3. If you are prompted whether to open or save the file, click Open.
4. The Nametags Report appears in PDF format in Adobe Acrobat Reader.
5. Close Adobe Acrobat Reader.

The valid format parameters are shown in Table 12-2.

In addition to the rs:Command and rs:Format parameters, several other report server parameters use the rs: prefix. Table 12-3 shows these.

Device information parameters can also be passed as part of the URL. These *device information parameters* are specific to the format being used to render the report. Because they modify rendering format-specific details, device information parameters can also be thought of as renderer control parameters. Therefore, they use an rc: prefix.

Format Parameter	Result
ATOM	Atom data feed
CSV	Comma-separated value text file
EXCEL	Excel spreadsheet
HTML4.0	HTML page using the HTML 4.0 standard
IMAGE	BMP, EMF, GIF, JPEG, PNG, or TIFF image
MHTML	Self-contained HTML document
NULL	None
PDF	Adobe PDF document
WORD	Microsoft Word document
XML	XML document

Table 12-2   *Values for the Format Parameter*

Parameter	Valid Values	Function
rs:ClearSession	True False	When true, this parameter prevents a report from being pinned in cache by forcing the report to be re-rendered.
rs:ParameterLanguage	A valid culture identifier, such as "en-us"	Used to specify a language for the parameters passed in the URL that is different from the browser's language setting. This defaults to the browser's language setting when it is not specified.
rs:SessionID	A unique session identifier	Used to maintain session state when the report server has been configured not to use session cookies.
rs:Snapshot	The date and time of a valid snapshot for the specified report	Used to render the requested report from a history snapshot.

Table 12-3 *Report Server (rs) URL Parameters and Their Possible Values*

Let's look at a couple of examples using device information parameters. When you receive a report rendered as HTML, you also receive the Report Viewer controls. This may not always be desirable. Several device information parameters enable you to specify what portion of the Report Viewer interface you want visible. For example:

1. Enter the following URL in the address bar:

```
http://localhost/ReportServer?/Galactic Delivery Services/Axelburg/
    Invoice-Batch Number Report&StartDate=11/1/2012&EndDate=11/30/2012
    &rc:Parameters=false
```

2. Press ENTER. The Invoice-Batch Number Report appears with data for November 2012. The parameter portion of the Report Viewer is not displayed, so the user cannot change the parameter values.

You can get rid of the entire Report Viewer interface as follows:

1. Enter the following URL in the address bar:

```
http://localhost/ReportServer?/Galactic Delivery Services/Axelburg/
    Invoice-Batch Number Report&StartDate=11/1/2012&EndDate=11/30/2012
    &rc:Toolbar=false
```

2. Press ENTER. The Invoice-Batch Number Report appears with data for November 2012.
3. Expand the 445 row heading and the Axelburg column heading.

Even when we expand the row and column headings, causing a new page to be sent from the report server, the Report Viewer does not reappear.

Setting	Valid Values	Function
rc:DataFeed		The feed name to be used for this Atom feed.
rc:Encoding	ASCII UTF-7 UTF-8 Unicode	The character encoding scheme to use. The default is UTF-8.

Table 12-4   *ATOM Format Device Information (rc) URL Parameters and Their Possible Values*

Table 12-4 shows the device information parameters for the ATOM format.

Table 12-5 shows the device information parameters for the comma-separated value (CSV) format.

Table 12-6 shows the device information parameters for the Excel format.

Setting	Valid Values	Function
rc:Encoding	ASCII UTF-7 UTF-8 Unicode	The character encoding scheme to use. The default is UTF-8.
rc:ExcelMode	True False	If True, assumes the target output is to be loaded into Excel. The output may not be in true CSV format, but will be more suitable for loading into Excel. The default is True. "ExcelMode" will violate CSV compliance in order to make the output more suitable for import into Excel. Basically, it renders top-level peer data regions as their own "blocks" in CSV.
rc:FieldDelimiter		The field delimiter to use in the file. The default is a comma.
rc:FileExtension		The file extension for the file. The default is .csv.
rc:NoHeader	True False	If True, no header is written with the data in the file. The default is False.
rc:Qualifier		The string qualifier to put around fields that contain the field delimiter. The default is a quotation mark.
rc:RecordDelimiter		The record delimiter to use in the file. The default is a carriage return and linefeed.
rc:SuppressLineBreaks	True False	If True, line breaks in the data are not included in the file. The default is False.
rc:UseFormattedValues	True False	If True, formatted strings are put in the file. The default is True when ExcelMode is True; otherwise, the default is False.

Table 12-5   *CSV Format Device Information (rc) URL Parameters and Their Possible Values*

Setting	Valid Values	Function
rc:OmitDocumentMap	True False	If True, the document map for the rendered report is not included in the Excel file. The default is False.
rc:OmitFormulas	True False	If True, formulas are not included in the Excel file. The default is False.
rc:SimplePageHeader	True False	If True, the report page header is placed in the Excel page header. Otherwise, the report page header is placed in the first row of the worksheet. The default value is False.

Table 12-6   *Excel Format Device Information (rc) URL Parameters and Their Possible Values*

The device information parameters for the HTML4.0 format are shown in Table 12-7. Table 12-8 shows the device information parameters for the image format. Table 12-9 shows the device information parameters for the MHTML format.

Setting	Valid Values	Function
rc:AccessibleTablix	True False	Determines whether to render with added accessibility metadata for use with screen readers. The default is False.
rc:ActionScript		The name of a JavaScript function to use when an action event occurs. If specified, an action event will trigger the specified function instead of a postback.
rc:BookmarkID	{BookmarkID}	Jumps to the specified Bookmark ID in the report.
rc:DocMap	True False	Specifies whether the document map is shown. The default is True.
rc:ExpandContent	True False	Determines whether the report is placed inside a table structure to limit its horizontal size.
rc:FindString	{TextToFind}	Searches for this text in the report and jumps to its first location.
rc:GetImage		A particular icon for the HTML Viewer user interface.
rc:HTMLFragment	True False	When this is set to True, the report is returned as a table rather than as a complete HTML page. This table can then be placed inside your own HTML page. The default value is False.
rc:ImageConsolidation	True False	Specifies whether to consolidate chart, map, gauge, and indicator images into one large image. The default value is True for most modern browsers.
rc:JavaScript	True False	If True, JavaScript is supported in the rendered report. The default value is True.

Table 12-7   *HTML4.0 Format Device Information (rc) URL Parameters and Their Possible Values* (continued)

Setting	Valid Values	Function
rc:LinkTarget	{TargetWindowName} _blank _self _parent _top	Specifies the target window to use for any links in the report.
rc:OnlyVisibleStyles	True False	If True, only shared styles for the currently rendered page are generated.
rc:OutlookCompat	True False	Specifies whether to include extra metadata to make the report look better in Outlook. The default is False.
rc:Parameters	True False	Specifies whether to show the parameters section of the Report Viewer. The default is True.
rc:PrefixId		When used with the HTMLFragment parameter, the specified prefix is added to all ID attributes in the HTML fragment.
rcReplacementRoot		This string is prepended to all drillthrough, toggle, and bookmark links in the report when rendered outside the ReportViewer control.
rc:ResourceStreamRoot		This string is prepended to the URL for all image resources.
rc:Section	{PageNumber}	The page number of the report to render.
rc:StreamRoot	{URL}	The path used to prefix the value of the src attribute of any IMG tags in an HTML rendering of the report.
rc:StyleStream	True False	If True, styles and scripts are created as separate streams rather than in the document. The default is False.
rc:Toolbar	True False	Specifies whether the Report Viewer toolbar is visible. The default is True.
rc:UserAgent		The user-agent string of the browser that is making the request, which is found in the HTTP request.
rc:Zoom	Page Width Whole Page 500 200 150 100 75 50 25 10	The zoom percentage to use when displaying the report. The default is 100.

Table 12-7   *HTML4.0 Format Device Information (rc) URL Parameters and Their Possible Values* (continued)

Setting	Valid Values	Function
rc:ColorDepth	Ignored	This setting can be specified without causing an error, but starting with this release of SQL Server Reporting Services, the value is ignored. TIFF images are always rendered with a 24-bit color depth.
rc:Columns		The number of columns to use when creating the image.
rc:ColumnSpacing		The column spacing to use when creating the image
rc:DpiX		The number of dots per inch in the x-direction. The default is 96.
rc:DpiY		The number of dots per inch in the y-direction. The default is 96.
rc:EndPage		The last page to render. The default value is the value for the StartPage parameter.
rc:MarginBottom	An integer or decimal followed by "in" (the abbreviation for inches)	The bottom margin to use when creating the image.
rc:MarginLeft	An integer or decimal followed by "in" (the abbreviation for inches)	The left margin to use when creating the image.
rc:MarginRight	An integer or decimal followed by "in" (the abbreviation for inches)	The right margin to use when creating the image.
rc:MarginTop	An integer or decimal followed by "in" (the abbreviation for inches)	The top margin to use when creating the image.
rc:OutputFormat	BMP EMF GIF JPEG PNG TIFF	The graphics format to create.
rc:PageHeight	An integer or decimal followed by "in" (the abbreviation for inches)	The page height to use when creating the image.
rc:PageWidth	An integer or decimal followed by "in" (the abbreviation for inches)	The page width to use when creating the image.
rc:StartPage		The first page to render. A value of 0 causes all pages to be rendered. The default value is 1.

Table 12-8   *Image Format Device Information (rc) URL Parameters and Their Possible Values*

The PDF format device information parameters are shown in Table 12-10. Table 12-11 shows the device information parameters for the Word format. Table 12-12 shows the device information parameters for the XML format.

Setting	Valid Values	Function
rc:JavaScript	True False	If True, JavaScript is supported in the rendered report. The default is False.
rc:OutlookCompat	True False	Specifies whether to include extra metadata to make the report look better in Outlook. The default is True.
rc:MHTMLFragment	True False	When this is set to True, the report is returned as a table rather than as a complete HTML page. This table can then be placed inside your own HTML page. The default value is False.

Table 12-9   *MHTML Format Device Information (rc) URL Parameters and Their Possible Values*

Setting	Valid Values	Function
rc:Columns		The number of columns to use when creating the PDF file.
rc:ColumnSpacing		The column spacing to use when creating the PDF file.
rc:DpiX		The number of dots per inch in the x-direction.
rc:DpiY		The number of dots per inch in the y-direction.
rc:EndPage		The last page to render. The default value is the value for the StartPage parameter.
rc:HumanReadablePDF	True False	Indicates whether the PDF source is in a more readable format. The default is False.
rc:MarginBottom	An integer or decimal followed by "in" (the abbreviation for inches)	The bottom margin to use when creating the PDF file.
rc:MarginLeft	An integer or decimal followed by "in" (the abbreviation for inches)	The left margin to use when creating the PDF file.
rc:MarginRight	An integer or decimal followed by "in" (the abbreviation for inches)	The right margin to use when creating the PDF file.
rc:MarginTop	An integer or decimal followed by "in" (the abbreviation for inches)	The top margin to use when creating the PDF file.
rc:PageHeight	An integer or decimal followed by "in" (the abbreviation for inches)	The page height to use when creating the PDF file.
rc:PageWidth	An integer or decimal followed by "in" (the abbreviation for inches)	The page width to use when creating the PDF file.
rc:StartPage		The first page to render. A value of 0 causes all pages to be rendered. The default value is 1.

Table 12-10   *PDF Format Device Information (rc) URL Parameters and Their Possible Values*

Setting	Valid Values	Function
rc:AutoFit	True False Never Default	If True, AutoFit is set to True on every Word table. If False, AutoFit is set to False on every Word table. If Never, AutoFit is not set on individual tables, so the behavior reverts to the Word default. If Default, AutoFit is set to True on all tables that are narrower than the physical drawing area.
rc:ExpandToggles	True False	If True, all of the drilldown items are rendered in their expanded state. If False, all of the drilldown items are rendered in their collapsed state. The default is False.
rc:FixedPageWidth	True False	If True, the page width property in the resulting Word document is expanded to accommodate the width of the largest report page. If False, Word's default page width is used. The default is False.
rc:OmitHyperlinks	True False	If True, hyperlinks are not included in the resulting Word document. If False, hyperlinks are included. The default is False.
rc:OmitDrillThroughs	True False	If True, drillthrough actions are not included in the resulting Word document. If False, drillthrough actions are included. The default is False.

Table 12-11   *Word Format Device Information (rc) URL Parameters and Their Possible Values*

Setting	Valid Values	Function
rc:Encoding	ASCII UTF-8 Unicode	The character encoding scheme to use. The default is UTF-8.
rc:FileExtension		The file extension for the XML file. The default is .xml.
rc:Indented	True False	If True, the XML file is indented. The default is False.
rc:MIMEType		The MIME type of the XML file.
rc:OmitSchema	True False	If True, the schema name and XML Schema Definition (XSD) are not included in the XML file. The default is False.
rc:Schema	True False	If True, the XSD is rendered in the XML file. Otherwise, the report itself is rendered in the XML file. The default is False.
rc:UseFormattedValues	True False	If True, the formatted value of each text box is included in the XML file. Otherwise, the unformatted value of each text box is included. The default is False.
rc:XSLT		The path in the report server namespace of an Extensible Stylesheet Language Transformation (XSLT) document to apply to the XML file. The XSLT must be a published resource on the report server, and it must be accessed through the report server itself.

Table 12-12   *XML Format Device Information (rc) URL Parameters and Their Possible Values*

Finally, you can specify the user name and password for data sources that prompt for credentials each time the report is run. This is done using the dsu: and dsp: prefixes. For example, to specify credentials for a data source called GalacticPrompt, you would add the following to the end of the URL:

```
dsu:GalacticPrompt=MyDBUser&dsp:GalacticPrompt=DBPassword
```

where MyDBUser is a valid database login and DBPassword is the password for that login.

URL Access Using an HTTP Post

The previous examples demonstrate the use of URL access using the HTTP Get method. This method has several limitations. First, all the parameter values are exposed in the URL itself. Second, the number of characters you can have in a URL is limited.

You can get around these limitations and still use URL access by employing the HTTP Post method. The *HTTP Post method* passes parameters as fields in an HTML form so they are not exposed in the URL. Also, the HTTP Post is not subject to the same length restrictions as the HTTP Get.

The following HTML page uses the HTTP Post to request the Transport Monitor Report for Transport Number 1310 in the HTML 4.0, TIFF image, or Excel format:

```
<HTML>
<Head>
<title>
Reporting Services URL Post Demo
</title>
</Head>
<Body>
<FORM id="frmRender" action="http://localhost/ReportServer?
            /Galactic Delivery Services/Chapter09/TransportMonitor"
            method="post" target="_self">
<H3>Transport Monitor Report</H3><br>
<b>For Transport 1310</b><br><br>
Render the Transportation Monitor Report in the following format:<br>
<Select ID="rs:Format" NAME="rs:Format" size=1>
<Option Value="HTML4.0">HTML 4.0</Option>
<Option VALUE="IMAGE">TIFF Image</Option>
<Option VALUE="EXCEL">Excel File</Option>
</Select>
<Input type="hidden" name="TransportNumber" value="1310">
<br><br>
```

```
<INPUT type="submit" value="Render Report">
</FORM>
</Body>
</HTML>
```

Not only can we use an HTML page like this on a website, we can also use it right within the Report Manager. As discussed in Chapter 10, we can upload any file to a report server folder, including an HTML page. This allows us to create a more polished user interface for gathering report parameters while still utilizing the organization, navigation, and security features of the Report Manager.

Let's give it a try:

1. Use a text editor to create a file called **TransportMonitorFrontEnd.HTML** that contains the code for the HTML page to do the HTTP Post.
2. Open the Report Manager in a browser, and navigate to the Galactic Delivery Services/Chapter09 folder.
3. Use the Upload File button in the Report Manager toolbar to upload the TransportMonitorFrontEnd.HTML file into the Chapter09 folder. Change the name to **Transport Monitor Front End**.
4. Select Transport Monitor Front End in the Chapter09 folder.
5. Select a rendering format from the drop-down list, and click the Render Report button. You will see the Transport Monitor Report for Transport 1310.

You could set the Hide in list view property of the Transport Monitor Report so the report itself is hidden in the list view of Chapter09. Now the user must utilize the front-end HTML page to execute the report.

Web Service Access

In addition to URL and HTTP Post access, you can access reports by using the web service interface. This is the same interface used by the Report Manager web application to interact with Reporting Services. This means anything you can do in Report Manager, you can also do through the web service interface.

The web service interface provides additional functionality not available through URL access. For example, the web service interface enables you to specify a set of credentials to use when executing a report. This allows your custom application to use a set of hard-coded credentials to access reports through the web service interface. This can be a big benefit in situations where you want Reporting Services reports to be exposed on an Internet or extranet site where each user does not have a domain account.

Using a Web Service Call to Execute a Report

This example takes you through the steps necessary to execute a report using the web service interface. In this example, you build a web application that acts as a front end for the Axelburg Invoice-Batch Number Report.

NOTE

Some basic knowledge of ASP.NET programming is assumed in the following discussion.

Creating a Project and a Web Reference   First, you need to create an ASP.NET project with a reference to the Reporting Services web service.

1. Start up Visual Studio.
2. Create a new project.
3. Select Visual Basic | Web in the Installed Templates area.
4. Select ASP.NET Web Application from the Templates area.
5. Type **AxelburgFrontEnd** for Name. Select an appropriate location for this project.
6. Click OK.
7. When the new project has been created, right-click the project folder for this new project in the Solution Explorer, and select Add Service Reference from the context menu. The Add Service Reference dialog box appears.
8. Click the Advanced button. The Service Reference Settings dialog box appears.
9. Click Add Web Reference. The Add Web Reference dialog box appears.
10. Enter the following address for the web reference:

    ```
    http://{computername}/ReportServer/ReportExecution2005.asmx
    ```

    where {computername} is the name of the computer hosting the report server. Click Go.
11. When the ReportExecutionService Description appears in the dialog box, replace the Web reference name with **RptExecSvc**. Click Add Reference.

To use a web service, you need to create code that knows how to send data to and retrieve data from that web service. Fortunately, this code is generated for you by Visual Studio through the process of creating a web reference. Once the web reference is in place, you can call the methods of the web service the same way you call the methods of a local .NET assembly.

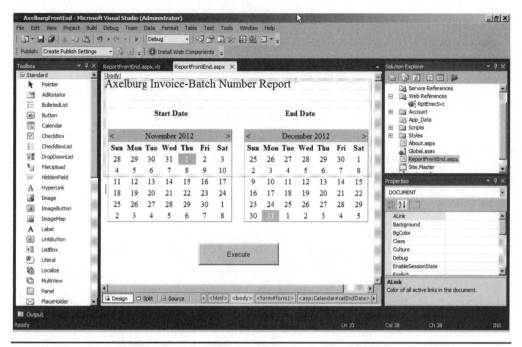

Figure 12-2 *The Axelburg Invoice-Batch Number Report front end*

Creating the Web Form   Now, we need to create the web form that is going to serve as our user interface.

1. Change the name of Default.aspx to **ReportFrontEnd.aspx**.
2. Using the Design view of the ReportFrontEnd.aspx form, place three labels, two calendar controls, and a button on the web form, as shown in Figure 12-2.
3. Change the Text property of each label to match Figure 12-2.
4. Change the ID property of the left calendar control to **calStartDate**.
5. Set the SelectedDate property and the VisibleDate property of calStartDate to **November 1, 2012**.
6. Change the ID property of the right calendar control to **calEndDate**.
7. Set the SelectedDate property and the VisibleDate property of calEndDate to **December 31, 2012**.

8. Change the ID property of the button to **cmdExecute**.
9. Change the Text property of the button to **Execute**.
10. Double-click the cmdExecute button to open the code window.
11. Enter the following code for cmdExecute_Click:

```
Protected Sub cmdExecute_Click(ByVal sender As Object, _
                               ByVal e As EventArgs) _
                               Handles cmdExecute.Click
    Dim report As Byte() = Nothing
    ' Create an instance of the Reporting Services
    ' Web Reference.
    Dim rs As RptExecSvc.ReportExecutionService _
                        = New RptExecSvc.ReportExecutionService
    ' Create the credentials that will be used when accessing
    ' Reporting Services. This must be a Windows logon that has
    ' rights to the Axelburg Invoice-Batch Number report.
    ' *** Replace "LoginName", "Password", and "Domain" with
    '      the appropriate values. ***
    rs.Credentials = New _
         System.Net.NetworkCredential("LoginName", _
         "Password", "Domain")
    rs.PreAuthenticate = True

    ' The Reporting Services virtual path to the report.
    Dim reportPath As String = _
    "/Galactic Delivery Services/Axelburg/Invoice-Batch Number Report"

    ' The rendering format for the report.
    Dim format As String = "HTML4.0"

    ' The devInfo string tells the report viewer
    ' how to display with the report.
    Dim devInfo As String = _
         "<DeviceInfo>" + _
         "<Toolbar>False</Toolbar>" + _
         "<Parameters>False</Parameters>" + _
         "<DocMap>True</DocMap>" + _
         "<Zoom>100</Zoom>" + _
         "</DeviceInfo>"

    ' Create an array of the values for the report parameters
    Dim parameters(1) As RptExecSvc.ParameterValue
    Dim paramValue As RptExecSvc.ParameterValue _
                        = New RptExecSvc.ParameterValue
    paramValue.Name = "StartDate"
    paramValue.Value = calStartDate.SelectedDate
    parameters(0) = paramValue
    paramValue = New RptExecSvc.ParameterValue
    paramValue.Name = "EndDate"
    paramValue.Value = calEndDate.SelectedDate
    parameters(1) = paramValue
```

```vb
    ' Create variables for the remainder of the parameters
    Dim historyID As String = Nothing
    Dim credentials() As RptExecSvc.DataSourceCredentials = Nothing
    Dim showHideToggle As String = Nothing
    Dim mimeType As String
    Dim warnings() As RptExecSvc.Warning = Nothing
    Dim reportHistoryParameters() As _
                        RptExecSvc.ParameterValue = Nothing
    Dim streamIDs() As String = Nothing

    Dim execInfo As New RptExecSvc.ExecutionInfo
    Dim execHeader As New RptExecSvc.ExecutionHeader
    rs.ExecutionHeaderValue = execHeader
    execInfo = rs.LoadReport(reportPath, historyID)
    rs.SetExecutionParameters(parameters, "en-us")

    Try
        ' Execute the report.
        report = rs.Render(format, _
                devInfo, "", mimeType, "", warnings, streamIDs)

        ' Flush any pending response.
        Response.Clear()

        ' Set the HTTP headers for a PDF response.
        HttpContext.Current.Response.ClearHeaders()
        HttpContext.Current.Response.ClearContent()
        HttpContext.Current.Response.ContentType = "text/html"
        ' filename is the default filename displayed
        ' if the user does a save as.
        HttpContext.Current.Response.AppendHeader( _
                "Content-Disposition", _
                "filename=""Invoice-BatchNumber.HTM""")

        ' Send the byte array containing the report
        ' as a binary response.
        HttpContext.Current.Response.BinaryWrite(report)
        HttpContext.Current.Response.End()
    Catch ex As Exception
        If ex.Message <> "Thread was being aborted." then
            HttpContext.Current.Response.ClearHeaders()
            HttpContext.Current.Response.ClearContent()
            HttpContext.Current.Response.ContentType = "text/html"
            HttpContext.Current.Response.Write( _
                        "<HTML><BODY><H1>Error</H1><br><br>" & _
                        ex.Message & "</BODY></HTML>")
            HttpContext.Current.Response.End()
        End If
    End Try
End Sub
```

12. Click Save All on the toolbar.

13. Select Debug | Start Debugging from the main menu. This executes your program.

14. When the browser window opens with the web application front-end page, click Execute. The report appears using the dates selected on the front-end page.

15. Switch back to Visual Studio, and select Debug | Stop Debugging from the main menu.

You can refer to the comments in the code sample for information on the purpose of each section of code.

NOTE

The items in the DeviceInfo XML structure are the same rendering-specific device information settings as those documented in the "URL Access" section of this chapter. Use the parameter name, minus the rc: prefix, as the element name.

Managing Reporting Services Through Web Services

In addition to executing reports through the web service interface, you can manage Reporting Services using the web services. If you choose, you can write an application that completely replaces the Report Manager web application for controlling Reporting Services.

The Report Viewer Control

The Report Server web service gives you a tremendous amount of control over report access. However, the web service simply provides our applications with a stream that contains the report. It is up to our applications to provide an appropriate method for viewing the content of that report stream.

The Report Viewer control in Visual Studio 2005, Visual Studio 2008, and Visual Studio 2010 takes things one step further. Not only does it provide access to the reports, it also provides a means to view them. In fact, the Report Viewer can even free you from the tether to the report server altogether. The Report Viewer control can be used in both Windows forms and web forms.

Displaying a Report from a Report Server

We first use the Report Viewer control to access a report on the report server. In this example, you build a Windows application that uses the Report Viewer to display the

Axelburg Invoice-Batch Number Report. For this application to function properly, it must have access to the report server whenever a report is executed.

NOTE

The web service example in the previous section works in any version of Visual Studio .NET. The Report Viewer examples in this section require Visual Studio 2005, Visual Studio 2008, or Visual Studio 2010.

Creating a Project and an Instance of the Report Viewer   First, you need to create a Windows application project in Visual Studio.

1. Start up Visual Studio.
2. Create a new project.
3. Select Visual Basic | Windows in the Installed Templates area.
4. Select Windows Forms Application from the Templates area.
5. Enter **AxelburgRVFrontEnd** for Name. Select an appropriate location for this project.
6. Click OK. A Windows application project with a Windows form, called Form1, is created.
7. Expand Form1 so it covers the design surface.
8. Select the Toolbox window.
9. Locate the Reporting section of the Toolbox and, if it is not already expanded, expand it.
10. Drag the ReportViewer control from the Toolbox, and drop it on Form1 (see Figure 12-3).
11. Click the Dock in parent container link in the ReportViewer Tasks dialog box.

NOTE

If you plan to put other controls on the same form with the Report Viewer, do not dock the viewer in the parent container.

Configuring the Report Viewer   Now we need to point the Report Viewer at a report. You need to make several selections from the ReportViewer Tasks dialog box. If this dialog box is not visible, click the small black triangle in the upper-right corner of the Report Viewer control, as shown in Figure 12-4.

1. In the ReportViewer Tasks dialog box, select <Server Report> from the Choose Report drop-down list.

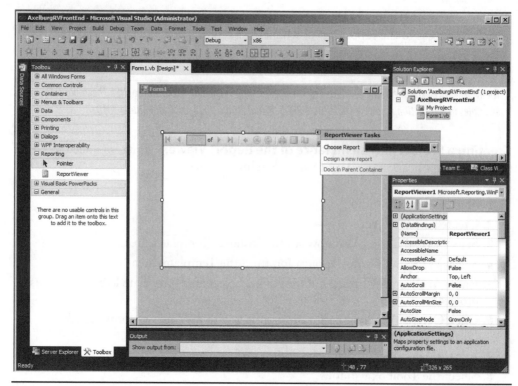

Figure 12-3 *Placing a Report Viewer control on a Windows form*

2. Enter **http://{computername}/reportserver** for Report Server URL, where {computername} is the name of the server hosting Reporting Services.
3. Enter **/Galactic Delivery Services/Axelburg/Invoice-Batch Number Report** for Report Path.

Figure 12-4 *Opening the ReportViewer Tasks dialog box*

NOTE

You can use the ServerReport.ReportServerUrl and ServerReport.ReportPath properties of the Report Viewer control to programmatically change the report that the Report Viewer displays. In this way, a single Report Viewer control can display different reports, depending on user selection.

   4. Click Save All on the toolbar.

   5. Select Debug | Start Debugging from the main menu. Form1 executes and displays the Invoice-Batch Number Report from the report server, as shown in Figure 12-5.

NOTE

The assembly necessary to support the ReportViewer control is not included in the standard Microsoft .NET framework. You need to download and install the ReportViewer redistributable on any computers that will be running applications utilizing the ReportViewer control that do not have Visual Studio installed. The ReportViewer redistributable is available, free of charge, from the Microsoft website.

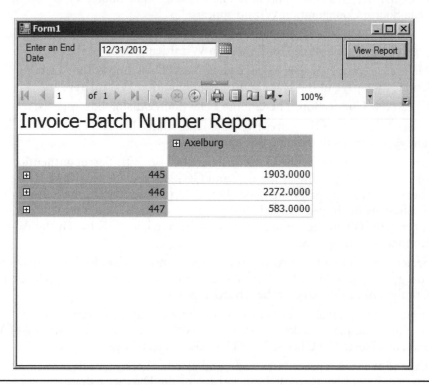

Figure 12-5 *The Report Viewer displaying a report with drilldown*

Displaying a Local Report in the Report Viewer

So far, all the methods of accessing reports we looked at in this chapter have required a report server. The report server provides a number of advantages for managing reports, including centralized control for updating report definitions and maintaining security. However, in some situations, it is impractical or undesirable for all installations of an application to pull reports from a report server.

The Report Viewer control provides an alternative. In addition to displaying reports rendered by a report server, the Report Viewer can render reports contained within the Visual Studio project. In this example, we create a simple report right in the Visual Studio project, and then display it with the Report Viewer.

Creating a Local Report   We begin by creating a report in the Visual Studio project.

1. Close Form1 containing the report to return to Visual Studio, if you have not already done so.
2. Open the ReportViewer Tasks dialog box.
3. Click the Design a new report link. The Choose a Data Source Type page of the Data Source Configuration Wizard appears.
4. Make sure Database is selected, and click Next. The Choose a Database Model page of the Data Source Configuration Wizard appears.
5. Make sure Dataset is selected, and click Next. The Choose Your Data Connection page of the Data Source Configuration Wizard appears.
6. Click New Connection. The Choose Data Source dialog box appears.
7. Select Microsoft SQL Server from the Data source list, and click Continue. The Add Connection dialog box appears.
8. Create a connection to the Galactic database. Use SQL Server authentication, with GalacticReporting as the user and G@l@ct1c as the password. Remember to check the Save my password check box. Select Galactic from the Select or enter a database name drop-down list. Test the connection to make sure you configured it correctly. When the connection passes the test, click OK to exit the Add Connection dialog box.
9. Select the radio button next to "Yes, include sensitive data in the connection string," and click Next. The Save the Connection String to the Application Configuration File page of the wizard appears.
10. In most cases, it makes sense to store the connection information in the configuration file to make maintenance easier. Leave the default setting of Yes, and click Next. The Choose Your Database Objects page appears.
11. Expand the stored procedures node, and place a check mark next to stp_EmployeeList. Enter **EmployeeList** for the DataSet name.

12. Click Finish. A typed dataset is created by the wizard for use with the report, and you are taken to the Dataset Properties page of the Report Wizard dialog box.

13. Enter **EmployeeList** for Name.

14. Click Next. You are taken to the Arrange fields page of the Report Wizard dialog box.

15. Drag all three fields to the Values area.

16. Click Next. The Choose the layout page of the Report Wizard appears.

17. Click Next. The Choose a style page of the Report Wizard appears.

18. Click Finish. Your report layout should appear similar to the layout shown in Figure 12-6.

19. Click Save All on the toolbar.

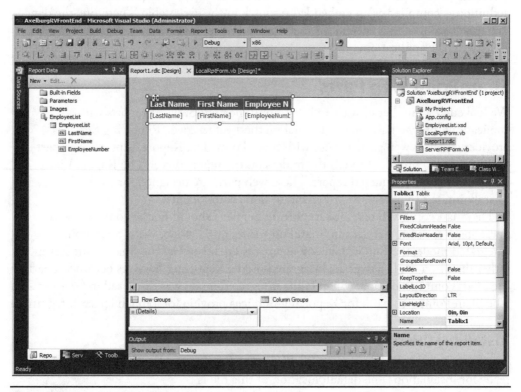

Figure 12-6   *Layout of the local report*

Point the Report Viewer at the Local Report   Now, we point the Report Viewer at the new local report.

1. Click the Form1.vb [Design] tab in the layout area of Visual Studio 2010.
2. Open the ReportViewer Tasks dialog box.
3. Select AxelburgRVFrontEnd.Report1.rdlc from the Choose Report drop-down list. Several items have been added to an area below the Form1 layout. Click Save All on the toolbar.
4. Select Debug | Start Debugging from the main menu. Form1 executes and displays the local report. The local report you just created shows a list of all Galactic employees.
5. Close Form1 when you finish viewing this report.

When you compile the AxelburgRVFrontEnd project, the Report1.rdlc report definition is compiled as an embedded resource in the executable. Therefore, the data source is the only thing needed for the report to be rendered. The report always goes along with the application.

SharePoint Web Parts

We looked at a number of ways to integrate Reporting Services reports with applications, but we have one additional method yet to cover. Reporting Services provides a pair of web parts for use with SharePoint. The Report Explorer web part enables users to browse through the folders on the report server. The Report Viewer web part displays a rendered report. These web parts are designed for use with SharePoint, but they can be used as stand-alone components.

The SharePoint web parts for Reporting Services should not be confused with operating Reporting Services in SharePoint Integrated mode. With SharePoint Integrated mode, the Report Catalog databases are hosted by the SharePoint server rather than by a SQL Server. In Integrated mode, Reporting Services becomes a part on the SharePoint installation. (SharePoint Integrated mode was discussed in Chapter 2.) The SharePoint web parts for Reporting Services provide for a much looser integration.

Installing the Web Parts

The SharePoint web parts come with Reporting Services in the RSWebParts.cab file, ready for installation. The default location of this file is

```
C:\Program Files (x86)\Microsoft SQL Server\110\Tools\Reporting Services\
SharePoint
```

This .cab file should be installed using the Stsadm utility. The Stsadm utility unpacks the web parts, installs them in the appropriate location, and creates entries in the SafeControls section of the web.config file for the SharePoint virtual server. Use the following command line to complete the installation using default locations:

```
"C:\Program Files\Common Files\Microsoft Shared\web server extensions\
        14\BIN\STSADM.EXE" -o addwppack -filename.
        "C:\Program Files\Microsoft SQL Server\110\Tools\
        Reporting Services\SharePoint\RSWebParts.cab"
```

NOTE

If you use the globalinstall switch with the Stsadm utility to install the web parts in the global assembly cache, you need to use the strong name for the assembly in place of the friendly name in the web.config file for the SharePoint virtual server.

Adding the Web Parts

Now that the web parts are installed, they need to be added to a web part page using the SharePoint window. Use the following steps:

1. Access the SharePoint site.
2. Go to the Libraries page, and click Create.
3. Scroll down the page, and select Web Part Page. Click the Create button.
4. Type a name for the web part page, and select a layout template.
5. Enter the document library where your web part page is to be saved.
6. Click Create at the bottom of the page.
7. Click "Add a Web Part" in the area where you would like to add this web part.
8. Click Modify Shared Page. Point to Add Web Parts, and then click Browse.
9. Select "SQL Server Reporting" from Categories. "SQL Server Reporting Services Report Viewer" will be selected in the Web Parts area.
10. Click Add.
11. Click Stop Editing in the toolbar.

When both the Report Explorer and Report Viewer web parts are placed on the same web part page, you can connect them together. This enables the user to browse to a report in the Report Explorer web part, and then view the report in the Report Viewer web part. If the two web parts are not connected, selecting a report in the

Report Explorer causes it to display in a new page. Use the following steps to connect the two web parts:

1. Click Modify Shared Web Part.
2. On the Report Explorer toolbar menu, click the down arrow, point to Connections, point to Show Report In, and then click Report Viewer.
3. Click OK.

Reporting Services Utilities

In addition to URL access, the web service interface, Report Viewer, and SharePoint web parts, you can interact with Reporting Services through several command-line utility programs. Like the other methods, these command-line utilities let you manage Reporting Services. These utilities enable you to control Reporting Services, as well as the encryption keys and encrypted values. The most capable of the utilities, the RS utility, lets you script and automate nearly any Reporting Services activity.

Each utility program is briefly described here. For more information, you can execute any of the utility programs followed by -? to view a listing of the valid parameters.

The RSKeyMgmt Utility

The *RSKeyMgmt utility* administers the encryption key used by Reporting Services. You can use the RSKeyMgmt utility to back up the encryption key. You can also use RSKeyMgmt to delete encrypted data and create a new encryption key in case of a problem.

When Reporting Services is installed, sensitive information stored in the configuration files, such as logon credentials, is encrypted for security. Also, any user names and passwords stored in reports or shared data sources are encrypted. The encryption key used to decrypt the information is stored in the Report Catalog (ReportServer) database. Making certain changes can cause problems with the Reporting Services installation. These changes include the following:

▶ Modifying the user account used by the Reporting Services web service

▶ Modifying the name of the SQL server used to store the Report Catalog

▶ Modifying the name of the computer hosting Reporting Services

A backup copy of the encryption key made with the RSKeyMgmt utility helps recover your Reporting Services installation in these situations.

The backup copy of the encryption key is protected by a password. You specify this password as a parameter to the RSKeyMgmt utility when you create the backup. You must have this password when you use the backup copy of the key.

NOTE

The encryption key can also be managed using the Reporting Services Configuration Manager. In fact, if you like a nice graphical user interface, the Reporting Services Configuration Manager is probably an easier way to complete these management tasks (see Chapter 2).

Creating a Backup of the Report Server Encryption Key   To make a backup of the report server encryption key, do the following:

1. Open a command window.
2. Enter the following at the command prompt, where {password} is the password used to protect the encryption key:

```
Rskeymgmt -e -f c:\temp\rsdbkey.txt -p {password}
```

3. Press ENTER.
4. Type **Y** to confirm.
5. When the backup process is complete, store the resulting file in a safe location.

Recovering a Reporting Services Installation   If your Reporting Services installation becomes disabled because of one of the situations described previously and you have a backup of the encryption key, follow this procedure:

1. Copy the backup of your encryption key onto the report server.
2. Open a command window.
3. Enter the following at the command prompt, where {location} is the path and filename for the backup file and {password} is the password used to protect the encryption key:

```
Rskeymgmt -a -f {location} -p {password}
```

4. Press ENTER.

If your Reporting Services installation becomes disabled because of one of the situations described previously and you do not have a backup of the encryption key, follow this procedure:

1. Open a command window.
2. Enter the following at the command prompt:

```
Rskeymgmt -d
```

3. Press ENTER.

4. Use the RSConfig utility to specify the connection information to the Report Catalog.

5. Reenter the user names and passwords for all reports and shared data sources stored on this report server that use stored credentials.

CAUTION

This process deletes all of the encrypted credentials stored in the ReportServer database. Use this process only if the encryption key becomes corrupted and cannot be recovered.

The RSConfig Utility

The *RSConfig utility* changes the credentials used by Reporting Services to access the Report Catalog (ReportServer) database. These credentials are encrypted in the configuration file, so they cannot be edited directly.

The following example changes the credentials used to access the Report Catalog on a SQL server called RSServer to use a SQL Server logon called RSCatLogon with a password of rscat37:

```
Rsconfig -c -s RSServer -d ReportServer -a Sql -u RSCatLogon
                                             -p rscat37
```

NOTE

The Reporting Services Configuration Manager can be used to perform the same functions as the RSKeyMgmt and RSConfig utility programs. The Configuration Manager provides a graphical user interface, which you may find preferable to the command-line interface of the other utility programs (see Chapter 2).

The RSReportServer.Config File

The RSConfig utility (as well as the Reporting Services Configuration Manager) modifies information stored in the RSReportServer.config file. Some of the information in this file, such as logon credentials, is encrypted for security purposes. This information must be edited using the utility program. Other configuration information in this file is in plain text and can be edited with Notepad or another text editor.

CAUTION

Always make a backup copy of the RSReportServer.config file before editing. The Reporting Services Windows service cannot restart if this configuration file is invalid.

The default location of this file is

```
C:\Program Files\Microsoft SQL Server\MSRS11.MSSQLSERVER\
                                 Reporting Services\ReportServer
```

Table 12-13 shows the values immediately under the Configuration element in the RSReportServer.config file. The settings are shown in the order they occur in the file.

Setting	Valid Values	Function
Report Server Database Connection Information	(Encrypted— use the RSConfig utility or the Reporting Services Configuration Tool to modify)	This is the information required by Reporting Services to access the ReportServer database. This includes DSN, LogonUser, LogonDomain, and LogonCred.
ConnectionType	Default Impersonate	The type of credentials being used by Reporting Services to access the ReportServer database.
InstanceId		The identifier for the Reporting Services instance. This is tied to a SQL Server instance.
InstallationID		A globally unique identifier (GUID) to identify this Reporting Services installation.
SecureConnectionLevel	0 to 3	The degree of security for the web service connection. 0—All requests processed. 1—Requests made over insecure connections and passing sensitive information, such as credentials, are rejected. 2—All rendered reports and web service calls require a secure connection. 3—All calls made to the Reporting Services SOAP API require a secure connection.
CleanupCycleMinutes		The number of minutes after which old sessions and expired snapshots are removed from the ReportServer database. A value of 0 disables the cleanup process. The default is 10.
MaxActiveReqForOneUser		The maximum number of simultaneous, in-progress connections a single user can have open. This setting is intended to thwart a denial of service (DoS) attack. A value of 0 indicates no limit. The default is 20.

Table 12-13   *RSReportServer.config Configuration Elements*

Setting	Valid Values	Function
DatabaseQueryTimeout		The number of seconds before a connection to the ReportServer database times out. A value of 0 results in no timeout. The default is 120.
RunningRequestsScavengerCycle		The number of seconds before orphaned and expired requests are canceled. The default is 60.
RunningRequestsDbCycle		The frequency, in seconds, at which the Manage Jobs page is updated and the running jobs are checked to determine if they have exceeded the report execution timeout. The default is 60.
RunningRequestsAge		The number of seconds after which a running job's status is changed from new to running. The default is 30.
MaxScheduleWait		The number of seconds Reporting Services waits for a schedule to be updated by the SQL Server Agent when a next run time is requested. The default is 5.
DisplayErrorLink	True False	If True, a link to the Microsoft Help and Support site is displayed when an error occurs. The default is True.
WebServiceUseFileShareStorage	True False	If True, the Reporting Services web service stores cached reports and temporary snapshots on the file system rather than in the ReportServerTempDB database. The default is False.
WatsonFlags		Specifies the type of dump sent with error reporting to Microsoft. 0x0430—Full dump 0x0428—Minidump 0x0002—No dump The default is 0x0428.
WatsonDumpOnExceptions		Do not change this setting.
WatsonDumpExcludeIfContainsExceptions		Do not change this setting.

Table 12-13   *RSReportServer.config Configuration Elements* (continued)

Below these items in the RSReportServer.config file are entries for URLReservations. These entries define the URLs used for HTTP access to the Report Server web service and the Report Manager web application. This information is created by your selections made through the Reporting Services Configuration Manager. You should *not* modify this information directly in the RSReportServer.config file. Instead, make all modifications using the Reporting Services Configuration Manager.

Setting	Valid Values	Function
AuthenticationTypes	RSWindowsNegotiate RSWindowsKerberos RSWindowsNTLM RSWindowsBasic Custom	One or more authentication types used by the report server. When Custom is specified, none of the other types may be used. Removing the RSWindowsNTLM entry may cause some browsers to be unable to authenticate to the report server. See the following entries for an explanation of each valid value. The default values are RSWindowsNegotiate and RSWindowsNTLM.
RSWindowsNegotiate		The user security token is passed to the report server on the request.
RSWindowsNTLM		The report server accepts HTTP requests over an NTLM-authenticated connection after the user identity is verified.
RSWindowsKerberos		The report server accepts Kerberos tokens.
RSWindowsBasic		Credentials are passed in the HTTP request in clear text. Secure Sockets Layer (SSL) encryption should always be used with this method of authentication.
Custom		This entry is used when a custom security extension is used.
LogonMethod	0 1 2 3	This entry specifies the logon type for RSWindowsBasic authentication. The valid logon types are: 0 - Interactive Logon (Default) 1 - Batch Logon 2 - Network logon 3 - Cleartext logon
Realm		This entry is used by RSWindowsBasic authentication to specify a resource partition that includes authorization and authentication features used to control access to protected resources.
DefaultDomain		This entry is used by RSWindowsBasic authentication to determine the domain to use.
EnableAuthPersistence	True False	If True, authentication is performed on connection and subsequent requests from that same connection impersonate the security context of the first request. If False, each request is authenticated separately. If you are using proxy server software such as ISA Server to access the report server, EnableAuthPersistence should be set to False to prevent all requests from impersonating the security context of the first request.

Table 12-14   *RSReportServer.config Authentication Elements*

Table 12-14 shows the values in the Authentication section of the RSReportServer.config file. The settings are shown in the order they occur in the file.

Table 12-15 shows the values in the Service section of the RSReportServer.config file. The settings are shown in the order they occur in the file.

Table 12-16 shows the values in the UI section of the RSReportServer.config file. The settings are shown in the order they occur in the file.

Setting	Valid Values	Function
IsSchedulingService	True False	If True, a thread is dedicated to making sure the schedules in the ReportServer database match the schedules in the SQL Server Agent. The default is True.
IsNotificationService	True False	If True, a thread is dedicated to polling the notification table in the ReportServer database to determine if there are any pending notifications. The default is True.
IsEventService	True False	If True, Reporting Services processes events in the event queue. The default is True.
PollingInterval		The number of seconds between polls of the event table. The default is 10.
WindowsServiceUseFileShareStorage	True False	If True, the Report Server Windows service stores cached reports and temporary snapshots on the file system rather than in the ReportServerTempDB database. The default is False.
WorkingSetMaximum		The point after which no new memory allocations are granted to report server applications. By default, this is the amount of available memory on the server. This setting does not appear in the RSReportServer.config file unless it is added manually.
WorkingSetMinimum		The lower limit of memory usage by the report server. The report server will not release memory if overall use is below this limit. By default, this value is calculated at service startup. This setting does not appear in the RSReportServer.config file unless it is added manually.
MemorySafetyMargin		The percentage of the WorkingSetMaximum value that causes the report server to switch from using low memory pressure operating scenarios to using medium memory pressure operating scenarios.
MemoryThreshold		The percentage of the WorkingSetMaximum value that causes the report server to switch from using medium memory pressure operating scenarios to using high memory pressure operating scenarios. Under high memory pressure operating scenarios, the report server slows down request processing and changes the memory allocated to each server application.
RecycleTime		The number of minutes for the recycling of the report server application domain. After this interval has elapsed, all new requests are sent to a new instance of the Reporting Services application domain. The default is 720.

Table 12-15   *RSReportServer.config Service Elements*

Setting	Valid Values	Function
MaxAppDomainUnloadTime		The number of minutes the report server application domain is allowed to unload during a recycle operation. The default is 30.
MaxQueueThreads		The maximum number of threads dedicated to polling the event table in the ReportServer database. The default is 0, which means there is no limit set.
UrlRoot		The URL root used by delivery extensions to create the URL for accessing items stored on the report server.
UnattendedExecutionAccount		The credentials for the Execution Account (see Chapter 2 for more information). These credentials are encrypted and should be set using the Reporting Services Configuration Tool.
PolicyLevel		The security policy configuration file for the report server.
IsWebServiceEnabled	True False	If True, the Report Server web service is enabled. This is set using the Surface Area Configuration for Reporting Services portion of Policy-Based Management. The default is True.
IsReportManagerEnabled	True False	If True, the Report Manager is enabled. The default is True.
FileShareStorageLocation		The path to the folder where cached reports and temporary snapshots are stored, if they are being stored on the file system. A Universal Naming Convention (UNC) path can be used, but it is not recommended. The default is C:\Program Files\Microsoft SQL Server\MSRS11.MSSQLSERVER\Reporting Services\RSTempFiles.

Table 12-15   *RSReportServer.config Service Elements* (continued)

Setting	Valid Values	Function
ReportServerURL		The URL of the report server that the Report Manager connects to.
ReportBuilderTrustLevel	FullTrust	The trust level the Ad Hoc Report Builder runs under. This must be set to FullTrust.
PageCountMode	Estimate Actual	The method used by the Report Manager for calculating page count. If set to Estimate, the page count will be initially set to 2, but adjusts upward as the user pages through the report. If set to Actual, the entire report is processed to calculate the actual page count. This setting will increase the wait time for displaying the first page of lengthy reports. The default value is Estimate.

Table 12-16   *RSReportServer.config UI Elements*

The next sections of the RSReportServer.config file deal with extensions to the report server for delivery, rendering, data processing, semantic query processing, model generation, custom security, and event processing. These extensions are beyond the scope of this book.

The RS Utility

The *RS utility* executes scripts that can interact with Reporting Services. The scripting language supported by the RS utility is Visual Basic .NET. This scripting language supports the complete web service interface to Reporting Services.

The RS utility automatically creates a reference to the web service interface. This predefined reference, called rs, means you do not need to instantiate the web service interface; it is simply ready to go. All the Reporting Services classes and data types are also available.

The following sample code lists the contents of the Galactic Delivery Services virtual folder:

1. Enter the following into Notepad or some other text editor:

```
Public Sub Main()
     Dim items() As CatalogItem
     items = rs.ListChildren("/Galactic Delivery Services", False)

     Dim item As CatalogItem
     For Each item In items
          Console.WriteLine(item.Name)
     Next item
End Sub
```

2. Save this to a file called **rstest.rss** in a convenient folder on the report server.
3. Open a command window on the report server.
4. Change to the folder where you stored the rstest.rss file.
5. Enter the following at the command prompt, where {userID} is a logon with administrative rights on the report server and {password} is the password for that logon:

```
rs -i rstest.rss -s http://localhost/ReportServer
                              -u {userID} -p {password}
```

6. Press ENTER. A list of the folders in the Galactic Delivery Services folder appears in the command window.

Using the RS Utility to Manage System Properties

In Chapter 11, we looked at the Site Settings page in the Report Manager. This page enables you to make configuration changes to Reporting Services system properties.

In addition to the settings exposed on the Site Settings page, Reporting Services has a number of other configuration options. Table 12-17 lists all these Reporting Services system properties.

Property	Valid Values	Function
EnableClientPrinting	True False	If True, users may download the ActiveX object and use client-side printing. The default is True.
EnableExecutionLogging	True False	If True, the execution of each report is recorded in a log table. The default is True.
EnableIntegratedSecurity	True False	If True, integrated security may be used in data sources. The default is True.
EnableLoadReportDefinition	True False	If True, the report server will generate clickthrough reports in the Ad Hoc Report Builder. The default is True.
EnableMyReports	True False	If True, a MyReports folder is created for each report server user. The default is False.
EnableRemoteErrors	True False	If True, remote users will receive error information when a report fails. The default is False.
EnableReportDesignClientDownload	True False	If True, a user with appropriate rights may use the Edit link in the Report Definition section of the report properties to download a copy of the report definition. The default is True.
ExecutionLogDaysKept	0 to 2,147,483,647	The number of days of log information kept in the report execution log. A value of 0 means an unlimited number of days is kept in the log. The default is 60.
ExternalImagesTimeout		The maximum number of seconds the report server attempts to retrieve an external image. The default is 600.
MyReportsRole	{Security Role}	The security role to assign to each user with their MyReports folder. The default is My Reports.
SessionTimeout	An integer value	The number of seconds a session remains active without any activity. The default is 600.
SharePointIntegrated	True False	This is a read-only property indicating the current operational mode of the report server. If True, the report server is operating in SharePoint Integrated mode. If False, the report server is operating in native mode.
SiteName	A string up to 8,000 characters in length	The title displayed at the top of the Report Manager pages. The default is Microsoft Report Server.

Table 12-17 *Reporting Services System Properties*

Property	Valid Values	Function
SnapshotCompression	All None SQL	If All, report snapshots are compressed when stored in all locations, including both the ReportServer database and the file system. If None, report snapshots are not compressed. If SQL, report snapshots are only compressed when stored in the ReportServer database. The default is SQL.
StoredParametersLifetime	−1 to 2,147,483,647	The maximum number of days a stored parameter can be saved. The default is 180. A value of −1 means there is no limit.
StoredParametersThreshold	−1 to 2,147,483,647	The maximum number of parameter values that can be stored by the report server. The default is 1500. A value of −1 means there is no limit.
SystemReportTimeout	−1 to 2,147,483,647	The maximum number of minutes a given report may execute. This value can be overridden for an individual report. A value of −1 means reports may execute for an unlimited amount of time. The default is 5.
SystemSnapshotLimit	−1 to 2,147,483,647	The maximum number of snapshots that can be saved for a given report. A value of −1 means there is no limit.
UseSessionCookies	True False	If True, the report server uses session cookies to track each session. If False, the rs:SessionID report server parameter must be used to pass the session ID. The default is True.

Table 12-17   *Reporting Services System Properties* (continued)

CAUTION

Using integrated security with a report exposes your SQL server to a security risk. If a user with administration rights on the SQL server executes a report with integrated security, that report then has administration rights on the server. A malicious query built into such a report could harm your SQL server when it is run with integrated security. This risk can be mitigated by using a careful quality assurance (QA) testing process before each report is deployed to the report server. If this is impossible and you want to eliminate the risk of this type of attack, set the EnableIntegratedSecurity system property to False.

One of the easiest ways to query and set the system properties that are unavailable on the Site Settings page is through the RS utility. The following script prints all the system properties and their current values:

```
Public Sub Main()
    Dim SSRSProperties() As [Property]
    Dim SSRSProperty As [Property]
```

```
      SSRSProperties = rs.GetSystemProperties(Nothing)
      For Each SSRSProperty In SSRSProperties
          Console.WriteLine(SSRSProperty.Name & " - " & SSRSProperty.Value)
      Next
End Sub
```

This script sets the SystemReportTimeout property to ten minutes:

```
Public Sub Main()
      Dim SSRSProperties(0) As [Property]
      Dim SSRSProperty As New [Property]

      SSRSProperty.Name = "SystemReportTimeout"
      SSRSProperty.Value = 600
      SSRSProperties(0) = SSRSProperty

      rs.SetSystemProperties(SSRSProperties)
End Sub
```

Log Files

The report server creates a set of trace log files that can be helpful for managing and troubleshooting. These trace logs are text files that can be viewed with Notepad or any other text editor. In a default installation, the trace log files created by Reporting Services are stored in the following folder:

```
C:\Program Files\Microsoft SQL Server\MSRS11.MSSQLSERVER\
                              Reporting Services\LogFiles
```

In addition to these trace log files is an ExecutionLogStorage table in the Report Catalog (ReportServer) database. A record is created in this table each time a report is executed. The date and time of the execution, as well as the user name of the logged on user, are recorded. Unfortunately, the report being executed is identified by a globally unique identifier (GUID) rather than by the report name. Fortunately, there is a view in the ReportServer database called ExecutionLog2 that denormalizes these GUID references and makes it easy to query meaningful information from the ExecutionLogStorage table.

NOTE

Report Execution Logging must be turned on to use the logging features.

Best Foot Forward

You should now have a good idea of how to not only create great reports with Reporting Services, but also how to manage those reports on the report server and how to integrate your reports with other applications. We'll wrap things up in Chapter 13 with a brief look at some Reporting Services best practices.

Chapter 13

Well Begun: Best Practices

In This Chapter

- ▶ **Report-Authoring Practices**
- ▶ **Report Deployment Practices**
- ▶ **Where Do We Go from Here?**

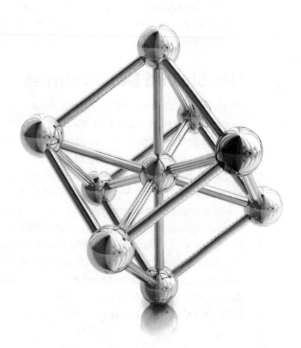

Before finishing, let's consider a few items that can make Reporting Services more efficient and easier to manage. These best practices are general rules of thumb that help things run smoother in most Reporting Services installations. As with all rules of thumb, exceptions exist. However, as you create your Reporting Services installation and the business practices to go with it, consider these practices and the benefits they can bring.

Report-Authoring Practices

The following practices can make your report-authoring process more efficient and more consistent. A standard look and feel is usually desirable as users move from one report to the next. The ability to be responsive to your users and create reports in a timely manner is always a plus.

Use Report Templates

A number of tasks in report authoring can be repetitive, such as placing the company name and logo at the top of the page and placing the page number and date of execution at the bottom. Rather than wasting time creating these items afresh on each report, use one or more report templates. The report templates enable you to start your report layout with these redundant items already present.

In addition, the report templates let you provide a common look and feel to your reports. Templates can help ensure that certain style elements, such as a logo image or a page number in a certain location, are always present. The templates can help to enforce this common look and feel across a number of report authors.

Use Shared Data Sources

Shared data sources can help cut down on management headaches. They centralize the storage of database credentials. If a database is moved to a new server, fewer places exist to change the connection information. If the database logon credentials are changed, fewer locations must be modified.

Shared data sources also facilitate the use of production and development database servers. Report development can be done using a shared data source pointing to the development database server. A shared data source with the same name can exist on the production report server pointing to the production database server. With the Overwrite Data Sources option turned off, the shared data source from the development environment does not overwrite the shared data source in the production environment. Instead, the report goes seamlessly from querying development data in the development environment to querying production data in the production environment. Isn't that the way it's supposed to work?

Use Views and Stored Procedures

Give your report authors rights to query views and execute stored procedures. Avoid giving them rights to the underlying tables. Having them operate with views and stored procedures makes it easier to enforce security and maintain privacy. It also prevents accidental data modifications and deletions.

Use Navigation Features

Take advantage of the document map, bookmark, drilldown, and drillthrough capabilities to make your reports more usable. These navigation features make it easier for your users to find the information they are looking for. *Drilldown* and *drillthrough* make it possible to hide complex detail until your user specifically requests it. Finally, drillthrough allows several reports to be linked together into a working unit.

Remember, the goal of reporting is to convey information to the end user. This is done best when a user can quickly navigate to desired information and follow the data intuitively from one level of detail to another or from one report to another. The Reporting Services navigation features make this possible.

Report Deployment Practices

The practices listed here can help you move reports from the development environment to the production report server. You need to make sure there is some level of control over which reports can access your production data. You also need to control who can do what on your production report server.

Create a Backup of the Encryption Key

This tip is not a report deployment practice, but it does help protect all the reports and shared data sources you have deployed to the report server. Occasionally, the key used to encrypt all the sensitive information stored on the report server becomes corrupt. When this happens, all that sensitive information is no longer accessible. The report credentials stored with each shared data source can no longer be decrypted and used. Worse yet, the credentials stored in the RSReportServer.config file cannot be decrypted, so the Report Server Windows service can no longer connect to the Report Catalog. In short, everything comes to a screeching halt.

If you do not have a backup copy of the encryption key, the only way to recover from this situation is to create a new encryption key and then reenter all the credential information. That is why the encryption key backup can be so important. With an encryption key backup, recovery from a corrupt key is trivial!

Review Reports Before Deploying

It is generally a good idea to have reports reviewed before they are put into production. This is especially true if you have nondevelopers creating their own reports. You need to make sure efficient queries are being used to extract the data so an undue burden is not placed on the database server. You also need some level of assurance the information the report claims to present is the information being pulled from the database.

Use Linked Reports

Rather than deploying duplicate copies of the same report to your report server, use linked reports. Each linked report can have its own default parameters and its own security. At the same time, updates to that report are done in one centralized location. This helps prevent the confusion that can arise from having multiple versions of the same report running in the production environment at the same time.

Use Folders and Descriptions to Organize Reports

If your Reporting Services installation is as successful as we all hope, soon tens or even hundreds of reports will reside on your report server. With this number of reports, organizing the reports properly to aid both the end users and the administrators is important. Otherwise, both the users and the administrators can become frustrated.

Organize your reports into logical groupings in folders. Use the tree structure of the folders to create a multiple-level structure. You should create enough folders so no folder contains too many reports, but not so many folders that the structure becomes cumbersome.

Use meaningful report names and add informational descriptions to each report. Remember, both the report name and the description are searchable in Report Manager. Then make sure your users know how to use this search function.

Assign Security at the Folder Level

Make your security role assignments at the folder level. Let the reports inherit their security from the folders they reside in. Assigning individual security roles to individual reports is cumbersome and easily leads to errors. Your security practices should be relatively easy to implement; otherwise, they will not be followed.

Assign Security to Domain Groups

By the same token, it makes more sense to assign roles to domain groups than try to assign roles to each individual user. Just as with assigning security at the report level, making assignments at the user level causes things to become very complex very rapidly. The simpler security policy is usually better, because it is the one more likely to be followed.

Assign Only the Rights Needed

Only give each user the rights they need to complete their required tasks. Assigning broad rights rather than narrow is easier, but this can lead to security breaches and problems managing the report server. Take the time to create custom security roles that provide users with only those rights they need. Then use these custom roles as you are granting access to domain groups. The additional time taken during setup is more than made up for in the time saved not having to clean up after users who were doing things they shouldn't have been able to do in the first place.

Hide Items

Keep the folders looking as clean and uncluttered as possible. Use "Hide in tile view" to hide items the user does not need to interact with. This might include shared data sources or subreports. If the user should not click an item, then the user has no reason to see it in the folder.

Remember, however, this is not a security measure. The user can easily click Details View to reveal any of these hidden items. Security rights provide security; "Hide in tile view" is a means of keeping things neat.

Deploy Supporting Items to the Report Server

The report server has the capability to store and serve supporting information. Documentation for your reports should be created as HTML pages, Word documents, PDF documents, Excel spreadsheets, and even PowerPoint presentations. These items can then be deployed to the report server right in the folders with the reports. This makes it easier for your users to understand the content and appropriate use of each report.

Use Caching and Snapshots

Use caching and snapshots to reduce the load on your report server and increase performance. Set up scheduled snapshots to execute long-running reports during off-hours. Believe me, users will not care if their data is eight hours old when they can get their reports back in seconds!

Where Do We Go from Here?

As Reporting Services continues to mature over the coming years, little doubt exists that it will remain an exciting product. With this new version of Reporting Services in SQL Server 2012, and third parties releasing alternative report-authoring environments and Reporting Services extensions, it is safe to say Reporting Services will continue to be in the news for some time to come. Based on current interest, it also looks like Reporting Services is going to have a rapidly growing user community.

It may be difficult to say exactly where Reporting Services is going from here, but all the signs point in a positive direction. It might be easier to answer the question, "Where does my business information go from here?" With a tool as capable, flexible, and extensible as Reporting Services, the answer is, "Anywhere you need it to go!"

Index

Master Microsoft® SQL Server® 2012 and Microsoft's Powerful Business Intelligence Tools

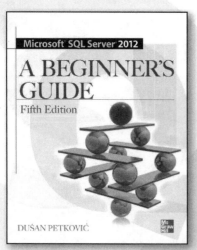

**Microsoft SQL Server 2012:
A Beginner's Guide, Fifth Edition**
Dušan Petkovic
Filled with real-world examples and hands-on exercises, this book makes it easy to learn essential skills.

**Microsoft SQL Server 2012
Reporting Services, Fourth Edition**
Brian Larson
Create, deploy, and manage BI reports using the expert tips and best practices in this hands-on resource.

**Delivering Business Intelligence
with Microsoft SQL Server 2012,
Third Edition**
Brian Larson
Equip your organization for informed, timely decision making with the expert tips in this practical guide.

**Visualizing Data with Microsoft
Power View**
*Brian Larson, Mark Davis, Dan English,
and Paul Purington*
Unlock the power of Microsoft Power View and build rich BI reports with just a few clicks.

**Microsoft SQL Server 2012 Master
Data Services, Second Edition**
Tyler Graham and Suzanne Selhorn
Learn best practices for deploying and managing Master Data Services (MDS).